ASPEN PUBLISHERS

WILLS, TRUSTS, AND ESTATES

KEYED TO DUKEMINIER/SITKOFF/LINDGREN
EIGHTH EDITION

Peter Wendel

Professor of Law
Pepperdine University

The *Emanuel Law Outlines* Series

Wolters Kluwer
Law & Business

AUSTIN   BOSTON   CHICAGO   NEW YORK   THE NETHERLANDS

Aspen Publishers
Attn: Permissions Department
76 Ninth Avenue, 7th Floor
New York, NY 10011-5201

To contact Customer Care, e-mail customer.care@aspenpublishers.com, call 1-800-234-1660, fax 1-800-901-9075, or mail correspondence to:

Aspen Publishers
Attn: Order Department
PO Box 990
Frederick, MD 21705

Printed in the United States of America.

2 3 4 5 6 7 8 9 0

ISBN 978-0-7355-7923-1

This book is intended as a general review of a legal subject. It is not intended as a source of advice for the solution of legal matters or problems. For advice on legal matters, the reader should consult an attorney.

Library of Congress Cataloging-in-Publication Data

Wendel, Peter T., 1956-
  Wills, trusts, and estates : keyed to Dukeminier/Sitkoff/Lindgren eighth edition/ Peter Wendel.
    p. cm. — (The Emanuel law outlines series)
  Includes index.
  ISBN 978-0-7355-7923-1
1. Wills—United States—Outlines, syllabi, etc. 2. Trusts and trustees—United States—Outlines, syllabi, etc. 3. Inheritance and succession—United States—Outlines, syllabi, etc. I. Dukeminier, Jesse. Wills, trusts, and estates. II. Title.

KF755.W46 2010
346.7305—dc22

2010010509

About Wolters Kluwer Law & Business

Wolters Kluwer Law & Business is a leading provider of research information and workflow solutions in key specialty areas. The strengths of the individual brands of Aspen Publishers, CCH, Kluwer Law International and Loislaw are aligned within Wolters Kluwer Law & Business to provide comprehensive, in-depth solutions and expert-authored content for the legal, professional and education markets.

CCH was founded in 1913 and has served more than four generations of business professionals and their clients. The CCH products in the Wolters Kluwer Law & Business group are highly regarded electronic and print resources for legal, securities, antitrust and trade regulation, government contracting, banking, pension, payroll, employment and labor, and healthcare reimbursement and compliance professionals.

Aspen Publishers is a leading information provider for attorneys, business professionals and law students. Written by preeminent authorities, Aspen products offer analytical and practical information in a range of specialty practice areas from securities law and intellectual property to mergers and acquisitions and pension/benefits. Aspen's trusted legal education resources provide professors and students with high-quality, up-to-date and effective resources for successful instruction and study in all areas of the law.

Kluwer Law International supplies the global business community with comprehensive English-language international legal information. Legal practitioners, corporate counsel and business executives around the world rely on the Kluwer Law International journals, loose-leafs, books and electronic products for authoritative information in many areas of international legal practice.

Loislaw is a premier provider of digitized legal content to small law firm practitioners of various specializations. Loislaw provides attorneys with the ability to quickly and efficiently find the necessary legal information they need, when and where they need it, by facilitating access to primary law as well as state-specific law, records, forms and treatises.

Wolters Kluwer Law & Business, a unit of Wolters Kluwer, is headquartered in New York and Riverwoods, Illinois. Wolters Kluwer is a leading multinational publisher and information services company.

To my students,
from whom I've learned so much

and

To Jesse, a teacher's teacher—and one of the kindest individuals
I've had the privilege of knowing

Summary of Contents

Table of Contents

CHAPTER 1

INTRODUCTION TO WILLS, TRUSTS, AND ESTATES

CHAPTER **2**

INTESTACY: THE DEFAULT DISTRIBUTION SCHEME

CHAPTER 3

TESTAMENTARY CAPACITY

CHAPTER 4

WILLS EXECUTION, REVOCATION, AND SCOPE

CHAPTER 5

CONSTRUING WILLS

CHAPTER 6

WILL SUBSTITUTES AND PLANNING FOR INCAPACITY

CHAPTER 7
LIMITATIONS ON THE TESTAMENTARY POWER TO TRANSFER

CHAPTER 8

TRUSTS: OVERVIEW AND CREATION

CHAPTER 9

TRUSTS: LIFE AND TERMINATION

CHAPTER 10

TRUST ADMINISTRATION AND THE TRUSTEE'S DUTIES

CHAPTER 11

CHARITABLE TRUSTS

CHAPTER 12

POWERS OF APPOINTMENT: DISCRETIONARY FLEXIBILITY

CHAPTER 13

CONSTRUING TRUSTS: FUTURE INTERESTS

CHAPTER 14
THE RULE AGAINST PERPETUITIES

CHAPTER 15
ESTATE AND GIFT TAXES

Preface

Wills, Trusts, and Estates is an intrinsically interesting class because it is all about who gets your property when you die. As law students, many of you may have a hard time connecting with that issue because (1) you still believe that you are going to live forever and (2) at this stage in your life, your debts probably exceed your assets so the issue in the course is moot as applied to you. To help bring the course and subject matter alive, envision your larger family situation and apply the issues in the course to various family members as appropriate. Sooner or later someone close to you will lose a loved one and you will want to be able to help that person through a very difficult time in his or her life. Even if you do not practice in this area, being able to explain the basics of a will, trust, or the probate process to the person will help him or her, at least from a property perspective, through this critical period.

If you have lost a loved one recently or if a family member is seriously ill, some of the issues in this course may be painful for you. If you are in that situation, I would advise you to let your professor know in advance so that both of you can avoid a potentially uncomfortable classroom situation.

As you progress through the material, you will see that most of the rules, viewed and analyzed individually, are fairly straightforward and easy to understand. The degree of difficulty in the course comes from the overwhelming volume of rules. To keep all the rules clear, I strongly recommend that you keep in mind the macro approach to the course. Even if your professor does not cover the first chapter of the book, you should read at least the Capsule Summary for Chapter 1. The flowchart in that summary section provides a roadmap for the whole course.

Individual students will use the outline in different ways. Ideally, each student should read the casebook, analyze the material, go to class and take good notes, and then create an outline. As you create your own outline, if you encounter problems with wording certain rules or understanding certain doctrines, refer to the appropriate sections of this outline (see the **Casebook Correlation Chart**) for well-written rule statements and further explanations. If, however, you find yourself struggling with the material itself (either because of the nature of the material or because of the way that your professor is presenting it), try reading the appropriate sections of the outline before you read the casebook and go to class. That should give you a better understanding of what you need to extract from the casebook and class discussions. In addition, some students need to see the "big picture" before they can fully understand the significance of the particular case or statute they are reading and analyzing. If you are that type of student, you might want to read the **Capsule Summary** of that topic before you turn to the material in the casebook. The Capsule Summary provides an overview that will help you absorb and understand the detailed information in the chapter as you read it the first time.

Learning psychologists emphasize that repeatedly covering material is the best way to move it from short-term memory to long-term memory. The **Quiz Yourself** section of each chapter is designed both to test your knowledge and understanding of the material and to help transfer that knowledge from your short-term memory to your long-term memory. Because there are so many rules in Wills, Trusts, and Estates, I strongly recommend that you answer the questions at the end of each chapter as you complete that chapter. Waiting until the end of the semester will not leave enough time for your long-term memory to absorb all the rules. Moreover, writing your answers to the Quiz Yourself questions will give you practice in exam-writing techniques. When you compose your essays, remember to write the rule before you apply it.

As the end of the semester approaches, you can review the Capsule Summary to refresh your recollection of the material and to spot those areas of the course where you are still weak. Use the outline to supplement your own outline and to fill any gaps in your understanding. Moreover, you should read the

Exam Tips to become sensitized to fact patterns, issues, and overlapping scenarios that commonly appear on Wills, Trusts, and Estates exams.

Many people have contributed to this project. I would like to thank the multitude of students I have taught at Pepperdine, UCLA, Santa Clara, and Loyola–Los Angeles for keeping the material fresh and challenging and for giving me so many insights into, and perspectives on, the material. I want to thank Barbara Roth and Barbara Lasoff at Aspen for their patience, support, and suggestions. I want to thank Taurean Brown and Tamara Kagel, research assistants extraordinaire. And lastly, I want to thank my good friend and colleague Robert Popovich for his invaluable help with Chapter 15; he truly is a tax guru.

I wish you the best in your Wills, Trusts, and Estates course. I think you will find it interesting, challenging, and enjoyable.

Peter Wendel
Pepperdine University School of Law

February 2010

Casebook Correlation Chart

Wills, Trusts, and Estates Emanuel Outline (by chapter heading)	Dukeminier/Sitkoff/ Lindgren: *Wills, Trusts, and Estates* (8th edition 2009)

CHAPTER 1
Introduction to Wills, Trusts, and Estates
  I. The Power to Transfer Property at Death
  II. "Dead Hand" Control
  III. Who Takes Decedent's Property: An Overview
  IV. The Probate Process: An Overview
  V. Estate Planning
	
	1-27
	27-38
	38-39
	39-49
	49-70

CHAPTER 2
Intestacy: The Default Distribution Scheme
  I. The Intestate Distribution Scheme
  II. Surviving Spouse: Who Qualifies
  III. Surviving Spouse: Calculating Share
  IV. Issue: Calculating Share
  V. Shares of Ancestors and Remote Collaterals
  VI. Descendants/Issue: Who Qualifies
  VII. Gifts to Children
  VIII. Bars to Succession
	
	71-75
	77-87
	75-77
	87-92
	92-97
	97-132
	133-145
	145-157

CHAPTER 3
Testamentary Capacity
  I. General Testamentary Capacity
  II. Insane Delusion
  III. Undue Influence
  IV. Fraud
  V. Duress
  VI. Tortious Interference with an Expectancy
	
	159-168
	168-180
	180-207
	207-210
	210-215
	215-221

CHAPTER 4
Wills Execution, Revocation, and Scope
  I. Executing a Valid Will
  II. Common Law Approach to Attested Wills
  III. Modern Trend Approach to Attested Wills
  IV. Notarized Wills
  V. Holographic Wills
  VI. Revocation
  VII. Scope of a Will
  VIII. Contracts Concerning Wills
	
	223-228
	228-246
	227-264
	265-267
	268-285
	286-307
	307-325
	325-334

CHAPTER 5
Construing Wills
  I. Admissibility of Extrinsic Evidence: General Rule
  II. Changes in the Beneficiary
  III. Changes in the Testator's Property
	
	335-358
	358-379
	380-392

Casebook Correlation Chart (Cont.)

Casebook Correlation Chart (Cont.)

Capsule Summary

This Capsule Summary can be used to provide an overview of the material in the course and/or for review at the end of the course. Reading the Capsule Summary, however, is not a substitute for mastering the material in the main outline. Numbers in brackets refer to the pages in the main outline where the topic is discussed.

CHAPTER 1
INTRODUCTION TO WILLS, TRUSTS, AND ESTATES

I. THE POWER TO TRANSFER PROPERTY AT DEATH

A. **Introduction:** The macro issue raised by the course is, "who gets your property when you die?" To the extent the answer is "whomever you intend," there are a number of theoretical and public policy issues inherent in that answer. [1–2]

B. **Right vs. privilege:** A decedent has the right to dispose of his or her property at death. Although the states have broad authority to regulate the process, the states cannot completely abrogate the right. [2–3]

C. **Public policy debate:** Some argue the power to transfer wealth at death is natural and good in that it encourages one to save and promotes family values, while others argue the power to transfer wealth at death perpetuates economic disparity and unfairly rewards those lucky enough to have been born to rich parents. [3–4]

II. "DEAD HAND" CONTROL

A. **"Dead hand" control defined:** A decedent may condition a beneficiary's gift on the beneficiary behaving in a certain manner as long as the condition does not violate public policy. [4]

B. **Validity:** "Dead hand" control is generally upheld unless the condition constitutes a complete restraint on marriage, requires a beneficiary to practice a certain religion, encourages divorce or family strife, or directs the destruction of property. [4–6]

III. WHO TAKES DECEDENT'S PROPERTY: AN OVERVIEW

A. **Overview:** Who takes a decedent's property depends first on whether the property is nonprobate or probate property. Nonprobate property is limited to (1) property held in joint tenancy, (2) life insurance contracts (modern trend expands this exception to include all contracts with a payable-on-death clause), (3) legal life estates and remainders, and (4) inter vivos trusts. Nonprobate property passes pursuant to the terms of the nonprobate instrument. Probate property passes pursuant to the terms of the decedent's will, otherwise through intestacy. [6–7]

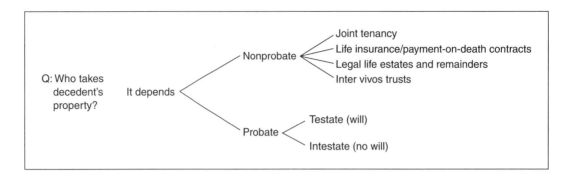

IV. THE PROBATE PROCESS: AN OVERVIEW

A. **Default:** Probate is the default. The decedent must take affirmative steps (execute a valid will or create a valid nonprobate instrument) to avoid having the property pass through probate. [7]

B. **Probate administration:** The probate court appoints a personal representative. He or she has the job of collecting the decedent's probate assets, paying off creditors' claims, and distributing the property to those who are entitled to receive the property. [8–10]

V. ESTATE PLANNING

A. **Key objectives:** In advising a party about his or her estate plan, the key objectives that an estate planning attorney should keep in mind typically are (1) honoring the party's intent, (2) avoiding estate taxes, and (3) avoiding probate. [11]

B. **Professional responsibility:** Under the common law approach, the attorney owes no duty of care to, and is not in privity of contract with, intended beneficiaries. Accordingly, intended beneficiaries have no standing to sue for malpractice. Under the modern trend, an attorney owes a duty of care to intended beneficiaries, and intended beneficiaries are third party beneficiaries with respect to the contract between the attorney and testator. Intended beneficiaries have standing to sue for malpractice. [11–14]

CHAPTER 2

INTESTACY: THE DEFAULT DISTRIBUTION SCHEME

I. THE INTESTATE DISTRIBUTION SCHEME

A. **Introduction:** The default distribution scheme is intestacy. If a decedent fails to dispose of all of his or her property through nonprobate instruments or a valid will, the decedent's property passes pursuant to the state's descent and distribution statute to the decedent's heirs. [20]

B. **A typical intestate distribution scheme:** Although the details vary from state to state, the basic order of who takes is fairly similar: (1) surviving spouse, (2) issue, (3) parents, (4) issue of parents, (5) grandparents/issue of grandparents, (6) next-of-kin, (7) escheats to the state. How much each takes is where the differences typically arise state to state. [20–22]

II. SURVIVING SPOUSE: WHO QUALIFIES

A. **Marriage requirement:** The term *spouse* assumes that the couple has gone through a valid marriage ceremony (most states include *putative spouses,* where the couple goes through what at least one spouse believes is a valid marriage ceremony, but the marriage is either void or voidable). Cohabitants do not qualify unless the jurisdiction recognizes common law marriage and the couple meets the requirements for common law marriage. Increasingly states are recognizing same-sex marriage or registered domestic partners. Such recognition grants qualifying same-sex couples some/all of the same rights (depending on the jurisdiction) as married heterosexual couples. Once married, even if a couple legally separates, for inheritance purposes they continue to qualify as spouses until a court enters its final order of dissolution. [22–23]

B. **Survival requirement:** At common law, to qualify as an heir one has to prove by a ***preponderance*** of the evidence that he or she survived the decedent by a millisecond. Under the modern trend, some jurisdictions require the heir to prove by ***clear and convincing*** evidence that he or she survived the decedent by a millisecond, while other jurisdictions require the taker to prove by clear and convincing evidence that he or she survived the decedent by 120 hours (5 days). [24–25]

Scope: The survival requirement applies to all parties who claim a right to take some of the decedent's probate testate or intestate property. The jurisdictions are split as to whether a survival requirement applies to nonprobate property. In some jurisdictions the survival requirement is the same for all types of property, while in other jurisdictions the survival requirement varies depending on the type of property. [25–26]

III. SURVIVING SPOUSE: CALCULATING SHARE

A. **Typical state statute:** Under a typical state descent and distribution statute, the surviving spouse takes 100 percent of the decedent's intestate property if the decedent has no surviving issue, parents, or issue of parents; 50 percent if the decedent has one child (alive or dead but survived by issue) or no surviving issue but surviving parent(s) or issue of parents; and 33 percent if more than one child (alive or dead but survived by issue). [26–27]

B. **Uniform Probate Code (UPC):** Under the UPC, the surviving spouse takes 100 percent of the decedent's intestate property if no issue or parents, or 100 percent if all of the decedent's issue are also issue of the surviving spouse and the latter has no other issue; $200,000 plus 75 percent of the rest if the decedent has no surviving issue but surviving parent(s); $150,000 plus 50 percent of the rest if all of the decedent's surviving issue are also issue of the surviving spouse but the latter has other issue; or $100,000 plus 50 percent of the rest if one or more of the decedent's surviving issue are not issue of the surviving spouse. [27–28]

IV. DESCENDANTS/ISSUE: CALCULATING SHARES

A. **Calculating shares:** The term *issue* includes not only one's children, but also all of one's blood descendants. The jurisdictions are split over what it means to divide the decedent's property equally among the decedent's issue when the issue are not equally related to the decedent. Depending on the jurisdiction, the property is divided per stirpes, per capita, or per capita at each generation (if the decedent dies testate or with nonprobate property, the written instrument can expressly provide for which approach applies). [28–30]

B. Per stirpes: Under the per stirpes approach, the first division of decedent's property always occurs at the first generation of issue (whether anyone is alive at that generation or not); the property is divided into one share for each party who is alive at that generation and one share for each party who is dead at that generation but who is survived by issue; and the shares for those who are dead but survived by issue drop by bloodline to their respective issue. [30–31]

C. Per capita with representation: Under the per capita approach, the first division of decedent's property always occurs at the first generation of issue where there is a live taker; the property is divided into one share for each party who is alive at that generation and one share for each party who is dead at that generation but who is survived by issue; and the shares for those who are dead but survived by issue drop by bloodline to their respective issue. [31–32]

D. Per capita at each generation: Under the per capita at each generation approach, the first division of decedent's property always occurs at the first generation of issue where there is a live taker; the property is divided into one share for each party who is alive at that generation and one share for each party who is dead at that generation but who is survived by issue; and the shares for those who are dead but survived by issue drop by the pooling approach (the shares are added together and then distributed equally among the issue of the deceased parties at the prior generation). [32–34]

V. SHARES OF ANCESTORS AND REMOTE COLLATERALS

A. Collateral relatives: The decedent, the decedent's spouse, and the decedent's issue are the decedent's immediate family. All of the decedent's other relatives are called his or her "collateral relatives." If the decedent has no spouse or issue, how the decedent's property is distributed to his or her collateral heirs varies by jurisdiction. There are three possible approaches: the parentelic approach, the degree of relationship approach, and the degree of relationship with a parentelic tiebreaker approach. [34–37]

VI. DESCENDANTS/ISSUE: WHO QUALIFIES

A. Qualifying as an issue: Establishing a parent-child relationship means each can inherit from and through the other. Such a relationship can be established naturally, whether the parents are married or not; by adoption, which severs the relationship with the natural parents as a general rule; or through equitable adoption. [37–38]

    1. Parents married: Where the natural parents are married, the general rule is both parties (the natural parents and the child) can inherit from and through each other (the 2008 amendments to the UPC permit the genetic parent to inherit from and through the child unless the child died before age 18 and there is clear and convincing evidence the parental rights could have been terminated).

    2. Adoption: Adoption establishes a parent-child relationship between the adopted child and the adoptive parents. As a general rule, adoption severs the relationship between the adopted child and his or her natural parent of the same gender as the adopting parent. In many jurisdictions, however, if the adoption is by a stepparent, following the adoption the child can still inherit from and through the natural parent of the same gender as the adopting stepparent, but the natural parent cannot inherit from or through the child.

3. **Equitable adoption:** Equitable adoption arises where (1) the natural parents and adoptive parents agree on the adoption, (2) the natural parents perform by giving up custody of the child, (3) the child performs by moving in with the adoptive parents, (4) the adoptive parents partially perform by taking the child in but failing to complete the adoption, and (5) the adoptive parent dies intestate. The child is entitled to a claim against the adoptive parent's estate equal to his or her intestate share.

4. **Child born out of wedlock:** Where the parents are unmarried, the general rule is the child can inherit from and through the natural parents (assuming paternity can be established), but for the natural parents or relatives of the natural parents to inherit from or through the child, the natural parents or relatives must acknowledge and support the child (the 2008 amendments to the UPC permit the genetic parent to inherit from and through the child unless the child died before age 18 and there is clear and convincing evidence the parental rights could have been terminated).

5. **Posthumously conceived child:** The emerging general rule is that posthumously conceived children qualify as a child of the deceased genetic parent (and thus can inherit from and through the parent) as long as (1) the parent authorized the use of his or her genetic material while alive; and (2) the child is conceived within a reasonable period (2-3 years) of the parent's death. Whether the authorization must be in writing, and the requisite time period, vary from jurisdiction to jurisdiction.

VII. GIFTS TO CHILDREN

A. **Advancements:** At common law, inter vivos gifts to a child are irrebuttably presumed to count against the child's share of the decedent's intestate estate. Under the modern trend, inter vivos gifts do not count against an heir's share of the decedent's intestate estate unless there is a writing by the donor contemporaneous with the inter vivos gift expressing such an intent or a writing by the donee acknowledging such an intent. [45–47]

Hotchpot: Where there is an advancement, the amount of the advancement is added back into the decedent's intestate estate, and then each heir's share of the hotchpot is determined. In distributing the decedent's intestate property, an heir who receives an advancement has the value of the advancement credited against his or her share (of the hotchpot amount). [45–48]

VIII. BARS TO SUCCESSION

A. **Introduction:** Even where an individual is otherwise entitled to take from a decedent (be it nonprobate or probate property, testate or intestate property), the taker is barred from taking under the homicide doctrine or if he or she disclaims. [48]

B. **Homicide doctrine:** If the taker killed the decedent, and the killing was felonious and intentional, as a general rule the killer is treated as if he or she predeceased the decedent for purposes of distributing the decedent's property. The doctrine applies to all types of property—nonprobate, probate testate, and intestate property (where the property is joint tenancy, by operation of law it is converted into tenancy in common). The issue is a civil issue subject to the preponderance of the evidence burden of proof. The jurisdictions are split as to whether the issue of the killer should be barred from taking the share that would otherwise go to the killer. [48–49]

C. Disclaimer: If a party properly executes a disclaimer, declining to accept a testamentary gift the taker otherwise would have received, the party who disclaimed is treated as if he or she predeceased the decedent for purposes of distributing the disclaimed property. [50–51]

CHAPTER 3
TESTAMENTARY CAPACITY

I. GENERAL TESTAMENTARY CAPACITY

A. Overview: The traditional method of opting out of intestacy is to execute a will. The first requirement for creating a valid will is testamentary capacity. The testator must have testamentary capacity at the time he or she executes or revokes a will. [62]

B. Testamentary capacity: The testator must be 18 years old and of sound mind. Sound mind is *the ability* to know (1) the nature and extent of his or her property, (2) the natural objects of his or her bounty, (3) the nature of the testamentary act he or she is performing, and (4) how all of these relate to constitute an orderly plan of disposing of his or her property. Absent evidence to the contrary, there is a strong presumption of testamentary capacity. (Testamentary capacity is higher than marriage capacity but lower than contractual capacity, so the appointment of a conservator does not, in and of itself, mean the testator lacks testamentary capacity.) [62–64]

C. Defects in capacity: Even if the testator has testamentary capacity generally, if the will or any part thereof is caused by a defect in capacity (insane delusion, undue influence, or fraud), the court strikes as much of the will as was affected by the defect. [64]

II. INSANE DELUSION

A. Defined: An insane delusion is a false perception of reality that the testator adheres to against all reason and evidence to the contrary. The jurisdictions are split over the test for what constitutes an insane delusion. [64–66]

1. **Majority approach:** If a rational person could not reach the same conclusion under the circumstances, the belief is an insane delusion.

2. **Minority approach:** If there is any factual basis to support the belief, the belief is not an insane delusion. (Notice this approach is more protective of testator's intent.)

B. Causation: Even where the testator has an insane delusion, the delusion must cause the testator to dispose of his or her property in a way that he or she would not have otherwise. Some jurisdictions apply a "might have affected" approach to causation, while other jurisdictions apply a "but for" approach. (Notice the "but for" approach is more protective of testator's intent.) [66–67]

III. UNDUE INFLUENCE

A. Defined: Undue influence occurs where another substitutes his or her intent for the testator's intent; where there is coercion (typically mental or emotional, not physical). [67]

B. **Traditional rule statement:** The plaintiff bears the burden of proving that (1) the testator was susceptible, (2) the defendant had the opportunity, (3) the defendant had a motive, and (4) causation. [67]

C. **Presumption doctrine:** Because undue influence is difficult to prove and the alleged undue influencer is in the best position to produce the relevant evidence, most jurisdictions have a "burden shifting" approach to undue influence where the burden shifts to the alleged undue influencer to show *no* undue influence if the plaintiff meets the requirements of the presumption doctrine. The details of the presumption approach vary from jurisdiction to jurisdiction, but in many jurisdictions if the plaintiff can prove (1) the defendant and the testator were in a confidential relationship, (2) the testator was of weakened intellect, and (3) the defendant takes the bulk of the testator's estate, then a presumption of undue influence arises and the burden of proof shifts to the defendant to rebut the presumption. [67–68]

D. **Gifts to attorney:** The general rule is that anytime an attorney who drafts an instrument receives a substantial gift under it, a presumption of undue influence arises unless the attorney is related to or married to the client. Most jurisdictions require clear and convincing evidence that the gift was truly the testator's intent to overcome the presumption; some jurisdictions create an irrebuttable presumption of undue influence. (Some jurisdictions apply the presumption regardless of the size of the gift; others apply the presumption to any gift to the testator's attorney, even if the attorney did not draft the instrument; and some jurisdictions require an independent attorney to consult the testator and determine the gift is the testator's true intent to overcome the presumption.) [69–71]

E. **No contest clauses:** If a testator suspects that someone may challenge his or her will (or other testamentary instrument), the testator may include a clause that provides that if the beneficiary challenges the will (or any provision in the will), the beneficiary is barred from taking under the will. No contest clauses are generally valid, but narrowly construed. Even if a beneficiary challenges a will (or clause) and loses, some jurisdictions will not enforce the clause if there is *probable cause* to support the challenge (whatever its basis), while other jurisdictions will not enforce the clause if the challenge is based on a claim of forgery, revocation, or misconduct by a witness or the drafter. [71–73]

IV. FRAUD

A. **Rule statement:** Fraud occurs where there is an intentional misrepresentation, made knowingly and purposely to influence the testator's testamentary scheme, that causes the testator to dispose of his or her property in a way in which he or she would not have otherwise. There are two types of fraud. [73–74]

   1. **Fraud in the inducement:** A person intentionally misrepresents a fact to the testator to induce the testator to execute a will (or amend a provision in a will or revoke a will) in reliance upon the misrepresentation.

   2. **Fraud in the execution:** A person intentionally misrepresents the nature of the document (either completely or in part) that the testator is signing.

V. DURESS

A. Rule statement: Where a wrongdoer performs, or threatens to perform, a wrongful act that coerces the donor into making a donative transfer he or she would not have otherwise made. Transfers procured by duress are invalid. [74]

VI. TORTIOUS INTERFERENCE WITH AN EXPECTANCY

A. Rule statement: Tortious interference with an expectancy is a tort action. The plaintiff still has to prove either fraud or undue influence. Nevertheless, bringing the claim as one of tortious interference with an expectancy has several advantages: (1) it is not a will contest for purposes of a no contest clause; (2) punitive damages may be available; and (3) the action is subject to the standard statute of limitations, not the shortened probate statute of limitations. [74–75]

CHAPTER 4

WILLS EXECUTION, REVOCATION, AND SCOPE

I. EXECUTING A VALID WILL

A. Overview: Assuming an individual has testamentary capacity, the next requirement for a valid will is that it has to be properly executed. Whether a will has been properly executed is a function of two variables: the jurisdiction's Wills Act formalities and how strictly the courts require the testator to comply with those formalities. [84]

II. COMMON LAW APPROACH TO ATTESTED WILLS

A. Attested wills: The three basic requirements for an attested will are (1) a writing that is (2) signed and (3) witnessed. Each jurisdiction, however, adds a variety of other, ancillary requirements. Great care must be paid to each jurisdiction's Wills Act statute to ascertain all the necessary execution formalities in each jurisdiction. [85–86]

B. Judicial approach: Historically the courts have required strict compliance by the testator with each statutory requirement. Strict compliance requires 100 percent absolute compliance. Even the slightest deficiency or error in the execution ceremony invalidates the will regardless of how clear the testator's intent is. [85–86]

C. Typical statutory requirements: Although the statutory requirements vary from jurisdiction to jurisdiction, a number are common to most states. These requirements have given rise to a number of ancillary rules. [86–88]

1. Signature: Anything the testator intends to be his or her signature constitutes his or her signature. (If the testator is interrupted while in the act of signing and thus does not complete his or her signature, the assumption is that the testator intended to write his or her whole signature and that the partial signature was not intended to constitute a valid signature.) Most states permit another to sign for the testator as long as the signature is made in the testator's presence and at the testator's direction.

2. **Witnesses:** Most jurisdictions require the testator to sign or acknowledge his or her signature in the presence of two witnesses present at the same time. The witnesses must sign the will (and, in most jurisdictions, must know they are signing a will).

3. **Presence:** A requirement in virtually every Wills Act statute is that one party must perform in the presence of another party (that is, the testator has to sign in the presence of the witnesses, and/or the witnesses have to sign in the presence of the testator). Under the traditional line of sight approach, the party in whose presence the act has to be performed must be capable of seeing the act being performed if he or she looks at the moment it is being performed. Under the modern trend conscious presence approach, the party in whose presence the act has to be performed has to understand, from the totality of the circumstances, that the act is being performed.

4. **Order of signing:** Many courts hold that there is an implicit order of signing requirement in that the testator must perform (sign or acknowledge) before either of the witnesses sign the will. The modern trend holds that it does not matter who signs first as long as the testator and witnesses all sign as part of one transaction (as long as no one leaves the room before all parties have signed the will).

5. **Writing below signatures:** Where there is writing (typed or handwritten) below the testator's and/or witnesses' signatures, the validity of the writing depends (1) on whether the state requires the testator and/or witnesses to subscribe the will (sign the will at the end) (in which case the gift is invalid), and (2) if the will need not be signed at the end, on temporally when the gift was added to the will (if before it was signed, valid; if after it was signed, invalid).

6. **Delayed attestation:** At common law, the witnesses have to sign the will immediately after the testator signs or acknowledges the will. Under the modern trend, delayed attestation is permitted as long as the witnesses sign within a reasonable time of the testator signing or acknowledging.

D. **Interested witness:** If one of the two witnesses to a will takes under the will, the witness has a conflict of interest. At early common law, the whole will was void. Today, the jurisdictions vary in their approach to the interested witness doctrine. Some void the entire gift to the witness, others purge the interested witness of the "excess" interest that he or she would take if this will were valid, while others say the interested witness scenario creates only a rebuttable presumption of wrongdoing on the part of the interested witnesses (and apply the purging approach if the witness cannot rebut the presumption). [88–90]

E. **Swapped wills:** Where two testators with the same testamentary scheme (typically husband and wife) accidentally sign each other's will, the traditional common law approach is that the wills are invalid. Some courts try to save the wills under the misdescription doctrine, where all incorrect references in the will are struck and then the will is read to see if the court can construe and give effect to what is left. Under the modern trend, the will may be probated under scrivener's error. [90–91]

III. MODERN TREND APPROACH TO ATTESTED WILLS

A. **Overview:** The modern trend tries to facilitate the execution of attested wills by reducing the number of statutory requirements and/or by reducing the degree of compliance the courts require with respect to the execution requirements. [91]

B. UPC execution requirements: The UPC has simplified the execution process by (1) reducing the number of execution requirements, and (2) loosening up on several of the requirements that remain. [92]

1. **Witnesses present at the same time:** At common law, the testator has to sign or acknowledge in the presence of two witnesses present at the same time. Under the UPC, the witnesses need not be present at the same time; the testator can sign or acknowledge in front of the witnesses separately.

2. **Acknowledgment:** At common law, if the testator uses the acknowledgment method of executing the will, the testator has to acknowledge his or her signature. Under the UPC, if the testator uses the acknowledgement method of execution, the testator can acknowledge either the signature or the will in front of the witnesses.

3. **Conscious presence:** The UPC expressly provides that where another signs for the testator, the conscious presence approach applies to the requirement that the party sign in the testator's presence and at his or her direction.

4. **Writing below signature:** The UPC does not require the testator or the witnesses to subscribe the will (sign at the bottom or end).

5. **Delayed attestation:** The UPC provides that the witnesses may sign the will within a reasonable time after witnessing the testator sign or acknowledge (this also implicitly rejects the requirement that the witnesses have to sign in the testator's presence).

C. Judicial approach—"curative doctrines": The UPC repudiates strict compliance. At first it advocated substantial compliance, but the most recent version of the UPC advocates the harmless error/dispensing power approach. [92–94]

1. **Substantial compliance:** Substantial compliance holds that a will was properly executed as long as (1) there is clear and convincing evidence that the testator intended the document to be his or her will, and (2) there is clear and convincing evidence that the testator substantially complied with the Wills Act formalities.

2. **Harmless error/dispensing power:** Harmless error/dispensing power holds that the will was properly executed as long as there is clear and convincing evidence that the testator intended the document to be his or her will.

D. Interested witnesses: The UPC has abolished the interested witness doctrine completely. [89]

IV. NOTARIZED WILLS

A. Notary option: Pursuant to the 2008 revisions to the UPC, a will is valid if signed by two witnesses *or a notary*. [94]

V. HOLOGRAPHIC WILLS

A. Rule statement: Holographic wills need not be witnessed, but (1) there must be a writing, (2) the writing has to be in the testator's handwriting (either completely or at least the material provisions—the jurisdictions are split), (3) the writing must be signed by the testator, and (4) the writing must express testamentary intent (the intent that the document be the decedent's will) (some jurisdictions also require (5) that the writing be dated). The jurisdictions are split over whether the testamentary intent must be expressed in the testator's handwriting or whether it can be expressed in printed material on the document. [94–97]

VI. REVOCATION

A. Introduction: A validly executed will (attested or holographic) can be revoked by act, by writing (if the writing qualifies as a will), by presumption, or by operation of law. [97]

B. Revocation by act: A testator can revoke a will by act if (1) the act is destructive in nature (tearing, burning, obliterating, scratching, and so on), and (2) the testator has the intent to revoke when the act is performed. Someone other than the testator can perform the act as long as it is performed in the testator's presence and at his or her direction. At common law, the act has to affect at least some of the words of the will. Under the modern trend, the act need not affect the words of the will as long as the act affects some part of the will. (The act of writing can be a destructive act for revocation purposes.) Some jurisdictions do not permit partial revocation by act. [97–98]

C. Revocation by writing: A testator can revoke a will by writing if the writing qualifies as a will (either attested or holographic). A subsequent will can revoke a prior will either expressly or implicitly (through inconsistency), and either in whole or in part (in which case it is a codicil). [97–98]

Codicils: A will that merely amends and/or supplements an existing will and that does not completely replace an existing will is called a codicil. [98]

D. Revocation by presumption: Where a will was last in the testator's possession and cannot be found after testator's death, a presumption arises that the testator revoked the will (by act). The presumption can be rebutted if the proponents prove by a preponderance of the evidence that a more plausible explanation exists for why the will cannot be found. If the presumption is rebutted, the will is not revoked, and under the lost will doctrine, the will can be probated if its terms can be established by clear and convincing evidence. [99–100]

E. Dependent relative revocation: Even where a will has been properly revoked, if (1) the testator revoked the will, in whole or in part, (2) based upon a mistake, and (3) the testator would not have revoked but for the mistake, the revocation will not be given effect under dependent relative revocation. The courts appear to also require that either (4) the mistake must be set forth in the revoking instrument and be beyond the testator's knowledge, or (5) there must be a failed alternative scheme (typically an attempt at a new will that failed). [100–102]

F. Revival: If a testator executes will #1, and thereafter executes will #2 (a will or codicil), and thereafter revokes will #2, the jurisdictions are split over what is necessary to revive will #1. Under the English approach, will #2 never revoked will #1, so when will #2 is revoked, will #1 is "uncovered" and can be probated. The majority American approach, however, is that will #2 revokes will #1 the moment will #2 is executed. The jurisdictions that follow the American approach are split over what is necessary to revive will #1 when will #2 is revoked. Some jurisdictions require that will #1 be reexecuted. Other jurisdictions provide that all that is necessary to revive will #1 is that the testator intended to revive will #1. Under this latter approach, however, the key is *how* was will #2 revoked. Where will #2 is revoked by act, the general rule is that the courts will take virtually any evidence of the testator's intent to revive will #1. Where will #2 is revoked by writing (will #3), the intent to revive will #1 must be expressed in will #3. (Under the

UPC, if will #2 is a codicil, revocation of the codicil automatically revives the provisions of the underlying will that the codicil had revoked.) [102–103]

G. Revocation by operation of law: Where the testator divorces, all of the provisions of the will in favor of the ex-spouse are automatically revoked by operation of law. (In some jurisdictions, the doctrine applies not only to the ex-spouse, but also to the ex-spouse's family members; and in some jurisdictions the doctrine applies not only to wills, but also to nonprobate instruments.) [103–104]

VII. SCOPE OF A WILL

A. Introduction: There are a handful of doctrines that define the scope of a will and permit intent not expressed in a will to be given effect. [104]

B. Integration: Those pieces of paper physically present when the will is executed and that the testator intends to be part of the will constitute the pages of the will. [104]

C. Republication by codicil: A codicil has the effect of reexecuting, republishing, and thus redating the underlying will, but if redating the underlying will appears inconsistent with the testator's intent, the courts do not have to redate the will. [104–105]

D. Incorporation by reference: A document not executed with Wills Act formalities may be incorporated by reference and given effect along with the will if (1) the will expresses the intent to incorporate the document, (2) the will describes the document with reasonable certainty, and (3) the document was in existence at the time the will was executed (the courts apply this last requirement strictly). [105–107]

E. Acts of independent significance: A will may refer to an act or event that is to occur outside of the will, and that act or event may control either who takes under the will or how much a beneficiary takes, as long as the referenced act has its own significance independent of its effect upon the will. [107–108]

VIII. CONTRACTS CONCERNING WILLS

A. Contracts relating to wills: A person may contract to execute a particular will, to make a particular devise, or not to revoke a particular will or devise. If the contract is valid under contract law, the contract will be enforced against the testator's estate before the decedent's estate is distributed. At common law, the alleged contract could be oral. Under the modern trend/UPC approach, there must be a writing signed by the decedent evidencing the contract. [108–112]

B. Joint will: A joint will is a will executed by two different people that each intends to constitute his or her will. The modern trend general rule is that the execution of a joint will does not give rise to even a presumption of a contract not to revoke. The intent to form a contract not to revoke must be express. [109–110]

C. Contract rights vs. spousal protection rights: Where a surviving spouse remarries and then dies, and the surviving spouse's spouse claims his or her spousal protection rights, if such rights constitute a breach of a contract not to revoke, the jurisdictions are split over whether the contract beneficiaries under the contract not to revoke come first (typically the children of the first marriage) or whether the spousal protection rights of the surviving spouse come first. [110-112]

CHAPTER 5

CONSTRUING WILLS

I. ADMISSIBILITY OF EXTRINSIC EVIDENCE: GENERAL RULE

A. Overview: Assuming a properly executed will, upon the testator's death it has to be probated. Probating a will means construing and giving effect to its provisions. [128]

B. Admissibility of extrinsic evidence: The starting assumption is that the written will is the best evidence of the testator's intent and extrinsic evidence should not be admissible to vary its meaning (but extrinsic evidence is admissible if it goes to the *validity* of the will). Consistent with this assumption, the traditional rule has been that extrinsic evidence is admissible to help construe a will only if there is a latent ambiguity in the will. The modern trend is to admit extrinsic evidence to help construe the will, and maybe even to reform the will, anytime there is clear and convincing evidence (1) that the will contains a mistake, and (2) its effect upon testator's intent. [129–132]

    1. Common law: Under the plain meaning rule, in determining whether there is an ambiguity in the will, the words of the will are given their usual plain meaning, and extrinsic evidence that the testator intended a different meaning is not admissible. If the will contains an ambiguity, under the common law approach extrinsic evidence is admissible to help construe the ambiguity only if it is a latent ambiguity (not apparent on the face of the will); extrinsic evidence is not admissible if the ambiguity is a patent ambiguity. Doctrines that evolved to permit the admissibility of extrinsic evidence to help resolve latent ambiguities were the misdescription doctrine, the equivocation doctrine, and the personal usage exception doctrine.

    2. Modern trend: Under the modern trend, the courts have repudiated the plain meaning rule and take evidence of the circumstances surrounding the testator at the time he or she executed the will to help determine if there is an ambiguity in the will. In addition, the modern trend has abolished the distinction between latent and patent ambiguities and admits extrinsic evidence anytime there is an ambiguity in the will. Increasingly the courts are taking extrinsic evidence to reform a will if there is clear and convincing evidence that (1) the will contains a mistake; and (2) its effect upon testator's intent (though the reformation approach is still a minority approach among courts).

C. Scrivener's error: Under the modern trend, if there is clear and convincing evidence of a scrivener's error, and clear and convincing evidence of its effect upon testator's intent, extrinsic evidence is admissible to establish and to correct the error. (Scrivener's error is a new doctrine, and the full scope of the doctrine has yet to be established.) [132–133]

II. CHANGES IN THE BENEFICIARY

A. Lapse: Where a beneficiary predeceases the testator, the gift is said to lapse and will fail. [133]

B. Failed gifts: Failed specific gifts and failed general gifts fall to the residuary clause, if one, otherwise to intestacy; failed residuary gifts fall to intestacy. If part of the residuary fails, under the common law that part falls to intestacy, while under the modern trend that part goes to the other residuary takers. [133–135]

WILIS, TRUSTS, AND ESTATES

C. **Anti-lapse:** Anti-lapse may save a gift that otherwise would lapse and fail. Anti-lapse provides that where there is a lapsed gift, if (1) the predeceased beneficiary meets the requisite degree of relationship to the testator (varies by jurisdiction), and (2) the predeceased beneficiary has issue who survive the testator, then (3) the gift to the predeceased beneficiary will go to the issue of the predeceased beneficiary (4) as long as the will does not express an intent that anti-lapse should not be applied (low threshold—historically, an express survival requirement or an express gift-over to an alternative taker constituted an express contrary intent). [135–137]

Spouses excluded: As a general rule, the anti-lapse doctrine does not apply to gifts to spouses where the spouse predeceases the testator because a spouse does not meet the requisite degree of relationship requirement.

D. **Class gifts:** The class gift doctrine may also save a gift that would otherwise fail. A class gift has a built-in right of survivorship so that if one member of the class predeceases the testator, his or her share is redistributed among the surviving members of the class. Whether a gift to a group is a class gift is a question of testator's intent. Where it is not clear whether a gift to multiple individuals is a class gift, courts focus on four factors: (1) how the beneficiaries are described, (2) how the gift is described, (3) whether all the individuals share a common characteristic, and (4) the testator's overall testamentary scheme. The more factors favoring a class gift, the more likely a court is to find the gift to be a class gift. [137–140]

Anti-lapse and class gifts: Where a member of a class gift dies survived by issue, the jurisdictions are split over which doctrine should be applied first to try to save the otherwise failed gift—anti-lapse or the class gift doctrine. The modern trend is to apply anti-lapse first (which saves the gift by giving it to the issue of the predeceased beneficiary) before applying the class gift doctrine (which saves the gift by giving it to the other members of the class).

III. CHANGES IN TESTATOR'S PROPERTY

A. **Types of gifts:** There are four different types of gifts that one can make in a will. A specific gift is where the testator intends to give a specific item (typically that the testator owns at time of execution). A general gift is a gift of a general pecuniary value, where any item or items matching the gift will satisfy the gift. A demonstrative gift is a general gift from a specific source; demonstrative gifts are a subset of general gifts and are treated the same as other general gifts. A residuary gift is a gift of all the testator's property that he or she has not given away specifically or generally. [140–141]

B. **Ademption:** Under the common law approach, if the testator makes a specific gift and the item that is the subject of the specific gift is not in the testator's estate at time of death, under the identity approach an irrebuttable presumption arises that the gift was revoked and the beneficiary takes nothing. Under the UPC, a presumption against revocation arises, and the beneficiary is entitled to any replacement property the testator owns at time of death or, if none, the monetary equivalent of the gift. [141–144]

1. **Avoidance doctrines:** Because ademption is such a harsh doctrine, a number of avoidance doctrines have arisen: (1) classify the gift as general, not specific, so the ademption doctrine does not apply; (2) if the item is still in the testator's estate but it has changed, argue that the change is merely one in form, not substance, in which case the beneficiary is still entitled to the item; or (3) construe the will at time of death, not execution, and give the beneficiary the

matching item in the testator's estate at death even if that is not the item to which the testator was referring when the will was executed.

2. **Softening doctrines:** A couple of "modified intent" doctrines that soften the impact of ademption have also arisen: (1) if, as a result of the transfer of the item that was the subject of the specific gift, at death the testator is owed an outstanding balance, the outstanding balance goes to the beneficiary; and (2) if the specific gift was transferred while a conservator or durable power of attorney agent was acting for the testator, the beneficiary is entitled to the monetary equivalent of the net sale price.

3. **UPC:** The latest version of the UPC presumes that where a specific gift is no longer in the testator's estate, the gift should not be adeemed. If the testator has acquired property to replace the original specific gift, the beneficiary gets the replacement property. If the testator has not acquired replacement property, the beneficiary is entitled to the monetary equivalent of the specific gift unless that is inconsistent with the testator's intent.

C. **Stocks:** At common law, the beneficiary receives the benefit of any change in the stock between time of execution and time of death if the gift of stock was a specific gift. The modern trend presumes the testator's intent was to give a percentage interest in the company and, in the event of a stock split or dividend, the only way to satisfy the testator's intent is to give the beneficiary the benefit of the change in stock, even if the gift is a general gift. The UPC gives the beneficiary the benefit of any change in the stock initiated by a corporate entity long as at the time of execution the testator owned stock that matched the description of the gift of stock given in the will. [144–145]

D. **Satisfaction:** At common law, if a beneficiary under a will receives an inter vivos gift from the testator of the same type of property as the gift in the will and the beneficiary is the testator's child, a rebuttable presumption arises that the inter vivos gift counts against the child's testamentary gift. Under the modern trend/UPC approach, if the testator makes an inter vivos gift to any beneficiary under his or her will, the gift does not count against the beneficiary's testamentary gift unless there is a writing evidencing such an intent. If the donor creates the writing, it must be contemporaneous with the gift; if the donee creates the writing, it can be created anytime. [145]

E. **Exoneration of liens:** At common law, if a specific gift is burdened with debt (that is, a mortgage or lien), absent contrary intent expressed in the will, it is presumed that the beneficiary of the specific gift is entitled to have the debt completely paid off (out of the residuary typically) so that the beneficiary takes the gift free and clear of any debt. Under the modern trend, the beneficiary takes subject to the debt absent an express clause directing that the debt is to be satisfied before the gift is made. [145–146]

F. **Abatement:** If at time of death the testator has made more gifts than he or she has assets, the doctrine of abatement states that residuary gifts should be reduced first, general gifts second, and specific gifts last. Some states permit the court to vary from this order if abating the residuary first appears inconsistent with the testator's overall testamentary scheme (the testator intended the residuary taker to take the bulk of his or her probate property and abating the residuary clause would be inconsistent with this intent). [146]

C
A
P
S
U
L
E

S
U
M
M
A
R
Y

CHAPTER 6

WILL SUBSTITUTES AND PLANNING FOR INCAPACITY

I. OVERVIEW TO THE WILL SUBSTITUTES

A. **Introduction:** One can opt out of intestacy either (1) by executing a valid will, or (2) by creating a valid nonprobate instrument. Historically, there were only four ways a decedent could pass property at time of death by using nonprobate arrangements (inter vivos trust; life insurance contracts; joint tenancy; legal life estates and remainders), though the modern trend has been to expand the scope of the nonprobate arrangements. [154–155]

II. INTER VIVOS TRUSTS

A. **Introduction:** The trustee holds legal title. The beneficiaries hold equitable title. Even if the trust is revocable and the settlor is the life beneficiary, there is no need to transfer legal title upon the death of the settlor. The property placed in the trust inter vivos passes pursuant to the terms of the trust and is nonprobate property. [155–159]

1. **Revocability:** Under the traditional common law approach, if a trust is silent as to its revocability, it is irrevocable. If the trust is revocable and expressly provides for a particular method of revocation, only that method suffices. If the trust is revocable and does not provide for a particular method of revocation, any method that adequately demonstrates the settlor's intent to revoke suffices (including the revocation methods that apply to wills). Under the modern trend Uniform Trust Code, if a trust is revocable unless is expressly provides that it is irrevocable. If the trust is revocable and expressly provides for a particular method of revocation, that method is *not* exclusive unless the trust expressly so provides. And a subsequently executed will can expressly or implicitly revokes the trust, in whole or in part.

2. **Creditor's rights:** When a life tenant's interest is extinguished, creditors of the life tenant have no right to reach the property. Under the modern trend, however, where the settlor is the life beneficiary of a revocable trust, creditors of the settlor can reach the property in the trust, even after the settlor's death.

III. CONTRACTS WITH PAYABLE-ON-DEATH CLAUSES

A. **Common law:** At common law, the only type of contract with a payable-on-death (P.O.D.) clause that qualified as a valid nonprobate transfer was a life insurance contract (even though the effect of the contract is to pass the insurance proceeds upon the insured's death immediately to the beneficiary identified in the contract). [160]

B. **Modern trend:** The modern trend/UPC expands the life insurance nonprobate exception to include all third party beneficiary contracts with a P.O.D. clause. [160–163]

IV. MULTIPLE PARTY ACCOUNTS

A. Multiple party accounts: Historically, banks and brokerage houses forced parties interested in creating multiple party accounts to use the joint tenancy account even if that is not what the parties intended. There are three possible intents the parties may have had when they created the account: (1) a true joint tenancy, (2) an agency account, or (3) a P.O.D. account. Upon the death of one of the parties, the courts take extrinsic evidence of the parties' true intent and treat the property accordingly if there is clear and convincing evidence of an intent other than a true joint tenancy (although at common law, the P.O.D. intent is invalid so the property passes into the depositor's probate estate). Under the modern trend, the presumption is that inter vivos the parties own in proportion to their contributions, and at death there is a right of survivorship. The presumption, however, can be rebutted if there is clear and convincing evidence of a different intent, and that intent will control the disposition of the funds in the account. [163–166]

V. POUR-OVER WILLS AND INTER VIVOS TRUSTS

A. Introduction: A pour-over will and trust combination is the most common estate planning combination today, though the property being poured over to the trust under the terms of the will does not avoid probate. Where a will has a pour-over clause giving probate property to the trustee of the testator's separate trust, the pour-over clause must be validated under incorporation by reference, acts of independent significance, or the Uniform Testamentary Additions to Trusts Act (UTATA). [166–167]

B. Acts of independent significance: Under acts of independent significance, the trust must have its own significance independent of its effect upon the decedent's probate property—that is, the trust must be funded inter vivos and have property in it when the testator dies. Subsequent amendments to the trust can be given effect regardless of when they are created, but many jurisdictions subjected the trust to probate court supervision (at least as to the probate property being poured into the trust). [167–168]

C. Incorporation by reference: Under incorporation by reference, the trust *instrument* is being incorporated by reference into the will. The critical requirement is that the trust instrument must be in existence when the will is executed. The trust need not be funded inter vivos, but the trust that is created is a testamentary trust subject to probate court supervision for the duration of its life, and subsequent amendments to the trust are not valid absent a subsequent codicil to the will. [168]

D. UTATA: Under the most widely adopted version of UTATA, the pour-over clause is valid as long as (1) the will refers to the trust, (2) the trust terms are set forth in a separate writing other than the will, and (3) the settlor signed the trust instrument prior to or concurrently with the execution of the will (under the most recent version of UTATA, the trust instrument need only be signed before the settlor/testator dies, not before or concurrently with the will). The trust need not be funded inter vivos, yet it will not be subject to probate court supervision after it is created; and amendments to the trust can be given effect regardless of when they are created. [169–173]

VI. JOINT TENANCIES IN REAL PROPERTY

A. Joint tenancies: The right of survivorship means that upon the death of one joint tenant, his or her share is extinguished and the shares of the remaining joint tenants are recalculated. No property is passed at death, so nothing passes through probate. [173–174]

VII. PLANNING FOR THE POSSIBILITY OF INCAPACITY

A. Overview: Good estate planning includes planning for the possibility that the person may become incapacitated before he or she dies. With respect to property issues, the most common tool to deal with that possibility is the durable power of attorney. With respect to personal decisions about one's health care, the tools are either a living will (medical directive) or a durable power of attorney for health care decisions. [174–176]

CHAPTER 7

LIMITATIONS ON THE TESTAMENTARY POWER TO TRANSFER

I. SPOUSAL PROTECTION SCHEMES: AN OVERVIEW

A. Introduction: Every jurisdiction has several doctrines that protect surviving spouses (and, to some degree, children) that have the effect of limiting one's power to transfer one's property at death. A surviving spouse has a right (1) to support, and (2) to a share of the couple's marital property. [186]

II. SURVIVING SPOUSE'S RIGHT TO SUPPORT

A. Spousal support: In virtually every state a surviving spouse has a right for support (typically for life) under (1) the social security system, (2) private pension plans pursuant to ERISA (Employee Retirement Income Security Act of 1974), (3) the homestead exemption, (4) the personal property set-aside, and (5) the family allowance. [186–188]

III. SURVIVING SPOUSE'S RIGHT TO A SHARE OF THE MARITAL PROPERTY

A. Separate property vs. community property: The scope of a surviving spouse's right to a share of the deceased spouse's property depends on whether the jurisdiction follows the separate property approach (in which case the right is called the elective or forced share) or the community property approach (in which case the right is part of the community property doctrine). [188–190]

IV. THE ELECTIVE SHARE DOCTRINE: POLICY CONSIDERATIONS

A. The elective (or forced) share: Under the separate property system, although each spouse owns his or her earnings acquired during marriage as his or her separate property, upon death the elective share doctrine provides that the surviving spouse is entitled to a share of the deceased spouse's property regardless of the terms of the deceased spouse's will. How much property the surviving spouse is entitled to (typically one-third of the estate subject to the elective share) and what property is subject to the elective share varies from jurisdiction to jurisdiction. [190–192]

V. THE ELECTIVE SHARE: DOCTRINAL CONSIDERATIONS

A. Property subject to the elective share: More than any other part of the elective share doctrine, the jurisdictions are split over what property is subject to the elective share. [192]

B. Common law: At common law and in a number of states, the elective share entitles the surviving spouse to a share of the deceased spouse's probate estate, regardless of the terms of the deceased spouse's will. A spouse can avoid the elective share, however, by putting his or her assets into nonprobate arrangements. [192–193]

C. Modern trend: The modern trend is to expand the reach of the elective share to limit the deceased spouse's ability to avoid the doctrine by using nonprobate arrangements. The jurisdictions are split, however, over how best to identify when the elective share doctrine should be expanded to cover nonprobate transfers. [193–196]

    1. Illusory transfer test: Under the illusory transfer approach, the courts analyze whether the nonprobate arrangement really constituted an inter vivos transfer or whether the decedent retained such an interest (life estate, right to revoke, right to appoint) in the property that the transfer is more testamentary than inter vivos (and thus the property in question is subject to the elective share).

    2. Intent to defraud test: Under the intent to defraud test, the issue is whether the decedent intended to defraud the surviving spouse of his or her elective share rights in the property. The jurisdictions that follow the intent to defraud approach are split over which approach should be taken to the intent to defraud: a subjective approach (did the decedent *actually intend* to defraud the surviving spouse of his or her elective share rights in the property in question) or an objective approach (focusing on a variety of factors).

    3. Present donative intent test: Under the present donative intent test, the courts focus on whether the deceased spouse really had a present donative intent at the time he or she created the nonprobate transfer.

    4. 1969 UPC augmented estate approach: The surviving spouse is entitled to receive one-third of the deceased spouse's augmented estate. The augmented estate includes not only the decedent's probate estate, but also certain nonprobate and gratuitous inter vivos transfers made during the marriage: (i) any transfers where the deceased spouse retained the right to possession or income from the property, (ii) any transfers where the deceased spouse retained the power to revoke or the power to use or appoint (dispose of) the principal for his or her own benefit, (iii) any joint tenancies with anyone other than the surviving spouse, (iv) gifts to third parties within two years of the deceased spouse's death in excess of $3,000 per donee per year, and

(v) property given to the surviving spouse either inter vivos or via nonprobate transfers (including life estate interests in trusts). Life insurance proceeds to someone other than the surviving spouse are expressly excluded.

5. **1990 UPC marital property approach:** The surviving spouse starts out entitled to only 3 percent of the deceased spouse's augmented estate, and the percentage increases 2 to 3 percentage points a year, reaching 50 percent after 15 years of marriage. The augmented estate includes *both* spouses' property, including property the deceased spouse transferred before marriage if he or she retained substantial control over the property, and life insurance proceeds paid to parties other than the surviving spouse.

6. **New York approach:** The New York approach gives the surviving spouse $50,000 or one-third of the decedent's augmented estate. The New York augmented estate includes not only the decedent's probate estate but also (i) gifts causa mortis; (ii) gifts to third parties within one year of the deceased spouse's death in excess of $10,000; (iii) Totten trusts (saving account trusts); (iv) joint tenancies and tenancies by the entirety (real or personal), to the extent of the deceased spouse's contributions; (v) payable-on-death transfers; and (vi) inter vivos transfers where the deceased spouse retained the right to possession or income from the property, or the power to revoke or the power to use or appoint (dispose of) the principal for his or her own benefit. Property that the surviving spouse receives by virtue of the deceased spouse's death, be it from nonprobate transfers or probate transfers (will or intestacy), is credited against the surviving spouse's elective share.

D. **Funding with life estates:** Where a surviving spouse claims an elective share, the general rule is that the property given to the surviving spouse under the will counts first against the elective share (so as to minimize the disruptive effect the elective share has on the deceased spouse's estate plan). Where, however, the deceased spouse left the surviving spouse only a life estate interest (which arguably constitutes only "support" for life and not an outright "share"), most states will not count the life estate interest against the elective share. [196–197]

VI. COMMUNITY PROPERTY

A. **Basics:** Under the community property system, property acquired before marriage and property acquired by gift, descent, or devise during the marriage is each spouse's separate property. Property otherwise acquired by either spouse during the course of the marriage (typically earnings) is community property. Each spouse has an undivided one-half interest in each community property asset. Upon the death of a spouse, the surviving spouse owns his or her one-half of each community property asset outright, and the deceased spouse's half of each community property asset goes into his or her probate estate where he or she can devise it to anyone. [197–198]

B. **Migrating couples:** Migrating couples pose special problems because (1) property is characterized as separate property or community property at the time it is acquired according to the laws of the jurisdiction where the parties are domiciled at time of acquisition, (2) changing domicile does not change the characterization of property, and (3) the applicable time of death spousal protection approach depends on the couple's domicile at time of death. [198–199]

1. **Migrating from separate to community property:** Where a couple migrates from a separate property state to a community property state, the risk is that the surviving spouse will be underprotected. The spousal protection doctrine at time of death will be the community property

approach, but if the couple spent most of their marriage in the separate property jurisdiction the risk is that the couple's assets will be primarily, if not exclusively, separate property. Quasi-community property attempts to deal with this problem by providing that upon the spouse's death, his or her separate property that would have been characterized as community property if the couple had been domiciled in a community property jurisdiction when the property was acquired is characterized as quasi-community property and is treated like community property for distribution purposes. But not all of the community property jurisdictions recognize quasi-community property.

2. **Migrating from community to separate property:** Where a couple migrates from a community property state to a separate property state, the risk is that the surviving spouse will be overprotected. The spousal protection doctrine at time of death will be the elective share approach. The risk is that the surviving spouse will "double dip" in the spousal protection schemes. Upon the death of the first spouse, the surviving spouse will get his or her half of the community property outright, and the deceased spouse's half will go into probate where the surviving spouse can claim an elective share in the deceased spouse's probate property. The Uniform Disposition of Community Property Rights at Death Act provides that a deceased spouse's share of the community property is not subject to the elective share doctrine. But not all separate property jurisdictions have adopted the Act.

VII. THE OMITTED SPOUSE

A. **Omitted spouse doctrine:** Where an individual executes a valid will, thereafter marries, and thereafter dies without revoking or revising the will, a presumption arises that the testator did not intend to disinherit his or her new spouse. The presumption, however, is rebuttable if (1) the will expresses the intent to disinherit that spouse, (2) the testator provided for that spouse outside of the will and intended for the transfer to be in lieu of the spouse taking under the will, or (3) the spouse waived his or her right to claim a share of the deceased spouse's estate. If the presumption is not rebutted, the omitted spouse generally receives his or her intestate share of the testator's probate estate. [199]

B. **Scope:** The courts generally hold that (1) a general disinheritance clause is not sufficient to constitute an intent to disinherit that spouse, and (2) a gift in a will to a party who ends up being the decedent's spouse does not bar the omitted spouse doctrine unless the testator made the gift in contemplation of the beneficiary being his or her spouse. [199–200]

C. **UPC:** The UPC broadens the evidence that can be used to prove that the spouse's omission from the will was intentional to include (1) evidence from the will, (2) other evidence that the will was made in contemplation of the testator's marriage to the surviving spouse, or (3) a general provision in the will that it is effective notwithstanding any subsequent marriage. The UPC also limits funding of the omitted spouse's share to property not devised to the decedent's issue (1) who were born before the testator married the surviving spouse, and (2) who are also not issue of the surviving spouse. [200]

D. **Revocable trusts:** In some states the omitted spouse doctrine has been extended to cover both probate property and property in a revocable inter vivos trust created by the deceased spouse. [200–201]

VIII. THE OMITTED CHILD

A. Omitted child doctrine: Where an individual executes a valid will, thereafter has a child, and thereafter dies without revoking or revising his or her will, a presumption arises that the testator did not intend to disinherit the child. The presumption, however, is rebuttable if (1) the will expresses the intent to disinherit that child, (2) the testator provided for the child outside of the will and intended for that transfer to be in lieu of the child taking under the will, or (3) the testator had one or more children when the will was executed and devised substantially all of his or her estate to the other parent of the omitted child. As a general rule, the omitted child receives his or her intestate share. [201–202]

B. Children alive when will executed: Some states expand the scope of the classic omitted child doctrine to include children alive when the will was executed but not named in the will. Some states even cover omitted issue of a child who died before the testator. [201–202]

C. Evidence of intent to disinherit: Under the Missouri-type statute, the intent to disinherit the omitted child must come exclusively from the terms of the will. Under the Massachusetts-type statute, extrinsic evidence is admissible to help determine if the disinheritance was intentional. [202–203]

D. Accidentally overlooked child: Some states provide that if a testator fails to provide for a child in a will because the testator mistakenly believes that the child is dead, the child receives the share he or she would under the omitted child doctrine. Some states also cover a child not provided for in a will because the testator did not know about the child. [203]

E. UPC: The UPC omitted child statute applies only to children born or adopted after execution of the will. Evidence of the intent to disinherit is limited to the express terms of the will. If the testator had no children when he or she executed the will, the child is entitled to his or her intestate share unless the testator left substantially all of his or her property to the surviving spouse and the omitted child is a child of the surviving spouse, in which case the omitted child is not entitled to a share. If the testator had one or more children living when the will was executed and the testator devised property to one or more of the children, the omitted child's share comes out of the gift to the other children and is determined by calculating what the children would have taken if each child received an equal share of the gifts to the children. The UPC covers children omitted because the testator thought the child dead, but not children omitted because the testator did not know about them. [203–204]

F. Revocable trusts: In some states the omitted child doctrine has been extended to cover both probate property and property in a revocable inter vivos trust created by the deceased parent. [204]

CHAPTER 8

TRUSTS: OVERVIEW AND CREATION

I. INTRODUCTION: CONCEPTUAL OVERVIEW

A. Bifurcated gift: A trust is a bifurcated gift. One party (the settlor) gives property to a second party (the trustee) to hold and manage for the benefit of a third party (the beneficiary). The trustee holds legal title to the trust property and manages the trust property. The beneficiaries hold equitable title. The trustee owes a fiduciary duty to the beneficiaries to manage the trust property in their best interests. The same party can be settlor, trustee, and beneficiary as long as there is another co-trustee or beneficiary. A trust is created the moment it is funded. As a general rule, a trust will not fail for want of a trustee; the court will appoint a trustee if necessary. The trust is an ongoing gift, often lasting for decades. This means that the trust property is bifurcated between the income and principal, and the equitable interest typically is bifurcated between a beneficiary who holds the possessory estate (typically a life estate) and the beneficiaries who hold the future interest(s) (typically a remainder). [214–218]

II. REQUIREMENTS TO CREATE A VALID TRUST

A. Trust requirements: To have a valid trust: (1) the settlor must have the intent to create a trust, (2) the trust must be funded, (3) the trust must have ascertainable beneficiaries, and (4) the terms of the trust may have to be in writing. [218–219]

B. Intent: The intent to create a trust arises anytime one party transfers property to a second party for the benefit of a third party. Use of any pertinent term of art (***trustee, trust,*** or ***in trust***) generally is deemed to express the intent. [219–221]

    1. Precatory trust: A precatory trust is where a donor makes a gift to a donee with the "wish" or "hope" that the donee will use the property for the benefit of another. ***A precatory trust is not a trust.*** There is no legal obligation to use the property for the benefit of the other party, only a moral obligation.

    2. Gifts that fail for want of delivery: Where a party makes a gratuitous promise to make a gift in the future but then dies before properly transferring the property, as a general rule the failed gift (for want of delivery) cannot be saved by converting the intent to make a gift in the future into a present declaration of an intent to create a trust with the declarant as trustee.

C. Funding: A trust is funded when property is transferred to the trust/trustee. Virtually any property interests except for future profits and expectancies qualify as adequate property interests. [221–224]

    1. Declaration of trust: Where the settlor is the trustee, if the trust property is personal property, the modern trend general rule is the settlor's expression of intent also transfers the property to the trust. No separate act is necessary to fund the trust. If the property being transferred to the trust is real property, as long as the declaration of trust is in writing and adequately references the real property, the modern trust deems the property transferred to the trust even without any additional writing.

    2. Deed of trust: Where a third party is trustee, the first key is how the deed of trust was expressed, oral or in writing. If oral, there must be physical or symbolic delivery of the property to the trustee. If written, and the writing expressly references the property subject to the trust, the jurisdictions are split as to whether this also transfers the property in question to the trustee or whether there must be a separate act of delivery.

D. Ascertainable beneficiaries: Beneficiaries are ascertainable if they are identified by name or if there is an objective method of identifying the beneficiaries. The only exception to the requirement that the beneficiaries must be ascertainable is where a trust is created for unborn children. In that case, the courts will monitor the trustee's actions. [224–227]

Honorary trusts: Where a private trust would otherwise fail for want of ascertainable beneficiaries, but the purpose of the trust is such that it is impossible to have ascertainable beneficiaries (for example, care of a pet or gravesite) and the purpose is specific and honorable, and not capricious or illegal, under the honorary trust doctrine the courts will permit the trust to continue as long as the "trustee" agrees to honor the terms of the trust. (Technically, such trusts are subject to the Rule against Perpetuities and that may cause the trust to fail, but under the modern trend to the Rule against Perpetuities courts usually find a way around the Rule against Perpetuities problem—at least for 21 years.)

E. **Writing:** The terms of the trust must be in writing if (1) the trust is an inter vivos trust that includes real property, or (2) the trust is a testamentary trust. [227–229]

1. **Remedy—failed inter vivos trust:** Where a settlor executes a deed transferring real property to a trustee, and the settlor and trustee orally agree on the terms of the inter vivos trust but the deed is silent as to the trust, the trust fails for want of writing. At common law, the "trustee" is permitted to keep the real property as his or her own because strict application of the Statute of Frauds bars evidence of the oral trust agreement to vary the terms of the deed. Under the modern trend, a constructive trust is imposed on the "trustee" to prevent unjust enrichment (particularly where the "trustee" procured the transfer as a result of fraud or undue influence or stood in a confidential relationship with the donor), and the trustee will be ordered to transfer the property to the intended beneficiaries.

2. **Remedy—failed testamentary trust:** Where a beneficiary under a will agrees to hold the property in question as a trustee for the benefit of others, but the terms of the testamentary trust are not in the will (or incorporated by reference), the testamentary trust fails for want of writing. Under the common law approach, the key is whether the failed testamentary trust is a secret or semi-secret trust. A secret trust is where the face of the will makes no reference to the testator's intent that the beneficiary identified in the will was to take in a fiduciary capacity as a trustee and not as an ordinary beneficiary. Where the failed testamentary trust is a secret trust, a constructive trust is imposed and the property is ordered distributed to the intended beneficiaries. A semi-secret trust is where the will hints at or expresses the testator's intent that the beneficiary is to take for the benefit of others, but the identity of the trust beneficiaries and/ or the terms of the trust are not set forth in a writing that can be given effect. Under the traditional common law approach, where a semi-secret trust failed, a resulting trust is imposed on the trustee and the property is ordered returned to the testator's probate estate. Under the modern trend, a constructive trust is typically imposed on both a secret and a semi-secret trust.

3. **Remedial trusts:** Constructive trusts and resulting trusts are remedial trusts that arise by operation of law as a matter of equity, and they are not subject to the traditional trust requirements. Constructive trusts typically arise and are imposed by courts to prevent unjust enrichment. The court will order the party currently holding title to the property to transfer the property to the party that the court concludes, as a matter of equity, is entitled to the property. Resulting trusts arise whenever a trust fails in whole or in part. The court will order the property transferred back to the settlor (or the settlor's estate if the settlor is dead).

CHAPTER **9**

TRUSTS: LIFE AND TERMINATION

I. LIFE OF TRUST: EXTENT OF BENEFICIARIES' INTERESTS

A. Trust life: Once a trust is validly created, the primary issue during the life of the trust is the extent of the beneficiaries' interest in the trust. Each beneficiary's interest can be either mandatory or discretionary, and each beneficiary's interest can be in the income and/or the principal. [236]

B. Mandatory trust: If the trustee must distribute all of the income to a beneficiary on a regular basis, the trust is a mandatory trust. [236]

C. Discretionary trust: If the trustee has discretion over when to distribute the income and/or principal, the trust is a discretionary trust. Because of the trustee's fiduciary duty to the beneficiaries, however, under a discretionary trust, the trustee still has a duty to inquire and a duty to act reasonably and in good faith in exercising his or her discretion. Courts generally hold that attempts at giving a trustee absolute or sole discretion are invalid (for that would no longer be a trust), but such language usually is construed as removing the duty that the trustee act reasonably—the trustee need only act in good faith. In exercising his or her discretion, the trustee should also take into consideration the settlor's intent as to the purpose of the trust or the purpose of the beneficiary's interest. (For example, a discretionary trust for a beneficiary's "comfortable support and maintenance" has become a term of art meaning that the beneficiary is to be kept at the standard of living he or she had upon becoming a beneficiary.) [236–239]

D. Spray/sprinkle trust: Where the trustee must distribute all of the income among a group of beneficiaries and the trustee has discretion as to how much each beneficiary is to take, the trust is known as a spray or sprinkle trust. [239]

II. LIFE OF TRUST: CREDITORS' RIGHTS

A. Creditors' rights: A creditor's rights depend on whether the creditor is a creditor of (1) a beneficiary other than the setttlor, or (2) a beneficiary who is also the settlor. [239]

B. Creditors of beneficiary (who is not the settlor): A creditor of a beneficiary steps into the beneficiary's shoes and acquires the exact same rights the beneficiary has, no more and no less. If the beneficiary's interest is mandatory, the creditors have the same right to receive the property. If the beneficiary's interest is discretionary, the creditors cannot force the trustee to exercise his or her discretion. [239–240]

C. Discretionary trust: Under the traditional approach, if a beneficiary's interest in a trust was discretionary, a creditor of the beneficiary could not reach the interest unless the creditor could show that it was an abuse of discretion not to make the distribution. In addition, in some states a creditor can get a court order that if and when the trustee decides to make a distribution, the trustee must make the payment to the creditor. The Restatement (Third) of Trusts adopts that approach, but the Uniform Trust Code provides that a creditor of a beneficiary may not compel a distribution that is subject to the trustee's discretion, regardless of the presence or absence of a spendthrift clause, even if there is a standard limiting the discretion or the trustee has abused the discretion, unless (1) the trustee has not complied with a standard of distribution or there has been an abuse of discretion; and (2) the distribution is ordered to satisfy a judgment or court order against the beneficiary for support or maintenance of a child, spouse, or former spouse. [240–241]

D. **Spendthrift trust:** If the settlor includes a spendthrift clause (a clause that prohibits beneficiaries from transferring their interest) in the trust, the general rule is that the beneficiary's creditors cannot step into the beneficiary's shoes—they cannot reach the beneficiary's interest in the trust. [241–243]

Exceptions: Not all creditors are subject to spendthrift clauses. As a general rule, there are four categories of creditors who are not subject to spendthrift clauses: children entitled to child support, ex-spouses entitled to alimony, creditors who provide basic necessities, and governmental entities entitled to taxes. These creditors can still step into the beneficiary's shoes and reach the beneficiary's interest to the extent it is mandatory, but they cannot force a trustee to exercise his or her discretion in favor of them. For the Uniform Trust Code approach, please see the last sentence of the prior paragraph C.

E. **Creditors of beneficiary (who is also the settlor):** It is against public policy to permit one to shield one's assets from creditors. Accordingly, creditors of a beneficiary who is also the settlor can reach the beneficiary's interest in the trust to the full extent that the trustee could use the trust property for the benefit of the beneficiary/settlor (that is, the creditors can reach the property whether the beneficiary/settlor's interest is mandatory or discretionary). Moreover, spendthrift clauses in favor of a beneficiary who is also the settlor are null and void. [243–245]

Self-settled asset protection trust: A handful of states recognize self-settled asset protection trusts in favor of a beneficiary who is also a settlor if (1) the trust is irrevocable, (2) the trust interest is discretionary, and (3) the trust was not created in fraud of creditors.

III. TRUST MODIFICATION AND TERMINATION

A. **Introduction:** A trust ends naturally when all of the trust principal is disbursed pursuant to the terms of the trust. Under special circumstances, however, the terms of the trust may be modified or the trust may be terminated prematurely. (The discussion implicitly assumes an irrevocable trust. If the trust is revocable, all that is necessary to modify or terminate the trust is for the settlor to revoke the trust.) [245–246]

B. **Settlor and beneficiaries consent:** If the settlor and all the beneficiaries consent, the trust can be modified or terminated, regardless of the trustee's objections. [246]

C. **Trustee and beneficiaries consent:** If the trustee and all the beneficiaries consent, the trust can be modified or terminated, regardless of the settlor's objections. [246]

D. **Beneficiaries consent but trustee objects:** Where all the beneficiaries consent but the trustee objects, the common law courts developed doctrines that permit the beneficiaries to overcome the trustee's objections under limited circumstances. [246–251]

1. **Modification:** At common law, courts order the terms of a trust to be modified if (1) all the beneficiaries consent, and (2) there is an unforeseen change in circumstances that materially frustrates settlor's intent. The trust is modified to promote the settlor's presumed intent under the circumstances. At common law, the courts construe what constitutes an "unforeseen" change and what constitutes "materially frustrating" very narrowly to protect settlor's intent. The modern trend construes those terms broadly to give the beneficiaries greater control over

the trust property. The mere fact that a proposed modification would be more advantageous to one or more beneficiaries, however, is not enough to warrant modifying a trust, even if all the beneficiaries consent. The UTC takes the modern trend further. First, the UTC permits modification if there are changes not anticipated by the settlor, even if the change does not defeat or substantially impair the settlor's intent. In addition, the UTC authorizes modification even if not all the beneficiaries consent if (1) the court could have been modified if all the beneficiaries had consented, and (2) the interests of the non-consenting beneficiaries are adequately protected.

2. **Termination—Claflin doctrine:** At common law, under the Claflin doctrine, courts order a trust to be terminated prematurely, even if the trustee objects, if (1) all the beneficiaries consent, and (2) there is no unfulfilled material purpose. What constitutes an "unfulfilled material purpose" is fact sensitive and turns on the wording and purpose of each trust, but there is a handful of trust purposes that almost all courts have held constitute an unfulfilled material purpose: (1) discretionary trusts, (2) spendthrift trusts, (3) support trusts, and (4) trusts where the property is not to be distributed to the beneficiary until he or she reaches a specific age. The Restatement (Third) of Property, Donative Transfers, termination of the trust over the objection of the trustee, even if there is an unfulfilled material purpose, as long as (1) all the beneficiaries consent, and (2) the court determines the reasons to terminate outweigh the unfulfilled material purpose.

3. **Securing consent of all beneficiaries:** Where some of the beneficiaries are minors or are unborn, one way to attempt to secure their consent is to petition the court to appoint a guardian ad litem to represent the interests of the minor or unborn beneficiaries. An alternative way to attempt to secure the consent of minor or unborn beneficiaries is under the doctrine of virtual representation. If the interests of the minor or unborn beneficiaries are virtually identical to those of living adult beneficiaries, a court may permit the latter to represent the interests of the former.

CHAPTER 10

TRUST ADMINISTRATION AND THE TRUSTEE'S DUTIES

I. TRUSTEE'S POWERS

A. Common law: At common law, the office of trustee has no inherent powers, only those that are either expressly granted to the trustee by the deed or declaration of trust or those implicitly provided in light of the express trust powers and purpose. [258–259]

B. Modern trend: At first, to simplify the granting of trust powers, states adopted long lists of statutory powers that the settlor could incorporate by reference to the statutory provision. More recently, the trustee has been granted automatically all the powers a prudent person would need to manage the trust in light of its purpose. [259–260]

II. DUTY OF LOYALTY

A. **Scope:** The trustee owes a duty of absolute loyalty to the beneficiaries. Everything the trustee does must be done in the best interests of the beneficiaries. The duty of loyalty means that the trustee must act reasonably and in good faith. [260–262]

1. **Duty against self-dealing:** Self-dealing arises where the trustee (or members of the trustee's family) transact with the trust. The trustee has an inherent conflict of interest where there is self-dealing. Where a trustee engages in self-dealing, an irrebuttable presumption of breach of the duty of loyalty arises. Under the "no further inquiry" rule, the reasonableness of the transaction and/or the trustee's good faith are irrelevant. Where, however, (1) the trust authorizes self-dealing, or (2) all the beneficiaries consent after full disclosure, then self-dealing is permitted if the transaction is reasonable and the trustee is acting in good faith.

2. **Uniform Trust Code:** For the most part the Uniform Trust Code adopts the traditional approach to self-dealing, except transactions by a trustee with a close relative or with the trustee's lawyer are no longer absolutely forbidden but are only presumptively voidable. If the trustee can prove that the transaction was objectively fair and reasonable, and not affected by a conflict, the trustee is not liable.

3. **Duty to avoid conflicts of interest:** A conflict of interest arises where the trust deals with another party with whom the trustee has an interest that may affect the trustee's assessment of the proposed transaction. The "no further inquiry" rule does not apply, but the transaction must be reasonable and the trustee must act in good faith.

III. DUTY OF PRUDENCE—TRUST INVESTMENTS

A. **Traditional approach—list of safe investments:** Traditionally, the presumed purpose of a trust was to preserve the trust property. Historically, the courts and legislatures would identify categories of investments that were presumed appropriate, but even then an investment in a particular entity or activity on the list had to be otherwise reasonable and proper. Moreover, each investment decision was analyzed in isolation. The risk level of other investments and the profits generated by other investments were irrelevant in assessing the propriety of a particular investment. [262–263]

B. **Model Prudent Man Investment Act:** The act, first adopted in 1940, abolished statutory lists and authorized any investment that a prudent man would make, barring only "speculative" investments. The most common statement of the prudent person standard is that the trustee should invest with the same care as a prudent person would with respect to his or her own property, taking into consideration the dual goals of preserving the principal while generating a reasonable stream of income. [263]

C. **Modern trend—Uniform Prudent Investor Act:** The modern trend view is that a trust is a vehicle for holding and managing assets. The modern trend, as reflected in the Restatement (Third) of Trusts and the Uniform Prudent Investor Act, adopts the prudent investor approach. The prudent investor approach requires the trustee to spread the risk of loss by diversifying the trust investments. The prudent investor approach abolishes the duty to segregate and permits pooling of trust funds to reduce transaction costs and to achieve economies of scale. The prudent investor approach adopts the portfolio approach to assessing trust investments. The performance of the trust's investments is assessed on a portfolio, not an individual, basis—the key is an acceptable level of risk at an aggregate level, not an investment-by-investment assessment of the level of risk. The focus is on total rate of return, not individual investment or investment decisions, or the return on a particular investment. [263–268]

D. **Delegation of duties:** Traditionally, a trustee could not delegate those activities and responsibilities that he or she could reasonably be expected to perform. Trustees could, however, delegate ministerial activities (those that do not require the exercise of discretion). [268–269]

1. **Modern trend duty to delegate:** The modern trend recognizes that some trustees are unqualified to undertake certain responsibilities inherent in holding and managing trust property—in particular, the duty to invest trust property properly. The Uniform Prudent Investor Act and the Restatement (Third) of Trusts provide that the trustee must act in the best interests of the beneficiaries in deciding whether to delegate discretionary responsibilities, including investment making responsibilities, and to whom to delegate them.

2. **Duty to supervise:** Where the trustee does delegate either ministerial or discretionary responsibilities, the trustee still has a duty to select carefully, to give adequate instructions, and an ongoing duty to monitor and supervise the actions of the agents to whom the responsibilities have been delegated.

IV. IMPARTIALITY—ALLOCATING PRINCIPAL AND INCOME

A. **Duty of impartiality:** A trustee has a duty of loyalty to all the beneficiaries. The trustee must balance the competing interests of the different beneficiaries. The trustee has a duty to produce a reasonable income for the life beneficiaries while preserving the principal for the remaindermen. [269–272]

1. **Principal and income allocation:** Historically whether property acquired by a trust was allocated to principal or income turned on the *form* of the property acquired. The modern trend (as reflected in the 1997 Principal and Income Act) modifies the traditional approach. Because the focus is on total return, and not on income vs. principal, the trustee is authorized to reassign some of the return (the power of equitable adjustment), if necessary, to make sure that both types of beneficiaries are treated fairly.

2. **Unitrust:** Under a unitrust, the life beneficiaries are entitled to a specified percentage of the value of the trust principal each year so there is no need to distinguish income from principal. All property generated is assigned to principal, and, at the appropriate intervals, the specified percentage of the trust principal is distributed to the appropriate beneficiaries.

V. SUB-DUTIES RELATING TO CARE OF TRUST PROPERTY

A. **Duty to take proper care:** The trustee must take proper care of the trust property. The trustee has (1) a duty to take secure possession of the trust property in a timely manner, (2) a duty to care for and maintain the trust property, (3) a duty to segregate the trust property from other property (particularly the trustee's own property—duty not to commingle), and (4) a duty to earmark (clearly identify the trust property as trust property). (At common law, if the trustee breaches the duty to segregate and earmark, the trustee is strictly liable. Under the modern trend, the breach must cause the damage before the trustee is liable.) [272]

VI. DUTY TO INFORM AND ACCOUNT

A. Duty to inform: The trustee has a duty to provide beneficiaries with complete and accurate information when requested. Even where the settlor expressly authorizes withholding information, at a minimum the beneficiary is entitled to information about his or her interest in the trust. Where the trustee proposes selling a significant portion of the trust assets, the trustee must notify the beneficiaries in advance unless the value of the assets is readily ascertainable or disclosure is seriously detrimental to the beneficiaries' interests. [272–273]

B. Duty to account: The trustee has a duty to account on a regular basis so that the trustee's performance can be assessed. If the trust is a testamentary trust, the trustee has a duty to account to the probate court. If the trust is an inter vivos trust, the trust may authorize the trustee to account directly to the beneficiaries. As a general rule, proper accounting starts the statute of limitations on any claim against the trustee for actions taken by the trustee that are disclosed in the accounting. If the trustee files a fraudulent accounting and the beneficiaries later discover the fraud, the beneficiaries are not barred from reopening the accounting. Under the doctrine of constructive fraud, where an accounting makes factual representations that turn out to be false, if the trustee makes the representations honestly and in good faith but fails to undertake reasonable efforts to ascertain the accuracy of the factual representations, such false factual representations in the accounting constitute a "constructive" or "technical" fraud and provide grounds for reopening an otherwise properly allowed accounting. [273–275]

CHAPTER 11

CHARITABLE TRUSTS

I. CHARITABLE PURPOSE

A. Charitable purposes: A charitable trust is one that has a charitable purpose. A purpose is charitable if it is for (a) the relief of poverty, (b) the advancement of education, (c) the advancement of religion, (d) the promotion of health, (e) governmental or municipal purposes, or (f) any other purpose the accomplishment of which is beneficial to the community at large. Benevolent trusts (trusts that perform "kind acts") are not charitable trusts unless they accomplish one of the specific charitable purposes. [281–282]

B. Benefits: There are two principal advantages, from a trust law perspective, of classifying a trust as a charitable trust: [282–283]

1. Not subject to the Rule against Perpetuities: Because charitable trusts serve charitable purposes for the community at large, charitable trusts are not subject to the Rule against Perpetuities.

2. No ascertainable beneficiaries requirement: Because charitable trusts have to serve the community at large, or at least a good segment of the community at large, there is no requirement that the trust have ascertainable beneficiaries. In fact, the trust cannot have ascertainable beneficiaries because that is inconsistent with the idea of the trust benefiting the community at large (or a subset of the community at large).

II. CY PRES

A. **Rule statement:** Where a trust with a general charitable purpose expresses a particular charitable purpose, and it becomes impossible, impractical, or illegal to carry out that particular charitable purpose, rather than imposing a resulting trust, courts modify the particular trust purpose to another particular charitable purpose within the trust's general charitable purpose. The Uniform Trust Code also authorizes application of cy pres if the particular charitable purpose has become wasteful – where the available funds so exceed the needs of the particular purpose that continued use for just that purpose would be wasteful. [283–285]

B. **Administrative deviation:** If accomplishing the trust purpose becomes impossible or impractical for administrative reasons, the courts are empowered to order, and should apply, administrative deviation to remove the obstacle before modifying the settlor's intent under cy pres. [285]

III. ENFORCING THE TERMS OF A CHARITABLE TRUST

A. **Enforcing charitable trust terms:** Each state's attorney general has the duty of supervising the administration of each charitable trust. Because most state attorneys general's offices are overwhelmed, many courts have granted standing to members of the community who have a special interest in the trust to bring suit against the charitable trustee for breach of trust. Increasingly, settlors of charitable trusts (and donors of charitable gifts) are being granted standing to enforce the terms of the gift. [285–286]

CHAPTER 12

POWERS OF APPOINTMENT: DISCRETIONARY FLEXIBILITY

I. INTRODUCTION

A. **Power of appointment:** An important tool that estate planners can use to add flexibility to the administration of a trust is a power of appointment. A power of appointment is similar to a power to revoke in the hands of a beneficiary other than the settlor. A power of appointment gives the donee the power to override the distributive terms of the trust and to direct the trustee to distribute some or all of the trust res outright to the appointees. A power is discretionary and imposes no fiduciary duty on the party who holds as a general rule. The power adds flexibility in that if circumstances change, the party holding the power of appointment has the discretionary power to change the distributive provisions of the trust by overriding the original terms (but the party also has the power to override the original distributive provisions even if circumstances do not change). [290–293]

B. **General power:** A power is a general power of appointment if the group of appointees in whose favor the power can be exercised (that is, the property can be appointed to) includes either the donee, the donee's estate, the donee's creditors, or creditors of the donee's estate. [291–293]

C. **Special power:** A power is a special power of appointment if the group of appointees in whose favor the power can be exercised excludes the donee, the donee's estate, the donee's creditors, *and* creditors of the donee's estate. [291–293]

D. Inter vivos vs. testamentary: In creating a power, the donor can also specify when the power may be exercised—only inter vivos, only upon the donee's death (testamentary), or either. [291–293]

E. Creditors' rights: If the power of appointment is a special power, the donee is treated like an agent, and creditors of the donee have no right to reach the property subject to the power. If the power of appointment is a general power, the donor's creation of the power is treated like an offer to make a gift to the donee. If the donee exercises the power, the donee is treated as having accepted the gift, and creditors of the donee can reach the appointed property regardless of to whom the property was appointed. If, however, the donee does not exercise the general power of appointment, as a general rule creditors of the donee cannot reach the property subject to the power. (In a few states, creditors of a donee holding a general power of appointment can reach the property subject to the power, even if the power is not exercised.) [291–293]

II. CREATING A POWER OF APPOINTMENT

A. Intent to create: If one party intends to give another party a discretionary power to appoint property, the first party has created a power of appointment. No technical words are necessary to create a power. [293–294]

B. Power to consume: If a beneficiary is given a life estate and a power to consume, the power to consume is deemed a general power of appointment unless it is limited to an ascertainable standard relating to health, education, support, or maintenance of the holder of the power to consume. [294]

III. EXERCISING A POWER OF APPOINTMENT

A. Exercise: A power of appointment is exercised anytime the donee intends to exercise the power. The instrument creating the power may stipulate how express the donee must be to exercise the power. [294]

B. Testamentary powers and residuary clauses: Where a testator holds a testamentary power of appointment and his or her residuary clause makes no express reference to a power of appointment (standard residuary clause), the jurisdictions are split as to whether the residuary clause exercises the power. [294–296]

1. **Majority rule:** The majority rule is that a standard residuary clause does not exercise either a general or special testamentary power of appointment, though some jurisdictions hold that where the testator held a testamentary power of appointment there is sufficient ambiguity to admit extrinsic evidence to help determine whether the testator intended the residuary clause to exercise the power.

2. **Minority rule:** In a minority of states, a standard residuary clause adequately expresses the testator's intent to exercise a general power of appointment that the testator held, but not a special power of appointment.

3. **UPC approach:** A standard residuary clause expresses the intent to exercise a power of appointment the testator held only if (1) the power is a general power of appointment and the creating instrument does not contain an express gift over in the event the power is not

exercised, or (2) the testator's will manifests an intention to include the property subject to the power.

4. **Blended residuary clause:** Many residuary clauses include a generic reference to any power of appointment the testator may hold ("I hereby give all my property, including any property over which I hold a power of appointment, to . . ."). Where the instrument creating the power does not require a specific reference to the power, the jurisdictions are split over whether such a generic reference is sufficient to exercise the power. The UPC requires the reference to be specific; such a blended residuary clause is not enough in and of itself.

5. **Lapse and anti-lapse:** Where the testamentary power is properly exercised but the appointee predeceases the donee, application of anti-lapse turns on the type of power. As a general rule, where the power is a general power of appointment, the courts apply anti-lapse—if the appointee meets the degree of relationship with the donee. Where the power is a special power of appointment, the traditional approach is not to apply anti-lapse if the issue of the predeceased appointee are not eligible members under the instrument creating the power, but the modern trend applies anti-lapse even if the issue of the predeceased appointee are not express members of the original class of eligible objects of appointment.

C. **Limitations:** Although general powers of appointment can be exercised as the donee sees fit (outright, in trust, or even subject to a new power of appointment), the general rule is that absent authority in the instrument creating the power to do otherwise, the holder of a special power of appointment must appoint the property outright. The modern trend, however, permits the holder of a special power to appoint either in trust or subject to a new power as long as both the donee and the objects of the new power were included in the original class of possible appointees. [296–297]

D. **Attempted appointment that fails:** Where the donee expresses the intent to exercise the power of appointment, but the expression is ineffective for one reason or another, the appointive property in question will be treated as if the power were not exercised unless it is saved by either allocation or capture. [297]

1. **Allocation:** Where the holder of a special power creates an instrument (typically a will) that purports to blend the appointive property with his or her own property (typically a blended residuary clause) and then gives all of the combined property to a group of beneficiaries, the allocation doctrine (1) "unblends" the property, and (2) allocates the appointive property first and only to eligible appointees and then allocates the rest of the holder's property as necessary to try to carry out the distribution scheme expressed in the instrument. This ensures that only eligible appointees take the appointive property while trying to give effect to the holder's distributive intent. Any appointive property that is not distributed to eligible takers under this doctrine passes as if the power had not been exercised. [297]

2. **Capture:** Where the holder of a general power creates an instrument (typically a will) that purports to blend the appointive property with his or her own property (typically a blended residuary clause) and then gives all of the combined property to a group of beneficiaries, if one or more of the gifts fail, the holder of the appointive property is deemed to have appointed the failed gift to him- or herself (or probate estate if the instrument is a will), and the appointive property is distributed accordingly. [297]

IV. RELEASING A POWER OF APPOINTMENT

A. Release: A donee may release a power of appointment, in whole or in part (either in whose favor the property may be appointed or when the power may be exercised). [297–298]

B. Inter vivos exercise of testamentary power vs. release: A testamentary power of appointment is one that can be exercised only upon the donee's death. An inter vivos attempt at exercising the power is invalid, as is an inter vivos contract as to how the donee will exercise the power at death. Where, however, the effect of the inter vivos contract is substantially the same as the effect of a release of the power, many courts will enforce the agreement not as a contract but as an inter vivos release of the testamentary power. [298]

V. FAILURE TO EXERCISE A POWER OF APPOINTMENT

A. Failure to exercise: If the donee fails to exercise the power of appointment, the appointive property is distributed pursuant to the donor's instructions in the event the power is not exercised. Where the donor has not made express provision for such an event, the property is be returned to the donor (or the donor's estate), unless the power is a special power of appointment to an ascertainable limited group, in which case the property may be distributed equally among the possible appointees if the court finds that was the donor's implied intent. [298–299]

CHAPTER 13

CONSTRUING TRUSTS: FUTURE INTERESTS

I. FUTURE INTERESTS

A. Overview: Almost invariably, the equitable interests in a trust are some combination of a possessory estate and future interest(s). A possessory estate is the right to possess the property right now; a future interest is the present right to possess and enjoy the property in the future. There are a number of construction issues that can arise in creating possessory estates and future interests. [306]

B. Future interest in grantor: If the grantor holds the future interest, the interest must be a reversion, a possibility of reverter, or a right of entry. The most common is the reversion—it follows a life estate, a fee tail, or a term of years where the future interest is expressly or implicitly retained by the grantor. [306–307]

C. Future interests in grantee: If the grantee holds the future interest, the interest must be a vested remainder, a contingent remainder, or an executory interest. The most common is the remainder—it follows a life estate, a fee tail, or a term of years where the future interest is given expressly to a party other than the grantor. A remainder is contingent unless it is vested; it is vested if (1) the holder is ascertainable, and (2) there is no express condition precedent (expressed in the same clause creating the remainder or the preceding clause) that the holder must satisfy before he or she has the right to take possession. [307–309]

II. PREFERENCE FOR VESTED REMAINDERS

A. Introduction: The common law courts favor construing an ambiguous remainder as vested as opposed to contingent. Vested remainders have a number of benefits over contingent remainders. [309]

B. Destructibility: At common law, if a contingent remainder does not vest before or at the moment the preceding finite estate ends, the contingent remainder is destroyed. (The modern trend abolishes the destructibility of contingent remainders doctrine.) Vested remainders are never subject to the doctrine. [309–310]

C. Accelerating into possession: Vested remainders are entitled to immediate possession regardless of how or when the preceding estate ends. At common law, a contingent remainder cannot become possessory until all of the express condition precedents are satisfied, and if the contingent remainder does not vest in time, it is destroyed under the destructibility of contingent remainders doctrine. [310–311]

Disclaimers: If a life tenant disclaims, under the common law approach, whether a remainder accelerates into possession turns on whether the remainder is contingent or vested. Under the modern trend, some courts have held that it depends on the testator/settlor's probable intent if he or she had known that the life tenant would disclaim. To reduce the high costs of administration associated with this rule, some disclaimer statutes expressly provide that the disclaiming party is treated as if he or she predeceased the decedent, and whether a remainder accelerates into possession depends on the effect of treating the disclaimant so.

D. Transferability: At common law, vested remainders are transferable but contingent remainders are not. Under the modern trend, both vested and contingent remainders are transferable. [311]

Transmissibility: If a party holding a remainder dies before the end of the preceding estate, the remainder passes to the remainderman's probate estate where he or she can devise it or it will pass to his or her heirs. (This rule, however, presumes that the remainder was not destroyed under the destructibility of contingent remainders when the remainderman died.)

Preference for early vesting: Where the language in an instrument is ambiguous as whether the remainder is to vest upon the death of the transferor or the death of the life tenant, the preference is to construe the language so that the remainder vests upon the death of the transferor/testator. [311–315]

1. **Remainderman predeceases life tenant:** If the remainderman predeceases the life tenant, at common law the remainder interest passes into the remainderman's probate estate where it is devisible and inheritable. Under the modern trend, lapse and anti-lapse applies where the remainderman predeceases the life tenant.

2. **Express survival requirement:** Where a grantor includes an express survival requirement, and the language is ambiguous as to whether the remainderman must survive the grantor, the life tenant, or one or more remaindermen, it is a question of grantor's intent. More often than not, however, the courts construe the language as requiring the party in question to survive to the moment he or she is entitled to possession.

3. **Implied survival requirement:** Courts tend to imply a survival requirement where a gift is to the grantor's heirs, issue, descendants, or similar "multiple-generation" gifts, but not where the gift is a "single-generation" gift (that is, to children or siblings).

4. **"Die without issue" divesting condition:** Where a remainderman's interest is expressly divested if he or she "dies without issue," but the instrument is ambiguous as to whether it applies only if the remainderman dies before the life tenant or whenever the remainderman dies, absent evidence of the grantor's preference the courts tend to construe the divesting condition as applying only if the remainderman dies before the life tenant.

5. **Rules in Clobberie's Case:** Clobberie's Case established three rules of construction concerning gifts with ambiguous language delaying delivery: (1) where the gift is "all the income to [the beneficiary's name], with principal to be paid when he or she reaches a specific age or upon marriage," if the beneficiary dies before marrying or reaching the specified age, his or her interest is transmissible; (2) where the gift is "to [the beneficiary's name] at [a specific age]," if the beneficiary dies before reaching that age the gift fails; and (3) where the gift is "to [the beneficiary's name], to be paid when the beneficiary reaches [a specific age]," if the beneficiary dies before reaching that age, his or her interest is transmissible.

6. **UPC approach:** The UPC has advocated applying a lapse/anti-lapse approach to *all* future interests in trusts (revocable or irrevocable), unless the instrument expressly provides otherwise. (This proposal has been widely criticized and has not been widely adopted.)

III. CLASS GIFTS

A. **Class gifts:** Where the possessory interest in the income is given to a class, a variety of construction issues can arise. [316]

B. **Income to class, single member dies:** A rebuttable presumption arises that the gift to the class is in joint tenancy with right of survivorship such that the income is to be redistributed among the surviving members of the class. The presumption is rebutted if the instrument expresses a contrary intent, either expressly or implicitly. The Restatement (Third) Property, however, rejects the traditional approach and presumes that the issue of deceased class member should receive the income. [316–317]

C. **Gifts to "issue":** Gifts to "issue" are intrinsically ambiguous where the instrument fails to indicate whether the property should be distributed per stirpes, per capita by representation, or per capita at each generation. The majority approach is to apply the jurisdiction's default approach. The Restatement (Second) of Property applies the per capita by representation approach. The UPC applies the jurisdiction's default approach, even if the express language is to the "issue by representation." [317–318]

D. **Gifts to "heirs":** Remainders to a designated party's "heirs" create problems concerning who is included (as a general rule surviving spouse are included) and when the class of heirs should be determined (when the designated individual dies or when the remainder becomes possessory). The common law preference for vested remainders favors determining the designated party's heirs when the party dies, regardless of when distribution is to occur. The modern trend/UPC determines who qualifies as an heir when the property is to be distributed to the heirs. [318–319]

1. **Doctrine of worthier title:** If a document purports to create a remainder in the settlor's heirs, the remainder is converted into a reversion in the grantor.

2. **Rule in Shelley's Case:** If a document purports to create a remainder in real property in the heirs of a life tenant, the remainder is given to the life tenant.

E. **Class closing:** Under the rule of convenience, a class closes automatically, by operation of law, as soon as one member of the class is entitled to possession of his or her interest. No one else can enter the class, even if he or she otherwise appears to be eligible to join the class. [319–322]

   1. **Outright gifts:** Where an instrument (typically a will) provides for outright gifts to a class of beneficiaries, the class closes upon the transferor's death.

   2. **Gifts of future interests:** Where an instrument creates a future interest in a class and the gift is a periodic payment of income, the class closes upon each periodic date for distribution of the income and reopens with the beginning of the next period for the duration of the period. Where the gift is a one-time distribution of principal, the earliest the class will close is upon the end of the preceding estate.

   3. **Gifts of a specific amount:** Where an instrument (typically a will) provides for an outright gift of a specific amount to each class member, the class closes at the time of distribution (typically at the death of the transferor).

CHAPTER 14

THE RULE AGAINST PERPETUITIES

I. INTRODUCTION

A. **The Rule against Perpetuities:** A future interest must vest, if at all, within the lives in being at the time of its creation plus 21 years, or the interest is void. [330]

B. **Traditional approach:** The rule is applied in the abstract the moment the interest is created, does not wait to see whether the interest vests within the perpetuities period, and is not concerned with probable scenarios. If there is but one scenario, no matter how implausible, where the interest would vest, but not until after the perpetuities period, the interest is void from the moment of its attempted creation. The party must show logically that the interest must vest, if at all, within the lives in being when the interest was created plus 21 years (the perpetuities period). [330–333]

C. **Scope:** The rule applies only to contingent remainders, vested remainders subject to open, executory interests, and powers of appointment. [331]

D. **Creation:** The future interest must vest within the lives in being when the interest is created plus 21 years. Interests are created under a deed when it is delivered, under a will when the testator dies, under an irrevocable trust when it is funded, and under a revocable trust when it becomes irrevocable. Special rules covered below apply to interests created under powers of appointment. [332–333]

II. CLASSIC RULE AGAINST PERPETUITIES SCENARIOS

A. **Introduction:** There are several Rule against Perpetuities scenarios that are both well known and which demonstrate the abstract nature of the doctrine. [333]

B. **The fertile octogenarian:** In applying the Rule against Perpetuities, the common law courts assume conclusively that a person is fertile until death, regardless of his or her age. For example, assume a settlor creates an irrevocable trust for the benefit of a woman, *W,* who is 80 years old.

The trust provides "to **W** for life, then to her children for life, then to her first grandchild." The woman has two children, and when the interest is created, neither of them has any children. The interest in the first grandchild violates the Rule against Perpetuities because the woman could have another child, **C** (who would not be a life in being at the time the interest was created), and more than 21 years later **C** could have a child who could be the first grandchild—thereby vesting the interest but not until after the perpetuities period. [333]

C. **The unborn widow:** A person's widow cannot be identified until the designated person dies, so any future interest following a future interest to a widow needs to be analyzed carefully to see if it violates the Rule against Perpetuities. For example, "to **H** for life, then to **H**'s widow for life, then to **H**'s children then surviving." If you assume **H**'s widow is living, the interest in **H**'s children then surviving would be valid, but because **H**'s widow could be unborn at the time the interest is created, the interest in **H**'s children surviving when the unborn widow dies violates the Rule against Perpetuities. [333–334]

D. **The slothful executor:** The potential for delayed and/or prolonged administration of a decedent's estate means that gifts to be made to unnamed generic takers upon distribution of the decedent's estate usually violate the Rule against Perpetuities. For example, if **T**'s will provides that she leaves her estate "to my heirs who are alive when the court orders distribution of my estate," that interest violates the Rule against Perpetuities because all the lives in being plus 21 years may pass before the court orders distribution of **T**'s probate estate. [334–335]

III. PERPETUITIES REFORM

A. **Saving clause:** Because of the difficulty in understanding the Rule against Perpetuities, the courts will enforce an express "saving clause" that provides that despite the express terms of the trust, the trust will terminate at the latest upon the running of the perpetuities period. [335]

B. **Cy pres:** Under the cy pres doctrine, where a future interest in a trust violates the Rule against Perpetuities, the court is empowered to modify the trust so that it will not violate the rule. [335]

C. **Modern trend:** Because of the harshness of the Rule against Perpetuities, in particular the fact that it is applied in the abstract regardless of real-life probabilities, the modern trend is to modify the rule. There are several different approaches to such modification. [335]

D. **Wait and see:** Instead of applying the Rule against Perpetuities in the abstract to see if there is one possible scenario where the future interest vests but not until after the running of the perpetuities period, the courts wait and see if the future interest in question actually does not vest until after the perpetuities period. Under the Uniform Statutory Rule Against Perpetuities, the analysis is simplified even further in that the perpetuities period is a set 90 years (as opposed to the traditional "life in being plus 21 years" perpetuities period). [335–336]

E. **Abolishing the Rule against Perpetuities:** Some states have abolished the Rule against Perpetuities, permitting trusts to last forever. [336–337]

IV. CLASS GIFTS AND THE RULE AGAINST PERPETUITIES

A. **Class gifts—all or nothing:** If a gift to a class violates the Rule against Perpetuities as to one member of the class, it violates the rule as to all members of the class. The class must close *and* vest (conceivably different events) completely or the gift to the class is invalid. The courts, however, have recognized a couple of exceptions to this rule. [337]

B. **Exception—gifts to subclasses:** If the future interest in question can be characterized as a gift to subclasses as opposed to a single class, although the gift may be invalid as to some subclasses, it may be valid as to other subclasses. [337–338]

C. **Exception—gifts of specific amounts:** If the future interest is to a class, but each class member's share is a specific sum not indeterminate upon the final number of class members, the courts have held that even though the gift to some members of the class may violate the rule, the gift is valid as to those members whose share is definitively ascertainable within the perpetuities period. [338]

V. POWERS OF APPOINTMENT AND THE RULE AGAINST PERPETUITIES

A. **Powers of appointment vs. interests created by exercise:** As long as a general inter vivos power of appointment becomes exercisable or fails within the perpetuities time period, the power is valid even if it is not exercised until after the perpetuities period. General testamentary powers of appointment and special powers of appointment are valid as long as there is no scenario under which the donee can exercise the power after the perpetuities period. With respect to any interests created by the exercise of a valid general inter vivos power of appointment, the perpetuities period starts with the exercise of the power. With respect to interests created by the valid exercise of a general testamentary power or special power, the interests created are analyzed as if they were created by the instrument that created the power. [338–340]

VI. OTHER RULES REGULATING TEMPORAL RESTRICTIONS

A. **Rule prohibiting suspension of the power of alienation:** The power to alienate cannot be suspended for a period of time longer than the Rule against Perpetuities. The power to alienate is deemed suspended when no one alive, either alone or in combination with others, can convey the property in question in fee simple. Under the Wisconsin view, as long as the trustee has the power to sell the trust assets, the power to alienate has not been suspended. Under the New York view, the power to alienate has been suspended if either (1) the trustee lacks the power to transfer legal title, or (2) the beneficiaries, acting together, lack the power to transfer the equitable title. A spendthrift clause is usually void under the rule against suspending the power to alienate if the clause restricts the power to transfer for more than one life estate. [340–341]

B. **Rule against accumulations of income:** The traditional rule against accumulations of income provided that accumulations of income must be limited to: (1) the settlor's life; (2) the settlor's life plus 21 years; (3) the remaining years of minority of anyone alive at the time of the settlor's death; or (4) the point in time when a minor beneficiary entitled to receive income being accumulated reaches the age of majority. [341]

Modern trend: The modern trend is to abolish a distinct rule against the accumulations of income and to apply the Rule against Perpetuities to the issue.

CHAPTER 15
ESTATE AND GIFT TAXES

I. OVERVIEW

A. **Introduction:** Gratuitous transfers of property, both inter vivos and testamentary transfers, may trigger tax consequences under the gift and estate tax system. [348–350]

II. THE FEDERAL GIFT TAX SCHEME

A. **Federal gift tax:** Inter vivos gifts that exceed the annual gift tax exclusion constitute a taxable gift during that year. Depending on the amount of cumulative taxable gifts, a donor may owe federal gift taxes. [350]

B. **Gift:** For gift tax purposes, the key is not the transferor's intent. It is instead whether the transferor has received adequate consideration and has abandoned sufficient dominion and control over the property to put it beyond recall or the right to demand the beneficial enjoyment of the property. Where the transferor has retained the power to revoke, appoint, or change the owner, the transferor has not abandoned sufficient dominion and control. [350–352]

C. **Annual exclusion:** The tax code provides that each donor can give up to $10,000 a year to each donee before a gift is considered a taxable gift (commonly known as the "annual gift tax exclusion"). The annual amount one can exclude now automatically increases to stay pace with inflation, and in 2009 was increased to $13,000. [352–354]

D. **Calculate the decedent's taxable estate:** To calculate the decedent's taxable estate, miscellaneous deductions are allowed from the decedent's gross estate. The principal deductions are for charitable contributions, a decedent's debts, loans, mortgages, and the marital deduction. [354]

III. THE FEDERAL ESTATE TAX: AN OVERVIEW

A. **Federal estate tax:** Depending on the value of a decedent's net property holdings at death and the amount of his or her inter vivos gifts, a decedent may owe a federal estate tax at death. There are several steps in determining whether a decedent owes a federal estate tax: (1) calculate the decedent's gross estate, (2) calculate the decedent's taxable estate, (3) calculate the estate tax, and (4) apply credits to determine estate tax liability. [354–355]

IV. CALCULATING THE DECEDENT'S GROSS ESTATE

A. **Decedent's gross estate:** The decedent's gross estate consists of the value of virtually all property the decedent owned and transferred at time of death via probate or nonprobate means. The nonprobate property includes property transferred by right of survivorship, transfers where the decedent retained a life estate or control of the beneficial rights, revocable transfers, transfers where the decedent retained a reversionary interest, selected transfers within three years of death, and property over which the decedent held a general power of appointment. [355–360]

V. THE MARITAL DEDUCTION

A. The marital deduction: One spouse can transfer an unlimited amount of property to the other spouse without any gift or estate tax consequences as long as the transfer meets the requirements for the marital deduction, the key requirement being that the interest must be something other than a life estate or other terminable interest. [360–363]

VI. THE GENERATION-SKIPPING TRANSFER TAX

A. Generation-skipping transfer tax: Where a transferor attempts to transfer property to a transferee who is more than one generation below the transferor, a federal generation-skipping transfer tax is imposed. The tax imposed is the highest possible federal estate tax rate, but various exemptions and exclusions apply. [363–365]

C
A
P
S
U
L
E

S
U
M
M
A
R
Y

CHAPTER 1

INTRODUCTION TO WILLS, TRUSTS, AND ESTATES

ChapterScope

This chapter focuses on the macro issue raised by the course: *"Who gets your property when you die?"* To the extent the answer is "whomever you intend," this chapter examines the theoretical and public policy issues inherent in that answer. In particular, the chapter examines:

- **The scope of the power:** Although a decedent has the right to dispose of his or her property at death, the *states have broad authority to regulate the process.*

- **Public policy considerations:** Academics disagree over whether the power to transfer wealth at death *is natural and good, or* whether it *perpetuates economic disparity* and unfairly rewards those lucky enough to have been born to wealthy parents.

- **"Dead hand" control:** A decedent may condition a beneficiary's gift on the beneficiary behaving in a certain manner as long as the condition does not violate public policy. Such "dead hand" control is generally upheld unless the condition constitutes a *complete restraint on marriage,* requires a beneficiary to *practice a certain religion, encourages divorce or family strife,* or directs the *destruction of property.*

- **Course overview:** *Who takes decedent's property at his or her death?* The answer depends first on whether the property is *nonprobate or probate* property. *Nonprobate property* passes pursuant to the terms of the nonprobate instrument, be it joint tenancy, life insurance/payment on death contracts, legal life estate and remainders, or inter vivos trusts. *Probate property* passes pursuant to the terms of the *decedent's will, otherwise through intestacy.*

- **Probate administration:** A personal representative is appointed, and he or she has the job of collecting the decedent's probate assets, paying off creditors' claims, and distributing the property to those who are entitled to receive the property.

- **Professional responsibility:** Under the *common law* approach, the attorney owes *no duty of care* to, and is *not in privity of contract* with, intended beneficiaries. They have no standing to sue for malpractice. Under the *modern trend,* an attorney owes a *duty of care* to intended beneficiaries, and intended beneficiaries are *third-party beneficiaries* with respect to the contract between the attorney and testator. Intended beneficiaries have standing to sue for malpractice.

I. THE POWER TO TRANSFER PROPERTY AT DEATH

A. Introduction

1. **Historical perspective:** The power to transfer one's property by passing it to one's heirs (spouse, children, family members) was recognized well before the power to transfer one's

property by will. The scope of one's power to transfer at death is generally considered to be a matter of civil law as opposed to natural right.

2. **Cultural differences:** The scope of one's power to transfer property at death varies greatly from society to society. In many countries, children cannot be disinherited. They are entitled to a share of the deceased's property, regardless of the deceased's attempts to dispose of his or her property otherwise. In some societies, one cannot will away his or her property; it can pass only to one's heirs.

3. **State variations:** While all states recognize the power to transfer one's property at death, the details of what constitutes a valid will, and to whom the property will pass if there is no valid will, vary greatly from state to state.

B. **Right vs. privilege**

1. **Governmental power to regulate:** It was generally presumed that the power to pass one's property at death was not a constitutionally protected right. In ***Irving Trust Co. v. Day,*** 314 U.S. 556, 562 (1942), the U.S. Supreme Court said as much: "Nothing in the Federal Constitution forbids the legislature of a state to limit, condition, or even abolish the power of testamentary disposition over property within its jurisdiction."

2. **Right to transfer—government cannot abrogate completely:** In ***Hodel v. Irving,*** 481 U.S. 704 (1987), however, the U.S. Supreme Court reversed itself and held that the "escheat" provision of the Indian Land Consolidation Act of 1983 constituted an unconstitutional "taking" of decedent's property without just compensation. The act completely deprived Indian landowners, without compensation, of the right to dispose of their fractional interests in Indian land by intestacy or devise if the decedent's interest represented 2 percent or less of the total acreage in the tract and earned less than $100 during the preceding year. The decedent's fractional interest would "escheat" to the tribe. The statute, however, permitted the owners of the land to convey the land at time of death through nonprobate arrangements (inter vivos trusts). Nevertheless, the Court found the statute overly broad and unconstitutional. Apparently, the Court was bothered that the statute virtually abrogated an important right (the power to transfer at death) and that the statute was not well drafted to achieve its stated goals. The statute applied even in cases where permitting the property to pass to one's heirs would have resulted in increased consolidation of the property, the goal of the statute.

Right to transfer vs. right to receive: To the extent constitutional protections apply to property transfers at death, the protections arguably apply only to the decedent's power to dispose of his or her property at death, not necessarily to a particular heir's or beneficiary's right to receive property from a decedent.

3. **Right to transfer—government's power to increase:** Historically, the rule was that any right of publicity that a celebrity had at time of death died with him or her. The right was not inheritable or devisable. In the 1980s, however, a number of states statutorily recognized a descendible postmortem right of publicity. The courts have generally ruled that this new property right applies not only to parties alive at the time the statute was adopted, but also to deceased celebrities. The only issue is with respect to deceased celebrities, does the new property pass per their residuary clauses or per intestacy even if they died testate. In ***Shaw Family Archives v. CMG Worldwide,*** 486 F. Supp. 2d 309 (S.D.N.Y. 2007), the court, rejecting the holding of two other federal district courts, (1) ruled that a will can devise only property owned by the testator at time of death, so any publicity rights created after Marilyn Monroe's

death were not devised as part of her will; and (2) construed the California and Indiana statutes being invoked by Monroe's estate as not permitting the will of a deceased celebrity to devise newly created right.

Epilogue: In response to the opinion, California amended its statutes to expressly provide that publicity rights are devisable at death, even by general residuary clauses in a will executed before the right was recognized. The court, however, concluded that Marilyn Monroe was domiciled in New York at the time of her death so New York law applied, not California.

C. Public policy debate

1. **Pro:** A person should have the power to transfer his or her property at death because such a policy is consistent with a system of private property; encourages and rewards a life of hard work; is consistent with and promotes family ties; encourages individuals to accumulate wealth for old age and to give to family; and encourages family members to love, serve, and protect their elders.

2. **Con:** A person should not have the power to transfer his or her property at death because such a policy perpetuates economic disparity and discrimination and constitutes an unearned windfall to those who happen to have wealthy relatives—and such unearned wealth creates powers and privileges that are undeserved and denies equal opportunity to all children.

3. **Rebuttal:** Inter vivos investments in "human capital"—health, education, "culture," and connections—arguably account more for disparity in opportunities and wealth than inherited wealth.

4. **Academic vs. public opinion:** Academics tend to favor stiffer inheritance taxes, arguing that such taxes are inherently fairer than other forms of taxation. The public in general, however, tends to oppose inheritance taxes. Whether this is because people believe that they will end up with great wealth, which they want to be able to transfer at their death, or whether this reflects some larger notion of the role of property rights and governmental rights, is unclear.

5. **Historical compromise—permit but tax:** Historically, the United States has tried to balance these competing public policy arguments by permitting wealth to be transferred upon death, but imposing an estate and gift tax at significantly higher rates than those applied to earned income.

6. **Modern trend—phased-in elimination of estate tax:** The anti-estate tax proponents currently hold the upper hand, as reflected by the most recent amendments to the federal estate and gift tax laws that increase the tax exemption over the next several years and the proposal to abolish the estate tax. The debate over the balance between maximizing one's ability to dispose of his or her property at death and using the estate and gift tax system to redistribute wealth and equality, however, is far from over.

D. State variations: While all states recognize the right to transfer one's property at death, the details of what constitutes a valid will, and to whom the property will pass if there is no valid will, vary greatly from state to state.

E. Shifting patterns

1. **Demographics:** Most state inheritance schemes are built around the notion of a family. To the extent the traditional American family is undergoing change, pressure is growing to recognize

nontraditional families and relationships within a state's inheritance scheme (who qualifies as a spouse? who qualifies as a child?). You should keep an eye on these issues as you cover the material.

2. **Property transfers:** Professor John H. Langbein has postulated that the field of wills and trusts is itself a dying field. Rather than parents spending their lives accumulating wealth to transfer to their children at their death, Prof. Langbein argues that the principal means of transferring wealth from one generation to the next will be by parents funding their children's education.

II. "DEAD HAND" CONTROL

A. **Definition:** To some degree, money is power. "Dead hand" control arises where a decedent *conditions a gift to a beneficiary upon a beneficiary behaving in a certain way.* By qualifying the testamentary gift, the decedent is attempting to exercise control over the beneficiary even after the transferor's death. Such conditional gifts are typically made in a trust commonly known as an *incentive trust.*

   1. **Arguments in support:** It is the decedent's property. Given that a decedent could have conditioned an inter vivos gift on a donee acting in a certain manner, the decedent should have the right to condition a testamentary gift on a beneficiary acting in a certain manner. A beneficiary has no right to receive the property. Given that a decedent can completely disinherit a beneficiary, the decedent should be able to condition or restrict an intended beneficiary's inheritance.

   2. **Arguments against:** Circumstances change, and where the donor is deceased, he or she no longer has the capacity or flexibility to take ever-changing circumstances into consideration in structuring his or her gifts. In addition, some conditions are so contrary to fundamental rights or generally accepted public policy they should be considered invalid conditions.

B. **Restatement (Third) of Property:** The Restatement (Third) of Property favors freedom of disposition. It takes a very protective approach to a donor's intent, providing in pertinent part that a "donor's intention is given effect to the maximum extent allowed by law." It also acknowledges, however, that a donor's intent is invalid where it is "prohibited or restricted by an overriding rule of law." Restatement (Third) of Property: Wills and Other Donative Transfers §10.1 (2003) (hereinafter "Restatement (Third) of Property, Donative Transfers").

C. **Valid conditions:** Testamentary conditional gifts ("dead hand" control) are valid unless they violate public policy, or judicial enforcement of the condition would constitute state action violating constitutionally protected fundamental rights. The courts have been reluctant to find that upholding conditional terms of the gift constitutes sufficient state action to offend the Constitution, and the courts have been very reluctant to hold conditional gifts as contrary to public policy.

D. **Invalid conditions:** There are a handful of conditions that generally have been held to be invalid as against public policy.

   1. **Absolute restraints on marriage:** Gifts conditioned on the beneficiary not marrying anyone—at least as to first marriages—generally are considered to violate the fundamental right to marry and are *void.*

a. **Exception—partial restraints:** Partial restraints on marriage that impose only reasonable restrictions generally are not contrary to public policy and are *valid.* What constitutes a "reasonable" restriction is very fact sensitive. The courts pay particular attention to the age of the intended beneficiary and the time frame of the intended restriction or condition.

b. **Exception—temporal/religion requirement:** Gifts requiring a beneficiary to marry within a reasonable time period, even to someone of a particular religious background, have been held *valid.* Such gifts arguably do not restrict an individual's right to marry; they merely encourage him or her to marry within a certain time frame and within a particular religion.

Example: In *Shapira v. Union National Bank,* 315 N.E.2d 825 (Ohio 1974), a father's testamentary gifts to his sons required each to be married within seven years of the father's death to "a Jewish girl whose both parents were Jewish." One son sued, claiming the condition: (1) violated his fundamental right to marry, a right protected by the Fourteenth Amendment to the Constitution, and (2) violated public policy generally. The court ruled that (1) enforcing the conditions did not constitute sufficient state action to offend the Constitution, and (2) gifts conditioned on a beneficiary marrying within a particular class or religion constitute only a partial restraint on marriage, which is reasonable and valid and not against public policy.

2. **Religion requirement:** Gifts that require a beneficiary to remain faithful to a particular religion generally are held to violate public policy concerning religious freedom and are *invalid.*

3. **Encouraging separation and/or divorce:** Gifts that require a beneficiary to separate or divorce before receiving the gift generally are deemed against public policy and are *void.* But gifts that provide for a beneficiary only in the event of separation and/or divorce are not necessarily deemed to encourage divorce. The controlling factor appears to be the decedent's dominant intent: to encourage the separation/divorce or merely to provide support in the event of separation/divorce.

4. **Promoting family strife:** Gifts conditioned upon family members ostracizing and/or not communicating with other family members generally have been held to violate public policy and are *void.*

5. **Property destruction directive:** Although individuals generally are free to destroy property while they are alive, individuals generally are not free to destroy property upon their death, and such directives are *invalid.* Destruction of property inter vivos carries with it an economic cost that deters owners. Destruction of property at death carries with it no meaningful economic cost for the decedent and deprives society of the opportunity to determine the best use of the property.

E. **Remedy:** Where there is a conditional gift that violates public policy, the critical variable is whether there is a "gift-over" clause: a clause in the instrument that provides where the gift is to go if the condition or restriction is not satisfied.

1. **Gift-over clause:** Where a gift-over clause exists and the conditional gift violates public policy, more often than not the courts will strike the condition as void as against public policy, but the courts will not give the property to the beneficiary subject to the condition. Instead, the property will be distributed to the alternative beneficiary under the express gift-over clause.

2. **No gift-over clause:** Where no express gift-over clause exists, if there is a conditional gift that violates public policy, most often the courts will simply strike the void condition/restriction and permit the beneficiary subject to the condition to take the property free and clear of any conditions.

III. WHO TAKES DECEDENT'S PROPERTY: AN OVERVIEW

A. **Macro issue:** The course can be boiled down to a single issue: Who gets the decedent's property when he or she dies? (For a summary of the material that follows, see tree diagram on p. 6)

B. **Macro answer:** First and foremost, the answer turns on what type of property is involved: nonprobate or probate.

C. **Probate vs. nonprobate property:** A will disposes of the decedent's probate property only. There are a number of ways to dispose of property without the property having to pass through probate. These property arrangements are referred to collectively as nonprobate property. Probate is the default.

D. **Nonprobate property:** The decedent has to take affirmative steps for the property to qualify as nonprobate property. Historically, only four types of property arrangements have qualified as nonprobate.

1. **Joint tenancy:** Joint tenants hold the property in question concurrently. They own it in whole and in fractional shares. The key characteristic of joint tenancy is its *right of survivorship.* Upon the death of one joint tenant, his or her fractional share is extinguished, and the shares of the surviving joint tenants are recalculated. Technically, no property interest "passes" upon the death of a joint tenant.

2. **Life insurance:** Life insurance is an agreement between the insured and the insurance company that, upon the insured's death, benefits will be paid to the beneficiary or beneficiaries selected by the insured. Life insurance proceeds are not probate property and are distributed directly to the beneficiaries without being subject to the probate process. At common law, life insurance contracts were the only type of contract with a payment on death (P.O.D.) clause that qualified as a valid will substitute.

   Modern trend—P.O.D. contracts: A life insurance policy is a contract with a P.O.D. clause. The modern trend recognizes *all* contracts with P.O.D. clauses as valid, nonprobate transfers exempt from the probate process.

3. **Legal life estates and remainders:** When the party who holds a legal life estate dies, although the right to possession passes to the party holding the remainder, that transfer is the result of the original grantor's division of the property between the life estate and remainder, not the result of the deceased life tenant passing a property interest. Properly created legal life estates and remainders avoid probate.

   Modern trend—transfer on death deed: A growing number of jurisdictions permit a transferor to create a revocable deed that does not pass any interest until the party dies. This arrangement permits a decedent to transfer his or her interest in real property upon death without the transfer being subject to the probate process.

4. **Inter vivos trusts:** A trust is an artificial legal entity that holds and manages the property placed in the trust. There are several different types of trusts: inter vivos trusts, testamentary trusts, and Uniform Testamentary Additions to Trusts Act (UTATA) trusts. Of the three, only property properly transferred to an inter vivos trust during the life of the party avoids passing through probate.

E. **Nonprobate property takers:** The decedent's nonprobate property goes to the transferees identified in the written instrument properly creating the nonprobate property arrangement. The property does not pass through probate.

F. **Probate property:** If the property in question does not qualify as nonprobate property, the property automatically falls to probate as the default system.

1. **Will vs. intestacy:** Who takes the decedent's probate property depends on whether the decedent had a valid last will and testament. A properly executed will constitutes an expression of a person's intent as to who should take his or her property when he or she dies. If a decedent does not have a will or if the will does not dispose of all the decedent's property, the property passes via intestacy to the decedent's heirs.

2. **Intestacy is the default:** If a decedent takes no steps to opt out of intestacy, all of his or her property will pass through intestacy.

3. **Opting out of intestacy:** One can opt out of intestacy by properly executing a will or by properly executing a will substitute—one of the recognized nonprobate methods of transferring property. If one properly executes a will substitute, the property in question totally avoids probate. If, however, one opts out of intestacy by executing a will, the property still passes through probate.

G. **Summary:** The tree diagram that follows summarizes the macro answer to the issue, "Who gets the decedent's property when he or she dies?" and it constitutes the "big picture" of the material to be covered in the course.

Who Takes the Decedent's Property?

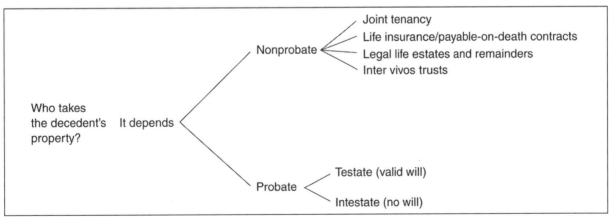

IV. THE PROBATE PROCESS: AN OVERVIEW

A. **Probate is the default:** Nonprobate property passes pursuant to the terms of the instrument in question to the transferees identified in the instrument without passing through the probate system. Probate property must pass through the probate system.

B. Probate administration: Probate is a very complex process. At many law schools, it is a separate course. While it is impossible to do justice to the probate process here, some sense of the process and terminology is helpful to understanding some of the issues in wills and trusts.

C. Terminology

- **Testate:** If the decedent dies with a valid last will and testament, the decedent is said to have died "testate," and his or her property will be distributed pursuant to the terms of the last will and testament.

- **Intestate:** If the decedent dies without a valid last will and testament, the decedent is said to have died "intestate," and his or her property will be distributed pursuant to the state statute on descent and distribution.

  The terms *testate* and *intestate* are not necessarily mutually exclusive. If a decedent dies with a will that disposes of some, but not all of the decedent's property, the decedent died both testate and intestate.

- **Testator:** A male who executes a valid will.

- **Testatrix:** A female who executes a valid will.

  Increasingly today, the term *testator* is gender neutral, referring to both males and females who die with a valid will.

- **Devise:** A gift of real property under a will. The word can also be used in its verb form: to devise; devises.

  Increasingly today, the term *devise* is being used to describe testamentary gifts of either real or personal property.

- **Devisee:** A beneficiary receiving real property under a will.

- **Bequest:** A gift of personal property under a will. The word can also be used in its verb form: to bequeath, bequeaths.

- **Legacy:** A gift of money under a will.

- **Legatee:** A beneficiary receiving money under a will.

- **Personal representative:** The person appointed by the probate court to oversee the administrative process of wrapping up and probating the decedent's affairs.

- **Executor:** What the personal representative is called if the decedent dies testate and the will names the personal representative.

- **Administrator:** What the personal representative is called if the decedent dies intestate or testate but the will fails to name a personal representative.

  Increasingly today, the more generic *personal representative* term is used without bothering to note if the person is an executor or administrator.

- **Probate court:** The state court with special jurisdiction over determining who is entitled to receive the decedent's probate property.

- **Statute of descent and distribution:** If a decedent dies intestate as to some or all of his or her property, such property will be distributed to those individuals identified to receive such property under the state's statute of descent and distribution.

- **Heirs:** At common law, if a decedent died intestate, the decedent's *real* property was said to "descend" to the decedent's heirs.

- **Next-of-kin:** At common law, if a decedent died intestate, the decedent's *personal* property was "distributed" to the decedent's next-of-kin.

  Today, the terms *heirs* and *next-of-kin* are used interchangeably to refer to anyone receiving property (real or personal) under a state's intestate scheme.

D. **The probate process:** Probating a decedent's estate is important because it (1) provides for an orderly transfer of title for the decedent's property; (2) ensures that creditors receive notice, an opportunity to present their claims, and payment; (3) extinguishes claims of creditors who do not present their claims to the probate court; and (4) ensures that the decedent's property is properly distributed to those who are entitled to receive it.

   1. **Opening probate:** The probate court in the county where the decedent was domiciled at time of death has primary (or domiciliary) jurisdiction over the decedent's probate estate. The court has jurisdiction over the decedent's personal property, and the decedent's real property located within that jurisdiction.

      Probate is opened by presenting the decedent's death certificate. Depending on the situation, the probate court issues "letters testamentary" appointing an executor or "letters of administration" appointing an administrator. A majority of the jurisdictions require notice to interested parties before selection and appointment of the executor or administrator.

      Ancillary jurisdiction: Ancillary jurisdiction may be necessary if the decedent owned real property located in a different jurisdiction from his or her domicile. Ancillary jurisdiction ensures (1) that local creditors in the jurisdiction where the real property is located receive notice and an opportunity to present their claims, and (2) that there is compliance with that jurisdiction's recording system.

   2. **Will contests:** If a party wishes to file a claim challenging the validity of a will offered for probate, most jurisdictions have a statute requiring that the contest be brought in a timely manner after probate is opened, or the claim is barred.

   3. **Probate administration:** Once the court issues its letters, the personal representative is authorized to begin his or her responsibilities.

E. **Personal representative's powers:** The jurisdictions are split as to the personal representative's powers to administer the estate. Some jurisdictions require probate court supervision and authorization at almost every step of the way, thereby incurring greater expense for the estate. Other states permit unsupervised administration under most circumstances, with one final accounting being filed with the probate court at the end.

F. **Personal representative's duties**

   1. **Inventory decedent's assets:** First, the personal representative has a duty to ascertain and take control of the decedent's probate property, which he or she inventories to the probate court.

2. **Give notice to and pay creditors:** Second, the personal representative gives notice (usually by publication, but known creditors may be entitled to actual notice) of the opening of probate and that creditors of the decedent are required to file any and all claims within a set statutory period or their claims will be forever barred. The personal representative must pay those creditors who present valid claims within the prescribed time period. In addition to paying creditors, the personal representative must file federal and state estate tax returns and, if necessary, pay any taxes due.

3. **Distribute decedent's probate property:** Whatever property is left over after paying creditors' claims is then distributed to those who are entitled to receive under the decedent's last will and testament and/or to those entitled to receive under the state's statute of descent and distribution, depending on whether the decedent died testate or intestate (or both).

G. **Costs and delays of probate:** Probating a typical estate is a costly process that ties up the decedent's probate assets during the process. The process is costly due to probate court fees, personal representative's fees, attorneys' fees, and miscellaneous other fees that may be applicable. On average, probate of even a fairly simple, uncontested estate takes anywhere from one to two years.

H. **Probate and "titled" property:** As a practical matter, probate is necessary to transfer title to those assets, real or personal, that were titled in the decedent's name. Where the probate asset has a written form of title in the decedent's name, a probate court order is needed to transfer title properly.

I. **Avoiding probate:** Due to the costs and hassles inherent in probate, more and more people are trying to avoid it. In theory, a person can avoid probate by putting all of his or her property in nonprobate property arrangements. In practice, however, it is very difficult to put all of one's property in nonprobate arrangements.

1. **"Nontitled" probate assets:** As a practical matter, probate can be avoided if all of the decedent's property is nontitled personal property. But if the takers opt not to open probate, those who take the decedent's property may take subject to creditors' claims.

2. **"Small estate" probate statutes:** All states have a small estate probate procedure that may be employed if the size and nature of the decedent's probate property permit. Such procedures basically permit expedited probate with minimal court supervision or involvement, thereby minimizing the attendant costs and delays.

3. **European approach of universal succession:** Universal succession provides that title to the decedent's property passes to the appropriate heirs or residuary devisees automatically and by operation of law without the need for a personal representative or probate. The heirs or residuary legatees who take title to the decedent's assets are then responsible for paying the decedent's creditors and the estate's tax liability and distributing the decedent's property to the appropriate takers.

Not widely adopted: While universal succession is the norm in Europe, Louisiana is the only state that has adopted it. The Uniform Probate Code (UPC) permits the decedent's heirs or residuary devisees to petition the probate court for universal succession, which is to be granted where the court determines administration appears unnecessary. Limited forms of universal succession are permitted in some states under certain circumstances. (California permits universal succession for property passing to a surviving spouse.)

V. ESTATE PLANNING

A. Objectives: Estate planning can be a very complicated process, depending on a person's personal and financial situation and on his or her intent. In advising a party about his or her estate plan, the key objectives discussed below should be kept in mind.

B. Decedent's intent: The principal purpose of estate planning is to ensure that the person's intent with respect to who gets what, and when, is honored. An estate planning attorney should consider the person's family situation, the person's financial situation (assets and liabilities), and the different ways in which the property can be transferred at death (through intestacy, a will, and/or the nonprobate arrangements).

C. Avoid estate taxes: One of the primary purposes of estate planning is to avoid or minimize state and/or federal estate taxes.

D. Avoid probate: Probate can be very costly and cumbersome, tying up the decedent's probate property for years. Estate planning to avoid probate is rather simple, at least as to the decedent's larger assets and/or those assets that the decedent does not use often. If those assets are held in a valid, nonprobate arrangement (joint tenancy, an inter vivos trust, or a payment-on-death contractual arrangement), the remaining probate assets may qualify for small estate probate treatment.

Couples: The typical couple (married or not, with or without children) can avoid probate upon the death of the first partner without too much difficulty by using nonprobate arrangements. Which nonprobate arrangement is best depends in large part upon the degree to which the couple is willing to share ownership inter vivos.

1. **Joint tenancy:** The typical estate plan for a couple is to leave all of the couple's property to the surviving partner. Joint tenancy is the simplest and cheapest way to achieve this goal and avoid probate. Joint tenancy works well for both real property and personal property such as bank accounts, certificates of deposit, retirement plans, and so on.

2. **Transfer on death deed:** A growing number of jurisdictions permit a transferor to create a revocable deed that does not pass any interest until the party dies, thereby permitting a decedent to transfer his or her interest in real property upon death without the transfer being subject to the probate process.

3. **Inter vivos trusts:** If property is placed in an inter vivos revocable trust, the party gets the benefits of avoiding probate, retains the discretion to give some or all of his or her property to someone other than the surviving partner, and maintains separate ownership inter vivos. Inter vivos trusts also work well for real property owned by one of the parties that is located in another jurisdiction. By placing the real property in an inter vivos trust, ancillary probate is not necessary to transfer the property upon the party's death.

4. **Payment-on-death (P.O.D.) contracts:** Depending on the jurisdiction, substantial personal property assets can be passed through P.O.D. contractual arrangements. Increasingly, a party's largest assets are his or her pension benefits. In an increasing number of states, pension benefits and other contractual benefits can be disposed of as a nonprobate transfer by identifying, in the contract governing the asset, to whom the asset is to go upon the party's death.

E. Professional responsibility: The scope of an attorney's professional responsibility is critical to determining who has standing to sue the attorney for malpractice.

1. **Tort theory:** To sue an attorney for malpractice based on a tort theory, one has to prove negligence. To prove negligence, one has to prove a duty of care existed between the defendant attorney and the plaintiff.

2. **Contract theory:** To sue an attorney for malpractice based on a contract theory, one has to show privity of contract.

3. **Common law approach:** Under the common law approach, the attorney-client relationship is construed very narrowly to protect attorneys from claims of malpractice from frustrated individuals who thought they were to take under the decedent's estate planning instruments but did not.

   a. **Tort—no duty:** Under the common law approach, the attorney owes a duty of reasonable care to only the client—the testator—but not to any intended beneficiaries. Only the testator, while alive, or the personal representative, after the testator's death, has standing to sue the drafting attorney for negligence.

   b. **Contract—no privity:** Under the common law approach, the attorney is in privity of contract only with the other party to the contract. Third-party beneficiary contracts are not recognized. An estate planning attorney is in privity of contract with the testator only, not with any intended beneficiaries. Only the testator, while alive, or the personal representative, after the testator's death, has standing to sue the drafting attorney for breach of contract.

   c. **Pro:** The common law approach protects attorneys from baseless and/or fraudulent claims from frustrated individuals who thought they were to take under the decedent's estate planning documents but did not.

   d. **Con:** The common law approach bars valid claims from intended beneficiaries where the attorney has erred.

4. **Modern trend—majority approach:** Under the majority modern trend approach, the attorney-client relationship is construed broadly such that intended beneficiaries have standing to sue the testator's attorney for malpractice.

   a. **Tort—duty:** Under the modern trend approach, a majority of courts that have considered the issue have extended the attorney's duty to intended beneficiaries based on the reasonable foreseeability of injury to the intended beneficiaries if the attorney fails to exercise due care.

   b. **Contract—privity:** Under the modern trend approach, a majority of courts that have considered the issue have held that a nonparty to a contract can sue for breach of contract if the nonparty qualifies as a third-party beneficiary. Once the client identifies to the estate planning attorney to whom the client wishes his or her property to go, the intended beneficiary achieves third-party beneficiary status and is in privity of contract with the attorney. The intended beneficiary has standing to bring a malpractice action if the attorney errs.

   c. **Pro:** The modern trend approach permits valid claims from intended beneficiaries where the attorney has erred.

   d. **Con:** The modern trend approach fails to protect attorneys from baseless and/or fraudulent claims from frustrated individuals who thought they were to take under the decedent's estate planning documents but did not. Such claims drive up malpractice insurance premiums for attorneys who practice estate planning, making the cost of obtaining a will more expensive for everyone.

5. **Example:** In *Simpson v. Calivas,* 650 A.2d 318 (N.H. 1994), the testator's will left all his real property to his son except for a life estate in "our homestead located at Piscataqua Road, Dover, New Hampshire," which was left to the testator's second wife (the son's stepmother). The probate court ruled that the will devised a life estate in *all* the real property located at Piscataqua Road (including a house, over 100 acres, and several buildings used in a family business), not just the house and a limited amount of land. The son sued the attorney who drafted the will, alleging negligence and breach of contract, claiming that the father intended that the stepmother receive a homestead only in the house, with the remaining land to go outright to the son (an intent supported by the attorney's own notes from his meeting with the testator).

   The lower court applied the traditional common law approach and dismissed the son's claims. The New Hampshire Supreme Court adopted the modern trend. The court reasoned that the reasonably foreseeable harm to the intended beneficiaries, if reasonable care were not exercised, justified extending the duty of care to include the intended beneficiaries.

6. **Modern trend—compromise approach:** A handful of jurisdictions, concerned that adopting the modern trend would subject attorneys who practice estate planning to too many baseless claims from frustrated beneficiaries, have adopted the modern trend approach of extending duty and privity beyond the client to include intended beneficiaries—but only those intended beneficiaries identified in the testator's estate planning instruments (typically a will or trust).

   a. **Pro:** The modern trend compromise approach permits some valid claims from intended beneficiaries who are identified in the will where the attorney has erred.

   b. **Con:** The compromise approach fails to provide a remedy for intended beneficiaries, no matter how clear the evidence, who fail to get mentioned in the will. The intended beneficiary becomes caught in a legal catch-22 where he or she has no standing unless mentioned in the will, yet it is the failure to include the intended beneficiary in the will which is the basis for the professional malpractice claim.

7. **Modern trend—curative doctrines:** Increasingly, courts are adopting doctrines that permit courts to cure defects in the will's execution and that permit courts to reform wills to correct attorney drafting errors. These developments reduce the risk of a malpractice claim because they permit the courts to correct the attorney's mistake.

8. **Conflicts of interest and duty to disclose:** The testator's attorney may owe a duty of care to another party if the attorney has an ongoing attorney-client relationship with the party. The lawyer may have a duty to disclose what otherwise would be considered testator's confidential information to the attorney's other client.

   Example: In *A. v. B.*, 726 A.2d 924 (N.J. 1999), a firm represented both husband and wife for estate planning purposes. Both parties signed a "Waiver of Conflict of Interest" form that expressly permitted the firm to disclose confidential information obtained from one party to the other, but failed to address confidential information obtained from other sources. Due to a typographical error in recording the matter in the firm's files, the firm's family law department did not realize the firm already represented the couple when it agreed to represent a woman who wanted to sue the husband claiming he had fathered her illegitimate child. When the firm realized the mistake, it immediately withdrew from representing the woman, but it also believed it had an ethical duty to disclose to the wife the existence of the husband's illegitimate child and the corresponding estate planning ramifications. The husband invoked the duty of confidentiality. The court ruled that New Jersey's Rules of Professional Conduct (RPC) 1.6(b), which *requires* disclosure of confidential information to prevent the client "from committing a criminal, illegal, or fraudulent act that the lawyer reasonably believes is likely to result in death or substantial bodily harm or substantial injury to the financial interest or property of another," did *not* apply because the possible inheritance of the wife's estate by the child was too remote. But the court found that RPC 1.6(c), which *permits* but does not require disclosure of confidential information where the lawyer reasonably believes necessary "to rectify the consequences of a client's criminal, illegal or fraudulent act in furtherance of which the lawyer's services had been used," permitted disclosure because the husband's deliberate decision not to disclose the existence of the illegitimate child constituted a fraud on his wife. (The court noted that while the ABA Model Rule 1.6 permits disclosure only where failure to do so would likely result in imminent death or substantial bodily harm, New Jersey's RPC are broader and permit disclosure to rectify the consequences of the client's fraudulent act as well.) In addition, the spirit of the Waiver of the Conflict of Interest Form supported disclosure.

Quiz Yourself on
INTRODUCTION TO WILLS, TRUSTS, AND ESTATES

1. Chelsea marries Ken, Jr. Chelsea's mother, Hillary, is outraged. Decades later, Hillary writes a will that provides as follows: "I leave all of my property to my daughter, Chelsea, if she is not married when I die; but if she is married, I leave all of my property as follows: one-quarter to my sister Ann; one-quarter to my brother Bob; and the rest to the National Democratic Party." Both Ann and Bob were married when Hillary executed the will. Hillary never told Chelsea about the provision in the will. Years later, when Hillary dies, Chelsea challenges the provision in the will conditioning the gift to her. What are Chelsea's strongest claims, and is the conditional gift valid? _____

2. Brad and Jennifer are happily married and live in a noncommunity property state. They purchase Nirvanacres as true joint tenants. Brad has a car, in his name alone, that he purchased before he married Jennifer. He has an insurance policy in the amount of $50,000 that he purchased before his marriage that designates his mom as the beneficiary. He has a checking account with $100,000 in it from a commercial he made during the marriage. Jennifer has a boat that she purchased before she married Brad. She has $500,000 in a checking account from a sitcom she made during the marriage. Tragically, Brad drowns while surfing when some of the locals, protecting their turf, bump him off his board. Brad dies with a valid will giving his car to his friend from Missouri, Sheryl. The will has no other provisions. What is the extent of Brad's property (what is nonprobate, what is probate testate, and what is probate intestate)?

   a. If your course covers community property, what would your answer be if they lived in a community property jurisdiction? _____

3. Bozo the attorney drafts a will and trust for the Smiths. Bozo sets up a "by-pass" trust in the trust to minimize the estate taxes upon the death of the couple. He forgets, however, to include a clause directing that the "by-pass" trust be funded so as to take advantage of the available tax benefits. As a result of his alleged failure, the estate is subject to estate and gift taxes, costing the estate $1 million. The beneficiaries sue, alleging malpractice. Do the beneficiaries have standing to sue?

Answers

1. The conditional gift is valid. Chelsea can claim that the clause is against public policy because: (1) it constitutes a complete restraint on marriage; and (2) it encourages divorce. Unfortunately for Chelsea, both claims will fail. Hillary apparently put the condition in the will because she did not like Chelsea's husband, not because she was against marriage in general. Both Ann and Bob were married at the time she executed the will making gifts to them, yet she did not condition her gifts to them on their being unmarried at the time of her death. The clause does not constitute a complete restraint on marriage, it merely reflects her misgivings about Chelsea's marriage to Ken, Jr. Nor is the clause invalid because it encourages divorce. There is no evidence that Hillary ever told Chelsea of the conditional terms of her will. Chelsea did not find out about the provision until Hillary died, when it was too late to change her marriage status to take advantage of the gift. Thus no attempt to induce Chelsea to divorce was made. The conditional gift is valid.

2. The first task is to check for any valid nonprobate assets. Brad and Jennifer owned Nirvanacres as joint tenants, one of the recognized nonprobate means of transferring property. Upon Brad's death, his interest is extinguished, and Jennifer now owns Nirvanacres as her separate property. Life insurance is another recognized nonprobate means of transferring property. Upon Brad's death, the $50,000 insurance proceeds will be distributed immediately to his mother. Brad's car and his checking account are his probate property. Brad's will validly devises his car to Sheryl. The rest of Brad's property (the money in his checking account) will fall to intestacy where it will be distributed pursuant to the state's descent and distribution statute to his heirs.

   a. Assuming Brad and Jennifer live in a community property jurisdiction, their nonprobate assets are the same as above (the insurance policy was purchased with earnings acquired premarriage so it is Brad's separate property; and the facts say they took the house as true joint tenants). Brad's car is still his separate property because it was acquired premarriage. He can devise it to Sheryl. But his earnings during marriage and Jennifer's earnings during marriage are community property assets. Upon his death, he has a half interest in his earnings during the marriage (half of $50,000 equals $25,000) that goes into his probate estate, and he has a half interest in Jennifer's earnings during the marriage (half of $500,000 equals $250,000) that goes into his probate estate. His will does not cover these assets, so they will fall to intestacy where they will be distributed pursuant to the state's descent and distribution statute.

3. Under the traditional common law approach, Bozo is not liable to the beneficiaries. Under the common law approach, an attorney owes no duty to the intended beneficiaries, only to the client. The beneficiaries have no standing to sue for malpractice. Under the modern trend approach, an attorney owes a duty of care to the intended beneficiaries as third-party beneficiaries of the attorney-client relationship. The beneficiaries have standing to sue Bozo for both negligence and breach of contract.

Under the compromise modern trend approach, standing depends on whether the beneficiaries are named in the estate planning instruments. If they are, they have standing. If not, they do not have standing.

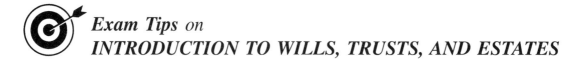

Exam Tips *on*
INTRODUCTION TO WILLS, TRUSTS, AND ESTATES

The first chapter is primarily an overview chapter that exposes you to some "mind stretching" concepts, gives you some background and context, introduces a number of themes that are touched on repeatedly throughout the book, and throws in a couple of traditional rules that do not really fit anywhere else in the book.

Study suggestion: keep the big picture in mind at all times

As you move through the course rule by rule, you will quickly realize that most of the rules are straightforward and logical. The problem is that a rule exists for virtually every conceivable scenario. The degree of difficulty in the course is not with any given rule, but rather with the volume of rules and plethora of overlaps that can arise. The key to keeping the material straight is to keep the big picture in mind.

Some rules apply to all types of property (nonprobate, probate testate, and probate intestate), while other rules apply to only one or two types of property. As you learn each rule, think about the scope of its application.

Analytical key: the material is presented in reverse analytical order

The material starts with the default and works its way up the distribution scheme. The material starts with intestacy, then it examines wills (the traditional method of opting out of intestacy), and then it examines nonprobate transfers (the modern preferred method of opting out of intestacy). Analytically, one should reverse the process.

☞ First, check for nonprobate property: If there is any nonprobate property, it will pass to the transferees properly identified in the nonprobate instrument.

☞ Whatever fails to qualify as nonprobate property is probate property. Who takes the decedent's probate property depends on whether the decedent died with a valid will. If the decedent died with a valid will that properly disposes all of his or her property, the decedent died testate. The decedent's property will pass to the beneficiaries identified in the will.

☞ If the decedent died without a will (intestate) or with a will that does not properly dispose of all of the decedent's property, the property will be distributed to the decedent's heirs pursuant to the jurisdiction's statute of descent and distribution.

The power to transfer one's property at death

The power to transfer property at death is rarely tested. If tested, it will be a pure theory question or you will need to see a statute that abrogates an individual's ability to transfer his or her property at death. Raise and address both the public policy considerations and the constitutional considerations.

"Dead hand" control

Of the material in the first chapter, this is one of the more tested areas. It can be overlapped with either a devise in a will or a gift in trust, though probably more often it is attached to a gift in trust.

☞ If you see a conditional gift, remember the general rule: Conditional gifts are valid unless the condition falls within one of the well-recognized exceptions. If the conditional gift does not fall squarely within one of the exceptions, argue by analogy to the closest exception. Focus on the nature of the beneficiary's affected right and the degree of unreasonableness caused by the requirements of the condition.

The probate process: an overview

The material on probate administration is intended to give you a sense of the process and some background, and to help you understand the context in which some of these issues arise. The most important part of this section is the terminology. You have to master the terminology before you can understand who the players are and what happened.

☞ If your professor is a stickler for terminology, you need to study the nuances of the different terms. Most professors do not sweat the details of the terminology as long as you understand what is going on and use the modern trend generic terms properly.

Estate planning

The material on estate planning is to give you some appreciation for what an estate planning attorney should take into consideration when meeting with a client and advising him or her. With the exception of the malpractice material, the material in this section is rarely tested directly.

The professional responsibility material presented in this section is critical. It is often a latent issue on a traditional fact pattern type exam. As you will see repeatedly throughout the book, if an attorney fails to comply with a wills and/or trusts rule (an issue that will be raised directly by the fact pattern), the latent follow-up issue is whether the party adversely affected by the attorney's conduct can sue the attorney for malpractice. You want to keep that issue in the back of your head as you move through the facts on an exam. If you conclude that a will has not been properly executed, that a will was not properly revoked, or that a will or trust was not drafted properly, consider whether the party adversely affected by the outcome can sue the attorney for malpractice.

☞ If a malpractice claim can be brought, the key is which approach the jurisdiction follows. If the fact pattern does not tell you, analyze in the alternative. First, state the common law approach and apply it, *and* then state and apply the modern trend.

CHAPTER 2

INTESTACY: THE DEFAULT DISTRIBUTION SCHEME

ChapterScope

This chapter examines the default distribution scheme—intestacy. If the decedent fails to dispose of all of his or her property through nonprobate instruments or a last will and testament, the decedent's property passes pursuant to the state's descent and distribution statute to the decedent's heirs. In particular, the chapter examines:

- **A typical intestate distribution scheme:** Although the details vary from state to state, the basic order of *who takes* is fairly similar: (1) surviving spouse, (2) issue, (3) parents, (4) issue of parents, (5) grandparents/issue of grandparents, (6) next-of-kin, (7) escheats to the state. *How much* each takes is where the differences typically arise state to state.

- **Surviving spouse:** To qualify as a surviving spouse, the couple must have gone through a valid marriage ceremony (or at least what one of them believes is a valid ceremony). Increasingly, states are extending "spousal" status to same-sex couples, but the conditions for such status vary from state to state.

  - **Survival requirement:** At common law, to qualify as a taker one has to prove by a preponderance of the evidence that he or she survived the decedent. Under the modern trend, some jurisdictions require the taker to prove by clear and convincing evidence that he or she survived the decedent, while other jurisdictions require the taker to prove by clear and convincing evidence that he or she survived the decedent by 120 hours.

- **Surviving spouse's share:** The surviving spouse's share varies greatly from jurisdiction to jurisdiction and depends in part on whether the decedent was survived by other family members (focusing primarily on the decedent's issue, parents, and issue of parents).

- **Calculating shares to issue:** The jurisdictions are split over what it means to divide the decedent's property equally among the decedent's issue when the issue are not equally related to the decedent. Depending on the jurisdiction, the property can be divided *per capita with representation, per stirpes,* or *per capita at each generation.*

- **Qualifying as an issue:** Establishing a parent-child relationship means each can inherit from and through the other. Such a relationship can be established (1) *naturally/genetically,* whether the parents are married or not; or (2) *by adoption,* which as a general rule severs the relationship with the natural parents—though there are increasingly exceptions to the severance rule; or (3) through *equitable adoption,* where the adoptive parent agrees to adopt, but fails to complete the adoption, yet the child has a claim against the adoptive parent's estate equal to his or her intestate share.

- **Advancements:** At common law, inter vivos gifts to a child are rebuttably presumed to count against the child's share of the parent's intestate estate. Under the modern trend, inter vivos gifts do *not* count against an heir's share of the decedent's estate absent a contemporaneous writing by the donor expressing such intent or a writing by the donee acknowledging such intent.

■ **Bars to taking:** Even where an individual is otherwise entitled to take from the decedent (non-probate or probate, testate or intestate property), the taker is barred from taking under the following circumstances:

■ **Homicide doctrine:** If the taker killed the decedent, and the killing was felonious and intentional, the killer is treated as if he or she predeceased the decedent.

■ **Disclaimer:** If a party properly executes a disclaimer, thereby declining to accept the testamentary gift the taker otherwise would be entitled to receive, the party who disclaimed is treated as if he or she predeceased the decedent.

I. THE INTESTATE DISTRIBUTION SCHEME

A. Introduction

1. **Intestacy the norm:** Despite the benefits of nonprobate transfers and wills, roughly half the population dies intestate. Any property not disposed of by nonprobate means falls to probate, and any probate property not disposed of by will falls to intestacy where it is distributed to the decedent's heirs.

2. **Heirs vs. heirs apparent:** To qualify as an heir (an intestate taker), the heir must survive the decedent. Though laypeople often refer to others as their "heirs," technically this usage is incorrect. Because an heir must survive the decedent, a person who is alive has no heirs, only "heirs apparent."

3. **Expectancies:** Most children expect to receive some property from their parents' estate when a parent dies (particularly after the death of the second parent). Such an expectation by an heir apparent is called an *expectancy.*

   a. **Not a property interest:** An expectancy is not a property interest. The heir needs to survive the decedent to take anything, and even if the heir survives the decedent, the decedent can defeat the expectancy by transferring the property inter vivos or by executing a will that devises the property to others.

   b. **Transferability:** Because an expectancy is not a property interest, the general rule is that it is not transferable. If, however, an heir apparent agrees to transfer his or her expectancy for valuable consideration and thereafter tries to avoid enforcement of the agreement on the grounds that an expectancy is not transferable, a court of equity will enforce the agreement if it finds it fair and equitable under the circumstances.

4. **Descent and distribution statute:** Under intestacy, a decedent's personal property is distributed according to the descent and distribution statute of the state where the decedent was domiciled at time of death, and the decedent's real property is distributed according to the law of descent and distribution of the state where the real property is located.

B. Overview—a typical intestate scheme: The basic structure of most descent and distribution statutes is the same. The statute provides a list, in order, of *who takes* in the event an individual dies intestate, and *how much* each individual is entitled to take. A typical intestate distribution scheme is as follows:

Who takes?	How much?
1. Surviving spouse	100% if no surviving issue, parents, or issue of parents; or
	50% if one child, or issue of one deceased child, or no child but parents, or issue of parents; or
	33% if > one child (alive or deceased with issue).

Any property not passing to a surviving spouse passes as follows:

2. Issue	Equally
3. Parents	Equally
4. Issue of parents	Equally
5. Grandparents	Equally
6. Issue of grandparents	Equally
7. Next-of-kin	By degree of relationship
8. Escheat to the state	100%

1. **Tiered approach:** The categories of possible takers are listed in order, in tiers. Any property not passing to the surviving spouse falls to the first tier where there is a live taker. Once that tier is determined, all the property that the surviving spouse did not take is distributed at that tier. No property falls to a lower tier.

   a. **Example:** Pete dies intestate survived by his wife, Gerri, his four children, and his mom. Under the typical intestate distribution scheme, his wife Gerri takes 33 percent of his property, and the rest is distributed equally among his four children. His mom does not receive any of his property.

   b. **Example:** Ann dies intestate survived by her children and her grandmother. Under the typical intestate distribution scheme, her property is distributed among her children. Her grandmother does not receive any of her property.

2. **State variations:** While the basic "order of takers" is the same in most states, even at the macro level some states differ. For example, California permits the issue of a predeceased spouse to take after issue of grandparents but before next-of-kin. Moreover, at the micro level, there is a plethora of minute details upon which different jurisdictions disagree.

3. **Community property:** The intestate distribution scheme above presumes that the jurisdiction does not recognize community property. If the jurisdiction recognizes community property, upon the first spouse's death the community property is immediately divided: 50 percent to the surviving spouse outright and 50 percent to the deceased spouse. The deceased spouse's 50 percent goes into probate. The deceased spouse may devise his or her half as he or she wishes. If, however, the deceased spouse dies intestate, typically all of the deceased spouse's half of the community property goes to the surviving spouse. The deceased spouse's separate property is distributed pursuant to the intestate distribution scheme set forth above.

4. **Coverage note:** Because individual treatment of each state's intestate scheme is beyond the scope of this outline, the material will focus on the key components of the typical scheme and of the Uniform Probate Code (UPC). Students need to pay close attention to whether their professor requires them to be responsible only for the UPC, the probate code of the state where the law school is located, or some combination thereof.

C. The UPC approach: The UPC intestate distribution scheme, UPC §§2-102 through 2-105, has fewer tiers of takers and a different method of calculating their respective shares:

Who takes?	How much?
1. Surviving spouse	100% if no issue or parents; or
	100% if all decedent's issue are also issue of surviving spouse and surviving spouse has no other issue; or
	$200,000 + 75% of rest if no issue but surviving parent; or
	$150,000 + 50% of rest if all issue are also issue of surviving spouse and surviving spouse has other issue;
	$100,000 + 50% of rest if one or more issue not issue of surviving spouse.

Any property not passing to a surviving spouse passes as follows:

2. Issue	Equally
3. Parents	Equally, or all to the survivor
4. Issue of parents	Equally
5. Grandparents/issue	50% to paternal grandparents or survivor; otherwise to their issue equally;
	50% to maternal grandparents or survivor; otherwise to their issue equally;
	If no surviving grandparents or issue on one side, all to the other side
6. Escheat to the state	100%

1. UPC favors surviving spouse: Compared to most state intestate schemes, the UPC gives the surviving spouse a larger share of the deceased spouse's intestate estate.

2. UPC favors state: Note the different philosophies about the propriety of the decedent's property going to the state. Under the UPC, the decedent's property escheats to the state much sooner than it would under most state statutes.

II. SURVIVING SPOUSE: WHO QUALIFIES

A. Marriage requirement: The term *spouse* as used in descent and distribution statutes assumes that the couple has gone through a valid marriage ceremony.

1. Cohabitants: Nonmarried couples who live together generally do not qualify as spouses and have no inheritance rights upon the death of one.

2. Common law marriage: Common law marriage doctrines generally provide that if a couple lives together for the requisite period of time and holds itself out as a married couple, the couple is treated as a married couple even though its members fail to go through a valid marriage ceremony. If cohabitants meet the requirements for common law marriage, they have the inheritance rights of a married couple. Not all jurisdictions recognize common law marriages.

B. Same-sex couples: The heated debate over whether same-sex couples should be permitted to marry or otherwise qualify for spousal-like status continues at the state level.

1. **Same-sex marriages:** At the time of publication, five states recognized and were permitting same-sex marriages: Connecticut, Iowa, Massachusetts, New Hampshire, and Vermont. In late 2009, the Council of the District of Columbia adopted a law authorizing same-sex marriages and the mayor signed it, but it is subject to mandatory Congressional review. If not reversed, Washington, D.C. will start permitting same-sex marriages in early 2010. For a period in 2008, following the California Supreme Court's ruling that the state's opposite-sex definition of marriage violated the state's constitution, California permitted same-sex marriages. In November 2008, however, California voters passed Proposition 8, reinstating the opposite-sex definition via constitutional amendment. The constitutionality of Proposition 8 was upheld, but same-sex marriages performed during that time are still recognized. Increasingly, states appear likely to permit same-sex marriages; which states, however, and how many, only time will tell.

2. **Civil unions/domestic partners:** An increasing number of states have granted same-sex couples many of the same rights as married couples, but without permitting them to marry. At the time of publication, California, the District of Columbia, New Hampshire, Nevada, New Jersey, Oregon and Washington permit same-sex couples a civil union/registered domestic partner option that grants same-sex couples essentially the same state (but not federal) rights and duties as married couples; in Colorado, Hawaii, Maine, and Wisconsin, same-sex couples can register with the state and receive many, but not all, of the same state rights and duties as married couples.

3. **Contract claim:** In some states, a surviving same-sex partner might have a claim against the deceased partner based on contract law. Whether the contract must be express (either oral or written—as opposed to implied) varies from jurisdiction to jurisdiction.

4. **Defense of Marriage Act:** In 1996, Congress enacted the Defense of Marriage Act. The Act defines "marriage" for federal purposes as applying only to heterosexual couples and provides that despite the Full Faith and Credit Clause of the Constitution, states are not required to recognize same-sex marriages entered into in other states. Nevertheless, at the time of publication, California, New Jersey, New Mexico, New York, Rhode Island, and the District of Columbia had decided to recognize same-sex marriages entered into in other states (though to varying degrees). Other states may do so as well in the future as same-sex marriages receive more acceptance.

C. **Putative spouses:** Putative spouses generally do qualify as spouses. Putative spouses exist where the couple goes through what at least one of the parties believes is a valid marriage ceremony, but for some reason the marriage is either void or voidable (e.g., one spouse is already married and not divorced; the marriage ceremony is not valid; the marriage violates the states' degree of relationship requirements). As long as one of the parties reasonably believes in good faith that the marriage is valid, the spouses qualify as putative spouses and are treated as spouses for purposes of most intestate schemes.

D. **Married but separated:** Spouses who are legally separated generally still qualify as spouses for purposes of the intestate distribution scheme. Even if the parties have filed for divorce, the parties remain legally married until the court enters the final judgment or decree of dissolution of marriage.

Spousal abandonment: In some states, if one spouse abandons the other, the abandoning spouse may be disqualified from inheriting from the other spouse.

E. Survival requirements: To be eligible to receive property from a decedent, a taker must "survive" the decedent. How long the taker must survive the decedent, and the burden of proof the taker has to satisfy, varies from jurisdiction to jurisdiction, and within any given jurisdiction it may vary based upon the type of property involved—probate intestate, probate testate, or nonprobate. If the claimant fails to meet the survival requirement, the claimant is treated as if he or she predeceased the decedent.

1. **Scope:** Historically, a survival requirement applied to anyone claiming a decedent's probate testate or intestate property, but not to nonprobate property. The modern trend applies a survival requirement to nonprobate property as well. Close reading of the controlling statute is necessary to determine a jurisdiction's approach, and whether the jurisdiction applies the same or different survival requirements to the different types of property.

2. **Common law:** Under the common law approach, to qualify as an heir the party had to prove by a preponderance of the evidence that he or she survived the decedent by a millisecond. Whether a person survived the decedent is a question of fact.

   Historical perspective: The preponderance of the evidence approach proved workable at early common law because the potential for simultaneous death scenarios was low. With the advent of the Industrial Revolution and the development of machines such as cars, trains, and airplanes that substantially increased the potential for simultaneous death scenarios, however, the preponderance of the evidence standard came under increasing criticism.

3. **Uniform Simultaneous Death Act:** As initially adopted, the Uniform Simultaneous Death Act (USDA) basically codified the common law rule. The act provided that where "there is no sufficient evidence" as to who survived whom, the party claiming a right to take is to be treated as having predeceased the decedent.

   a. **Criticism of common law and USDA:** Under a typical intestate distribution scheme, if both spouses die intestate with no children, all of the couple's probate property ends up on the second-to-die spouse's side of the family. If both spouses die together, the issue becomes which spouse survived the other. Instead of the two families grieving together, they end up in court suing each other to see which family receives all of the couple's property. The common law rule has been criticized (1) for its high costs of litigation (the "winner take all" outcome coupled with the low burden of proof invites litigation in simultaneous or near simultaneous death situations), (2) for its unfairness (all of the couple's property ends up on one side of the family), and (3) because it encourages unseemly behavior (families suing each other when they should be comforting each other).

   b. **Example:** In *Janus v. Tarasewicz,* 482 N.E.2d 418 (Ill. App. 1985), Stanley and Theresa Janus returned from their honeymoon to learn that Stanley's brother had died unexpectedly. The couple was distraught and unknowingly took some Tylenol laced with cyanide. Stanley collapsed first, Theresa a short time later. Although there was conflicting medical evidence, Stanley's vital signs arguably disappeared during the ambulance ride to the hospital, and he was pronounced dead shortly after arrival. Theresa arguably still had a palpable pulse and blood pressure upon arrival at the hospital, and she was put on a mechanical respirator for approximately 48 hours before being removed and pronounced dead. Stanley had a life insurance policy that named Theresa as primary beneficiary; in the event that she failed to survive him, his mother was named as contingent beneficiary. Stanley's mother sued her family claiming that there was insufficient evidence that Theresa survived him. Applying the USDA standard, the court held that there was sufficient evidence to support the finding that Theresa survived Stanley.

   c. Determining time of death: To determine whether one person survived another, one needs to know when each party died.

- **Common law:** Under the common law approach, a person is dead when there is irreversible cessation of circulatory and respiratory functions.

  - **Criticism:** With the advent of modern medical technology, the common law standard became unworkable. Artificial life support systems now keep patients' hearts beating and lungs breathing.

- **Modern trend:** Under the modern trend, where circulatory or respiratory functions are maintained artificially, death occurs when there is irreversible cessation of total brain activity.

4. The clear and convincing evidence standard: To minimize simultaneous death litigation, some states have raised the bar on the survival requirement. In those states, to qualify as a survivor, a claimant must prove by clear and convincing evidence that he or she survived the decedent.

Criticism: The clear and convincing evidence survival standard has been criticized for not raising the bar enough. The difference between preponderance of the evidence and clear and convincing evidence arguably is not enough to deter family members from suing each other when a substantial amount of money is at stake.

5. UPC 120-hour approach: The UPC requires that to qualify as a taker (surviving heir, devisee, or life insurance policy beneficiary), the taker must prove by clear and convincing evidence that he or she survived the decedent by 120 hours (five days). UPC §§2-104 and 2-702. The most recent version of the USDA requires the same.

6. The mechanics of the survival requirement: The mechanics of applying the survival requirement is a two-step process: (1) Did the claimant *actually* survive the decedent? (2) Did the claimant *legally* survive the decedent? The first step is purely a question of fact based upon the fact pattern. The second prong is an artificial analysis based upon the statutory requirement that the heir must survive by a requisite period of time. Even if the claimant actually survives the decedent, if the claimant does not legally survive the decedent (that is, meet the statutory survival requirement), the claimant is treated as if he or she predeceased the decedent.

   a. Apply separately to each decedent: In applying the survival requirement, be sure to start the analysis all over again when analyzing who gets the second-to-die decedent's property. Otherwise you may get caught in an abstract catch-22 where you reason that because the second-to-die is treated as predeceasing the first-to-die, the first-to-die must take the second-to-die's property.

   b. Example: Pete and Gerri are married with no children. While taking a romantic drive down the Big Sur coastline, Gerri looks a bit too long at the sunset and drives off the road. The car sails off the cliff onto the rocks below. Pete is killed instantly. Gerri dies two days later. Assume both Pete and Gerri died intestate. Pete is survived by his father, Frank. Gerri is survived by her mother, Maude.

Analytical steps: Start with the decedent who died first. Check to see if the claimant actually and legally survived the decedent. Then, when analyzing who gets the second-to-die's property, start the analysis all over again.

Common law/USDA approach: Pete died first. Because Gerri can prove by a preponderance of the evidence that she survived him (here, by two days), she takes his probate intestate property. When Gerri dies two days later, because Pete failed to survive her, Gerri's intestate property (including the property she took from Pete) goes to her mother, Maude.

The clear and convincing evidence approach: Pete died first. Because Gerri can prove by clear and convincing evidence that she survived him (here, by two days), she takes his probate intestate property. When Gerri dies two days later, because Pete failed to survive her, her property (including the property she took from Pete) goes to her mom, Maude.

UPC approach: Analyze the spouses in the order of their actual deaths.

i. **Analysis of the first spouse to die:** Pete died first. (1) Can Gerri prove that she *actually* survived Pete? Yes; she survived by two days. (2) Can Gerri prove that she *legally* survived Pete—that is, can she prove by clear and convincing evidence that she survived Pete by 120 hours (five days)? No; she died two days later. For purposes of distributing Pete's estate, Gerri is treated as if she predeceased him. All of Pete's probate property passes to his father, Frank.

ii. **Analysis of second spouse to die:** Who takes Gerri's probate property? Because we treated her as predeceasing Pete, does she have a surviving spouse? No. Start the analysis all over again when analyzing who gets a decedent's property. When analyzing who gets Gerri's probate property, ask whether Pete (1) actually survived Gerri, and (2) legally survived Gerri. Here, Pete did not actually survive Gerri, so she has no surviving spouse. Her probate property passes to her mother, Maude.

7. **Failure to meet survival requirement:** Whichever standard is applied, if the claimant fails to meet the survival requirement, the claimant is treated as if he or she predeceased the decedent.

8. **Wills and nonprobate instruments:** As applied to probate testate and nonprobate property, the statutory survival requirement is a default rule that applies if the written instrument does not have its own express survival requirement. If the written instrument has an express survival requirement, it applies.

III. SURVIVING SPOUSE: CALCULATING SHARE

A. **Policy concerns:** How much the surviving spouse takes turns on the details of each state's descent and distribution scheme. The key policy issue is how much the surviving spouse ***should*** take. In particular, (1) should the surviving spouse take ***all*** of the deceased spouse's intestate property if there are surviving issue, and (2) should the surviving spouse take ***all*** of the deceased spouse's intestate property if there are surviving parents or issue of parents (siblings and their issue)?

B. **Traditional intestate distribution scheme:** Under the traditional intestate distribution scheme, a surviving spouse takes 100 percent of the deceased spouse's intestate property only in the absence of any surviving issue, parents, or issue of parents.

If surviving issue: If the predeceased spouse had surviving issue, the surviving spouse's share often depended on how many surviving "children" (alive or dead but survived by issue) survived the decedent.

1. **If one surviving child:** If the deceased spouse is survived by one child (alive or dead but survived by issue), typically the surviving spouse takes 50 percent of the predeceased spouse's intestate property.

2. **If more than one surviving child:** If the deceased spouse is survived by more than one child (alive or dead but survived by issue), typically the surviving spouse takes 33 percent of the predeceased spouse's intestate property.

3. **If surviving parent(s) or issue of parent(s):** If the predeceased spouse has no surviving issue, but has surviving parent(s) or issue of parent(s), typically the surviving spouse takes 50 percent of the deceased spouse's intestate property.

4. **Small estates:** Some states give the surviving spouse the first $50,000 or $100,000 of the deceased spouse's intestate estate and then the appropriate fraction of the rest of the deceased spouse's probate intestate estate. The effect is to give the surviving spouse all of the deceased spouse's intestate estate where the estate is small enough.

C. **UPC approach:** A surviving spouse is better off under the UPC than under the typical intestate distribution scheme. UPC §2-102.

    If surviving issue: Unlike most state statutes, the UPC gives the surviving spouse 100 percent of the decedent's property, even if the decedent has surviving issue, if (1) the surviving spouse is also the parent of the surviving issue, and (2) the surviving spouse has no other issue. UPC §2-102(1)(ii).

    1. **Rationale:** The assumption is that most spouses trust the surviving spouse to determine how best to use the property for the benefit of the surviving issue, as opposed to giving the surviving issue their own shares outright (and incurring the administrative hassles and expenses if any of them are minors).

    2. **Whose surviving issue:** The surviving spouse takes less than 100 percent of the deceased spouse's intestate property if the deceased spouse has surviving issue and either (1) not all of them are also issue of the surviving spouse, or (2) all are issue of the surviving spouse, but the surviving spouse also has issue of his or her own who were not issue of the predeceased spouse.

        a. **Not all issue are issue of surviving spouse:** Where the deceased spouse has surviving issue, but not all of them are also issue of the surviving spouse, the surviving spouse takes the first $100,000 þ 50 percent of the rest of the predeceased spouse's intestate property. The remaining 50 percent is distributed equally among the deceased spouse's issue. UPC §2-102(4).

        b. **Surviving spouse has own issue:** Where the deceased spouse has surviving issue, and all of them are issue of the surviving spouse, but the surviving spouse has issue of his or her own who were not issue of the predeceased spouse, the surviving spouse takes the first $150,000 + 50 percent of the rest of the predeceased spouse's intestate property. The remaining 50 percent is distributed among the deceased spouse's issue. UPC §2-104(3).

    c. Stepparent syndrome: The UPC is more concerned about the surviving spouse properly taking care of the deceased spouse's issue where not all of the deceased spouse's issue are issue of the surviving spouse. In that case, the surviving spouse takes less and the issue take more. The potential for the dreaded "Cinderella evil stepparent" syndrome arguably is present where not all of the predeceased spouse's issue are issue of the surviving spouse.

    3. No issue but surviving parent(s): Where the deceased spouse has no issue but is survived by one or more parents, the UPC gives the surviving spouse the first $200,000 + 75 percent of the rest of the deceased spouse's property. UPC §2-102(2). Surviving parents are worse off under the UPC than under a typical state statute.

    4. No surviving issue or parent(s), but surviving issue of parents: Most states give the surviving spouse 100 percent of the deceased spouse's property only if there are no surviving issue, parents, or issue of parents. The UPC gives the surviving spouse 100 percent of the deceased spouse's property if there are no surviving issue or parents. The UPC does not consider issue of parents when determining the surviving spouse's share. UPC §2-102(1)(i).

    5. Tiered approach to takers: Just like with the typical intestate distribution scheme, any property not passing to a surviving spouse falls to the first tier where there is a live taker, and all the falling property is distributed at that tier.

  D. State's spousal share: Each state's intestate distribution statute must be read with great care to determine (1) the different possible *fractional shares* of the surviving spouse, and (2) *what determines* which fractional share the surviving spouse receives.

IV. DESCENDANTS/ISSUE: CALCULATING SHARES

  A. Property to descendants/issue: If there is no surviving spouse, or there is a surviving spouse but he or she does not take all of the decedent's property, both the typical intestate scheme and the UPC give the property to the decedent's issue equally.

    Descendants/issue vs. children: The term *descendants/issue* is much broader than the term *children.* One's *descendants/issue* are all of one's offspring—one's children, their children, their children, and so on. One's *children* are one's immediate offspring, that is, only the first generation of one's issue.

  B. Calculating shares—analytical steps: If a decedent's issue take under intestacy, they take equally. But this statement is overly simplistic and masks a number of subtle issues.

    1. Taking equally: Where all of the decedent's children survive the decedent, what constitutes taking "equally" is rather straightforward. For example, suppose the decedent dies survived by three children, *A, B,* and *C:*

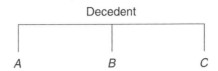

The decedent's property should be divided equally among his or her three children, one-third each. The question becomes more complicated if one or more of the children have issue of their own:

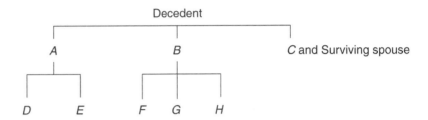

2. **Determining which issue take:** Three fundamental principles need to be kept in mind when distributing property to a decedent's issue.

   - **Issue of predeceased children take in their place:** If the decedent had a child who predeceased the decedent but is survived by issue, his or her issue will share in the distribution of the decedent's property. It is often said that the surviving issue of the predeceased child take "by representation"—they step up and represent the predeceased relative. In the example above, if *A* predeceased the decedent, *A*'s issue who survive the decedent would take *A*'s share by representation. *A*'s one-third would be split equally by *A*'s issue.

   - **If a person takes, his or her issue do not:** In the example above, if *B* survives the decedent, *B* would receive a share but *B*'s issue *(F, G, and H)* would not receive a share of the decedent's estate.

   - **Absent adoption, only blood relatives qualify as heirs:** If *C* predeceases the decedent, survived by his wife and her children from a prior marriage, neither *C*'s surviving wife nor her issue from the prior relationship are entitled to share in the distribution of the decedent's *intestate* property. As a general rule, sons-in-law, daughters-in-law, and stepchildren do not qualify as eligible takers under the intestate distribution scheme.

3. **Taking equally where issue of unequal degree:** It is easy to calculate equal shares when all the surviving issue are of equal degree of relationship to the decedent. It is more difficult to determine what constitutes equal shares when the issue are of unequal degree. There are three different approaches to how to calculate the shares when the surviving issue are of unequal degree. To understand the three approaches, it is necessary to understand the subissues inherent in the problem. For example:

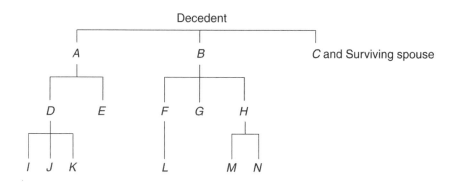

Assume *A, B, C, D, F,* and *G* predecease the decedent (you might want to draw a line through those who predeceased the decedent), who dies intestate. Assuming no surviving spouse, the issue is who takes the decedent's property.

4. **Analytical steps in calculating shares:** Analytically, there are three distinct subissues that need to be answered in calculating the shares of the takers where one or more of the decedent's children predecease the decedent survived by issue.

   First, at which generation should the decedent's property be divided first? At the first generation, even if there are no live takers in the first generation, or at the first generation where there is a live taker?

   Second, at whichever generation the estate is divided first, how many shares should the estate be divided into? The answer to this step is always the same: one share for each descendant who is alive at that generation, and one share for each descendant at that generation who is dead but survived by issue.

   Third, how are the "dropping" shares distributed? The "dropping shares" are the shares for the descendants who are dead but survived by issue. Should the dropping shares drop by bloodline to the issue of that party, or should the dropping shares be "pooled" and distributed equally among the eligible takers at the next generation?

   Although the answer to the second step is always the same, there are different possible answers to the first and third steps. Three different doctrines have developed that correspond to three of the different possible combinations of possible answers to the different steps: the ***per stirpes*** approach; the ***per capita with representation*** approach; and the ***per capita at each generation*** approach.

5. **Distributions to issue of collaterals:** Where a decedent's property is distributed to the issue of collateral relatives (see section V), the per stirpes, per capita, and per capita at each generation doctrines apply as well in calculating the shares.

C. **Per stirpes:** Under the per stirpes approach (also known as the old English approach), *always* make the first division of the decedent's property at the first generation of descendants, whether there are any live takers or not; the dropping shares then drop by bloodline.

Mechanics of the per stirpes approach:

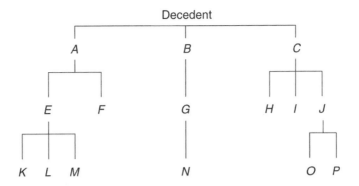

Assume *A, B, C, E, H,* and *J* all predecease the decedent, who then dies intestate. Who takes the decedent's property assuming no surviving spouse?

- Step 1: Under per stirpes, always divide the decedent's property at the first generation (among decedent's children), even if everyone at that generation is dead.

- Step 2: One share is given to each party who is alive, and one share is given to each party who is dead but survived by issue. Here, although *A, B,* and *C* are all dead, *A, B,* and *C* are all survived by issue, so each receives a one-third share.

- Step 3: Under per stirpes, the shares for each party who is dead but survived by issue drop by bloodline. Each share drops only to the issue of the predeceased party. *A*'s one-third drops to his or her issue; *B*'s one-third drops to his or her issue; and *C*'s one-third drops to his or her issue.

  When distributing *A*'s one-third, drop to the next generation of *A*'s descendants and divide it one share for each party who is alive at that level and one share for each party who is dead but survived by issue. *A*'s one-third is divided equally between *E* and *F*, one-sixth each, and *E*'s one-sixth drops by bloodline to *E*'s issue, *K, L,* and *M,* to be shared equally, one-eighteenth each.

  B's one-third drops by bloodline to *B*'s issue, *G*. Because *G* is alive and takes, *N* takes nothing.

  C's one-third drops by bloodline to *C*'s descendants. Dividing up *C*'s share at the next generation, the formula is one share for each party who is alive and one share for each party who is dead but survived by issue. *H* predeceased *C* and is not survived by issue, so *H* does not take a share. *I* is alive, so *I* takes a share. *J* is dead but survived by issue, so *J* takes a share. *C*'s one-third is split one-sixth to *I*, one-sixth to *J*. *J*'s one-sixth drops by bloodline to *O* and *P,* one-twelfth each.

D. Per capita with representation: Under the per capita with representation approach (also known as the per capita approach or the modern American per stirpes approach, though the latter name is more confusing), make the first division of the decedent's property at the first generation where there is a live taker; the dropping shares then drop by bloodline.

1. **Mechanics of the per capita with representation approach:**

Assume *A, B, C, E, H,* and *J* all predecease the decedent, who then dies intestate. Who takes the decedent's property assuming no surviving spouse?

- Step 1: At which generation should the decedent's property be divided first? Under per capita with representation, always divide at the first generation where there is a live taker. Here, divide at the second generation, *E*'s generation.

- Step 2: How many shares should the property be divided into? One share is given to each party who is alive, and one share is given to each party who is dead but survived by issue. Here, *F, G,* and *I* are alive (three shares), and *E* and *J* are dead but survived by issue (two shares), so one-fifth each (no share for *H*).

- Step 3: How are the dropping shares (the shares for the dead parties survived by issue) distributed? Under per capita with representation, they drop by bloodline. *E*'s one-fifth will drop by bloodline to O and P, one-tenth each.

2. **Criticism:** Under both per stirpes and per capita with representation, there is the potential for descendants of equal degree to the decedent to take unequally.

   Under the per stirpes approach, although *K, L, M, O,* and *P* are all the decedent's grandchildren and thus equally related to the decedent, they take unequally. *K, L,* and *M* took one-eighteenth, and *O* and *P* took one-twelfth each. Under the per capita with representation approach, although *K, L, M, O,* and *P* are all great-grandchildren of the decedent and thus related to the decedent by the third degree, they take unequally. *K, L,* and *M* took one-fifteenth each, while *O* and *P* took one-tenth each.

3. **Benefit of per capita at each generation:** The per capita at each generation approach ensures that all descendents who are equally related to the decedent take equally. Per capita at each generation "pools" the dropping shares (the shares for descendants who are dead but survived by issue). The "pooling" terminology is just an artificial way of saying that the dropping shares are added together and then divided equally among all of the eligible takers at the next generation.

E. **Per capita at each generation:** Under the per capita at each generation approach, always make the first division of the decedent's property at the first generation where there is a live taker, and the dropping shares drop by pooling—combine them and distribute them equally among the eligible takers at the next generation.

Mechanics of the per capita at each generation approach:

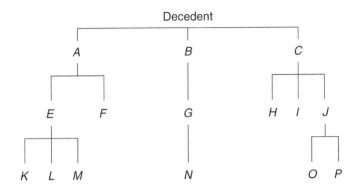

Assume *A, B, C, E, H,* and *J* all predecease the decedent, who then dies intestate. Who takes the decedent's property assuming no surviving spouse?

- Step 1: At which generation should the decedent's property be divided first? Under per capita at each generation, always divide at the first generation where there is a live taker. Here, divide at the second generation, *E*'s generation.

- Step 2: How many shares should the property be divided into? One share is given to each party who is alive, one share is given to each party who is dead but survived by issue. Here, *F, G,* and *I* are alive (three shares), and *E* and *J* are dead but survived by issue (two shares), so one-fifth each (no share for *H*).

- Step 3: How are the dropping shares (the shares for the dead parties survived by issue) distributed? Under per capita at each generation, pool the dropping shares. There are two dropping shares. Add them together (*E*'s one-fifth + *J*'s one-fifth = two-fifths) and divide the total equally among the eligible takers at the next generation. *K, L, M, O,* and *P* are the eligible takers at the next generation (*N* is not eligible because her parent took already).

  Dividing the pool (two-fifths) among the eligible takers (two-fifths divided by five) results in *K, L, M, O,* and *P* each taking two-twenty-fifths. Under the per capita at each generation approach, all descendants at a generation who take will take equally.

Summary of Distribution to Issue

	Per Stirpes	**Per Capita with Representation**	**Per Capita at Each Generation**
Where is the estate divided first?	First generation always	First generation live taker	First generation live taker
How many shares is the estate divided into at that generation?	One share each party alive; one share each party dead but survived by issue	One share each party alive; one share each party dead but survived by issue	One share each party alive; one share each party dead but survived by issue
How to treat dropping shares?	Drop by bloodline	Drop by bloodline	Drop by pooling

F. Miscellaneous rules

1. **Power to opt out:** Each jurisdiction has a default approach as to how to distribute a decedent's property among his or her issue. The default approach always applies to intestate distributions. But an individual can opt out of a jurisdiction's default approach by executing a valid will or nonprobate instrument that expressly provides for an alternative method of distributing the decedent's estate.

2. **UPC approach:** The original version of the UPC (the 1969 version) adopted the per capita with representation approach. The revised version of the UPC has adopted the per capita at each generation approach. UPC §2-106. Most jurisdictions, however, are split between the per stirpes and the per capita with representation approaches.

3. **Negative Disinheritance:** Assuming one does not want a particular heir to take any of his or her intestate property, what must one do to disinherit that particular heir?

   a. **Common law:** The only way a decedent can disinherit an heir is to execute a valid will that disposes of all of the decedent's property so that nothing passes through intestacy (thereby depriving the heir of any chance of taking). If the decedent's will expresses an intent to disinherit the heir, but some or all of the decedent's property is distributed through intestacy and the heir in question qualifies to receive a share, the heir takes despite the decedent's clear intent.

   b. **Modern trend/UPC:** Under the modern trend/UPC approach, a decedent can disinherit an heir by properly executing a will that expresses such an intent, even if some or all of the decedent's property passes through intestacy and the heir otherwise would have qualified to take some of the property. The heir is treated as if he or she predeceased the decedent. (If the heir is survived by issue, they take by representation unless the will expressly disinherits them as well.) UPC §2-101(b).

V. SHARES OF ANCESTORS AND REMOTE COLLATERALS

A. **Introduction:** Each person sits in the middle of a family tree. An individual may have his or her own family (spouse, issue), while at the same time being part of a number of other families (child of parents, grandchild of grandparents, and so forth). When a decedent dies intestate, his or her property is distributed first to his or her immediate family. If, however, there is no surviving spouse or issue, the property flows "up" to the decedent's ancestors and collateral relatives. There are three different major approaches to how the decedent's property should be distributed when it flows "up" to ancestors and remote collaterals: (1) the parentelic approach, (2) the degree of relationship approach, and (3) the degree of relationship with a parentelic tiebreaker approach.

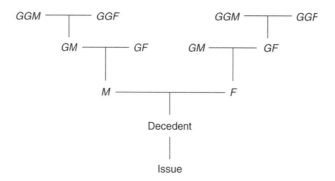

Collateral relatives: The decedent, the decedent's spouse, and the decedent's issue are the decedent's immediate family. All of the decedent's other relatives are technically called "collateral relatives." The decedent's parents (*M* for mother and *F* for father) and their other issue are called first-line collaterals, because their line is the first line removed from the decedent's immediate family. The decedent's grandparents (*GM* for grandmother and *GF* for grandfather) and their other issue (other than the decedent's parents) are called second-line collaterals. Great-grandparents (*GGM* for great-grandmother and *GGF* for great-grandfather) and their other issue (other than the decedent's grandparents) are called third-line collaterals, and so on.

B. Parentelic approach: At the macro level, every intestate scheme starts with the decedent's immediate family and then moves out along collateral lines, starting with the closer lines and moving to the more remote. This is known as the parentelic approach. This distribution approach keeps going out by collateral lines until there is a line in which there is a live taker. The property is then distributed to the decedent's relatives in that parentelic line. In distributing the property, the per stirpes, per capita, or per capita at each generation doctrines apply, depending on the default approach in the state.

C. Degree of relationship approach: The degree of relationship approach focuses on the degree of relationship between the decedent and claiming relative, regardless of which parentelic line the taker is in. Under the degree of relationship approach, one simply counts the degrees of relationship between the decedent and the relative, and those relatives of the closest degree (lower degree) take to the exclusion of those of a more remote degree (higher degree). Some jurisdictions start with the parentelic approach but at some point (either after the first collateral line or the second collateral line) switch to the degree of relationship approach.

1. Determining the degree of relationship: To determine a person's degree of relationship, count from the decedent up to the closest common ancestor (the head of a parentelic line—a grandparent or great-grandparent, or so on), and then down to the live relative.

2. Example: Assume the decedent dies intestate survived by only *A, B, C,* and *D.*

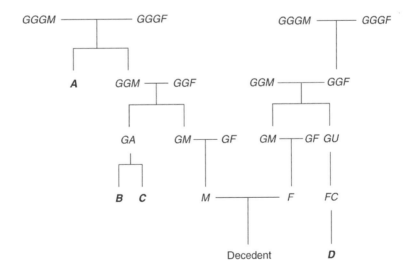

(*M* = Mother; *F* = Father; *GM* = Grandmother; *GF* = Grandfather; *GGM* = Great-grandmother; *GGF* = Great-grandfather; *GGGM* = Great-great-grandmother; *GGGF* = Great-great-grandfather; *GA* = Great Aunt; *GU* = Great Uncle; *FC* = First Cousin)

To calculate the degree of relationship between *A, B, C,* and *D* to the decedent, the key is to identify the closest common ancestor (the closest grandparent) who both parties share. Count the steps up from the decedent to that common ancestor and then down from the common ancestor to the party in question.

Degree of relationship for A: The closest common ancestor for both the decedent and *A* are the *GGGP*s. Count up from decedent to the *GGGP*s. From decedent to *M* is one, from *M* to *GP*s is two, from *GP*s to *GGP*s is three, from *GGP*s to *GGGP*s is four, and then down from *GGGP*s to *A* is five. *A* is related to the decedent by the fifth degree.

Degree of relationship for B: The closest common ancestor for both the decedent and *B* are the *GGP*s. Count up from decedent to the *GGP*s. From decedent to *M* is one, from *M* to *GP*s is two, from *GP*s to *GGP*s is three, from *GGP*s down to *GA* is four, and then from *GA* to *B* is five. *B* is related to the decedent by the fifth degree.

Degree of relationship for C: The closest common ancestor for both the decedent and *C* are the *GGP*s. Count up from decedent to the *GGP*s. From decedent to *M* is one, from *M* to *GP*s is two, from *GP*s to *GGP*s is three, from *GGP*s down to *GA* is four, and then from *GA* to *C* is five. *C* is related to the decedent by the fifth degree.

Degree of relationship for D: The closest common ancestor for both the decedent and *D* are the *GGP*s. Count up from decedent to the *GGP*s. From decedent to *F* is one, *F* to *GP*s is two, *GP*s to *GGP*s is three, from *GGP*s down to *GU* is four, and then from *GU* to *FC* is five, and from *FC* to *D* is six. *D* is related to the decedent by the sixth degree.

Degree of relationship approach: Under the degree of relationship approach, those relatives of a closer degree take to the exclusion of those of a more remote degree. Here, *A, B,* and *C* are of the fifth degree, and *D* is of the sixth degree. *A, B,* and *C* take to the exclusion of *D. A, B,* and *C* split the estate equally.

Parentelic approach: Under the parentelic approach, one simply keeps going out by parentelic lines until one finds the first collateral line with a live taker. The property is then distributed to the takers in that line. Here, there are no live takers in the parents' line (the first-line collaterals). There are no live takers in the grandparents' line (the second-line collaterals). But there are live takers in the great-grandparents' line (the third-line collaterals). Under the parentelic approach, once a collateral line with a live taker is found, the property is distributed in that line. Here, the property goes to the issue of the great-grandparents, *B, C,* and *D.*

(How much *B, C,* and *D* take turns on the particulars of the state's intestate distribution scheme. Some jurisdictions split the property 50-50 between the maternal and paternal common ancestors and then distribute to their issue—in that case, *B* and *C* take 25 percent each, and *D* takes 50 percent. Other jurisdictions apply the per stirpes/per capita with representation/per capita at each generation default approach and make the first division below the common ancestor tier.)

D. **Degree of relationship with a parentelic tiebreaker approach:** The third approach to property passing to collateral relatives is the degree of relationship with a parentelic tiebreaker. As the name indicates, the first step is to determine the degree of relationship of the possible takers. Those of a closer degree take to the exclusion of those of a higher, more remote degree. Then, if there are multiple takers sharing the lowest degree of relationship, under the parentelic tiebreaker, those in the closer parentelic/collateral lines take to the exclusion of those in the more remote parentelic/collateral lines.

Application: Analyzing the above fact pattern under the degree of relationship with a parentelic tiebreaker approach, *A, B,* and *C* are of the fifth degree of relationship, and *D* is of the sixth degree.

A, B, and *C* prevail initially. But because *B* and *C* are of a closer parentelic line (the *GGPs'* line; *D* is in the *GGGPs'* line), *B* and *C* take to the exclusion of *A* under the parentelic tiebreaker. *B* and *C* split the estate 50-50.

E. Half-bloods: Half-bloods are relatives who share only one common parent as opposed to the traditional relationship where siblings share both parents.

Classic scenario: *H* and *W* are married with two children, *A* and *B. H* either dies or *H* and *W* divorce, and *W* remarries *H2. W* and *H2* have a child, *C. A* and *B* are whole-blooded siblings (have identical genetic makeup, half from *H* and half from *W*), and *A* and *B* are half-blooded siblings with *C* (having only half the same genetic makeup, the half from *W*).

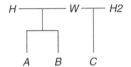

If *H, W,* and *H2* die, and then *A* dies intestate with no surviving spouse or issue, *A*'s property passes to his or her siblings (*H2* has no right to inherit from *A* absent additional evidence of adoption or attempted adoption). Inasmuch as *B* is a whole-blooded sibling, and *C* is only a half-blooded sibling, the issue is whether *B* takes more than *C*.

1. **Common law:** At common law, only whole-blooded relatives are entitled to inherit. Only *B* inherits from *A*.

2. **UPC and modern trend majority:** The UPC and the majority of the American jurisdictions have abolished the old common law rule and treat half-bloods the same as whole-bloods. UPC §2-107. *A*'s intestate estate is distributed equally between *B* and *C*.

3. **Modern trend minority:** A handful of American jurisdictions permit a whole-blooded relative to take more than a half-blood (typically the half-blood takes either half a share or takes only if there are no full-blooded relatives).

VI. DESCENDANTS/ISSUE: WHO QUALIFIES

A. Descendants/issue as takers: The basic intestate distribution scheme gives a decedent's probate property first to his or her surviving spouse and second to his or her descendants/issue. Often, the decedent's issue receive a share even if there is a surviving spouse. One qualifies as an issue in several ways.

Descendants/issue as chain of parent-child relationships: Issue are all generations of decedents from an individual—children, grandchildren, and so forth. But a line of issue is nothing more than a line of parent-child relationships:

Parent (*P*)   *P*

Child (*C*)   *C* = *P*

Grandchild   *C*

B. **Qualifying as a descendant/issue:** To qualify as a descendant/issue, a party must establish a parent-child relationship.

C. **Establishing parent-child relationship:** The starting point for analyzing whether a parent-child relationship exists is to apply the traditional biological test. The woman who contributes the egg *and* gives birth to the child is the child's natural mother. The man who contributes the sperm is the natural father.

1. **Parents married:** Both at common law and under the modern trend, if a child is born and the natural parents are married, a parent-child relationship arises for inheritance purposes.

2. **Inheriting "from and through":** A parent-child relationship establishes inheritance rights in both directions as a general rule. A child can inherit *from* a parent if the parent dies intestate, and a parent can inherit *from* a child if the child dies intestate. Moreover, as a general rule, inheritance rights are not only from a person, but also *through* a person. If a child's parent dies, and thereafter the parent's mother (the child's grandmother) dies intestate, the child can inherit *through* the deceased parent. Likewise, a parent can inherit not only from a child, but also *through* a predeceased child under the appropriate circumstances. When discussing inheritance rights, the general rule is that a person can inherit from and through the other party.

    a. **Presumption:** A child born to a married couple is presumed to be the child of that couple. The wife is presumed to be the natural mother. The husband is presumed to be the natural father. As a general rule, the child can inherit from and through either natural parent (*NP*), and either natural parent can inherit from and through the child (*C*).

    b. **UPC approach:** A handful of jurisdictions and the UPC require the natural parent (or, in some jurisdictions, the relatives of the natural parent) to openly treat the child as his or her own and not to refuse to support the child before that parent or relatives of that parent can inherit from and through the child, *even if the natural parents are married.* UPC §2-114(c) (1969).

        2008 revisions: The 2008 revisions to the UPC delete subsection (c) and provide instead that a genetic parent can inherit from and through the child unless the child died before reaching age 18 and there is clear and convincing evidence that immediately before the child's death the parental rights of the parent could have been terminated based on nonsupport, abandonment, abuse, neglect, or other actions or inactions of the parent toward the child. UPC §2-114(a)(2) (2008).

    c. **Posthumously born child:** A posthumously born child is a child conceived while the natural father is alive, but born after he dies. If the couple was married, the posthumously born child doctrine applies. It is an offshoot of the presumption that a child born to a married couple is a child of that couple. As long as the wife gives birth to a child within 280 days of a husband's death, a rebuttable presumption arises that the child is a natural child of the predeceased husband. If the child is born more than 280 days after the husband's death, the burden is on the child to establish that he or she is a child of the predeceased husband. (The Uniform Parentage Act §4 provides that any child born to a woman within 300 days of her husband's death is presumed to be a child of that husband.)

D. Adoption: The jurisdictions are split as to what effect, if any, adoption has on (1) a child's right to inherit from his or her natural parents, and (2) a child's right to inherit from his or her adopting parents. Pay careful attention to the statute you are covering. The focus here is on the 1969 UPC approach, which is the general approach, but references will also be made to the new 2008 amendments to the UPC which expand the parent-child relationship for inheritance purposes. Be sure to take note of which UPC version your professor is teaching.

1. **General rule:** If a child is adopted, the general rule is that the adopting parents step into the shoes of the natural parents, and a parent-child relationship is established between the adopted child and the adopting parents. Moreover, adoption severs the parent-child relationship between the natural parents and the child. The child (*C*) can no longer inherit from and through the natural parents (*NP*), and the natural parents can no longer inherit from and through the child. Instead, the child inherits from and through the adopting parents (*AP*), and the adopting parents inherit from and through the child. UPC §2-114(b) (1969); UPC §§2-118(a), 2-119(a) (2008).

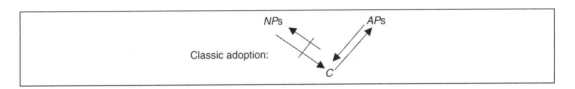

2. **Stepparent adoption exception:** A number of jurisdictions and the UPC modify the general rule concerning adoption when the adoption is by a stepparent (a spouse of a natural parent): (1) The adoption does not affect the parent-child relationship (and the inheritance rights) between the adopted child and the natural parent who is married to the adopting stepparent. (2) The adoption establishes a parent-child relationship between the adopting stepparent and the child, with full inheritance rights in both directions. (3) The adoption does not completely sever the parent-child relationship with the natural parent of the same gender as the adopting stepparent. The natural parent loses his or her right to inherit from and through the child, but the child retains the right to inherit from and through the natural parent of the same gender as the adopting stepparent. UPC §2-114(b) (1969); UPC §2-119(b) (2008).

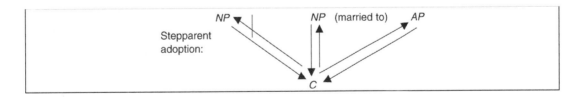

   a. **Rationale:** While at first blush the rule may appear unfair to the natural parent of the same gender as the adopting parent, under family law, as a general rule, a natural parent must consent to his or her child being adopted if the child is a minor (the typical situation). A natural parent's consenting to the stepparent adopting his or her child is tantamount to the natural parent waiving his or her right to inherit from and through the child. The child, on the other hand, has no say in the adoption if he or she is a minor. Accordingly, the child's ability to inherit from and through the natural parent is not affected.

b. **Example:** *H* and *W* are married. They have four children, *A, B, C,* and *D. H* dies. *W* remarries *H2. H2* adopts *A, B, C,* and *D*. Thereafter, *H*'s brother dies intestate, with no surviving spouse, issue, or parents. Are *H*'s children entitled to participate in the distribution of their deceased natural uncle's estate?

In *Hall v. Vallandingham,* 540 A.2d 1162 (Md. App. 1988), the court construed the Maryland descent and distribution statute as applying the general adoption rule to the stepparent adoption scenario. Under the general rule, the adopting parent steps into the shoes of the natural parent of the same gender, and the parent-child relationship with the natural parent is ***completely*** severed. The court reasoned that absent clear legislative intent, adopted children should be no better off than nonadopted children and should have only two parents from whom they can inherit.

Under the modern trend/UPC approach, because the adoption was by a stepparent (the spouse of one of the natural parents), the children can still inherit from and through the natural parent of the same gender as the adopting stepparent. *A, B, C,* and *D* would participate in the distribution of their uncle's estate.

3. **Adoption by relative of parent:** Under the 2008 revisions to the UPC, where a child is adopted by a relative of either natural/genetic parent, or the spouse or surviving spouse of a relative, the child retains the right to inherit from and through *both* natural/genetic parents. UPC §2-119(c) (2008).

4. **Post-death adoption:** Under the 2008 revisions to the UPC, where a child is adopted after the death of both natural/genetic parents, the child retains the right to inherit through *both* natural/genetic parents. UPC §2-119(d) (2008). California permits the adoptee to continue to inherit from and through both natural/genetic parents where the adoption occurs after the death of *either or both* natural/genetic parents.

5. **Adult adoptions:** When one thinks of an adoption, one naturally assumes that the adoptee is a minor child. Adoption is not limited to minors, however. As a general rule, adopted adults are treated the same as adopted children for inheritance purposes.

6. **Construction of wills, trusts, and other written instruments:** Technically, whether an adopted child qualifies as a "child" or "heir" for purposes of a will, trust, or other written instrument is a question of the intent of the decedent—not a question of intestate rules. The written words of the instrument are presumed to be the best evidence of the decedent's intent. But often the instrument fails to address the issue. Historically many courts ruled that an adopted child had the right to inherit ***from, but not through***, his or her adoptive parents; the modern trend and general rule is to permit an adopted child to inherit both ***from and through*** his or her adoptive parents, unless the written instrument expresses a contrary intent. Some courts, however, are reluctant to apply this rule where the adopted party is an adopted adult.

Example: In *Minary v. Citizens Fidelity Bank & Trust Co.,* 419 S.W.2d 340 (Ky. App. 1967), the testator's will devised her estate in trust, income to her husband and three children for life, and, upon the death of the last surviving beneficiary, the principal was to be distributed to the testator's then-surviving heirs according to the descent and distribution laws then in force. The husband died, the first child to die died without surviving issue, and the second child to die died with two surviving issue. The third child adopted his wife and then died without other surviving issue. As to whether an adopted person can inherit "through" an adopting parent, the court noted that Kentucky had adopted the modern trend both judicially and statutorily. Because, however, the adopted person was an adopted adult, adopted solely to qualify the person as an heir entitled to take from a remote ancestor's estate, the court ruled that although such an adoption technically fell within the express terms of the statute, such an adoption was a subterfuge that thwarted the remote ancestor's intent and should not be permitted.

E. Equitable adoption: Equitable adoption applies where the natural parents transfer custody of their child to a couple (or individual) who promises to adopt the child but who then fails to complete the proper paperwork to adopt the child legally. The doctrine is based on the equitable maxim that "equity regards as done that which ought to be done." As applied in this scenario, equity treats the child as a child of the adoptive parent for purposes of distributing the adoptive parent's *intestate* property.

   1. Traditional requirements: Although the rationale for the doctrine is based in equity, the doctrinal requirements are based in contract. Equitable adoption requires (1) an agreement between the natural parents and the adoptive parents to adopt the child, (2) that the natural parents fully perform by giving up custody of the child, (3) that the child fully performs by moving in and living with the adoptive parents, (4) that the adoptive parents partially perform by taking the child in and raising the child as their own, and (5) that the adoptive parents die intestate (a handful of states, however, apply the doctrine even where the decedent died testate).

   2. Child's right to take: If the requirements of the doctrine are established, the child is entitled to receive his or her intestate share of the adoptive parent's probate estate.

   3. Agreement to adopt: The agreement to adopt, the first requirement, need not be in writing. It can be either oral or implied.

   4. Theoretical perspective: There are two ways to view the equitable adoption doctrine. The first is that it establishes a parent-child relationship, but one that differs from a legally adopted parent-child relationship. As a general rule, under equitable adoption the child can inherit from, but not through, the adoptive parent. The adoptive parent cannot inherit from or through the child. Moreover, the doctrine does not affect the child's relationship or inheritance rights with his or her natural parents. If one argues equitable adoption establishes a parent-child relationship, the inheritance rights that accompany it look very little like the inheritance rights that accompany the typical parent-child relationship.

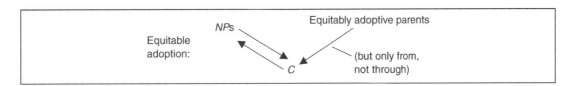

In light of the limitations on the parent-child relationship that arises from the equitable adoption doctrine, one way to think of the doctrine is that it does not establish a parent-child relationship; rather, it merely provides a cause of action for the child against the adoptive parent for breach of contract (the promise to adopt), with damages measured by the intestate share the child would have received if the parent had adopted the child.

   5. Modern trend: In *O'Neal v. Wilkes,* 439 S.E.2d 490 (Ga. 1994), the court applied equitable adoption in a very technical manner and denied the claim. The court held the first requirement was not satisfied because the aunt who had physical custody of the child and who entered into the agreement with the adopting parents lacked legal custody and authority to enter into the agreement. The dissent argued (1) that in applying the doctrine, courts should remember its equitable nature and apply it to promote equity; and (2) that the doctrine should apply ***any time the child is led to believe that he or she was adopted***. A number of law review articles support the dissent's approach, and not all courts are as strict in requiring a contract.

F. Child born out of wedlock: The inheritance rights of a child born out of wedlock vary depending upon whether the jurisdiction applies the common law or the modern trend.

   1. Common law: At common law, a child born out of wedlock was considered an "illegitimate" child. As such, the child was considered a child of no one. The child could not inherit from or through either natural parent, and neither natural parent could inherit from or through the child.

   2. Modern trend/UPC approach: The modern trend repudiates the common law approach. A child has a parent-child relationship with both natural/genetic parents regardless of their marital status. UPC §2-117. But a child born out of wedlock is still not treated the same as a child born to a married couple. Under the modern trend, a child born out of wedlock automatically has a parent-child relationship with his or her natural mother (assuming no surrogate mother) and can inherit from and through the natural mother. Inheritance from and through the natural father, however, typically requires proof of paternity.

   a. Paternity issues: Proving paternity is primarily a family law issue that naturally overlaps with inheritance rights. Without going into all of the details of paternity law, the following briefly summarizes the different ways one can establish paternity. Because issues of paternity tend to take the course into family law, professors vary on how far they want to venture into paternity. Take your cue from your professor's classroom discussion of paternity issues and whether he or she distributes all or parts of the Uniform Parentage Act.

   b. Establishing paternity: Jurisdictions vary as to what is necessary to establish paternity. In most states, paternity can be established in any of the following ways:

   - Subsequent marriage between the natural mother and the natural father

   - Acknowledgment of the child by the natural father (typically by taking the child into his home and holding the child out as his own)

   - Adjudication of paternity during the father's lifetime based on a preponderance of the evidence

   - Adjudication of paternity after the father's death based on clear and convincing evidence

   c. Uniform Parentage Act: The Uniform Parentage Act automatically establishes a parent-child relationship between the child and the natural mother, with the child being entitled to inherit from and through the natural mother. But the Uniform Parentage Act requires proof of paternity between a child and natural father before the child is entitled to inherit from and through the natural father. Proving paternity turns on whether a presumption of paternity arises.

   - If a presumption of paternity arises, the child can bring an action to establish paternity (and inheritance rights) at any time.

   - If no presumption of paternity arises, the action to establish paternity must be brought within three years of the child reaching the age of majority or it is barred.

- A presumption of paternity arises if the father acknowledges the child by taking the child into his home while the child is a minor and holding the child out as his own or if the father acknowledges his paternity in writing and files the writing with the appropriate administrative agency or court.

    d. UPC/modern trend: With respect to a child born out of wedlock, under the modern trend, a majority of jurisdictions and the UPC require the natural parent (or, in some jurisdictions, the relatives of the natural parent) to openly treat the child as his or her own and not to refuse to support the child before that parent or relatives of that parent can inherit from and through the child. UPC §2-114(c) (1969).

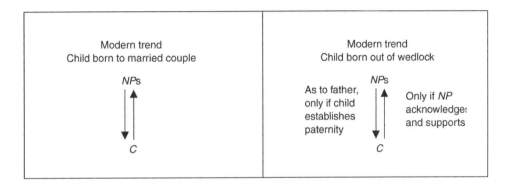

    2008 revisions: The 2008 revisions to the UPC delete subsection (c) and provide instead that a genetic parent can inherit from and through the child unless the child died before reaching age 18 and there is clear and convincing evidence that immediately before the child's death the parental rights of the parent could have been terminated based on nonsupport, abandonment, abuse, neglect, or other actions or inactions of the parent toward the child. UPC §2-114(a)(2) (2008).

G. Nontraditional parent-child relationships—reproductive technology

    1. Introduction: Medical advancements in the area of reproductive possibilities (donated sperm, donated eggs, surrogate mothers) greatly complicate the issue of who legally is the parent. These issues are primarily family law issues, but to the extent inheritance rights traditionally are attached to the parent-child relationship, the family law issues naturally overlap into wills and trusts. Whether inheritance rights should be altered to take into account children conceived and/or birthed with the help of reproductive technology is unsettled and open for debate.

    2. Posthumously conceived children: Common law treats a posthumously ***born*** child (conceived while the natural father is alive but born after his death) as alive from the moment of conception if it were to the child's benefit. With the development of modern reproductive technology, it is now possible to have a posthumously ***conceived*** child (conceived after a natural parent's death). The issue is whether the posthumously conceived child should be treated as a child of the predeceased natural parent for purposes of distributing his or her estate.

    a. Intestacy—caselaw: In ***Woodward v. Commissioner of Social Security***, 760 N.E.2d 257 (Mass. 2002), after learning that the husband had leukemia, the Woodwards "banked" some of the husband's sperm, concerned that the leukemia treatment might leave him sterile. Unfortunately, the treatment was unsuccessful, and he died. Two years later, using the husband's preserved semen, the wife conceived through artificial insemination, giving birth to twin girls. She applied for surviving "child" benefits and surviving "mother" benefits under two Social Security survivor benefits programs. The Social Security Administration rejected the claims based on its interpretation of Massachusetts law on inheritance rights. The issue was certified to the state court. The Massachusetts Supreme Judicial Court ruled that posthumously conceived children may enjoy inheritance rights of "issue" under the state's intestacy scheme where the surviving parent or child's legal representative demonstrates (1) a genetic relationship between the child and the decedent; and (2) that the decedent affirmatively consented to the posthumous conception and to the support of any resulting child. The court also noted that the action to establish paternity inheritance rights is brought in a timely manner and that notice is given to all interested parties.

b. **Intestacy—uniform law:** The Uniform Status of Children of Assisted Conception provides that a natural parent who dies before the artificial conception of a child is not treated as a parent of the child; more recently enacted uniform laws, however, favor permitting posthumously conceived children to qualify as an heir of the decedent. The 2008 revisions to the UPC provide that a posthumously conceived child inherits from the deceased parent if (1) while the parent was alive he or she authorized the posthumous use of the genetic material in a signed writing, or there is clear and convincing evidence of such consent; and (2) the child is in utero within 36 months of, or born within 45 months of, the parent's death. UPC §2-120 (2008). The trend appears to favor this latter approach, but the details of the statutory requirements vary from state to state.

c. **Probate testate and nonprobate:** If a natural parent wants a posthumously conceived child to be treated as his or her child, the parent can expressly so provide in his or her will or nonprobate instrument (inter vivos trust).

d. **Construction of wills, trusts, and other written instruments:** Technically, whether a posthumously conceived child qualifies as a "child" or "heir" for purposes of a will, trust, or other written instrument is a question of the intent of the decedent—not a question of intestate rules. The written words of the instrument are presumed to be the best evidence of the decedent's intent. But often the instrument fails to address the issue. In such cases, the modern trend is to treat the child as a child of the decedent.

Example: In *In re Martin B.*, 841 N.Y.S.2d 207 (Sur. Ct. 2008), grantor established 7 trusts for the benefit of his "issue/descendants." Grantor's son died six months earlier of Hodgkins lymphoma, with no children, but before he died he banked sperm and authorized his wife to use it. Using his sperm, three years later she gave birth to a son, and then two years later to a second son. The trust gave the trustees the discretion to use the principal for the settlor's issue during the grantor's wife's life, and upon her death, to distribute the principal to their issue. The issue was whether the posthumously conceived children could receive any of the trust property. The court ruled that "where a governing instrument is silent, children born of this new biotechnology with the consent of their parent are entitled to the same rights 'for all purposes as those of a natural child.'"

UPC: The 2008 revisions to the UPC expressly provide that a posthumously conceived child is included in a class gift in a trust or will of a third party (someone other than the predeceased donor parent) as long as (1) the predeceased parent authorized the posthumous use of the genetic material in a signed writing or there is clear and convincing evidence of such consent (§§2-705(b) and 2-120(f)), and (2) the child is living on the distribution date or is in utero within 36 months of or is born within 45 months of the distribution date (§2-705(g)).

3. **Surrogacy:** Surrogate motherhood arises where a married couple contracts with a woman to bear a child for them (the child *may or may not* be the product of the husband's sperm and/or the wife's *egg*) and the woman agrees that the child will be the couple's. Where one or more of the parties change their mind, a number of difficult legal issues arise. The courts disagree over who qualifies as the child's parents under these circumstances. Typically resolution of child custody and support issues has res judicata effect on what constitutes the parent-child relationship for inheritance purposes. Under the 2008 revisions to the UPC, a surrogate mother has no rights in the child (absent a court order to the contrary) unless the surrogate mother is the genetic mother and no one else has a parent-child relationship with the child. UPC §2-121.

4. **Same-sex couples:** Where a woman has a child through artificial insemination, and then her lesbian partner adopts the child (if permitted in the jurisdiction), the same-sex couple adoption scenario poses problems. The general adoption rule provides that the adopting parent steps into the shoes of the natural parent of the same gender, and the adoption completely severs the parent-child relationship between the child and the natural parent of the same gender as the adopting parent (no doubt assuming a traditional heterosexual couple). In the same-sex couple scenario, however, the effect is that the adopting partner knocks out the natural mother—not the intended effect. To avoid this outcome, some courts permit the natural mother to adopt along with the adopting lesbian partner, thereby coming back in as an adopting parent—creating a full parent-child relationship (including inheritance rights) between the child and both lesbian partners.

   UPC: The 2008 revisions to the UPC provide that a child conceived by assisted reproduction other than surrogacy has a parent-child relationship with the birth mother and another if the other party either (1) consented in writing to the birth mother's assisted reproduction with the intent to be the other parent, or (2) functioned as a parent of the child within two years of the child's birth. UPC §§2-102(c), (f).

VII. GIFTS TO CHILDREN

A. **Advancements:** The doctrine of advancement addresses the issue of whether inter vivos gifts a decedent made to an heir should count against the heir's share of the decedent's probate estate. (If the donor dies testate, the doctrine of satisfaction applies; the issue and policy considerations are very similar. Satisfaction is covered in Chapter 5.)

1. **Common law:** Under the common law approach, if a parent makes an inter vivos gift to a child, a rebuttable presumption arises that the gift constitutes an advancement that counts against the child's share of the parent's intestate estate.

   a. **Hotchpot:** All inter vivos gifts to the child are added back (on paper, the child is not forced to give the gift back) into the parent's probate intestate estate to create the "hotchpot." Then the hotchpot is divided equally among the decedent's heirs. Any advancement received by a child is counted against that child's share of the hotchpot. The child actually receives from the parent's intestate estate only their share of the hotchpot minus any advancement the child has received.

   b. **Rationale:** Intestate property passes to one's children equally because it is assumed the parent loved his or her children equally and wanted to treat them equally upon his or her death. While that assumption is reasonable as applied to a parent's probate property, it is questionable whether it should it be extended to include inter vivos gifts a parent made to his or her children. The logic underlying the advancement doctrine is that only by including inter vivos gifts can it be said that the children were truly treated equally.

c. **Example:** Decedent died intestate with three children, *A, B,* and *C.* Decedent gave *A* inter vivos gifts totaling $25,000. Decedent gave *B* inter vivos gifts totaling $50,000. Decedent gave *C* inter vivos gifts totaling $75,000. Decedent died with a probate estate of $150,000. How much does each child take?

Analysis: Assuming the presumption that the gifts count as an advancement is not rebutted (there is no evidence to rebut it), under the traditional approach to the advancement doctrine, the inter vivos gifts are added back, on paper, to the actual probate estate to create the hotchpot. The hotchpot here is $300,000 (the actual probate estate, $150,000, plus the inter vivos gifts: $25,000 + $50,000 + $75,000). Then the hotchpot is divided equally among the children. $300,000 divided by three *(A, B,* and *C)* is $100,000 each. Because *A* received $25,000 inter vivos, *A* receives only $75,000 from the actual probate estate (leaving $75,000 in the actual probate estate). Because *B* received $50,000 inter vivos, *B* receives only $50,000 from the actual probate estate (leaving $25,000 in the actual probate estate). And because *C* received $75,000 inter vivos, *C* receives only $25,000 from the actual probate estate (exactly what is left, leaving nothing in the probate estate).

d. **Advancement exceeds share:** If a child receives inter vivos gifts that exceed what he or she is entitled to receive from the hotchpot, the child does not have to give any of the inter vivos gifts back to the parent's probate estate—but the child will not be permitted to share in the distribution of the parent's estate.

e. **Child predeceases:** If a child predeceases the parent, and the child received an inter vivos gift, under the common law approach the advancement doctrine still applies to the share of the parent's estate going to a child's issue.

f. **Criticisms:** The common law advancement doctrine has been heavily criticized. It inherently involves a high cost of administration (hearings to calculate exactly what was given to whom, when, and how to value it) that invariably leads to siblings fighting with siblings when they should be consoling each other.

2. **Modern trend/UPC approach:** The modern trend/UPC approach modifies the advancement doctrine to reduce the potential for litigation, costs of administration, and family fighting. Inter vivos gifts do not constitute an advancement unless a writing indicates that the donor intended the gift to constitute an advancement. UPC §2-109.

a. **Writing requirement:** (a) If the *donor* creates the writing, the writing must be made *contemporaneously* with the inter vivos gift; (b) if the *donee* creates the writing, the writing may be made *any time.* UPC §2-109(a).

b. **Donee predeceases:** Unlike the common law approach, if the donee predeceases the donor, and the inter vivos gift to the donee qualifies as an advancement, the advancement does not count against the share of the donor's estate going to the donee's issue unless the writing expressly provides so. UPC §2-109(c).

    c. Scope: Although the modern trend/UPC approach arguably reduces the scope of the doctrine by providing that it applies *only* if a writing expresses or acknowledges such intent, the modern trend also expands the doctrine by providing that it may apply to any heir, not just to a child. UPC §2-109(a).

    d. Valuation: If an inter vivos gift qualifies as an advancement, it is valued as of the time the donee receives possession or enjoyment of the property, whichever occurred first. UPC §2-109(b).

B. Transfers to minors: Under the intestate distribution scheme, if a decedent dies intestate and is survived by issue, there is a good chance that some of the property may be distributed to a minor. The problem is that minors lack the legal capacity to hold property. The law has devised a number of options for managing property for a minor.

    1. Guardianship: The first option, and arguably the oldest, is guardianship—also known as guardian of the property. The guardian's job is exactly as its name implies: to guard and preserve the ward's property until the minor reaches the age of capacity.

    Criticisms: Guardians have minimal powers over the property. They have to go to court for authorization to deal with the property. If the minor needs help, the guardian is permitted to use only the income generated from the property, not the property itself, absent court approval. Guardians have to account regularly to the probate court. The result is a very inefficient arrangement with high administrative costs due to the frequent need for trips to the court for authorization or to account.

    Modern trend: The modern trend has modified guardianship and transformed it into a conservatorship. Under a conservatorship, the conservator takes title as trustee for the minor and has all the powers a trustee would have over the property. The conservator still has to account to the court, but usually only once a year. The result is a far more efficient arrangement for managing a minor's property. UPC Article V.

    2. Uniform Gifts/Transfers to Minors Act: A second arrangement for managing a minor's property is as a custodian under the Uniform Gifts to Minors Act or its successor, the Uniform Transfers to Minors Act. Under either, a custodian has discretionary power to use the property for the benefit of the minor, as the custodian deems appropriate, without court approval. UPC §2-109(a); UTMA §14(a). Upon the minor's turning 21, the custodian must disburse any remaining property to the minor. The custodian has no duty to account to the court, only to the minor upon turning 21. A custodianship arguably is more efficient than a guardianship, but it is most appropriate for small to moderate-size gifts.

    3. Trusts: The third arrangement used to hold and manage a minor's property is a trust. The terms of the trust control the scope of the trustee's powers over the property, the trustee's ability to use the principal and/or income for the benefit of the child, the trustee's duty to account, and when the trust is to terminate and the property to be distributed. The trust is the most flexible way to hold and manage property for a minor, but typically it has higher up-front costs involved in creating the trust and may have high administrative fees depending on the trustee's fees. It is most appropriate when the size of the gift to the minor is large.

    4. Comparisons: Of the three possible arrangements, the trust and custodianship have substantial benefits over guardianship. Both the trust and the custodianship arrangements, however, require a written instrument expressly opting for that arrangement. Absent such a writing, the default in a jurisdiction will be either guardianship or, if the jurisdiction follows the modern trend, conservatorship.

VIII. BARS TO SUCCESSION

A. **Introduction:** The material so far has focused on determining who takes the decedent's property when he or she dies intestate and how much they get. The doctrines in this section address the issue of whether there are situations where an otherwise eligible taker is nevertheless barred from taking.

B. **Homicide:** Where a party who otherwise is entitled to take from a decedent kills the decedent, the equitable principle that one should not profit from one's own wrongdoing argues against permitting the killer from taking.

1. **Judicial approaches:** If the jurisdiction does not have a statute addressing the issue, the courts are split over how to treat the issue:

a. The decedent's property passes to the killer because the statutory probate scheme so instructs. If the court alters the scheme, the court is legislating.

b. The killer is barred from taking the decedent's property because equity demands that one should not profit from one's own wrongdoing.

c. Legal title to the decedent's property passes to the killer, but a constructive trust is imposed to prevent unjust enrichment, and the court orders the property to be distributed to the next in line to take.

2. **Example:** In *In re Estate of Mahoney,* 220 A.2d 475 (Vt. 1966), the wife was convicted of manslaughter in the death of her husband. The husband died intestate, and the wife claimed her intestate share. Vermont had no homicide statute, yet the court said that it would be inequitable to permit the wife to profit from her own wrongdoing and adopted the constructive trust approach to the issue to ensure that the killer did not profit from her own wrongdoing.

3. **Statutory/UPC approach:** A majority of the jurisdictions and the UPC have an express statute that provides that a killer shall not take from his or her victim. UPC §2-803. Most of the statutes treat the killer as if he or she predeceased the decedent.

4. **Intentional and felonious killing:** The general rule, both judicially and statutorily, is that for the killing to bar (either outright or through the constructive trust) the killer from taking from the decedent, the killing must be intentional and felonious.

a. **Manslaughter:** In cases of manslaughter, it is critical to distinguish the two types of manslaughter. *Voluntary* manslaughter is intentional killing and comes within the scope of the homicide doctrine—the killer is barred from taking. *Involuntary* manslaughter is unintentional killing and does not come within the scope of the homicide doctrine—the killer is not barred from taking. In *In re Estate of Mahoney,* above, although the court adopted the constructive trust approach to the homicide issue, the wife was convicted of manslaughter and not murder, and the conviction did not indicate whether it was voluntary or involuntary manslaughter. The court remanded for further hearings on the degree of the manslaughter.

b. Self-defense: Killing in self-defense is not felonious and does not trigger the homicide doctrine.

c. Assisted suicide: Mercy killings and assisted suicides technically are intentional and felonious killings and come within the scope of the homicide doctrine, though whether the doctrine should include such acts is greatly debated.

5. **Burden of proof:** Whether a killer takes from his or her victim is a civil issue, not a criminal issue. A criminal conviction has res judicata effect upon the civil issue (UPC §2-803(g)), but an acquittal is not the final word because the burden of proof in a criminal case is proof beyond a reasonable doubt, while the burden of proof in a civil case is merely preponderance of the evidence. If the defendant is acquitted on homicide charges but civilly found liable for the decedent's intentional and felonious wrongful death, the killer is barred from participating in the distribution of the victim's estate.

6. **Remedy:** The general rule is that if the doctrine applies, in distributing the victim's property, treat the killer as if he or she predeceased the victim.

7. **Killer's issue:** The general rule is that application of the homicide doctrine means that the killer is treated as if he or she predeceased the victim. If a relative predeceases the decedent, and the relative is survived by issue, often the relative's share passes to his or her issue. With respect to property passing under intestacy, this occurs pursuant to the per stirpes/per capita doctrines. With respect to probate testate property (and, in some jurisdictions, nonprobate property), this occurs pursuant to the lapse and anti-lapse doctrines (see Chapter 5). The jurisdictions are split over whether the homicide doctrine should apply to the killer's issue to bar them from taking if they would otherwise take under these doctrines (and in some states, such as California, it varies depending on whether the victim died testate or intestate).

   UPC approach: The UPC treats the killer as if he or she had disclaimed the property (UPC §2-803), which arguably permits the killer's issue to take the killer's share under anti-lapse and the per stirpes/per capita doctrines if they would otherwise qualify (that is, if they meet the requirements of those doctrines).

8. **Scope of doctrine:** The general rule is that the homicide doctrine applies to all types of property: nonprobate, probate testate, and probate intestate. UPC §2-803.

   Joint tenancy: If the victim and the killer held property in joint tenancy, by operation of law the joint tenancy is converted into tenancy in common. The killer keeps his or her interest, and the victim's interest is distributed as if the killer had predeceased the victim.

9. **Statute covers probate property only:** Where the statute expressly covers probate property only, one can argue that a constructive trust should be imposed on the nonprobate property. This argument is based on the equitable principle that one should not benefit from one's own wrongdoing. The constructive trust would be in favor of those who would have taken if the killer had predeceased the victim.

C. **Abandonment/elder abuse:** A number of states have other doctrines that bar a taker from receiving if the taker is guilty of misconduct short of homicide. Some states bar a taker if he or she is guilty of abandonment. Other states bar a taker from receiving if he or she is guilty of the new offense of elder abuse. Elder abuse involves acts that amount to physical abuse, neglect, or fiduciary abuse of the decedent while he or she was an elder or dependent adult. Cal. Prob. Code §259.

Chinese approach: The Chinese system looks at the conduct of those surrounding the decedent to determine who is worthy to take and who is not. Such an approach is extremely fact sensitive, has high costs of administration, and arguably creates an incentive for, and therefore a potential for, fraud.

D. **Disclaimers:** Distributions under intestacy, devises under a will, and nonprobate transfers are simply different ways of making a gift. What makes these gifts unique is that for all practical purposes these gifts are testamentary gifts—gifts made by the donor at time of death. A valid gift requires three elements: intent to make a gift, delivery, and acceptance. While acceptance is generally presumed, a disclaimer is simply a way of expressing one's intent that he or she declines to accept a testamentary gift.

1. **Treat as if predeceased:** If a party disclaims, as a general rule the legal significance is that the party disclaiming is treated as if he or she predeceased the decedent. The property in question is then distributed as if the party who disclaimed predeceased the decedent. The property is distributed to the next eligible taker under the various rules governing who takes in the event a taker predeceases the decedent.

2. **Benefits of disclaiming:** A party may disclaim his or her testamentary gift for a variety of reasons:

   a. **Redistribute property:** Disclaimers are often called a form of post-mortem estate planning. Disclaimers can be used to adjust who takes and how much they take after the death of the decedent. For example, if a decedent dies intestate survived by a spouse and two children, in many states the children are entitled to receive at least 50 percent of the decedent's estate. If the children are both adults, they may disclaim their interests to increase the share going to the surviving spouse. If both disclaim, they are treated as if they predeceased the decedent. As long as the children have no issue, the decedent is now treated as if he or she had no surviving issue, in which case more (potentially all) of the decedent's property passes to his or her surviving spouse.

   b. **Avoid gift tax consequences:** One of the benefits of disclaiming is that it can avoid estate and gift tax consequences. If one accepts the property and then gives it to the next taker in line, gift tax consequences to the transfer may result. If, however, one disclaims and the legal effect is simply to pass the property in question to the next taker in line, the disclaimer has no gift tax consequence.

   c. **Avoid creditors:** As a general rule, creditors are entitled to reach any transferable property that the debtor holds. If an heir or devisee is facing creditors' claims, such that any inheritance or devise would, for all practical purposes, go directly to the creditors, the heir or devisee can elect to disclaim the property in question to avoid the property going to the creditors. If the taker disclaims, the legal significance is that the disclaimer is tantamount to rejecting the gift. If the gift is rejected, it was never accepted, so the taker never had a property interest in the property in question. If the taker never held a property interest in the property, the taker's creditors never had a right to reach it.

   Federal government as creditor: Where the federal government is a creditor of the disclaimant (for tax purposes or under Medicaid reimbursement provisions), the property disclaimed often is subject to the claim of the federal government.

3. **Scope:** Pay careful attention to a disclaimer statute to see if it applies to only probate property (traditional approach) or if it also applies to nonprobate property (modern trend approach).

4. **Execution requirements:** Most disclaimer statutes have technical rules concerning what must be done for the disclaimer to be effective. Most require that the party disclaiming do so in writing within nine months of the decedent's death.

Quiz Yourself on
INTESTACY: THE DEFAULT DISTRIBUTION SCHEME

Where the question is split to reflect different jurisdictional approaches, you only need to answer the approach(es) that you are expected to know for your exam.

4. Goldie and Curt have been living together for 15 years. They have two children, and Goldie has a child from a prior relationship. Many years from now, Goldie drowns accidentally while filming a sequel entitled *On Silver Pond*. She is survived by Curt and her three children.

   a. Who takes Goldie's probate property under the typical statute of descent and distribution if she dies intestate? _____

   b. Who takes Goldie's probate property under the UPC statute of descent and distribution if she dies intestate? _____

5. Juwon and Leslie met while serving in the armed forces. They were married a few years later but never got around to executing wills. Both were killed in a training accident. Leslie was killed instantly. Juwon suffered severe burns over 90 percent of his body and died three days later. Leslie was also survived by her mother, Mae. Juwon was survived by his father, Freddie.

   a. Who takes Leslie's and Juwon's property under the traditional common law approach?
   _____

   b. Who takes Leslie's and Juwon's property under the modern trend/UPC approach?
   _____

6. In the following family tree, assume that *A, B, C, D, F,* and *X* predecease the decedent.

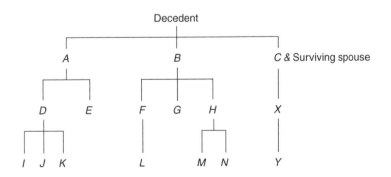

   a. Who takes how much under the per capita approach? _____

   b. Who takes how much under the per stirpes approach?   _____

   c. Who takes how much under the per capita at each generation approach?   _____

   d. Do you need to answer all three of the subquestions, or only the one concerning the approach that your jurisdiction follows?

7. Assume the following family situation. The only people alive when the decedent dies are those identified by the underlined letters: *A, B, C,* and *D.*

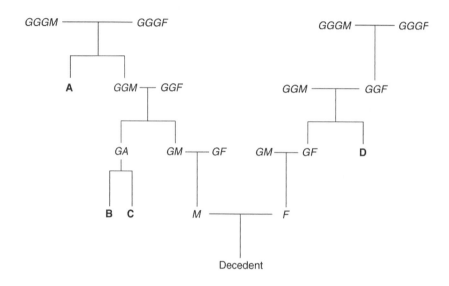

   a. Who takes the decedent's estate if he or she dies intestate and the jurisdiction applies the degree of relationship with a parentelic tiebreaker approach?   _____

   b. Who takes the decedent's estate if he or she dies intestate and the jurisdiction applies the UPC approach?   _____

8. *H* and *W* are married and have two children, *A* and *B.* They divorce, and *H* marries *W2. W2* adopts *A* and *B,* and thereafter becomes pregnant. *H* dies unexpectedly during the seventh month of *W2*'s pregnancy, and *W2* dies two months later while giving birth to *C.* One year later, *A* dies intestate, with no surviving spouse or issue. Who takes *A*'s property under the modern trend/UPC approach? _____

9. Tracy is a wild and crazy kind of guy, enlisting in the navy so he can have them pay to ship him around the world. He is an "old-fashioned" kind of sailor, liking to believe that he has a girl in every port. Lulu claims that Tracy is the father of her child, but Tracy refuses to acknowledge that the child is his. Tracy moved on, and Lulu raised the child, Sunshine, on her own without any help from Tracy. Sunshine grew up to have a very successful musical career, only to die intestate recently in a plane crash. Tracy has stepped forward and now asserts his right to inherit from his daughter. Who takes Sunshine's property under the modern trend/UPC approach?   _____

10. Molly is a single mom. Her husband died many years back, and she has struggled in raising their two children, Alice and Bob. Alice has been an ideal child, excelling throughout her years in school and attending and graduating from college. Molly gave Alice $100,000 to help offset the expenses of attending a private college. Bob, on the other hand, has been an underachiever, not even graduating from high school. Molly died unexpectedly last week, with an estate of $300,000. How should Molly's estate be distributed?   _____

a. Under the common law approach?   _____

b. Under the modern trend/UPC approach?   _____

11. Assume Howard and Wendy are married. They own Suburbacres as joint tenants. They both have life insurance policies, with the other as sole beneficiary. And they have wills leaving all of their probate property to their surviving spouse. One day Wendy is found dead. She had been murdered, and the circumstances surrounding her death are not clear. Wendy is survived by Howard and her parents. Howard is tried for her murder, but he is acquitted. In a related civil case, however, he is found responsible for her wrongful death. What is the most likely result as to who gets her property?

_____

12. Harry and Whilma are married. They have two grown children, Ann and Bill. Ann has two children, Ned and Mary. Bill has one child, Fred. Harry also has a child, Pat, from a prior marriage. Pat has one grown child, Tom. Harry dies intestate. Pat always liked Whilma and is concerned that she might not have enough money to get by now that Harry is dead. Pat disclaims his right to take any property from Harry's estate. Who takes how much under the modern trend/UPC approach?   _____

Answers

4a. When a decedent dies intestate, the order of takers is: (1) surviving spouse, and (2) issue. Although Curt survives her, he does not qualify as a spouse unless the jurisdiction recognizes common law marriage. If the jurisdiction recognizes common law marriages, Goldie and Curt's relationship probably qualifies as a common law marriage. Assuming it does, under a typical descent and distribution statute, Curt takes 33 percent of her property because more than one child also survives her. The remaining 66 percent is divided equally among her three children. If the jurisdiction does not recognize common law marriages, Goldie has no surviving spouse and all of her property passes equally to her three children.

4b. Under the UPC approach, the threshold question is still whether the jurisdiction recognizes common law marriage. If the jurisdiction recognizes common law marriages, Goldie and Curt's relationship probably qualifies as a common law marriage. Assuming it does, Curt qualifies as a surviving spouse. Under the UPC approach to intestate distribution, how much Curt takes is determined by who Goldie's surviving issue are and who Curt's surviving issue are. Here, all of her issue are not also his issue because one has a different father. Accordingly, under the UPC, Curt takes the first $100,000 and 50 percent of the rest. The three children split the remaining 50 percent equally. If the jurisdiction does not recognize common law marriages and has adopted the UPC approach to intestate distribution, Curt does not qualify as a surviving spouse. All of Goldie's probate property passes equally to her three children.

5a. At common law, to qualify as a taker one has to prove by a preponderance of the evidence that he or she survived the decedent by a millisecond. Under the common law approach, Juwon qualifies as a surviving spouse. Because Leslie is also survived by her mother, Juwon takes 50 percent of Leslie's property, with the remainder going to Leslie's mom, Mae. When Juwon dies three days later, he does not have a surviving spouse. Leslie actually died three days before he did. All of Juwon's property (including the 50 percent that he took from Leslie's estate) goes to his father, Freddie.

5b. Under the modern trend/UPC approach, to qualify as a taker under intestacy, one has to prove by clear and convincing evidence that he or she survived the decedent by 120 hours (five days). Although

Juwon actually survived Leslie, he did not legally survive her—he cannot meet the statutory survival requirement. Juwon is treated as if he predeceased Leslie, and all of Leslie's property passes to her mother, Mae. When Juwon died, Leslie had actually predeceased him. He has no surviving spouse, so all of his property passes to his father, Freddie.

6a. Under the per capita approach, you divide at the first generation where there is a live taker. All of the decedent's children, *A, B,* and *C,* predeceased the decedent, so the first division is at the grand-children's generation. The number of shares is one share for each party who is alive at that tier and one share for each party who is dead at that tier but survived by issue. *E, G,* and *H* take shares because they are alive. *D, F,* and *X* take shares as deceased but survived by issue. Divide the estate into six shares. Under per capita, the dropping shares drop by bloodline. *D*'s one-sixth drops to *I, J,* and *K* equally (one-eighteenth each). *E* keeps his one-sixth. *F*'s one-sixth drops to *L. G* keeps her one-sixth. *H* keeps her one-sixth. And *X*'s one-sixth drops by bloodline to *Y.*

6b. Under the per stirpes approach, always divide at the first generation, whether anyone is alive at that tier or not. The number of shares is one share for each party who is alive at that tier and one share for each party who is dead at that tier but survived by issue. *A, B,* and *C* each take a share. Under per stirpes, the dropping shares drop by bloodline. *A*'s one-third falls to *D* and *E* (one-sixth each), and *D*'s one-sixth falls to *I, J,* and *K,* who each take one-eighteenth. *E* takes one-sixth. *B*'s one-third falls to *F, G,* and *H* equally (one-ninth each) because each is either alive or dead but survived by issue. *F*'s one- ninth falls by bloodline to *L. G* keeps her one-ninth. *H* keeps her one-ninth. *C*'s one-third falls to *X,* who is dead but survived by issue, so the one-third falls to *Y.*

6c. Under the per capita at each generation approach, divide at the first generation where there is a live taker. All of the decedent's children, *A, B,* and *C,* predeceased the decedent so the first division is at the grandchildren's generation. The number of shares is one share for each party at that tier who is alive and one share for each party who is dead at that tier but survived by issue. *E, G,* and *H* take shares as alive; *D, F,* and *X* take shares as dead but survived by issue. Under per capita at each generation, pool the dropping shares and divide them equally among the eligible takers at the next tier (the issue of the predeceased issue). The three dropping shares are those for *D, F,* and *X.* Their three one-sixth shares are pooled so that one-half of the decedent's estate drops to the great- grandchildren. That one-half is divided equally among their collective issue: *I, J, K, L,* and *Y* take one-tenth each.

6d. Although each jurisdiction has a statutory default approach, an individual can opt out of that approach by expressing an intent for a different approach in a written instrument that validly passes property at death (a valid will or will substitute). You need to be able to apply all three approaches, regardless of which approach your jurisdiction has adopted, because the testator/transferor can always opt out of the default.

7a. Under the degree of relationship with a parentelic tiebreaker approach, the first step is to count the degree of relationship between each claimed taker and the decedent. *A* is related to the decedent by the fifth degree (decedent to *M* = 1; *M* to *GM* = 2; *GM* to *GGM* = 3; *GGM* to *GGGM* = 4; and *GGGM* to *A* = 5). *B* and *C* are related to the decedent by the fifth degree (decedent to *M* = 1; *M* to *GM* = 2; *GM* to *GGM* = 3; *GGM* to *GA* = 4; and *GA* to *B/C* = 5). *D* is related to the decedent by the fourth degree (decedent to *F* = 1; *F* to *GF* = 2; *GF* to *GGF* = 3; *GGF* to *D* = 4). *D* takes all of the decedent's property as the closest relative under the degree of relationship approach (there is no need to use the tiebreaker component here because there is only one relative claiming in the closest degree).

7b. Under the UPC approach, if there is not a live taker within the grandparents' line or closer, the property escheats to the state. The state takes it all.

8. The order of takers under intestacy is surviving spouse, issue, parents, and issue of parents. Here, the facts say that *A* has no surviving spouse or issue. *A*'s natural parents are *W* and *H*. *H* predeceases *A*, so *H* is not an eligible taker. *W* survives *A*, but *W2* adopted *A* and *B*. Normally adoption establishes a parent-child relationship between the adoptive parent and the child and severs completely the relationship between the natural parent and the child. But if the adoption is by a stepparent, a widely recognized exception provides that the adoption severs the right of the natural parent who is not married to the stepparent to inherit from the child, but the child can still inherit from that natural parent. Here, though, because it is the child who predeceased the natural parent, the exception is not applicable, and the general adoption rule controls. *W*, the natural parent, cannot inherit from *A*, and both of *A*'s legal parents (*H* and *W2*) predeceased *A*. The next possible takers are the issue of *A*'s parents. *B* is a whole-blooded sibling. Although *H* died before *C* was born, because *H* and *W2* were married, it is presumed that *C* is *H*'s child. Relative to *A* and *B*, *C* is a half-blooded sibling. Under the modern trend/UPC approach, there is no distinction between half-blooded and whole-blooded siblings. *B* and *C* split *A*'s estate equally.

9. Under the modern trend/UPC approach (1969), before a natural parent or relative of a natural parent can inherit from or through a child, the natural parent must acknowledge and support the child. Tracy neither acknowledged nor supported the child. He is not entitled to take from her estate if she dies intestate. Lulu takes all of her property.

Under the 2008 revisions to the UPC, a genetic parent can inherit from and through the child unless the child died before reaching age 18 and there is clear and convincing evidence that immediately before the child's death the parental rights of the parent could have been terminated based on nonsupport, abandonment, abuse, neglect, or other actions or inactions of the parent toward the child. It would appear that Sunshine is over the age of 18, so Tracy would be entitled to inherit his share of Sunshine's property.

10a. Under the common law approach, any inter vivos gifts made from parent to child are presumed to be advancements that count against the child's share of the parent's estate. Here, assuming Alice cannot rebut the presumption, the $100,000 qualifies as an advancement. The advancement amount is added back into the decedent's estate ($100,000 + $300,000) to create the hotchpot ($400,000). The hotchpot is then divided among the heirs, with the advancement amount credited against the share of the recipient of the advancement. Here, the hotchpot is split 50-50 between Alice and Bob, $200,000 each. Alice's advancement is counted against her share of the hotchpot, and she takes only $100,000. Bob takes the remaining $200,000.

10b. Under the modern trend, there is a presumption against inter vivos gifts counting as advancements unless a writing expresses such intent on the donor's part. Here, there is no evidence of any such writing. The $100,000 was merely an inter vivos gift. Molly's estate of $300,000 is divided equally between Alice and Bob, with each taking $150,000.

11. Under the homicide doctrine, as a general rule, a killer who is civilly responsible for the intentional and felonious murder of the decedent is not entitled to receive any of the decedent's property, be it nonprobate, probate testate, or probate intestate. The general rule is to treat the killer as if he or she predeceased the decedent. The issue of whether someone intentionally and feloniously killed the decedent, for purposes of determining distribution of the decedent's property, is a civil issue to be determined by a preponderance of the evidence. The civil finding that Howard was responsible for Wendy's wrongful death is probably sufficient to bar Howard from taking the proceeds of her life insurance policy or from taking under her will. As for the joint tenancy, it is converted into tenancy in common. Howard keeps his half, and her half falls into probate where it will be distributed with the rest of her probate property as if he predeceased her.

12. Under the modern trend/UPC approach, one of the variables in determining the surviving spouse's share is whether the decedent has surviving issue and, if so, whose issue they are. Where not all of the decedent's issue are also the surviving spouse's issue, the surviving spouse takes the first $100,000 plus 50 percent of the rest of the decedent's probate estate. The issue splits the remaining 50 percent.

Here, Whilma takes the first $100,000 and 50 percent of the rest of Harry's probate property. Ann, Bill, and Pat split the remaining 50 percent. But Pat has disclaimed. The question becomes what effect, if any, Pat's disclaimer has on who takes how much. The legal effect of a disclaimer is to treat the party who disclaims as if he or she predeceased the decedent. At first blush, it might look like all of Harry's surviving issue are now issue of Whilma, so she should take all of Harry's property. But Pat's child, Tom, steps up to take Pat's share by representation. Pat's disclaimer does not have the consequences Pat intended because Pat did not take into consideration that Pat's child would take Pat's share by representation. Whilma still takes only the first $100,000 and 50 percent of the rest, and the other 50 percent is split equally among Ann, Bill, and Tom.

Exam Tips on
INTESTACY: THE DEFAULT DISTRIBUTION SCHEME

The intestate distribution scheme is core wills and trusts material. The intestate distribution scheme is the default. On an exam, intestacy issues can be raised expressly by the facts telling you that the decedent died intestate (without a will) or implicitly as a result of you properly analyzing that the will the decedent purported to execute is invalid (or was properly revoked). The doctrines that affect how much a taker takes are also tested often. These issues must be raised expressly by the facts and should be easy to spot and analyze.

The intestate distribution scheme

☞ You need to be very comfortable with who takes when, and how much they take. The order of takers is straightforward. Focus on how to calculate how much they take and the variables that control how much they take.

Surviving spouse: who qualifies

☞ The survival requirement material is core wills and trusts material that is tested often. The rules in this area vary, so you need to know which approach applies to which type of property in your jurisdiction.

☞ A survival issue should be easy to spot. Either you will see two or more people dying within seven days of each other or you will see a written instrument that has an express survival requirement.

☞ If you spot a survival issue, always deal with the person who actually died first. Lead with the appropriate rule for that type of property. Analytically, in applying the rule, the party claiming that he or she survived (1) has to actually survive, and (2) has to legally survive, the latter being where the statutory survival requirement comes in.

☞ Start the whole process all over again when dealing with the second person to die and determining who takes his or her property. Even if you treated the second-to-die as predeceasing the first-to-die for purposes of distributing the first person's property, when you analyze who takes the second-to-die's property start the process all over again. Do not treat the person as predeceasing anyone.

Surviving spouse: calculating share

The surviving spouse's share varies from jurisdiction to jurisdiction, so you should take great care to read the controlling statutory language. Start with the different possible shares that the surviving spouse can take, and then for each possible share, couple it with the variable or variables that determine when he or she takes that amount.

☞ How much the surviving spouse takes usually turns on who else survives the deceased spouse—children/issue, parents, or issue of parents. Be particularly careful to see if the word *child* or *issue* is used in your statutory scheme.

☞ If the statutory shares turn on the number of children, check to see if predeceased children count if issue survive them.

In most statutes, in determining the surviving spouse's share, the only issue who are relevant are the deceased spouse's issue, not the surviving spouse's issue. The UPC, however, changes that approach. You have to sweat the details of the statutory language that controls how much a surviving spouse takes. There are no short cuts.

Issue: calculating shares

Where a decedent dies intestate and more than one of his or her children predecease the decedent (or one actually predeceases and one or more are treated as if they predeceased the decedent), state and apply the default approach in your jurisdiction for who takes (per capita, per stirpes, or per capita at each generation). If the decedent dies testate or with a nonprobate instrument, look to see if he or she expressed an intent to apply an approach other than the jurisdiction's default.

Your analysis has three steps: (1) Where do you divide the property first? (2) How many shares should you divide it into? (3) Who takes the dropping shares?

☞ If your professor includes multiple-choice questions on the exam, these are core doctrines that are tailor-made for multiple-choice type questions.

Shares of ancestors and remote collaterals

This material is rarely tested on a traditional essay-type fact pattern. If your professor spends time in class showing you how to calculate degrees of relationships and parentelic lines, this is easy to test in a multiple-choice question.

Issue: who qualifies

This material is tested fairly often because it overlaps nicely with calculating a surviving spouse's share. If the surviving spouse's share turns on the number of issue or children, this material goes directly to that variable.

☞ Although this material is tested fairly often, most professors do not get too creative because this material has the potential of crossing over too far into family law.

To raise this issue, watch for either a nontraditional family situation or a nontraditional birth situation. In particular, watch for (1) a child who is born out of wedlock, (2) a child who is born after the death of his or her parent, (3) a parent who refuses to acknowledge or support the child, (4) a child who is adopted (and by whom), or (5) an incomplete adoption.

☞ Think in terms of the parent-child relationship. How one establishes such a relationship varies from jurisdiction to jurisdiction. Specific rules go with each of the scenarios set forth above.

☞ The inheritance rights of posthumously conceived children is a new, cutting-edge issue which increases the likelihood of it being tested. Know the different approaches and your jurisdiction's approach.

Equitable adoption is a favorite rule to test in this area. Do not forget that it applies only if the claimed equitably adoptive parent died intestate. If he or she died testate or with a nonprobate instrument, the question is a question of the testator/transferor's intent, arguably not an equitable adoption doctrine question (though it may be relevant if there is no clear evidence of the testator/transferor's intent). In addition, as a general rule equitable adoption permits the party invoking it to inherit from but not through the equitably adoptive parent. (Remember to argue the modern trend approach in the alternative if the doctrine fails under the traditional approach.)

Gifts to children

Advancement is easy to test and to spot. You have to see the decedent making an inter vivos gift to someone who later qualifies as an heir when the donor dies intestate.

☞ Lead with the rule your jurisdiction follows (common law vs. UPC). The UPC approach requires a writing for the doctrine to apply. If the donor creates the writing, it need not be signed, but it must be contemporaneous. Watch for a nice crossover issue/argument-in-the-alternative here. If the writing is by the donor, is not contemporaneous, but is signed and in the donor's handwriting, while it will fail for advancement purposes, it may qualify as a holographic will in its own right. Raise this issue and analyze whether the writing qualifies as a holographic will (covered in Chapter 4).

Bars to succession

If homicide is tested, it is easy to spot—the decedent had to have been murdered. The tricky part of homicide is remembering some of the nuances of the doctrine: It applies only to voluntary manslaughter, not involuntary; it is a civil issue, so the burden of proof is preponderance of the evidence; it generally applies to all types of property—nonprobate, probate testate, and probate intestate.

☞ If the doctrine applies, treat the killer as if he or she predeceased the decedent (except for the special ruling covering joint tenancy).

☞ Pay special attention to whether the killer has surviving children. If so, you need to analyze whether the killer's issue take his or her share. The jurisdictions are split, so pay special attention to the statutory language in your jurisdiction. Some jurisdictions permit the killer's issue to take, some do not, and some distinguish between whether the victim died testate or intestate.

Disclaimers often appear on exams because it is a great overlap issue. Disclaimers are easy to spot on an exam because they include a writing that expresses the intent to disclaim the property in question.

☞ Rarely is creation of the disclaimer an issue. Few professors spend much time on the requirements for validly creating one. The key is their effect.

☞ Lead with the legal effect of a disclaimer—treat the party disclaiming as if he or she predeceased the decedent. Disclaimers typically apply to all types of property—nonprobate, probate testate, and probate intestate, but read your statute carefully.

☞ Watch for overlap issues. For example, assume the decedent had two children. One of the children predeceased the decedent and was survived by a child. The other child survives the decedent and has three children. The decedent died intestate, and the surviving child disclaims. As applied to that child, the issue is simple. The disclaiming child is treated as predeceasing the decedent, and his or her share goes to his or her children. But the disclaimer raises a tough overlap issue. In light of the disclaimer, the decedent now has no surviving child. Assuming the jurisdiction applies the per capita or per capita at each generation approach, where should the court make the first division? The per capita doctrines answer, at the first division where there is a live taker. But where is that where the only live child disclaims? Disclaimers can be used to raise a number of challenging overlapping issues.

☞ The party disclaiming has no right to direct where the disclaimed property goes. It passes pursuant to the appropriate principles regardless of what the disclaiming party thinks. Just because the fact pattern says that the party disclaimed because he or she wanted the property to go to *X,* that does not necessarily mean that *X* will take the property. Go through the steps in the analysis to determine who will take the property following the disclaimer.

CHAPTER 3

TESTAMENTARY CAPACITY

ChapterScope ━━━━━━━━━━━━━━━━━━━━━━━━━━━━━━━━━━━━━━

The traditional method of opting out of intestacy is to execute a will. This chapter examines the first requirement for creating a valid will: testamentary capacity. Even if a testator has testamentary capacity generally, if the will or any part thereof is caused by a defect in capacity (insane delusion, undue influence, or fraud), the court will strike that part of the will. In particular, the chapter examines:

- **Testamentary capacity:** The testator must be 18 years old and of sound mind. Sound mind requires the testator to have the ability to know (1) the nature and extent of his or her property, (2) the natural objects of his or her bounty, (3) the nature of the testamentary act he or she is performing, and (4) how all of these relate to constitute an orderly plan of disposing of his or her property.

- **Insane delusion:** A false perception of reality that the testator adheres to against all reason and evidence to the contrary. A *majority* of courts hold that if a *rational person* could not reach the same conclusion under the circumstances, the belief is an insane delusion. A *minority* of courts holds that if there is *any factual basis to support* the belief, the belief is *not* an insane delusion.

- **Undue influence:** Where another substitutes their intent for the testator's intent. Plaintiff bears burden of proving (1) the testator was susceptible, (2) the defendant had the opportunity, (3) the defendant had a motive, and (4) causation.

  - A *presumption of undue influence* arises in many jurisdictions and shifts the burden of proof to the defendant if the plaintiff can prove (1) the defendant and the testator were in a confidential relationship, (2) the testator was of weakened intellect, and (3) the defendant takes the bulk of the testator's estate.

  - **No contest clauses:** A testator may include a clause in the will (or other testamentary instrument) that provides that if a beneficiary challenges the will or any provision in the will, the beneficiary is barred from taking under the will. No contest clauses are generally valid but narrowly construed, and they may not be enforced, depending on the jurisdiction, if (1) there is probable cause to support the challenge, or (2) the challenge is based on forgery, revocation, or misconduct by a witness or the drafter.

- **Fraud:** An intentional misrepresentation, made purposely to influence the testator's testamentary scheme, which causes the testator to dispose of his or her property in a way which he or she otherwise would not have (causation).

  - *Fraud in the execution* occurs if a person intentionally misrepresents the nature of the document that the testator is signing (either completely or in part). *Fraud in the inducement* occurs if a person intentionally misrepresents a fact to the testator to induce the testator to execute a will (or amend a provision in a will or revoke a will) in reliance upon the misrepresentation.

- **Duress:** Duress occurs where a wrongdoer performs, or threatens to perform, a wrongful act that coerces the donor into making a donative transfer he or she would not have otherwise made.

■ **Tortious interference with an expectancy:** Tortious interference with an expectancy requires (1) an expectancy; (2) a reasonable certainty that the expectancy would have been realized but for the interference; (3) intentional interference with the expectancy; (4) tortious conduct involved with the interference, such as fraud, duress, or undue influence; and (5) damages.

I. GENERAL TESTAMENTARY CAPACITY

A. **Introduction:** To the extent one dislikes the intestate distribution scheme, the traditional method of opting out is to execute a will. The first requirement for a valid will is that the testator have the requisite testamentary capacity.

1. **Policy justifications:** It is so well accepted that a testator must have capacity that it often goes unquestioned. The policy justifications are primarily intuitive.

   ■ A person who lacks capacity is not recognized as an individual for a whole host of purposes. Consistency dictates that capacity be required to execute a legal document as important as a will. A legal system that did not require capacity would run afoul of public opinion.

   ■ The aging process involves the risk that one may lose mental capacity and no longer understand the nature of his or her thoughts or actions. Requiring capacity at time of execution assures testators that the intent expressed when they have capacity will be protected from the risk that they may lose capacity later in life.

   ■ The requirement of capacity protects family members. Most people assume that testators normally will provide for their families. If a testator fails to leave most or all of his or her property to family members, that *may* be evidence that the testator lacked capacity. The capacity requirement has been criticized for elevating family protection above testamentary freedom.

   ■ The requirement of capacity protects testators from unscrupulous third parties who may try to take advantage of a testator of weakened capacity.

   For all these reasons, and no doubt others, every jurisdiction requires that the testator have the requisite mental capacity to create a valid will.

2. **Temporal application:** The testator must have the requisite capacity at the time he or she performs a testamentary act—executes or revokes a will.

   Lucid interval: If a person who usually lacks testamentary capacity executes a will during a lucid moment, the will is valid even though the testator lacked capacity for some period of time before and/or after executing the will (though the testator's condition immediately before and after executing the will is relevant to the issue of testator's capacity at the moment of execution).

B. **Requirements:** To execute or to revoke a will, the testator must be *at least 18 years old and of sound mind.*

1. **Sound mind:** Sound mind requires that the testator have the *ability* to know (a) the nature and extent of his or her property, (b) the natural objects of his or her bounty, (c) the nature of the

testamentary act he or she is performing, and (d) how all of these relate together to constitute an orderly plan of disposing of his or her property.

a. *Ability* **to know:** The testator need only have the ability to know the information covered by the requirements. He or she need not actually know the information.

b. **Low threshold:** When viewed from the perspective of the ability to know, it becomes readily apparent that the test for sound mind is extremely low. De facto, there is a strong presumption that one has testamentary capacity.

c. **Burden of proof:** The majority approach is that once a proponent offers prima facie proof that a will was duly executed, it creates a rebuttable presumption the testator had testamentary capacity and the burden is on the contestant to prove a lack of testamentary capacity. *See Wilson v. Lane*, 614 S.E.2d 88 (Ga. 2005); *Breeden v. Stone*, 992 P.2d 1167 (Co. 2000). The minority approach is the will proponent bears the burden of proving testamentary capacity. *See In re Estate of Washburn*, 690 A.2d 1024 (N.H. 1997). Where the issue of testamentary capacity is at issue, it can be an extremely soft, fact-sensitive analysis with different triers of fact and courts analyzing nearly identical fact patterns differently. Who bears the burden of proof can affect the outcome.

2. **Standing:** The general rule is that a party has standing to contest the validity of a will, or provision in a will, only if that party will financially benefit if his or her challenge is successful.

3. **Testamentary capacity vs. contractual capacity:** One must have contractual capacity to enter into a valid and binding contract. Contractual capacity is higher than testamentary capacity.

a. **Rationale:** Contractual capacity is concerned with one improvidently disposing of one's assets during one's lifetime. The risk is that the person may become destitute and therefore dependent on the state for support. The state has a legitimate interest in not wanting to pay the cost of caring for those who could have cared for themselves. Testamentary capacity, on the other hand, is concerned with the level of capacity necessary to transfer one's assets at time of death. The state has less of an interest in the possible consequences of testamentary transfers. If one improvidently transfers his or her assets at death, there is no risk that the state will have to care for the transferor because he or she is dead. Hence, the level of capacity necessary for testamentary capacity is lower than the level of capacity necessary for contractual capacity.

b. **Appointment of conservator:** If a person lacks contractual capacity, a conservator is appointed to handle the person's affairs. Because testamentary capacity is lower than contractual capacity, the mere appointment of a conservator does not mean that the person necessarily lacks testamentary capacity. More facts would be necessary to determine if the person lacked testamentary capacity.

4. **Testamentary capacity vs. marriage capacity:** Testamentary capacity is higher than the capacity necessary to marry. The right to marry is a fundamental right. It is accorded special status that limits the state's ability to regulate it. Accordingly, the level of capacity necessary for a valid marriage is below testamentary capacity.

> Summary: Contractual capacity > testamentary capacity > capacity to marry

5. **Attorney's ethical duty:** A lawyer has an ethical duty to assess the capacity of an individual before drafting his or her will. It is unethical to draft a will for a person who lacks capacity. But the attorney is authorized to rely upon his or her own judgment in determining whether the person has the requisite testamentary capacity.

6. **Defects in capacity:** Even if a person has general testamentary capacity, a person may suffer from a defect in capacity that may invalidate part or all of the will. Four possible defects in capacity may nullify part or all of the will: (1) insane delusion, (2) undue influence, (3) fraud, or (4) duress.

7. **Remedy:** If the testator suffers from a defect that causes him or her to dispose of his or her property in a way that the testator otherwise would not have, the general rule is the court will strike as much of the will as was caused by the defect.

II. INSANE DELUSION

A. **Definition:** An insane delusion is a false sense of reality to which a person adheres despite all evidence to the contrary.

   1. **Delusion:** A delusion is a false perception of reality. At one level, a delusion is nothing more than a form of a mistake.

   2. **Mistake:** As a general rule, courts do not correct mistakes. If they did, every time a person was left out of a will that he or she expected to be in, the person could claim there must have been a mistake and ask the court to rewrite the testator's will to include the person. There is general agreement that courts should not rewrite testators' wills. The process is too speculative, involves high costs of administration, and opens the door to fraudulent claims.

B. **Jurisdictional split:** Two different doctrinal approaches have evolved with respect to what constitutes an insane delusion.

   1. **Majority:** A majority of jurisdictions apply the *rational person test* to determine what constitutes an insane delusion. If a rational person in the testator's situation could not have reached the same conclusion, the belief is an insane delusion.

   2. **Minority:** A minority of the jurisdictions apply the *any factual basis to support test* to determine what constitutes an insane delusion. If there is any factual basis to support the testator's belief, it is not an insane delusion.

   3. **Differences:** At first blush, the two approaches appear quite different. The majority arguably is broader and less protective of a testator's intent, permitting a finding of insane delusion even if some evidence supports the testator's position.

   4. **Similarities:** On the other hand, one could argue that the two tests are closer than one might think. The majority test is that the belief has to be one that a rational person in the testator's position *could* not reach (not *would* not). Under the minority approach, the belief is not an insane delusion if there is some factual basis to support the belief. If there is some factual basis to support the testator's belief, then arguably a reasonable person could reach the same conclusion as the testator based on the factual support. The majority and minority approaches may not be as different as they first appear.

5. **Traumatic event:** Although not an explicit part of either test, the cases tend to indicate that if a traumatic event in a person's life alters how he or she views the world, or at least part of the world, the contestant has a better chance of convincing the court that the testator suffered from an insane delusion. The doctrine is extremely fact-sensitive. Courts and juries appear more likely to conclude that an insane delusion was caused by something traumatic that happened to a testator during his or her life than that an insane delusion just occurred.

6. **Protection of testator's intent:** The any factual basis approach is more protective of testator's intent. If there is any factual basis that supports testator's belief, no room exists for a jury to substitute its belief. Under the rational person approach, even if some factual basis supports the testator's belief, if the jury thinks the belief is too bizarre, the jury can substitute its belief.

7. **Example:** In *Breeden v. Stone*, 992 P.2d 1167 (Co. 2000), testator Spicer Breeden regularly abused alcohol and cocaine and suffered from delusions, mood swings, and paranoia, including that everyone was spying on him—including family, friends, and repairmen working in the area (it turned out that one of his friends, Crow, was an FBI informant). Testator cut off his TV antennae and his cable service because he thought the FBI could monitor his conduct through the TV screen. After a particularly hard and long weekend of using cocaine and alcohol with his friends from Friday, March 15, 1996, to early Sunday morning, March 17th, later that day while driving 110 mph he hit another car, killing the driver (testator did not stop but switched cars and continued to party, consuming more alcohol and cocaine). When the police came to his house on March 19th, to question him about the accident, he barricaded himself inside, scribbled out a will that cut out his family (from whom he was estranged) and left all his property to one of his friends, shot his dog (wounding it), and then shot and killed himself. The court held the proof of due execution of the will created a presumption of general testamentary capacity that the contestants did not overcome, shifting the issue to the insane delusion claim.

   a. **Rational person analysis:** Under the majority approach, it is rather easy to conclude that a rational person could not hold the delusions and paranoia that the government, the testator's family, and his friends were all out to get him.

   b. **Any factual basis:** Under the minority approach, it came out in a later proceeding that one of the testator's friends may have been an FBI informant. It is unclear, however, whether the probate court was aware of this or whether it would have found that fact alone supported testator's delusions and paranoia.

   c. **Court's holding:** The court found that testator suffered from an insane delusion but that there was not sufficient evidence that it materially affected the provisions of his will.

8. **Example:** In *In re Honigman,* 168 N.E.2d 676 (N.Y. App. 1960), testator and his wife were faithfully married for 40 years. At the age of 70, after undergoing surgery for prostate cancer, he became obsessed with the belief that his wife was being unfaithful. He told anyone who would listen that she was having sex with every man she met, that she hid men in the closet and under the bed, and that she hauled men up into their second-floor bedroom window by tying bedsheets together and pulling them up. Testator executed a will that left his wife the bare minimum permitted under the law and the rest to his siblings. He told his attorney that his wife was independently wealthy and he wanted to take care of his siblings. After his death, his wife challenged the will claiming that his belief that she was being unfaithful was an insane delusion. In support of the belief, the siblings presented evidence that the wife always answered the phone; that she received a sentimental anniversary card addressed only to her from a male

friend on a day that was not the testator and his wife's anniversary; and one day when the testator was leaving, the wife asked when he would be back. The testator became suspicious, so he hid near the house and watched the same male friend of theirs who sent the anniversary card enter the house.

    a. **Rational person analysis:** The question is whether a rational person in the testator's position could reach the same conclusion. After 40 years of faithful marriage, the testator's belief appears to be the result of his coming out of the surgery not quite the same man. While it is theoretically possible that his wife may suddenly have begun a life of promiscuous and wild sex, the testator's claims seem rather preposterous under the circumstances.

    b. **Any factual basis analysis:** The question is whether there is any factual basis to support the testator's belief. The key here is how much nexus there must be between the belief and the allegedly supportive evidence. The testator's siblings offered three bits of evidence that arguably support the belief, but only indirectly at best. The siblings have an argument, though.

    c. **Court's holding:** Applying the rational person test, the court held that the contestants had presented sufficient evidence from which the jury could conclude that the testator suffered from an insane delusion.

  9. Dead man's statutes: An issue that often arises in probate proceedings is whether it is appropriate to permit a witness who has an interest in the outcome of the probate proceedings to testify about alleged oral statements the decedent made when the decedent is not alive to respond to the testimony. Historically, many states had "dead man's statutes" that prohibited such testimony. Today only a minority of states still have such statutes. Some states have completely abolished them, while others permit such testimony if corroborated by other evidence or if the court finds such testimony reliable.

C. Causation: Even if the testator suffers from an insane delusion, the insane delusion is irrelevant unless it is shown that the belief caused the testator to dispose of his or her property in a way that the testator would not have otherwise.

  1. Majority: Most jurisdictions require ***"but for" causation:*** but for the insane delusion, the testator would not have disposed of his or her property as he or she did. Some courts soften the standard a bit, requiring instead that the insane delusion ***materially affect*** the will's provisions.

  2. Minority: A minority of jurisdictions requires only that the insane delusion ***might have affected*** the disposition of the testator's property.

  3. Protection of testator's intent: The "might have affected" test for causation is so low as to be almost always satisfied. The "but for" test arguably is more protective of testator's intent, requiring a showing that the testator would not have disposed of his or her property as he or she did if the testator did not have the insane delusion. The "materially affected" test is something of a compromise between these two more extreme standards.

  4. Fact-sensitive: Both the majority and the minority approaches to whether a belief constitutes an insane delusion are extremely soft, fact-sensitive doctrines. Insane delusion issues are more about knowing how to marshal the facts and making the arguments pro and con than about predicting with 100 percent certainty whether a particular belief constitutes an insane delusion. The more preposterous the belief, the more likely it is to be called an insane delusion.

5. **Religious or spiritual beliefs:** Although not explicitly part of the doctrine, the cases indicate that generally courts and juries are reluctant to apply the doctrine to religious or spiritual beliefs. This is intuitively understandable. In light of the principle of separation of church and state, many people are uncomfortable with the idea of courts and juries evaluating how "reasonable" a person's religious or spiritual beliefs are or whether any factual basis supports these religious or spiritual beliefs.

III. UNDUE INFLUENCE

A. **Introduction:** The second defect in testamentary capacity that may render a will invalid is undue influence.

B. **Definition:** Undue influence is difficult to define. It is "substituted intent"—when one influences the testator to the extent that the will expresses the influencer's intent, not the testator's intent. Others have defined it as coercion, though not necessarily coercion of a physical nature, but more of a mental, emotional nature.

   Proof: Rarely is there direct evidence of undue influence. At best, there is circumstantial evidence.

C. **Traditional rule statement:** The prevailing view is that the traditional undue influence doctrine has four elements:

   ■ **Susceptibility:** Was the testator susceptible to the undue influence?

   ■ **Opportunity:** Did the defendant have the opportunity to exert undue influence?

   ■ **Motive:** Did the defendant have a motive for exerting undue influence?

   ■ **Causation:** Did the undue influence cause the testator to dispose of his or her property in a way that the testator would not have otherwise?

   1. **Burden of proof:** Under this approach, the party challenging the will bears the burden of proof.

   2. **Causation:** Note the nature of the four elements. The first three are, by nature, factual. It is relatively easy to marshal facts that reflect directly upon them. Invariably, the analysis comes down to the final requirement—causation. It is the toughest to prove. Rarely are there facts that go directly to it. The issue is whether the alleged facts combined to cause the testator to dispose of his or her property in a way that the testator would not have otherwise. That is more of a legal conclusion than a question of fact. It is usually the determining element.

D. **Burden-shifting approach:** Because there is rarely direct evidence of undue influence, and the defendant is in the best position to present whatever evidence is available, most jurisdictions have a "burden-shifting approach" to undue influence. If the elements of the burden-shifting doctrine are satisfied, a presumption of undue influence arises, and the burden shifts to the defendant to rebut the presumption.

   1. **Rule statement:** The burden-shifting doctrine varies from jurisdiction to jurisdiction. In many jurisdictions, the presumption of undue influence arises if:

   ■ there was a ***confidential relationship*** between the defendant and the testator;

- the defendant *receives the bulk of the testator's estate;* and

- the testator was of *weakened intellect.*

(Some jurisdictions put more emphasis on whether the defendant was *active in the procurement or execution of the will,* either substituting it for the third requirement or adding it as a fourth requirement.)

Example: In *Estate of Lakatosh*, 656 A.2d 1378 (Pa. Super. Ct. 1995), Roger Jacobs befriended Rose Lakatosh, a 70-year-old woman who lived alone, was easily distracted, and was having trouble remembering things. She quickly became dependent on Roger. He visited her daily, sometimes several times a day, and took her on errands. A few months after first meeting Roger, Rose gave him a power of attorney over her affairs ("to protect her") and executed a will giving all but $1,000 of her $268,000 estate to him. Roger was not present when the will was drafted or executed, but the attorney was his cousin (to whom Roger had referred Rose for a different matter). Roger used the power of attorney to use Rose's money for his own benefit and that of his friends (whom Rose did not know). Rose's living standards deteriorated, and shortly before her death she revoked the power of attorney, but not the will. The court found that there was a confidential relationship between Roger and Rose, that Rose was of weakened intellect, and that Roger was to receive the bulk of her estate. Roger was unable to overcome the presumption of undue influence.

2. **Restatement (Third) of Property, Donative Transfers:** The Restatement (Third) provides that while a confidential relationship is not enough to raise a suspicion of undue influence, a confidential relationship coupled with suspicious circumstances are sufficient to raise an inference of abuse of the confidential relationship. All relevant facts may be taken into account in considering what constitutes suspicious circumstances.

3. **Burden of proof:** If these requirements are satisfied, a presumption of undue influence arises and the burden shifts to the defendant to rebut the presumption.

4. **Confidential relationship:** There is no bright line for what constitutes a confidential relationship, but at a minimum the testator has to confide in the other party.

5. **Comparison:** In essence, the presumption doctrine provides that where the plaintiff can prove the first three elements of the traditional doctrine *by this particular evidence,* then a presumption of causation arises, and the burden shifts to the defendant to show no undue influence.

6. **Fact-sensitive:** Just as with insane delusion, undue influence is an extremely soft, fact-sensitive doctrine. Often the analysis is more about marshaling the facts and making the arguments pro and con than it is about the conclusion one reaches because it is so difficult to predict with much certainty how a court would rule.

7. **Nontraditional relationships:** Because undue influence is such a soft, fact-sensitive doctrine, there is the potential for abuse. In applying the doctrine, juries may be affected by how they perceive the testator's relationship with the party alleged to have committed undue influence. The more nontraditional the relationship, the more potential the jury will impose its own values in assessing the nature of the relationship. Just as with insane delusion, a fairly high percentage of jury findings of undue influence are reversed on appeal.

E. Gifts to attorneys: Gifts to the client's attorney, particularly if the attorney drafted the instrument, smack of impropriety. Such gifts naturally raise questions as to whether it was truly the client's wishes or whether the gift was the result of undue influence or fraud on the part of the attorney. Attorneys are skilled in the subtle art of persuasion, so the client may never realize what is happening; the attorney owes a fiduciary duty to the client, and such gifts appear to conflict with that duty; and as the drafter-taker it would be easy for the attorney to fraudulently slip the gift into the will.

1. **Majority approach:** The general rule is that any time an attorney who drafts an instrument receives a substantial gift under it, a *presumption of undue influence* arises unless the attorney is related to or married to the client.

   Heightened burden: Most jurisdictions require a heightened burden of proof to overcome the presumption, requiring clear and convincing evidence that the gift was truly the testator's intent.

2. **Minority approach:** Some jurisdictions are so concerned about gifts to the drafting attorney that they create an *irrebuttable presumption of undue influence.*

   Exceptions: The irrebuttable presumption of undue influence generally cannot be overcome by evidence that the client freely and independently wanted to make the gift. The presumption can only be avoided. The attorney must come within one of two exceptions to the presumption: (1) the attorney is related to or married to the testator, or (2) the will was reviewed by an independent attorney who advised the testator about the potential for undue influence to make sure the gift was the free and voluntary act of the testator.

3. **Example:** In *In re Will of Moses,* 227 So. 2d 829 (Miss. 1969), the testatrix, an older woman, was having sexual relations with her younger male attorney. The testatrix decided to change her will to leave the bulk of her estate to her attorney. She went to an independent attorney, who drafted a will that she properly executed that expressed her wishes, but the drafting attorney failed to investigate the nature of her relationship with the beneficiary or to advise her about the appearance of undue influence. The court held that due to the fiduciary relationship between the testatrix and the beneficiary (attorney-client), a special presumption of undue influence arose even though he did not draft the will. Moreover, the presumption was not overcome because although the testatrix went to an independent attorney, the attorney did not advise her about the potential for undue influence to make sure the gift was indeed her free and voluntary act.

   Criticism: Critics have argued that in *Moses* the court was more concerned with the non-traditional sexual relationship than it was with the attorney abusing his fiduciary relationship with a client by receiving a gift. Note again the potential for improper use of the doctrine due to its soft, fact-sensitive nature.

4. **Rationale:** Most jurisdictions found it necessary to create a special presumption of undue influence for the attorney who takes because the existing doctrines (the four-element approach to undue influence, and the burden-shifting presumption of undue influence) did not do a good job of covering the problem.

   a. **Presumption of undue influence doctrine:** Under the general presumption of undue influence doctrine, the attorney-client relationship constitutes a confidential relationship. It is easy to argue that the testator is of weakened intellect, relative to the attorney, particularly if the client is elderly or physically debilitated. But the gift must constitute the bulk of the testator's estate. A shrewd attorney could avoid application of the presumption of undue influence doctrine by making sure he or she did not get too greedy—that is, by making sure that the gift, while substantial, did not constitute the bulk of the testator's estate.

b. **Basic undue influence doctrine:** Under the basic undue influence doctrine, where the attorney who drafts a will takes under it, it is relatively easy to prove susceptibility (testator confided in attorney and relied upon attorney's advice in drawing up will), opportunity (attorney had access to client's innermost thoughts about estate plans and finances, had a fiduciary relationship with client, and had the ability to influence testator's thinking), and motive (money). As usual, however, the difficult element is causation. The attorney would argue there was no substituted intent—that the gift was the client's true intent in appreciation of years of service.

5. **Example:** In *Lipper v. Weslow,* 369 S.W.2d 698 (Tex. App. 1963), testatrix's will left her estate to her two surviving children and disinherited the issue of her predeceased son. The issue of the predeceased son sued claiming undue influence on the part of the surviving son, Frank. He lived next door to the testatrix, he was the attorney who drafted the will, he bore malice toward his predeceased half-brother, and he had a key to the house. Testatrix was 81 years old when she signed the will. She did not read the will or discuss its terms when she signed it. She died only 22 days later. The will contained a paragraph that stated that the testatrix disinherited the grandchildren because they and their mother had been "most unfriendly" to her since the death of her son, though there was conflicting evidence as to the accuracy of this assertion. Although there was evidence that showed the testatrix was susceptible (due to her age and dependency upon her son), that the son had the opportunity (he lived next door, he was an attorney, he drafted the will, and he had a key to the house), and motive (he disliked his deceased half-brother and he took more under the will), the court ruled there was no causation. The court noted that for years the testatrix had told a number of different people, on different occasions when the son was not present, that she intended to disinherit her grandchildren because of their behavior.

a. **Presumption approach:** In the *Lipper* case, it is unclear whether the presumption would arise. There was a confidential relationship—Frank was her son and attorney. It is unclear whether he took the "bulk" of her estate. He received more than he otherwise stood to receive, though he took only half the estate. It is questionable whether the testatrix was of weakened intellect. She was 81 years old, but the court noted that she was a person of strong will and physically active until the day she died. On the other hand, she lived alone and was dependent on her son, who lived next door, for a number of activities. But even if the presumption of undue influence arose, the evidence that for years the testatrix had told a number of different people that she intended to disinherit her grandchildren arguably overcomes the presumption.

b. **Interested drafter approach:** The interested drafter doctrine does not apply if the attorney is related to the testator. In *Lipper,* Frank, the attorney who drafted the will and who took under it, was the testator's son, so the doctrine would not apply.

6. **Ethical considerations:** An interested drafter may also be subject to ethical discipline. Rule 1.8(c) of the Model Rules of Professional Conduct provides that a lawyer "shall not prepare an instrument giving the lawyer or a person related to the lawyer . . . any substantial gift from a client, . . . except where the client is related to the donee." The comments to the rule recognize

that before a client makes a gift to his or her attorney, the client should have the detached advice of an independent attorney. Disciplinary actions for violating the rule range from suspension to disbarment.

7. **No contest clause:** A no contest clause is a clause that says if a beneficiary under the instrument sues contesting the instrument, or a provision in the instrument, the beneficiary loses whatever he or she is taking under the instrument.

   a. **Public policy considerations:** No contest clauses are something of a double-edged sword. No contest clauses may deter frivolous suits and protect testator's intent, which are good. But no contest clauses may actually be shielding a party's wrongful conduct, which is bad.

   b. **Construction:** Because of the mixed public policy concerns, the general rule is that no contest clauses are valid but are construed narrowly and are not enforceable in certain situations. An action to construe a will generally is not considered a will contest.

   c. **Enforceability:** To say that a no contest clause is unenforceable means that even if a beneficiary contests and loses, the beneficiary still takes his or her original gift under the will. The jurisdictions are split as to when a no contest clause is unenforceable.

      i. **Majority/UPC approach:** A majority of jurisdictions and the UPC refuse to enforce a no contest clause if there is probable cause to support the will contest, whatever the nature of the contest. UPC §§2-517 and 3-905.

         Rationale: If there is probable cause to support the claim, the risk that the no contest clause is being used to shield wrongful conduct is too great to ignore. The legal system wants such contests brought and investigated to ensure that the will is not the product of wrongful conduct.

      ii. **Minority approach:** In a minority of jurisdictions, a no contest clause is unenforceable, regardless of the amount of evidence supporting the claim, if the claim is one of forgery, revocation, or misconduct by one active in the procurement or execution of the will. This approach arguably is more protective of no contest clauses, creating a narrower exception to their enforcement

F. **Anticipating and deterring challenges:** Alleged defects in capacity (lack of capacity generally, insane delusion, undue influence, and fraud) are among the most common grounds for challenging a will (or trust). Because these doctrines are so fact-sensitive, they are easy to bring and easy to litigate before a sympathetic jury.

   1. **"Unnatural" disposition:** Because these doctrines are so fact-sensitive, some have argued that it permits juries to substitute their intent for the testator's intent. This is particularly true where the testator's intent constitutes an "unnatural" disposition—that is, not what a typical person would do under the circumstances. Although an unnatural disposition does not itself constitute a defect in capacity, at a minimum it opens the disposition to attack, thereby forcing the estate to defend against the claim.

      a. **Trial vs. appeal:** At least one study found that where there is an unnatural disposition, a jury is likely to find the testator lacked capacity for one reason or another, only to have the court of appeals reinstate the will in approximately half of the cases where the jury found the will invalid.

    b. Potential for litigation: Anytime there is an unnatural disposition in the testator's will, the will arguably is subject to attack for lack of capacity or defect in capacity. Because the capacity and defect in capacity doctrines are so fact sensitive, it is virtually impossible to defeat a will contest on a motion for summary judgment. At a minimum, the beneficiaries under the will are looking at the costs of trial, the potential embarrassment of the testator's eccentric beliefs being made public, and, in light of the jury's natural sympathy with the contestants, the possible costs of an appeal. In light of the inevitable costs of defending the will, many beneficiaries will agree to settle rather than litigate under the cost-benefit analysis that even if they were to prevail, the costs of defending the will would be greater.

    c. Family protection: In light of the jury's sympathy for family members where there is an unnatural disposition in the testator's will, many argue for a stronger approach to family protection doctrines. Many European countries grant children a right to take from a parent's probate estate.

2. Deterring will contests: Assuming one were anticipating a challenge, there are a number of estate planning tools that one might consider using to reduce the likelihood of such a suit and to decrease the chances that such a suit would be successful.

    a. Explanatory statement: If one anticipates a will contest, the urge is natural to include a statement in the will explaining why the testator did what he or she did in the hope that such a statement would either deter a will contest or help to convince the jury that the provisions in the will truly are the testator's intent. Including such a statement in the will, however, probably increases the possibility of a lawsuit:

- If the statement portrays a family member poorly, the person may feel the need to contest the will just to defend him- or herself.

- If the statement gives reasons for the testator's actions, the testator needs to be absolutely sure that each and every reason given is accurate and defensible. Any inaccuracy can be used to raise issues of capacity and/or undue influence.

- If the statement libels a person, the statement can be the basis for a claim of testamentary libel.

        Recommendation: If an explanatory statement is appropriate, it should *not* be included in the will, which becomes a public document. Instead, the client should handwrite a letter to the attorney setting forth his or her testamentary scheme, the lawyer then should write the client noting its effect upon family members, then the client should write another letter to the attorney explaining the reasons for the 'unnatural' disposition. The lawyer can then disclose the letters during probate to those who need the explanation. This reduces the chances that anyone will feel the need to sue to clear one's name and minimizes any possible damages if the statement is libelous. Moreover, the letters should favor general statements of explanation as opposed to details and incidents. The same can be achieved through a video, or the testator can hold a family meeting to explain his or her wishes before he or she dies.

    b. Extra precautions: The lawyer may also wish to have the testator's capacity assessed by a medical expert; have a third witness at the will execution ceremony; and/or include a no-contest clause.

2. **Inter vivos trusts:** Another way a person can try to protect his or her estate plan is to use an inter vivos trust instead of a will. As a practical matter, using an inter vivos trust increases the chances that the testamentary scheme will survive a challenge.

Benefits: The principal advantage of using an inter vivos trust, as opposed to a will, is its temporal nature. Because the trust is established inter vivos and engages in inter vivos transactions with third parties during the settlor's lifetime, it is harder to strike down. If a will is challenged and held invalid, no transfers have to be undone. All that happens is that the transfers proposed in the will are not given effect. If an inter vivos trust is challenged after the settlor's death and held invalid, the court faces the daunting task of undoing potentially years' worth of inter vivos transaction. Courts are more unlikely to hold an inter vivos trust to be invalid years after its creation than they would be to hold a will invalid before it is given effect.

IV. FRAUD

A. **Rule:** Fraud occurs where someone intentionally misrepresents something to the testator, with the intent of influencing the testator's testamentary scheme, and the misrepresentation causes the testator to dispose of his or her property in a way that he or she would not have otherwise.

Misrepresentation: A person must intentionally misrepresent something to a testator, knowing it to be false when he or she makes the misrepresentation.

B. **Fraud in the inducement:** Fraud in the inducement occurs when a person misrepresents a fact to the testator for the purpose of inducing the testator to execute a will with certain provisions, or for the purpose of inducing the testator to revoke a will. The key is that the misrepresentation does not go to the terms of the will per se, but rather concerns a fact that is important to the testator and may induce the testator to dispose of his or her property differently in light of the misrepresentation.

C. **Fraud in the execution:** Fraud in the execution occurs when a person misrepresents the nature of a document the testator is signing. Fraud in the execution occurs when either a person tricks another into signing a document that purports to be the signer's will, but the signer does not realize it, or when the testator realizes he or she is signing his or her will, but the person misrepresents some of the contents of the will.

D. **Elements:** The claim of testamentary fraud is different from the tort-based fraud claim.

1. **Mens rea:** The misrepresentation must be made knowingly and for the purpose of influencing testator's testamentary scheme. If the misrepresentation is made as a practical joke, with no purpose other than a practical joke, and the testator changes his or her testamentary scheme based upon the misrepresentation, technically the fraud doctrine should not apply.

Significance: The requirement that the misrepresentation be made with the *purpose* of influencing the testator's testamentary scheme arguably is more of a theoretical requirement than a practical requirement. There rarely is direct evidence of the party's intent at the time he or she makes the misrepresentation. The jury is free to draw whatever inferences it thinks appropriate from the circumstances surrounding the making of the misrepresentation. The jury is even free to disbelieve self-serving statements made by the party who made the misrepresentation.

2. **Causation:** The fraud must cause the testator to dispose of his or her property in a way that he or she would not have otherwise.

3. **Remedy:** The remedy for fraud depends on the effect of the fraudulent misconduct.

   a. **Fraudulent provisions:** The norm is that the fraud will cause the testator to execute a will he or she otherwise would not have. In such cases, the remedy is to strike as much of the will as was affected by the fraud or, if necessary, to strike the whole will.

   b. **Fraudulent failure to revoke:** If the fraud causes the testator not to revoke a will (or clause) that he or she otherwise would have revoked, the appropriate remedy is to strike the will (or clause) that the testator would have revoked but for the misconduct.

   c. **Fraudulent failure to execute:** If the fraud causes the decedent not to execute a will that he or she otherwise would have, although the court will not execute the will for the decedent, the court can impose a constructive trust on the parties who take the decedent's probate property and order the property distributed to the parties who would have taken the property had the decedent executed the will that the misconduct prevented the decedent from executing.

      Constructive trust: The practical effect of this remedy is to give effect to the will that the decedent did not execute. The constructive trust remedy is rare, but courts have imposed it, where appropriate, to prevent unjust enrichment by those who would otherwise receive the decedent's property. As a general rule, the unjust enrichment must result from some party's misconduct.

V. DURESS

A. **Introduction:** The Restatement (Third) of Property, Donative Transfers, provides that duress occurs where a wrongdoer performs, or threatens to perform, a wrongful act that coerces the donor into making a donative transfer he or she would not have otherwise made. Transfers procured by duress are invalid. Duress can also be viewed as a subset—and extreme example of—undue influence.

B. **Example:** In *Latham v. Father Divine,* 85 N.E.2d 168 (N.Y. App. 1949), testatrix's will left almost all of her estate to Father Divine. The plaintiffs alleged that the testatrix intended to revoke that will and execute a new will leaving her estate to them, but the testatrix was prevented due to Father Divine and his followers' fraud, undue influence, and physical force. The court ruled that the plaintiffs' complaint stated a case for relief in equity and, if proved, entitled the plaintiffs to a *constructive trust* ordering the beneficiaries under the testatrix's will to transfer the property to the plaintiffs.

VI. TORTIOUS INTERFERENCE WITH AN EXPECTANCY

A. **Introduction:** Where a third party has intentionally committed tortious conduct in the testamentary process (undue influence, fraud, or duress), those who would have taken but for the misconduct can also sue the third party for tortious interference with an expectancy.

B. **Rule statement:** The plaintiff typically has to prove (1) the existence of an expectancy; (2) a reasonable certainty that the expectancy would have been realized but for the interference; (3)

intentional interference with the expectancy; (4) tortious conduct involved with the interference, such as fraud, duress, or undue influence; and (5) damages.

C. **Advantages:** Inasmuch as the plaintiff must prove fraud or undue influence, the plaintiff could just sue under those doctrines, but the tort action has advantages over a suit in probate for fraud or undue influence.

1. **Not a will contest:** If a will contains a no contest clause, and a beneficiary sues for fraud or undue influence, the challenge would come within the scope of the no contest clause and the beneficiary may lose his or her gift under the will if he or she were to lose the challenge. If, however, the beneficiary sues claiming tortious interference with an expectancy, that tort action does not challenge the validity of the will and thus does not trigger the no contest clause. By suing in tort, even if the plaintiff were to lose, he or she could still take under the will as a beneficiary despite a no-contest clause.

2. **Punitive damages:** By suing in tort, the plaintiff is eligible to claim punitive damages. If the plaintiff sues for fraud or undue influence, the typical remedy is simply to strike those parts of the will affected by the fraud or misconduct.

3. **Longer statute of limitations:** As part of the probate process, notice is given to creditors to bring their claims within a shortened statute of limitations or their claims will be forever barred. Claims against a will likewise must be brought within a shortened time period or they are forever barred. The tort statute of limitations, however, does not begin to run until the party discovers or should have discovered the misconduct.

D. **Procedural issues:** Some jurisdictions require the claim to be brought in the probate court; some permit it to be brought in civil court. In ***Schilling v. Herrera***, 952 So. 2d 1231 (Fla. App. 2007), Schilling, the decedent's brother, sued Herrera, the decedent's caretaker, claiming tortious interference with an expectancy. Decedent's health began to fail, and she executed a Durable Power of Attorney naming her brother as her attorney-in-fact. Decedent lived in Florida, and her brother in New Jersey. When the decedent was in a rehabilitation center, Herrera began to care for her, and she continued to care for her when the decedent was released, visiting her in her apartment as needed, and then converting her garage into a bedroom and decedent moved in with her. The brother helped pay for the care. Herrera convinced decedent to execute a new Power of Attorney naming Herrera and a new will naming Herrera personal representative and sole beneficiary. When the decedent died, Herrera did not inform the decedent's brother until after she probated the will and probate had closed. The decedent's brother claimed that he called Herrera during this time but that she intentionally refused to answer or return his calls. The trial court dismissed the brother's claim because (1) Herrera owed the decedent's brother no duty, and (2) the brother had failed to exhaust his probate remedies. The court of appeals reversed, emphasizing that it is *the testator who was defrauded or unduly influenced by the defendant, not the claimant*. The court ruled the brother did state a claim because he alleged that Herrera's "fraudulent actions" and "undue influence" were what caused the decedent to change her will leaving all her property to Herrera and revoking a prior will that left her estate to her brother. The court of appeals also ruled that while the claim must be brought in probate court if adequate relief is available in probate court, an exception exists where the circumstances surrounding the tortious conduct effectively preclude adequate relief in the probate court. Such circumstances existed here because of Herrera's refusal to answer or return the brother's calls.

Quiz Yourself on
TESTAMENTARY CAPACITY

13. George is an elderly gentleman and very successful businessman, but he has been very lonely since the death of his wife. His children are grown and live out of town. One evening, George meets Anna Nicoli, a woman young enough to be his daughter. Anna Nicoli, an ex-Playboy bunny, uses her persuasive powers to convince George that what he feels is true love. George proposes to Anna Nicoli, and she agrees. They run off to Las Vegas where they are married. They spend the rest of the night celebrating. George drinks enough champagne to get so drunk he does not know what he is doing. Anna Nicoli pulls out a will, has George declare that it expresses his testamentary wishes, and has him sign it in front of two of her bridesmaids (her best friends). Later that night, George slips into a coma and never recovers, dying several days later. Who takes George's probate property?

_____

14. While vacationing in Scotland, Ned is out boating on Loch Ness, when out of the blue his boat capsizes and he almost drowns. When he comes to, he tells everyone that the Loch Ness monster caused the accident. He swears until he is blue in the face that he saw the beast as the boat capsized. His buddies razz him that he just can't handle a boat in choppy waters. When he dies, his wife and kids are shocked to learn that he left all of his property to the Society for the Discovery of the Loch Ness Monster. His wife wants to challenge the will. What is the wife's best claim for challenging the will, and what are her chances of succeeding?   _____

15. Pattie is kidnapped by a group of ecosystem revolutionaries called the Redwood Liberation Army. During her kidnapping, she is subjected to a series of psychological brainwashing techniques, including beatings and food and light deprivation. After weeks of such torture, Pattie becomes a follower of the movement and denounces her family's publishing empire as being a waste of our natural resources. She properly executes a will leaving all of her property, including her share of the family's publishing empire, to Ima Treehugger, the leader of the Redwood Liberation Army. Sadly, during a "tree sit-in," Pattie is stung to death by a swarm of killer bees. Ima offers Pattie's will for probate. Pattie's family wants to challenge the will. What are their best arguments, and what is the most likely result?   _____

16. Nogood Nolan is an attorney. His office is across the street from Retirement World, a seniors-only retirement community. Every day Nolan goes to Retirement World for breakfast, lunch, and dinner, befriending little old men and woman who have been moved there by their children, who do not have enough time to care for them. After befriending them, he convinces them that their children really do not care for them and that he is their best friend. He persuades them to execute a new will, giving a substantial gift to him. He refers them to a good friend of his whose office is in the same suite as Nolan's. The attorney has a standard "Nogood Nolan" will that gives the testator's family half of the estate and Nolan the other half. The will includes a no-contest clause. After one elderly woman dies and her family learns of her new will and gift to Nolan, the family considers suing to challenge the gift to Nolan.

a. What is their best claim?   _____

b. What else should they argue in the alternative?   _____

c. If they lose, is the no-contest clause enforceable?   _____

17. Jill loves animals. She has a will that leaves everything to the Humane Society (an organization that takes care of lost pets), but she is very concerned about what is going to happen to her pets when she dies. She is "pet guardian" of two dogs (she prefers that term to "pet owner," thinking that the latter implies that pets are mere property with no rights). Knowing of Jill's opinions about animals, one of her neighbors, Jim, tells Jill that if she leaves her property to him, he will use her money to take care of her dogs until they die, and then he will give what is left to the Humane Society. Jill executes a new will that leaves all of her property to Jim. When Jill dies, Jim has the dogs put to sleep and uses the money to buy a new house for himself. The Humane Society wants to sue. What is their best claim, and what is the most likely result? _____

Answers

13. The threshold issue is whether George has a valid will. George arguably lacked general testamentary capacity at the time that he executed the will. If George was so drunk that he did not know what he was doing when he signed the will, he did not have the ability to know the nature and extent of his property, who were the natural objects of his bounty, the nature of the testamentary act that he was performing, and how all of that fit together to form an orderly plan of disposition. The court is likely to hold that George lacked testamentary capacity at the time he executed the will. The will is invalid. Assuming this is George's only will, he dies intestate. The first taker under intestacy is the decedent's surviving spouse. While George's will is invalid, it is much harder to set aside a marriage. Marriage is a fundamental right. The mental capacity necessary for a valid marriage is lower than that necessary for a valid will. Moreover, there is no evidence that George was drunk when he got married. The most likely result is that the court will find that the marriage is valid. Although Anna Nicoli is not able to take under the will because it is invalid, she is entitled to take a surviving spouse's share under intestacy. Assuming that the court applies the UPC approach, because George has surviving issue who are not Anna Nicoli's issue, Anna Nicoli takes the first $100,000 and 50 percent of the remainder, and George's issue split the remaining 50 percent.

14. While there is no evidence that Ned lacks testamentary capacity generally, a strong argument can be made that he was suffering from an insane delusion. Under the majority approach, an insane delusion is a belief that a reasonable person in the testator's situation could not reach. A strong argument can be made that a reasonable person could not reach the conclusion that the Loch Ness monster really exists. In addition to showing that the testator suffered from an insane delusion, those challenging the will must also show causation—that the insane delusion caused the testator to dispose of his or her property in a way that he or she otherwise would not have. Ned's belief in the Loch Ness monster appears to be the only reason that he left his property to the Society for the Discovery of the Loch Ness Monster, so if the belief constitutes an insane delusion, causation is not a problem. Under the minority approach, a belief is not an insane delusion if there is any factual basis to support it. People claim to have seen the Loch Ness monster, and photographs that purport to show it even exist. Under the minority approach, arguably there is evidence to support the belief that the Loch Ness monster really exists. Ned's wife and children have a stronger argument and a better chance of prevailing under the majority approach to insane delusion than they do under the minority approach.

15. The best chance Pattie's family has to have the will declared invalid is to claim undue influence. Undue influence is substituted intent, arguably a form of mental coercion. Pattie's family bears the burden of proving undue influence. They could proceed first under the presumption of undue influence doctrine. The typical burden-shifting approach requires that (1) the testator was of weakened intellect, (2) the alleged undue influencer received the bulk of the testator's property, and (3) the alleged undue influencer was in a confidential relationship with the testator. Pattie arguably was in a state of weakened mental capacity and intellect as a result of her kidnapping and captivity. Ima received all of Pattie's property. The issue is whether Ima and Pattie had a confidential relationship. That is questionable, though one could argue that Ima forced a confidential relationship upon Pattie during her captivity. If the court were to find a confidential relationship existed between the parties, a presumption of undue influence would arise and Ima would have the burden of rebutting it.

In the alternative, Pattie's family could argue the basic four-factor undue influence doctrine. They would have to show that Pattie was susceptible to undue influence, that Ima had both the opportunity and motive to exert undue influence, and causation. Pattie was susceptible to undue influence as a result of her kidnapping, captivity, and treatment. Ima had the opportunity to unduly influence Pattie by secluding her during her kidnapping and wielding great control over Pattie, including whether Pattie was fed. Ima had sufficient motive to exert undue influence, both money and the public relations coup of being able to say that the daughter of such a well-known industrialist had turned on her family's operations. And lastly, Ima's actions caused Pattie to dispose of her property in a way that she otherwise would not have. Before Ima kidnapped and brainwashed Pattie, there is no evidence that Pattie ever had any dealings with the Redwood Liberation Army or that she would have left her property to them.

In the alternative, Pattie's family could also argue that Pattie lacked testamentary capacity generally, but that is a more difficult argument because Pattie appeared able to be functional and to otherwise understand what she is doing.

16a. Because of the no-contest clause, the family's best claim is to sue for tortious interference with an expectancy. One of the principal benefits of the doctrine is that it does not constitute a will contest, so it does not come within the scope of a no-contest clause. Even if the family were to lose, they would still be entitled to take their half of the estate.

To succeed under a tortious interference with an expectancy claim, however, the family would have to show undue influence. This is a close call. Under the burden shifting approach, although Nolan and the testatrix were friends, it is unclear whether their relationship was close enough to qualify as a confidential relationship. It is also unclear whether the testatrix was of weakened intellect. The testatrix is elderly, but no other evidence shows that her mind had deteriorated. And lastly, although Nolan received a substantial gift, arguably he did not receive the bulk of the testatrix's estate. Meeting the requirements under the burden shifting approach to undue influence would be difficult.

Under the traditional approach to undue influence, susceptibility is tough to show under these facts even though the testatrix was elderly, lived alone, and was somewhat isolated from her family. Opportunity is similar; other than the time he spent with her at breakfast, lunch, and dinner, Nolan's contacts with her were minimal. As an attorney, however, he is trained in the art of subtle persuasion, a factor that might be relevant to both opportunity and susceptibility. Motive is the easiest to prove; Nolan stands to gain financially. But causation is tough. It is unclear whether Nolan substituted his intent for hers or whether she simply wanted to thank him for his friendship. Close call that could go either way.

The family might also assert a claim of interested drafter, if the jurisdiction recognizes it. The doctrine varies from jurisdiction to jurisdiction. There is no evidence that Nolan actually drafted the will, but he arguably was active in the procurement of the will (it is unclear what the relationship is between Nolan and the drafting attorney, but if they are partners or closely affiliated professionally, that might be enough to come within the scope of the interested drafter doctrine). No evidence shows that the drafting attorney inquired as to the nature of the relationship or advised the testatrix about her testamentary scheme to ensure that it was her independent wish.

Though there are several arguments the family can make, the outcome is far from clear.

16b. See the different claims raised and discussed in answer *a*.

16c. As discussed in answer *a*, if the claim is one of tortious interference with an expectancy, even if the family loses, the no contest clause would not be enforced against them because the claim is not a will contest. If the claim is a straight undue influence claim and they lose, whether the no contest would be enforced against them depends on which approach the jurisdiction takes to the exceptions to no contest clauses. Under the majority/UPC approach, the no contest clause is unenforceable as long as probable cause supports the claim. Because most courts find that testamentary gifts to an attorney raise at least the appearance of impropriety, it is likely that a court would find probable cause to support the family's claim here and would not enforce the no-contest clause. Under the minority approach, the no-contest clause is enforceable unless the claim is one of forgery, revocation, or misconduct by one active in the procurement or execution of the will. If the jurisdiction recognizes the last ground, the no contest clause should not be enforced because Nogood encouraged the woman to have a new will executed. The family should not lose their gifts under the will.

17. The Humane Society's best claim would be to claim fraud, fraud in the inducement in particular. To prove fraud in the inducement, the claimant must show that someone knowingly made a false statement to the testator with the intent of inducing the testator to execute a will that disposed of his or her property based on the statement, and the misrepresentation caused the testator to dispose of his or her property in a way that he or she would not have otherwise. Here, the key is whether at the time that Jim represented to Jill that he would use the money to care for the dogs and then give the money to the Humane Society, he did not intend to honor that statement. If he never intended to honor the statement, he knowingly made a false representation. He arguably made such a statement to induce Jill to leave her property to him, and arguably that is what caused her to change her will and leave her property to him. The most likely result is that the court will find that Jim's statements amounted to fraud in the inducement and will impose a constructive trust, ordering Jim to transfer the money to the Humane Society.

Exam Tips on
TESTAMENTARY CAPACITY

There is such a strong presumption of testamentary capacity, you should raise and discuss the material in this chapter only if you think one of the parties to the fact pattern could bring a claim involving testamentary capacity in good faith.

Unlike most of the wills and trusts doctrines, the doctrines in this chapter are very soft, fact-sensitive doctrines that usually can go either way. From an exam writing perspective, it is more important to focus on how you marshal the facts and make your arguments pro and con than it is to worry about reaching a "right" conclusion.

General testamentary capacity

☛ If general testamentary capacity is an issue, remember the testator only has to have the *ability to know* those requirements.

☛ An easy-to-test doctrine within the general testamentary capacity is the rule that the mere appointment of a conservator does not mean, in and of itself, that the testator automatically lacks testamentary capacity.

    ☞ If you see facts raising capacity concerns, the key is whether the testator had the requisite capacity *at the moment* he or she performed the testamentary act. (Capacity applies to executing wills and codicils and performing acts of revocation.)

☛ If testamentary capacity is going to be tested, much more often it is tested through one of the defects in capacity doctrines.

Insane delusion

☛ There is some overlap among the defect doctrines. One way to distinguish an insane delusion is that both undue influence and fraud involve misconduct by a third party, while an insane delusion usually arises independently from the testator's own beliefs.

☛ Watch for a belief that is unusual or extreme. The more extreme, the more likely the professor expects you to raise and analyze it as a possible insane delusion.

    ☞ If you have an insane delusion issue, lead with the rule statement for your jurisdiction. The majority reasonable basis test is a more intrusive doctrine than the more protective minority approach of the any-factual-basis test.

    ☞ Be sure to raise and analyze *causation.* Even if there is an insane delusion, without causation there is no defect in capacity justifying judicial intervention. The jurisdictions are split on what constitutes causation. Just as with the underlying doctrine, raise and argue the different approaches on behalf of the competing parties.

Undue influence

☛ Undue influence is another soft, fact-sensitive doctrine. Lead with the rule statement and then apply the different doctrinal requirements to the facts. How well you marshal and argue the facts pro and con and analyze them are the keys.

☛ There are arguably four different ways to claim undue influence (depending on the jurisdiction): (1) the traditional four-element approach, (2) the three-element burden-shifting approach, (3) the interested witness doctrine, and (4) the interested drafter doctrine. On an exam, a party asserting undue influence would probably analyze the doctrines in the exact opposite order, because that order gives the claimant the best chances of the result he or she wants. Argue in the alternative if the facts permit.

☞ Juries tend to find a defect in capacity where there is an unnatural disposition and questionable facts, but appellate courts tend to overrule the juries in a high percentage of cases. Include this judicial observation in your analysis.

☛ No-contest clauses are tested often and are easy to spot in a traditional fact pattern. There has to be an express no-contest clause. Lead with the basic rule statements concerning enforceability. Sweat the details of the approach your jurisdiction applies. These typically are statutory rules, so there is no need to argue in the alternative.

Fraud

☛ Fraud is fairly simple to spot. Someone has to knowingly lie to the testator. If you see that, raise and analyze the fraud issue.

☞ State whether it is fraud in the execution or fraud in the inducement.

☞ Although rarely an issue in the real world, a nice nuance issue is the requirement that the intentional lie ***has to be made with the purpose of influencing the person's testamentary scheme.*** An intentional lie for a different purpose arguably will not constitute fraud in the execution or inducement.

☞ Even if there is fraud, there also has to be causation.

Duress

☛ Duress is fairly simple to spot. Someone has to threaten to perform or does perform a wrongful act that coerced the testator. It is an extreme form of undue influence.

Tortious interference with an expectancy

☛ Tortious interference with an expectancy is a doctrine that you should raise and analyze whenever you claim either undue influence or fraud. Raise it and argue it in the alternative. Include in your discussion of the rule the advantages of this tort doctrine over the pure wills doctrines (in particular, if there is a no-contest clause in the document).

WILLS EXECUTION, REVOCATION, AND SCOPE

ChapterScope _____

This chapter examines some of the core issues in the course: the requirements for a validly executed will, a validly revoked will, and the scope of a will. In particular, the chapter examines:

- **Attested wills:** To have a valid attested will, the will must be in *writing, signed,* and *witnessed.* Each jurisdiction adds a plethora of other detailed requirements.

    - The jurisdictions are split over how strictly the testator must comply with Wills Act formalities. Most jurisdictions require *strict compliance,* but the modern trend favors either *substantial compliance* or the *harmless error/dispensing power* approach.

- **Holographic wills:** Holographic wills need not be witnessed, but they must be handwritten, be signed by the testator, and express testamentary intent (the intent that the document be the decedent's will).

- **Codicils:** A will that merely amends an existing will is called a codicil.

- **Revocation of wills:** A validly executed will (attested or holographic) can be revoked *by a subsequent will, by act, by presumption,* or *by operation of law.*

    - **Dependent relative revocation:** If the testator revokes a will, in whole or in part, based upon a mistake, and the testator would not have revoked but for the mistake, the revocation is not given effect.

    - **Revival:** If testator executes will #1, and thereafter executes will #2, which revokes will #1, and thereafter revokes will #2, will #1 is revived, if (1) will #1 is reexecuted with Wills Act formalities, or (2) in some jurisdictions, evidence shows that the testator intended to revive will #1.

- **Scope of the will:** Several doctrines permit testamentary intent that is not expressed in a will to be given effect as long as a validly executed will exists.

    - **Integration:** Those pieces of paper physically present when the will is executed and that the testator intends to be part of the will constitute the pages of the will.

    - **Republication by codicil:** A codicil has the effect of reexecuting, republishing, and thus, as a general rule, redating the underlying will.

    - **Incorporation by reference:** A document not executed with Wills Act formalities may be given effect along with the will if the document was in existence at the time the will was executed, the will expresses an intent to incorporate the document, and the will adequately identifies the document.

■ **Acts of independent significance:** A will may refer to an act or event that is to occur outside of the will, and that act or event may control either who takes under the will or how much a beneficiary takes, as long as the referenced act has its own significance independent of its effect upon the will.

■ **Contracts relating to wills:** A person may contract to execute a particular will, to make a particular devise, or not to revoke a particular will or devise. If the contract is valid under contract law (that is, includes consideration), it will be enforced against the testator's estate before the decedent's estate is distributed.

I. EXECUTING A VALID WILL

A. Overview: Whether a will has been properly executed is a function of two variables: (1) the jurisdiction's statutory Wills Act formalities, and (2) the jurisdiction's judicial philosophy as to what degree of compliance with the Wills Act formalities is acceptable.

B. Statutory requirements: Every jurisdiction has a statute that sets forth the requirements that an individual must comply with to execute a valid will. These statutory requirements are commonly referred to as the jurisdiction's Wills Act formalities. The Wills Act formalities vary from state to state, and the requirements depend upon whether the will is a traditional attested (that is, witnessed) will or a holographic will. A traditional attested will, at a minimum, includes a writing that is signed and witnessed.

Functions served: The writing, signing, and witnessing requirements serve a number of different functions to ensure that the document expresses the decedent's final wishes and is the document the testator intends to be probated as his or her will.

1. **Evidentiary:** The Wills Act formalities serve an evidentiary function by ensuring that the document offered for probate truly reflects the testator's last wishes as to who should take his or her property.

2. **Protective:** The Wills Act formalities serve a protective function by making it more difficult for fraudulent claims to be brought and by protecting testator's intent as expressed in the properly executed will.

3. **Ritualistic:** The Wills Act formalities serve a ritualistic function by impressing upon the testator the finality of the act he or she is performing.

4. **Channeling:** The cumulative effect of the Wills Act formalities serve a channeling function by encouraging individuals to consult an attorney to draft and supervise the execution of their wills, thereby facilitating the probating of the will and decreasing administrative costs.

C. Judicial philosophy: The other variable that controls whether a will has been validly executed is the judicial philosophy as to how strictly the testator must comply with the Wills Act formalities. The jurisdictions are split over the degree of compliance required. Common law requires strict 100 percent compliance with the Wills Act formalities, while the modern trend favors either substantial compliance or a harmless error/dispensing power approach.

II. COMMON LAW APPROACH TO ATTESTED WILLS

A. Introduction: The traditional common law approach to an attested will is (1) statutorily to have lots of detailed and technical Wills Act formalities, and (2) judicially to require strict compliance with each and every one of those Wills Act formalities.

B. Statutory requirements: An attested will is a will whose signing is witnessed. All states permit attested wills as valid wills. At a minimum, an attested will includes a writing that is signed and witnessed. Invariably, jurisdictions have a number of other ancillary requirements. How many and what they are vary from state to state.

1. Typical statute: The typical common law Wills Act takes the basic three requirements (writing, signature, and witnesses) and expands them into a plethora of requirements.

2. Example: The following is a typical common law Wills Act broken down to show its large number of formalities:

(1) A writing (2) signed (3) at the foot or end thereof (4) by the testator, (5) or by another (6) in his presence (7) and by his direction, (8) such signature made or acknowledged (9) by the testator (10) in the presence (11) of two or more witnesses (12) present at the same time (13) and such witnesses shall attest [sign] (14) and shall subscribe [sign at the end of] the will (15) in the presence of the testator.

C. Judicial approach: The common law judicial approach to the statutory Wills Act formalities is to require *absolute* strict compliance with each Wills Act requirement, no matter how clear the testator's intent that this document be his or her last will. If there is *any* deficiency in the execution ceremony, the document is not a valid will.

1. Testator's intent: The common law combination of statutorily having numerous, detailed Wills Act formalities and judicially requiring strict compliance means that a testator who is not careful could end up with his or her clear testamentary intent not being given effect for failure to comply perfectly with each Wills Act formality.

2. Example: In *In re Groffman,* 2 All E.R. 108 (P. 1968), the testator had his will prepared by an attorney but decided to execute it on his own. The testator, his wife, and two other couples were socializing one evening when the testator gestured towards his coat and asked the two gentlemen to witness his will. The coffee table in the lounge was covered with food, so one of the men escorted the testator into the adjacent dining room. The testator took the will from his pocket, unfolded it, and showed the first witness his signature, after which the witness signed the will. The second witness, who had a leg ailment, was still in the lounge at the time. The first witness returned to the lounge and encouraged the second witness to hurry, as it was cold in the dining room. The second witness went into the dining room and repeated the signing ceremony while the first witness remained in the lounge.

The court acknowledged that it had no doubt the testator intended the document to be his will. Yet the court ruled that the decedent did not acknowledge the signature in the presence of two witnesses present at the same time. The court's holding typifies the traditional common law strict compliance approach to the Wills Act formalities.

3. Example: In *Steven v. Casdorph*, 508 S.E.2d 610 (W. Va. App. 1998), the testator (Mr. Miller) took his will to a bank where he signed in the presence of Ms. Pauley, a bank employee who was a notary, who then took the will to two other bank employees (tellers who worked in the same small lobby) who signed as witnesses. The latter two did not see the testator sign the will nor did the testator acknowledge his signature or will in their presence. The will left the bulk of his estate to the Casdorphs (his nephew and his wife), who had driven the testator to the bank. After the testator's death, his heirs challenged the will claiming improper execution. The West Virginia statute required the testator to sign or acknowledge the will in the presence of two witnesses, present at the same time, who must also sign the will in the presence of the testator. The appellate court applied strict compliance and invalidated the will.

The dissent (and lower court) emphasized that there was no evidence of fraud, coercion, or undue influence and argued that substantial compliance with the statutory requirements should be sufficient to validate the will.

D. Typical formalities: Although the Wills Act formalities vary from jurisdiction to jurisdiction, a number of requirements are common to most of the statutes. These requirements have given rise to a number of ancillary rules.

1. **Writing:** As a general rule, oral wills are not permitted. To have a valid will, there must be a writing.

2. **Signature:** The writing must be signed. A signature is anything the testator intends as his or her signature. There is no requirement that the individual sign his or her full name, but if a person intends to sign his or her full signature and does not complete it, the general rule (at least under the strict compliance approach) is that the partial signature does not qualify as the person's signature.

   A mark: Any mark, even an *"X"*, may qualify as the testator's signature if that is what the testator intends as his or her signature. In ***Taylor v. Holt***, 134 S.W.3d 830 (Tenn. App. 2003), in the presence of two witnesses, the testator typed his name in cursive font into a word processing file containing his will and then printed the document out for the witnesses to sign. The testator did not "re-sign" the document. The Tennessee statute authorized "any . . . symbol or methodology executed or adopted by a party with intention to authenticate a writing or record. . . ." The court upheld the will as validly signed.

3. **Signing by another:** The will may be signed by someone other than the testator, as long as the person signs the testator's name, in the testator's presence, and at the testator's direction. The testator's direction must be express; it will not be implied.

4. **Witnesses:** Most jurisdictions require that the testator sign or acknowledge in the presence of at least two witnesses, who are present at the same time. The witnesses must sign the will, and, in some jurisdictions, the witnesses must know that what they are signing is the testator's will.

   Acknowledgment: Under most statutes, the testator need not sign in front of the witnesses as long as the testator acknowledges, in front of the witnesses present at the same time, that the signature already present on the document is the testator's signature.

5. **Presence:** The testator must sign or acknowledge in the *presence* of the witnesses, and, under the traditional approach, the witnesses must sign in the *presence* of the testator. The presence requirement thus needs to be defined very carefully to take into account *who* has to perform *what* in the presence of *whom.* There are two approaches to the presence requirement.

   a. **Line of sight test:** Under the traditional approach, the actor who has to perform in the presence of the second party has to perform the specified act so that the second party either *sees or has the opportunity of seeing* the act. The latter means that the second party would have **actually seen** the specified act if the second party had looked at the right moment. As applied to a typical traditional statute, the witnesses, present at the same time, must see or have the opportunity of seeing the testator sign or acknowledge his or her signature, and the testator must see or have the opportunity of seeing the witnesses sign the will.

Example: In the *Groffman* case, when the testator acknowledged his signature to the first witness, the second witness was still in the lounge and could not see the signature being acknowledged. When the second witness made his way into the dining room and witnessed the testator acknowledge his signature, the first witness was back in the lounge and could not see the signature being acknowledged. Under the line of sight approach, the testator did not acknowledge his signature in the presence of two witnesses present at the same time.

    b. Conscious presence test: Under the modern trend approach, *presence* is defined by whether the party, in whose presence the act has to be performed, can tell from sight, sound, and general awareness of the events that the required act is being performed. The conscious presence approach is broader than line of sight, opening up the temporal and physical scope of the presence doctrine. In applying the conscious presence test, however, the courts still appear to require some interaction between the testator and the witnesses so that the witnesses are in a position to fulfill their evidentiary and protective functions.

    c. Modern trend/UPC: The modern trend and UPC approach (UPC §2-502(a)(3)) is to abolish the requirement that the witnesses sign in the presence of the testator. Under such statutes, there is only one "presence" requirement: that the testator sign or acknowledge the will in the presence of the witnesses.

6. Order of signing: Because the witnesses are required to witness the testator sign or acknowledge his or her signature, there appears to be an implicit order of performing.

    a. Traditional approach: A number of courts construe this implicit order of performing as mandatory. The testator has to sign the will before either witness can sign. If either witness signs before the testator, the witness has to resign after the testator signs or acknowledges. Otherwise, the witness's signature is not valid for purposes of the execution ceremony.

    b. Modern trend: A witness may sign the will before the testator signs or acknowledges, as long as all the parties sign the will as part of one ceremony—and as long as no one leaves the room during the execution ceremony. (This argument may be difficult to make under the UPC approach because it expressly requires the witnesses to sign "after" witnessing the testator perform. UPC §2-502(a)(3)—but if the jurisdiction has also adopted the UPC harmless error doctrine, as long as there is clear and convincing evidence that the decedent intended the document to be his or her will, the order of signing is irrelevant. UPC §2-503, *see below*.)

7. Writing below signature: With respect to attested wills, if writing appears physically below the testator's signature, two variables must be analyzed: (1) whether the jurisdiction requires the will to be "subscribed"—that is, signed at the end; and (2) *temporally,* when was the writing added.

    a. Subscribe + added *after* will signed: If the jurisdiction requires that the will be subscribed, writing below the signature raises the issue of whether the will was subscribed. The key is *when* the writing below the signature was added. If it was added temporally after the will was properly executed and subscribed, the original will is valid, and only the writing that was added later in time and physically below the signature is null and void (assuming it does not qualify as a codicil in its own right—an issue discussed later).

b. **Subscribe + added *before* will signed:** If the jurisdiction requires that the will be subscribed, and the writing below the signature was added temporally before the will was signed, the will was not signed at the end. Under the traditional strict compliance approach, the whole will would be invalid. (Under the modern trend, a court might be willing to simply strike the provision below the signature and hold that whatever is above the signature is still valid.)

c. **Need not subscribe + added *after* will signed:** If the jurisdiction does not require that the will be subscribed, and the writing below the signature was added temporally after the will was executed, the writing is not considered a part of the will. The will as it existed when it was executed can be given effect, but the writing added later cannot be given effect (unless it qualifies as its own codicil).

d. **Need not subscribe + added *before* will signed:** If the jurisdiction does not require the will to be subscribed, as long as the writing below the signature was added temporally before the will was executed, the whole will is valid, including the writing physically below the signature.

8. **Delayed attestation:** If the statute requires the witnesses to sign in the testator's presence, the witnesses must sign the will at the same time as the testator, in the testator's presence. If the statute does not expressly require the witnesses to sign in the testator's presence, the modern trend and UPC permit the witnesses to sign the will later (delayed attestation), even after the death of the testator, as long as the witnesses sign within a reasonable time period. UPC §2-502(a)(3)(A).

   Reasonable time period: What constitutes a reasonable time period is open to debate. The witnesses should sign the will while their recollection of the execution ceremony is still fresh enough that they can remember whether the execution ceremony was valid. A general recollection that they thought it was valid, arguably, is not sufficient.

9. **Videotaped wills:** Although arguments exist on both sides of the issue, to date no court has upheld a videotaped will. One of the biggest concerns is the potential for litigation over idle comments a person made as to who should take his or her property when he or she died, comments that happened to be captured on videotape in the presence of others. The typical videotaping scenario lacks any ritualistic function, lacks direct evidence as to whether the person intended the taped statement to constitute his or her last will and testament, and has the potential for high administrative costs.

10. **Electronic wills:** Nevada permits electronic wills executed under very strict requirements. Otherwise it is presumed that an electronic will would not satisfy the traditional Wills Act formalities unless the jurisdiction were to apply substantial compliance or harmless error/ dispensing power (see section III.D *infra*).

E. **Interested witness:** The witnessing requirement implicitly assumes that the witnesses assess the testator's capacity at the time of execution, assess the execution ceremony, and protect the testator. These functions arguably require that the witnesses be "disinterested"—that they not take under the will. If a witness has a financial interest under the will, the witness has a conflict of interest in assessing whether the testator has the requisite capacity, in assessing the execution ceremony, and in protecting the testator. Historically the requirement has been that there must be at least two disinterested witnesses. If there are not, the scope of the remedy has evolved over time, with jurisdictions split over which remedy is appropriate.

1. **Invalidate will:** At common law, an interested witness is not permitted to testify in court. If the interested witness is one of the necessary witnesses to the will, without his or her testimony the whole will fails. But invalidating the whole will arguably is harsh since it deprives other beneficiaries in the will of their gifts.

2. **Void interested witness's gift:** By voiding the gift to the interested witness, the witness's ability to testify is restored. With the witness's credibility restored, the will can be probated, but the witness's gift is voided. But even this remedy arguably is harsh. The witness has a conflict of interest only to the extent that the witness stands to take more under this will than he or she would take if this will were not valid.

3. **Purging approach:** The purging approach adopts the argument that a witness has a conflict of interest only to the extent he or she stands to take *more* under the will than he or she would otherwise and purges the interested witness only of his or her *excess* interest under the will. To determine the excess interest, calculate (1) how much the witness would take if the will were not valid, and (2) how much the witness stands to take under the will. If the latter amount is greater, purge the witness of the excess interest. (When calculating how much the witness would take if the will were not valid, do not automatically use the intestate scheme. The testator may have a prior will that would control who takes how much.) The old version of UPC §2-505, adopted in a significant number of states, adopted the purging approach.

4. **Rebuttable presumption of misconduct:** An interested witness gives rise to only a rebuttable presumption of misconduct. If the interested witness rebuts the presumption, he or she gets to keep the whole gift under the will. If the interested witness cannot rebut the presumption, apply the purging approach. The rationale for this approach is that the interested witness scenario arises most often when a testator executes his or her will at home. The testator often asks those closest to him or her to serve as witnesses, yet these are the very same people most likely to be beneficiaries under the will. The interested witness doctrine is more likely to trap innocent, well-intentioned witnesses than to catch parties engaged in misconduct. Under this logic, at worst only a rebuttable presumption of wrongdoing should arise.

5. **Abolish the doctrine:** The UPC and a substantial minority of states take the analysis above to its logical extreme and completely abolish the interested witness doctrine on the theory that it does more harm than good by trapping innocent interested witnesses. If one suspects that an interested witness is guilty of wrongdoing, the party can still challenge the gift under the appropriate doctrines (undue influence, fraud). Revised UPC §2-505.

Example: In *Estate of Morea,* 645 N.Y.S.2d 1022 (Sur. Ct. 1996), of the three witnesses to decedent's will, two took under the will. Because there were not two disinterested witnesses, an issue arose under the interested witness doctrine. One of the witnesses who took under the will was the decedent's son. Under the New York interested witness statute, a party who is both a witness and a beneficiary takes the lesser of his or her intestate share or his or her legacy under the will. Inasmuch as the son had nothing to gain under the will, the court declared him to be a disinterested witness, thereby (1) satisfying the statutory requirement that the will be witnessed by two disinterested witnesses, and (2) permitting the other/third witness to keep his gift under the will.

F. Swapped wills: In the swapped wills scenario, two individuals (typically spouses) have "mirror" wills prepared. Mirror wills are wills that have parallel testamentary schemes. For example, each may say, "all my property to my surviving spouse, but if my spouse fails to survive me, all to *X*" (*X* could be anyone, but both identify *X* as the alternative taker if the other spouse predeceases the testator). When the two execute their wills, the wills are accidentally switched, so each party signs the will that was intended for the other party. The mistake often is not discovered until after the death of the first party. The issue is whether the will the person signed, but which was not drafted for him or her to sign, can be probated as a valid will.

1. **General rule:** Although there is a writing, signed by the testator, and witnessed, the general rule, particularly under the traditional common law approach, is that the will is invalid. The testator signed the wrong document. The printed words of the will state that it is someone else's will. Although one can discern testator's intent from the larger picture, the testator did not intend for that document to be his or her will. He or she intended the document that was drafted for him or her to sign to be his or her will. Most courts apply the strict compliance approach and rule the will is a nullity and refuse to probate it. This approach is consistent with the general rule that courts will not correct mistakes.

2. **Example:** In ***In re Pavlinko's Estate,*** 148 A.2d 528 (Pa. 1959), Vasil and Hellen Pavlinko had mirror wills drafted for them. Each will left all of the testator's estate first to the surviving spouse, if there was one, and otherwise to Hellen's brother, Elias Martin. The Pavlinkos' wills were written in English, but their native language was "Little Russian," nowadays known as Ukrainian. When it came time to execute the wills, Vasil executed the will drafted for Hellen, and she executed the will drafted for him. Hellen died first, but Vasil did not bother to probate her will. When Vasil died, the problem was discovered. Elias offered the will Vasil executed, but the court held that the document was not properly executed because it was not his will.

3. **Modern trend:** Under the modern trend, the courts are more concerned with testator's intent and less concerned with Wills Act formalities. Under the modern trend, a number of courts have stretched some existing doctrines to validate an accidentally swapped will.

   a. **Misdescription doctrine:** The misdescription doctrine was developed to help construe a validly executed will that contains a misdescription. Under the misdescription doctrine, the court takes extrinsic evidence to determine the extent of the misdescription and then strikes the words that constitute the misdescription. The court does not, however, insert any words or rewrite the will. The court only strikes the words that constitute the misdescription and then checks to see if enough words are left to give effect to testator's intent.

   In the swapped will scenario, a few courts have used the misdescription doctrine as just described—to strike all the words that do not make sense in light of the fact that the wrong testator signed the document, and then to check to see if enough words are left to make sense of the document and to determine who is to take. Most courts do not apply the misdescription doctrine to the swapped wills scenario, however, because in such cases the doctrine is being used to ***validate*** a will, which is not the doctrine's intended use of ***construing*** an otherwise valid will.

      i. Example: In *In re Pavlinko's Estate*, misdescription did not apply because the wording of the clause conditioning the gift to Elias read as follows: "If my . . . husband, Vasil Pavlinko, should predecease me, then and in that event, I give and bequeath . . . the rest, residue and remainder of my estate . . . to my brother, Elias Martin." Although misdescription could be used to strike the reference to Elias as Vasil's brother (Elias was Vasil's brother-in-law), when the misdescription doctrine is applied to the conditional language preceding Elias' gift ("if my . . . husband, Vasil Pavlinko, should predecease me"), both ***husband*** and ***Vasil*** would have to be struck, making the sentence unintelligible.

      ii. Which will: Where the parties signed the wrong wills, it is best to offer for probate the will the decedent signed. It arguably meets all of the Wills Act formalities (a writing that is signed and witnessed). If the document that was drafted for, but not signed by, the decedent is offered, the proponents are asking the court to validate a document that on its face fails to meet the Wills Act formalities—the decedent did not sign it—a greater stretch for the court.

    b. Two wills as one: In *In re Snide*, 418 N.E.2d 656 (N.Y. 1981), Harvey Snide, the decedent, and his wife, Rose Snide, intended to execute mutual wills at a common execution ceremony, but each accidentally executed the will prepared for the other. Rose offered the instrument Harvey actually signed for probate. A guardian ad litem appointed to represent a minor child objected to the probate of the will asserting that it lacked testamentary intent. The court acknowledged that a valid will requires testamentary intent, but declined to accept the view that this intent attaches irrevocably to the document prepared, rather than the testamentary scheme it reflects. The court emphasized the obvious nature of the mistake and noted that the two wills constituted reciprocal elements of a unified testamentary scheme which were executed as part of one unified execution ceremony. The court ruled that the will had been properly admitted to probate.

    c. Scrivener's error doctrine: Scrivener's ***error*** has the same effect upon testator's intent as scrivener's ***fraud.*** If the attorney intentionally swaps the wills, that represents fraud in the execution. A court would impose a constructive trust to protect and give effect to the testator's intent. Academics have argued that it should not matter whether the will is accidentally or intentionally swapped—either way, testator's intent is frustrated unless a court imposes a constructive trust to save it. Just recently, a court adopted the scrivener's error doctrine for the first time, but in a different context (see Chapter 5), though the doctrine appears to cover swapped wills as well.

III. MODERN TREND APPROACH TO ATTESTED WILLS

  A. Introduction: The modern trend has tried to make it easier for testators to execute a valid attested will by addressing both of the variables that control whether a document has been properly executed. First, the modern trend approach, as typified by the UPC, reduces the number of requirements in the Wills Act. Second, the modern trend, as typified by the UPC, encourages courts not to require strict compliance, but rather to apply substantial compliance or harmless error/dispensing power as the judicial approach to the degree of compliance with the Wills Act formalities.

B. UPC statutory provision: The UPC has tried to simplify the execution process for attested wills by (1) reducing the number of requirements, and (2) loosening up on several of the requirements that remain. UPC §2-502 requires:

> (1) a writing; (2) signed (3) by the testator or (4) in the testator's name by another (5) in the testator's conscious presence (6) and by the testator's direction; and (7) signed (8) by at least two individuals, each of whom (9) signed within a reasonable period after he [or she] witnessed either (10) the signing of the will or (11) the testator's acknowledgment of the will. [This is not an exact version of the UPC, but is paraphrased a bit to highlight differences with the traditional common law approach.]

C. UPC requirements: The UPC eliminates several common law Wills Act formalities and loosens up on several other requirements.

1. **Need not sign at end:** The UPC does not require that the testator sign the will at the end or foot of the will.

2. **Signed by another:** The UPC expressly provides that where another signs for the testator, in the testator's presence and at the testator's direction, the test for the requirement that the other sign in the testator's presence is the conscious presence test—a looser standard than the line of sight approach to presence. UPC §2-502(a)(2).

3. **Acknowledgment:** The UPC loosens the acknowledgment option by providing that the testator may acknowledge either his or her signature *or the will.* UPC §2-502(a)(3). At common law, if the testator is going to acknowledge, the testator has to acknowledge his or her signature. The testator has to open the will to where he or she had previously signed the will so that the witnesses can see the signature. This burden sometimes trips up the careless testator. The UPC significantly lowers the threshold for a valid acknowledgment by permitting the testator to acknowledge the signature or the will.

4. **Separate witnesses:** The UPC does not require the witnesses to be present at the same time for any reason, even when the testator signs or acknowledges. UPC §2-502(a)(3).

5. **Witnesses' execution:** The UPC provides that the witnesses need to sign within a reasonable time after witnessing the testator sign or acknowledge. UPC §2-502(a)(3). This language implicitly rejects the requirement that the witnesses have to sign in the presence of the testator and arguably endorses the delayed attestation approach.

6. **Witnesses' presence:** The UPC does not require the witnesses to sign the will in either the testator's presence or the presence of each other. UPC §2-502(a)(3). Many traditional Wills Act statutes require the witnesses to sign the will in each other's presence.

D. Curative doctrines—UPC judicial philosophy: The modern trend, as reflected by the UPC, encourages the courts not to insist on strict compliance with the Wills Act formalities requirements, but rather to apply a substantial compliance approach or even a harmless error/dispensing power approach if the execution ceremony fails to meet the Wills Act requirements.

1. **Substantial compliance:** Under substantial compliance, even if a will is not executed in strict compliance with the jurisdiction's Wills Act formalities, the court is empowered to probate the will if (1) clear and convincing evidence shows that the testator intended this document to constitute his or her last will and testament, and (2) clear and convincing evidence shows that the will substantially complies with the statutory Wills Act formalities. UPC §2-503 (1990).

a. **Example:** In *In re Will of Ranney,* 589 A.2d 1339 (N.J. 1991), the testator properly signed the will in front of two witnesses present at the same time, but the witnesses signed the self-proving affidavit instead of the will. (At common law, the courts would call the witnesses into court to testify as to the validity of their signatures and the attestation clause. The self-proving affidavit is presented to the court in lieu of the witnesses being called to testify.) The self-proving affidavit technically is not a part of the will. Applying strict compliance, the New Jersey Supreme Court held that the will was not properly executed, but the court went on to adopt the substantial compliance doctrine and remanded the case for further consideration.

UPC self-proving affidavit: The UPC permits a combined attestation clause and self-proving affidavit that requires the testator and witnesses to sign their names only once, thereby avoiding the potential for the mistake that occurred in the *Ranney* case. UPC §2-504. (Only a minority of jurisdictions has adopted it.)

b. **Example:** In *In re Estate of Hall*, 51 P.3d 1134 (Mont. 2002), testator and his wife (the Halls) went to their attorney's office, modified a draft of their joint will, and then signed it on the advice of their attorney that it would constitute a valid will until they signed the final version. The Halls executed the modified draft, the attorney signed it (there was no one else in the office at the time), and then the Halls returned home where they destroyed their original wills. Montana had adopted the harmless error doctrine, and the court applied it to validate the will on the ground that there was clear and convincing evidence that the testator intended the document to be his will. Testator died before executing the final version.

c. **Criticism:** Professor Langbein, arguably the father of substantial compliance in the United States, rather quickly criticized his own proposal. After studying its use in Australia, Professor Langbein concluded that the courts put too much emphasis on the second prong of the test (that clear and convincing evidence shows that the will substantially complied with the Wills Act formalities). Professor Langbein advocated a dispensing power/harmless error approach as a better alternative.

2. **Dispensing power/harmless error:** Under the dispensing power/harmless error approach, if a will is not executed in strict compliance with the jurisdiction's Wills Act formalities, the court is empowered to probate the will if clear and convincing evidence shows that the decedent intended the document to constitute his or her last will and testament. UPC §2-503 (1997). (As applied to attested wills, the dispensing power/harmless error approach is substantial compliance without the second prong.)

a. **Scope:** As its name implies, the dispensing power/harmless error doctrine authorizes courts to "dispense" with those Wills Act formalities that they deem appropriate as long as there is clear and convincing evidence the decedent intended the document to be his or her will. As applied to the three basic requirements (writing, signed, and witnessed), many have argued that (a) the witness requirement is the least important (and thus the easiest to dispense with), and (b) the writing requirement is the most important and the one that cannot be dispensed with under almost any scenario.

b. **Pros and cons:** Although strict compliance may have its weaknesses (occasionally frustrating the testator's intent even where clear), it has its strengths (bright line test, easy to apply, lower costs of administration, and less potential for fraud). Substantial compliance, and even more so than the dispensing power/harmless error doctrine, increases the power of the courts to give effect to testator's intent. But both doctrines have their own weaknesses (softer, more fact-sensitive doctrines that increase costs of administration and the potential for fraud).

    c. Scope: The UPC version of the harmless error doctrine applies to validate a writing as long as there is "clear and convincing evidence the decedent intended the writing to constitute (i) the decedent's will, (ii) a partial or complete revocation of the will, (iii) an addition to or an alteration of the will, or (iv) a partial or complete revival of his [or her] revoked will or a formerly revoked portion of the will."

3. Majority approach: Although the academic community favors substantial compliance and dispensing power/harmless error (the Restatement (Third) of Property, Donative Transfers, adopts the harmless error doctrine), the states favor strict compliance. A minority of jurisdictions has followed the UPC lead and adopted the dispensing power/harmless error approach, though some of them have modified the doctrine to statutorily indicate that the signature requirement cannot be dispensed.

IV. NOTARIZED WILLS

A. Revised UPC: Pursuant to the 2008 revisions to UPC §2-502(a)(3), a will is valid if signed by two witnesses *or a notary*. The logic behind the new provision is that (1) a single notary can serve the functions underlying the Wills Act formalities (evidentiary, protective, ritualistic) as well as a pair of witnesses, and (2) under the harmless error doctrine, such a will would be valid even without the notarization.

V. HOLOGRAPHIC WILLS

A. Distinguishing feature: The distinguishing feature of holographic wills is that they do not require that the will be witnessed. To offset the lack of witnesses, however, a number of other requirements are added, the most important of which is that the will must be in the testator's handwriting.

1. Jurisdictional split: Only about half the states, primarily in the West and South, recognize holographic wills because the absence of witnesses raises a number of concerns: whether the testator had capacity when the will was executed; increased potential for fraud and undue influence; whether the decedent really intended for this writing to be his or her last will; how to resolve conflicts between multiple wills; and higher costs of administration.

2. UPC approach: The UPC recognizes holographic wills. UPC §2-502(b).

B. Requirements: In light of the concerns raised by the lack of witnesses, most states compensate by adding additional requirements for holographic wills.

1. Writing: As with attested wills, holographic wills must be in writing.

2. Signed: As with attested wills, holographic wills must be signed. Anything the testator intends as his or her signature qualifies as a valid signature. Unlike attested wills, however, only the testator can sign a holographic will. Most states do not require the holographic will to be signed at the end (but if it is not, it raises questions about whether the person wrote his or her name intending it to be his or her signature or for identification purposes only).

3. **Dated:** Some states require that holographic wills be dated. The UPC does not require the holographic will to be dated to be valid. UPC §2-502.

4. **Handwritten:** To offset the lack of witnesses, holographic wills must be in the testator's handwriting. This decreases the potential for fraud in the execution. The jurisdictions are split over how much must be in the testator's handwriting. Some jurisdictions require that the *entire* document must be in the testator's handwriting; most require only that the *material provisions* be in the testator's handwriting.

   a. **Entirely:** If the jurisdiction requires that the holographic will be entirely in the testator's handwriting, any printing or other marks on the document may invalidate the whole will under a strict compliance approach to the requirements.

   b. **Material provisions:** The material provisions are those provisions that affect the disposition of testator's property: the "who gets what," any administrative provisions (that is, appointment of a personal representative or guardian), and *maybe* testamentary intent (the intent that this document constitutes the person's last will and testament).

   c. **UPC approach:** The UPC requires only that the material provisions, not the entire instrument, be in the testator's handwriting. UPC §2-503(b).

5. **Example:** In *Kimmel's Estate*, 123 A. 405 (Pa. 1924), decedent handwrote a letter to two of his children. The letter talked about some family matters and the weather. Near the end of the letter he wrote *"I have some very valuable papers I want you to keep fore me if enny thing hapens all the scock money in the 3 Bank liberty lones Post office stamps and my home on Horner St. goes to George Darl & Irvin Kepp this letter lock it up it may help you out. . . . Father."* The decedent mailed the letter and died suddenly that afternoon. Some of his children offered the letter for probate. The court held the document qualified as a holographic will.

   Conditional wills: Conditional wills are those that contain an express clause conditioning their being given effect upon some event occurring. Although conditional wills are valid and permitted, it is often unclear whether a clause in a will was intended to be an express condition precedent to the will being given effect or merely an explanation for why the person got around to executing a will. Courts tend to view conditional wills with disfavor and favor construing such clauses, when possible, as mere explanations for why the decedent executed the will as opposed to an express condition precedent to the will being given effect. Such clauses tend to appear more often in holographic wills than in attested wills because attested wills are usually drafted by attorneys, most of whom know better than to include such ambiguous clauses.

6. **Testamentary intent:** Testamentary intent is the intent that the document constitutes the person's last will and testament—the intent that this document be probated as the decedent's will. Because holographic wills are not witnessed, there is no ritualistic function. The requirement that the document express testamentary intent is meant to ensure that only writings that the decedent intended to serve as a will—as opposed to drafts or idle thoughts—are probated. The key is the use of words that indicate the document is to have significance following the person's death. Words such as *save this* support a finding of testamentary intent, though the word *estate,* standing alone, has been held too ambiguous to establish testamentary intent.

   a. **Material provisions:** If the jurisdiction requires only that the material provisions be in the testator's handwriting, a subissue is whether testamentary intent is a material provision. If it is, testamentary intent must be discernible exclusively from the handwritten portions of the document. This issue arises most often with commercially printed form wills where the decedent merely fills in the blanks indicating who is to get what, but does not write in his or her own handwriting any words that independently express the intent that the document serve as his or her will (because the preprinted words clearly express such an intent).

    i.   Strict compliance: Some courts have held that testator's intent must be discernible exclusively from the testator's handwriting. The court "whites out" any material not in the testator's handwriting and then assesses what is left to see if testamentary intent can be established.

    ii.   UPC approach: The UPC has expressly disavowed, as overly formalistic, the approach that the testamentary intent must be discernible exclusively from the testator's handwriting. Under the UPC, testamentary intent can be derived from the handwritten material, the non-handwritten provisions, or other extrinsic evidence. UPC §2-502(c).

  b.   Example: In *Estate of Gonzalez,* 855 A.2d 1146 (Me. 2004), the decedent purchased a commercially printed form will, filled in the blanks giving his estate to three of his five children, and then signed the form will. The decedent showed the document to his brother and his brother's wife, and then told them he intended to re-write it more neatly on a second blank commercially printed form will. The brother signed the first form will, but no one else signed as a witness. The brother, his wife, and her mother signed the second form will, but the decedent fell ill and died before copying the testamentary provisions over to the second form will or signing it. The first document was offered for probate. The issue was whether the writing expressed the requisite testamentary intent. The court acknowledged the jurisdictions are split on how to treat the printed words on the commercially printed form will. Some jurisdictions consider testamentary intent a material provision that must be in the testator's handwriting and thus will *not* consider the printed words on the form will. Other jurisdictions do consider the printed words on the form will when analyzing whether the document has testamentary intent. The court concluded that the printed words were incorporated by reference and should be considered when analyzing whether the document has testamentary intent. The court ruled the document was a valid holographic will.

    Under the UPC approach, testamentary intent may be established from either the handwritten words, the portions of the document that are not in the testator's handwriting, or other extrinsic evidence. Under the UPC approach, there is no doubt the commercially printed form will in *Gonzalez* expresses testamentary intent and would be probated as a valid holographic will.

  c.   Attested wills: Testamentary intent is a requirement for traditional witnessed wills. The typical execution ceremony for attested wills, however, includes such a strong ritualistic component that it virtually guarantees that the executed document has testamentary intent. In the appropriate fact pattern, however, testamentary intent can be the determining element even for traditional, witnessed wills. (See *In re Pavlinko's Estate*, *supra*, and *Fleming v. Morrison*, *infra*, for two examples where traditionally executed and witnessed wills were held invalid arguably because they lacked testamentary intent.)

C.   Judicial approach: Holographic wills present an interesting dilemma for courts in terms of what degree of compliance with the holographic requirements the court should demand. On the one hand, because holographic wills eliminate the witness requirement, the remaining requirements are so important that absolute strict compliance arguably should be required. On the other hand, because holographic wills are intended to permit the layperson to execute his or her will without the cost of an attorney, the courts arguably should apply a looser standard. The courts appear torn between the two approaches.

Example: In ***In re Estate of Kuralt***, 15 P.3d 931 (Mont. 2000), Charles Kuralt was married to Suzanne Baird ("Petie"), but he also had a long-term and intimate relationship with Pat Baker (later known as Pat Shannon). In 1989, he executed a valid holographic will leaving all of his property in Twin Bridges, Montana, to Pat. In 1994, he executed an attested will that left all of his property to his wife and children. In 1997, he began the process of transferring inter vivos the Montana property to Pat, only he was hospitalized and died before finishing the process. While in the hospital, he handwrote and signed a document which he sent to Pat. The document discussed his health problems and concerns and provided in pertinent part, "I'll have the lawyer visit the hospital to be sure you ***inherit*** the rest of the place in MT if it comes to that." After Kuralt's death, Pat offered the letter for probate. His estate opposed the letter on the grounds it expressed only a future intent to make a will. The court emphasized that the bedrock principle was to honor testator's intent, that Kuralt's underlying word "inherit" indicated his intent to make a testamentary transfer of the property, and determined there was sufficient evidence to conclude that the document was a holographic codicil to his will. (A codicil is a will that amends an existing will; see section VI.C.3 *infra*.)

VI. REVOCATION

A. **Revocability of wills:** Wills are executed inter vivos but are not effective until death. If the testator changes his or her mind after executing a will, the testator can revoke it, replace it, or amend it at any time. A will may be revoked (1) by act, (2) by writing, (3) by presumption, and (4) by operation of law.

B. **Revocation by act:** A will may be revoked by a ***physical*** act as long as the act is destructive in nature (burning, tearing, and so forth) and is performed with the intent to revoke. The act may be performed by the testator or by another, but, if by another, the act must be performed in the testator's presence and at the testator's direction. UPC §2-507(a)(2).

  1. **Common law:** The traditional and majority rule requires the destructive act to affect some part of the written portion of the will.

  2. **Modern trend/UPC approach:** The UPC rejects the common law approach. The UPC requires only that the destructive act affect some part of the will. UPC §2-507(a)(2).

C. **Revocation by writing:** A will may be revoked by a subsequent writing expressing the intent to revoke, but only if the subsequent writing qualifies as a valid will. The subsequent writing must be executed with Wills Act formalities. The subsequent writing must qualify either as an attested will or a holographic will. UPC §2-507(a)(1). A subsequent will can revoke a prior will expressly or implicitly by inconsistency.

  1. **Express revocation:** Express revocation is when there is a clear and express statement of the intent to revoke the prior will ("I hereby revoke my prior will"). A properly executed instrument that does no more than express the intent to revoke a prior will is a valid will.

2. **Revocation by inconsistency:** Revocation by inconsistency occurs when the subsequent will disposes of the decedent's property in a way that is inconsistent with the prior will. Because the later expression of the testator's intent controls over the prior in time expression of intent, the prior will is deemed revoked to the extent of any inconsistencies. UPC §2-507(a)(1).

3. **Will vs. codicil:** If a subsequent will completely revokes the prior will, either expressly or by inconsistency, the subsequent will becomes the testator's sole will. If, however, the subsequent will only partially revokes or amends the prior will, either expressly or by inconsistency, the subsequent will is called a *codicil.* The prior will still stands and is valid to the extent it is not revoked by the codicil.

    a. **Codicils—execution:** First and foremost, a codicil is a will—it must be executed with the requisite Wills Act formalities. A codicil is a will that merely amends an existing will rather than completely replacing it. UPC §2-507(b)-(d).

    b. **Exception—codicils to holographic wills:** An important exception to the general rule that codicils must qualify as a valid will in their own right is that handwritten amendments *(interlineations)* to a holographic will constitute a valid holographic codicil, even if the interlineations (the handwritten amendments) do not qualify as a valid holographic will in their own right.

4. **Mixed wills and codicils:** Holographic codicils to attested wills are valid, and attested codicils to holographic wills are valid.

5. **Revocation of codicil/will:** Revocation of a codicil does not revoke the underlying will. Revocation of a will revokes all codicils thereto.

6. **Writing as revocation by act:** The act of writing can qualify as revocation by act. If a testator takes out her typed, attested will and writes "VOID" across the first page of it but does not sign the document after writing "VOID" across it, the act of writing "VOID" does not qualify as a valid revocation by writing because it does not qualify as a valid will (neither attested nor holographic because not signed). But the act of writing "VOID" across the will does qualify as a destructive act. Assuming the testator had the intent to revoke at the time she performed the act, which is implicit in the nature of the act, the act of writing qualifies as revocation by act.

7. **Example:** In *Thompson v. Royall,* 175 S.E. 748 (Va. 1934), testatrix had her attorney take out her will and codicil to revoke them. The attorney suggested that rather than destroying them, she keep them as memoranda. So on the back of the manuscript cover to the will, the attorney handwrote, in the presence of the testator and another, the following notation: "This will null and void." The testatrix then signed the notation. The testatrix died three weeks later. The will and codicil were offered for probate. The court held that the writing did not qualify as *revocation by writing* because the notation did not qualify as a valid will (not attested because not witnessed and not holographic because the material provisions were not in the testator's handwriting). The court held that the writing did not qualify as *revocation by act* because the handwriting did not touch any of the written portions of the will as required under the traditional common law approach.

    Modern trend: The writing in *Thompson* may qualify as a valid *revocation by act* because the act arguably affected some portion of the will (if the manuscript cover were construed to be part of the will). The writing may also qualify as *revocation by writing.* The testatrix died three weeks after creating the writing in the presence of two witnesses. Under the modern trend, delayed attestation is permitted as long as it occurs within a reasonable time period. Most courts construe reasonable time period to be up to six months. Here, the witnesses could be brought in and asked to sign the notation as witnesses. The notation may qualify as a valid attested will under the modern trend.

D. Revocation by presumption: If a will was last in the testator's possession and cannot be found following testator's death, a rebuttable presumption arises that the testator revoked the will by act. If the presumption is not overcome, the will is deemed revoked. If the presumption is rebutted, the will is deemed "lost," and extrinsic evidence is admitted to prove its terms. If the terms are established, the "lost" will is probated (the jurisdictions are split over the burden of proof—preponderance vs. clear and convincing; almost any evidence is admissible).

1. **Rationale:** Testators know that their will is a very important document. If the testator takes the will home with him or her, the presumption is that he or she will safeguard the will by keeping it in a safe place with other important papers. If the will is not found after the testator's death, the more likely explanation is that the testator revoked it by act rather than that the testator lost it.

2. **Weak presumption:** The presumption that the testator revoked the will is a rather weak presumption. If those challenging the will offer a more plausible explanation for why the will is found, the issue becomes one for the trier of fact.

3. **Duplicate originals:** Duplicate originals are multiple originals of the same will, each one properly executed. A photocopy of an executed will is not a duplicate original. The testator must properly execute each version of a duplicate original. Often the attorney keeps one duplicate original, and the testator takes the other duplicate original home with him or her.

   a. **Revocation by act or by writing:** Affirmative evidence that the testator properly revoked one duplicate original by act or by writing automatically revokes all duplicate originals.

   b. **Revocation by presumption:** The jurisdictions are split over whether the presumption doctrine applies to revoke all duplicate originals if the one the testator took home is not found, but the other duplicate original is found.

      i. **Revokes all duplicate originals:** If the presumption doctrine applies to one duplicate original, it applies to all duplicate originals. The reasoning underlying this approach is that revocation by presumption is a subset of revocation by act. Valid revocation by act revokes all duplicate originals, so valid revocation by presumption of one duplicate original revokes all duplicate originals, even if the other duplicate original is found.

      ii. **Not revoke all duplicate originals:** The presumption doctrine does not revoke duplicate original wills unless *none* of the duplicate originals are found following the testator's death. The reasoning underlying this approach is that revocation by presumption is based on the assumption that testators who take their wills home with them take care to safeguard them. If there is a duplicate original (say, at the attorney's office), however, the testator is less likely to safeguard the duplicate original he or she takes home. If the will the testator took home is not found, it is just as likely that the testator lost it as that he or she destroyed it with the intent to revoke.

4. **Example:** In *Harrison v. Bird,* 621 So. 2d 972 (Ala. 1993), testatrix executed duplicate wills, leaving one with her attorney and taking the other home with her. Thereafter, testator called the

attorney and advised him that she wanted to revoke her will. The attorney tore the will into pieces in the presence of his secretary and mailed the pieces to the testatrix. The court held that the attorney's act of tearing one of the duplicate originals into pieces was not a valid revocation by act because it was not done in the presence of the testatrix. The court went on to rule, however, that because the pieces of the will that were mailed to the testatrix were not found after her death, the presumption doctrine applied. The court applied the approach that the presumption doctrine revokes all duplicate originals even if one or more are found following the testatrix's death.

5. **Partial revocation by physical act:** The jurisdictions are split over whether partial revocation by physical act is permitted. There are two concerns. First, it increases the potential for fraud, though it is difficult to see how the potential for fraud is any greater where the revocation is partial as opposed to complete. The other concern is more theoretical. A partial revocation intrinsically is also a new gift. By revoking only part of a will, the revoked part has to go somewhere. If it goes anywhere else in the will, it arguably is a new gift. New gifts should be executed with Wills Act formalities—so the reasoning goes. Due to these concerns, not all jurisdictions recognize partial revocation by physical act.

   a. **If jurisdiction does not recognize:** Those jurisdictions that do not recognize partial revocation by physical act simply ignore the act in question and give effect to the will as originally written.

   b. **Modern trend/UPC approach:** Many states and the UPC do recognize partial revocation by physical act (UPC §2-507), but the states are split over how to treat the revoked gift. The majority permits the revoked gift to fall to the residuary and to increase the residuary, but the partial revocation cannot increase a gift outside of the residuary. A few states, concerned that the "new gift" was not made with Wills Act formalities, hold that the revoked gift may pass via intestacy only. The UPC provides that the will should be given effect as it reads with the partial revocation by act regardless of where that means the revoked gift goes.

E. **Dependent relative revocation:** Even if a will is validly revoked (in whole or in part), it may yet be possible to probate the will if the revocation was based upon a mistake (of fact or law) and if the testator would not have revoked if testator had known the truth. At first blush the doctrine appears rather straightforward. The doctrine becomes much more difficult, however, when one overlaps the added observation that the courts tend to apply the doctrine only if (1) there is a failed alternative testamentary scheme, or (2) if the mistake is set forth in the writing that revoked the will and the mistake is beyond the testator's knowledge.

1. **Revocation by act:** The classic dependent relative revocation scenario is where the testator revokes a gift by act (valid revocation) on the belief that a new will or codicil is valid, but the new will or codicil is not valid (mistake of law). The intended beneficiary stands to take nothing because the original gift was validly revoked and the new gift fails due to the mistake of law. Dependent relative revocation reasons that it is better to save the original gift if that is what the testator would have wanted if he or she had known that the new will or codicil was invalid.

   a. **Example:** Pete has a valid typed will that provides in part as follows: "I give $10,000 to Lulu." Thereafter, Pete decides that Lulu deserves more. He takes out the will and draws a line through the $10,000 and handwrites above the lined out gift "$20,000." Thereafter he dies. How much, if anything, does Lulu take?

b. Analysis: When Pete drew the line through the original gift of $10,000, he validly revoked the gift by act (destructive act, with the intent to revoke, that affected the printed portion of the will). When Pete handwrote in "$20,000," he was attempting a holographic codicil that fails because it is not signed, not all of the material provisions are in his handwriting (one cannot tell who is supposed to take from the handwriting), and, depending on the jurisdiction, testamentary intent is in question. At this point, Lulu stands to take nothing. She should invoke dependent relative revocation. There was a valid revocation (the line through the "$10,000"), based upon a mistake (the belief that the holographic codicil would be valid), and arguably the testator would not have revoked but for the mistake (Pete was trying to increase the gift, so clearly he would prefer the original gift over no gift). The failed alternative testamentary scheme is the attempt at a new will or codicil that failed due to a mistake of law. The mistake and the failed alternative testamentary scheme usually go hand in hand. Where the revocation is by act, almost invariably the mistake is a mistake of law because the testator's attempt at a new will or codicil fails for some legal reason.

2. Revocation by writing: The less common dependent relative revocation scenario is where the revocation is by writing. Intrinsically then, there cannot be a failed alternative testamentary scheme because the new will or codicil had to be valid for there to be a successful revocation by writing. Instead, where the revocation is by writing, almost invariably the mistake is a mistake of fact. For dependent relative revocation to apply, the courts require that the mistake be set forth in the writing and that the mistake be beyond the testator's knowledge.

a. Example: Pete has a valid typed will that provides in part as follows: "I hereby give $10,000 to Lulu." Thereafter, Pete hears that Lulu married Fred, a marriage that angers Pete. Pete properly executes a codicil that provides as follows: "I hereby revoke my gift to Lulu in light of her marriage to Fred." In fact, Lulu never married Fred.

b. Analysis: Pete validly revoked the original gift to Lulu when he properly executed the codicil. Because the revocation is by writing, the norm is that the mistake is one of fact, not of law. Here, the alleged mistake is that Pete thought Lulu married Fred. In fact, she did not. Where the revocation is by writing, the mistake of fact must be set forth in the revoking writing and must be beyond the testator's knowledge. Here, the codicil expressly states that the reason Pete was revoking was because of his belief that Lulu had married Fred. The mistake of fact is set forth in the writing, and the mistake is beyond Pete's knowledge. There is no reason to believe that Pete should have known whether Lulu and Fred were actually married.

3. Tendencies: Almost invariably, where the revocation is *by act,* the mistake is a *mistake of law* in that the testator attempted a new will or codicil that is invalid. Almost invariably, where the revocation is *by writing,* the mistake is a *mistake of fact* that must then be set forth in the valid revoking instrument. It is possible, however, to have a valid revocation by writing where the mistake is a mistake of law. But the mistake still has to be set forth in the writing (the new gift fails because it violates the Rule against Perpetuities, it violates public policy, and so forth).

Example: In *LaCroix v. Senecal*, 99 A.2d 115 (Conn. 1953), testatrix executed a valid will leaving the residue of her estate half to her nephew (identified by nickname) and half to Senecal, a friend. Thereafter, testatrix executed a codicil which revoked the residuary clause and substituted an almost identical clause except this time she referred to her nephew by both his nickname and his proper name. The codicil, however, was witnessed by Senecal's husband. Under the applicable interested witness statute, this voided the gift to Senecal. The court applied dependent relative revocation: There was a valid revocation (the codicil) based upon a mistake (the belief that the gift to Senecal in the codicil was valid), testatrix would not have revoked but for the mistake (as evidenced by the void gift in the codicil), and because the revocation is by writing, the mistake must be set forth in the writing (the gift to Senecal as set forth in the codicil—evidencing the testatrix's mistaken belief that the gift in the codicil was valid). The court gave effect to the gift to Senecal under the original will.

F. **Revival:** Assuming a testator validly executes will #1, and thereafter validly executes will #2 that expressly or implicitly revokes will #1, and thereafter validly revokes will #2 intending to give effect to will #1, the jurisdictions are split over what the testator must do to "revive" will #1.

   1. **English approach:** Under the English approach, will #1 was never really revoked so it could be probated. The English approach takes literally the statement that a will is not effective until the testator dies. Taken literally, will #2 would have revoked will #1 only if will #2 had remained in effect until the testator died. Because the testator revoked will #2 before he died, will #2 never became effective, so it never revoked will #1; therefore, there is no need to "revive" will #1. Will #2 merely "covered" will #1 temporarily. Because will #2 was revoked, will #1 was automatically "uncovered" and was still valid without the testator having to do anything other than revoking will #2. A handful of states follow the English approach.

   2. **The American approach:** Despite the general rule that a will is not effective until the testator dies, for purposes of revoking an existing will, the general American rule is that a will is effective the moment it is properly executed. The moment the testator properly executes will #2, will #1 is revoked—it is null and void. If thereafter the testator revokes will #2, unlike the English approach, revoking will #2 does not automatically give effect to will #1. The testator must do something to "revive" will #1. The jurisdictions are split over what the testator must do to revive will #1.

   3. **Minority approach:** A minority of states requires the testator to reexecute will #1 to revive it (or incorporate it by reference into a valid new will). Only by going through the Wills Act formalities again is testamentary life given to will #1.

   4. **Majority/UPC approach:** A majority of the states and the UPC think that requiring the testator to go through the Wills Act formalities again is too burdensome. Instead, all the testator has to do to revive will #1 is to intend to revive will #1. UPC §2-509. This statement is a bit misleading, however, because the states limit what evidence the courts can take of the testator's intent to revive depending on how the testator revoked will #2.

      Proving intent to revive: The key to proving the testator's intent to revive is how the testator revoked will #2. If the testator revoked will #2 by act, the courts take almost any evidence of testator's intent to revive will #1, even the testator's own alleged statements. UPC §2-509(a). If, however, the testator revoked will #2 by writing a new will (will #3), the intent to revive will #1 must be set forth in the new will (will #3). UPC §2-509(c).

   5. **Example:** In *Estate of Alburn*, 118 N.W.2d 919 (Wis. 1963), testatrix executed will #1 while living in Milwaukee (the Milwaukee will). Thereafter testatrix moved to Kankakee and executed will #2 (the Kankakee will) that revoked the Milwaukee will. Thereafter testatrix moved back to Wisconsin, destroyed the Kankakee will, and told people she wanted her property to pass pursuant to the Milwaukee will. The court applied the minority American approach and held that the testatrix did not properly revive the Milwaukee will because she did not reexecute it with Wills Act formalities.

The beneficiaries under the wills then invoked dependent relative revocation (with respect to will #2, the Kankakee will) to avoid intestacy. The Kankakee will was validly revoked by act (torn up). The beneficiaries had to prove that (1) the revocation was based upon a mistake, (2) there was a failed alternative testamentary scheme, and (3) the testatrix would not have revoked but for the mistake. The beneficiaries proved that (1) the testatrix revoked the Kankakee will based on the belief that the Milwaukee will had been revived (a mistake of law), (2) the Milwaukee will was not revived, thus constituting the failed alternative testamentary scheme (the attempt at a "new" will that failed), and (3) by comparing who took under the Milwaukee will, who took under the Kankakee will, and who took under intestacy, that the Milwaukee will (what testator wanted but could not have) was closer to the Kankakee will than it was to intestacy, and that testator would not have revoked but for the mistake. The court applied dependent relative revocation and probated the Kankakee will.

Analysis under the majority/UPC approach: Under the majority/UPC approach to revival, will #1 is revived as long as the testator intends to revive it, but the key to establishing testator's intent is how the testator revoked will #2. Here, the testatrix revoked the Kankakee will (will #2) by act (tore it up). Where will #2 is revoked by act, the court takes any evidence of testator's intent to revive. Here, the testatrix orally told people that the reason she revoked the Kankakee will is that she wanted her property to pass pursuant to the Milwaukee will (will #1). Under the majority/UPC approach to revival, the testatrix properly revived the Milwaukee will.

6. **Will #2 as will vs. codicil:** Where will #2 wholly revokes will #1, the UPC follows the majority American approach set forth and discussed above. Where will #2 only partially revokes will #1, however (that is, where will #2 is a codicil), the UPC follows more the English approach. The part of will #1 that was revoked by will #2 is presumed to be automatically revived and the burden of proof is on the party trying to prove that the testator did ***not*** intend to revive the revoked provisions of will #1. UPC §2-509(b).

G. **Revocation by operation of law—divorce:** The overwhelming majority rule is that divorce automatically and irrebuttably revokes all provisions in a testator's will in favor of the ex-spouse, unless the will expressly provides otherwise. UPC §2-804.

1. **Rationale:** After a typical divorce, the law presumes that the ex-spouses no longer love each other, they no longer consider each other natural objects of their bounty, and they no longer wish to leave any of their property to each other.

2. **Traditional scope:** The traditional approach, and still majority approach, is to apply the revocation by operation of law doctrine only to wills, not to the will substitutes—life insurance, joint tenancy, pension plans, and other nonprobate arrangements.

3. **Modern trend/UPC scope:** The UPC applies the revocation by operation of law doctrine not only to wills, but also to the will substitutes—life insurance, joint tenancy, pension plans, and other nonprobate arrangements. UPC §2-804.

4. **Beneficiaries affected:** The jurisdictions are split over which beneficiaries come within the scope of the revocation by operation of law doctrine—just the ex-spouse or also the ex-spouse's relatives. The UPC takes a fairly broad approach, revoking provisions in favor not only of the ex-spouse, but also revoking provisions in favor of the ex-spouse's relatives. UPC §2-804(b)(1).

5. **Domestic partners:** Some states permit domestic partners to obtain inheritance rights by registering. Some of those states apply the revocation by operation of law doctrine to domestic partners.

   If the domestic partners terminate their partnership, the termination automatically revokes all provisions in the testator's will in favor of the ex-domestic partner.

6. **Revocation by marriage, birth of child:** Two other "life altering" events can be analogized to the revocation by operation of law upon divorce doctrine: marriage and/or birth of a child. These events trigger special public policy concerns to make sure that the new spouse and/or child is provided for. The omitted spouse and omitted child doctrines (discussed in Chapter 7) cover these situations, and the effect of these doctrines is to give the new spouse or child a share of the testator's property before giving effect to the will. To that extent, the doctrines indirectly act as a revocation by operation of law. But in those scenarios, it is not so much that any particular provision of the will is being revoked, but rather a "new gift" is being read into the will that may have the effect of reducing or eliminating some of the gifts already in the will.

VII. SCOPE OF A WILL

A. **Integration:** The scope of a will starts with the threshold issue of determining what constitutes the pages of the will. The doctrine of integration provides that those pieces of paper that are physically present at the time of execution and that the testator intends to be part of the will constitute the pages of the will.

B. **Republication by codicil:** Executing a codicil to a will "reexecutes" and "republishes" the underlying will.

   1. **Republication by codicil:** As a general rule, a codicil automatically redates the underlying will. Redating the will may be significant for a variety of reasons, one of which is the doctrine of incorporation by reference (see section C *infra*). The codicil can either redate the underlying will expressly (via an express clause expressing such an intent) or implicitly (in the absence of an express clause, the courts presume that the testator intended to redate the underlying will).

      Exception: In a handful of scenarios redating the underlying will may be counterproductive to testator's apparent wishes. In such situations, the parties can argue to the court that the testator must not have intended to redate the underlying will in light of the adverse consequences that would follow. Courts are generally receptive to this argument where there is no express republication clause in the will, but not where there is an express republication clause (although one can argue that such clauses are boilerplate clauses thrown in by the drafting attorney and do not really express the testator's intent).

   2. **Preexisting will:** Classifying a will as a codicil implicitly presumes a preexisting valid will. If the underlying will is not valid, however, the "codicil" is not a codicil, but rather is its own freestanding will (even if it does not dispose of all the testator's property). As a will, it does not automatically reexecute and republish the invalid will, but it may still be possible to use the valid will to give effect to the testamentary wishes expressed in the invalid will through incorporation by reference (see section C *infra*).

Exception: A handful of jurisdictions do not recognize incorporation by reference (New York among them). In those states, some courts will stretch republication by codicil to reexecute and republish an invalid underlying will, but only if the invalid will went through a valid execution ceremony but is invalid for some other reason (for example, lack of or defect in capacity at the time the underlying instrument was executed).

3. **Curative powers:** If there were potential problems with the original will execution ceremony that do not affect its validity in whole (for example, interested witness or undue influence claim as to part of the will), these problems may be cured by the republication by codicil doctrine. As long as the problem is not present when the codicil is executed, the codicil's execution is deemed to reexecute and republish the underlying will, thereby curing the possible problem in the will.

C. **Incorporation by reference:** A valid will can incorporate by reference a document that was not executed with Wills Act formalities, thereby giving effect to the intent expressed in the incorporated document, as long as: (1) the will expresses the intent to incorporate the document, (2) the will describes the document with reasonable certainty, and (3) the document being incorporated was in existence when the will was executed. UPC §2-510.

1. **Intent and describe requirements:** The courts apply a rather low threshold for the first two requirements. If the will makes reference to another document, arguably that is enough to constitute the intent to incorporate it. If the will's description of the document is not 100 percent accurate, but the court is persuaded that this is the document to which the testator was referring, the court will find that the will describes the document with reasonable certainty.

2. **Document in existence requirement:** The courts strictly apply the requirement that the document has to have been in existence at the time that the will was executed. Exact dating is not necessary, but the plaintiff bears the burden of proving by a preponderance of the evidence that the document was in existence when the will was executed. If the document changes over time, only the document as it existed at the time the will was executed is incorporated by reference (unless the will is reexecuted under republication by codicil).

   Example: In *Simon v. Grayson,* 102 P.2d 1081 (Cal. 1940), the testator's will left $4,000 to his executors "to be paid by them as directed by me in a letter that will be found in my effects and which will be addressed to my executors and dated March 25, 1932." The testator's will was dated March 25, 1932. Upon testator's death, a letter addressed to the testator's executors was found in the testator's safe deposit box. The letter provided, "In my will I left you $4,000 to be paid to a person named in a letter. I direct you to pay the $4,000 to Esther Cohn." The letter, however, was dated July 3, 1933. Despite the discrepancy in the dates, the court concluded that this was the document that the testator intended to incorporate by reference and that the will described the document with reasonable certainty. Because the letter was created ***after*** the will was executed, the document could not have been incorporated into the will as initially executed. On November 25, 1933, however, the testator executed a codicil to the will. The codicil automatically republished the underlying will and redated it to a date after the date of the letter, thereby satisfying the requirement that the document to be incorporated must be in existence when the will is executed.

3. **Example:** In *Clark v. Greenhalge,* 582 N.E.2d 949 (Mass. 1991), testatrix's 1977 will named Greenhalge as executor and principal beneficiary, and provided that he was to receive all of her tangible personal property except for those items designated to be given to others "by a

memorandum" she would create and make known to Greenhalge. Thereafter testatrix created a memorandum *and* a notebook in which she made entries giving certain items of tangible personal property to certain beneficiaries. The memorandum was created in 1972 and amended in 1976. The notebook was titled "List to be given [testatrix] 1979" and contained an entry giving a picture to Ms. Clark. The testatrix told Ms. Clark of her intent to add the picture to the list in early 1980. Testatrix died in 1986, and Greenhalge refused to honor the purported gift of the picture via the list. Greenhalge argued that the will expressed the intent to incorporate *only* the memorandum. The court held that the language of the will was broad enough to include both the memorandum *and* the notebook, and that the will described the notebook with reasonable certainty. As for whether the entry in question had been entered in the notebook when the will was executed, the court noted that the testatrix executed two codicils to her will, one on May 30, 1980, and a second on October 23, 1980. (The court did not analyze whether the precise entry had been made in the notebook by the date of the second codicil, apparently because it was displeased with the way the executor had behaved.)

UPC's tangible personal property list: The UPC's tangible personal property list permits a testator to give away his or her tangible personal property via a list not executed with Wills Act formalities, even if the list is created *after* the will is executed, as long as the will expressly states such an intent. UPC §2-513. In essence, the doctrine modifies incorporation by reference by waiving the requirement that the document be in existence at the time the will is executed as long as the document only disposes of the testator's tangible personal property.

In *Clark v. Greenhalge,* if Massachusetts had adopted the tangible personal property list doctrine at the time, the doctrine would have mooted the issue of whether the entry in the notebook giving the picture to Ms. Clark had been made in the notebook at the time the will was republished by the codicil.

4. **Example:** In *Johnson v. Johnson,* 279 P.2d 928 (Okla. 1955), a single-page instrument was offered for probate as the decedent's will. The instrument (which was not signed or witnessed) consisted of three typed paragraphs giving away property. At the bottom of the page, in the decedent's handwriting, was the following: "To my brother James I give ten dollars only. This will shall be complete . . . D.G. Johnson." The typed portion of the paper did not qualify as a will. The bottom, handwritten portion did qualify as a valid holographic will. The issue was whether the scope of the valid holographic will could be expanded to give effect to testamentary intent expressed in the typed paragraphs that did not qualify as a will.

   a. **Republication by codicil:** In light of the fact that the underlying will was never properly executed, the holographic will cannot be a codicil, and republication by codicil cannot be applied to give effect to the typed provisions of the paper. (Even in jurisdictions that do not recognize incorporation by reference, republication by codicil should not be stretched to save the typed material because the typed material was never executed.)

   b. **Integration:** The general rule is that typed material cannot be integrated into a holographic will (because this violates the requirement that the material provisions must be in the testator's handwriting), but typed material can be incorporated by reference into a holographic will (technically the incorporated material does not become part of the will; the incorporated document is simply given effect as part of the probate process). Pursuant to the general rule, the typed material cannot be integrated into the holographic will at the bottom of the page.

    c. Incorporation by reference: Incorporation by reference is the best argument if one is inclined to stretch the doctrine to give effect to the typed material under these facts. The reference to "This will shall be complete . . ." arguably constitutes an adequate reference to the typed portions of the page to satisfy the low threshold for the will expressing the intent to incorporate and describing the document (that is, treating the typed material as a separate document) with reasonable certainty. It is safe to assume that the typed portion of the page was in existence when the handwritten provisions were added, thus satisfying the requirements for incorporation by reference. (A strong dissent argued that this instrument was one will, that part of a will cannot be incorporated into another part of the same will, and that the typed material could not be given effect.)

D. Acts of independent significance: Under the doctrine of acts of independent significance, a will may dispose of property by reference to acts outside of the will (the referenced act can control either who takes or how much a beneficiary takes) as long as the referenced act has significance independent of its effect upon the testator's probate estate. UPC §2-512.

    1. Conceptually difficult: Conceptually, acts of independent significance is one of the most difficult doctrines in wills and trusts. In essence, it permits a testator to "change" the provisions of his or her will without having to execute a codicil. The counterargument is that the will is not really being "changed" because the language of the will referenced an act that occurred outside of the will and was performed for reasons independent of its effect upon the testator's will. Although the act may affect either who takes or how much a beneficiary takes under the testator's will, the act has its own significance independent of its effect upon the will.

    2. Example: The testatrix's will provides: "I give $1,000 to each of my son-in-laws, I give all of the stuff in my garage to my brother, Bob, and I leave $10,000 to each of the persons I will identify in a letter I will leave for my executor." At the time the testatrix executed her will, she had two daughters, neither of whom were married. Thereafter, both daughters married, the testatrix bought a new lawnmower that she stored in the garage, and the testatrix wrote a letter to her executrix telling her to give $10,000 to Carolyn and $10,000 to Kristin. When the testatrix dies, who takes what?

    Analysis: One could argue that after each of the testatrix's daughters got married, the testatrix should have executed a codicil expressly stating that the new son-in-law was to take $1,000 and naming the son-in-law. But the acts of independent significance doctrine provides that as long as the act referenced in the will has its own significance independent of its effect upon testator's probate property, the referenced act can control who takes how much without the testator having to execute a codicil.

    a. First clause: The referenced act in the first clause is each daughter getting married. The act of getting married carries with it all sorts of ramifications. It is an act that has its own independent significance apart from the fact that it also permits the new son-in-law to receive $1,000 under the testatrix's will. The gifts to the sons-in-law are valid without the testatrix having to execute a codicil.

    b. Second clause: The referenced act in the second clause is the act of putting things in and taking things out of the testatrix's garage. Every time that the testatrix puts something in the garage or takes something out, in essence she is changing her testamentary gift. As long as the referenced act has its own inter vivos significance, however, she need not execute a codicil. Storing items and using items are legitimate, inter vivos purposes that show that the referenced act has its own independent significance apart from its effect upon who takes what under the testatrix's will. Bob would get the new lawnmower without testatrix having to execute a codicil.

    c. Third clause: The referenced act in the third clause that controls who will take $10,000 is the creation of a letter addressed to the executor. The letter does ***not*** have its own independent significance apart from its effect upon who takes under the testatrix's will. The referenced act, the letter, is intended to and actually does serve only one purpose, to control who takes under the testatrix's will. The letter has no independent significance. Carolyn and Kristin do not take any money.

3. Writing as independent act: The creation of a writing, even a testamentary writing (especially if it is someone else's testamentary instrument), qualifies as an act of independent significance as long as the referenced writing has its own independent significance apart from its effect on the will.

    Example: Testatrix's will leaves $10,000 to each of the persons listed as beneficiaries in her brother's will. Thereafter her brother creates a will. Each beneficiary in his will qualifies to take $10,000 under her will under acts of independent significance. The referenced act is the creation of her brother's will. He created his will to dispose of his probate property. The brother's will has its own significance (disposing of the brother's property upon his death) independent of its effect upon the sister's will (identifying who takes the $10,000 gifts).

E. Temporal perspectives: Republication by codicil, incorporation by reference, and acts of independent significance are doctrines that expand the scope of the will by giving effect to writings or events outside of the will. The doctrines, however, have different "temporal" perspectives.

1. Backward looking: Republication by codicil and incorporation by reference look back in time. Republication by codicil looks back in time by requiring that a valid will be executed ***before*** the codicil is executed. The codicil then republishes and redates the underlying will. Incorporation by reference likewise looks back in time. Incorporation by reference looks back in time by requiring that the document to be incorporated be created ***before*** the will was executed.

2. Forward looking: Although acts of independent significance can look back in time, typically the doctrine looks forward. With rare exception, the referenced act is an act to occur in the future, after the will is executed. Whenever a will references an act to occur in the future that affects who takes or how much they take, acts of independent significance is the only doctrine that can give effect to the gift.

VIII. CONTRACTS CONCERNING WILLS

A. Introduction: Under probate administration, creditors take first before beneficiaries under a will or heirs under intestacy. Creditors have extended valuable consideration to the decedent and are entitled to recover before beneficiaries or heirs, who are merely donees.

1. Potential for fraud: The principle that creditors take before beneficiaries or heirs creates a potential for fraudulent claims in that someone who mistakenly expected to be a beneficiary under a testator's will might claim that the testator "promised" to leave him or her a gift in exchange for his or her doing something for the testator. The frustrated individual may turn the frustration from not having received a gift into a claim that he or she "contracted" with the testator and is entitled to receive the expected "gift" as a creditor.

2. **Contract requirements:** Contracts relating to wills—contracts to make a will (or provision) or not to revoke a will (or provision)—must meet the standard contract requirements of offer, acceptance, and consideration.

> **Example:** Bob is terminally ill. Pat and Bob enter into an agreement that Pat will care for Bob in exchange for Bob leaving all of his property to Pat. Pat cares for Bob until his death, only to discover a will that leaves all of Bob's property to his father, Fred. Pat sues for breach of contract. If Pat and Bob are married, there is no consideration because spouses have a duty to care for each other. If Pat and Bob are not married, there is consideration, and Pat may take all Bob's property.

3. **Remedy—constructive trust:** If a contract concerning a will is established and the testator breaches the agreement by executing a different will, the probate court still probates the will the testator executed, but a constructive trust based on the contract typically is imposed on the testator's probate property. The devisees or heirs, as the case may be, are ordered to give the property to the contract beneficiary.

B. **Writing requirement:** Under contract law, the Statute of Frauds generally controls whether a contract needs to be in writing. As applied to contracts concerning wills, however, because of the potential for fraudulent claims and the fact that the other party to the alleged contract is dead, some jurisdictions require contracts concerning wills to be in writing even if not required under the Statute of Frauds.

1. **Equitable estoppel:** Under traditional common law principles, oral agreements between parties that one will leave property to the other upon the former's death do not have to be in writing. This approach, however, facilitates fraudulent claims of contracts concerning wills and increases the potential for "strike" suits where the claiming party hopes that the beneficiaries under the will or the heirs will settle for a percentage of the claim rather than litigate the issue.

2. **Clear and convincing evidence:** Some states have tried to reduce the potential for fraudulent claims concerning wills by requiring clear and convincing evidence to establish contracts concerning wills.

3. **Modern trend/UPC approach:** The UPC has tried to reduce the potential for fraudulent claims even further by requiring that contracts concerning wills must be evidenced by some writing signed by the decedent. UPC §2-514.

C. **Contracts not to revoke a will:** A contract not to revoke a will arises when a party agrees not to revoke a will or a provision in a will. Contracts not to revoke raise some issues not raised by contracts to make a will.

1. **Joint wills:** A joint will is a single will properly executed by two parties that serves as the last will and testament for each of the two parties, typically husband and wife. The joint will typically provides that upon the death of the first party, all of his or her property goes to the surviving party to the joint will, and upon the death of the surviving party, all of the second-to-die's property goes to some agreed upon beneficiary or beneficiaries.

2. **Mutual wills:** Mutual wills, also known as mirror wills, are similar to joint wills except that there are two wills, each having the same testamentary distribution scheme. Like joint wills,

mutual wills typically arise between husband and wife. Each spouse has his or her own separate will that typically provides that upon the spouse's death, all property goes to the surviving spouse, if one, and otherwise to their children (or some other agreed upon beneficiary).

a. **Ambiguity:** The issue that naturally arises out of joint and/or mutual wills is whether the will(s) implicitly contain a contract not to revoke, so that upon the death of the first party, the testamentary scheme the parties agreed upon becomes binding on the surviving party. Ultimately it is a question of the parties' intent. In the absence of good drafting, at a minimum, there is the potential for litigation.

b. **Modern trend/UPC approach:** In the interest of minimizing litigation and promoting testamentary freedom, the UPC provides that executing a joint will or mutual wills does not create even a presumption of a contract not to revoke. UPC §2-514. The surviving party is free to dispose of all of his or her property, including the property received by virtue of the first party's death, as the surviving party sees fit.

3. **Contract rights vs. spousal protection rights:** Where there is a contract not to revoke and the parties to the contract are husband and wife, if after the first spouse's death the surviving spouse remarries, the contract not to revoke comes into conflict with two statutory protection schemes.

a. **Spousal protection doctrines:** The ***pretermitted spouse doctrine*** provides that where a will is executed premarriage and the testator marries and dies without changing the will to provide for the new spouse, in essence the statute presumes that the testator wanted to provide for the new spouse but failed to get around to it before dying. The statute gives the new spouse his or her intestate share before any other beneficiaries take under the will. The ***elective share doctrine*** permits a surviving spouse to claim a share of the deceased spouse's estate regardless of the terms of the will and before any beneficiaries take under the will. (Both of these doctrines are covered in much more detail in Chapter 7.)

b. **Order of takers:** As a general rule: (1) creditors take before beneficiaries in the will, (2) spouses claiming spouse protection take before beneficiaries in the will, and (3) creditor's claims (other than creditors claiming under a contract not to revoke) are satisfied before spousal protection claims are satisfied. The issue is whether creditors claiming under a contract not to revoke are entitled to the same status as other creditors, or whether spouses are entitled to protection before the beneficiaries of the contract not to revoke.

c. **Contract beneficiaries:** The complexity of this issue stems from the fact that the third party beneficiaries of the contract not to revoke are also beneficiaries under the will. If the surviving spouse dies without remarrying, the beneficiaries take under the will in their capacity as beneficiaries. If, however, the surviving spouse remarries and breaches the contract not to revoke, the will beneficiaries who are also beneficiaries of the contract not to revoke can now claim as creditors. The breach of the contract not to revoke actually helps their claim because it permits them to try and change their place in line from mere will beneficiaries (who normally take last) to creditors (who normally take first). Inasmuch as the will/contract not to revoke beneficiaries wear two hats, their place in line depends first on whether there was a breach of the contract not to revoke.

d. **Breach:** Some contracts not to revoke state that ***anything*** that alters the agreed-upon distribution scheme constitutes a breach of the contract. Under this language, the mere act of remarrying may constitute a breach because it alters the agreed-upon testamentary distribution scheme by subjecting the estate to spousal protection claims. Other contracts not to revoke are worded such that the contract is breached only if the surviving spouse revokes the will. Under this language, the surviving spouse's remarriage does not, in and of itself, constitute a breach of the contract not to revoke. Arguably the new spouse is entitled to take before the will/contract not to revoke beneficiaries because, in the absence of a breach, the will/contract not to revoke beneficiaries can claim only in their capacity as will beneficiaries.

e. **Jurisdictional split:** The jurisdictions are split over who should take first where the surviving spouse remarries and the new spouse's claims constitute a breach of the contract not to revoke.

   i. **Majority:** A majority of jurisdictions enforces the terms of the contract not to revoke and let the contract beneficiaries take before the new spouse. These jurisdictions justify their approach on a number of different grounds: (1) the spousal protection claims apply only to property the surviving spouse owns legally and equitably, and the contract not to revoke places the equitable title in the beneficiaries of the contract not to revoke; (2) once the surviving spouse accepts the benefits of the contract, an equitable trust is imposed on the surviving spouse, reducing his or her interest in the property to a mere life estate with the remainder in the beneficiaries of the contract not to revoke; (3) once the surviving spouse accepts the benefits of the contract, he or she is estopped from altering the agreed-upon testamentary disposition scheme; or (4) under general creditors rights principles and the probate code, once the surviving spouse breaches the contract not to revoke, the beneficiaries become creditors entitled to protection before the surviving spouse.

   ii. **Minority:** A minority of the jurisdictions invokes the principle that contracts that discourage or restrain the right to marry are void as against public policy. The courts protect the new surviving spouse and let the new spouse take first by voiding the contract not to revoke because it violates public policy.

f. **Example:** In *Via v. Putnam,* 656 So. 2d 460 (Fla. 1995), husband and wife executed mutual wills that provided, upon the death of the first spouse, all to the surviving spouse, and upon the death of the surviving spouse, all to their children. Each will contained a contract not to revoke that provided that the surviving spouse would not do anything to change the agreed-upon testamentary scheme. Following the husband's death, the wife remarried. Upon her death, her surviving spouse claimed his spousal protection rights in her property. The children sued, claiming that the surviving wife's remarriage breached the contract not to revoke and, as creditors, they were entitled to take before the new husband's spousal protection claims. The court adopted the minority approach and held that as a matter of public policy spousal protection trumped the claims of creditors claiming under a contract not to revoke. The husband took first.

4. **Property affected:** The scope of the property subject to the contract not to revoke should be addressed in the contract, but in the absence of clear drafting, the courts tend to hold that the standard contract not to revoke applies not only to the property the surviving party received from the deceased party, but also to the surviving party's property—both the property the surviving party held at the time of death of the first party and the property subsequently acquired by the surviving party.

5. **Right to use:** The surviving spouse has a life estate in the property subject to the contract not to revoke, with the right to use and consume such property reasonably.

6. **Survival requirement:** Under general wills doctrines, a beneficiary has to survive the testator or the beneficiary does not take. Under general contracts doctrines, the beneficiary to a contract does not have to survive the other party to the contract to claim his or her benefits under the contract. As applied to beneficiaries of the contract not to revoke who wear two hats—one as will beneficiaries and the other as beneficiaries of the contract not to revoke—as a general rule the courts hold that the beneficiaries claim in their capacity as will beneficiaries unless and until there is a breach of the contract not to revoke. If there is a breach, at that moment their status changes to creditors claiming under the contract. If there is no breach, the beneficiaries must survive the decedent to take. If there is a breach, under general contract principles they do not need to survive the decedent to claim their benefits under the contract.

Quiz Yourself on
WILLS EXECUTION, REVOCATION, AND SCOPE

18. Arash is hit by a car and rushed to the hospital. He is lucid but has sustained serious internal injuries, and it is not clear whether he will make it. Pamela, his girlfriend, hears about the accident and rushes to his side—bringing with her a draft of his will that leaves everything to her. Pamela calls in two nurses, and in front of both of them, Arash declares that the document is his last will and testament and disposes of his property as he wishes. He picks up the pen and starts to sign his first name when suddenly the door to his hospital room opens and his wife, Alexandra, walks in. She is livid to see Pamela there. All hell breaks loose, and, in the commotion, Arash forgets to complete his signature. Pamela takes the document out to the nurses' station, where she has the nurses sign their names.

   a. Is the will valid under the traditional common law approach? _____

   b. Is the will valid under the modern trend approach? _____

19. Tess has a properly executed, typed will. When the will is found after her death, it is discovered that physically below her signature line is a handwritten sentence that provides as follows: "I also give $1,000 to my friend Betty." Is the will valid? Is the gift to Betty valid? _____

20. Tim has a heart attack. He remains conscious and alert. His girlfriend, Wi, and his neighbor, Joe, put him in the back seat of his car (in the seat behind the driver's seat). Joe gets in back with Tim. Wi jumps in front and starts driving to the hospital. Tim's attorney had sent Tim a draft of a new will. His old will gave all of his money to UCLA, his alma mater. His new will gives half to Wi and half to UCLA. As Wi was running around the house looking for the car keys, remarkably, she had the presence of mind to grab the draft of the new will. While racing Tim to the hospital (but keeping her eyes on the road at all times), Wi passes the new will back to Tim and asks him to execute it. Tim declares that the document is his last will and testament and signs it. Joe, who is sitting next to Tim and watching all this, then signs it. Joe then passes it up to the front seat, where Wi signs it at the first stop light. Tim survives the heart attack, only to die from food poisoning after ingesting his first hospital meal. Who takes his property? _____

21. Gerri and Dick have been married for years. Her will leaves everything to Dick, or, in the event he predeceases her, to her mom. Gerri thought she and Dick were happily married, until she discovers that he is having an affair with Bambi. Gerri is crushed. She handwrites her mom a dated letter in which she pours out her heart, describing the anguish she is going through as she debates filing for divorce. The letter has several sentences that read: "And to think that I have a will that leaves all of my property to that jerk. It should go to you." Gerri signs the letter, "your loving daughter." A week later, Bambi kills Gerri. Who gets Gerri's property? _____

22. Dude is deathly afraid to fly. Anna Nicoli asks him to go to Hawaii with her. She promises to make it worth his while. Dude decides the offer is too good to pass up. Before getting on the plane, he handwrites, dates, and signs the following instrument: "If the plane crashes and I die, I want all my property to go to my alma mater, Chico State." Dude successfully makes it to Hawaii and back, only to drive off the road while daydreaming about the time he spent with Anna Nicoli in Hawaii. Dude dies from his injuries. Chico State offers the writing for probate. Dude's heirs oppose it. Assuming the jurisdiction recognizes holographic wills, who gets Dude's property? _____

23. Gerri and Dick have been married for years. Her typed will leaves everything to Dick, or, in the event he predeceases her, to her mom. Gerri thought she and Dick were happily married, until she discovers that he is having an affair with Bubu. Gerri takes out the envelope containing the will and writes across the envelope, in big letters, "VOID." Gerri is killed in car crash a week later. Who takes her property? _____

24. Tami executes a will leaving her property to her alma mater, Loyola, and takes it home with her. A month later, a violent earthquake strikes the area, totally destroying Tami's house and killing her. Following her death, her family cannot find her will. Who takes Tami's property? _____

25. What difference, if any, would it make if Tami had executed duplicate original wills in the previous question? _____

26. Tom properly executes a will. The will provides in part as follows: "I give $10,000 to my favorite research assistant, Raquel, and I give the rest, residue, and remainder of my estate to my church." Following Tom's death, his will is found, but a line is drawn though the sentence giving the gift to Raquel. Who takes what? _____

27. Toni has a properly executed will that provides in part as follows: "I give my best friend Gail, $10,000. I give the rest of my estate to my alma mater, the University of Chicago." Thereafter, Toni hears that her best friend is dating her ex-boyfriend, Frankie. Toni takes out her will and, with a pen, draws a line through her gift to Gail. She tells everyone she revoked the gift to Gail because she is dating her ex-boyfriend. Toni is so depressed she commits suicide. It turns out that although Gail is dating someone named Frankie, it is not the Frankie Toni used to date. What is Gail's best argument that she is entitled to take? What are her chances of prevailing? _____

28. Jalo had a valid will that left all of her property to Puffy. Thereafter, she broke up with Puffy and started seeing Ben. Shortly after she started seeing Ben, she properly executed a new will that left all of her property to Ben. Not long thereafter, however, she grew tired of Ben and went back to Puffy. At the time, she handwrote, dated, and signed an instrument that provided as follows: "I hereby revoke my will leaving my property to Ben. Jalo." She tells everyone that the reason she revoked her second will is that she really loves Puffy and wants him to have her property. Shortly thereafter, she dies on the operating table during elective surgery. Who takes her property? _____

29. Surfer Dude has a valid will that leaves his "surfboard to Jane, and the rest of my property shall go as directed in a letter I will send to my executor, Hulama." Surfer Dude then types and signs a letter telling Hulama that he wants all of his property to go to the Heal the Bay organization. Thereafter, Surfer Dude executes a valid codicil appointing Jake his executor. After making this change, Surfer Dude dies from an infection he contracts as a result of surfing in polluted waters. Who takes his property? _____

30. Paul and his sister Kristin went to UCLA, and they hated their dreaded rival USC. They often talked about how they would leave their estates to the UCLA Athletic Department to help fight their rivals. Paul is several years older than his sister and wants to make sure that she is taken care of first. Paul properly executes a will that provides that he leaves everything to his sister Kristin for life, and upon her death his property should be distributed according to the residuary clause of Kristin's will. Unbeknownst to Paul, Kristin has not drafted her will yet. It is not until two years after Paul executes his will that Kristin properly executes her will leaving everything to UCLA. Who takes Paul's property when he dies? _____

31. Arash promises to leave all of his property to Lulu if she takes care of him for the rest of his life. Lulu does for six months, only to discover when Arash dies at the end of the six months that his properly executed will leaves all of his property to his family—Hamid, Farideh, Benny, and Ashley. Lulu sues to enforce the terms of her agreement with Arash. Who takes Arash's property? _____

32. Pete and Gerri are married. They have four lovely children. They execute mirror wills that have an express clause waiving the testator's right to revoke the will. Each will leaves all of the testator's property to the surviving spouse, if one, and otherwise to the children equally. Many years later, Pete dies, and Gerri moves in with Rick—fulfilling his lifelong dream. Gerri executes a new will leaving all of her property to Rick. Who takes her property when she dies? _____

Answers

18a. Under the traditional common law approach, Arash's will was not validly executed. There are a couple of problems with the document Pamela is offering as Arash's will under the common law approach. First, it arguably was not properly signed. Although anything the testator intends to qualify as his signature constitutes a valid signature, there is a general presumption that when a person begins to sign his or her name, he or she intends to sign the whole name. If the person does not sign his or her whole name but stops voluntarily, then arguably whatever the person wrote, he or she intended to constitute his or her whole signature. Where, however, the person is interrupted during the signing of their name, the presumption is that the person intended to sign his or her whole name and did not intend for anything short to qualify as their signature. Here, it is assumed that Arash intended to sign his whole name. When his wife walked in and interrupted the signature, Arash may have reconsidered and decided not to sign the document. Under the traditional common law approach, the more likely result is that the court would hold that Arash did not properly sign the document.

Moreover, under the traditional common law approach, witnesses are required to sign the will in the testator's presence. Here, the nurses did not sign the will in Arash's room; they signed the document back at the nurses' station. There is no evidence that Arash was anywhere nearby when they signed the will. Because the nurses did not sign the document in Arash's presence, the will was not properly executed and is invalid.

18b. Under the modern trend approach, the will arguably is still invalid, though a much stronger argument can be made that it should be considered a valid will. Under the modern trend, the witnesses do not have to sign the will in the testator's presence. Delayed attestation is permitted as long as the witnesses sign within a reasonable time of witnessing the testator perform. Under the modern trend, the fact that the nurses signed the document a bit later at the nurses' station is acceptable.

The issue under the modern trend is whether the will was properly signed. Just as is true at common law, whatever the testator intended to qualify as his signature qualifies. The issue with respect to a partial signature, however, is still the same. Where the testator is interrupted during signing, a presumption arises that he or she did not intend for the partial signature to constitute a full signature because when the person started to sign he or she intended to sign his or her full name. That is particularly applicable here where the reason the testator stopped signing is because his wife, who would have been disinherited to the full extent permitted by law, entered the room. Maybe seeing her made him reconsider. Under the modern trend, if one were to apply strict compliance, most likely the will would be invalid.

In some jurisdictions, the modern trend favors substantial compliance and/or dispensing power. Under both of those doctrines, however, the will proponents still have to prove by clear and convincing evidence that the decedent intended this document to be his or her last will. Because we presume Arash intended to sign his whole name, it is questionable whether there is clear and convincing evidence that he intended this document to be his last will. What constitutes clear and convincing evidence, however, is fact sensitive and somewhat subjective. Different people disagree over what constitutes clear and convincing evidence. Arash did start to sign his name, which arguably constitutes clear and convincing evidence that he intended the document to be his will. But when his wife, who was being disinherited, entered the room, he stopped and did not complete his name. Arguably he did not complete his signature because he had second thoughts and no longer wanted to disinherit her. It is unclear how the case would come out. Although the will proponents have a stronger argument under these doctrines, the equities and public policy considerations favoring a spouse may be the deciding factor.

19. The analysis depends on (1) whether the jurisdiction follows the common law approach to the Wills Act formalities (which typically requires that the will be signed at the end) or the modern trend approach (which does not require the will to be signed at the end), and (2) when the handwritten clause was added to the document—that is, before or after the document was signed.

If the jurisdiction requires the will to be "subscribed" (signed at the end), and the handwritten sentence was added temporally **before** the testator signed the will, the whole will is invalid because the will was not signed at the end. If the jurisdiction requires the will to be subscribed, and the handwritten sentence was added temporally **after** the testator signed the will, the original will should be valid, but the handwritten material added temporally after the will was executed is invalid.

If the jurisdiction follows the modern trend and does not require the will to be signed at the end, and if the handwritten sentence was added temporally **after** the testator signed the will, the will is valid, but the handwritten sentence was not part of the original will and is not valid unless it qualifies as a holographic codicil. Because it was not signed, it most likely does not qualify as a holographic codicil (an argument can be made under the dispensing power approach that it might qualify as a valid holographic codicil).

If the jurisdiction does not require the will to be signed at the end, and if the handwritten sentence was added temporally **before** the testator signed the will, the handwritten material is a valid part of the original will, and both the will and the handwritten material are valid and can be given effect.

20. The first issue is whether the will was properly executed. The testator has to sign the will in the presence of two witnesses. The traditional common law approach to the presence requirement is the line of sight approach. The modern trend takes the conscious presence approach. Here, Joe satisfies either test, but Wi arguably does not satisfy the line of sight test. Sitting in the driver's seat, she was not capable of seeing what Tim was doing in the back seat right behind her. The facts specifically say that she kept both eyes on the road at all times because she was speeding Tim to the hospital. Under the line of sight test, the will arguably was not properly executed.

Under the modern trend approach, the will arguably was properly witnessed. Although Wi did not actually see Tim sign the will, from the totality of the circumstances she realized that Tim was executing the will: She knew that Tim had had a heart attack, she knew that when she passed the will back to him it had no signatures on it, she heard him declare that he wanted the document to be his will, and that when the document was passed back up to her it had Tim's signature on it. Under the modern trend, the will arguably was signed in her presence even though she did not see it being signed.

But Wi is an interested witness. At early common law, this voids the whole will. Tim's property therefore passes to UCLA pursuant to the prior will. The general rule, however, is that an interested witness does not void the will, but rather an interested witness creates an irrebuttable presumption of wrongdoing on the part of the interested witness. Some jurisdictions void the whole gift to the witness; others take the purging approach. Under the purging approach, the interested witness is purged of the excess interest he or she stands to gain if this will were valid. Here, Wi stands to take nothing under the prior will and half of Tim's estate under the new will, so she is purged of the full 50 percent that she stands to take under this will. Under these approaches, the issue then becomes what happens to the failed gift to Wi. Under the common law approach, when part of the residuary clause fails, the failed gift falls to intestacy—here to Tim's heirs under intestacy. Under the modern trend approach to partial failure of the residuary clause, the failed part passes to the other residuary takers—here to UCLA.

Under the modern trend, in some jurisdictions an interested witness creates a rebuttable presumption of wrongdoing. Here, Wi probably could rebut the presumption, thereby entitling her to take the full gift, half of Tim's estate. The UPC abolishes the interested witness doctrine. The burden is on the parties who suspect wrongdoing to bring a claim of wrongdoing and prove it. Under this approach, Wi takes her devise in the will.

21. Gerri's property goes to Dick unless the writing she sent to her mother qualifies as a holographic will. Assuming the jurisdiction recognizes holographic wills, there is a writing (the letter), it is dated (if the jurisdiction requires), the whole document is in her handwriting (so it does not matter if the jurisdiction requires only the material provisions or the whole document to be in the testator's handwriting) and it is signed (it is assumed the testatrix intended "your loving daughter" to be her signature). The issue is whether the document has testamentary intent—the intent that this document be taken down and probated as the decedent's will. Although testamentary intent is a rather soft, fact-sensitive doctrine, here it appears the document falls short. It is unclear whether Gerri's comment that her property

"should" go to her mother is enough to indicate an intent to change her testamentary scheme and to have this document qualify as her new will. The letter describes the anguish she was going through. Arguably Gerri had not made up her mind as to how she wanted to react, both inter vivos (whether she should file for divorce) and at time of death (whether she wanted to revoke her gift to Dick). In cases where the courts have held such letters to have adequate testamentary intent, usually there is also a phrase indicating the intent that the document is to have future significance (such as "save this" or "keep this, it may help you in the future"). Although a close call, arguably the letter lacks the necessary testamentary intent to qualify as a valid holographic will. *Note:* The homicide doctrine is not applicable. It applies only to the killer. Here, Bambi killed Gerri, not Dick, and there is no evidence that Dick was in any way involved in Gerri's death. If evidence did support that Dick were involved, Gerri's heirs might be able to invoke the homicide doctrine against him.

22. The writing qualifies as a valid holographic will. It is dated, completely in the testator's handwriting, is signed, and expresses testamentary intent (the document expresses the intent that it controls who takes Dude's property when he dies, that Dude intended for this to be his will). The issue is whether this is a conditional will that was to be effective only if Dude died in a plane crash. Most courts construe such clauses more as an explanation of why the testator is executing the will, rather than a condition precedent to the will being valid. The more likely result is that the will is valid.

23. The issue is whether the will was properly revoked. The two principal means of revoking a will are by act or by writing. If by writing, the writing has to qualify as a valid will. Here, the word *void* is not enough to qualify as a valid will. There were no witnesses, so it cannot qualify as a traditional attested will. There is no signature, so it cannot qualify as a holographic will (there also is an issue as to whether it adequately expresses testamentary intent that is moot because it is not signed). For revocation by act, the act has to be destructive in nature and done with the intent to revoke. Here, the act of writing "VOID" arguably is sufficiently destructive, and it was performed with the intent to revoke (Gerri no longer wanted her estate to go to Dick in light of his affair). The issue is whether the act qualifies because it is on the envelope. In the common law approach, the act has to affect the printed words of the will. Writing on the envelope fails to affect the printed words of the will. Under the modern trend, the act need only affect some part of the will. The envelope is not part of the will. Even under the modern trend, the most likely result is that the will was not revoked. Dick takes Gerri's property.

24. Here, because the will was last in Tami's possession and cannot be found following her death, the presumption that she revoked it arises. The presumption, however, is rebuttable if a more plausible explanation exists for why the will cannot be found. Here, the explanation is that the will was destroyed when Tami's house was destroyed. That is probably sufficient to overcome the presumption. Although the presumption is overcome, no will exists to probate. Under the lost will doctrine, the court takes extrinsic evidence as to the terms of the will, and, if the terms are established, the court probates the lost will.

25. Although some jurisdictions apply the presumption doctrine only if none of the duplicate originals can be found, others apply it even if other duplicate originals can be found. Here the presumption doctrine does not apply at all, so the question is irrelevant.

26. Under a variation on the presumption doctrine, when the will was last in the testator's possession and is found after the testator's death with a destructive or mutilating mark on it, a presumption arises that the testator made the mark with the intent to revoke. Here, the presumption arises that the testator made the mark. Inasmuch as the mark affects only part of the will, the issue arises as to whether the jurisdiction recognizes partial revocation by act. If the jurisdiction does not, Raquel takes $10,000,

and the residue passes to the testator's church. If the jurisdiction recognizes partial revocation by act, a subtle issue remains. The facts do not indicate if the mark was made with pen or pencil. Some courts have held that a pencil mark does not show enough finality of intent to constitute the intent to revoke. If Tom's mark appears in pencil, Raquel might still take her gift of $10,000. If the mark appears in pen, and the jurisdiction recognizes partial revocation by act, the gift to Raquel is revoked. Because a partial revocation is inherently a new gift, those jurisdictions that strictly apply the Wills Act formalities reason that where there is partial revocation, the gift that is revoked must pass through intestacy. The general rule, however, is that the gift falls to the residuary clause. The testator's church takes the revoked gift as well as the rest of the residuary.

27. Gail will claim that she is entitled to take under dependent relative revocation. Under this doctrine, the claimant must show that there was a revocation based upon a mistake, and but for the mistake, the testator would not have revoked. In addition, the courts typically apply the doctrine only where there is either a failed alternative scheme or the mistake is set forth in the revoking instrument. Here, Toni validly revoked the gift by drawing a line through the gift with the intent to revoke. The revocation was based upon a mistake, the wrongful belief that the Frankie Gail was dating was Toni's ex-boyfriend. Because that appears to be the only reason Toni revoked the gift to Gail, it is reasonable to conclude that but for the mistake, Toni would not have revoked the gift to Gail. But the courts typically apply the doctrine only where there is a failed alternative scheme or where the revoking instrument sets forth the mistake. Therefore, Gail is not entitled to relief under dependent relative revocation. Toni revoked by act, so the only way Gail can prevail under the prevailing judicial approach to dependent relative revocation is if there is a failed alternative scheme. There is no failed alternative scheme here. Gail's claim therefore fails. Under the majority approach to partial revocation by act, the gift falls to the residuary clause. Under the minority approach, the revoked gift passes through intestacy.

28. The handwritten instrument qualifies as a valid holographic will. There is a writing, all of the terms of the writing are in the testator's handwriting, the document expresses testamentary intent (the intent to revoke an existing will affects a testator's testamentary scheme and thereby expresses testamentary intent), and it is signed. The holographic will here is will #3 and it revokes will #2—the classic revival scenario. Under the English approach, will #1 is effective because will #2 never revoked will #1, it just "covered" it. The general American approach is that the moment will #2 was executed it revoked will #1. The jurisdictions are split on what is necessary to revive will #1 if will #2 is revoked. If the jurisdiction requires the testator to reexecute will #1, will #1 cannot be revived under these facts, and Jalo died intestate. If all the testator has to do to revive will #1 is to intend to revive will #1 when he or she revokes will #2, the key is how the testator revoked will #2. If the testator revoked will #2 by act, the courts will take any evidence of the testator's intent to revive will #1. If, however, the testator revoked will #2 by will #3, the intent to revive will #1 must be set forth in will #3. Here, Jalo revoked will #2 by will #3. The intent to revive will #1 must be set forth in will #3, which it is not. Despite Jalo's oral declarations as to her intent to revive will #1, the document would not be revived under revival (nor would the court give effect to will #2 under dependent relative revocation).

29. The issue is whether the court can give effect to Surfer Dude's testamentary wishes as expressed in his letter to Hulama. The letter does not qualify as a will. No evidence supports that any witnesses saw its execution, so it does not qualify as a valid attested will. The letter is typed, so it does not qualify as a valid holographic will. The Heal the Bay organization can argue incorporation by reference. Although the reference in the will to the letter satisfies the intent to incorporate and describe with reasonable certainty requirements, the letter was created after the will was executed, so it cannot be incorporated by reference. But Surfer Dude executes a codicil. Under republication by codicil, the codicil is presumed to reexecute and redate the underlying will to the date of the

codicil. By redating the will to the date of the codicil, the letter to Hulama is now in existence when the will is republished and can be incorporated by reference. Jane gets Surfer Dude's surfboard. The Heal the Bay organization gets the rest of his property. (Acts of independent significance cannot be used to give effect to the letter because it has no independent significance apart from its effect upon Surfer Dude's probate estate.)

30. UCLA will not be able to claim Paul's property under incorporation by reference. Although the reference in Paul's will that his property should be distributed pursuant to the residuary clause of his sister's will arguably satisfies the intent to incorporate requirement and it describes the document with reasonable certainty, Kristin's will was not in existence when Paul executed his will. Nor did Paul execute any codicils to his will that permit redating the will. Under acts of independent significance, however, the will may refer to acts outside of the will that may control who takes or how much they take as long as the referenced act has its own significance independent of its effect upon the will. Here, the referenced act is the residuary clause of Kristin's will. Kristin's will has its own significance independent of its effect upon Paul's will—disposing of Kristin's property. The court can give effect to the clause in Paul's will referencing the clause in Kristin's will under acts of independent significance.

31. Who takes Arash's property turns on whether the jurisdiction follows the common law approach or the modern trend/UPC approach. At common law, oral contracts to make a will are enforceable (some jurisdictions require clear and convincing evidence). Here, the agreement between Arash and Lulu arguably is enforceable. Under the modern trend/UPC approach, however, there must be a writing signed by the decedent evidencing the terms of the agreement. Here, there is no such writing. Lulu therefore is not entitled to enforce the terms of their agreement, but she is entitled to bring a claim for quantum meruit for the value of the services she did render.

32. Although the mere execution of mutual wills or a joint will does not give rise to a contract not to revoke, here the mirror wills expressly provide that the parties agreed to waive their power to revoke. When Gerri executes a new will in favor of Rick, she breaches her contract not to revoke. The children are able to sue as third party beneficiaries under the contract not to revoke in the original will. The court will probate the new will in favor of Rick, but the court will impose a constructive trust on Rick ordering him to transfer Gerri's property to the children under the contract not to revoke.

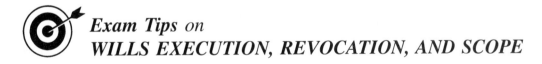

Exam Tips on **WILLS EXECUTION, REVOCATION, AND SCOPE**

This chapter presents core wills material. This chapter might be the most important chapter in the book, both doctrinally and theoretically.

Executing a valid will

☞ Two variables control whether a will has been properly executed: the jurisdiction's statutory Wills Act formalities and the jurisdiction's approach to what degree of compliance is required. In most jurisdictions, the latter is a judicial (nonstatutory) doctrine. If you get a will execution issue, remember to raise and discuss each variable.

Common law approach to attested wills

☛ You should be very familiar with every requirement of the Wills Act in your jurisdiction. Every requirement is a potential issue. There are, however, a few scenarios that are tested more often.

☛ If you see anything other than the testator's full name, you have a signature issue.

  ☞ It is presumed that the testator intended whatever he or she wrote to be his or her signature, unless there is evidence that the testator was interrupted while signing. If the testator was interrupted, the issue is whether the testator intended what is on the paper to be his or her signature. The presumption is that if the testator did not complete what he or she intended when he or she started, whatever appears is not a complete signature. Otherwise, whatever is on the paper should qualify as a valid signature.

☛ The witness requirement is tested often. Several aspects to the witnessing requirement make it a favorite.

  ☞ Know whether your jurisdiction applies the line of sight or the conscious presence test (the former is more bright line, the latter more fact sensitive). Know *who* has to do *what* in *whose* presence. Under the common law approach, both parties have to perform in the presence of each other. The testator has to sign in the physical presence of the witnesses, and the witnesses have to sign in the physical presence of the testator. Under the modern trend, most jurisdictions have eliminated the latter requirement.

    ☞ Watch for a delayed attestation scenario where one witness signs the will and the second witness fails to sign right away. Under the modern trend, that does not necessarily mean the will is invalid. If the testator dies within a relatively short time thereafter, raise and note that the second witness can still be called in to sign the will to save it.

    ☞ Under the strict common law approach, if a witness steps away for any part of the testator's performance and then returns, most likely you will have to start the whole execution analysis all over again. If the whole execution ceremony was not completed before the witness left, whatever the parties do after the wayward witness returns has to qualify as a valid execution ceremony in its own right.

  ☞ If a witness signs the will before the testator, at common law that act is a nullity, and the analysis would have to start all over beginning with the testator signing the will.

  ☞ A fairly common execution scenario is when a typed will is found with handwritten material appearing physically below the testator's signature block. This simple scenario is deceptive in that it can raise a plethora of issues: (1) where on the will the signature must appear; (2) when the material was added; (3) assuming the material does not qualify as part of the original will, whether it qualifies as its own holographic will; and (4) whether the court can use the typed material in analyzing whether the holographic instrument has testamentary intent.

    ☞ Inasmuch as there are five different approaches to the interested witness doctrine, know which approach your jurisdiction has adopted and its effect when applied.

    ☞ Under the purging approach, do not automatically assume the witness takes whatever he or she would take under intestacy. Check to see if there are other testamentary instruments (for example, a prior will).

☞ The swapped wills scenario is a nice overlap testing scenario because it can test the common law approach (invalid), the misdescription doctrine (to try to cure the defect in the execution ceremony), and the scrivener's error doctrine.

Modern trend approach to attested wills

☛ Know the key modern trend changes to the typical common law Wills Act formalities. Witnesses typically do not have to sign in the presence of the testator (permitting delayed attestation). There is no order of signing requirement as long as no one leaves the room before all have signed the will.

☛ Unless your jurisdiction has adopted substantial compliance or dispensing power by statute, lead with strict compliance when analyzing whether the testator has complied with the modern trend Wills Act formalities. If the execution ceremony fails, be sure to argue and apply in the alternative that the court should adopt substantial compliance or dispensing power (unless strict compliance has been legislatively adopted in your jurisdiction).

☞ Under both curative doctrines, there still must be clear and convincing evidence that the testator intended the document to be his or her will. While the doctrines permit the court to slide on the execution ceremony, they do not permit the court to slide on the testator's state of mind. If you have doubt as to whether the testator intended this to be his or her will, arguably the will is not valid.

Holographic wills

☛ If your jurisdiction recognizes holographic wills, you need to sweat the details of the statute because they can vary greatly from jurisdiction to jurisdiction.

☛ The most litigated and tested element of the holographic will doctrine is the requirement that the document have testamentary intent. Define the requirement before applying it.

☞ In applying it, be sure to include whether the jurisdiction takes the UPC approach (if your jurisdiction has not taken a position on the issue, argue it in the alternative). Testamentary intent is a very fact-sensitive issue. Include the key words from the writing that you think are relevant to the issue. Always include the alternative characterization of the instrument (what would the party opposing the instrument call it if not a will?).

☞ Remember that holographic codicils to holographic wills have their own special rule.

Revocation

☛ Revocation by writing requires a writing that qualifies as a valid will. Be able to distinguish a codicil from a new will. This is important under both the common law and the modern trend in a whole host of different contexts (for example, scope of revocation effected by second instrument, effect of revocation of second instrument).

☞ If the subsequent will has a residuary clause, invariably it is a whole new will. If, however, the subsequent will does not have a residuary clause but the prior will had one, the subsequent will invariably is a codicil.

☛ Revocation by act is easy to spot—some destructive act must be performed to some part of the will. Make sure there is evidence of the intent to revoke. Revocation is a testamentary act that requires capacity at the time the act is performed.

☞ Watch the facts carefully to see which part of the will is affected (tests the common law vs. modern trend approach to this issue).

☛ If someone other than the testator performs the revocation by act, the same "presence" concerns and issues can arise as discussed under the execution material.

☛ Strict compliance is applied to the revocation by act requirements, just as it is to the execution requirements. If the revocation fails under strict compliance, you can argue that the court should adopt substantial compliance and dispensing power judicially.

☛ If the will was last in the testator's possession and is not found after his or her death, this gives rise to a presumption that the will was destroyed by act.

☞ If the will was last in the testator's possession and is found following his or her death, but with destructive marks across the will, based upon the presumption doctrine, the presumption arises that the testator made the marks with the intent to revoke.

☛ Many students get confused over the relationship between the revocation by presumption doctrine and the lost will. If the presumption doctrine applies and the presumption is not rebutted, the will is revoked (the lost will doctrine does not apply then). If the presumption doctrine does not apply, or it applies but the presumption is rebutted, the will is not revoked—but it cannot be found. The lost will doctrine then applies, and the will should be probated if there is the requisite evidence of its terms.

☞ Partial revocation by physical act is a subset of the revocation material that is often tested. Know whether your jurisdiction recognizes the doctrine, and, if so, what happens to the revoked gift (or be prepared to argue all three approaches in the alternative).

☛ Dependent relative revocation is one of the most difficult doctrines covered in the course. The doctrine is fairly easy to spot. The triggering facts are that you have to see a valid revocation based upon a mistake (whether of fact or law does not matter).

☞ If you see a dependent relative revocation issue, as always, begin by stating the basic rule statement and then give the rule elaboration: Almost invariably the courts apply the doctrine only where there is either a failed alternative scheme or where the mistake is set forth in the revoking instrument.

☞ As a practical matter, the failed alternative scheme means that the testator attempted to execute a new will (or codicil), but the instrument is invalid for some reason, so the "failed will" constitutes the failed alternative scheme. But the decedent thought the "failed will" was valid, so that constitutes the mistake—a mistake of law. So where the revocation is by act, watch for an attempt at a new will that fails. If the testator revoked the original will because he or she thought the new will was valid, you have both your mistake (of law) and your failed alternative scheme. Assuming you can show causation, apply dependent relative revocation to give effect to the original will (disregard the valid revocation).

☞ If you see a valid revocation by writing but the revocation is based upon a mistake, the mistake must be set forth in the revoking will. The norm is for the mistake to be a mistake of fact. If the mistake of fact is not set forth in the writing, dependent relative revocation does not apply.

☞ Where the revocation is by writing and the mistake is a mistake of law (the new will expressly revokes the old, but the new gift violates the Rule against Perpetuities and is void), the mistake typically is not patent but is implicit in the wording of the doctrine. This is the least common way of testing dependent relative revocation.

☛ Dependent relative revocation applies equally well to partial revocations. This is the classic dependent relative revocation scenario. Watch for testators who scratch out part of a typed will and then handwrite on the original will an "interlineation" (a handwritten clause or sentence on the original will purporting to amend the will). Analyze the act of scratching out part of the typed will as a revocation. Analyze the handwritten interlineations as a possible holographic codicil. If not a valid codicil, analyze the revocation under dependent relative revocation. The failed codicil constitutes the failed alternative scheme and the mistake (of law). Apply dependent relative revocation if the testator would not have revoked if he or she had known that the codicil was going to be invalid.

☞ The final requirement of dependent relative revocation is that the testator would not have revoked the original will but for the mistake. Under dependent relative revocation, the court has only two options: give effect to the valid revocation or ignore the revocation and give effect to the original gift. If the testator's true intent is closer to the original gift than it is to giving effect to the revocation, apply dependent relative revocation (assuming the other requirements are met). If the testator's true intent is closer to the result that would occur if the court gave effect to the valid revocation, do not apply dependent relative revocation even if all the other requirements are met.

☛ Revival is a fairly simple doctrine that is generally easy to spot. You must have at least two wills, and the testator must revoke will #2. When the testator revokes will #2, that automatically gives rise to a revival issue.

☛ The subtle way to raise the revival issue is to make will #2 a codicil. Students tend to overfocus on the will #1/will #2 terminology and forget that a codicil is a will. If there is a will and a codicil to the will, and the testator revokes the codicil, you have a revival issue.

☞ Remember the UPC rule that where the second will is a codicil and the codicil is revoked, a presumption arises that the testator intended to revive the terms of the original will that were revoked by the codicil; the burden is on those opposed to revival to show that the testator did not intend to revive the original terms.

☛ Under the "revive as long as intended" approach to revival, ***how*** the testator revoked the second will determines what evidence is admissible to prove the intent to revive.

☛ The revocation by operation of law issues tested most often go to its scope: Does it also apply to will substitutes? The common law approach applies it only to wills. Does it apply to other family members? The majority approach applies it only to the ex-spouse.

Scope of the will

☛ Republication by codicil, incorporation by reference, and acts of independent significance are core doctrines that are heavily tested.

☛ Republication by codicil not only redates the underlying will, it also reexecutes it. If there is a problem with the will that does not invalidate it (for example, an interested witness problem), republication by codicil may clean up that problem.

  ☞ While republication by codicil generally redates the underlying will to the date of the codicil, if that is inconsistent with the testator's apparent testamentary intent, argue against redating the will. (This argument is less viable where the codicil expressly states that it republishes and redates the underlying will, but even there the argument can be made that such language represents the attorney's boilerplate language.)

☛ If there appears to be a republication by codicil issue but the underlying document does not qualify as a valid will, switch to incorporation by reference. Usually you can reach the same result—being able to give effect to the intent expressed in both documents.

☛ Incorporation by reference is another basic doctrine often tested. Because the courts apply such a low threshold to the first two requirements, almost invariably the element at issue is whether the document to be incorporated was in existence at the time the will was executed.

  ☞ The burden of proof is on the party trying to incorporate the document. If the document is undated, the party trying to incorporate fails unless something about the codicil shows its "relative" date is before the will.

  ☞ The document can be incorporated only as it existed on the date the will was executed.

  ☞ If there is difficulty showing that the document was in existence on the date the will was executed, or if the document was revised after execution, watch for a codicil that redates the will and thereby clears up the apparent problem with the dates.

☛ Acts of independent significance is one of the toughest doctrines in the course. If you see generic language in a will that refers to something outside of the will that affects either who takes or how much they take, that is the classic scenario for acts of independent significance.

  ☞ Analytically, the key is to identify the controlling "referenced" act in the will. Then ask if that act has its own independent significance (usually its own inter vivos significance) apart from its effect upon the property passing under the will. If the reference act has its own significance, apply the doctrine and permit the clause to dispose of the property. If the act does not have its own significance, the clause is invalid regardless of the clarity of the testator's intent.

  ☞ If the referenced act occurs after execution of the will, typically the only way the referenced act can affect who takes or how much a beneficiary takes is if it qualifies as an act of independent significance.

Contracts relating to wills

☛ Know which approach your jurisdiction takes to whether contracts relating to wills must be in writing.

☛ If you see a joint will (and, to a lesser extent, mirror wills), probably a contract not to revoke issue is involved. The key is to spot the issue because application is fairly easy. Most jurisdictions apply the modern trend that the mere execution of a joint will (or mirror wills) does not give rise to even a presumption of a contract not to revoke.

 ☞ The contract not to revoke and the spousal protection material overlap is a very difficult area of the course. Know which approach your jurisdiction takes to which doctrine prevails, and read the fact pattern very carefully to see what is necessary for a breach of the contract not to revoke.

 ☞ If there is a valid contract not to revoke and the surviving party to the agreement breaches it, remember which will the court will probate (the will that breaches the agreement). Then the third party beneficiaries to the contract not to revoke have to assert the breach and ask the court to impose a constructive trust ordering that the property that they are entitled to under the contract be transferred to them.

CHAPTER 5

CONSTRUING WILLS

ChapterScope ━━━━━━━━━━━━━━━━━━━━━━━━━━━━━━━━━━━

This chapter examines issues inherent in probating and giving effect to a will. In particular, the chapter deals with doctrines that address the fact that changes can occur between the time a will is executed inter vivos and when it becomes effective at time of death. In particular, the chapter examines:

■ **Admissibility of extrinsic evidence:** The general rule is that extrinsic evidence is admissible only if there is an ambiguity in the will or if the evidence goes to the validity of the will.

- ■ **Patent vs. latent ambiguities:** Common law distinguishes between patent and latent ambiguities and admits extrinsic evidence to help construe the ambiguity only if the ambiguity is a latent ambiguity. The modern trend not only abolishes the distinction between latent and patent ambiguities and admits extrinsic evidence anytime there is any mistake.

- ■ **Modern trend:** Under the modern trend, if there is clear and convincing evidence of a mistake, and clear and convincing evidence of its effect upon testator's intent, some courts will admit extrinsic evidence to establish the mistake and reform the will in view of testator's true intent. This general approach has been adopted by one court as a specific doctrine in the case of scrivener's error.

■ **Lapse:** Where a beneficiary predeceases the testator, the gift is said to lapse and it fails. Failed specific gifts and failed general gifts fall to the residuary clause; failed residuary gifts fall to intestacy.

■ **Anti-lapse statutes:** Anti-lapse statutes provide that where there is a lapsed gift, if (1) the predeceased beneficiary meets the requisite degree of relationship to the testator, and (2) the predeceased beneficiary has issue who survive the testator, then the gift will go to the issue of the predeceased beneficiary (3) as long as the will does not express an intent that anti-lapse should not be applied.

■ **Class gifts:** A class gift has a built-in right of survivorship so that if one member of the class predeceases the testator, his or her share is simply redistributed among the surviving members of the class. When it is not clear whether a gift to multiple individuals is a class gift, courts focus on four factors: (1) how the beneficiaries are described, (2) how the gift is described, (3) whether all the individuals share a common characteristic, and (4) the testator's overall testamentary scheme.

■ **Ademption:** Under the common law approach, if the testator makes a specific gift and the item that is the subject of the specific gift is not in the testator's estate at time of death, under the identity approach an irrebuttable presumption arises that the gift was revoked. Under the modern trend/UPC approach, a presumption against revocation arises, and the beneficiary is entitled to any replacement property the testator owns at time of death or, if none, the monetary equivalent of the gift.

- ■ **Avoidance doctrines:** Because ademption is such a harsh doctrine, a number of avoidance doctrines have arisen: (1) classify the gift as general, not specific; (2) change in form, not substance; (3) construe the will at time of death, not execution.

- ■ **Softening doctrines:** In addition, doctrines that soften the impact of ademption have arisen: (1) if the testator is owed an outstanding balance as a result of the transfer of the specific gift, the outstanding balance goes to the beneficiary; (2) if the specific gift was transferred while a conservator or durable power of attorney agent was acting for the testator, the beneficiary is entitled to the monetary equivalent of the net sale price.

■ **Satisfaction:** At common law, if a testator makes an inter vivos gift to his or her child, and the child is also a beneficiary in the testator's will, a rebuttable presumption arises that the inter vivos gift counts against the child's testamentary gift. Under the modern trend/UPC, if a testator makes an inter vivos gift to anyone who is also a beneficiary under his or her will, the gift does not count against the beneficiary's testamentary gift unless a writing evidences such an intent.

■ **Exoneration of liens:** At common law, if a specific gift is burdened with debt (a mortgage or lien), absent contrary intent expressed in the will, it is presumed that the beneficiary of the specific gift is entitled to have the debt completely paid off (out of the residuary clause) so that the beneficiary takes the gift free and clear of any debt. Under the modern trend, the beneficiary takes subject to the debt absent an express clause directing that the debt is to be satisfied before the gift is made.

■ **Abatement:** If at time of death the testator has made more gifts than he or she has assets, the doctrine of abatement states that residuary gift should be reduced first, general gifts second, and specific gifts last.

I. ADMISSIBILITY OF EXTRINSIC EVIDENCE: GENERAL RULE

A. **Scope of chapter:** The chapter is titled Construing Wills, and it focuses on wills. The modern trend, however, applies the will construction doctrines examined in this chapter to nonprobate instruments as well, particularly trusts and contracts with payable-on-death (P.O.D.) clauses. If your jurisdiction adopts the modern trend, remember that the scope of the chapter is not just the construction of wills, but rather the scope is the construction of wills, trusts, and other testamentary instruments.

B. **Admissibility—validity vs. construction:** The key to analyzing whether extrinsic evidence should be admitted is to ask *why* the extrinsic evidence is being offered. If it is being offered to help determine the validity of a will (whether it was properly executed, whether the decedent had the requisite testamentary capacity, whether the decedent suffered from a defect in capacity, whether the will was properly revoked, and so on), the extrinsic evidence is admissible. If, however, the extrinsic evidence is being offered to help construe an admittedly valid will, the courts are reluctant to admit such evidence absent an ambiguity.

Example: In *Fleming v. Morrison,* 72 N.E. 499 (Mass. 1904), Francis Butterfield properly executed a document that purported to be his will, leaving all of his property to Mary Fleming. At the time Francis executed the document, he told his attorney that the document was a "fake" made to induce Ms. Fleming to sleep with him. Although the document was clear on its face, the court admitted the offered extrinsic evidence because it went to the validity of the will—that Francis never intended the document to be his will and thus the document lacked testamentary intent.

C. Common law: At common law, courts are very reluctant to admit extrinsic evidence to help construe a will. To the extent the testator had gone to all the trouble and expense of executing a will, the will arguably constitutes the best evidence of testator's intent.

> **Policy considerations:** The common law position was that once the testator had properly executed a will, the court's job is to protect that intent. Admitting extrinsic evidence only increases the potential for fraudulent claims and increases the costs of administration.

D. Plain meaning rule: The common law bias against admitting extrinsic evidence manifests itself in the plain meaning rule: in construing and giving effect to a will, the words used in the will should be given their plain meaning. As a general rule, extrinsic evidence is not admissible to show that the testator used the words to mean something other than their plain meaning. Extrinsic evidence is admissible to help construe a word or phrase in a will if there is an ambiguity.

  1. Majority approach: Although the plain meaning rule is coming under increasing criticism, and there is a modern trend approach that rejects it, the plain meaning rule remains the majority approach.

  2. Example: In *Mahoney v. Grainger,* 186 N.E. 86 (Mass. 1933), the testatrix instructed her attorney that she wanted to leave the residue of her estate to her 25 or so first cousins equally. She told her attorney her first cousins were her nearest relatives. In fact, her maternal aunt was her nearest relative. Rather than naming each of the testatrix's first cousins by name, the attorney drafted the testatrix's will so that it left the residue of her estate to her "heirs at law," thinking that the first cousins would take as the nearest relatives. The testatrix properly executed the will. Following the testatrix's death, the maternal aunt claimed the residue as the nearest heir at law. The first cousins offered extrinsic evidence to show that the testatrix intended that the residue was to go to the first cousins. The court applied the plain meaning rule and found that the phrase *heirs at law* was not ambiguous. The extrinsic evidence was not admissible to establish a meaning for the phrase *heirs at law* that was inconsistent with the plain meaning of that phrase.

    a. Criticism: The assumption underlying the plain meaning rule is that the meaning a reader attributes to a word is the same meaning the testator attributed to the word. Moreover, if the meaning the reader attributes to the word is different from the meaning the testator attributed to the word, the plain meaning rule means that the reader's meaning trumps. Inasmuch as the testator wrote the will and probate is about determining and giving effect to the testator's intent, the testator's meaning arguably should control, not the reader's construction.

    b. Counterargument: Admitting extrinsic evidence opens the estate to fraudulent claims and increases costs of administration (increased litigation).

  3. Personal usage exception: If the testator has always referred to a person by a name other than the person's true name (for example, by a nickname), and the testator uses that name in the will, courts take extrinsic evidence to show that the testator always called the person by that name and to show that the person called by the nickname is the person who is supposed to take the gift, not the person whose true name actually matches the name used in the will (assuming someone else has that name).

E. Patent vs. latent ambiguity: At common law, the courts admit extrinsic evidence to help construe a latent ambiguity, but not to help construe a patent ambiguity.

1. **Patent ambiguity:** A patent ambiguity is an ambiguity that is apparent from the face of the will. It is apparent from the four corners of the will; no extrinsic evidence is necessary to realize that there is an ambiguity.

2. **Extrinsic evidence:** At common law, if an ambiguity is a patent ambiguity, extrinsic evidence is not admissible to help construe the ambiguity.

3. **Latent ambiguity:** A latent ambiguity is an ambiguity that is not apparent from the face of the will. Recourse to circumstances outside of the will is necessary to realize that there is an ambiguity. Often the latent ambiguity does not become apparent until the court attempts to give effect to the decedent's will and to determine who is to take what.

4. **Extrinsic evidence:** The very nature of a latent ambiguity is such that extrinsic evidence is necessary to establish the ambiguity. At common law, the courts admit extrinsic evidence to both establish and to help construe a latent ambiguity.

5. **Construing vs. rewriting:** Although a court takes extrinsic evidence to establish and help construe a latent ambiguity, as a general rule courts do not add words to a will or "rewrite" the will. The courts draw a subtle but very important distinction between construing wills and rewriting wills. As long as the extrinsic evidence clarifies the express language in the will, the extrinsic evidence is admissible and the court uses it to help it construe the ambiguity in the will. If, however, the extrinsic evidence is inconsistent with the language in the will or requires the court to add words to the will or rewrite the will, the court does not admit the extrinsic evidence. If the ambiguity cannot be resolved, the gift fails.

6. **Latent ambiguity doctrines:** A number of latent ambiguity scenarios arose with such frequency that specific ambiguity doctrines were developed to deal with them.

   a. **Equivocation:** An equivocation is where the language in the will fits more than one object or person equally well. The court takes extrinsic evidence to determine which of the objects or people was the intended object or person.

      Example: Professor's will provides as follows: "I leave $1,000 to my favorite research assistant, Mr. Brown." During the course of his teaching career, the professor had two research assistants named Mr. Brown. The court will take extrinsic evidence to determine which Mr. Brown was the intended beneficiary. Resolving which Mr. Brown is the appropriate recipient does not require the court to add any words to the will, only to construe the ambiguous identification that is express in the will.

   b. **Misdescription:** Misdescription arises where the description of an object or person in the will appears fine on the face of the will, but when the court goes to apply it, no object or person matches the exact description, but one exists that almost matches the description. The classic example of a misdescription is a typographical error when numbers or names get inverted.

      i. **Mechanics:** Consistent with the courts' general rule that they do not rewrite wills, courts take extrinsic evidence to establish the misdescription and to determine which words in the will to strike, but courts do not insert any words to correct the description. The court strikes the misdescription and then looks to see if the remaining words adequately describe the object or person so that the clause in the will can be given effect.

> **ii. Example:** The decedent's will reads, "I give my house at 432 Tuxedo Blvd. to my cousin Lisa." The decedent does not own the house at 432 Tuxedo; she owns the house at 234 Tuxedo Blvd. Applying the misdescription doctrine, the court takes the extrinsic evidence to establish the misdescription and strikes "432" from the will. The will then reads, "I give my house at Tuxedo Blvd. to Lisa." Which house on Tuxedo Blvd. becomes an ambiguity that the court takes extrinsic evidence to help resolve. Assuming the testator owned only one house on Tuxedo Blvd., that is an adequate description for the court to give effect to the gift.

c. Personal usage exception: One can argue that the personal usage exception is a form of a latent ambiguity. It is analogous to an equivocation except that the court treats the personal usage that the testator gave to the object or person as equal to the proper name of the object or person.

F. Modern trend—migrating toward reformation: The modern trend is much more open to trying to ascertain and give effect to the testator's intent. Accordingly, it repudiates a number of the common law doctrines.

1. Plain meaning rule repudiated: The modern trend repudiates the plain meaning rule. The modern trend considers extrinsic evidence of the circumstances surrounding the testator at the time he or she executed the will in analyzing what the testator's intent was when he or she executed the will and whether there is an ambiguity in the will.

2. Latent vs. patent repudiated: The modern trend also repudiates the patent vs. latent distinction, admitting extrinsic evidence anytime there is an ambiguity.

3. Correcting mistakes: Increasingly courts are admitting extrinsic evidence not only to resolve ambiguities but to correct mistakes in light of the testator's true intent—to reform the will.

4. Arguments supporting reformation: Several arguments have been advanced in support of the modern trend approach migrating toward reformation.

a. Theoretical argument: For years academics have argued that it was incongruous to distinguish intentional wrongdoing (undue influence, fraud, duress) from mistakes (unintentional acts). In both cases, the effect of the action is to frustrate the testator's intent. But if the third party intentionally committed the act in question, the courts will admit extrinsic evidence to prove the wrongdoing and impose a constructive trust to correct it; if the third party merely negligently committed the act, the courts will fail to correct the mistake and leave the frustrated beneficiaries to sue for malpractice. To the extent the two scenarios are functionally equivalent, they should be treated the same. The courts should take extrinsic evidence and come to the aid of the testator's intent in both situations.

b. Testator's intent: While there is a risk that admitting extrinsic evidence may undermine the testator's intent if fraudulent claims are brought, excluding extrinsic evidence may undermine the testator's intent if the document as offered for probate does not accurately reflect the testator's intent due to a mistake.

c. Will execution: When a testator validly executes a will, it creates a strong presumption that the will accurately reflects the testator's testamentary intent. The presumption, however, is rebuttable. If there is clear and convincing evidence of a mistake, and clear and convincing evidence of its effect upon the testator's true intent, extrinsic evidence should be admissible to overcome the presumption and to reform the will accordingly.

    d. Potential for litigation: In contract law, the parol evidence rule has undergone considerable erosion without a resulting proliferation of groundless litigation. There is no reason to believe the effect of adopting the reformation doctrine will be any different. Moreover, by requiring clear and convincing evidence of both the mistake and its effect upon the testator's intent, the high threshold should help to control any potential increase in the number of will contests.

5. Example: In *Arnheiter v. Arnheiter*, 125 A.2d 914 (N.J. Super. 1956), the testatrix's will directed her executor to sell her interest in "304 Harrison Avenue" and to use the proceeds to establish trusts for her nieces. But the testatrix did not own any interest in 304 Harrison Avenue either at the time the will was executed or at her death. At the time she executed the will and at her death, she owned a one-half interest in 317 Harrison Avenue. The court applied the misdescription doctrine, admitting extrinsic evidence to establish the misdescription, striking the misdescription, and then construing the ambiguity as referring to the only property on Harrison Avenue in which she had an interest—317 Harrison Avenue.

6. Scrivener's error doctrine: Where there is clear and convincing evidence that there was a scrivener's error, and clear and convincing evidence of its effect upon the testator's intent, extrinsic evidence is admissible to establish and correct the mistake. The doctrine of scrivener's error is a new doctrine that was adopted for the first time in 1998 in the *Erickson* case.

    a. Example: In *Erickson v. Erickson,* 716 A.2d 92 (Conn. 1998), the testator executed a will leaving the residue of his estate to Dorothy, and two days later he married her. Under the state's laws, however, if after making a will a testator gets married, the marriage automatically revokes the will unless the will expressly provides for the marriage. The testator died without changing his will, and his children from his first marriage invoked the statute to void the will, thereby taking a share of his estate through intestacy. Dorothy, the testator's wife, offered extrinsic evidence to establish the attorneys erred in having the will executed two days before the marriage and not expressly acknowledging the impending wedding in the will. The testator's children opposed admission of the evidence on the grounds that there was no ambiguity in the will. The court adopted the scrivener's error doctrine, ruling that if there is clear and convincing evidence of the scrivener's error and clear and convincing evidence of its effect upon the testator's intent, the evidence should be admitted.

    b. Scope: The *Erickson* case arguably raises more questions about the scope of the doctrine than it answers. Is the case an aberration or the wave of the future? Is the doctrine limited to cases involving the validity of the instrument, or does it also apply to construction cases? Is the doctrine limited to situations where it can be applied without rewriting the will, or will it open the doors to courts rewriting wills to correct scrivener's error? Will the doctrine be applied only to instruments that were validly executed but are invalid for other reasons, or will it also be applied to wills that were not validly executed because of the scrivener's error? Will the doctrine be limited to situations where the scrivener is an attorney, or will it apply regardless of who the scrivener is (for example, the writer of a holographic will)?

7. Other examples of reformation: Although the cases are fairly isolated, a handful of cases have ignored the traditional rule that courts do not correct mistakes and have corrected drafting mistakes by attorneys. Most have done so simply based on the equities of the case and the evidence of the mistake, without articulating a broad doctrine to explain or justify their actions. An exception is the doctrine of probable intent adopted by New Jersey.

Probable intent: The doctrine of probable intent provides that if an unforeseen change in circumstances occurs after a will is executed that is not provided for in the will, and the unforeseen change materially frustrates the testator's intent as expressed in the will, the court takes extrinsic evidence of the circumstances surrounding the testator, with particular attention being paid to family considerations. The court puts itself in the testator's situation and decides what it thinks the testator probably would have done under the circumstances. (The doctrine is similar to cy pres, a well-established charitable trust doctrine covered in Chapter 12 concerning modification of trusts.)

8. **Restatement (Third) adopts reformation:** The Restatement (Third) of Property, Donative Transfers, authorizes courts to reform any donative document, even where there is no ambiguity, to conform to the donor's intent if there is clear and convincing evidence (1) that a mistake of fact or law affected the specific terms of the document, and (2) of the donor's intent. Restatement (Third) of Property, Donative Transfers §12.1. The language of the Restatement (Third) arguably includes wills, trusts, and other testamentary instruments. How the Restatement (Third) provision will be received is yet to be determined.

II. CHANGES IN THE BENEFICIARY

A. **Survival requirement:** All jurisdictions require that anyone taking from a decedent must survive the decedent. This default rule is true whether the decedent dies testate or intestate. Where a will exists, however, the will may expressly opt out of the survival requirement and permit the beneficiary to take even if he or she predeceases the testator.

   1. **Common law:** At common law, a beneficiary under a will has to prove by only a preponderance of the evidence that he or she survived the decedent by a millisecond.

   2. **Modern trend/UPC approach:** Under the modern trend/UPC approach, a beneficiary under a will or trust must prove by clear and convincing evidence that he or she survived the decedent by a millisecond.

   3. **Transferor's intent:** Whatever approach the jurisdiction takes to the survival requirement, that approach is a default standard. If the will expressly imposes a longer survival requirement, the beneficiary must prove that he or she meets the survival requirement imposed by the express terms of the will.

B. **Lapse:** If a beneficiary fails to survive the testator, the gift is said to lapse. A lapsed gift fails.

   1. **Rationale:** It is presumed that the testator intended the beneficiary personally to benefit from the gift. If the beneficiary predeceases the testator and there is no lapse doctrine, the gift passes to the beneficiary's estate to be distributed either to a beneficiary under the predeceased beneficiary's will or to the predeceased beneficiary's heirs—neither of whom the original testator may have met. The reasonable presumption is that if the named beneficiary predeceases the testator, the testator would prefer that the gift be revoked.

   2. **Void gift:** A gift is void if the beneficiary is dead when the will is executed; a gift lapses if a beneficiary is alive when the will is executed, but dies before the testator. A void gift is treated the same as a lapsed gift for most purposes under the modern trend.

C. **Failed/void gift—default takers:** A gift may fail for a variety of reasons: it may be void, it may lapse, the gift may be to an ineligible taker (pets are not eligible takers, so all gifts to pets fail), or the gift may violate the Rule against Perpetuities. Whatever the reason, if a gift fails and it is not "saved," it falls in a cascading scheme.

1. **Specific gifts:** If a specific gift fails, it falls to the residuary clause, if there is one, or otherwise to intestacy.

2. **General gifts:** If a general gift fails, it falls to the residuary clause, if there is one, or otherwise to intestacy.

3. **Residuary gift:** If a residuary gift fails **completely,** it falls to intestacy.

4. **Part of residuary gift:** If there are multiple takers in the residuary clause, and the gift fails as to one or more of them but not as to all of them, the jurisdictions are split as to what happens to the part of the residuary clause that fails.

    a. **Common law:** Under the "no residue of a residue" rule, if part of the residuary clause failed, that part falls to intestacy.

        Rationale: The common law visualizes the residuary clause as a safety net. If a specific gift or general gift fails, it falls, and the residuary clause is there to catch it. If the residuary clause fails, however, there is no safety net below the residue; it falls to intestacy. If only part of the residuary clause fails, there is still no safety net below it. If part of the residuary fails, that part falls to intestacy.

    b. **Example:** In *Estate of Russell,* 444 P.2d 353 (Cal. 1968), the testator's valid holographic will provided in pertinent part as follows: "I leave everything I own Real & Personal to Chester H. Quinn & Roxy Russell." The testator's heirs offered extrinsic evidence to prove that Roxy Russell was a dog. The court ruled that the fact that Roxy Russell was a dog was a latent ambiguity, and extrinsic evidence was admissible to establish that fact. Dogs, however, are not eligible beneficiaries, so the gift to Roxy failed. The gift to Roxy was in the residuary clause. The court applied the "no residue of a residue" rule and held that Roxy's half fell to intestacy to the testator's heirs.

        Court's treatment of admissibility of extrinsic evidence: Many would argue that the court's treatment of the admissibility of extrinsic evidence constitutes the majority modern trend approach. The court repudiated the plain meaning rule and the patent-latent distinction and ruled that extrinsic evidence is admissible to help construe a will anytime there is an ambiguity. An ambiguity is any express language in a will that is reasonably susceptible to two or more interpretations. Just because an ambiguity exists in the will, not all extrinsic evidence is admissible. Only extrinsic evidence that is consistent with one of the possible reasonable interpretations of the ambiguity is admissible. The court held that the express words of the will were not reasonably susceptible to the interpretation that Chester's extrinsic evidence attempted to put on them and that the extrinsic evidence in question should not have been admitted.

    c. **Modern trend/UPC approach:** The modern trend reasons that if the testator included a residuary clause, the testator's intent was for **all** of the testator's property to pass via the will and for nothing to pass through intestacy. As long as any part of the residuary clause is valid, that part catches whichever part of the residuary clause fails.

> **Rule statement:** If part of the residuary clause fails, the other part catches it. The part that fails is distributed among the other beneficiaries in the residuary clause. UPC §2-604(b).

5. **Saving failed gifts:** Two principal doctrines are used to try to save a failed gift: the anti-lapse doctrine and the class gift doctrine.

D. **Anti-lapse statutes:** The presumption that the testator would prefer that the gift fail where the beneficiary predeceases the testator arguably does not apply where the beneficiary is sufficiently related to the testator and the beneficiary has issue who survive the testator. In that situation, anti-lapse statutes presume that the testator would prefer that the gift go to the predeceased beneficiary's issue rather than fail. The presumption can be rebutted, but only by an express contrary intent expressed in the will. Virtually all states have adopted the anti-lapse doctrine statutorily, but the details of the statutes vary greatly from state to state, as discussed below.

1. **Basic rule statement:** Anti-lapse statutes provide that (1) where there is a lapse, and (2) the predeceased beneficiary meets the statutory degree of relationship to the testator, and (3) the predeceased beneficiary has issue who survive the testator, the lapsed gift goes to the issue of the predeceased beneficiary (4) unless the will expresses a contrary intent. UPC §2-605 (1969).

    UPC rule statement: The UPC drafters have adopted several different versions of the anti-lapse doctrine, the most recent of which is extremely complicated and not well received to date. The UPC discussion below focuses on the 1969 version. It is widely adopted and representative of what most states are doing.

2. **Lapse requirement:** While the basic lapse doctrine arose to cover scenarios where the beneficiary *actually* predeceased the decedent, it has been expanded to cover scenarios where the beneficiary *is treated as* predeceasing the decedent: if the beneficiary disclaims the interest, if the will has an express survival requirement that the beneficiary fails to meet, if the beneficiary feloniously and intentionally kills the testator, etc.

    a. **Common law:** As originally developed, the anti-lapse doctrine applies to lapsed gifts only, not to void gifts.

    b. **Modern trend/UPC approach:** The modern trend/UPC approach is to apply the anti-lapse doctrine to any qualifying beneficiary who predeceases the testator regardless of whether the beneficiary dies before or after execution of the will. UPC §2-605 (1969).

3. **Requisite degree of relationship:** Although virtually all states have adopted the anti-lapse doctrine, the scope of the doctrine varies from state to state depending on how closely related the predeceased beneficiary has to be to the testator. Some states limit the doctrine to devises to beneficiaries who are descendants of the testator, while other states define the requisite degree of relationship broadly to include a much larger pool of beneficiaries. (California, for example, includes any beneficiary who is related to the testator or the testator's spouse, current or former.) Careful attention must be paid to the degree of relationship required by each statutory articulation of the doctrine.

    UPC: The UPC requires that the predeceased beneficiary be a grandparent or a lineal descendant of a grandparent to qualify for the anti-lapse doctrine. UPC §2-605 (1969). A 1990 amendment expanded the scope of predeceased beneficiaries covered to include stepchildren.

4. **Survived by issue:** The predeceased beneficiary must have issue who survive not only the predeceased beneficiary, but also the testator. The UPC requires that the issue survive the testator by 120 hours. UPC §2-605 (1969).

5. **Contrary intent:** The anti-lapse doctrine is based on presumed intent. If the beneficiary is related closely enough to the testator and is survived by issue, the testator is presumed to have preferred that the gift go to the issue of the predeceased beneficiary rather than fail. This presumption is a rebuttable presumption, but the contrary intent *must be expressed in the will* under most anti-lapse statutes.

   a. **Low threshold:** Most courts and/or statutes have created a very low threshold for what constitutes an express contrary intent. The general rule is that (1) *any* express words of survival or (2) any express gift-over in the will to another beneficiary in the event of the first beneficiary's death constitutes a sufficient "express contrary intent" to bar application of the anti-lapse doctrine.

   b. **Criticism:** Increasingly wills are boilerplate documents. The boilerplate language typically includes an express survival requirement: "[T]o, if he/she survives me." If the express survival requirement is simply part of the drafting lawyer's form will, it arguably should not be sufficient to bar anti-lapse. The testator did not expressly request the language, and even if the testator read the will before executing it, the average testator has no idea that the express survival requirement has the effect of knocking out the anti-lapse doctrine.

   c. **UPC:** The 1990 version of the UPC agrees with the criticism of the general rule and provides that mere words of survival ("if he survives me" or "my surviving issue"), without more, are not sufficient to constitute an express contrary intent barring application of anti-lapse. UPC §2-603(b)(3) (1990).

      Criticism: The 1990 version of the UPC has been heavily criticized by commentators and practicing attorneys alike for imposing the UPC's presumptions as to what an individual would want over the express words of the testator's own will, thereby exposing practicing attorneys to an increased potential for malpractice claims when drafting such clauses.

   d. **Example:** In *Ruotolo v. Tietjen,* 890 A.2d 166 (Conn. App. 2006), the testator devised half of his property "to Hazel Brennan of . . . , if she survives me." Hazel was his stepdaughter, a beneficiary covered by the state anti-lapse statute. She died 17 days before the testator, survived by a daughter. The issue was whether the language "if she survives me" constituted an express contrary intent to the application of anti-lapse. The court reasoned that anti-lapse was adopted to overcome the harsh effects of lapse and therefore should be applied broadly and liberally, placing on those who oppose such application the burden of proving a contrary intent. The court expressed concern that such language is merely boilerplate language in many wills, that there was no express gift-over in the event the beneficiary predeceased, and the effect under the facts of the case would be the gift would pass through intestacy (in contrast to the constructional preference for avoiding intestacy). The court adopted the UPC approach and held that the bare words of survivorship are not sufficient, standing alone, to constitute an express contrary intent.

6. **Scope:** The traditional and still majority approach applies the lapse and anti-lapse doctrines to wills only. Under the modern trend, however, a few states have statutes that apply the doctrines to most of the will substitutes—trusts, insurance policies, and contracts with payable-on-death clauses generally, but not joint tenancies.

7. Spouses: The general rule (and UPC approach) is that anti-lapse does ***not*** apply to spouses.

    a. Rationale: One possible reason spouses are excluded is that although the norm is for the issue of the predeceased spouse to also be the issue of the testator, this is not always the case.

        Worst case scenario: The norm is for the gift to a spouse to be the residuary clause. If the spouse predeceases, the gift lapses and fails. If a residuary clause fails, the gift falls to intestacy where the ***testator's issue*** take. On the other hand, if anti-lapse applies to spouses and the spouse predeceases, the ***spouse's issue*** take the residuary gift. Where all of the issue are the issue of both spouses, the ultimate takers are the same regardless of whether anti-lapse applies. Where, however, the predeceased spouse has issue who are not issue of the testator, the predeceased spouse's issue take to the exclusion of the testator's issue. That result arguably is even more illogical than not applying anti-lapse to spouses.

    b. Example: In ***Jackson v. Schultz,*** 151 A.2d 284 (Del. Ch. 1959), the testator's will devised all of his property to his wife, Bessie—"to her and her heirs and assigns forever." Bessie died, survived by issue, none of whom were issue of the testator. Thereafter the testator died with no known surviving relatives. Although the state's anti-lapse doctrine did not cover spouses, the court reasoned that the words ***and*** and ***or*** are interchangeable when construing wills. Rather than the testator's will devising his property to "Bessie ***and*** her heirs" (which is classic drafting language to indicate that Bessie took a fee simple absolute but no interest passes to her heirs), the court construed the express language of the will to read "to Bessie ***or*** her heirs" (thereby giving Bessie's heirs a gift-over in the event Bessie predeceased the testator). The court's construction had the same effect as applying anti-lapse to Bessie.

        Commentary: The court's opinion has been heavily criticized and not followed. If the court had not held as it did, the testator's property would have escheated to the state under intestacy. One way to view the opinion is that it shows how far some courts will go to prevent the state from taking property under intestacy. It should also be noticed that the action was one for specific performance. Bessie's children had entered into a contract to sell some of the testator's real property, and the purchasers apparently had balked when they realized that there were serious doubts as to the quality of the children's title. The real party in interest, the state, was not even a party to the action.

    c. "Residue of the residue" overlap: The modern trend "residue of the residue" rule can cause trouble when overlapped with the general anti-lapse rule. If the residuary clause is to multiple beneficiaries, and one of the beneficiaries is the testator's spouse, if the spouse predeceases the testator, the gift to the spouse lapses. Assuming the spouse is not covered by the anti-lapse rule, the gift fails. Under the common law "no residue of a residue" rule, the predeceased spouse's share of the residuary clause falls to intestacy where the testator's heirs take the gift. But under the modern trend "residue of the residue" rule, the predeceased spouse's share passes to the other residuary takers. This scenario highlights the risk of not covering spouses in the anti-lapse doctrine.

E. Class gift: A class gift is a gift to more than one individual that intrinsically includes a right of survivorship. The right of survivorship means that if the gift fails as to one member of the class, his or her share does not "fall" out of the class, but rather the failed share is re-divided among the other members of the class. The shares of the surviving members of the class are recalculated.

1. **Transferor's intent:** Whether a gift to multiple individuals is a class gift with a built-in right of survivorship or just a gift to multiple individuals is determined by testator's intent. Ideally, the testator indicates clearly whether he or she intends the gift to multiple individuals to be a class gift. Unfortunately, quite often the will is ambiguous. Courts admit extrinsic evidence to help in their analysis.

2. **Analysis:** Where it is not clear whether the testator intended a gift to multiple individuals to be a class gift, courts typically look to four factors to help construe testator's intent: (1) How did the testator describe the beneficiaries? (2) How did the testator describe the gift? (3) Do the beneficiaries share a common characteristic? (4) What is the testator's overall testamentary scheme?

   a. **Description of beneficiaries:** Typically a gift to multiple beneficiaries refers to them either collectively (as a group) or individually by name. Where the reference is to the beneficiaries collectively, that argues in favor of finding that the testator intended the gift to be to a class gift. Where the testator identifies each of the beneficiaries by name, that argues against finding that the testator intended the gift to be a class gift.

   b. **Description of gift:** Typically a gift to multiple beneficiaries describes the gift either in the aggregate or in separate shares. Where the gift is described in the aggregate, that argues in favor of finding that the testator intended the gift to be a class gift. Where the gift is described in distinct shares, that argues against the finding that the testator intended the gift to be a class gift.

   c. **Common characteristic:** Intrinsic to the notion of a class gift is that there is something special about those individuals that separates them from other individuals—that they share a common characteristic that distinguishes them and separates them from everyone else. If they all share a common characteristic, that argues in favor of finding that the testator intended the gift to be a class gift. If there is no common characteristic, that argues against finding that the testator intended the gift to be a class gift.

      Prevalence: Even where there is a common characteristic, if there are others who share the same common characteristic and they are not included in the gift, some courts have concluded that their exclusion from the gift cuts against a finding that the testator intended the gift to be a class gift.

   d. **Overall testamentary scheme:** This factor asks whether, in light of everything else the testator tried to do with his or her property, it makes more sense to apply a right of survivorship to the gift (that is, to find that the gift is a class gift). This factor is extremely fact sensitive. The court has to take the totality of the testator's testamentary scheme into consideration. Sometimes this factor sheds no insight into the testator's possible intent with respect to the specific gift in question. But two aspects of the testator's estate plan should be examined in particular under this factor.

      i. **Express right of survivorship:** A number of courts have held that if there is a gift in the will to multiple individuals that has an express right of survivorship in the gift, the failure to include an express right of survivorship in another gift to multiple individuals indicates that the testator did not intend for the latter gift to be a class gift. The counterargument, however, is that the testator thought it so obvious that the latter gift was a class gift that he or she thought there was no need to include an express right of survivorship.

ii. **Alternative takers:** It is always important to determine who would take the failed gift if it were not a class gift. Once that is determined, the courts analyze whether there is anything about the testator's overall testamentary scheme that indicates that the testator would not want that person to take the property in question. If so, that argues in favor of finding that the testator intended the gift to be a class gift.

3. **Factors, not requirements:** The four factors the courts focus on are only factors. All four do not have to be satisfied for the court to conclude that the testator intended the gift to be a class gift. The more factors that cut in favor of finding that the testator intended a class gift, the better. But in the end, it is a question of testator's intent, and the factors are relevant only to the extent they shed light on that issue. Whether a gift to multiple individuals is a class gift is usually very fact sensitive, and the outcome is often difficult to predict.

4. **Restatement (Third):** The Restatement (Third) of Property, Donative Transfers, focuses on how the beneficiaries are described. If the gift describes the beneficiaries (1) only by a group label, a rebuttable presumption arises that the gift is a class gift; (2) only by name, the gift is not a class gift; and (3) by both a group label and individual names (or the number of beneficiaries), a rebuttable presumption arises that the gift is not a class gift. The rebuttable presumption may be rebutted by language in the instrument or circumstances indicating the testator intended a class gift.

5. **Example:** In *Dawson v. Yucus,* 239 N.E.2d 305 (Ill. App. 1968), clause two of testatrix's will stated that she wanted the one-fifth interest in a farm, which she inherited when her husband died, to revert to his side of the family. To such end, she devised her interest in the farm one-half to Stewart Wilson and one-half to Gene Burtle, both nephews on her husband's side of the family. She gave the residue of her estate to her friends Ina Mae Yucus and Hazel Degelow, or to the survivor or survivors of them, should either predecease her. Gene Burtle predeceased the testatrix. Anti-lapse did not apply because the state required the predeceased beneficiary to be a descendant. The issue was whether the gift was a class gift. The gift described the two nephews by name, not collectively, which cut against a class gift. The gift to the nephews was made in separate shares, not collectively, which cut against a class gift. The two beneficiaries shared a common characteristic, nephews on the husband's side of the family, but there were other nieces and nephews on his side of the family that were not included. Lastly, the last clause of the testatrix's will was to more than one individual, and it contained an express right of survivorship. The court reasoned that where the testatrix wanted a right of survivorship, she showed that she knew how to create one. The absence of one in the gift of the farm cut against finding that she intended a class gift. Despite the express statement that the testatrix wanted her interest in the farm to return to her husband's side of the family, the court held that the gift of the farm to the two nephews was not a class gift. The gift to Gene lapsed and fell to the residue.

6. **Anti-lapse and class gifts:** Both anti-lapse and the class gift doctrine can be applied to save a lapsed gift to a class member, but the doctrines save the gift in favor of different takers. With anti-lapse, the saved gift goes to the issue of the predeceased beneficiary. With the class gift doctrine, the saved gift goes to the other members of the class. The overwhelming majority of states and the UPC apply anti-lapse first to class gifts. UPC §2-605 (1969). If anti-lapse cannot save the gift, then apply the class gift doctrine.

Exception for void gifts: A number of states do not apply anti-lapse to class gifts where a member of the class is dead at the time the will is executed (some apply the exception only if the testator also knows the party is dead when the will is executed).

III. CHANGES IN TESTATOR'S PROPERTY

A. **Introduction:** A will is executed inter vivos but does not take effect until the testator dies. In between, changes in the testator's property can create a number of construction issues. Most of the doctrines that have developed to deal with the more common scenarios turn on the type of gift involved.

1. **Characterization of gift:** A testator can make three basic types of gifts: a specific gift, a general gift, or a residuary gift. Which type of gift a devise is, ultimately, is a question of testator's intent. The issue is often very fact sensitive and open to debate. Nevertheless, there are fairly well-accepted definitions for the different types of gifts that reduce the debate over the characterization of most gifts.

2. **Specific gifts:** A specific gift is a gift where the testator has a specific item in mind when he or she makes the gift, typically an item that he or she currently owns. The testator intends for that specific item, and arguably only that specific item, to satisfy the gift. Almost invariably the gift is modified by the word *my*.

    Example: If the will says, "I give my car to Alice," the gift is construed as a specific gift of the car that the testator owned when he or she executed the will.

3. **General gifts:** A general gift is a gift of a general pecuniary value that is satisfied by using *any item* that fits the description of the gift.

    a. **Example:** The classic example of a general gift is a gift of money. If the will says, "I give $1,000 to Bill," the gift is construed as a general gift. The testator is making a pecuniary gift of $1,000. Any $1,000 will do—no specific bills were intended. A general gift is measured by any means the testator selects. For example, if the will says, "I give a 1995 Saturn GLS to Cindy," that gift would probably be construed as a general gift. If the testator owns a 1995 Saturn GLS when he or she dies, that car is used to satisfy the gift. If the testator does not have an item that matches a general gift in his or her estate at the time of his or her death, the executor has a legal duty to purchase an item that matches the general gift and give it to the beneficiary.

    b. **Demonstrative gifts:** Demonstrative gifts are general gifts from a specific source, for example, if the wills says, "I give Dave $1,000 from my checking account at Wagon Wheel Bank." The gift starts out looking like a general gift ($1,000), but then it looks like a specific gift ("from *my* checking account at Wagon Wheel Bank"). Demonstrative gifts are classified as a subset of general gifts and are treated as a general gift for construction purposes.

4. **Residuary gifts:** A residuary gift is a gift that gives away all of the testator's property that has not otherwise been given away. The classic example of a residuary gift is, "I give the rest, residue, and remainder of my property to Elaine." While that is the classic way to state a

residuary gift, no magic words are necessary. Any clause that gives away all the testator's property except whatever was given away specifically or generally is a residuary gift ("I give all of my property to Bob").

B. Ademption: The most common construction issue concerning the testator's property arises when the testator makes a specific gift in his or her will and thereafter the item in question is transferred. The issue is what, if anything, should the beneficiary take?

    1. Common law/identity approach: The common law doctrine of ademption states that where the testator makes a specific gift, and thereafter the specific item that is the subject of the specific gift is transferred, an irrebuttable presumption arises that the testator intended to revoke the gift.

        a. Identity approach: Under the traditional identity approach to ademption, if the will makes a specific gift, the executor is to go through the testator's probate estate to see if he or she can "identify" that item in the estate. If he or she can, the beneficiary takes the item. If the executor cannot find the item, the gift is adeemed (revoked), and the court will not take any extrinsic evidence as to why the item cannot be found or what was (or might have been) the testator's intent with respect to the item.

        b. Voluntary vs. involuntary transfer: Under the identity approach, it does not matter why the property that was the subject of the specific gift is no longer in the testator's probate estate. Where the testator voluntarily transfers the item, knowing that it is the subject of a specific gift in his or her will, the presumption that the testator intended to revoke the gift arguably makes sense. But if the item was involuntarily transferred (stolen or destroyed accidentally), the identity approach arguably is unreasonable; nevertheless, it is efficient.

        c. Efficiency vs. intent: The traditional identity approach arguably exalts efficiency over the testator's intent. The concern is that opening up the probate process to self-serving extrinsic evidence as to what the testator allegedly intended every time property that is subject to a specific gift is transferred would increase costs of administration and increase the potential for fraudulent claims. The identity approach to ademption might be harsh, but the bright line rule is easy to apply and puts the burden on the testators to revise their wills if they transfer a specific gift but want the beneficiary still to take a gift.

        d. General rule: The identity approach to the doctrine of ademption is the traditional and still majority approach to the doctrine.

        Incomplete disposal: Remember, if any part of the specific gift remains in the testator's estate when the testator dies, the beneficiary is entitled to receive whatever is left of the specific gift.

    2. Modern trend/judicial "modified intent" approach: Some states have adopted a "modified intent" approach to ademption. Under this approach, the jurisdiction still follows the identity approach but exempts property that was transferred through an act that is involuntary as to the testator, and/or that was made without the testator's knowledge and consent. The beneficiary of the gift gets either the full pecuniary value of the gift, or whatever is left of it minus proceeds that were used to support the testator, depending on the jurisdiction.

        Example: In *In re Estate of Anton*, 731 N.W.2d 19 (2007), Gretchen Coy deeded a piece of real estate to her father (Herbert Anton) and stepmother (Mary Anton), who built a duplex on the property. After Herbert's death, Mary became the sole owner. She executed a deed that devised half of it to her stepdaughter Gretchen and the other half to her son Robert. Thereafter, Mary was in a bad accident, her health deteriorated, and she was placed in a nursing home. Mary executed a durable power of attorney authorizing her daughter Nancy to run her affairs. Nancy tried to hold off selling the duplex, but after depleting almost all of Mary's other assets, and unable to secure a loan, she sold the duplex for $133,263 to help cover Mary's living expenses. When Mary died the remaining balance was $104,317. The court acknowledged that although Iowa historically followed the identity approach to ademption, more recently it had adopted a "modified intention" approach to exclude transfers through an act that is involuntary as to the testator. Under that approach, Iowa courts had recognized exceptions to ademption where (1) the sale was by a guardian or conservator without the knowledge and consent of an incompetent testator; or (2) the property was destroyed contemporaneous with the testator's death. The court extended the modified intention approach to include transfers by an attorney-in-fact without the knowledge of the testator. The court ruled, however, that where the proceeds are used for the testator's support, the beneficiary is entitled to only half of the remaining proceeds.

C. **Avoidance/softening doctrines to identity approach:** Because ademption is such a harsh doctrine, courts have developed a number of avoidance and softening doctrines (varying from jurisdiction to jurisdiction) to justify not applying ademption where one might think it would otherwise apply.

   1. **Characterize gift as general, not specific:** The ademption doctrine applies only to specific gifts. Where the wording of a gift is ambiguous, if the beneficiary can convince the court that the gift is a general gift, the executor has a legal duty to go out and acquire the item to satisfy the gift, thereby avoiding ademption.

   2. **Change in form, not substance:** The "change in form, not substance" doctrine provides that if the item that is the subject of the specific gift is in the estate but has suffered a change that goes to its form, but not its substance, the court should give the beneficiary the item. This doctrine gives some flexibility to the ademption doctrine. If the change is not that significant, ademption should not apply because the item arguably is still in the estate. Moreover, where the change is merely one in form, not substance, the testator would not have thought it necessary to revise his or her will because he or she would have assumed that the "new" item was still the same old item subject to the specific gift.

      a. **Example:** Testatrix's will provides that she gives her "checking account at Megabank to Alice." Thereafter, testatrix grows tired of the endless fees at Megabank and moves the checking account to Wagon Wheel Bank where she gets truly free checking. When testatrix dies, Alice should take the checking account at Wagon Wheel Bank because moving the checking account from one bank to another is merely a change in form, not substance.

      b. **Example:** Testatrix's will provides that she gives her "checking account at Megabank to Alice." Thereafter, testatrix closes the checking account and puts all the funds into a certificate of deposit to get a better return on her money. If testatrix were to die without changing her will, most courts would hold that the gift is adeemed—the change is one of substance, not form.

   3. **Construe at time of death:** The general rule is that a will should be construed relative to the circumstances surrounding the testator at time of execution. If testator's will says, "I give my car to Alice," the gift is construed to be a specific gift of the car that testator owned at the time

he or she executed the will. If testator sold the car and purchased a new car, under a strict application of the ademption doctrine, the specific gift is adeemed. If, however, the beneficiary can persuade the court to construe the gift at time of death, the beneficiary would take the car that the testator owned at time of death.

Change in value: Courts are reluctant to construe the will at time of death if the effect is to give the beneficiary a gift that is worth substantially more.

4. **Fact-sensitive:** Each of the traditional avoidance doctrines is a very soft, fact-sensitive, judicial doctrine. If a court dislikes the ademption doctrine, the avoidance doctrines often are construed broadly to avoid application of the ademption doctrine. If a court likes the ademption doctrine, the avoidance doctrines often are construed narrowly to enforce the ademption doctrine.

5. **Conservatorship/Durable power of attorney exception:** Under the modern trend, states are increasingly providing by statute that if the property subject to the specific gift was transferred during conservatorship or by an agent acting under a durable power of attorney for an incapacitated principal, the ademption doctrine does not apply. The beneficiary receives the general pecuniary value of the specific gift. The exception applies whether the transfer by the agent/conservator was voluntary or involuntary.

   a. **Effect:** The effect of the exception for acts by conservators or agents acting under a durable power of attorney for an incapacitated principal is to convert all specific gifts into general gifts. The beneficiary is entitled to the general pecuniary value of the specific gift measured as of the moment it is transferred.

   b. **Rationale:** To the extent the identity approach to ademption is based on the rationale that it is better to put the burden on the testator to revise his or her will when a specific gift is transferred than to take extrinsic evidence on what the testator intended, the exception for transfers during conservatorship/agents acting for incapacitated principals implicitly recognizes that it is unfair to require a testator to revise his or her will under these circumstances. If a conservator has been appointed, or if an agent is acting under a durable power of attorney for an incapacitated principal, there is a strong probability that the testator lacks the requisite testamentary capacity to revise his or her will. Because the testator cannot revise his or her will to indicate what he or she intended, the benefit of the doubt goes to the beneficiary.

6. **Outstanding balance doctrine:** A softening doctrine to ademption provides that (1) if the item that is the subject of the specific gift is transferred, voluntarily (sale/gift) or involuntarily (fire, theft, and so on), and (2) when the testator dies, there is still an outstanding balance due the testator as a result of the transfer, then (3) the beneficiary of the specific gift that was adeemed takes the outstanding balance in lieu of the specific item.

7. **Jurisdictional differences:** The identity approach to the ademption doctrine represents the traditional and still majority approach to the doctrine. Not all states, however, have adopted all of the modern trend avoidance, exception, and softening doctrines. Careful attention needs to be paid to the law in each jurisdiction to determine the exact scope of the ademption doctrine and to determine which avoidance, exceptions, and softening doctrines the jurisdiction has adopted.

D. UPC/intent approach: The UPC rejects the identity approach to ademption and instead adopts the intent approach to ademption. It accepts extrinsic evidence on what the testator intended, or would have intended, as to the specific gift in question. In addition, the most recent version of the UPC adopts a replacement property doctrine, along with the other modern trend avoidance and softening doctrines. The net effect is to limit greatly the scope of the ademption doctrine to the point where it is arguably more likely that the specific gift will ***not*** be adeemed even where it cannot be found in the testator's estate at time of death. The comments to the UPC acknowledge this change when they state that the new version of the UPC creates a "mild presumption" against ademption.

1. **Replacement property exception:** The UPC expressly provides that where a testator owns property at death that was acquired to replace property that was a specific gift in his or her will, the beneficiary of the specific gift gets the replacement property. UPC §2-606(a)(5).

2. **Outstanding balance doctrine:** The UPC expressly adopts the outstanding balance doctrine. Whether the property is transferred voluntarily or involuntarily, if the testator is owed money at time of death as a result of the transfer of the property subject to the specific gift, the outstanding balance is given to the beneficiary of the specific gift. UPC §2-606(a)(1)-(3).

3. **Testator's intent approach:** If neither the replacement property doctrine nor the outstanding balance doctrine apply, the UPC provides that the beneficiary of the specific gift is entitled to money equal to the value of the specifically devised property as of the date of its disposition if the beneficiary can establish (a) ademption would be inconsistent with the testator's plan of distribution, or (b) that the testator did not intend for ademption to apply. UPC §2-606(a)(6).

4. **Conservatorship exception:** The UPC also adopts the modern trend exception that if the property subject to the specific gift was transferred during conservatorship or by an agent acting under a durable power of attorney for an incapacitated principal, the ademption doctrine does not apply. UPC §2-606(b).

5. **Extrinsic evidence:** With the adoption of the replacement property doctrine and the testator's intent doctrine, the UPC has opened the ademption doctrine up to extrinsic evidence to a much greater extent than the avoidance/exceptions/softening doctrines. These latter doctrines are much narrower in scope, and the nature of the evidence that would be relevant is much more in line with the traditional common law preference for "circumstances surrounding the testator"—evidence that is hard to fabricate.

   Public policy considerations: The UPC approach is willing to accept increased costs of administration and increased potential for fraud for the sake of trying to ascertain the testator's true intent. To date, not many jurisdictions have adopted the new version of the UPC.

E. Stocks: Gifts of stock are challenging because of the nature of stock. With most forms of property, the owner has exclusive control over the property so that any changes in the property are largely within the owner's control. With stock, that is not the case. The corporate entity, and even other corporate entities, can influence the stock owned by the testator through stock splits, stock dividends, mergers, acquisitions, and so on.

1. **Common law:** The traditional, common law approach focuses on whether the gift of stock is a specific or general gift. If the gift of stock is specific and the change is due to a stock split, the beneficiary takes the additional shares. If the gift of stock is a general gift, the beneficiary does not take the additional shares following a stock split.

2. **Modern trend:** The modern trend rejects the separate vs. general gift analysis, reasoning that even if the gift of stock is a general gift, the intent was to give a percentage interest in the company. The only way to give the intended percentage interest is to take into consideration stock splits and to give the beneficiary the increased number of shares to achieve the desired percentage interest in the company.

3. **UPC:** The UPC approach rejects the common law specific vs. general gift distinction (based on the language used in the will) and instead focuses on whether at the time the testator executed the will he or she owned stock that matched the description of the gift of stock in the will. If so, and thereafter the testator acquired additional stock as a result of his or her ownership of the devised stock and action initiated by a corporate entity, the beneficiary gets the benefit of whatever changes occurred between date of execution of the will and date of death of the testator, even if the stock in the estate is stock of a completely different corporate entity. UPC §2-605.

4. **Stock dividends:** Some courts treat stock dividends the same as cash dividends and rule that the devisee is not entitled to a stock dividend because he or she would not be entitled to a cash dividend. Most courts and the UPC, however, adopt the modern trend "percentage of ownership" theory and award the stock dividend to the devisee.

F. Miscellaneous construction doctrines

1. **Satisfaction:** If, after executing a will, the testator makes an inter vivos gift to a beneficiary under the will, the issue is whether the inter vivos transfer should count against the beneficiary's testamentary share of the estate.

   a. **Common law:** If the beneficiary is a child of the testator and the property transferred inter vivos were of "like kind" to that devised under the will, a rebuttable presumption arises that the testator wanted the inter vivos gift to count against the child's share under the will (either complete or partial satisfaction).

   b. **Modern trend/UPC approach:** The modern trend/UPC approach reverses the presumption. Inter vivos gifts to beneficiaries under a will (any beneficiary, not just to the testator's children) are presumed *not* to be in satisfaction (partial or complete) absent a writing expressing such an intent. The writing can be the will making the testamentary gift, a writing by the testator at the time of the inter vivos gift, or a writing created by the donee anytime. UPC §2-609.

   c. **Scope:** Satisfaction applies to general gifts only. If the gift in question is a specific gift, where the testator gave the specific gift inter vivos to the beneficiary under the will, ademption applies.

   d. **Advancement vs. satisfaction:** The doctrines of advancement and satisfaction address the same generic issue: whether inter vivos gifts to one taking from the decedent's estate should count against the party's testamentary share. Advancement deals with the issue where the decedent dies intestate; satisfaction deals with the issue where the decedent dies testate.

2. **Exoneration of liens:** Where a will devises property that is burdened by debt (a mortgage or lien, typically), the issue that arises is whether the beneficiary should take the devised property free and clear of the debt (thereby reducing the gift to the residuary taker) or whether the beneficiary should take the gift subject to the debt. The issue is one of testator's intent. If the will fails to indicate testator's intent on the issue, a default rule is needed.

a. **Common law:** At common law, the presumption is that the beneficiary is to take the devised property free and clear of any debt.

b. **Modern trend/UPC approach:** The modern trend/UPC approach reverses the presumption. The presumption is that the testator intended the beneficiary to take the property subject to the accompanying debt (that is, to receive only the testator's equity in the devised property). A general clause in a will to pay all the testator's just debts is not enough to overcome the modern trend presumption. An express reference to the debt in question is necessary. UPC §2-607.

3. **Abatement:** If the testator gives away more in his or her will than he or she has to give, the doctrine of abatement provides for which gifts are to be reduced first.

a. **General approach:** The general approach, based upon testator's presumed intent, is that the residuary clause is reduced first, then general gifts, and specific gifts last. This order is based on the assumption that the more precise the nature of the gift, the more important it must have been to the testator.

Criticism: Often the testator presumes that the residuary clause will be the biggest gift and saves it for the most important beneficiary. Where the testator is married, typically the residue is left to the surviving spouse. Reducing the residuary gift first arguably is inconsistent with the testator's overall testamentary scheme in such situations.

b. **Minority approach:** Some states' abatement statute and the UPC adopt the general approach, but then include a provision giving the courts the flexibility to alter the order of abatement where it appears inconsistent with the testator's overall testamentary wishes. UPC §3-902. Careful attention must be paid to the wording of each abatement statute to see if the legislature has granted the courts such flexibility.

Quiz Yourself on CONSTRUING WILLS

33. Anna wants to leave her velvet pink couch to the nice lady who works at the local pastry shop in Beverly Hills. Anna fondly refers to her as "Mrs. Sugar," and the woman at the pastry shop has grown to adore the name and answers to it when Anna comes in. Anna dies one night after overeating at a Hollywood party. Her properly executed will devises "my pink velvet couch to Mrs. Sugar." The real name of the woman who works at the pastry shop is Mrs. Jones. A woman named Patty Sugar comes forward and claims she is entitled to the pink velvet couch because she is Mrs. Sugar. Mrs. Jones wants to offer as evidence a birthday card that Anna gave to her a few months before she died addressed to "Mrs. Sugar." Is the evidence admissible, and who takes the couch? _____

34. While being treated at the New Beginnings rehabilitation center in Malibu, Chandler forms a close friendship with a woman named Jennifer. A week after his discharge from the center, Chandler dies. His properly executed will devises "$100,000 to Jennifer from New Beginnings." There are five women named Jennifer enrolled at New Beginnings, and all five claim the money. What result? _____

35. Rachel's properly executed will states, "my engagement ring to my sister Monica, if she survives me, everything else to Phoebe." Monica dies, survived by two sons, Ross and Joey. Thereafter, Rachel dies. Who gets the ring? _____

36. Homer, a single father, has a will that states, "all of my property to my children." Homer has three children, Bart, Lisa, and Maggie. Tragically, Bart dies in a skateboarding accident. Upon hearing of Bart's death, Homer has a heart attack and dies. Bart is survived by two children, Crusty and Bob. Who takes Homer's estate? _____

37. Justin's will states, "my custom-made red leather pants to Britney." After wearing the red leather pants a few times, Justin's stylist tells him that red leather is "out" and off-white is "in." Justin does not want to be out of style, so he burns the red leather pants and has off-white leather pants custom-made to replace them. Thereafter, Justin has a heart attack at dance practice and dies. What, if anything, does Britney take? _____

38. Martha's will leaves "300 shares of IBM stock" to her stockbroker, Bob. After some tough times in the stock market, IBM stock goes up dramatically and splits 3 for 1. The next day, Martha accidentally dies after inhaling toxic potpourri with which she was experimenting. How many shares of IBM stock does Bob take? _____

Answers

33. Under the common law approach, the general rule of construction is the plain meaning approach. The words of a will are to be given their usual and plain meaning, and extrinsic evidence is not admissible to prove a different meaning was intended. An exception to the common law, plain meaning rule is the personal usage exception. Where the testator uses a personal phrase or name to refer to a person, and uses that personal phrase or name in the will, extrinsic evidence is admissible to show that the testator used that phrase or name to mean something different from what it appears. Here, Anna called the woman in the pastry shop by a personal phrase that only they understood. Extrinsic evidence should be admissible to show the personal usage and to establish the identity of the woman that Anna wanted to take the couch—Mrs. Jones. Under the modern trend, the plain meaning is rejected and extrinsic evidence is admissible anytime there is an ambiguity, be it patent or latent. The extrinsic evidence should be admissible to help construe the words of the will in light of the circumstances surrounding the testator at time of execution—that Anna used the nickname "Mrs. Sugar" to refer to the woman in the pastry shop. Mrs. Jones should take the couch under the modern trend as well.

34. Under the common law approach, extrinsic evidence is admissible if there is a latent ambiguity in the will, but not if there is a patent ambiguity. A latent ambiguity is one that is not apparent from the face of the will. Typically it becomes apparent when the court attempts to give effect to the will. Here, although the reference to "Jennifer from New Beginnings" appears clear upon first reading, when the probate court attempts to give effect to the clause it discovers that there were five women named *Jennifer* enrolled at New Beginnings. Where more than one person or thing matches the language used in the will, that is called an equivocation. An equivocation is a latent ambiguity. Even at common law, extrinsic evidence is admissible to prove the latent ambiguity and to help the courts construe the language in the will. Under the modern trend, extrinsic evidence is admissible anytime there is an ambiguity, latent or patent. An ambiguity is language in the will that is reasonably susceptible to two or more interpretations. Here, the reference to "Jennifer from New Beginnings" is reasonably susceptible to multiple interpretations. The court will take extrinsic evidence of the circumstances surrounding the testator at time of execution in an attempt to help construe the language and determine which Jennifer was intended to take the gift.

35. A beneficiary under a will must survive the testator. If the beneficiary does not, the gift lapses—it fails, unless it can be saved. Anti-lapse provides that where there is a lapse, but the beneficiary is sufficiently related to the testator and has issue who survive the testator, it is presumed that the testator would rather the gift go to the issue of the predeceased beneficiary, unless there is a contrary intent expressed in the will. Here, Monica predeceases Rachel, so the gift lapses unless it can be saved by anti-lapse. The requisite degree of relationship between testator and beneficiary depends on the wording of each state's statute, but most states cover siblings. If the statute covers descendants only, anti-lapse does not apply. Assuming Monica meets the statute's degree of relationship requirement, she is survived by issue. Unfortunately, there is an express contrary intent that blocks the anti-lapse doctrine. The express phrase "if she survives me" has been construed by the courts applying the common law approach as an express intent that anti-lapse not apply. Under the modern trend/UPC approach, however, such an express survival clause is not sufficient to constitute an express intent that anti-lapse not apply. Under the modern trend/UPC approach, the court would apply anti-lapse and give the ring to Monica's issue, Ross and Joey.

36. When Bart dies before Homer, Bart's gift lapses and the gift fails. There are two ways a failed gift can be saved—by anti-lapse or by the class gift doctrine. In most jurisdictions, anti-lapse applies to class gifts, so check for anti-lapse first. Under anti-lapse, there must be a lapse, the predeceased beneficiary must meet the statutory degree of relationship requirement (varies by jurisdiction), the predeceased beneficiary must have issue who survive the testator, and there must be no express intent in the written instrument that anti-lapse not apply. Bart's death before Homer, the testator, constitutes a lapse. Bart is Homer's son, so he meets the degree of relationship requirement in every state. Bart has issue who survive Homer, Crusty and Bob. And there is no express intent in the will that anti-lapse should not be applied. Crusty and Bob take Bart's share. Maggie takes one-third; Lisa takes one-third; and Crusty and Bob split one-third (one-sixth each).

If the jurisdiction does not apply anti-lapse to class gift, the class gift doctrine may save the gift for the other members of the class. Whether a gift constitutes a class gift depends on the testator's intent. Where that intent is not clear, the courts typically look at four factors: (1) how the beneficiaries are described—by name or by group; (2) how the gift is described—in the aggregate or in shares; (3) whether the beneficiaries share a common characteristic; and (4) the testator's overall testamentary scheme. Here, Homer described the beneficiaries as a group—"my children"—which favors a class gift. Homer described the gift in the aggregate—"all my property"—which favors a class gift. The beneficiaries share a common characteristic—they are all Homer's children, and there is no evidence Homer has any other children who were excluded—which favors a class gift. And Homer's overall testamentary scheme appears to have been to leave all his property to his children, which arguably favors a class gift here. Most likely, the gift will be construed to be a class gift, and under the right of survivorship that is built into each class gift, Bart's share goes to the other members of the class, Maggie and Lisa (one-half each), if the jurisdiction does not apply anti-lapse to class gifts.

37. Justin's gift of "my custom-made red leather pants" constitutes a specific gift. He intends for one specific item to satisfy that gift. When he burns the pants, the question is what effect, if any, that has on the gift. Under the traditional common law approach to ademption, there was an irrebuttable presumption that by disposing of the item subject to the specific gift before he died, Justin intended

to revoke the gift. Under ademption, Britney takes nothing. Because of the harshness of the ademption doctrine, however, many jurisdictions have developed avoidance doctrines. One such doctrine is the "change in form, not substance" doctrine. Under that doctrine, the beneficiary can argue that the gift, changed slightly in form but not in substance, is still in the testator's estate. Here, though, Justin burned the pants. Although there is another pair of custom-made leather pants in Justin's estate, they are a different pair, not the same pair that has changed slightly. Under the traditional, strict approach to ademption, Britney probably fails on her "change in form, not substance" argument and she takes nothing (though if she can convince the court that the change from red to off-white is merely a change in form, not substance, and the court overlooks the fact that it is a completely different pair of pants, she might prevail).

The modern trend/UPC approach to ademption makes a slight presumption against ademption. The UPC has adopted the replacement approach to ademption. If the testator disposes of the item that was the subject of the specific gift, but acquires property to replace the specifically devised property, the beneficiary takes the replacement property if still owned at death. Here, Justin burned the red pants and replaced them with off-white pants. Britney takes the replacement pants.

38. Under the traditional common law approach, where there is a stock split, whether the beneficiary gets the additional shares owned at the testator's death as a result of the stock split depends on whether the gift of stock was construed as a specific gift or general gift of stock. If specific, the beneficiary tends to take the additional shares. If general, the beneficiary does not take the additional shares. Here, there is no evidence that Martha owned any shares of IBM stock at the time she executed her will, and the wording of the gift does not refer to any specific shares of IBM stock. The gift would most likely be construed a general gift, and under the traditional, common law approach, Bob takes only 300 shares of IBM stock upon Martha's death. Under the modern trend, the courts tend to give the beneficiary the additional shares whether the gift is specific or general. Bob would take 900 shares as a result of the stock split to ensure that he takes the same proportional interest in IBM that Martha intended prior to the stock split. The UPC approach focuses on whether, at the time the testator executed the will, the testator owned stock that matched the description of the stock being devised in the will. If so, the beneficiary gets the benefit of any change in the stock initiated by a corporate entity. Here, there is no evidence that Martha owned any shares of IBM stock when she executed the will, so Bob takes only 300 shares of IBM.

 *Exam Tips on*
CONSTRUING WILLS

The modern trend applies the material in this chapter not only to wills, but also to the will substitutes. If your jurisdiction has adopted the modern trend approach, a good way to test your understanding of the modern trend is to go back and analyze each of the cases in the prior chapter (on the will substitutes) under the modern trend approach.

Admissibility of extrinsic evidence

☛ The threshold issue is *why* is the extrinsic evidence being offered. If the evidence goes to the validity of the will, invariably the courts admit the evidence. If the evidence goes to the construction of the will, it is not admissible unless there is an ambiguity in the will.

☛ If your jurisdiction still follows the common law approach, raise, define, and analyze whether the ambiguity is a latent or patent ambiguity. Under the common law approach, extrinsic evidence is admissible only if the ambiguity is a latent ambiguity.

☞ Common law applies the plain meaning rule when reading the will.

☛ If your jurisdiction follows the modern trend, the courts have generally repudiated the plain meaning rule. Extrinsic evidence is admissible if there is an ambiguity, latent *or* patent. If you see a possible ambiguity, lead with the rule statement for what constitutes an ambiguity: The language in question in the will must be reasonably susceptible to two or more interpretations.

☞ Assuming an ambiguity exists, only extrinsic evidence that is consistent with one of the possible reasonable interpretations is admissible, and the courts favor evidence of the circumstances surrounding the testator at time of execution as opposed to alleged oral declarations (easy to fabricate).

☛ Even where extrinsic evidence is admissible to help construe a will, as a general rule the courts do not rewrite wills; they only construe the ambiguous language. What constitutes "construing" and what constitutes "rewriting" is sometimes a very difficult question. The interpretation desired by the claimant must not vary too far from the express words of the will, or it is subject to being called a rewrite, not a mere construction.

☛ The scrivener's error doctrine is a new doctrine. Only one case has adopted and applied the doctrine so far, and that case can be spun a number of different ways, so a whole plethora of questions remains.

Changes in the beneficiary

☛ Core wills material—lapse/anti-lapse/class gifts/failed gifts. These doctrines constitute some of the most tested material in the course (lapse in particular, because it is a great overlap issue).

☛ However you conclude on the lapse issue, be sure to check to see if it affects your analysis of another issue raised by the fact pattern. (Examples: overlap between lapse and the per capita doctrine, or lapse and the advancement doctrine.)

☛ Watch for the more subtle ways to raise the lapse issue: the beneficiary dies before the will is executed (lapse vs. void, common law vs. modern trend); or the beneficiary dies after execution of the will, but then the testator executes a codicil; or the beneficiary survives the testator but is treated as if he or she predeceased the testator for one reason or another.

☞ If you have a lapse issue, be sure to raise and discuss anti-lapse. The final element, no express contrary intent, is a particularly tricky element. Watch for an express contrary intent expressed in an instrument other than the instrument making the gift. Such an expression of contrary intent is not enough to knock out anti-lapse.

☛ Failed gifts can also be saved by the class gift doctrine. If you see a gift to more than one individual, you should pause and ask whether the gift constitutes a class gift.

☞ Focus on the four factors in analyzing whether the gift is a class gift: how the gift is described, how the beneficiaries are described, whether the beneficiaries all share a common characteristic; and the testator's overall testamentary scheme.

☞ Remember these are just factors, not requirements. Three is probably good enough to qualify the gift as a class gift, and sometimes two is all that it takes. Whether a gift is a class gift or not is a rather soft, fact-sensitive issue. Be prepared to make detailed, fact-sensitive arguments.

☛ If a gift to a class member lapses, know which approach your jurisdiction takes to which doctrine should be applied first to try to save the gift: anti-lapse or the class gift doctrine.

☛ If a gift is not saved by anti-lapse or the class gift doctrine, or the "residue of the residue" rule, the gift fails. You need to know the cascading scheme of who takes if a gift fails because it underlies this whole batch of material and is necessary to ascertain who will argue which approach when it appears that a gift is failing.

Changes in testator's property

☛ Ademption is another key doctrine that every student should know and that shows up frequently on exams.

☞ A particularly tricky area of the law of gifts is where language in the will arguably indicates a general gift, but when the testator executed the gift, he or she owned a specific item that matched the gift exactly. If you get such a scenario, be prepared to argue both sides. The outcome may turn on which legal conclusion is most beneficial to the beneficiary. In the more common scenario, the item is no longer in the testator's estate, so classifying the gift as a general gift is more beneficial (that is, avoids ademption). Sometimes, however, it is more beneficial to classify the gift as specific (if the gift is of stock and thereafter there is a stock merger). (This is also a good overlap issue for whether extrinsic evidence should be admitted to help resolve the conflict.) Be prepared to argue and analyze in the alternative.

☛ Ademption applies only to specific gifts. Know which approach your jurisdiction takes to ademption: the harsh common law approach or the kinder modern trend approach.

☞ If your jurisdiction applies the harsh identity approach to ademption, run through the avoidance and softening doctrines. One or more can usually be argued in good faith.

☞ If your jurisdiction applies the kinder UPC/modern trend approach, look first to see if there is any replacement property in the testator's estate at time of death. If not, then argue for the monetary equivalent. Be prepared to use extrinsic evidence to support your claim that the testator did not intend for the gift to be adeemed.

☛ If you see a beneficiary under a will receiving an inter vivos gift from the testator, there is a high probability that either ademption or satisfaction applies, depending on whether the gift was specific or general.

☛ Gifts of stock is another area that is tested often. At common law, the key is whether the gift is characterized as specific (beneficiary receives the additional shares usually) or general (beneficiary takes only the original number of shares usually). The modern trend rejects the specific vs.

general distinction and focuses on whether the change is one of form, not substance—giving the beneficiary the benefit of a stock split or merger even where the gift is general. The UPC focuses on whether the testator owned stock at the time he or she executed the will that matched the description in the will. If so, the beneficiary receives the benefit of any increase or change in the form of the stock.

☛ The wrinkle in the abatement area to watch for is whether your jurisdiction grants the flexibility to vary the normal abatement order if it appears inconsistent with the testator's overall testamentary scheme.

CHAPTER 6

WILL SUBSTITUTES AND PLANNING FOR INCAPACITY

ChapterScope ━━━━━━━━━━━━━━━━━━━━━━━━━━━━━━━━━━━━━━━

This chapter briefly examines the traditional methods of avoiding probate and planning for incapacity before death. In particular, the chapter examines:

- **Revocable trusts:** The trustee holds legal title. The beneficiaries hold equitable title. There is no need to transfer legal title upon the death of any of the beneficiaries, even if the trust is revocable and the settlor is the life beneficiary. The property placed in an inter vivos trust is nonprobate property.

  - **Revocability:** If a trust is silent as to its revocability, it is irrevocable. If the trust is revocable and it expressly provides for a particular method of revocation, only that method will suffice (if the trust does not provide for a particular method of revocation, any method that demonstrates settlor's intent to revoke should suffice).

  - **Creditor's rights:** When a life tenant's interest is extinguished, creditors of the life tenant have no right to reach the property. Under the modern trend, however, where the settlor is the life beneficiary of a revocable trust, creditors of the settlor can reach the property in the trust even after the settlor's death.

- **Life insurance contracts/contracts with payable-on-death clauses:** Although life insurance contracts effectively pass property at time of the insured's death, the insurance proceeds are deemed "nonprobate" assets. The modern trend/UPC approach extends this nonprobate exception to all third-party beneficiary contracts with payable-on-death clauses.

  - **Multiple party accounts:** Banks and brokerage houses often force multiple parties to use the joint tenancy account even if that is not what the parties intended. Upon the death of one of the depositors, the courts will take extrinsic evidence of the parties' true intent and treat the account accordingly. The modern trend presumes that inter vivos the parties own in proportion to their contributions and at death there is a right of survivorship.

- **Pour-over wills:** Where a will has a pour-over clause giving probate property to the trustee of the testator's inter vivos trust, the pour-over clause must be validated under either the Uniform Testamentary Additions to Trusts Act (UTATA), acts of independent significance, or incorporation by reference.

  - **Revocable trusts and estate planning:** Revocable trusts are increasingly becoming a part of an individual's estate planning documents because of their benefits, but there are situations where they should not be used.

- **Joint tenancies:** The right of survivorship means that upon the death of one joint tenant, his or her share is extinguished and the shares of the remaining joint tenants are recalculated. No property passes, so there is nothing to pass through probate.

■ **Planning for incapacity:** Good estate planning includes planning for the possibility that the person may become incapacitated before he or she dies. With respect to property issues, the most common tool to deal with that possibility is the durable power of attorney. With respect to personal decisions about one's health care, the tools are either a living will/medical directive or a durable power of attorney for health care decisions (or some hybrid of the two).

I. OVERVIEW TO THE WILL SUBSTITUTES

A. **Introduction:** Historically, four types of legal arrangements, for all practical purposes, passed property at time of death but were not subject to the Wills Act formalities: life insurance contracts, joint tenancies, certain possessory estates and future interests (legal life estates and remainders), and inter vivos trusts.

Justification: Why these four particular property arrangements were deemed not subject to the Wills Act formalities is debatable. Some argue that with respect to each arrangement, the property interest technically passes inter vivos and nothing really passes at time of death, so there is no testamentary transfer that would be subject to the Wills Act formalities. Others argue that the formalities associated with the creation of each of these arrangements adequately serves the functions underlying the Wills Act formalities and thus it is not necessary to subject them to the Wills Act formalities. And still others argue that other public policy and legal considerations justify exempting these particular property arrangements from the Wills Act formalities.

B. **Controlling law:** Each of the four recognized will substitutes arguably falls within a particular area of law other than the law of wills. Life insurance policies are a subset of the law of contracts. Joint tenancies and possessory estates and future interests are a subset of the law of property. Inter vivos trusts are a subset of the law of trusts.

1. **Creation:** Inasmuch as these will substitutes do not have to be created with Wills Act formalities, the issue of whether any of these will substitutes are properly created is beyond the coverage of the law of wills and thus beyond the scope of this outline (except for the inter vivos trust, which is covered in greater detail in Chapter 8).

2. **Construction:** There is a growing debate over whether the will substitutes should be subject to the *"wills-related" doctrines*—in particular the will construction doctrines. A number of wills-related doctrines cover a whole host of ancillary issues that can arise with respect to instruments created inter vivos that purport to transfer a property interest at time of death. For example, if the beneficiary of an insurance contract dies before the insured, should contract law control the issue of whether the beneficiary has to survive the transferor, or should the wills-related doctrines control (the doctrines of lapse and anti-lapse, covered in Chapter 5)?

   a. **Common law:** The traditional common law approach held that inasmuch as these will substitutes are subsets of other areas of law, the rules and doctrines of those other areas of law control. As applied to the example above, contract law would apply, and the beneficiary would not have to survive the transferor to claim his or her interest under the contract.

   b. **Modern trend:** The modern trend is to subject the will substitutes to the wills-related construction doctrines.

Rationale: Most people use the will substitutes to avoid the costs, hassles, and delays of probate. People do not use the wills substitutes to avoid the wills-related doctrines. The wills-related doctrines were specifically developed to deal with issues that arise between the time of creating an instrument that purports to transfer property at time of death and the time of death of the party creating the instrument (change in the property, change in the beneficiary, or change in the party who created the legal arrangement). The wills-related doctrines are better suited to deal with these particular issues than the more general principles of contract law, property law, or trust law, none of which were developed with an eye toward time-of-death issues.

C. **Scope:** At common law, there are only four will substitutes: life insurance policies, joint tenancies, possessory estates and future interests (legal life estates and remainders), and inter vivos trusts. If the written instrument does not qualify as one of these four types of property arrangements, the written instrument has to qualify as a valid will. If the written instrument does not qualify as a will substitute or as a valid will, the written instrument is an invalid attempt to transfer property at time of death without complying with the Wills Act formalities, no matter how clear the individual's intent in the instrument. The modern trend is to recognize a whole plethora of will substitutes.

II. INTER VIVOS TRUSTS

A. **Introduction:** A trust is nothing more than another way to make a gift. Conceptually, the key to understanding a trust is to remember that it is a bifurcated gift. (Trusts are covered in detail in Chapter 8.)

Parties: While the traditional gift involves only two parties, a donor and a donee, a gift in trust involves three parties: a settlor, a trustee, and the beneficiaries. There are three parties because when a gift is made in trust, title to the property in question is bifurcated. Legal title is given to the trustee, who holds and administers the property for the benefit of the beneficiaries, who hold the equitable title. The donor is called the settlor.

B. **Theoretical perspective:** There are several different types of inter vivos trust that arguably run the gamut from those that clearly are inter vivos transfers to those that look very testamentary in nature. Whether all inter vivos trusts should be recognized as valid will substitutes has been an issue of much litigation over the years.

1. **Classic trust:** Assuming the settlor, trustee, and beneficiaries are all different parties, and assuming the trust is irrevocable, the settlor must transfer the property to the trust inter vivos. Once the settlor transfers the property to the trust, the settlor no longer has any interest in the property. The trust holds legal title to the property, not the settlor. When the settlor dies, legal title does not have to be transferred because the trust continues to hold the legal title.

   Example: Sally transfers $1,000 to Tess, as trustee, to hold for the benefit of Bob during his lifetime; upon his death, any remaining money is distributed outright to Betty. Assuming the transfer is irrevocable, Sally, the settlor, retains no interest in the property. It is like any other inter vivos gift Sally may make. Moreover, when Bob dies, any property distributed to Betty is not a testamentary transfer because the future interest is given to her when the trust is created.

2. **Settlor as trustee and life beneficiary:** Even if the settlor is both trustee and life beneficiary, as long as the trust is irrevocable, and the remainder interest has been conveyed to another beneficiary, the trust is still like any other inter vivos gift. The future interest (a vested remainder, typically) passes inter vivos to the beneficiary holding the future interest. The party holding the future interest receives certain rights inter vivos the moment the trust is created, even though the right to receive full enjoyment of their interest is delayed until the possessory interest has ended. The transfer is an inter vivos transfer, and because the trust holds legal title, there is no need to transfer title upon the settlor/life beneficiary's death.

3. **Revocable trust + settlor as life beneficiary:** Whether a gift in trust is a testamentary transfer that should be subject to the Wills Act formalities becomes more complicated when the settlor is also life beneficiary and retains the power to revoke the trust. While this arrangement bothered some courts initially, all jurisdictions now recognize it as a valid will substitute.

4. **Revocable trust + settlor as trustee and life beneficiary:** The issue of whether a gift in trust is a testamentary transfer that should be subject to the Wills Act formalities is taken to the limit where the settlor is also trustee, life beneficiary, and retains the power to revoke the trust.

   a. **Instrument constitutes a will:** To the extent the settlor wears all three hats (settlor, trustee, and life beneficiary) and retains the power to revoke, arguably the trust instrument is functionally indistinguishable from a will. If it is indistinguishable from a will, it should be subject to the Wills Act formalities.

   b. **Instrument constitutes a trust:** Even where the settlor is also trustee and life beneficiary and retains the power to revoke, a property interest is still conveyed inter vivos to the beneficiaries holding the future interest. Unlike a will, where the beneficiaries receive no rights or interest inter vivos, beneficiaries in a trust are owed a fiduciary duty, and they immediately receive rights that they can enforce against the trustee if the trustee breaches any of the numerous onerous burdens the trustee owes the beneficiaries. The fact that the trust is revocable does not defeat the fact that a property interest has been conveyed inter vivos. Typically, the future interest is a remainder. Where the trust is revocable, the remainder is a contingent remainder—but a contingent remainder is still a property interest the moment it is created, even though full enjoyment is delayed until the interest becomes possessory.

   Wills Act formalities: In the alternative, some argue that even if a revocable trust where the settlor is also trustee and life beneficiary is functionally indistinguishable from a will, the process one has to go through to create such a revocable inter vivos trust satisfies the functions underlying the Wills Act formalities and therefore should qualify as a will substitute.

C. **Traditional doctrinal perspective:** Revocable inter vivos trusts are widely recognized as valid will substitutes that do not have to comply with the Wills Act formalities, even where the settlor is also the trustee and life beneficiary.

Example: In *Farkas v. Williams,* 125 N.E.2d 600 (Ill. 1955), Farkas purchased stock on four different occasions, each time taking title in his name "as trustee for Richard J. Williams." Concurrently with each purchase, Farkas signed four declarations of trust where he conveyed himself the life interest, remainder to Williams, and retained the power to revoke by selling the stock. Farkas died intestate. His heirs claimed the inter vivos trusts were invalid testamentary dispositions that failed to comply with the Wills Act formalities. The court upheld the inter vivos trusts, reasoning that some interest passed inter vivos to Williams even though the trusts were revocable, and, in the alternative, the process Farkas went through in creating the inter vivos trusts adequately served the functions underlying the Wills Act formalities.

D. UTC approach: The Uniform Trust Code moots the traditional academic arguments. The UTC provides that while a trust is revocable, the rights of the beneficiaries are subject to the control of and the duties of the trustee are owed *exclusively* to the settlor. UTC §603.

Standing: Consistent with the UTC/modern trend approach, courts have held beneficiaries under a revocable trust have no standing to contest amendments to the trust because a beneficiary's interest is, at best, contingent and unenforceable during the settlor's lifetime. *See **Linthicum v. Rudi**,* 148 P.3d 746 (Nev. 2006).

E. Revocability: The traditional and still general majority rule is that inter vivos trusts are presumed to be irrevocable unless the terms of the trust expressly state that the trust is revocable.

UTC/modern trend: The new Uniform Trust Code reverses the traditional default rule and provides that a settlor may revoke or amend an inter vivos trust unless the trust expressly states it is irrevocable. UTC §602(a). (The provision does not apply to trust instruments executed before the effective date of the Code in that jurisdiction.) The UTC approach arguably is more consistent with a typical settlor's intent, but the traditional rule is true to the origin of trust law—the law of gifts. The traditional and still general rule reasons that gifts are irrevocable, and because trusts are simply another way of making a gift, trusts should be irrevocable unless expressly stated otherwise.

F. Revocation—particular method expressed: Where a trust sets forth an express, *particular* method of revocation, *only* that method of revocation is valid.

1. **Rationale:** The guiding principle of trust law is that settlor's intent controls. If the settlor sets forth a particular method of revoking a trust, it is presumed that the settlor intends that to be the exclusive method of revoking the trust. The issue is how particular must the method be before it is deemed the exclusive method.

2. **Example:** In *In re Estate and Trust of Pilafas,* 836 P.2d 420 (Ariz. App. 1992), the decedent executed an inter vivos trust and a will. The trust expressly provided that it was revocable by instrument in writing delivered to the trustee. Thereafter, the decedent expressed to his attorney and to family members the intent to revise his estate planning documents (to provide for certain family members who previously had been omitted). The decedent died before executing any new estate planning documents. Following his death, the will and trust that he took home with him could not be found. The omitted family members argued that the will and trust were revoked pursuant to the revocation by presumption doctrine. The court held that the express terms of the trust set forth an exclusive method of revocation (by writing delivered to the trustee) that precluded application of the presumption doctrine. The court concluded that the will was revoked, but not the inter vivos trust.

3. **Criticism:** The standard revocation clause, that the trust is revocable by writing delivered to the trustee, arguably is boilerplate language thrown in by drafting attorneys more to protect the trustee from claims of improperly distributing trust assets after the trust was revoked than it is to limit the settlor's ability to revoke the trust. Nevertheless, most courts presume that the settlor read and intended every clause of the trust and hold the clause to constitute the exclusive method of revoking.

4. **UTC/modern trend:** The modern trend is to minimize the differences between the law of trusts and the law of wills, particularly with respect to revocability. The Uniform Trust Code provides that where the trust sets forth a particular method of revocation, it should *not* be construed as the exclusive method *unless* the trust provision expressly makes it exclusive. UTC §602(c)(2). Substantial compliance with the particular method of revocation is sufficient. UTC §602(c)(1). A will executed after the trust, which specifically refers to the trust or the power to revoke, can revoke a revocable trust if the trust terms do not specify an exclusive method of revocation and if the will is not thereafter revoked. UTC §602(c)(1). Moreover, where the trust is not revoked, if the settlor retained a life estate interest in the revocable trust, following the settlor's death the settlor's creditors can reach the assets in the trust if the probate estate is insufficient to pay off the creditors.

5. **Example:** In *State Street Bank & Trust Co. v. Reiser,* 389 N.E.2d 768 (Mass. App. 1979), Dunnebier created a revocable inter vivos trust and transferred to the trust the stock of five closely held corporations. Thereafter, Dunnebier obtained an unsecured loan for $75,000. During the loan application process, Dunnebier represented to the bank that he held controlling interest in the five closely held corporations. (The court found that Dunnebier had not done so fraudulently.) Shortly thereafter, Dunnebier died unexpectedly. His probate assets were insufficient to pay his creditors. The bank sued to reach the assets in his revocable inter vivos trust. The court adopted the modern trend and held that to the extent Dunnebier had power over the assets in the revocable inter vivos trust during his lifetime, those assets should be available to creditors following the settlor's death. The court required the creditors to exhaust the decedent's probate assets first.

G. **Revocation—no particular method expressed:** If the trust is revocable, but silent as to the method of revocation, the power may be exercised in any manner that adequately expresses the intent to revoke. The trust can be revoked by writing (even if the writing does not qualify as a will), by act (destructive act coupled with intent), by presumption (arguably), and even orally (unless real property is involved).

Divorce: In many jurisdictions, an inter vivos revocable trust is not revoked by divorce, while a will is automatically revoked by operation of law. The modern trend is to treat inter vivos revocable trusts like wills and apply the revocation by operation of law doctrine and automatically revoke the provisions in the trust in favor of the ex-spouse. The Uniform Probate Code adopts this approach, UPC § 2-804. The Uniform Trust Code does not expressly adopt this approach, but section 112, Rules of Construction, provides that "[t]he rules of construction that apply in this State to the interpretation of and disposition of property by will also apply as appropriate to the interpretation of the terms of a trust and the disposition of the trust property." The official Comment to the section expressly references the issue of revocation by operation of law upon divorce, further supporting the argument that the UTC has implicitly adopted the modern trend through its rules of construction.

H. **Rights of creditors of the settlor:** The general rule is that one should not be able to shield one's assets from one's creditors. If one has a property interest in a trust, one's creditors should be able to reach that property interest. (The rights of creditors of beneficiaries *other than the settlor* are different and are covered in Chapter 8.)

1. **Common law:** At common law, the power to revoke is not a property interest—it is merely a "power." As such, creditors of a settlor of a revocable trust cannot reach the power or force the settlor to exercise the power in their favor.

2. **Modern trend:** The modern trend expands creditors' rights to permit creditors to reach a settlor's power to revoke.

   Rationale: A settlor's power over trust property subject to a power to revoke is functionally indistinguishable from one's power over one's money in the bank. The act of writing a check is functionally indistinguishable from the act of writing an instrument revoking a trust. As a matter of public policy, the modern trend also thinks it unfair to permit one to shield all of one's assets merely by putting them in a revocable trust that benefits others (typically the settlor's family members).

3. **Creditors of settlor:** Consistent with the principle that one should not be permitted to shield one's assets from one's creditors, during the settlor's lifetime, regardless of the terms of the trust, creditors of the settlor can reach the trust property to the full extent the trustee *could* have used the property in the trust for the settlor's benefit—whether the settlor's interest is mandatory or discretionary.

4. **Spendthrift clause:** If the settlor is also the life beneficiary and the trust has a spendthrift clause, the clause is null and void as to the settlor's creditors.

5. **Post-death:** Where a settlor retains a life estate in his or her revocable trust, the jurisdictions are split over whether settlor's creditors can reach his or her interest in the trust following the settlor's death.

   a. **Common law:** Under the traditional common law approach, if a settlor retains a life estate, upon the settlor's death, the life estate is extinguished. When the life estate ends, the settlor no longer has an interest in the trust, so there is nothing for the settlor's creditors to reach.

   b. **Modern trend:** The modern trend analogizes the assets in a revocable inter vivos trust to the settlor's other assets and reasons that to the extent the settlor had the right to use and benefit from those assets during his or her lifetime, his or her creditors should have a right to reach those assets following settlor's death. Under the modern trend, the settlor's creditors are permitted to reach the property in the trust to the extent the settlor had the power to use those assets during his or her life. If the settlor retained the power to revoke the whole trust, all of the trust assets are subject to the claims of the settlor's creditors.

      i. **Judicial vs. statutory:** Most jurisdictions that have adopted the modern trend have done so statutorily, though a few have done so judicially. The Uniform Trust Code adopts the modern trend.

      ii. **Probate estate:** Most jurisdictions that have adopted the modern trend require the settlor's creditors to exhaust the settlor's probate assets before being able to reach the settlor's trust assets. Only when the settlor's probate assets are insufficient to satisfy the claims can the creditors reach the assets in the settlor's revocable trust.

6. **Example:** In *State Street Bank & Trust Co. v. Reiser,* above, after Dunnebier died unexpectedly, his probate assets were insufficient to pay his creditors. His creditors sued to reach the assets in his revocable inter vivos trust. The court adopted the modern trend and held that to the extent Dunnebier had power over the assets in the revocable inter vivos trust during his lifetime, those assets should be available to creditors following the settlor's death. The court required the creditors to exhaust the decedent's probate assets first.

III. CONTRACTS WITH PAYABLE-ON-DEATH CLAUSES

A. Life insurance: The classic example of a contract with a payable-on-death (P.O.D.) clause is a life insurance policy. The insured enters into an agreement with an insurance company. The agreement provides that if the insured dies while covered by the policy, the company will pay the benefits under the policy to a beneficiary designated in the policy. For all practical purposes, the agreement effectively transfers property from the insured to a designated beneficiary upon the insured's death, but the written agreement between the insured and the insurance company need not be created with Wills Act formalities.

   1. Whole life: Whole life insurance (also known as ***ordinary*** or ***straight*** insurance) is where the insured purchases coverage for his or her whole life at an up-front purchase price (with fixed payments typically spread over a number of years). Often the policy will be completely paid off (in which case the policy is said to be "paid up" or "endowed") before the insured dies. Nevertheless, the insured has purchased insurance for his or her whole life so he or she is still insured. There is a "forced savings" component to whole life.

   2. Term life: Term life insurance (also known as ***pure*** insurance) is where the insured purchases coverage for a fixed period of time (for a term of years typically). Premiums are usually fixed for the term, but upon the expiration of the term the premiums typically increase to reflect the increased risk of death with age. There is no "forced savings" component to term life—the insured pays as he or she goes.

B. Common law: Although there is a plethora of different types of contracts with P.O.D. clauses, under the common law approach only life insurance contracts are exempt from the Wills Act formalities. If the contract is any other type of contract with a P.O.D. clause, no matter how clear the party's intent that the property in question should be transferred to the identified beneficiary upon the party's death, if the written instrument does not qualify as a will, it is an invalid attempt to transfer property at time of death.

   Example: In ***In re Estate of Atkinson,*** 175 N.E.2d 548 (Prob. Ct. Ohio 1961), the decedent made a deposit in a local bank and took the certificate of deposit as follows: "Walter S. Atkinson, P.O.D. Mrs. Patricia Burgeois." He created two other accounts with the same language but designating two other P.O.D. beneficiaries. After his death, his wife claimed her statutory share of his probate estate and argued that the monies in all three accounts should be included in his probate estate as invalid attempts at nonprobate transfers. The court agreed that despite the decedent's clear intent, the state did not recognize such payment on death accounts as valid nonprobate transfers.

C. Modern trend/UPC approach: The modern trend/UPC approach expands the historical will substitute exemption for life insurance contracts and applies it to ***any and all*** contracts and instruments with P.O.D. clauses (employment contracts, promissory notes, deposit agreements, pension plans, retirements accounts, and so on). UPC §6-101.

   1. Example: In ***Atkinson,*** under the modern trend/UPC approach, the deposit agreement between the decedent and the bank would have been a valid will substitute and the money would have passed to the P.O.D. designees, even though each account was not a life insurance policy and was not executed with Wills Act formalities.

   2. Example: In ***Estate of Hillowitz,*** 238 N.E.2d 723 (N.Y. App. 1968), the husband was a member of an "investment club." The terms of the written partnership agreement included an express P.O.D. clause that provided that upon his death, his share of the club was to go to his wife. The executors of his estate challenged the validity of the P.O.D. clause, claiming it was an invalid testamentary transfer (invalid because it did not qualify as a life insurance policy nor was it executed with Wills Act formalities). The court applied the modern trend and held the clause valid as a valid contract with a P.O.D. clause.

3. **Revocability:** Beneficiaries of a P.O.D. clause do not receive an irrevocable property interest inter vivos. The transferor who creates the P.O.D. clause is presumed to have the right to cancel or change the P.O.D. clause (absent consideration).

4. **Construction:** The modern trend/UPC approach generally applies the wills-related rules to the will substitutes, including life insurance policies. The wills-related rules are primarily those rules of construction that arise out of changes that can occur between when the instrument is created and when the transferor/testator dies.

5. **Example:** In *Cook v. Equitable Life Assurance Society,* 428 N.E.2d 110 (Ind. App. 1981), Douglas Cook purchased a life insurance policy and designated his then wife, Doris, as beneficiary. Thereafter, he and Doris divorced, and he married Margaret. The insurance policy expressly provided that the owner of the policy may change the beneficiary by written notice to the company. Douglas never gave written notice to the company, but after his marriage to Margaret he executed a holographic will that expressly stated that he was giving the insurance policy to his wife Margaret and his son. The court held that the divorce did not revoke the contractual provisions in favor of Douglas' ex-spouse and awarded the life insurance proceeds to Doris as the contractual beneficiary designation controlled.

   a. **Common law:** The *Cook* case typifies the traditional approach. The revocation by operation of law (divorce) doctrine applies to wills only.

   b. **UPC/modern trend:** Under the UPC and many jurisdictions, the revocation by operation of law doctrine applies to all will substitutes, including life insurance policies. Under this approach, in *Cook* Doris' status as beneficiary of his life insurance policy would have been revoked upon their divorce and, absent a substitute beneficiary in the life insurance policy, the proceeds would have defaulted to his probate estate where his will provision in favor of Margaret would have been given effect.

   Exception: Some jurisdictions that have adopted the modern trend exempt life insurance policies. You should check your state's approach. Whether there are good reasons to except out life insurance policies, or whether it is a testament to the lobbying power of the life insurance industry, is beyond the scope of this material.

   c. **UPC/modern trend survival requirement:** Although the modern trend/UPC approach is generally to apply the wills-related rules to the will substitutes, an exception to this trend is the survival requirement. While the UPC applies an express survival requirement to life insurance contracts, it is silent as to contracts with P.O.D. clauses generally. UPC §§2-104, 2-702, 6-101.

D. **Transfer on death (T.O.D.) deeds:** The modern trend nonprobate movement has led to the development of the transfer on death deed (TODD). About a dozen states have adopted statutes permitting TODDs, and the Uniform Law Commission is reportedly considering endorsing the development by promulgating a uniform TODD statute. While the details currently vary from state to state, the key characteristics of a TODD typically are (1) the deed must be executed and recorded inter vivos, but it does not become effective until the death of the grantor—i.e., absolutely no interest is transferred to the grantee until the grantor dies; (2) the deed is revocable during the grantor's life (but typically only by recording another deed that revokes the initial deed); and (3) the transfer is effective immediately upon the grantor's death and avoids probate.

E. **Superwills:** If a will is permitted to change the terms of a will substitute, such a will is known as a "superwill." Under the modern trend, an individual might have a plethora of written instruments that could qualify as valid will substitutes. For example, the individual might have an insurance policy, a pension plan, and a bank account—all with P.O.D. clauses identifying a particular beneficiary to take upon the individual's death. Inasmuch as these written instruments constitute will substitutes, the issue is whether a subsequently executed will should have the power to revise these instruments.

   1. **Argument in support:** A will substitute should be treated just like a will for purposes of revising the will substitute. A subsequent will controls over a prior will, so a subsequent will should control over a prior will substitute.

   2. **Intent:** Those in favor of recognizing superwills tend to favor restricting the doctrine to wills that make specific reference to the will substitute.

   3. **General rule:** For public policy reasons, most jurisdictions have rejected the idea of a superwill.

      a. **Rationale:** One of the principal benefits of the will substitutes, particularly life insurance contracts, is that they permit the quick and relatively easy transfer of property to the intended beneficiary upon the transferor's death. There are none of the hassles, delays, and expenses associated with probate. If, however, the nonprobate instrument were subject to change by a superwill, the nonprobate transfer could not occur until the party responsible for making the transfer was confident that there was not a valid superwill changing the beneficiary or the gift.

      b. **Counterargument:** The party responsible for making the transfer could still make the transfer immediately upon the death of the transferor, but the recipient could be required to post a letter of credit or be required to execute an indemnity agreement protecting the party responsible for making the transfer. This would permit the immediate transfer of the property in question, the nonprobate benefit, while recognizing the paramount public policy of giving effect to the decedent's intent.

   4. **Example:** In *Cook*, above, after Douglas married Margaret, he executed a holographic will that expressly stated that he was giving the insurance policy to his wife Margaret and his son. The court declined to adopt the superwill doctrine. Because Douglas had failed to comply with the terms of the insurance policy for how the policy beneficiary could be changed, the original designation of Doris as beneficiary controlled.

   5. **UPC:** The UPC adopts the superwill doctrine *only* if the contract permits the beneficiary of the policy to be changed by a subsequently executed will. UPC §6-101. The UPC is silent as to what the rule should be if the contract does not address the issue, arguably leaving it open for debate, though the stronger view appears to be that the beneficiary may be changed by a subsequent superwill only if the terms of the will substitute expressly permit such modification.

F. **Pension plans:** Pension plans vary greatly, so generalizations are difficult, but typically they involve the creation of a property right in a fund of money to be used by the individual upon retirement. If the benefits are not completely exhausted by the time the party dies, the party typically has a right to designate a third-party beneficiary who shall receive the remaining proceeds (subject to family protection doctrines).

1. **Defined benefits plan:** Typically a defined benefits plan is funded by the employer, there is no individual account, and the employee is entitled to receive a fixed benefit (i.e., a percentage of their highest annual salary) for the remainder of his or her lifetime—an annuity.

   a. **Annuities:** An annuity is a stream of income for the remainder of one's lifetime, paid monthly at a fixed amount. Annuities can be purchased separately or are an option as to how one can receive benefits from a pension plan.

   b. **Joint and survivor annuity:** Many couples purchase a joint and survivor annuity. It guarantees fixed payments not only for the life of the employee, but also for the life of his or her spouse.

2. **Defined contribution plan:** Under a defined contribution plan, the level of "back end" benefits is not fixed; rather the level of "front end" contributions is fixed. Typically, each month the employer and the employee will contribute a fixed percentage of the employee's salary to an individual account set up for the individual. Upon retirement, the individual has rights to the funds in his or her account.

3. **Federal regulation:** Private pension plans are heavily regulated by federal statutes and regulations—most notably by the Employee Retirement Income Security Act of 1974 (ERISA). As a general rule, federal law preempts state law on time-of-death issues.

   Example: In *Egelhoff v. Egelhoff*, 532 U.S. 141 (2001), David and Donna Egelhoff were married. David worked for Boeing and his employee benefits included a life insurance policy and a pension plan. Both plans were covered by ERISA. David designated his wife as the beneficiary of both. Thereafter they divorced, and David died four months later without changing his beneficiary designation. Washington statute provided that divorce automatically revokes the beneficiary designation in favor of an ex-spouse in all revocable nonprobate arrangements. ERISA expressly preempts all state laws insofar as they may "relate to any employee benefit plan." In determining whether a state law has connection with or references such a plan, the Court has focused on the objective of ERISA. The Court ruled that the Washington statute had an impermissible connection with an ERISA plan and was preempted because it (1) would control who is to receive benefits under an ERISA plan, and (2) interfered with the nationally unified plan of administration.

IV. MULTIPLE PARTY ACCOUNTS

A. **Introduction:** Multiple party accounts can take many forms—bank accounts, brokerage accounts, Totten trusts, etc. There are latent issues inherent in such arrangements: What are the rights of the respective parties to the property in the account inter vivos, and what are the rights of the parties to the property in the account upon the death of one of the parties?

B. **Intent vs. paperwork:** The courts have long recognized that a person might have several different reasons for opening a multiple party account, but historically banks and brokerage houses offered the depositor only one option: a joint tenancy account. Even at common law, courts would take extrinsic evidence to determine the depositor's true intent and treat the property in the multiple party account consistent with the depositor's true intent.

C. **Depositor's intent:** Three possible reasons explain why a depositor (or depositors) might open a multiple party account (or add another party's name to an existing account, thereby making the account a multiple party account):

1. **Joint tenancy account:** A depositor may create a multiple party account because he or she intended to create a joint tenancy account. If so, the moment the account is opened, or the moment the other party's name is added to an existing account, the other party takes a proportional interest in the account inter vivos, and upon death, a right of survivorship exists such that the property will pass nonprobate.

2. **Convenience/agency account:** A convenience or agency account is where a depositor adds a second party to an account as a convenience to the depositor, to facilitate paying bills, for example. As such, the second party is acting as an agent for the depositor; the second party is merely helping out. The depositor does not intend that the second party receive any interest in the account. Inter vivos, the second party can access the account, but only to use it for the benefit of the depositor (not for the second party's own benefit), and upon death, there is no right of survivorship.

3. **P.O.D. account:** The depositor may intend a P.O.D. account to avoid probate. The depositor does not intend for the other party on the account to take any interest inter vivos, but at time of death, the depositor intends a right of survivorship. Any money remaining in the account is to go to the other party.

   a. **Common law:** Even if the depositor's true intent is to create a P.O.D. account, at common law P.O.D. accounts are an invalid attempt at a testamentary transfer without complying with Wills Act formalities. The assets remaining in the account upon the depositor's death fall to probate and are distributed pursuant to the depositor's will, if one exists, or otherwise according to the state's intestate distribution scheme.

   b. **Modern trend/UPC approach:** P.O.D. accounts are one of the many possible P.O.D. arrangements permitted under the modern trend/UPC approach.

D. **Bank's/Brokerage house's perspective:** While there are three possible reasons that a depositor might want to create a multiple party bank account, historically banks and brokerage houses offered only one multiple party account option—a joint tenancy account.

1. **P.O.D. accounts:** At common law, banks and brokerage houses cannot offer P.O.D. accounts, even if that is what a depositor wants, because they are not valid will substitutes.

2. **Agency accounts:** While banks and brokerage houses can offer a convenience or agency account, such an account exposes the bank/brokerage house to liability in the event it knew or should have known that the agent was misappropriating funds or if the bank/brokerage house permitted the agent to continue to access the account after the agency was terminated (an agent's authority typically is terminated upon the principal becoming incapacitated or dying).

3. **Joint tenancy accounts:** As long as the paperwork provides that the account is a joint tenancy account, the bank/brokerage house is protected. Thus, banks and brokerage houses often force depositors interested in creating multiple party accounts to use the paperwork stating the account is a joint tenancy account even if that is not the depositor's true intent.

E. **Extrinsic evidence:** Even at common law, the courts quickly realized that banks and brokerage houses routinely forced depositors interested in creating multiple party accounts to use a joint tenancy account, even if that was not the depositor's true intent. Because the joint tenancy account may have been involuntarily created, the courts take extrinsic evidence to determine the depositor's true intent and then treat the account accordingly.

1. **Temporal focus:** The key is to distinguish the depositor's intent at the time the multiple party account was created (either at the time the account was opened if multiple names were put on the account from its inception, or at the time a second party's name was added to an existing account).

   Subsequent comments/actions: Although the depositor's intent at the time the multiple party bank account is created controls, the depositor's subsequent comments and/or actions may be relevant to the issue of his or her intent at the time the account was created.

2. **Burden of proof:** If the depositor executes paperwork that expressly states that the account is a joint tenancy account, the paperwork creates a presumption that the account is a "true" joint tenancy account. To overcome the presumption, most jurisdictions require clear and convincing evidence of a different intent.

3. **Example:** In *Varela v. Bernachea,* 917 So. 2d 295 (Fla. Dist. Ct. App. 2005), Bernachea, a retired attorney, fell in love with Varela. After a year of traveling together, Varela moved into his condo in Florida and he paid all of her expenses. Bernachea added Varela to his bank account as a joint tenant with a right of survivorship. Varela received a check card for the account which she freely used. Bernachea then suffered a heart attack, and while in the hospital, she wrote a check that transferred the entire $280,000.00 in the joint account into an account in her name alone. Two weeks after Bernachea returned from the hospital, he demanded the bank return the money to the original account and the bank complied and initiated proceedings to settle ownership status. Bernachea alleged that he did not have donative intent and that Varela had restricted access to the account because she only had a check card and not paper checks. The court ruled when a joint bank account is established with the funds of one person, a true joint tenancy is presumed and may be rebutted only by clear and convincing evidence to the contrary. The Court determined that a check card with no limit on its withdrawal abilities had the same significance as a check so Varela's access to the account was unrestricted. This, coupled with the fact that the only other evidence to rebut the presumption was an attorney of 30 years saying he did not understand the meaning of a right of survivorship, was insufficient to provide clear and convincing evidence Bernachea did not have donative intent. Varela was entitled to half of the money in the account.

F. **Criticism:** The common law approach of taking extrinsic evidence to determine the true intent of the depositor has been widely criticized for promoting litigation. Almost anytime there is a multiple party account there is the potential for litigation, usually between family members. At a minimum, the common law approach creates the potential for strike suits filed just for their settlement value.

   Paperwork conclusive: Some courts have gone so far as to hold that the joint tenancy paperwork is conclusive and extrinsic evidence is inadmissible to show a contrary intent.

G. **UPC approach:** The UPC provides that, inter vivos, it is presumed that the parties to a multiple party account own in proportion to their contributions, and that upon the death of any party, it is presumed that there is a right of survivorship. The presumptions control the distribution of the money in the account unless clear and convincing evidence of a contrary intent exists. UPC §§6-201–6-227.

1. **Survival requirement:** The UPC imposes an express survival requirement for parties to a multiple party account. UPC §6-212. There is no express survival requirement for other contracts with P.O.D. clauses.

   P.O.D. accounts: The UPC permits P.O.D. multiple party accounts. If the account is a P.O.D. account, the UPC applies the wills-related doctrines of lapse and anti-lapse to the beneficiary. UPC §§6-212, 2-706. In addition, if the account is a P.O.D. account, the beneficiary cannot be changed by will. UPC §6-213(b).

2. **Criticism:** The UPC "presumption" approach does little to reduce the potential for litigation; it merely changes the presumed characterization of the account from a joint tenancy account to what amounts to a P.O.D. account; it also has the effect of changing who has the burden of proof.

3. **Example:** In *Varela*, under the UPC approach, the presumption would arise that Varela did *not* receive any interest in the bank account inter vivos. Varela would have had the burden of proving by clear and convincing evidence that Bernachea intended a true joint tenancy when he added her name to the account.

H. **Totten trusts:** Although common law refuses to recognize P.O.D. bank accounts, most jurisdictions recognize "Totten trust savings accounts." For all practical purposes, Totten trust accounts are very similar to P.O.D. accounts. Totten trusts are rationalized as a form of inter vivos trusts (though not subject to the general trust rules). The depositor sets up a Totten account by depositing money in the account in the name of the depositor "for the benefit of" the beneficiary. Legal title is in the name of the depositor, but equitable title is in the name of the beneficiary. The bifurcation of the legal and equitable title constitutes an intent to create a trust.

   1. **Revocability:** The trust is deemed revocable so that depositor withdrawals are permitted without constituting a breach of trust (though general trust law holds a trust is irrevocable unless an express clause states that it is revocable).

   2. **Testamentary modification:** An express clause in a will changing the beneficiary is permitted (though generally wills cannot change the terms of a will substitute).

   3. **Survival requirement:** Most jurisdictions require the beneficiary of a Totten trust account to survive the depositor (though generally at common law there is no survival requirement for beneficiaries claiming under trusts or other will substitutes).

   4. **Commentary:** Totten trusts are unique. They should be segregated from the other nonprobate property arrangements because of their unique rules.

V. POUR-OVER WILLS AND INTER VIVOS TRUSTS

A. **Introduction:** The inter vivos trust and pour-over will combination is the most common estate planning scheme today. The revocable inter vivos trust has the principal advantage of avoiding probate, but only as to those assets placed in the trust inter vivos. Unlike a will, which automatically reaches out and applies to all of the decedent's probate assets at death, an inter vivos trust applies only to those assets transferred to the trust inter vivos. It is virtually impossible to put all of one's assets in an inter vivos trust, even if one is so inclined. People acquire and dispose of assets on such a rapid basis it is impossible to put all of one's assets in an inter vivos trust. Most settlors put their larger assets, and those assets that they do not use on a regular basis, in the trust.

They use a pour-over will for their other assets and for their newly acquired assets that they did not have time to put in the trust before they died.

B. Pour-over wills: A pour-over will is a will that contains an express clause giving some or all of the decedent's probate property to the trustee of the decedent's inter vivos trust, to hold and distribute pursuant to the terms of the trust. Typically the pour-over clause is the residuary clause, but it need not be. The clause can transfer to the trust a specific gift or a general gift, but the norm is either the residuary clause or a general gift of money.

Standard clause: A typical pour-over clause reads something like the following: "I give the rest, residue, and remainder of my estate to the trustee of my inter vivos trust, to hold and distribute pursuant to its terms."

C. Validity: The effect of a pour-over clause is that a document that was not executed with Wills Act formalities (the inter vivos trust) controls who takes some or all of the decedent's probate property. This violates both the spirit and the letter of the Wills Act formalities that any disposition of the decedent's probate property must comply with the Wills Act formalities. Before a pour-over clause can be given effect, the pour-over clause must be validated.

Inter vivos vs. testamentary funding: As to those assets transferred to the inter vivos trust during the settlor's lifetime, the inter vivos trust is a well-recognized will substitute and its terms are given effect regardless of the validity of any pour-over clause. As to the decedent's probate assets being transferred to the trust via a pour-over clause, that transfer constitutes a testamentary transfer that is subject to the Wills Act formalities. Before the inter vivos trust can apply to the decedent's probate property, the pour-over clause must be validated.

D. Common law: At common law, two possible "will-expanding" doctrines are used to try to validate a pour-over clause: acts of independent significance and incorporation by reference.

   1. Acts of independent significance: The doctrine of acts of independent significance provides that a will can reference an act outside of the will, and the act can control either who takes or how much they take, as long as the referenced act has its own significance apart from its effect upon the disposition of the decedent's probate property.

      a. Pour-over clause: As applied to a pour-over clause scenario, the "act" referenced in the will is the reference to the trust. The question becomes whether the trust has its own significance apart from its effect upon the decedent's probate property. As long as the trust is funded inter vivos and has some property in it at the time of the decedent's death, the trust has its own significance—holding and managing of the property placed in the trust inter vivos.

      b. Temporal sequence: Under acts of independent significance, it does not matter when the inter vivos trust is created (before or after the execution of the will), as long as the trust is created inter vivos (that some property is placed in the trust inter vivos) and has property in it at the time of the decedent's death.

      c. Trust amendments: Under acts of independent significance, amendments to the trust are valid and can be given effect, regardless of when they are created.

      d. Probate court supervision: Inter vivos trusts generally *are not* subject to probate court supervision. Testamentary trusts generally *are* subject to probate court supervision. With acts of independent significance, as for the property placed in the trust while the party is alive, the trust is an inter vivos trust. As for the property being poured into the trust via the pour-over clause, arguably those assets likewise should be treated as an inter vivos trust not subject to probate court supervision. But some probate courts retain jurisdiction over the assets being poured over, in essence treating the trust as a testamentary trust, subjecting it to the court's supervision and requiring the trustee to account to the court.

Costs: As a general rule, greater costs and administrative burdens are associated with testamentary trusts as opposed to inter vivos trust. Typically the trust is subject to probate court supervision for the life of the trust, and the trustee has a duty to account to the probate court on a regular basis.

2. **Incorporation by reference:** Incorporation by reference permits a will to incorporate and give effect to the provisions of a document that was not executed with Wills Act formalities as long as (1) the will expresses the intent to incorporate the document, (2) the will describes the document with reasonable certainty, and (3) the document was in existence at the time the will was executed.

   a. **Pour-over clause:** As applied to a pour-over will scenario, incorporation by reference incorporates the inter vivos trust *instrument* into the will and gives effect to it, thereby permitting the terms of the inter vivos trust instrument to control who takes the decedent's probate property and how much they take.

   b. **Temporal sequence:** Although there are three requirements for incorporation by reference, as applied to the pour-over will scenario, invariably the element at issue is whether the inter vivos trust *instrument* (as opposed to the trust itself) was in existence at the time the will was executed.

      Analysis: The courts apply a low threshold to the first two requirements. By stating in the will that the testator gives whatever the gift is "to the trustee of my inter vivos trust, to hold and administer pursuant to the terms of the trust," the testator has adequately expressed the intent to incorporate the trust instrument into the will and has described it with reasonable certainty (assuming the decedent has only one trust instrument). In the typical pour-over clause setting, the only element at issue is whether the trust instrument was in existence at the time the will was executed. The burden of proof is on the party seeking to incorporate the inter vivos trust instrument.

   c. **Funding:** Incorporation by reference incorporates the trust *instrument,* not the *trust,* so there does not have to be any funding in the trust. If there is property in the trust inter vivos, one should probably use acts of independent significance to validate the pour-over clause because it has more benefits associated with it.

   d. **Trust amendments:** One of the disadvantages of using incorporation by reference to validate a pour-over clause is that the doctrine incorporates the trust instrument *as it existed at the time the will was executed.* Any subsequent amendments to the inter vivos trust instrument cannot be incorporated and given effect (1) unless the will is re-executed or (2) a codicil is executed that redates the will under republication by codicil.

   e. **Probate court supervision:** If incorporation by reference is used to validate a pour-over clause, the trust instrument is incorporated into the will. The effect is that the trust is deemed a testamentary trust, with the added costs and administrative burdens inherent in a testamentary trust.

E. UTATA: In light of the benefits of the pour-over will and inter vivos trust combination, and the hassles and limitations of the common law validation doctrines, estate planners brought pressure for legislative action to facilitate validating the pour-over will and inter vivos trust testamentary scheme. The result was UTATA—the Uniform Testamentary Additions to Trusts Act. UTATA arguably gives the estate planner and client the best of both worlds. As long as the transferor meets the UTATA requirements, the transferor does not have to put a penny into his or her trust inter vivos; the pour-over clause is valid; all amendments to the trust are valid even if executed after the date of the will; and, after the probate property is poured over to the trust pursuant to the pour-over clause, the trust is treated as an inter vivos trust that is not subject to probate court supervision.

   1. UTATA requirements—original version: The original (and widely adopted) version of UTATA required (1) that the will refer to the trust, (2) that the terms of the trust be set forth in a writing separate from the will, and (3) that the trust instrument be executed ***prior to or concurrently with*** the execution of the will.

   a. Observation: The original UTATA requirements are basically the same as incorporation by reference, only with the added requirement that the trust instrument must be signed prior to or concurrently with the execution of the will.

   b. Analysis: In analyzing the UTATA requirements and the typical pour-over will scenario, the key element typically is the requirement that the trust be executed (signed) prior to or concurrently with the execution of the will. The pour-over clause by its nature satisfies the first requirement, that the will refer to the trust. The requirement that the terms of the trust be set forth in a separate document provides a bright line between a testamentary trust and a UTATA/inter vivos trust. If the settlor wants a testamentary trust, which is subject to probate court supervision, the settlor should put the terms of the trust in the will. If, however, the settlor wants the benefits of a trust but without the costs and administrative burdens of probate court supervision, the settlor has to put the terms of the trust in a document separate from the will. The requirement is easy to apply and analyze. The key requirement then is that the trust instrument must be signed prior to or concurrently with the execution of the will.

   c. UTATA benefits: First and foremost, if the settlor/testator meets the requirements of UTATA, the trust is deemed an inter vivos trust for purposes of probate court supervision, thereby saving the trust money and facilitating its administration, even though not a penny is put in the trust inter vivos. Second, all amendments to the trust are valid regardless of when they are executed.

   2. Revised UTATA: The revised version of UTATA eliminates the requirement that the trust instrument must be executed ***prior to or concurrently with the execution of the will,*** thereby making it even easier to validate a pour-over clause under UTATA. As long as the trust instrument is signed by the settlor anytime before he or she dies, and the will refers to the trust instrument and the terms of the trust are set forth in a separate document, the pour-over clause is valid and the trust is considered a UTATA trust not subject to probate court supervision. The UPC has adopted the revised version of UTATA. UPC §2-511.

   3. UTATA trust—inter vivos vs. testamentary trust: Before the adoption of UTATA, when classifying a trust based upon when it was created, there were only two possible types of trusts: inter vivos trusts and testamentary trusts. To have an inter vivos trust, property had to be transferred to the trust inter vivos. The traditional testamentary trust was set forth in the decedent's will and was funded when the settlor/testator died. UTATA is a hybrid trust in that it can be wholly unfunded until time of death (which makes it look like a testamentary trust), yet the express provisions of UTATA state that, for purposes of probate court supervision, it is treated like an inter vivos trust and is not subject to probate court supervision. To the extent other doctrines draw a distinction between inter vivos trusts and testamentary trusts, the issue is how the UTATA trust should be classified and treated for purposes of those doctrines.

a. **Divorce:** All jurisdictions have statutes that provide that upon divorce all provisions in each spouse's will in favor of the ex-spouse are automatically revoked by operation of law. Most statutes apply only to the ex-spouse's wills and not to any will substitutes. Because a testamentary trust is considered part of the will, the doctrine applies to testamentary trusts. Inasmuch as inter vivos trusts are will substitutes, the statute does not apply to inter vivos trusts. The issue is whether a UTATA trust should be treated like a testamentary trust, which is subject to the divorce doctrine, or an inter vivos trust, which is not.

b. **Example:** In ***Clymer v. Mayo,*** 473 N.E.2d 1084 (Mass. 1985), Clara Mayo properly executed a will and inter vivos, revocable trust instrument. The will gave her personal property to her husband and the residue of her probate property to the trustee of her trust, to hold and distribute pursuant to the terms of the trust. Clara also changed her life insurance policy and pension plans to make the proceeds payable to the trustee, to hold and distribute pursuant to the terms of the trust. Thereafter Clara and her husband divorced, and Clara died without revising any of her estate planning documents. Clara's heirs at law claimed that the pour-over clause was invalid because the trust was wholly unfunded at time of death and therefore they were entitled to receive her property. Clara's ex-spouse admitted that he was not entitled to take under her will due to the revocation by operation of law doctrine, but claimed that he was still entitled to take under the terms of the trust because the revocation by divorce doctrine in that jurisdiction applied to wills only. First, the court applied UTATA and held it proper to validate the pour-over clause and trust. The trust was executed concurrently with the will and did not have to be funded inter vivos. Second, the court held that because the decedent considered the will and trust one integrated testamentary scheme, the UTATA trust should be treated like a testamentary trust—that is, subject to the revocation by operation of law doctrine, at least where the trust was wholly unfunded at time of death.

4. **Common law doctrines post-UTATA:** UTATA does not render the common law validation doctrines meaningless. The key is to validate the pour-over clause to give effect to the testator's intent that the property be distributed pursuant to the terms of the trust. UTATA facilitates validating a pour-over clause and has the most benefits associated with it, but if the pour-over will cannot be validated under UTATA, the pour-over clause fails unless the clause can be validated using one of the common law doctrines. If the trust was funded inter vivos, use acts of independent significance. If the trust was not funded inter vivos, try incorporation by reference.

Example: Tom calls his attorney, Alice, and asks her to prepare an inter vivos trust and pour-over will. The pour-over clause gives the residue of his estate to his trustee to hold and distribute pursuant to the terms of the trust. Alice does as Tom requests. Tom properly executes the will but forgets to sign the trust instrument. Shortly thereafter Tom is killed in a car crash. Because the trust instrument was never signed, the pour-over clause cannot be validated under

UTATA (either the original version or the revised version). Because Tom did not transfer any property to the trust inter vivos, the pour-over clause cannot be validated under acts of independent significance. Because the will refers to the trust and the trust instrument is in existence, the pour-over clause can be validated under incorporation by reference. The trust is considered a testamentary trust subject to probate court supervision, but the probate property will be held and distributed pursuant to the terms of the trust.

5. **Failure to validate pour-over clause:** If the pour-over clause cannot be validated under UTATA, acts of independent significance, or incorporation by reference, the pour-over clause fails. If the pour-over clause fails, the property in question cannot be distributed pursuant to the terms of the trust. If the pour-over clause is the residuary clause of the will, and it fails, the property falls to intestacy. If the pour-over clause is not the residuary clause, and it fails, the property in question falls to the residuary clause if there is one or, if not, to intestacy.

   Example: Tom handwrites a valid, dated holographic will that gives all of his property to the trustee of his inter vivos trust, to hold and distribute pursuant to the terms of the trust. A week later, Tom types up a dated trust instrument, but he fails to sign it or to transfer any property to the trust. Tom dies without doing anything else. Because the trust instrument was never signed, the pour-over clause cannot be validated under UTATA (either the original version or the revised version). Because Tom did not transfer any property to the trust inter vivos, the pour-over clause cannot be validated under acts of independent significance. Because the trust instrument was not in existence when the will was executed, the pour-over clause cannot be validated under incorporation by reference. The pour-over clause fails, which means the residuary clause fails. The property passes via intestacy to Tom's heirs.

F. **Revocable trusts:** A number of pros and cons are associated with using revocable inter vivos trusts, though the pros outweigh the cons for the typical individual.

1. **Inter vivos:** Using an inter vivos trust to hold and manage one's assets while one is alive offers a variety of potential benefits, though at a cost.

   a. **Professional management:** While a settlor can appoint him- or herself as trustee to hold and administer the trust property, a settlor may appoint a professional trustee. This option is particularly attractive if (1) the settlor anticipates impending incapacity (creating an inter vivos trust is cheaper and easier than initiating guardianship or conservatorship proceedings), or (2) the settlor wants to transfer property to minors who lack capacity to hold title. Putting property in trust, however, increases costs (trustee's fees) and administrative expenses in dealing with the assets (increased paperwork).

   b. **Segregating assets:** Trusts are a good way of segregating assets to ensure that assets are not commingled. This option is particularly attractive to spouses or partners who want to make sure their assets are not mixed with other assets.

   c. **Taxes:** As long as the settlor retains the power to revoke the trust, for tax purposes the trust property is legally treated as if it were still the settlor's property regardless of the terms of the trust.

2. **Time of death:** The principal benefit of using a revocable, inter vivos trust is that the property transferred to the trust inter vivos avoids probate. Avoiding probate raises a number of different considerations.

a. **Costs:** Avoiding probate saves probate court costs, executor's fees, and attorneys' fees, but offsetting these future savings are the present fees inherent in having the trust drafted, in transferring assets to the trust, and possibly in paying trustee's fees to administer the trust.

b. **Tying property up:** Probating even a simple estate typically takes 12 to 24 months. Property passing through probate is tied up during the probate process. Property placed in an inter vivos trust avoids probate, thereby avoiding the hassles and delays associated with probate. Putting property in trust, however, does increase somewhat the administrative difficulties of dealing with the property.

c. **Creditors' claims:** If one anticipates a number of creditors' claims against a decedent's property, it may be better to have the decedent's property pass through probate. The probate process requires creditors to bring their claims within a fairly limited time frame or be forever barred. In contrast, if a decedent's property is in a revocable inter vivos trust, there is no shortened time period within which creditors have to bring their claims; creditors get the full benefit of the standard statute of limitations to bring their claims.

d. **Privacy:** When a decedent dies, an inventory of the decedent's probate assets and creditor's claims is public information. Moreover, when a will is offered for probate, it becomes a public document revealing the testator's wishes as to "who got what" that anyone can access. Inter vivos trusts, on the other hand, are private legal documents not subject to public inspection.

e. **Ancillary probate:** If the decedent owned real property in a jurisdiction other than the jurisdiction where probate is opened, "ancillary" probate in the jurisdiction where the real property is located is necessary, thereby further adding to the costs and hassles of probate. By placing the real estate in question in a revocable, inter vivos trust, ancillary probate can be avoided.

f. **Family protection doctrines:** A number of doctrines are designed to protect a decedent's family members from intentionally or unintentionally being disinherited (elective share, pretermitted spouse, pretermitted child, overlooked child). The details of each doctrine vary from jurisdiction to jurisdiction, but in some jurisdictions the protective doctrine applies only to the decedent's probate property. In such jurisdictions, an individual can shield his or her assets from such claims by putting the property in a revocable, inter vivos trust.

g. **Testamentary trusts:** Testamentary trusts are typically created as part of the probate process. Probate courts usually maintain supervision over the trust, even after probate has otherwise closed, for the life of the trust, requiring the trustee to account to the court on a regular basis. Such probate court supervision adds costs and administrative burdens that are avoided by using an inter vivos trust.

h. **Choice of law options:** When a settlor creates an inter vivos revocable trust of personal property, he or she has the power to choose which state's laws will govern the trust—the law where the trust is administered (which can be almost any state if the settlor sets it up right), the law where the settlor is domiciled, or the law where any beneficiary is domiciled. The choice of law option permits settlers to select whatever state's laws best support the settlor's overall testamentary scheme. (Where the trust contains real property, the law of the state where the real property is located controls. Where the trust is a testamentary trust, courts typically apply the law where the probate estate is opened regardless of the terms of the trust.)

UPC: The UPC permits testators to choose which state's laws will govern the administration of their will and probate estate on the same basis as inter vivos trusts—except for the state's family protection doctrines. The UPC approach gives testators the same flexibility as settlors in choosing the controlling state law, arguably reducing one of the incentives for using an inter vivos trust.

i. **Challenges to testamentary scheme:** Although an inter vivos trust can be challenged on the same capacity grounds as a will (lack of capacity generally, insane delusion, undue influence, fraud), as a practical matter it is much more difficult to challenge a trust. While the settlor is alive, it is much more difficult to challenge a trust—challengers have to assert their claims face to face against the settlor, and the settlor has the chance to defend him- or herself in court. And if the challenge is not brought promptly, once the inter vivos trust has been interacting with third parties, it becomes much more difficult as a practical matter for a court to set aside weeks, months, or maybe even years' worth of transactions. Using an inter vivos trust reduces both the chances that the testamentary scheme will be attacked and the chances that the claim will be successful.

j. **Estate taxes:** Because the federal government treats the settlor of an inter vivos revocable trust as the owner of the property in the trust as long as it is revocable, there are no federal estate tax benefits to using an inter vivos revocable trust.

k. **"Dead hand" control:** Using a trust facilitates "dead hand" control. A will typically devises property to the beneficiary in fee simple absolute. The beneficiary then is free to use the property as he or she sees fit. A trust, on the other hand, facilitates conditional gifts to beneficiaries. Beneficiaries may be entitled to receive property from the trust only as long as they behave in a certain manner. Trusts can also be used to ensure that a surviving spouse complies with a mutually agreed upon estate plan. Both spouses can put their assets in an inter vivos trust with an agreed-upon testamentary disposition scheme that becomes irrevocable upon the death of the first spouse.

VI. JOINT TENANCIES IN REAL PROPERTY

A. **Introduction:** A joint tenancy (or tenancy by the entirety) is a form of concurrent ownership where multiple parties own the property in question both in whole and in shares. The key characteristic is the right of survivorship. Under the right of survivorship, upon the death of one party, his or her share is *extinguished* and the shares of the surviving joint tenants are recalculated. In the case of a joint tenancy with more than two parties, this process of recalculating shares continues until only one party is surviving, at which time the concurrent ownership ends and the party owns it outright with no right of survivorship. When only one party remains, the property is no longer nonprobate property. Upon that party's death, it falls into his or her probate estate, unless he or she takes the appropriate steps to create a new nonprobate arrangement.

B. **Probate avoidance:** If a joint tenant (or tenant in the entirety) dies, his or her share is extinguished. His or her share was tantamount to a life estate. The deceased tenant has no interest in the property that can fall to probate. No interest *passes* when a joint tenant or (tenant by the entirety) dies. The tenants owned in whole from the outset. The surviving tenant(s)' shares are simply recalculated.

C. Devisability: Although a joint tenancy can be severed inter vivos and converted into a tenancy in common (with inheritable and devisable shares), the mere execution of a will does not sever a joint tenancy (or tenancy by the entirety for that matter). Even if the will makes express reference to the deceased tenant's interest in the property, execution of the will does not sever the joint tenancy. The right of survivorship extinguishes the joint tenant's interest before a will has any effect upon the property.

D. Creditor's claims: Because a joint tenant's interest in the property is extinguished upon his or her death, nothing is left for creditors of a deceased joint tenant to reach. Each joint tenant's interest is tantamount to a life estate, and when the life estate is extinguished, the party has no remaining interest in the property for creditors to reach. Creditors of a joint tenant must assert their claims while the joint tenant is alive. (The rights of creditors of tenants by the entirety is beyond the scope of this material.)

VII. PLANNING FOR THE POSSIBILITY OF INCAPACITY

A. Introduction: Humans are living longer and longer, and with the evolution of modern medicine, it is becoming increasingly likely that one may lose legal capacity well before one's death. Proper estate planning should include planning for the possibility of incapacity. Such planning should take into consideration the individual's wishes with respect to how his or her property should be managed, and the individual's wishes with respect to his or her health care and disposition of his or her body.

B. Asset management: Estate planners can use several tools to plan for managing their assets during incapacity.

    1. Inter vivos revocable trust: As noted above, arguably the best legal tool available for providing for the possibility of one's incapacity is the inter vivos revocable trust. The settlor can appoint him- or herself as the initial trustee, and then expressly appoint a successor trustee in the event the settlor is unable or unwilling to serve as trustee. This can avoid the expense and emotional stress often involved in instituting guardianship or conservatorship proceedings.

    2. Durable power of attorney: A power of attorney authorizes one to act for another. It creates a principal-agent relationship where the terms of the power dictate the scope of the agent's power to act for the principal. The standard power of attorney automatically terminates upon the incapacity of the principal party. The durable power of attorney continues despite the incapacity of the principal. It is a relatively simple and cheap method of planning for one's incapacity.

        a. Differences from trust: Unlike a trustee, an agent's power under a durable power of attorney automatically terminates upon the principal's death. The property subject to the durable power of attorney does not avoid probate. And an agent does not have legal title to the property subject to the power, making many third parties more reluctant to deal with an agent.

        b. Scope: Most states require that a durable power of attorney be created in writing. The writing can either incorporate by reference a statutory list of powers or it can be drafted to suit a principal's particular wishes. A power of attorney that gives an agent broad authority to act should be construed in light of the surrounding circumstances. Even if a power of attorney is worded broadly enough to appear to authorize actions that may be inconsistent with the principal's interests or intent, the instrument should be construed narrowly to prohibit such actions absent express authorization for the questionable action. What constitutes express authorization for questionable actions has proved to be a fertile source of litigation.

   c. **Example:** In *In re Estate of Kurrelmeyer*, 895 A.2d 207 (Vt. 2006), Louis Kurrelmeyer executed two durable general powers of attorney in favor of his wife, Martina, and his daughter, Nancy. Pursuant to these powers Martina transferred real estate owned by her husband, including the Clearwater property, into a trust she created. Later, Louis died and his will designated that the Clearwater property would be given to Martina in life estate and upon her death pass to Louis's children. Her trust, however, gave Martina additional rights in the property, including the ability to sell the house. Louis's son objected to the exclusion of the Clearwater property from the inventory of Louis's estate. The court found first that the durable power of attorney did authorize the creation of a trust because the express words in the instrument included the conveyance of real estate and a clause to "do and perform all and every act and thing whatsoever necessary to be done . . . as [Louis] could do." Furthermore, the fact that the trust was created by an agent, an attorney-in-fact, did not affect the trust's legitimacy as a trust does not require personal performance such as an affidavit does. Finally, the Court remanded the case to the lower court to determine whether or not Martina's actions in this instance breached her fiduciary duty of loyalty to Louis or violated the power of attorney instrument which prohibited the agent from making gifts to herself. (On remainder, the court upheld the validity of the trust and Martina's actions, a decision that was further appealed.)

C. Health care management: Modern medicine is steadily prolonging the dying process. This development raises serious financial and ethical issues. Some experts claim that the day is not far off when the dying process will consume all of one's assets, thereby depleting the individual's net worth and leaving nothing to pass on to one's heirs. Others have ethical and personal objections to artificially prolonging the dying process. While one has capacity, one has the power to control the health care one receives, including the right to refuse medical treatment. Prudent estate planning now includes planning for incapacity to ensure that one's wishes with respect to one's health care are respected.

1. **Living wills:** A living will (also known as an advance directive, an instructional directive or a medical directive) is a document that directs that no extraordinary medical treatment be undertaken when there is no reasonable expectation of recovery. Living wills are heavily regulated by statute, and care should be taken in drafting and executing living wills to ensure compliance with such statutes.

   Disadvantages: The principal disadvantage of living wills is that they have to anticipate possible scenarios and provide in advance for what the individual would want done under the situation. Living wills lack flexibility when the actual situation does not fit neatly into the express terms of the instrument.

2. **Durable power of attorney for health care decisions:** The durable power of attorney for health care decisions appoints an agent to make health care decisions for one after one becomes incapacitated. The instrument can give general directives to the agent that must be followed (in which case some authorities refer to it as a hybrid or combined directives approach), but the durable power of attorney for health care decisions has the added benefit of flexibility. By

giving the power to an agent, the agent can take the principal's wishes and all of the circumstances into consideration before making a decision as to what the principal would have wanted under the particular circumstances.

3. **Decision maker for incompetent:** In the absence of a living will or a durable power of attorney, most states authorize an incompetent person's immediate family to make health care decisions for him or her. Although the details vary from state to state, the typical order parallels the order of intestate takers—spouse, children, parents, etc.

4. **Example:** In ***Bush v. Schiavo***, 885 So. 2d 321 (Fla. 2004), Theresa Schiavo was married to Michael in 1990 when she suffered a cardiac arrest and never regained consciousness. In 1998, Michael petitioned the guardianship court to terminate life-prolonging measures. The Schindlers, Theresa's parents, opposed the petition. Following a hearing at which both sides presented evidence, the guardianship court found by clear and convincing evidence that Theresa was in a persistent vegetative state and that she would elect to cease life-prolonging measures if she were competent to make her own decision. Six days after nutrition and hydration were withdrawn, the Florida legislature passed a statute authorizing the governor to stay the removal where a person has no written medical directive, is in a persistent vegetative state, has had nutrition and hydration withdrawn, and a member of the patient's family opposes the removal. The court ruled that the statute was invalid because it violated the separation of powers provisions of the state constitution. For the legislature to pass a law that authorizes the executive branch to interfere with the final determination in a case unconstitutionally invades the power of the judicial branch.

5. **Physician-assisted suicide:** Only one state, Oregon, permits physician-assisted suicide.

6. **Disposition of one's body:** All states have adopted some form of the Uniform Anatomical Gift Act, permitting one to give one's body, or any part thereof, to any authorized health care provider for medical research or transplantation. The act permits the decedent to identify a specific individual who is to receive his or her body or any part thereof for transplantation. The gift may be made by will or by a donor card signed by the individual (some states require that the card be witnessed).

Quiz Yourself on WILL SUBSTITUTES AND PLANNING FOR INCAPACITY

39. Luke and Hans decide to make a movie together as partners. Their signed, typewritten agreement includes a provision that in the event of the death of one, all of his interest goes to the surviving partner, if one, or otherwise to his parents equally. During filming, Hans falls in love with Lea and marries her. Unfortunately, shortly thereafter Hans accidentally trips over some little green character and hits his head, killing Hans instantly. Hans died testate with a will giving all of his property to his wife Lea. Who takes Hans's interest in the movie? _____

40. Ozzie and Sharon are married. He has a life insurance policy that designates Sharon as beneficiary. Thereafter, Ozzie and Sharon develop marital problems, and Ozzie moves out. He meets Anna Nicoli and is immediately captivated by her abilities. He properly executes a new will that expressly provides

that he leaves the proceeds of his life insurance policy to Anna Nicoli, and the rest of his property to his children. Thereafter Ozzie dies. Who takes the proceeds of his insurance policy? _____

41. Pete is a single wills and trusts professor. He is invited to teach in Europe for the coming year. Before leaving the country, he puts his colleague's name (Bob) on his bank account as a joint tenant so that Bob can pay Pete's bills while Pete is out of the country. Unfortunately, Pete is killed while participating in the running of the bulls (he is trampled by the people running—even in death denied the glory of saying that he was gored to death). Pete had no will. Who takes the money in his bank account? _____

42. Bubba and Emily own Malibuacres as joint tenants with right of survivorship. Bubba properly executes a valid will that provides in part that he devises his interest in Malibuacres to his mom, Mia, and the rest of his property to his grandmother, Gia. When Bubba dies, who takes his interest in Malibuacres? _____

43. Bill properly creates an inter vivos trust for the benefit of his intern, Monica. Thereafter, Bill tears up the trust, declaring that he does not want "that woman" to take any of his property. Bill dies in a freak accident (he accidentally chokes on a cigar). Was the trust properly revoked? _____

44. Sally creates an inter vivos revocable trust and funds it with her house. The trust is for Sally's benefit during her life, and, upon her death, the property is to go to her dad. The terms of the trust provide that it may be amended or revoked by a writing delivered to the trustee expressing the intent to revoke. The trust appoints her sister, Toni, as trustee. Thereafter Sally's dad abandons her mom. Sally is livid at her dad and concerned about her mom's financial situation. Sally properly executes a will that expressly provides that she revokes her trust and gives her house to her mom. A few days later, Sally dies unexpectedly in a car crash. Who takes the house? _____

45. George W. is the son of a widely respected family. A couple of years ago, the family had George W. put all of his principal assets (including his profits from some questionable stock deals) in an inter vivos revocable trust that provides for his benefit during his lifetime, and, upon his death, for the benefit of his parents. George W. has been surprisingly successful, so successful that he decides to purchase a baseball team. When George W. applies for the loan to purchase the baseball team, he lists his assets as his own, forgetting to mention that the assets had been transferred to the inter vivos revocable trust. (George W. did not intend to defraud the bank. He has always had trouble remembering names and details.) Shortly after the bank gives George W. a substantial unsecured loan, George W. cuts his finger on a dangling chad. The cut becomes infected, and, before the doctors can do anything, he dies. There are not enough assets in George W.'s probate estate to repay the loan to the bank. Can the bank reach his assets in the inter vivos revocable trust? _____

46. Jerry executes a will that provides that it leaves all of his property to the trustee of his trust, to hold and distribute pursuant to the terms of the trust. Thereafter, Jerry has his attorney draw up a trust instrument that is for the benefit of Elaine during her lifetime, and, upon her death, the property is to be distributed outright—one half to George, and the other half to Kramer. Jerry executes the trust instrument at his attorney's office, but on his way to his accountant's to transfer property to the trust, Jerry is hit and killed by a mail truck. Who takes Jerry's property? _____

47. Groucho properly executes a valid will that leaves all of his property to the trustee of his trust, to hold and distribute according to the terms of this trust. A month later, Groucho drafts (but does not sign) a trust instrument that provides that the trust is for Harpo's benefit during his life, and, upon his death,

the principal is to be split between Chico and Zeppo. A month later, Groucho executes a codicil to his will, changing his executor to Zeppo. A month later, Groucho drafts (but does not sign) an amendment to his trust, giving an outright gift of $100,000 to Mrs. Claypool. A week later, Groucho makes an appointment with his attorney to sign the trust and trust amendment (and fund it), but the night before his appointment he falls asleep while smoking a cigar and dies from the ensuing fire. Who takes his property?   _____

Answers

39. At common law, a written agreement that purports to transfer a property interest at time of death is valid only if it qualifies as a valid will or as a valid nonprobate transfer. The partnership agreement between Luke and Hans is not a valid will because no evidence supports that there were any witnesses, so it cannot be an attested will, and it was typed, so it cannot be a holographic will. While one might try to argue that it qualifies as a joint tenancy, the alternative gift-over in each partner's parents shows that the parties did not intend to create a joint tenancy. The agreement is a contract with a P.O.D. clause. At common law, such contracts and clauses are valid will substitutes only if they qualify as a life insurance contract. Because the partnership agreement is not a life insurance agreement, the P.O.D. clause is invalid. Hans's interest in the movie falls into probate where it will be distributed to Lea pursuant to the terms of his will. Under the modern trend/UPC approach, all contracts with P.O.D. clauses are valid. Here, the court will enforce the partnership agreement and give Hans's interest to Luke as a valid nonprobate transfer.

40. The life insurance policy is a valid will substitute. The general rule is that the beneficiary of a life insurance policy can be changed only in accordance with the terms of the life insurance contract. The standard life insurance contract does not permit change of beneficiary by a properly executed will. The attempt to change the beneficiary is an attempt at what has been called a superwill. The general rule is that such superwills are not effective to change the beneficiary of a P.O.D. clause. Sharon still takes. The UPC permits superwills where the contract permits the will to change the beneficiary of the P.O.D. clause, but there is no evidence here that the contract permitted Ozzie to change the beneficiary by will. The couple did not divorce, they only separated, so there is no issue of revocation by operation of law.

41. Because banks routinely ask people to use the paperwork for a joint tenancy bank account, even if that is not what the parties intend, the courts take extrinsic evidence to determine the true intent of the parties when a multiple party bank account is created. At common law, the paperwork creates a presumption that the depositor intends a joint tenancy account, but if extrinsic evidence supports that the depositor intends a different account (either an agency account or a P.O.D. account), the court treats the account accordingly. (Some jurisdictions require clear and convincing evidence of an intent other than that indicated by the paperwork.) Here, Pete put Bob's name on the account so that Bob could pay Pete's bills while Pete was gone. Pete intended to create an agency account, not a true joint tenancy. Bob was to have no interest in the account inter vivos or upon Pete's death. The money in the account will fall into Pete's probate estate where it will pass to his heirs.

Under the modern trend/UPC approach, it is presumed that the parties own in proportion to their contributions to the account inter vivos, and upon the death of one of the parties to a multiple party bank account, it is presumed that there is a right of survivorship. The presumption can be overcome only by clear and convincing evidence. Here, arguably there is clear and convincing evidence that Pete intended only an agency account, which has no right of survivorship. Even under the modern trend/UPC approach, the money in the account should fall into Pete's probate estate where it will pass to his heirs.

42. The key characteristic of joint tenancy is the right of survivorship—when one joint tenant dies, his or her interest is extinguished. When one joint tenant dies, nothing "passes" to the surviving joint tenants; rather, their shares are merely recalculated to reflect that the deceased joint tenant's share has been extinguished. Executing a will does not sever a joint tenancy. Here, Bubba's will has no effect on the joint tenancy in Malibuacres. When Bubba dies, his interest in Malibuacres was extinguished, and Emily owns it outright. Bubba's will passes no interest in Malibuacres.

43. Where a trust is silent as to its revocability, the general rule is that the trust is irrevocable (though California is a notable exception; California assumes a trust is revocable unless it expressly provides that it is irrevocable). Here, the facts do not say if the trust is revocable. Applying the general rule, the trust would be irrevocable. Despite Bill's intent and his actions, the trust was not revocable and thus was not revoked.

44. Where a trust is revocable, if the terms of the trust set forth a particular method of revocation, under the traditional approach only that method of revocation is effective. Here, the trust specifically provided that the trust was revocable upon delivery of a written instrument expressing that intent to the trustee. Although Sally properly executed a valid will that expressed the intent to revoke the trust, there is no evidence that the will was delivered to Toni, the trustee, during Sally's lifetime. Absent evidence that the will was delivered to Toni during Sally's lifetime, under the traditional approach Sally has not complied with the terms of the trust concerning revocation, and the trust was not validly revoked. The house goes to Sally's dad.

Under the Uniform Trust Code, where the terms of a trust set forth a particular method of revocation, that method is deemed *not* to be the exclusive method unless the trust expressly so provides. There is no evidence Sally's trust so provided. The Uniform Trust Code also authorizes a will executed after the trust, which specifically refers to the trust, to revoke a revocable trust. Here, Sally's will expressed the intent to revoke the trust. Under the UTC, the trust would be revoked and the house goes to Sally's mom.

45. George W.'s interest in the trust was a life estate, with a remainder in his parents. Under the traditional common law approach, when a life estate ends, the party no longer has any interest in the asset in question. Under the common law approach, when George W. died, he no longer had any interest in the trust for the bank to reach in an attempt to satisfy his debt. The modern trend and Uniform Trust Code, however, provide that where a settlor retains a life estate in his or her inter vivos revocable trust, such an interest is analogous to one's interest in the rest of one's property. If the settlor could enjoy the benefits of the property during his or her lifetime, his or her creditors should be able to reach the property even after the settlor's death. Under the modern trend and UTC, the bank could reach the assets in George W.'s inter vivos trust.

46. The issue is whether the pour-over clause in the will is valid. There are three possible ways to validate a pour-over clause: UTATA, acts of independent significance, or incorporation by reference. If the jurisdiction has adopted the revised version of UTATA, the will must reference the trust, the terms of the trust must be set forth in a document other than the will, and the trust must be signed. The trust need not be funded inter vivos. Here, the will references the trust, the trust terms are set forth in a deed of trust separate from the will, and Jerry executed the trust, so the pour-over clause can be validated under the revised version of UTATA. Even though the trust was not funded inter vivos, the trust will

not be subject to probate court supervision. Elaine takes a life estate in the trust, and, upon her death, the property will be distributed outright—one-half to George and one-half to Kramer.

If the jurisdiction follows the original (and widely adopted) version of UTATA, the will must reference the trust, the trust terms must be set forth in a document other than the will, and the trust must be signed prior to or contemporaneously with the will. Here, the will references the trust and the terms are set forth in a deed of trust separate from the will, but Jerry did not execute the trust instrument until after he executed the will. The pour-over clause cannot be validated under the original version of UTATA. Acts of independent significance will work only if the trust was funded inter vivos. Jerry was on his way to his accountant's to transfer some property to the trust when he was hit and killed. No property was transferred to the trust inter vivos, so the pour-over clause cannot be validated under acts of independent significance. Under incorporation by reference, the will must express the intent to incorporate the document, the will must describe the document with reasonable certainty, and the document must be in existence when the will is executed. Here, the pour-over clause expresses the intent to incorporate the trust instrument and describes the trust instrument with reasonable certainty. But the trust instrument was not in existence when the will was executed. The pour-over cannot be validated. Because the pour-over clause is the residuary clause of his will, the property will fall to intestacy where it will be distributed to Jerry's heirs.

47. The issue is whether the pour-over clause in the will is valid. There are three possible ways to validate a pour-over clause: UTATA, acts of independent significance, or incorporation by reference. Under UTATA, the will must reference the trust, the terms of the trust must be set forth in a document other than the will, and the trust must be signed (the original and widely adopted version of UTATA requires that the trust be signed prior to or concurrently with the execution of the will). Here, Groucho never executed the trust. Acts of independent significance will work only if the trust was funded inter vivos. No property was transferred to the trust inter vivos, so the pour-over clause cannot be validated under acts of independent significance. Under incorporation by reference, the will must express the intent to incorporate the document, the will must describe the document with reasonable certainty, and the document must be in existence when the will is executed. Here, the pour-over clause expresses the intent to incorporate the trust instrument and describes the trust instrument with reasonable certainty. The trust instrument was not in existence when the will was executed, but Groucho executed a codicil to the will. Under republication by codicil, the codicil is deemed to reexecute and redate the will to the date of the codicil. By redating the will, the trust instrument was in existence when the codicil was executed. The trust instrument can be incorporated by reference. The amendment to the trust, however, cannot be given effect because it was not in existence when the codicil was executed. The pour-over clause can be given effect under incorporation of reference, the trust will be a testamentary trust subject to probate court supervision, and the beneficiaries under the trust will take the property pursuant to the terms of the trust (but Mrs. Claypool takes nothing).

Exam Tips on
WILL SUBSTITUTES AND PLANNING FOR INCAPACITY

Overview to the will substitutes

☞ At the macro level, the key to the nonprobate transfer issues is that if the transfer qualifies as a valid nonprobate transfer, give the property to the intended beneficiary. If the transfer does not qualify as a valid nonprobate transfer, the property falls to probate where it will be distributed pursuant to the testator's will, if one, or otherwise via intestacy.

☞ A second potential issue is whether the wills-related construction doctrines (covered in Chapter 5) apply to the will substitutes in your jurisdiction. If so, professors often overlap these areas by testing the wills-related rules in a nonprobate setting.

Inter vivos trusts

☞ Inter vivos trusts are valid will substitutes, even where the settlor is also life beneficiary and trustee, and holds a power to revoke. The method of revocation material is tested often because it differs from the wills revocation material.

    ☞ Just because you see a settlor tearing up an inter vivos trust and declaring his or her intent to revoke it, that does not necessarily mean the trust is revoked. Remember the split between the traditional approach and the modern trend with respect to whether a trust is revocable where the trust fails to cover the issue.

☞ If there is a provision stating that the trust is revocable, read carefully to see if it sets forth an exclusive method of revocation, an important issue under both the traditional approach and the Uniform Trust Code, though the standard of what constitutes an exclusive method is different under the two approaches.

☞ Watch for issues of creditors' rights where the beneficiary is the settlor. You should overlap and contrast this material with the material in Chapter 8 on the rights of creditors of a beneficiary where the beneficiary is not the settlor.

Contracts with payable-on-death clauses

☞ The principal issue with contracts with P.O.D. clauses is whether your jurisdiction recognizes them as a valid will substitute. The transferor's intent is usually very clear, but if the jurisdiction does not permit them, the transfer fails, and the property falls to probate despite the clarity of the transferor's intent.

☞ Watch for a will that makes an express reference to property subject to a valid will substitute, particularly a P.O.D. beneficiary. As a general rule, a will cannot change the beneficiary of a nonprobate instrument, though the UPC permits it for life insurance contracts if the contract expressly permits it.

Multiple party accounts

☛ Start with the presumption (common law vs. modern trend) and then analyze whether there is sufficient evidence of a contrary intent to overcome the presumption.

Pour-over wills and inter vivos trusts

☛ The pour-over wills material is critical. Not only is it the most common estate planning technique used today, it also overlaps the two major parts of the course—wills and trusts.

☛ Pour-over clauses always constitute an issue—they must be validated. The pour-over will is easy to spot. There must be a clause in the will expressly giving the property in question to the trustee of the testator's trust, to hold and distribute pursuant to the terms of the trust.

☞ If the will goes on to state the terms of the trust, the clause is not a pour-over will but rather the clause is creating a testamentary trust. There is no pour-over issue to analyze.

☞ If the will does not set forth the terms of the trust, but rather the terms are set forth in a separate document, the clause constitutes a pour-over clause that must be validated.

☛ In attempting to validate a pour-over clause, lead with UTATA; if that fails, try acts of independent significance; if that fails, try incorporation by reference last; if that fails, the pour-over clause is invalid and that gift fails.

☞ In applying UTATA, the key element typically is whether the trust instrument is signed. Pay close attention to which version of UTATA your jurisdiction follows.

☞ If the pour-over clause qualifies under UTATA, state the benefits: The trust does not have to be funded at all inter vivos, yet for purposes of probate court supervision, it is treated as an inter vivos trust; and all subsequent amendments to the trust are valid regardless of when they are executed.

☞ In applying acts of independent significance to validate a pour-over clause, the key requirement typically is whether the trust is funded inter vivos. In applying incorporation by reference to validate a pour-over clause, the key requirement typically is whether the trust *instrument* was in existence at the time the will was executed. (The trust instrument need not be signed at that time, nor must the trust be funded inter vivos.)

☛ While UTATA clearly states that a UTATA trust is not subject to probate court supervision, and thus is treated more like an inter vivos trust than a testamentary trust for purposes of probate court supervision, that does not necessarily mean that a UTATA trust is treated like an inter vivos trust for all doctrines where it makes a difference whether the trust is an inter vivos trust or a testamentary trust.

☞ If a doctrine distinguishes between inter vivos and testamentary trusts, whether a UTATA trust is treated as an inter vivos trust or a testamentary trust is a question of first impression where the courts consider the public policy considerations underlying the doctrine in question. The best way to handle the issue is to start by whether the UTATA trust was wholly unfunded until time of death. If so, absent countervailing public policy considerations, the UTATA trust should be treated as a testamentary trust. If the UTATA trust was funded inter vivos and has property in it at time of death, the UTATA trust should be treated as an inter vivos trust, absent countervailing public policy considerations.

Joint tenancies in real property

☛ If you have a joint tenancy issue, state (1) that the key characteristic is the right of survivorship, and (2) that upon the death of one joint tenant his or her interest "is extinguished" and the shares of the surviving joint tenants are recalculated (as opposed to saying that upon the death of one joint tenant his or her interest "passes" to the surviving joint tenants). Thus, a will does not sever a joint tenancy.

Planning for the possibility of incapacity

☛ Where there is a durable power of attorney, the issue typically is whether the attorney's actions are consistent with the principal's directives as set forth in the instrument. Even if the durable power of attorney instrument appears to authorize the action in question, if the action is inconsistent with the principal's overall testamentary scheme or arguably not in his or her best interests, the action must be expressly authorized by the durable power of attorney instrument to be permitted.

CHAPTER 7

LIMITATIONS ON THE TESTAMENTARY POWER TO TRANSFER

ChapterScope

This chapter examines spousal protection and family protection doctrines that limit one's power to transfer one's property at death. In particular, the chapter examines the surviving spouse's right to support and the surviving spouse's right to share in the marital property:

- ■ **The elective share (or forced share):** Under the separate property system, although each spouse owns his or her earnings acquired during marriage, upon death the surviving spouse is entitled to a share of the deceased spouse's property regardless of the terms of the deceased spouse's will. How much property the surviving spouse is entitled to, and what property is subject to the elective share, varies from jurisdiction to jurisdiction.

  - ■ **Common law:** At common law, the elective share entitles the surviving spouse to a share of the deceased spouse's *probate* estate, regardless of the terms of the deceased spouse's will. A spouse can avoid the elective share by putting his or her assets in a nonprobate instrument.

  - ■ **Modern trend/UPC approach:** The modern trend/UPC approach expands the reach of the elective share to permit the surviving spouse to claim an elective share against not only the deceased spouse's probate estate, but also against the deceased spouse's "augmented estate"—the deceased spouse's nonprobate assets and possibly even inter vivos gifts.

- ■ **Community property:** Under the community property system, earnings acquired by either spouse during the course of the marriage are owned equally by the spouses. Each spouse owns an undivided one-half interest in each community property asset. Upon the death of a spouse, the surviving spouse owns his or her one-half of each community property asset outright, and the deceased spouse's half of each community property asset goes into probate where he or she can devise it to anyone.

- ■ **Omitted spouse:** Where an individual executes a valid will, thereafter marries, and thereafter dies without revoking or revising the will, a presumption arises that the testator did not intend to disinherit the new spouse. The presumption is rebuttable, if (1) the will expresses the intent to disinherit that spouse; (2) the testator provided for that spouse outside of the will and intended for the transfer to be in lieu of the spouse taking under the will; or (3) the spouse waived his or her right to claim a share of the deceased spouse's estate.

- ■ **Omitted child:** Where an individual executes a valid will, thereafter has a child, and thereafter dies without revoking or revising his or her will, a presumption arises that the testator did not intend to disinherit the new child. The presumption is rebuttable if (1) the will expresses the intent to disinherit that child; (2) the testator provided for the child outside of the will and intended for that transfer to be in lieu of the child taking under the will; or (3) the testator had one or more children when the will was executed and devised substantially all of his or her estate to the other parent of the omitted child.

■ **Child mistakenly thought dead:** If the testator fails to provide for a child in a will because the testator mistakenly believes that the child is dead, the child receives the share he or she would under the omitted child doctrine.

I. SPOUSAL PROTECTION SCHEMES: AN OVERVIEW

A. **Introduction:** There are two different types of spousal protection: (1) *support* for the rest of the surviving spouse's life, and (2) an outright *share of the marital property,* regardless of who acquired the marital property.

1. **Support:** Through a combination of state and federal law, in virtually every state, a surviving spouse has rights for support under (1) the social security system, (2) ERISA (Employee Retirement Income Security Act of 1974), (3) the homestead exemption, (4) the personal property setaside, and (5) the family allowance.

2. **Share of marital property:** There are basically two property approaches to marital property—the separate property approach and the community property approach. The overwhelming majority of the jurisdictions follow the separate property approach. Only eight jurisdictions follow the traditional community property approach.

   a. **Separate property approach:** Under the separate property approach, any property acquired by either spouse, including his or her earnings, are that spouse's separate property. A spouse has no rights in the other spouse's separate property absent divorce or death. The spousal protection doctrine that grants a surviving spouse a share of the marital property in separate property jurisdiction is called the elective share. Upon the death of one spouse, under the elective share doctrine, the surviving spouse has a right to claim a share of the deceased spouse's property regardless of the terms of the deceased spouse's will.

   b. **Community property approach:** Under the community property approach, while property acquired before marriage and gifts acquired during marriage by either spouse are his or her separate property, all earnings acquired (and any property acquired with such earnings) during the marriage by either spouse are community property. Each spouse has an undivided one-half interest in each community property asset. Upon one spouse's death, each community property asset is divided in half. The surviving spouse's half is his or hers immediately and outright, thereby insuring that each spouse has a share of the marital property regardless of which spouse acquired it. The deceased spouse's half goes into probate where he or she can devise it to whomever he or she wishes.

   Rationale: Under the community property approach, the spouses are considered partners. Any property acquired as a result of the time, energy, and/or labor of either spouse is considered owned by the partnership.

II. SURVIVING SPOUSE'S RIGHT TO SUPPORT

A. **Spousal support:** Although the states are split over the surviving spouse's right to *share* in the deceased spouse's property (the elective share approach vs. the community property approach), the jurisdictions agree that surviving spouses, and maybe dependent children, are entitled to *support* from the deceased spouse. The surviving spouse is entitled to the following despite attempts by the deceased spouse to defeat such rights.

1. **Social security:** One way to think of social security is that it is a public pension plan. All workers are required to participate in it, and it provides benefits upon retirement to the worker and his or her surviving spouse. Only a surviving spouse can receive the worker's survivor's benefit (a stream of income for life—that is, support). The worker spouse cannot transfer the benefit to anyone else.

2. **Private pension plans:** Under ERISA, a surviving spouse must have survivorship rights in the worker spouse's retirement benefits, typically an annuity (a stream of income for life—that is, support). Unlike social security, under ERISA a surviving spouse can waive his or her rights in the worker spouse's private pension plan. But such waivers are not favored, and strict requirements apply to such waivers (prenuptial agreements do not qualify).

3. **Homestead:** The homestead right is to ensure that a surviving spouse has somewhere to live. The details of the homestead exemption, however, vary greatly from state to state. Some states grant the surviving spouse a life estate (support) in the family home or farm, while other states merely grant the surviving spouse a sum of money to provide for housing. (The UPC recommends a lump sum payment of only $15,000.) Some states require the decedent to claim the homestead exemption while alive by filing certain documents, while other states permit the homestead exemption to be claimed as part of the probate process.

4. **Personal property set-aside:** The surviving spouse is entitled to claim certain tangible personal property items regardless of the deceased spouse's attempts to devise them. Again, the details of the right vary from state to state. Some states have a statutory list of tangible personal property to which the surviving spouse is entitled; other states have a monetary limit on how much the surviving spouse may claim.

5. **Family allowance:** Probating the decedent's assets is often a long, drawn-out affair that can take one to two years even for fairly simple estates. A surviving spouse (and minor children, depending on the jurisdiction) needs money to live on during probate. The surviving spouse has a right to receive a family allowance during probate (but not for life). The amount of the allowance varies from jurisdiction to jurisdiction. Some states give a fixed allowance to all surviving spouses, some jurisdictions give an amount that takes into consideration the standard of living the surviving spouse was accustomed to at the time the deceased spouse died.

   a. **Commonwealth approach:** England and a number of its former colonies provide that surviving spouses (and others who were dependent upon the decedent for financial support) are entitled to support for life. Surviving spouses are entitled to a "reasonable" amount of support, regardless of their level of need. The English approach has been criticized as being too discretionary, involving too high a cost of administration, and denying the surviving spouse a right to share in the deceased spouse's property.

   b. **Dower and curtesy:** At early common law, the principal method of providing spousal support was either dower or curtesy.

      i. **Dower:** Dower provides a surviving wife with a life estate in one-third of all of her husband's qualifying real property—property in which the husband held an inheritable and/or devisable interest during the marriage. Once dower attaches to a parcel of land, the husband cannot unilaterally terminate it by transferring the land. The right springs to life upon the husband's death unless the wife also consents to the transfer by signing the deed, even if title is held in only the husband's name.

    ii. Curtesy: Curtesy provides a surviving husband with a life estate in all of the wife's qualifying real property, but only if children were born to the couple. What constitutes qualifying real property is the same as with dower—it must be inheritable and/or devisable.

    iii. Modern trend: Virtually all jurisdictions have abolished dower and curtesy in favor of the elective share. In the handful of jurisdictions that still retain the doctrines, curtesy is identical to dower. Moreover, in the few states that retain dower, the elective share is also available and almost always results in a greater financial award for the surviving spouse.

    iv. Transfers of real property: For all practical purposes, the doctrines of dower and curtesy are nonfactors. Nevertheless, to avoid any possible claims and possible clouds on the title, both spouses should sign any deed transferring real property, even if title is held in one spouse's name, to ensure that no dower or curtesy interest may be asserted after the transfer.

III. SURVIVING SPOUSE'S RIGHT TO A SHARE OF THE MARITAL PROPERTY

    A. Overview: If an unmarried individual acquires property, it is his or her separate property. If the individual marries, many argue that marriage is a partnership, and that by getting married the parties agree to share, to some degree, the burdens and benefits of marriage, including the property acquired by either spouse during the marriage.

    B. Traditional scenario: Even assuming that marriage is a legal sharing of burdens and benefits, in practice the sharing usually is not a true 50-50. Often children are an integral part of a marriage. Because only women can give birth to children, historically this led most couples to agree, either expressly or as a result of custom, that the wife would focus more of her time and labor within the home, while the husband would focus more of his time and labor outside of the home. To the extent the efforts outside of the home generate more material recognition (earn more money), the norm is for the husband to acquire more money and property than the wife.

    C. Policy issues: The issue is (1) *what* credit, if any, the non-wage-earning spouse (historically the wife) should receive for contributing to the partnership and enabling the wage-earning spouse (historically the husband) to focus on earning money, and (2) *when* that credit should be recognized.

    D. Overview of the elective share: The traditional English common law view is that the act of marriage has no effect upon the characterization of the property acquired by either spouse. Any and all property earned by either spouse during the marriage remains his or her separate property. Only upon termination of the marriage (divorce or death), if the non-wage-earning spouse is not adequately provided for does the state intervene and "force" the wage-earning spouse to give a share of his or her property to the non-wage-earning spouse. The separate property system's "at time of death" spousal protection scheme is commonly known as "the elective share" or "the forced share."

E. Overview of community property: While England embraced the separate property system, the rest of Europe embraced the community property system. Community property arguably is truer to the "marriage is a partnership" model. The moment any marital property is acquired, the community owns the asset. Each spouse owns an undivided one-half interest in each marital property asset. Upon the death of one spouse, the surviving spouse owns his or her half outright, and the deceased spouse's half goes into probate estate where he or she can devise it to whomever he or she wishes.

Marital property: Community property applies only to marital property. Marital property is property acquired as a result of the time, energy, or labor of either spouse during the marriage. Property acquired before marriage and gifts acquired by either spouse during the marriage are that spouse's separate property.

F. Temporal differences: One could argue that the principal difference between the elective share and community property is timing. Under community property, the spousal protection scheme attaches the moment the marital property is acquired. Under the elective share approach, the spousal protection doctrine does not arise until one of the spouses dies and the surviving spouse elects to claim his or her statutory amount instead of taking under the deceased spouse's will (hence the name "elective" share—the surviving spouse "elects" to take his or her statutory share under the elective share doctrine as opposed to the amount the deceased spouse left the surviving spouse in his or her will).

G. Fundamental differences: There are, however, a number of key differences between the two approaches, at least as developed historically, that should be noted up front.

1. Rights during marriage: The difference in the timing arguably affects the relationship between the spouses during the marriage. Under the separate property approach, the non-wage-earning spouse is dependent upon the wage-earning spouse to share properly, and if the wage-earning spouse does not, the non-wage-earning spouse's only recourse is divorce—not a particularly attractive option, at least historically. Under the community property approach, the moment each dollar is earned during the marriage, the non-wage-earning spouse enjoys an equal right to half of it. This arguably puts the spouses on a more equal status during the marriage, while the separate property approach arguably keeps the non-wage-earning spouse at a weaker position during the marriage.

2. Scope of property covered: Historically, the elective share applied to *all* of the deceased spouse's property, not just to the spouse's marital property. Community property, on the other hand, applies only to marital property acquired during the marriage, and not to either spouse's separate property acquired before marriage or to any gifts acquired by either spouse during marriage.

3. Fractional shares: Historically, the elective share was limited to one-third of the deceased spouse's property (though many states increased the share to one-half if there are no surviving issue). Community property, on the other hand, grants an immediate 50 percent interest in each marital asset to the non-wage-earning spouse the moment the community property asset is acquired.

Short marriage: Although community property appears to be the better approach for the non-wage-earning spouse, this assumes a traditional marriage where neither spouse has any assets at time of marriage, and the marriage is a long and productive marriage. If the marriage is very short and the deceased spouse had a sizeable separate property estate when he or she got married, the surviving spouse is better off under the elective share approach.

4. **Order of deaths:** Because the historical norm is for the wage-earning spouse to be the husband and for men to die before women, the norm is for the wage-earning spouse to die first. This makes the elective share an important right that the widow has to ensure that she gets a share of the deceased spouse's estate to live on and to devise as she sees fit when she dies. If the non-wage-earning spouse dies first, however, under the elective share approach she has no right to devise any of the marital property acquired by the wage-earning spouse. All she can devise is her own separate property. Under this scenario, the elective share looks more like a form of support than a true sharing of the marital assets. Under community property, even if the non-wage-earning spouse dies first, she can still share in the marital property and devise her half of the community property as she deems appropriate.

H. **Partnership model:** Many argue that community property is truer to the principles underlying the "marriage is a partnership" model. Under community property, the spouses are held to have agreed that the community owns any and all property acquired during the marriage by the labor of either spouse, with each spouse having an undivided half interest in each asset. The partnership, however, does not extend to the spouse's separate property.

Counterargument: The elective share is truer to the partnership model of marriage in that it extends not only to marital property but also to separate property. A true partnership entails a blending of *all* of each spouse's assets, not just the marital assets.

IV. THE ELECTIVE SHARE: POLICY CONSIDERATIONS

A. **Jurisdictional variations:** More than any other area of wills and trusts, the jurisdictions vary over the exact details of their elective share doctrines. The differences can be in the amount that the surviving spouse is entitled to under the elective share doctrine, the variables that determine the amount (length of marriage, family situation, surviving spouse's net worth, property subject to the elective share doctrine, and so on), or the property subject to the elective share.

1. **Coverage note:** If your professor is teaching your jurisdiction's probate code, read and analyze your elective share statute very carefully. The discussion here focuses on the UPC provisions and the major aspects of the doctrine that you should keep in mind when reading your jurisdiction's particular elective share statute.

2. **Share vs. support:** Virtually all elective share statutes grant the surviving spouse a *share* of the deceased spouse's property, but a handful permit the deceased spouse to satisfy his or her statutory requirements by granting the surviving spouse a life estate in a specific fraction of the deceased spouse's property. In such cases, arguably the elective share is nothing more than an enhanced support right, not a true share in the deceased spouse's property.

B. **Recap:** The elective share doctrine is the "at time of death" spousal protection approach adopted by the separate property system. During the marriage, each spouse owns all of his or her earnings as his or her separate property. The separate property system assumes that the spouses will care for each other and treat each other properly, and it intervenes only when the marriage is terminated at divorce or death. The elective share typically gives the surviving spouse the right to claim one-third of the deceased spouse's probate property (if the deceased spouse did not leave the surviving spouse at least that much in his or her will). The elective share applies regardless of the length of the marriage.

C. Personal right: The general rule, and UPC approach, is that only the surviving spouse can claim the elective share. If the surviving spouse dies before asserting the claim, the surviving spouse's estate, heirs, and creditors have no standing to claim the share even if the time to assert the claim has not expired. Because the elective share has to be "claimed," and because only the surviving spouse can claim it, the elective share looks more like a form of support than a true sharing of the marital property.

    1. Incompetent spouse: If the surviving spouse lacks the capacity to decide whether to exercise the elective share, a guardian of the spouse can decide "in the best interests" of the surviving spouse, with the probate court's approval. In some jurisdictions, what constitutes "the best interests" of the surviving spouse is a purely economic question—whether the spouse takes more under the elective share. In a majority of jurisdictions, however, the guardian is given greater discretion and is permitted to take the totality of the circumstances surrounding the deceased spouse and the surviving spouse into consideration.

    2. UPC approach: The 1969 version of the UPC authorized the probate court to claim the elective share for an incompetent spouse only if necessary to provide adequate support for the surviving spouse for the rest of his or her life. This approach reflects a support approach to the elective share. In 1990, the UPC was amended to provide that if the elective share is exercised for an incompetent spouse, the share of the elective share that exceeds the share the spouse was taking under the deceased spouse's will is placed in a custodial trust, with the surviving spouse having a life estate, and a remainder in the devisees under the will (so as to minimize the effect upon the deceased spouse's estate plan). UPC §2-212.

D. Life estates: For a variety of reasons, it is not uncommon for the first-spouse-to-die to leave the surviving spouse only a life estate in all or part of his or her property. Many spouses feel that their only duty is to support their surviving spouse for life, but upon the surviving spouse's death, the predeceased spouse wants to have the final say over who takes "their" property. In addition, the estate tax system and the marital deduction create incentives for the predeceased spouse to leave the surviving spouse a life estate.

    1. Estate taxes: A decedent's estate tax depends on the size of his or her estate. Assume a traditional marriage, where (1) the husband is the wage earner, and (2) he dies first with virtually all of the property in his name. Under community property, the husband owned only half of the property, resulting in a lower estate tax. Under the separate property approach, the husband owned all the property in his name, resulting in a higher estate tax. Even assuming the husband left all of his property to his wife, the wife is worse off under the separate property approach because the after-tax amount passing to her is less.

    2. Marital deduction: To equalize the surviving spouse (typically the wife) under the two property approaches, Congress adopted the estate tax marital deduction. The marital deduction provides that no estate taxes apply to any and all transfers from the deceased spouse to the surviving spouse, even if the transfer is the whole estate; all that needs to be transferred to qualify is a life estate interest (typically this is done in a trust and is called a QTIP trust). The marital deduction arguably requires the deceased spouse only to support the surviving spouse as opposed to truly sharing marital property.

E. **Medicaid eligibility:** Although the general rule is that the elective share is personal to the surviving spouse and cannot be exercised by anyone other than the surviving spouse, an exception exists when it comes to Medicaid eligibility. The elective share and the property that satisfies the elective share are assets that may be included in determining an individual's eligibility for Medicaid. Courts have ordered guardians of an incompetent spouse to claim the elective share so as not to jeopardize the spouse's Medicaid eligibility (thereby acting in the "best interests" of the spouse).

Example: In *In re Estate of Cross,* 664 N.E.2d 905 (Ohio 1996), the husband left a will devising all of his property to his son, who was not a child of his surviving wife. The decedent's wife was almost 80 years old and hospitalized at the time of his death, too incompetent to decide whether to exercise her elective share. The trial court appointed a commissioner to decide for the wife, and, after taking the totality of circumstances into consideration, including that the wife's care was being covered by Medicaid and that her eligibility would be compromised if she did not claim the elective share, the commissioner asserted the wife's elective share. The court agreed.

F. **Spousal abandonment:** The general rule is that spousal abandonment is not grounds for barring the surviving spouse from claiming an elective share. A handful of states, however, bar the abandoning spouse from claiming an elective share.

G. **Malpractice liability:** An attorney who fails to advise a client about the elective share and the effect it would have upon the client's testamentary scheme can be liable under malpractice for any damages caused.

H. **Same-sex couples:** To date, no court has extended the elective share doctrine to include same-sex couples who lived in a spousal-like relationship, but with states increasingly recognizing same-sex marriages, such partners should have the right to claim the elective share (in both the states that permit same-sex marriages and other states that recognize such marriages). *See supra* Chapter 2, II.B for further discussion of the rights of spouses in a same-sex marriage.

V. THE ELECTIVE SHARE: DOCTRINAL CONSIDERATIONS

A. **Scope of doctrine:** Inasmuch as the elective share doctrine gives the surviving spouse the right to a forced share, if necessary, of the deceased spouse's property, the issue becomes how much of the deceased spouse's property is subject to the elective share.

B. **Traditional scope:** The original formulation of the elective share, and the formulation still in effect in a number of states, provides that the surviving spouse is entitled to a share (typically one-third) of the deceased spouse's *probate* estate only.

Rationale: Historically most of a decedent's property passed via probate, so tying the elective share to the deceased spouse's probate estate made sense. In addition, under the separate property system, absent cause (divorce or death), each spouse is free to do with his or her property whatever he or she wants, including making inter vivos transfers.

C. **Nonprobate avoidance:** The traditional approach to the elective share doctrine accepts that inter vivos transfers by the deceased spouse are not subject to the elective share, only the decedent's testamentary transfers—property that the decedent owns at time of death. This distinction, however, arguably assumes a classic inter vivos transfer made to a third party, with the transferor retaining no interest in the property following the transfer.

1. **Nonprobate transfers:** Property placed in an inter vivos trust does not pass through probate, thus avoiding the elective share under the traditional approach. Yet the deceased spouse could retain a life estate interest in the trust and continue to benefit from the property until his or her death.

2. **Example:** Assume a spouse creates an inter vivos trust, transfers substantially all of his or her property to the trust, and retains a life estate interest in the trust (and possibly even the power to revoke or appoint the property). Despite the fact that the spouse has virtually the same right to enjoy the property in the trust that he or she would have if the property were not in trust, under the traditional approach the property in the trust is deemed not subject to the elective share because the future interest in trust property passed inter vivos pursuant to the terms of the trust, not through probate and not at time of death.

D. **Judicial responses:** As the use of such nonprobate avoidance arrangements grew, pressure increased for changes to the elective share doctrine to close such loopholes. The courts have struggled with articulating a workable response—to identify those inter vivos transfers that are not really inter vivos transfers for purposes of the elective share doctrine. Different jurisdictions have articulated different approaches. All of them have been criticized as being either incomplete or having high administrative costs.

1. **The illusory transfer test:** The most widely adopted judicial response to the nonprobate avoidance problem is the illusory transfer test approach. The essence of the illusory transfer test is to ask whether the inter vivos property arrangement that permits the property to avoid probate is really an inter vivos transfer, or whether the deceased spouse retained such an interest in the arrangement that the transfer is more testamentary than inter vivos. The problem is that how much of an interest the deceased spouse must retain varies from jurisdiction to jurisdiction, and often each case turns on its particular facts. If the transfer is deemed an illusory transfer, the transfer is still valid but the property in question is included in the decedent's estate subject to the elective share.

2. **The intent to defraud test:** While the illusory transfer test focuses on the amount of interest the deceased spouse retained in the property, the intent to defraud test focuses on the deceased spouse's state of mind: Did the deceased spouse intend to defraud his or her surviving spouse by creating the nonprobate property arrangement in question? The jurisdictions are split on how to determine whether the deceased spouse intended to defraud the surviving spouse of his or her elective share rights in the property.

   a. **Subjective approach:** Some jurisdictions take a subjective approach: Did the deceased spouse *actually intend* to defraud the surviving spouse of his or her right to an elective share in the property by creating the nonprobate transfer?

   b. **Objective approach:** Some jurisdictions take an objective approach to whether the nonprobate transfer in question defrauded the surviving spouse of his or her right to an elective share in the property, focusing on a variety of factors: the amount of property in question relative to the party's overall property, when the nonprobate arrangement was created relative to the party's death and relative to the party's marriage, how much of an interest the deceased spouse retained, and so on.

3. **The present donative intent test:** Some jurisdictions focus on whether the deceased spouse really had a present donative intent at the moment that he or she created the nonprobate transfer. (One could argue this is very similar to the intent to defraud test, only phrased slightly differently.)

4. **Example:** In *Sullivan v. Burkin,* 460 N.E.2d 572 (Mass. 1984), the husband and wife separated but did not divorce. The husband created an inter vivos trust, to which he transferred his real estate (his principal asset). He retained a life estate interest in the income generated by the property in the trust, the right to withdraw principal upon written request to the trustee, and the right to revoke. Upon his death, any and all property in the trust was to be distributed to two friends. His will (disposing of only 15 percent of his wealth) likewise made no provision for his separated wife. She invoked her right to an elective share and argued that it included the property in the trust. The court held that the trust was a valid inter vivos trust, but announced that henceforth, assets in an inter vivos trust created during the marriage would be subject to the elective share if the deceased spouse retained a power to revoke or general power of appointment (exercisable by deed or will).

5. **Conflict of laws:** The standard conflict of laws rule is that the laws of the state where the real property is located control disposition of the real property. The laws of the state where the real property is located therefore control whether the surviving spouse is entitled to receive an elective share in the real property. The UPC, however, provides that the laws of the state where the decedent was domiciled at time of death control whether the surviving spouse is entitled to receive an elective share in real property located in another state. UPC §2-202(d).

E. **Statutory/UPC response:** In many states, the legislature addressed the problem by drafting legislation that expands the scope of the property subject to the elective share.

1. **1969 UPC augmented estate:** The 1969 version of the UPC adopted what became known as the "augmented estate" approach to the elective share. The surviving spouse was entitled to receive one-third of the deceased spouse's augmented estate.

   a. **The augmented estate:** The augmented estate included not only the decedent's probate estate, but also certain nonprobate and gratuitous inter vivos transfers *made during the marriage:* (i) any transfers where the deceased spouse retained the right to possession or income from the property; (ii) any transfers where the deceased spouse retained the power to revoke or the power to use or appoint (dispose of) the principal for his or her own benefit; (iii) any joint tenancies with anyone other than the surviving spouse; (iv) gifts to third parties within two years of the deceased spouse's death in excess of $3,000 per donee per year; and (v) property given to the surviving spouse either inter vivos or via nonprobate transfers (including life estate interests in trusts). Life insurance proceeds to someone other than the surviving spouse were expressly excluded.

   Property given to surviving spouse: Property given to the surviving spouse inter vivos or through nonprobate transfers is included in the augmented estate to prevent a surviving spouse who has been provided for adequately via inter vivos gifts and/or nonprobate transfers from using the elective share doctrine to take more than his or her fair share.

   b. **Funding:** To protect the deceased spouse's estate plan as much as possible, the augmented estate is funded first by crediting any property he or she received under the will against the elective share amount. Any remaining property due is taken pro rata from the other will beneficiaries (though a few jurisdictions take it from the residuary gift).

c. **Community property component:** The 1969 version of the UPC limited the augmented estate to those nonprobate transfers made ***during the marriage.*** If the transfer occurred prior to marriage, even if the transfer otherwise would have constituted a transfer subject to the augmented estate, the property subject to the premarriage transfer was not included in the augmented estate. By limiting the augmented estate to transfers made during the marriage, the 1969 version of the UPC arguably began to introduce community property principles into the separate property system. Property acquired premarriage could successfully be exempted from the elective share, thus limiting the elective share more to the notion of marital property used in community property jurisdictions than that historically used in separate property jurisdictions.

2. **1990 UPC marital property approach:** The 1990 version of the UPC elective share doctrine (as amended in 2008) strove to achieve an elective share that would result in approximately the same amount of the deceased spouse's property going to the surviving spouse as would have gone under community property. Several major changes were adopted to the elective share doctrine to try to achieve this result under separate property rules. The augmented estate combines the property of both spouses and gives the surviving spouse a share of the combined, "augmented" estate that depends on the duration of the marriage.

   a. **Sliding scale:** The 1990 version of the UPC abandons the fixed percentage elective share and provides instead a gradually increasing share depending on the length of the marriage. The surviving spouse starts out entitled to 3 percent of the couple's marital property, and the share increases approximately 3 percentage points a year until the spouse is entitled to 50 percent of the couple's marital property after 15 years of marriage. UPC §2-203(a) (as amended in 2008).

   b. **Augmented estate:** The 1990 version of the UPC augmented estate no longer focuses only on the deceased spouse's property, but includes both spouses' property. If neither couple had any separate property when they married, this approach mirrors community property. Unlike the 1969 version of the UPC, however, the 1990 version includes transfers made before marriage if the deceased spouse retained substantial control over the property. The 1990 version of the UPC also reverses the 1969 UPC and expressly includes life insurance proceeds paid to someone other than the surviving spouse.

   c. **Community property differences:** The 1990 version of the UPC augmented estate arguably is broader than the community property notion of marital property. Under community property, the core concept of marital property is earnings acquired by either spouse during the marriage. Property acquired before marriage and gifts acquired during marriage are that spouse's separate property, and the other spouse has no rights in that property (unless the spouse commingles it with community property). Under the 1990 UPC approach to the augmented estate, property acquired before marriage and gifts acquired during marriage may be subject to the elective share.

3. **New York approach:** The New York approach gives the surviving spouse $50,000 or one third of the decedent's augmented estate. The augmented estate is narrower than the UPC's augmented estate. The New York augmented estate includes not only the decedent's probate estate but also (i) gifts *causa mortis*; (ii) gifts to third parties within one year of the deceased spouse's death in excess of $10,000; (iii) Totten trusts (savings account trusts); (iv) joint tenancies and tenancies by the entirety (real or personal), to the extent of the deceased spouse's contributions; (v) payment-on-death transfers; (vi) inter vivos transfers where the deceased

spouse retained the right to possession or income from the property, or the power to revoke or the power to use or appoint (dispose of) the principal for his or her own benefit. Property that the surviving spouse receives by virtue of the deceased spouse's death, be it from nonprobate transfers or probate transfers (will or intestacy), is credited against the surviving spouse's elective share. N.Y. Est. Powers & Trusts Law §5-1.1-A (1998).

4. **Delaware approach:** Delaware rejects the UPC approach in favor of the federal government's estate tax approach. All property includible in the decedent's gross estate for federal estate tax purposes (regardless of whether any tax is due) constitutes the deceased spouse's estate that is subject to the surviving spouse's elective share.

F. **Funding the elective share with a life estate:** The general rule is that if the surviving spouse claims the elective share, the elective share is satisfied first by counting the property the deceased gave under his or her will to the surviving spouse. The rationale is to minimize the disruption the elective share causes to the deceased spouse's overall estate plan. The rest of the property due the surviving spouse under the elective share is taken pro rata from the other beneficiaries (a minority of jurisdictions take it from the residuary clause). The issue is whether permitting a life estate interest to count toward the elective share is incompatible with the principle of the elective share. A life estate is intrinsically "support" in nature, while the elective "share" is intended to ensure that the surviving spouse receives a fair, outright share of the marital property.

1. **General rule:** If the surviving spouse elects to claim the elective share and takes against the will, most jurisdictions do ***not*** permit any life estate interests left in the will to the surviving spouse to count against the elective share.

2. **UPC:** Under the 1969 version of the UPC, if the surviving spouse claimed an elective share, any life estate left to the surviving spouse did ***not*** count against the elective share amount. In 1975, the UPC was revised to provide that any life estate interests left in the will to the surviving spouse ***did*** count against the surviving spouse's elective share. In 1993, the UPC reversed itself yet again and returned to the original position that any life estate interests left to the surviving spouse in the rejected will do ***not*** count against the elective share. UPC §2-209.

   Valuation: If the life estate counts toward the elective share, under the 1975 version of the UPC the life estate was valued at 50 percent of the property in which the surviving spouse was granted the life estate. In 1990, the UPC was amended to remove the 50 percent valuation method, and no substitute method was inserted.

G. **Waiver:** The general rule is that a surviving spouse may waive his or her right to an elective share (and to the homestead allowance, personal property exempt property, and the family allowance) at any time, as long as the waiver is in writing and signed by the waiving spouse. The waiver is not enforceable if the surviving spouse can prove (1) that it was not made voluntarily, or (2) that it was unconscionable when executed, and, before executed, the surviving spouse did not know nor reasonably could have known the deceased spouse's financial situation and the surviving spouse did not voluntarily and expressly waive the right to know such information.

1. **Example:** In ***Reece v. Elliot***, 208 S.W.3d 419. (Tenn. Ct. App. 2006), Reece and Elliot signed a prenuptial agreement before marrying as both had children from a previous marriage and both wanted to ensure that their assets would pass to their children. Both parties had independent counsel and created a list of their assets. Reece listed all of his properties and bank accounts but values were not listed for every item, including Reece's stock in his former employer's company. Elliot alleged that the prenuptial agreement was invalid because she did not enter the

agreement with "full knowledge" of the value of the deceased's assets because she did not know the value of the stock. "Knowledgeably" means the proponent of the agreement must prove that a full and fair disclosure of the nature, extent, and value of the party's holdings was provided. Elliot was not misled and was provided with the opportunity to ask questions and discover the extent of the other's holdings but failed to do so. The prenuptial agreement was held valid.

2. **Modern trend:** By statute, California now requires that for a properly executed prenuptial agreement to be valid (1) each party must have their own independent counsel, and (2) seven days' notice to each party before signing.

VI. COMMUNITY PROPERTY

A. **Overview:** Community property is a very complicated property system that is its own course. The essence of community property is that all marital property is owned by the community the moment it is acquired. Marital property is any property acquired during marriage as a result of the time, energy, or labor of either spouse. As a practical matter, community property is any earnings acquired by either spouse during the marriage (and any property purchased with community property earnings). Property acquired by gift, devise, or inheritance during marriage or by either spouse before marriage is separate property.

1. **Commingled property:** Commingled property arises when separate property is mixed with community property. A number of different formulas are used to determine the separate property share vs. the community property share.

2. **Transmutation:** The spouses can convert the legal characterization of property by agreement. Separate property can be converted to community property and vice versa. The jurisdictions are split over what evidence is necessary to prove a transmutation (writing vs. clear and convincing nonwritten evidence, and so on).

3. **Stepped-up basis:** Upon the death of a spouse, his or her property receives a stepped-up basis for purposes of calculating capital gains following subsequent sale of the property. If the property is held concurrently but not as community property (that is, joint tenancy or tenancy in common), only the deceased spouse's share receives a stepped-up basis to its fair market value at the time of the spouse's death. If, however, the property is held as community property, the whole asset receives a stepped-up basis (both the deceased spouse's half and the surviving spouse's half).

4. **Death:** Upon the death of one spouse, each community property asset is divided 50-50. The surviving spouse holds his or her share outright. The deceased spouse's share goes into probate, where the deceased spouse can devise it as he or she wishes.

B. **"Putting a spouse to an election":** Community property jurisdictions do not recognize an elective share, but they do permit a deceased spouse to put a surviving spouse to an election. Despite the similarity in terminology, which can cause confusion to the uninitiated, the doctrines are not similar at all. Putting a spouse to an election is simply a variation on the idea that a decedent can make a conditional gift. The deceased spouse conditions a devise to the surviving spouse on the surviving spouse agreeing to the deceased spouse being permitted to give away some of the surviving spouse's property. One of the principal issues is how clear the deceased spouse must be that he or she is putting the surviving spouse to an election. Historically, spouses were put to an implied election anytime the deceased spouse's will appeared to give away some of the surviving spouse's property. Under the modern trend, the courts have tightened up the intent necessary to put the surviving spouse to an election, holding that the intent must be clear.

C. **Migrating couples:** Migrating couples pose problems for the spousal protection doctrines. The problems arise because (1) real property is governed by the laws of the state where it is located, (2) personal property is characterized at the time it is acquired as either separate or community property based on the laws of the spouses' domicile at the time of acquisition, and (3) the "at time of death" spousal protection a surviving spouse is entitled to depends on the spouses' domicile at the time of death of the first spouse.

   1. **Separate to community example:** Assume a traditional relationship where all the couple's marital property is acquired by and titled in the wage-earning spouse's name. If the couple lives in a separate property jurisdiction, the property is the wage-earning spouse's separate property. If the couple retires and moves to a community property state, and shortly thereafter the wage-earning spouse dies, the spousal protection scheme is community property. The surviving spouse is entitled to 50 percent of their community property, but they have no community property. The characterization of their property is not changed because the couple moved to a community property jurisdiction. Legally, the spouse is protected, but as a practical matter there is no protection. The non-wage-earning spouse slips through the cracks of the spousal protection systems.

      a. **Quasi-community property:** Quasi-community property is separate property that would have been characterized as community property if the couple had been domiciled in a community property jurisdiction when the spouse acquired the property. When a spouse with quasi-community property dies, the quasi-community property is treated like community property for distribution purposes. The surviving spouse immediately receives a one-half interest in the quasi-community property that is his or hers outright. The deceased spouse can devise only half of the quasi-community property. Quasi-community property protects the migrating couple. Not all community property states recognize quasi-community property.

      b. **Order of deaths:** Quasi-community property is not the same as community property. Quasi-community property applies only to the property owned at death by the deceased spouse, not by the surviving spouse. If the nonacquiring spouse dies first, he or she has no right to devise any of the surviving spouse's property (even if the surviving spouse has property that would have been characterized as quasi-community property if he or she had died first). Quasi-community property gives the non-wage-earning spouse property rights in the property acquired during the marriage by the other spouse only if the wage-earning spouse dies first.

   2. **Community to separate example:** Assume a traditional relationship where all of the couple's marital property is acquired by and titled in the wage-earning spouse's name. If the couple lives in a community property jurisdiction, the property is treated as community property. Each spouse owns an undivided one-half interest in the property regardless of how it is titled. If the couple retires and moves to a separate property jurisdiction, and shortly after moving the wage-earning spouse dies, the spousal protection scheme is the elective share. The non-wage-earning spouse receives his or her half of the community property outright, and the deceased spouse's half goes into probate. The surviving spouse can then claim an additional one-third or one-half interest in the deceased spouse's probate property (depending on the jurisdiction

and family situation). When moving from community property jurisdictions to separate property jurisdictions, the surviving spouse may be able to "double dip" in the spousal protection schemes.

   a. **Legislative reform:** The Uniform Disposition of Community Property Rights at Death Act, adopted in many, but not all, separate property jurisdictions, provides that a deceased spouse's community property that is brought into the state is not subject to the elective share doctrine.

   b. **Transmute property:** One might think that the couple should transmute their community property to separate property upon moving from a community property to a separate property jurisdiction. That avoids the potential problem of the surviving spouse double dipping in the spousal protection doctrines. But by transmuting the property, the couple loses the tax benefits of the double stepped-up basis that community property receives upon the death of the first spouse. The lost tax savings could be huge.

VII. THE OMITTED SPOUSE

A. **Overview:** People disagree over whether the omitted spouse doctrine, historically known as the pretermitted spouse doctrine, is a spousal protection doctrine or a corrective doctrine, a doctrine designed to correct what is presumed to be a mistake by the decedent.

B. **Traditional scenario:** The omitted spouse doctrine applies where a testator executes a will, thereafter gets married, and dies without revising or revoking his or her will. The issue that arises is whether the testator intended to disinherit his or her spouse, or whether the testator intended to revise his or her will to provide for his or her new spouse, but died before getting around to it.

   Spousal vs. non-spousal capacity: The classic omitted spouse scenario assumes that the testator's will does not provide at all for the person who ends up being his or her spouse. But even if the will does provide for the person who ends up being the testator's spouse, unless the testator thought the person was going to be his or her spouse when he or she executed the will, the gift in the will to the person who became the testator's spouse does not defeat the doctrine.

C. **Omitted spouse presumption:** Where the testator (1) marries after executing his or her will and (2) dies without revising or revoking his or her will, this combination creates a presumption that the testator accidentally disinherited his spouse—that is, meant to amend his or her will to provide for his or her new spouse, but died before doing so.

D. **Rebuttable presumption:** The presumption that the testator accidentally disinherited his or her spouse is rebuttable, but the traditional omitted spouse doctrine provides that the presumption can be rebutted only by showing that: (1) the failure to provide for the new spouse was intentional and that intent appears from the will; (2) the testator provided for the spouse outside of the will and the intent that the transfer outside of the will be in lieu of the spouse taking under the will is established by any evidence, including oral statements by the testator and/or the amount of the transfer; or (3) the spouse validly waived the right to share in the testator's estate.

   Will evidences intent to omit: The courts have construed the first method of rebutting the presumption, that the will evidences the intent to disinherit, very narrowly. A general disinheritance clause, and even a general clause disinheriting any future spouse, is insufficient to defeat the presumption. The will must demonstrate the express intent to omit this specific spouse, and the clause must have been executed when the testator was contemplating marrying this specific spouse.

E. Omitted spouse's share: If the presumption that the failure to provide for the new spouse was not intentional is not rebutted, the typical omitted spouse statute gives the omitted spouse his or her intestate share of the testator's probate estate.

F. UPC: The UPC tracks the basic provisions of the traditional pretermitted spouse doctrine, but it has a few revisions worth noting.

   1. Intent to omit: The UPC broadens the evidence that can be used to prove that the spouse's omission from the will was intentional to include evidence (1) from the will, or (2) other evidence that the will was made in contemplation of the testator's marriage to the surviving spouse, or (3) a general provision in the will that it is effective notwithstanding any subsequent marriage.

   2. Omitted spouse's share: The UPC grants an omitted spouse the right to receive no less than his or her intestate share of the deceased spouse's estate from that portion of the testator's estate, if any, that is not devised to a child of the testator or the child's descendants (directly or through anti-lapse) if (1) the child is not a child of the surviving spouse, and (2) the child was born before the testator married the surviving spouse. The effect of this provision is that if the testator devises all of his probate estate to his child or descendants from a prior relationship or marriage, the surviving spouse will not receive an omitted spouse's share despite otherwise meeting the requirements of an omitted spouse.

G. Modern trend: A few states have modified their omitted spouse statutes to recognize that increasingly the inter vivos revocable trust is being used much like a will. In those states, the omitted spouse doctrine arises only if the marriage occurs after execution of all the deceased spouse's wills and revocable trusts, and the surviving spouse's share is of the property included in the probate estate and revocable trusts.

   Example: In ***In re Estate of Prestie,*** 138 P.3d 520 (Nev. 1006), the plaintiff (the son and primary beneficiary under the decedent's estate plan) asked the court to expand the scope of the doctrine *judicially* to take into consideration the decedent's revocable trust. The decedent amended his revocable trust just a few weeks before he married to grant his new spouse a life estate in his real property. The son argued that the new spouse should not qualify as an omitted spouse because the deceased spouse provided for her in his revocable trust. The court refused to consider the gift in the revocable trust in applying the doctrine, however, because the state statute made express reference only to the decedent's will.

H. Elective share vs. omitted spouse: It is hard to make too many detailed comments about the difference between the elective share and the omitted spouse share because the elective share varies so much from jurisdiction to jurisdiction, but close attention should be paid to the differences between the two in your jurisdiction. In particular, you should watch for the following:

   1. Overlap: The typical omitted spouse also qualifies for an elective share. If the spouse's decision is based solely on the bottom line, it is important that you know how to calculate the exact amount of the share he or she would receive under the respective doctrines. The modern trend approach to the elective share often includes nonprobate property as well, making it look more attractive, unless the UPC sliding scale has been adopted and the marriage has been a short one.

2. UPC: Under the UPC approach to the omitted spouse doctrine, where the testator has a will that devises all or substantially all of his or her property to a child or descendants of a child not of the surviving omitted spouse, for all practical purposes the surviving spouse is forced to claim an elective share because the omitted spouse's share under these circumstances will be so small.

I. Malpractice liability: If the client advises the attorney during the estate planning process that he or she is planning on getting married, and the attorney fails to expressly note that the will was made in contemplation of marriage, the beneficiaries whose shares are reduced to fund the omitted spouse's share can sue the attorney for malpractice. Moreover, if the attorney does not know that the client is contemplating marriage when the will is drafted and executed, but learns thereafter the testator has married, the attorney has an ethical obligation to advise the client of the omitted spouse doctrine and of the effect the doctrine would have upon the testamentary scheme expressed in the will. ABA Model Code of Responsibility, D.R. 2-104(A)(1).

VIII. THE OMITTED CHILD

A. Overview: The omitted child doctrine parallels the omitted spouse doctrine. Because a testator can completely and intentionally disinherit a child (except in Louisiana) but not a spouse (due to the elective share/community property spousal protection doctrines), the omitted child doctrine arguably is more of a presumed intent/corrective doctrine than a protective doctrine.

1. Louisiana approach: In 1995, Louisiana amended its constitution so that the protection against disinheritance now applies only to children under 23, the mentally infirm, and the disabled. In addition, a child can be disinherited if there is "just cause."

2. Commonwealth approach—the family maintenance model: In many commonwealth countries (England, Australia, and some of the Canadian provinces), a surviving spouse has no elective share rights, but a surviving spouse and children (and anyone else who was dependent upon the decedent during his or her lifetime) have the right to petition the probate court for maintenance. The court may, in its discretion, award maintenance out of the decedent's estate if the dependent is without adequate provision for his or her proper maintenance, education, or advancement in life. Some have argued that the United States should adopt the family maintenance doctrine.

Example: In *Lambeff v. Farmers Co-operative Executors & Trustees Ltd.*, 56 S.A.S.R. 323 (Sup. Ct. S. Australia. 1991), George Lambeff married in 1945 and had a daughter in 1946. Ten years later, he and his wife separated and George established a relationship with Barbara Lambeff, his de facto wife, shortly thereafter. George and Barbara had two sons. He died in 1989 with an estate of just over $200,000, which he left in trust to his two sons equally (each was married with young children). His single daughter petitioned the court for a share of the estate as her maintenance share. She noted that she had regularly attempted to establish ties with her father but had been repeatedly rebuffed by him. The court noted that she was significantly better off financially (more assets) and professionally (better job) than the two sons but nevertheless awarded her $20,000.

B. **Unintentional disinheritance of child—traditional scenario:** The omitted child doctrine applies where a testator executes a will, thereafter has a child, and dies without revising or revoking his or her will. The issue is whether the testator intended to omit his or her new child, or whether the testator intended to revise his or her will to provide for his or her new child, but died before getting around to it.

1. **Gift:** The classic omitted child scenario assumes that the testator did not provide at all in his or her will for the child born after execution of his or her will. If the will contains a provision that gives a share to children born after execution of the will, as a general rule that child does not qualify as an omitted child.

2. **Children alive at execution:** Some states extend the omitted child statute to include not only children born after execution of the will, but also children born before execution of the will but not named in the will.

   Affirmative disinheritance: Where the omitted child statute covers living children as well, most courts require affirmative disinheritance (specific reference to the child). A negative disinheritance (a blanket statement that the testator has no children or that no children are to take under the will) is generally held not to be sufficient. Generic clauses giving a nominal amount to any child who might qualify to take are likewise generally held insufficient to bar the doctrine.

C. **Omitted child presumption:** Where the testator has a child after executing his or her will and dies without revising or revoking his or her will, this combination creates a presumption that the testator meant to amend his or her will to provide for his or her new child, but died before getting around to it.

D. **Rebuttable presumption:** The presumption that the testator accidentally disinherited his or her child is rebuttable, but the traditional omitted child doctrine provides that the presumption can be rebutted only by showing that: (1) the failure to provide for the new child was intentional and that intent appears from the will; (2) the testator provided for the child outside of the will and the intent that the transfer outside of the will be in lieu of the child taking under the will is established by any evidence, including the amount of the transfer; or (3) the testator had one or more children when the will was executed and devised substantially all of his or her estate to the other parent of the omitted child.

1. **"Missouri" type statute:** Under what is known as the "Missouri" type of omitted child statute, the intent to omit the child must be determinable solely from the terms of the will. Extrinsic evidence is not admissible.

2. **"Massachusetts" type statute:** Under what is known as the "Massachusetts" type of omitted child statute, extrinsic evidence is admissible to help determine whether the omission of the child was intentional.

E. **Omitted child's share:** If the presumption that the failure to provide for the new child was not intentional is not rebutted, the typical omitted child statute gives the omitted child his or her intestate share of the testator's probate estate.

F. **Example:** In *Gray v Gray*, 947 So. 2d 1045 (Ala. 2006), John Gray executed a will while married to Mary, and although he had two children from a previous marriage, he left all of his estate to Mary. Three years later, John and Mary had a son, Jack. Five years later, John and Mary divorced. John died without changing his will. Under Alabama's revocation by operation of law doctrine,

Mary was treated as if she predeceased John due to the divorce and did not take. Jack petitioned the probate court to determine if he was entitled to a share of John's estate under Alabama's omitted child doctrine. The court said although the presumption arose that the omission was accidental, it could be overcome by the exception that the testator had one or more children when the will was executed and he left substantially all of his estate to the other parent of the omitted child. The court stated that it did not matter that John's other children were from a prior marriage; Jack was excluded from a share of the estate. The dissent argued that the exception was meant to apply where the child could look to inherit down the road from the other parent who took from the decedent, and here, where the other parent was ineligible to take due to the divorce, the exception should not apply.

G. Overlooked child: A number of states have expanded the traditional omitted child doctrine to include a living child who is omitted if the child is omitted because (1) the testator does not know about the child, or (2) the testator mistakenly believed the child was dead. (More states cover only the latter; a handful cover both.) As a general rule, the overlooked child receives his or her intestate share just like a pretermitted child.

H. UPC: The UPC tracks the basic provisions of the traditional pretermitted child doctrine, but it has a few revisions worth noting.

     1. Adopted children: The UPC expressly provides that it applies to children born or adopted after execution of the will.

     2. Intent to omit: Unlike the UPC omitted spouse doctrine, the UPC omitted child doctrine does not broaden the scope of the evidence that can be used to prove the intent to omit a new child. The UPC sticks with the traditional rule that the evidence that the failure to provide for the child was intentional must come *from the will.*

     3. Other children: Under the traditional approach, if the presumption arises that a child was accidentally omitted, the presumption is overcome if the testator had one or more children when the will is executed and devised substantially all of his or her estate to the other parent of the omitted child. The UPC, however, does not permit such evidence to defeat the child's claim to an omitted share, but rather uses it in calculating how much the child should receive.

     4. Omitted child's share: The omitted child's share under the UPC depends on whether the testator has other children living at the time he or she executes the will.

         a. No children: If the testator had no children when he or she executed the will, the omitted child receives his or her intestate share, unless the testator devised all or substantially all of his or her estate to the other parent of the omitted child and the other parent survives the testator and is entitled to take, in which case the omitted child takes nothing.

         b. One or more children: If the testator has one or more children living at the time he or she executes the will, and the will devised property to one or more of the then-living children, the omitted child's share (1) is taken out of the portion of the testator's estate being devised to the then-living children, and (2) should equal the share or interest the other children are receiving, had the testator included all omitted children with the children receiving shares and given each an equal share. (Gifts to the then-living children are to abate pro rata.)

5. **Overlooked child:** The UPC expressly includes a child who is overlooked in the will because the testator thought the child was dead when he or she executed the will. The UPC does not extend omitted child status to the child overlooked because the testator does not know about the child.

I. **Omitted issue of deceased child:** Most omitted child statutes cover omitted children only. Some statutes, however, expressly provide that they apply not only to omitted children, but also to the omitted issue of a child who died before the testator. The omitted issue of the child who died before the testator take their intestate share.

J. **Modern trend:** A few states have modified the omitted child doctrine to recognize that increasingly the inter vivos revocable trust is being used much like a will. In those states, the omitted child doctrine arises only if the birth occurs after execution of all the deceased spouse's wills and revocable trusts, and the omitted child's share is of the property included in the combined probate estate and revocable trusts.

Example: In **Kidwell v. Rhew**, 268 S.W.3d 309 (Ark. 2007), Irene Winchester created a revocable, inter vivos trust, transferred real property to the trust, and named her daughter, Margie Rhew, as successor trustee upon Irene's death. Irene never executed a will and another daughter, Rhenda Kidwell, petitioned the court to apply Arkansas's pretermitted-heir statute to the revocable trust. Kidwell argued that the pretermitted-heir statute should apply to dispositions made by testamentary will substitutes, such as an inter vivos trust. Although Kidwell would have had rights to the real property if the testamentary transfer had been created in a will, Irene did not dispose of her property through a will. She transferred the real property through a trust. The statute speaks only in terms of the execution of a will and therefore the court declined to apply the pretermitted-heir statute to the inter vivos trust. Kidwell was not entitled to a share of the estate.

Quiz Yourself on
LIMITATIONS ON THE TESTAMENTARY POWER TO TRANSFER

48. List the five different rights to support to which a surviving spouse is entitled as a general rule upon the death of his or her spouse. _____

49. Bob marries Carol. They have one child, Sunshine. On April 1, 2008, Bob dies intestate with a gross probate estate of $200,000. Bob's funeral expenses, administration expenses, and debts total $50,000. Carol is trying to determine what she would get if she claimed her elective share. As a result of Bob's death, Carol received $600,000 in life insurance proceeds from a policy on which Bob had paid the premiums. In addition, prior to his death, and during the marriage, Bob made the following transfers:

- 1/1/1993 Transferred $150,000 in trust for the benefit of Mom, but he retained the power to revoke the trust during his lifetime.

- 1/1/2003 $600,000 Purchased Malibuacres—Bob put up all the consideration but took title in joint tenancy with his brother, Bill.

- 6/1/2005 Irrevocable gift to Lulu $20,000.

- 1/1/2006 Irrevocable gift to Lulu $20,000.

■ 6/1/2006 Irrevocable gift to Lulu $28,000.

■ 1/1/2007 Irrevocable gift to Lulu $30,000.

■ 5/1/2007 Transferred $150,000 in trust for his benefit for life, remainder to Lulu, and retained the power to revoke.

■ 6/1/2007 Irrevocable gift to Lulu $33,000.

■ 1/1/2008 Irrevocable gift to Lulu $35,000.

(Answer the question below that constitutes the approach your jurisdiction takes. If your jurisdiction's approach is not among the possible questions, do your best to answer it on your own and then check the answer for the approach closest to your state's approach.)

a. What is Carol's right to an elective share if (1) the elective share is one-third of the net estate if the decedent is survived by one or more children, otherwise one-half of the net estate; and (2) the jurisdiction limits the elective share to the deceased spouse's probate estate? _____

b. What is Carol's right to an elective share if (1) the jurisdiction follows the same fractional shares as above, and (2) it also follows the "illusory transfer" approach to what constitutes the decedent's estate? _____

c. What is Carol's right to an elective share if (1) the jurisdiction follows the same fractional shares as above, and (2) it also follows the 1969 UPC approach to what constitutes the decedent's estate? _____

50. Suzie and Kevin are starving students. They get married and live in Missouri, a noncommunity property state. Suzy works outside the home earning their marital property, and Kevin stays at home raising the children. They decide to retire. At the time, they have a total of $500,000 in savings in Suzy's name alone. Shortly after moving to a community property state, Suzy dies with a will devising all of her property to the American Heart Association. Assuming the state has no special statute governing migrating couples and their property, and assuming Kevin asserts his rights to a share of the marital property, how much does the American Heart Association take? _____

51. In the previous problem, what if after moving to the community property jurisdiction, it was Kevin who died with a will devising all of his property to the American Heart Association? Suzy survives him, and the jurisdiction has adopted quasi-community property. How much does the American Heart Association take? _____

52. Sunshine and Dude, two penniless hippies residing in a community property state, get married. Dude hits it big on the surfing circuit. During the marriage, he earns $1 million in his name alone. Sunshine spends all her time volunteering to fight global warming. Concerned that the melting icebergs will submerge the coastal state where they live, the two retire to Missouri, a separate property jurisdiction. Shortly after establishing domicile in Missouri, Dude dies of boredom. His will devises all of his property to the Heal the Bay Association. Assuming Missouri has no special statute governing migrating couples and their property, and assuming Sunshine asserts her rights to the couple's marital property, how much will the Heal the Bay Association take? _____

53. In the previous problem, what if Missouri has adopted the Uniform Disposition of Community Property at Death Act? _____

54. Gloria has a will that devises all of her property to the National Organization of Women. The will includes an express clause disinheriting any and all other individuals who might claim they are entitled to a share of her estate, including any future spouses. Thereafter, to the shock of everyone, she marries Fred. Thereafter she dies without revoking or revising her will, but she takes out a $1 million life insurance policy that provides that the proceeds are to be paid to Fred upon her death. Following Gloria's death, Fred claims he is an omitted spouse entitled to a share of Gloria's property. Is Fred entitled to a share of Gloria's property:

a. Under the traditional approach to the omitted spouse doctrine?   _____

b. Under the UPC approach to the omitted spouse doctrine?   _____

55. Peter and Carolyn are married with no children. Peter executes a will leaving all of his property to Carolyn. Thereafter, Carolyn gives birth to a child, Chad. Soon after, Peter dies without revising his will. Is Chad entitled to any of Peter's probate property:

a. Under the traditional approach to the omitted child doctrine?   _____

b. Under the UPC approach to the omitted child doctrine?   _____

56. What if in the previous problem, Peter and Carolyn had two children (Ali and Benji) at the time Peter executed his will, and Peter's will left 70 percent of his estate to Carolyn and the rest to Ali and Benji. Thereafter, Peter and Carolyn had another child, Chad. Is Chad entitled to any of Peter's probate property:

a. Under the traditional approach to the omitted child doctrine?   _____

b. Under the UPC approach to the omitted child doctrine?   _____

Answers

48.   As a general rule, a surviving spouse's rights to support include (1) rights under social security, (2) rights under ERISA, (3) rights under the homestead exemption to a place to live, (4) rights under the personal property set aside to certain tangible personal property, and (5) rights to a family allowance to live on during probate (either a set statutory amount or an amount tied to the family's standard of living at the time the deceased spouse died).

49a. This approach represents the traditional elective share approach because it is limited to the deceased spouse's probate estate. The share depends upon the family situation. Here, Bob is survived by one child, so his wife, Carol, is entitled to 33 percent of his net probate estate. Bob's gross probate estate is $200,000, but he has expenses and debts totaling $50,000. Bob's net probate estate is $150,000. Carol can claim 33 percent of that, or $50,000.

49b. There is no consensus as to what constitutes an illusory transfer. The essence of the doctrine is that inter vivos transfers that, as a practical matter, do not transfer any *real* interest until the transferor dies should not be treated as inter vivos transfers for purposes of the elective share doctrine (that is, considered part of the decedent's estate when calculating the elective share). As applied to this fact pattern, the most likely result is that in addition to Bob's net probate estate ($150,000), the 5/1/2007 revocable trust, in which Bob retained a life estate interest, remainder to Lulu, would be brought back in and added to the net probate estate (to total $300,000 now). Whether the 1/1/1993 trust in favor of his mother would be brought back in is less clear. On the one hand, he retained the power to revoke, so he had control over the assets until he died (like a will, he could have changed the beneficiaries until death). On the other hand, Bob had no interest in the income or principal, only the power to revoke. He established the trust for the benefit of his mother. (These considerations begin to raise the arguments that led to the development of the intent to defraud test—the property is brought back in only if the decedent had the intent to defraud his or her surviving spouse of his or her elective share, though the jurisdictions are split over whether this is a subjective or objective test.) If the court were to conclude that the revocable trust in favor of Mom constitutes an illusory transfer, for purposes of the elective share doctrine his estate would be $450,000, and Carol would take one-third or $150,000. If the court were to conclude that the trust should not be brought back in, Bob's estate for elective share purposes would be $300,000, and Carol would be entitled to $100,000. (Property held in joint tenancy is generally held not to constitute an illusory transfer—the other party acquires substantive and substantial inter vivos right, and the gifts to Lulu were completed inter vivos transfers that generally would not be considered part of Bob's assets still under the illusory transfer approach.)

49c. The 1969 UPC approach takes the augmented estate approach. In addition to the probate estate, the augmented estate includes a number of transfers made without consideration, including: (1) transfers where the decedent retained the power to revoke, (2) any transfer in joint tenancy where the other joint tenant is not the spouse, (3) any transfers within two years of death exceeding $3,000 per donee, and (4) property received by the surviving spouse as a result of the decedent's death. Here, in addition to Bob's net probate estate ($150,000), under the 1969 UPC approach, the augmented estate would include: (1) both of his revocable trusts—to Mom and Lulu ($300,000); (2) Malibuacres, the joint tenancy with his brother ($600,000); (3) the gifts to Lulu within two years of Bob's death that exceeded $3,000 a year (6/1/2006 $28,000 + 1/1/2007 $30,000 + 6/1/2007 $33,000 + 1/1/2008 $35,000 = total $126,000 minus $6,000 ($3,000 per donee per year) equals $120,000); and (4) the life insurance proceeds Carol received ($600,000). The total augmented estate is $1,770,000. Carol's one-third is $590,000. Property that passes to the surviving spouse (the life insurance and probate estate share) is counted first in funding her share. Because Carol has already received more than her elective share amount, she takes no additional property under the 1969 UPC approach.

50. Because Missouri is a noncommunity property jurisdiction, all of the money that Suzy earns is her separate property. When they move to the community property jurisdiction, the characterization of the property does not change. Assuming the jurisdiction has no special statutes governing migrating couples (that is, no quasi-community property doctrine), when Suzy dies, Kevin is entitled to half of their community property. Because they have no community property, Kevin takes none of the property. The American Heart Association takes all $500,000.

51. Quasi-community property gives the surviving spouse community property rights in the deceased spouse's property that would have been characterized as community property if the couple had been domiciled in a community property jurisdiction when the property was acquired. Here, Kevin has no property in his name. Quasi-community property does not attach to Suzy's separate property. The American Heart Association takes nothing under Kevin's will because he has no property in his name and no rights to the property in Suzy's name.

52. When a couple moves from a community property jurisdiction to a separate property jurisdiction, there is the potential for the surviving spouse to "double dip." Here, because Dude's $1 million was earned during marriage in a community property state, it is community property. When they move to Missouri, a noncommunity property state, the characterization of the property does not change. Upon his death, Sunshine takes her half of the community property outright, and Dude's half goes into probate. Because the couple's marital domicile at time of death was a separate property jurisdiction, Sunshine can also claim her elective share rights in Dude's probate property. Assuming the share is 50 percent of the deceased spouse's probate estate, Sunshine could claim another $250,000. The Heal the Bay Association takes only $250,000.

53. Under the Uniform Disposition of Community Property at Death Act, the deceased spouse's share of their community property is not subject to the elective share doctrine. Here, Dude's half of the community property in his probate estate is not subject to Sunshine's elective share claim. The Heal the Bay Association takes $500,000.

54a. Under the omitted spouse doctrine, because Gloria married Fred after she executed her will and she died without revoking or revising her will, a rebuttable presumption arises that Fred's disinheritance was accidental. One way to rebut the presumption is to show that the decedent provided for the spouse outside of the will and the transfer was intended to be in lieu of the surviving spouse taking under the will. Here, shortly after she married Fred, Gloria took out a $1 million life insurance policy and designated Fred as the beneficiary. When Gloria died, Fred received the $1 million. A strong argument can be made that Gloria intended this transfer outside of the will to be in lieu of Fred's taking under her probate estate. Although there is no direct evidence that this is what Gloria intended, the size of the nonprobate transfer and the fact that she purchased the policy shortly after marrying Fred should be enough to convince the court that Gloria intended the life insurance proceeds to be in lieu of Fred taking under her will.

54b. Under the UPC, if the will expressly provides that the testator is intentionally omitting all future spouses, this clause effectively overcomes the presumption that the spouse was omitted accidentally. Fred is barred from claiming an omitted spouse's share under the UPC approach because of the express general disinheritance clause in the will.

55a. Under the traditional approach, Chad is entitled to his intestate share of Peter's estate. Under the omitted child doctrine, when Chad was born after Peter had executed his will, and Peter died without revising or revoking his will, a presumption arises that Chad was accidentally omitted. The traditional methods of rebutting the presumption do not apply here (the will does not express a specific intent to omit this child, there is no transfer outside of the will to Chad, and although Peter transferred all of his property to the other parent of the omitted child, he had no children at the time he executed the will).

55b. Under the UPC, Chad is not entitled to any of Peter's estate as an omitted child. Under the UPC, if the testator has no children at the time he or she executes the will, and the testator leaves all or substantially all of his or her property to the other parent of the omitted child, and the other parent survives the decedent and takes under the will, the child does not take a share of the decedent's probate estate.

56a. Under the traditional approach, although the presumption arises that the child was accidentally omitted, the presumption is rebutted here. The testator had one or more children when the will was executed, and the testator devised substantially all of his or her estate to the other parent of the omitted child. It is presumed that the testator decided to let the other parent of the child decide how best to care for the omitted child.

56b. Under the UPC approach, the presumption arises that Chad is an accidentally omitted child. Under the UPC approach, if the testator had one or more children when the will was executed, and the testator devised property to one or more of the then-living children, the omitted child is entitled to a share of the property being distributed to the then-living children. The omitted child's share is the share the child would have received if all omitted after-born (or adopted) children are included with the children who are taking under the will. Here, Chad would take one-third of the property being devised to Ali and Benji (30 percent of Peter's estate). Each child would end up with 10 percent of the estate.

Exam Tips on LIMITATIONS ON THE TESTAMENTARY POWER TO TRANSFER

The material in this chapter can be divided into three major areas: (1) a surviving spouse's right to support, (2) a surviving spouse's right to share in the couple's marital property (elective share and community property), and (3) the omitted spouse/omitted child doctrines.

Surviving spouse's right to support

☛ The details of a surviving spouse's right to support are generally beyond the scope of the typical wills and trusts course. If you see a spouse die with a surviving spouse, state that the surviving spouse has a right to support, and then quickly list the five forms of support.

Surviving spouse's right to share in the couple's marital property

☛ The key is coverage. When most professors reach this section of the book, they cover only that material that corresponds to the approach in their jurisdiction. Pay close attention to your professor's classroom coverage of this material.

 ☞ If the professor covers some of the comparative material, close attention in class will tell you how much of the "other" approach you need know.

The elective share

☛ More than any other doctrine, the elective share varies from state to state. The core concepts of the elective share doctrine are its temporal component (no inter vivos rights, just testamentary), its fractional share, and the property subject to it (probate estate only vs. augmented estate—if the latter, focus on what is included in the augmented estate).

Community property

☛ The core concepts of the community property approach are the scope of community property (property/earnings acquired during marriage, not premarriage property or gifts during marriage) and that at death community property is treated much like tenancy in common (split the property 50-50, the deceased's half goes into probate where he or she is free to devise it as he or she sees fit).

☞ Putting a spouse to an election is a bizarre doctrine. Watch for facts where the deceased spouse clearly tried to give away not only his or her own property, but also some property of the surviving spouse.

☞ A subtle way to test the doctrine is to include a no contest clause in the will. The general rule is that if the surviving spouse asserts his or her rights to take the property that he or she owns but the deceased spouse is trying to give away, the surviving spouse's claim to the property still constitutes a challenge to the testator's testamentary scheme that comes within the scope of a standard no-contest clause.

☞ Migrating couples are a great way to test how well the students understand some of the key differences between the two systems.

☞ If you are in a community property jurisdiction, the details of quasi-community property are important—it is not the same as treating the property as community property. Quasi-community property applies only to the property owned by the deceased spouse, not the surviving spouse.

Omitted spouse/omitted child

☛ This is core wills and trusts material and is tested often. These issues should be easy to spot, because the triggering fact is either marriage or birth of a child after execution of the will, and then the testator dies without revoking or revising his or her will.

☞ Watch for codicils and republication by codicil overlaps. Republication is not necessarily automatic, but if the terms of the codicil expressly republish the will, the court may feel compelled to republish.

☞ Watch out for the subtle way to raise the issue—where there appears to be a new will validly executed after the marriage/birth, but for some reason the "new will" is invalid. Not only will this mean that the original will still controls, but also because the attempted new will is invalid, the omitted spouse/child doctrine will still apply.

☛ If the presumption arises, give the rules for how it can be overcome (the limited ways), and then check to see if any apply.

☞ If the will purports to disinherit all future spouses/children, the general (non-UPC) rule is that the disinheritance must be specific—it must be written with an eye toward this particular person. Conversely, just because a spouse takes a gift, if he or she does not take in a spousal capacity, the presumption still arises.

☞ Pay close attention to whether your jurisdiction permits extrinsic evidence concerning whether the omission was intentional (the UPC permits for omitted spouses, not for omitted children).

☛ If the testator provided for the spouse/child outside of the will, the amount of the transfer can be relevant to whether the testator intended that to be in lieu of the person taking under the will.

☞ With respect to omitted children, the jurisdictions are split over the significance of whether the testator had one or more children at the time he or she executed the will. Pay close attention to how your jurisdiction deals with this situation.

☞ With respect to omitted children, pay close attention to how the share is calculated and funded. Some states permit the child to take his or her intestate share from the decedent's probate estate, while the UPC approach limits the share to a share of the property being devised to the other children.

CHAPTER 8

TRUSTS: OVERVIEW AND CREATION

ChapterScope

This chapter examines (1) what a trust is conceptually, and (2) how to validly create one doctrinally. In particular, the chapter examines:

- **Trust conceptually:** A trust is an abstract legal entity. One way to conceptualize a trust is to think of it as a bifurcated gift.

  - **Outright gift:** A traditional gift has two parties, a donor and a donee. The donor transfers legal and equitable title to the property being gifted to the donee.

  - **Gift in trust—bifurcated gift:** A trust is a bifurcated gift. The donor is re-named the settlor. The donee is bifurcated into the trustee and beneficiaries. The settlor transfers legal title to the trustee and equitable interest to the beneficiaries. The trustee holds and manages the property for the benefit of the beneficiaries. Because the trustee holds and manages the trust property, the property needs to be bifurcated into the property transferred to the trust (the trust principal or res) and the income it generates over time. Lastly, at the equitable level, almost every trust is some combination of possessory estate and the future interest. The simplest combination at the equitable level is a life tenant, who typically has a greater interest in the trust income, and a remainderman, who typically has a greater interest in the trust res (or principal).

- **Trust requirements:** To have a valid trust: (1) the settlor must have the intent to create a trust, (2) the trust must be funded, (3) the trust must have ascertainable beneficiaries, and (4) the terms of the trust must be in writing if the trust property includes real property or if the trust is a testamentary trust.

  - **Intent:** The intent to create a trust requires one party to transfer property to a second party for the benefit of a third. The same party can wear more than one hat as long as he or she is not the sole trustee and sole beneficiary.

  - **Funding:** A trust is not created until some property is delivered to the trust/trustee to hold and manage. What constitutes adequate evidence of delivery depends on (1) whether the trustee is the settlor or a third party, and (2) whether the property is personal property or real property.

  - **Ascertainable beneficiaries:** Beneficiaries are ascertainable if there is an objective method of determining their name, i.e., of determining who has standing to come into court and enforce the terms of the trust against the trustee.

  - **Writing:** If the trust is a testamentary trust, the terms of the trust must be in writing. If the trust is an inter vivos trust, the terms need to be in writing only if it involves real property.

I. CONCEPTUAL OVERVIEW

A. **Introduction:** Most students begin the course with no conceptual understanding of what a trust is or does. Without some conceptual understanding, it is difficult to understand the law of trusts. As you cover the material, focus on the conceptual nature of a trust as much as the law of trust.

B. **Terminology:** The law of trust has developed its own terminology that is critical to understanding trusts:

- **Settlor:** The party who creates the trust (also known, though less commonly, as a trustor).

- **Trustee:** The party to whom the settlor transfers the trust property; the trustee holds legal title to the trust property and manages the property for the duration of the trust.

- **Beneficiaries:** The parties who hold the equitable interest in the trust (typically bifurcated over time); the parties to whom the trustee owes a fiduciary duty.

- **Declaration of trust:** If the settlor is also the trustee, the expression of the intent to create the trust, along with the terms of the trust, is called a declaration of trust. (Although the term *declaration of trust* implies the expression is oral, it must be in writing if the trust holds real property or is testamentary.)

- **Deed of trust:** If someone other than the settlor is the trustee, the expression of the intent to create the trust, along with the terms of the trust, is called a deed of trust. (Although the term *deed of trust* implies the expression is written, at common law it can be oral if the trust is created inter vivos and involves only personal property.)

- **Res/corpus:** The trust property is often referred to as the trust res, or trust corpus, or more modernly, simply the trust property.

- **Inter vivos trust:** If the trust is created while the settlor is alive, it is an inter vivos trust. A trust is created when it is funded—when property is transferred to the trust/trustee.

- **Testamentary trust:** If the trust is created when the settlor dies (either in the settlor's will or funded via the settlor's will), it is a testamentary trust.

C. **Trust purpose:** One of the reasons why it is so hard for students to conceptualize the prototypical trust is that a trust serves so many different purposes. A will has but one principal purpose—to dispose of the testator's property upon his or her death. A trust, on the other hand, serves an endless number of purposes. A trust serves the settlor's intent, whatever that intent may be. It is the most flexible legal instrument available. Each trust must be read carefully to determine its purpose. But while there is no prototypical trust purpose, there is a prototypical trust structure, and it is that structure that defines the essence of a trust.

D. **Trust structure:** The prototypical trust structure is that *A* transfers property to *B* for the benefit of *C* (and possibly others). That is a trust. One party (the settlor) transfers property to a second party (the trustee), who holds and manages the property for the benefit of one or more third parties (the beneficiaries).

E. **Bifurcated gift:** A trust is merely another way of making a gift. A gift occurs when a donor transfers property to a donee. A trust is a "bifurcated gift." The gift in trust is bifurcated in that legal title to the property is given to one party (the trustee), while the equitable interest is given to another party (the beneficiary). The equitable interest is the right to use and benefit from the property. The extent of the beneficiary's equitable interest in the property is defined by the terms of the trust, and the terms of the trust are determined by the settlor when he or she sets up the trust.

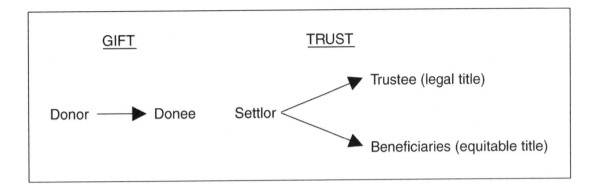

The trustee holds and manages the trust property for the benefit of the trust beneficiaries. Once title is bifurcated between the legal and the equitable interests, the trustee owes the beneficiaries a whole host of fiduciary duties.

F. **Ongoing gift:** The statement that the trustee "holds and manages" the trust property implicitly indicates another difference between the classic gift and a gift in trust. The classic gift is a two-party transaction. The moment the property is given to the donee, the gift is over. It has no "on-going" life. A trust, on the other hand, is a three-party transaction. The statement that the trustee "holds and manages" the trust property implicitly indicates that a trust has an on-going life after the settlor transfers the property to the trust. The trustee holds and manages the trust property during the life of the trust.

1. **Bifurcate trust property:** Because the trustee holds and manages the trust property over time, the trust property typically becomes bifurcated between the trust principal (the property the settlor transferred to the trust) and the trust income (the money generated by the trust principal while the trustee is holding and managing the trust). A beneficiary's interest can be in the trust income and/or the trust principal.

2. **Bifurcate equitable interests:** In addition, at the equitable level, invariably the equitable title is bifurcated over time. The beneficiary who currently holds the right to benefit from the trust right now holds the possessory equitable interest. The party who currently holds the right to benefit from the trust in the future holds the future equitable interest. The simplest bifurcation is a life estate and remainder.

   "Equitable" vs. "legal" possessory estates and future interests: If someone wants to break up property interests over time, doing so in trust (equitable possessory estates and future interests) is much preferred to doing so by deed (legal possessory estate and future interests). By bifurcating the interests in trust, one party, the trustee, holds legal title to the property in trust and power to manage the property. This greatly facilitates dealing with the property with respect to a whole host of possible legal issues where bifurcating the interests legally only needlessly complicates dealing with the property.

G. **Example—gift vs. trust:** Alice gives Betty $1,000. That is a classic inter vivos gift. Betty can do whatever she wants with the gift. On the other hand, if Alice gives Betty $1,000, to use for the benefit of Cindy during her lifetime, and, upon her death, any remaining principal is given to Deb, that is a classic trust. Betty cannot use the property for her own benefit. She can use the property only for the benefit of Cindy and Alice. Cindy has a life estate interest, and Deb has the remainder interest.

H. **Visualize:** One way to visualize a trust is that it is nothing more than a legal receptacle, a legal "bucket," that holds the trust property during the life of the trust. The settlor creates the bucket by expressing the intent to create a trust. The settlor funds the trust by putting property into the trust, the legal bucket. The trustee holds the bucket, managing the property in the bucket for the benefit of the beneficiaries. The trustee reaches into the bucket and distributes income or disburses principal to one or more of the beneficiaries, pursuant to the terms of the trust (that is, pursuant to the settlor's intent). Typically, the life beneficiary is entitled to the income, and the remainder beneficiary is entitled to the principal.

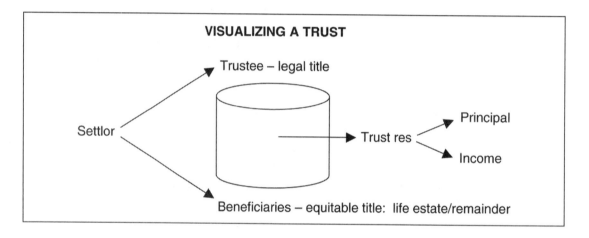

VISUALIZING A TRUST

Settlor → Trustee – legal title

Settlor → Trust res → Principal / Income

Settlor → Beneficiaries – equitable title: life estate/remainder

I. **Historical origin:** The trust evolved out of the law of "uses" at common law. Uses initially arose as a way to permit Franciscan friars, whose vow of poverty prevented them from owning property, to use property held by another. The use quickly spread to other purposes (avoiding the rule of primogeniture and feudal death taxes). King Henry attempted to abolish the use, but the Statute of Uses of 1535 ended up leading to the law of trusts. If the feoffee had affirmative duties to hold and manage the property for the benefit of another, that constituted an "active" trust (as opposed to a use) and was permitted under the Statute of Uses. (The requirement that the trustee must have active duties continues to the present day; if the trustee has no duty, the trust fails and the beneficiaries take the property.)

J. **Trust purposes:** The trust may be the most flexible instrument the law has conceived. A trust can be used for virtually any purpose. A trust can be used to avoid probate; it can be used to hold property for a minor; it can be used for a variety of estate planning/tax purposes; it can be used to try and influence the beneficiaries' behavior; it can be used for an endless variety of purposes. The key is to read each trust carefully to ascertain the particular purpose of each trust.

Commercial trusts: Although trusts typically are used for gratuitous property transfers between individuals (typically family members) and/or for protective purposes (to care for individuals who cannot care for themselves), trusts are also used for commercial purposes: business trusts instead of incorporating; mutual funds to hold collective investments; pension funds; and asset securitization—sale of equitable interests in a stream of payments. These scenarios bring added complexity to the already complex trust structure. Accordingly, the material will focus on the noncommercial trust scenarios.

K. Basic trust rules: There are a few basic rules relating to trusts that are critical to understanding the larger law of trusts.

1. Same party can wear all three hats: Although there are three distinct parties to a trust—settlor, trustee, and beneficiary—the same person can wear all three hats at the same time—can be settlor, trustee, and beneficiary at the same time—as long as there is another trustee or another beneficiary.

Merger: If the same party is both trustee and beneficiary, and there is no other trustee or beneficiary, the legal title and the equitable title are said to merge, and the trust is terminated (bifurcation of the legal and equitable titles is essential to a trust). Bifurcation creates a fiduciary duty between the trustee and the beneficiaries. If the same person is both trustee and beneficiary, one cannot hold oneself to a fiduciary duty, so the trust merges and terminates.

2. A trust is not created until it is funded: A trust is not created until it is funded. A trust is not funded until property is transferred to the trust/trustee. Funding is distinct from the expression of the intent to create a trust. Where the trustee is a third party (someone other than the settlor), property has to be transferred to the trustee, with the intent that the trustee hold and manage it for the benefit of someone else. Executing a deed of trust does not constitute funding.

3. A trust will not fail for want of a trustee: Where the settlor clearly expresses the intent to create a trust and provides for funding, a trust will not fail for want of a trustee. If the trustee declines to serve (a named trustee is not required to serve but rather must accept the appointment), dies, or is unable to continue, or if the settlor forgot to name a trustee, a court will appoint a successor trustee. (Once a trustee accepts the position, due to the fiduciary duties inherent in the office, the trustee can leave the position only with court approval or the consent of all beneficiaries.) Where a will creates a trust but fails to name the trustee, the general rule is to appoint the executor as trustee.

Exception: If the court concludes that the powers given to the trustee were personal, to be exercised by only that trustee (that the settlor intended the trust to last only as long as the named trustee served as trustee), the court will decline to appoint a successor trustee, and the trust will fail. The courts construe this exception narrowly, however, and rarely apply it.

4. Co-trustees must agree on action: If a private trust appoints co-trustees, the general rule is that all the trustees must consent to any proposed action. An individual trustee or subgroup cannot act alone. The trust instrument, however, can provide that the trust can act upon a vote of a majority of the trustees.

Uniform Trust Code: The Uniform Trust Code rejects the common law rule and permits action based on the vote of a majority of the co-trustees.

L. Remedial trusts: Remedial trusts arise by operation of law and thus are not subject to the requirements to create a valid trust. They are used as equitable remedies by courts to order one party who is currently holding property to transfer the property to another party whom the court concludes has a stronger equitable claim to the property.

1. **Resulting trust:** A resulting trust arises anytime a trust fails in whole or in part. The courts use it to require the party holding the property (typically the trustee) to return the property to the settlor (or the settlor's estate if the settlor is dead).

2. **Constructive trust:** Constructive trusts are used to prevent unjust enrichment. Historically, the courts required (1) a confidential or fiduciary relationship between the transferor and the transferee, (2) a promise (express or implied) by the transferee, (3) that the transferor transferred property to the transferee in reliance upon the promise, and (4) that the transferee refuses to honor the promise, thereby constituting unjust enrichment. Under the modern trend, the courts tend not to emphasize the elements as much as the equitable notion that the constructive trust is used to prevent unjust enrichment.

II. REQUIREMENTS TO CREATE A VALID TRUST

A. **Overview:** There are four requirements to create a valid trust: (1) the settlor must have the intent to create a trust; (2) there must be funding—property transferred to the trust/trustee; (3) the beneficiaries must be ascertainable; and (4) possibly a writing.

   Practical application: Just as the requirements for a valid inter vivos gift are easy to satisfy, as a general rule, so too are the requirements for the creation of a valid trust.

B. **Theoretical comparison:** The requirements to create a valid trust are very similar to the requirements to make a gift. In fact, the requirements arguably are the same, only altered slightly to reflect the differences between an outright gift and a gift in trust.

1. **Gift requirements:** To make an outright gift, there must be the intent to make a gift and delivery (acceptance is presumed). At common law, if manual delivery was practical, manual delivery was required. If manual delivery was impractical or impossible, constructive or symbolic delivery was acceptable. (Constructive delivery is delivery of something that gives control over the property being gifted; symbolic delivery is delivery of something that stands for or symbolizes the property.)

2. **Trust requirements:** The trust requirements arguably are the same as for a gift, only altered slightly to reflect the inherent nature of a trust.

   a. **Intent:** To make a gift in trust, the settlor must have the intent to make a gift in trust. The only difference in the intent requirement is that the intent must be that the gift be in trust—a transfer to one person who holds and manages it for the use and benefit of another—as opposed to the intent to make an outright gift.

   b. **Delivery:** The second requirement for a gift, delivery, has to be altered to reflect the fact that a gift in trust is a bifurcated gift. As applied to the trust, the delivery requirement is that the property must be delivered to the trustee (funding). Where the property is delivered to the trustee with the intent that the gift be a trust, equitable title is automatically transferred to the beneficiaries by operation of law. This helps to explain the third requirement for a valid trust: The beneficiaries must be ascertainable.

   c. **Ascertainable beneficiaries:** The beneficiaries must be ascertainable so the court knows who has standing to enforce (1) the terms of the trust, and (2) the fiduciary duties the trustee owes the beneficiaries.

    d. Writing: The final possible requirement, writing, is not really a trust requirement. If the trust involves real property, the Statute of Frauds requires that the trust be in writing. If the trust is a testamentary trust, the Wills Act requires that the terms of the trust be in writing. The writing requirement is no different than it is for an outright inter vivos gift of real property or any other testamentary gift.

C. Observation: The doctrinal requirements for a valid trust are rather straightforward. There are, however, a handful of challenging conceptual issues with respect to some of the elements, particularly the first two—intent and funding. Because these issues can be a bit confusing, they tend to distort some students' perception of the material. Trust law is easier to understand if you keep these issues in perspective.

D. Intent: The first requirement for a valid trust is the intent to create a trust. The intent to create a trust (to make a gift in trust) exists anytime one party transfers property to another party with the intent to vest the beneficial interest in a third party. No technical words are necessary, but if the settlor uses any of the basic trust terms (***in trust, trustee***) that is presumed indicative of the intent to create a trust.

    1. Example: In ***Lux v. Lux***, 288 A.2d 701 (R.I. 1972), paragraph 2 of the testatrix's will left the residue of her estate to her grandchildren. Paragraph 3 provided that her real estate "shall be maintained" for the benefit of the grandchildren and "shall not be sold" until the youngest reached age 21. The court ruled that the use of the phrases "shall be maintained" and "shall not be sold" indicated the intent to create a trust. The court appointed the executor of the estate trustee.

    2. Example: In ***Jimenez v. Lee,*** 547 P.2d 126 (Or. 1976), a daughter sued her father for breach of trust. The daughter claimed that two gifts to the father for the benefit of the daughter to be used for her education constituted trusts. Although the grantors did not use any technical terms or expressly state that the gifts were in trust, the grantors clearly indicated that the money being given to the father was to be used for the daughter's educational needs. The court held that because the grantors intended to vest the beneficial interest in the daughter, the grantors had the intent to create a trust and the father held the money in question as a trustee.

    3. Fuzzy at the margins: Because the intent to create a trust is merely a variation on the intent to create a gift, sometimes it is hard to tell the difference between the two. There are two scenarios where it is particularly difficult to draw the line between the intent to create a trust and the intent to create a gift: (1) precatory trusts, and (2) failed gifts.

        a. Precatory trust: A precatory trust arises where there is an outright gift from a donor to donee, but the donor includes some language that expresses the ***hope,*** or the ***wish***—but ***no legal obligation***—that the property be used for the benefit of another. A precatory trust is not a trust at all, but merely a "gift with a wish." The key is whether the language used in conjunction with the transfer indicates the intent to vest the beneficial interest in the third party (in which case the transfer is a trust) or whether the language expresses merely the ***hope or wish*** that the recipient of the property use it for a third party (in which case the transfer is merely a gift with a wish, a precatory trust). Where the language is ambiguous, the court will take into consideration all the circumstances surrounding the situation.

        Example: Andy gives Betty $1,000 and tells her that he "hopes she uses it to pay for her daughter's music lessons." Instead, Betty goes to Las Vegas and gambles it away. There is no breach of trust because when Andy made a gift with a wish the language did not vest the beneficial interest in the daughter. At most the gift was a precatory trust, which is no trust at all.

b. Failed gifts: Where a donor has the intent to make a gratuitous inter vivos gift, but the gift fails for want of delivery (typically the donor dies before making delivery), the donee may try to save the failed gift by recharacterizing the donor's intent as the intent to create a trust. The donee will argue that when the donor expressed the intent to create a trust, the donor also appointed him- or herself trustee, thereby "delivering" the property from him- or herself as settlor to him- or herself as trustee. Because a trust will not fail for want of a trustee, the donee will then ask the court to appoint a successor trustee and instruct him or her to transfer the property to the donee, thereby satisfying the delivery requirement for the gift, but only by recharacterizing the failed inter vivos gift as an intent to create a trust.

   i.   General rule: A leading trust authority (1 Austin W. Scott, Trusts §31 (William F. Fratcher ed., 4th ed. 1987)) and the Restatement (Third) of Trusts §16(2) (T.D. No. 1, 1996), along with most courts, reject the argument that an inter vivos gift that fails for want of delivery can be saved by recharacterizing the donor's intent as an intent to declare a trust.

   ii. Example: In *Hebrew University Association v. Nye,* 169 A.2d 641 (Conn. 1961), the Hebrew University Association claimed that Ethel Yahuda had effectively transferred a library of rare books and manuscripts to the Association. The Association's complaint alleged only that Ethel was the rightful owner of the books and that she had "gifted" them to the Association. The complaint contained no theory as to how the gift was completed. The court noted that although Ethel clearly expressed the intent to make a gift of the books to the Association, there was no evidence in the record of delivery before Ethel died. As for the argument that the failed gift could be saved by recharacterizing Ethel's intent as a declaration of trust, the court rejected the fiction that equity can transform a donor into a trustee to save a gift that fails for want of delivery. Although one can create an oral trust of personal property and deliver the personal property to oneself as a trustee, the intent to create a trust, as opposed to make a gift, must be present. Ethel never referred to herself as a trustee nor acted like a trustee with respect to the property. The court found no evidence to support a declaration of trust.

   iii. Epilogue: In *Hebrew University Association v. Nye,* 223 A.2d 397 (Conn. 1966), following remand and a new trial, the Association brought forth evidence that when Ethel expressed her intent to make an inter vivos gift of the library to the Hebrew University Association, she gave the Association a memorandum containing a list of most of the contents of the library. The court held that in light of her intent to make a gift of the library, the memorandum constituted constructive delivery constituting an inter vivos gift.

   iv. Reliance: Where a donee changes his or her position in reliance upon a promised gift such that it would be inequitable not to enforce the gift, a court of equity will compel the donor to complete the gift, not because the incomplete gift is being converted into a declaration of trust, but rather because a constructive trust is being imposed on the donor to prevent unjust enrichment. 1 Austin W. Scott, Trusts §31.4 (William F. Fratcher ed., 4th ed. 1987).

v. Death: Where a gift fails for want of delivery, if the donor dies thinking that he or she did all that was necessary to complete the gift, and if the donee was a natural object of the donor's bounty (wife or child), the courts will impose a constructive trust on the donor's estate to complete the gift—though the court will not treat the gift as a declaration of trust.

E. Funding: The second requirement for a valid trust is that the trust must be funded—some property must be transferred to the trust/trustee. There are two key components to the funding requirements: (1) the act of funding, and (2) what type of property interest will qualify as an adequate property interest for purposes of funding the trust.

1. **The importance of funding:** A trust is not created until some property is transferred to the trust (to the trustee), and only property transferred to the trust is part of the trust.

2. **Traditional approach:** Historically, the act of funding the trust was viewed as a completely separate and distinct act from the creation of the trust. The act of funding was a function of the law of property. The asset had to be delivered to the trust/trustee, and the Statute of Frauds governed whether there had to be written evidence of the transfer/funding. If the property being delivered to the trust was real property, there had to be a grant deed, separate from the declaration of trust or deed of trust, transferring the real property from the settlor to the trust/trustee. If the property was personal property, either (1) the item itself had to be manually delivered to the trust/trustee or (2) there had to be a written instrument manually delivered to the trust/trustee that listed the personal property in question and evidenced the symbolic/constructive delivery of the item(s) to the trust.

3. **Modern trend approach:** The modern trend approach to funding, and general rule, focuses much more on settlor's intent and much less on the formalities of property law and/or the Statute of Frauds. Under the modern trend approach, the creation of the trust and delivery requirements overlap and can be one and the same, depending on the facts. This is particularly true where the settlor is also the trustee. Most courts and authorities have concluded that it is impossible for a settlor to transfer property to him- or herself, reasoning instead that the settlor-trustee retains legal title (not as settlor but rather as trustee) regardless of delivery, but equitable title must be transferred to a beneficiary. What is necessary to properly transfer the equitable interest to a beneficiary is a more nebulous question based on the settlor's intent.

    a. **Written declaration of trust and real property:** Where the settlor is the trustee, if the declaration of trust is in writing and identifies the real property the trust holds, the general rule is the declaration of trust will also transfer the real property interest into the trust, thereby funding the trust without a separate writing. UTC §401. A handful of jurisdictions, however, still follow the traditional approach and require a separate writing to transfer title to the real property from the settlor as nontrustee to the settlor as trustee (although the writing does not have to be recorded).

    b. **Written declaration of trust and personal property:** Where the settlor is the trustee, if the declaration of trust is in writing and it specifically identifies the personal property the trust holds, the general rule is the writing will be sufficient to simultaneously create the trust, transfer the personal property interests into the trust, and transfer the equitable interest to the beneficiary. UTC §401. If, however, the trust property is stock or other titled property, a handful of jurisdictions require the settlor to change the registration of the trust property from the settlor as nontrustee to the settlor as trustee to transfer the property to the trust.

c. Oral declaration of trust and personal property: Where the settlor is the trustee, if the declaration of trust is oral and the settlor specifically identifies the personal property the trust holds, the general rule is the oral declaration will be sufficient to create the trust and to transfer the personal property interests into the trust.

   i. Overlap with intent: Where there is no writing evidencing the declaration of trust and/or the transfer of the property to the trust the risk of questionable claims of trust creation and/or funding increases significantly. With respect to creation, the courts tend to require clear and convincing evidence of the intent to create a trust; with respect to funding, the courts require (1) that the claimed "declaration of trust" expressly identify the property subject to the trust and/or (2) evidence that the settlor separated the "trust" property from the rest of his or her other property (as required under the trustee's duty to segregate the trust property from the rest of the trustee's property). Because the two elements overlap, often the evidence of each may as well (failure of the party to segregate an asset, if that is the only claimed asset in the trust, may be evidence of both the lack of intent to create a trust and the failure to fund any claimed trust).

   ii. Contrast failed gift: Where a donor promises to make a gift of a particular asset but then dies before delivering it, the frustrated donee may try to save the gift by re-characterizing the promise as a declaration of trust that also constituted funding and then ask the court to appoint a successor trustee and order delivery to complete the gift. Most courts will carefully scrutinize the evidence of the party's intent, and if they conclude the intent was to make a gift that failed for want of delivery, they will not save the gift by recharacterizing it as a declaration of trust.

   iii. Example: In *Unthank v. Rippstein,* 386 S.W.2d 134 (Tex. 1964), C.P. Craft handwrote a letter to Iva Rippstein in which he stated that he would send her "$200.00 cash the first week of each month for the next 5 years, provided I live that long." Then, Mr. Craft crossed out the words "provided I live that long" and wrote in the margin that he was binding his estate to make the payments. Mr. Craft died three days later. In an attempt to save the promised payments to her, Iva Rippstein argued that the letter constituted a declaration of trust. The court ruled that (1) there was insufficient evidence of the intent to create a trust or of any funding, and (2) the letter expressed merely a gratuitous promise to make gifts in the future that failed for want of delivery.

d. Written deed of trust and real property: Where the trustee is a third party (someone other than the settlor), if the deed of trust is in writing and identifies the real property the trust holds, jurisdictions are split on whether a reference to the property in a list attached to the deed of trust is sufficient to constitute delivery in all cases or whether the settlor must do more if the property is real property (i.e., execute a separate grant deed transferring title from the settlor to the trust/trustee).

e. Written deed of trust and personal property: Where the trustee is a third party, if the deed of trust is in writing and it specifically includes a list that identifies the personal property the trust holds, jurisdictions are split on whether a reference to the property in a list attached to the deed of trust is sufficient to constitute delivery in all cases or whether the settlor must do more if the property is stock (i.e., reregister the stock) or other titled property.

f. Oral deed of trust and personal property: Where the trustee is a third party, if the deed of trust is oral, even if the settlor specifically identifies the personal property the trust holds, the general rule is the oral declaration will be insufficient to create the trust and to transfer the personal property interests into the trust. There must be some other evidence of delivery, either actual delivery of the personal property in question to the trust/trustee or delivery of a written list of the personal property assets being transferred to the trust/trustee.

g. Uniform Trust Code: The Uniform Trust Code expressly permits oral trusts unless otherwise prohibited by state law (i.e., the Statute of Frauds), but heightens the required proof of the terms to clear and convincing evidence. UTC §407.

4. Adequate property interest: Funding requires that *some* property interest must be transferred to the trustee. Virtually anything one thinks of as a property interest will qualify: real property, personal property, money (even as little as a dollar or a penny), leasehold interests, possessory estates, future interests (even contingent remainders), life insurance policies, etc. There are two interests, however, that as a general rule the courts have held do not constitute an adequate property interest for purposes of holding that the trust has been funded: expectancies and future profits.

a. Future profits: Although the courts are in agreement that for purposes of funding a trust, future profits *do not* constitute an adequate property interest, a number of courts have held that for purposes of making an inter vivos gift, future profits *do* constitute an adequate property interest.

b. Trusts: In ***Brainard v. Commissioner,*** 91 F.2d 880 (7th Cir. 1937), in December 1927, the taxpayer orally declared, in the presence of his wife and mother, a trust of his stock trading during 1928 for the benefit of his family. Taxpayer agreed to assume personally any losses, but any profits were to be distributed to his family members after paying himself reasonable compensation for his services. There was no evidence that taxpayer owned any stock at the time he declared the alleged trust, and he had no property interest at that time in any possible future profits. The court held that the declaration constituted nothing more than a gratuitous undertaking to create a trust in the future when the profits were realized and were coupled with the intent to create a trust. There being no validly created trust in December 1927, when the profits were realized in 1928 they were taxable to the taxpayer as his property before being transferred to the trust.

c. Inter vivos gifts: In ***Speelman v. Pascal,*** 178 N.E.2d 723 (N.Y. App. 1961), Pascal wrote a letter to his secretary in which he stated that he gave her 5 percent of his share of the profits of the play ***Pygmalion*** as a present for her loyal work. He died shortly after writing the letter. The issue was whether the note was sufficient to constitute a present transfer, as an outright gift, of his future royalties. The court held that the note did transfer his future profits.

d. Debate: Academics love to debate whether these two cases/rules are reconcilable. To the extent a trust is merely another way of making a gift, if future profits constitute an adequate property interest for purposes of making an outright gift, future profits arguably should constitute an adequate property interest for purposes of creating a trust. There are three possible grounds that can be argued to reconcile the arguably conflicting cases:

i. Potential for tax fraud: Some have argued that in ***Brainard*** the court's real concern was the potential for tax fraud. By shifting the profits to the trust, and then giving the profits to his family members, the taxpayer was trying to shift the income generated by his labor to his dependents who were in a lower tax bracket. The only witnesses to this claimed trust creation were his wife and mother—interested witnesses. Upholding this arrangement would open the door to taxpayers who had a good year claiming (fraudulently) that they had created an oral trust in the prior year that transferred the income interest to other family members in a lower tax bracket. The problem with this possible explanation is that in *Brainard* the court does not even mention tax fraud or the potential for tax fraud as the basis for its opinion.

  ii. **Writing:** A second possible explanation that arguably reconciles these cases is that in *Speelman,* the intent to transfer the future profits was in writing, while in *Brainard,* the intent to transfer the future profits to the trust was oral. The problem with this explanation is that it should not matter whether the intent to transfer the property interest in question was in writing. Future profits are personal property that can be transferred without a written instrument. The counterargument is that there has to be delivery and how can one deliver future profits without a writing. (In *Brainard,* the absence of a writing also heightens the potential for fraud.)

  iii. **Means of producing the profits:** A third possible explanation that arguably reconciles the conflicting cases is that in *Speelman,* the donor currently owned the means of producing the future profits. Pascal owned the rights to produce the play that was to generate the profits. In contrast, in *Brainard,* there is no evidence in the record that Brainard owned any stock at all when he orally declared that he was creating a trust and funding it with the future profits from his stock trading. The problem with this explanation is that future profits have been held an adequate property interest for purposes of an inter vivos gift even where the donor does not currently own the means of producing the profits in question—and most commentators assume that Brainard probably did own the stock, the record just failed to reflect it.

e. **Judicial consensus:** Although the academics are bothered by the apparent inconsistency, the courts are not. The courts routinely hold that future profits are not an adequate property interest for purposes of funding a trust.

f. **Realized profits:** Although future profits are not an adequate property interest to create a trust, once the profits are realized, if the party still has the intent to hold them in trust, the moment the profits are realized they will be deemed transferred to the trust and will be sufficient to fund and create the trust at that moment.

g. **Grantor trusts—taxation:** In *Brainard,* the taxpayer was trying to avoid taxes by shifting the income generated by his stock trading from himself, as settlor, to the income beneficiaries, who were in lower tax brackets. Such tax avoidance is no longer available. Where the settlor/grantor retains sufficient dominion and control over the trust, under what are known as the "Clifford regulations," the trust is known as a grantor trust and the settlor is deemed owner of the income generated by the trust for tax purposes.

F. **Ascertainable beneficiaries:** The third requirement for a valid trust is that there must be ascertainable beneficiaries. The moment a settlor intends to create a trust and transfers property to the trustee, the equitable interest is transferred to trust beneficiaries automatically, by operation of law. The trustee needs to know to whom he or she owes a fiduciary duty; the courts need to know who has standing to enforce the terms of the trust and the fiduciary duty. Thus the requirement that the beneficiaries must be ascertainable.

1. **Unborn children exception:** Trusts created in favor of the settlor's unborn children are upheld despite the fact that the settlor's unborn children are not ascertainable when the trust is created.

   The public policy justification is to encourage settlors to create such trusts. The courts monitor the trustee's actions until the children are born to ensure that he or she is properly performing his or her fiduciary duties.

2. **Charitable trusts exception:** The requirement that trust beneficiaries have to be ascertainable applies to private trusts, not to charitable trusts. Because charitable trusts by their nature need to be for the good of the community, arguably the requirement is the exact opposite for charitable trusts—there cannot be ascertainable beneficiaries. If the beneficiaries are ascertainable, then the trust is not for the benefit of the community at large (this is covered in greater detail in Chapter 12).

3. **Ascertainable:** Ascertainable means that you must be able to *identify the beneficiaries by name*. If their names are not expressly set forth in the trust, the trust must contain a formula or description of the beneficiaries that permits the court to determine by *objective* means who they are.

   a. **Example:** In *Clark v. Campbell,* 133 A. 166 (N.H. 1926), the testator left his tangible personal property to his trustees, in trust, to give to his friends as his trustees shall select. The provision was challenged on the grounds that the trust failed for want of ascertainable beneficiaries. The court ruled that the testator intended to create a trust due to the use of the terms *trustee* and *in trust* (rejecting the argument by the trustees that this was a precatory trust, a gift to them with the *hope* that they would distribute the property among the testator's friends). The court held that *friends* was not an objectively ascertainable formula. The trust failed for want of ascertainable beneficiaries.

      i. **Power of appointment:** The testator's intent in the *Clark* case probably was not to create a trust, but rather to create a power of appointment. Powers of appointments are covered in Chapter 9, but two key differences are that (1) with a power of appointment, the holder owes no fiduciary duty to the possible appointees; and (2) exercise of the power is purely discretionary. In *Clark,* the court ruled that use of the terms *trustees* and *in trust* evidenced an intent to create a trust, not a power, and that the clause imposed a mandatory duty upon the trustees to dispose of the property in question. If the testator had not used the terms *trustees* and *in trust,* the more likely construction would have been that the testator intended to create a power. The possible appointees of a power do not have to be ascertainable. All that is necessary under a power is that the person to whom any property is distributed has to reasonably meet the description set forth in the power.

      ii. **Transform failed trust into power:** Professor Scott, one of the top scholars on the law of trusts, argued that anytime a trust in favor of a class that was not ascertainable failed, the trust should automatically be transformed into a power of appointment. The Restatement (Second) and (Third) of Trusts have adopted Scott's argument, but only a handful of courts have adopted the rule.

b. Familial terms: Courts routinely hold that familial terms such as *children*, *issue*, *nephews*, and *nieces* are objectively ascertainable. Some courts have even held that the terms *relatives* and *relations* refer to one's heirs under the state's descent and distribution scheme and thus are objectively determinable.

4. Honorary trusts: Trusts for the benefits of a pet or trusts to maintain one's gravesites, while honorable, technically fail for want of ascertainable beneficiaries. One of the principal purposes for the ascertainable beneficiaries requirement is to determine who has standing to come into court and hold the trustee accountable. Neither a pet nor a gravesite has standing to come into court and sue a trustee. If the beneficiary of a trust is not an ascertainable person, the trust fails for want of ascertainable beneficiaries. But the trust may be saved as an honorary trust.

   a. Rule statement: Where the purpose of a trust is such that it is impossible to have ascertainable beneficiaries, so that the trust should fail for want of ascertainable beneficiaries, if the purpose is specific and honorable, and not capricious or illegal, the trust may continue as long as the "trustee" is willing to honor the terms of the "honorary trust." If the trustee stops honoring the terms of the honorary trust, he or she is not permitted to keep the property. A resulting trust is imposed, and the property is ordered distributed to the proper takers.

   b. Rationale: While honorary trusts technically fail to meet the requirements for a valid trust, the courts decided to permit such trusts because of the honorable purpose of the trust (to care for one's pets, to maintain one's gravesite), but only as long as the party designated as the "trustee" is willing to "honor" the terms of the trust, even though there is no beneficiary to enforce the terms of the trust.

   c. Example: In *In re Searight's Estate,* 95 N.E.2d 779 (Ohio App. 1950), testator's will left his dog, Trixie, to Florence Hand, and he directed his executor to deposit $1,000 in the bank to be used to pay Florence 75 cents a day to care for the dog for its life. The money being paid to Florence was for the benefit of the dog, not for her own benefit, and as such the testator's intent was to create a trust for the benefit of Trixie, the dog. Although technically the trust should fail for want of ascertainable beneficiaries, because the trust was for a specific purpose that was honorable and not capricious or illegal, the court held that the trust qualified as an honorary trust and could continue as long as Florence was willing to honor the terms of the trust—to use the money to care for Trixie.

   d. Rule against Perpetuities: One problem with honorary trusts is that in theory such trusts are subject to the Rule against Perpetuities (covered in Chapter 11). If the administration of the trust can continue for longer than the maximum period allowed under the Rule against Perpetuities, the trust is invalid *from the moment of its attempted creation*. Under the traditional application of the Rule against Perpetuities, most honorary trusts are invalid.

      i. Modern trend: A variety of modern trend approaches to the Rule against Perpetuities soften the impact of the rule. Under the wait-and-see approach, the rule is not tested in the abstract, but rather the courts actually let the time period run and wait and see if the administration of the trust actually continues for longer than the maximum period allowed under the Rule against Perpetuities. Under the wait-and-see approach, the honorary trust is allowed to continue for at least 21 years. The Uniform Trust Code embraces this latter approach. UTC §409(1).

ii. **Example:** In *In re Searight's Estate,* the court "fudged" on the Rule against Perpetuities by computing how long the trust would last based on the payment plan and a reasonable rate of interest. The court found that the trust principal would be exhausted within three to five years. The court read this construction into the terms of the trust to find that the settlor had provided a time limit that would terminate the trust before it violated the Rule against Perpetuities.

e. **Honorary vs. charitable:** Charitable trusts are not subject to the Rule against Perpetuities; so if the trust qualifies as a charitable trust, favor the latter characterization. But charitable trusts have to be for the good of the community at large, or a large subset thereof, and most honorary trusts are for the benefit of a *particular* pet or gravesite. As such, most honorary trusts do not qualify as charitable trusts, but one should always check. (The Uniform Trust Code and an increasing number of states specifically recognize and permit a trust for the benefit of pets as distinct from an honorary trust. UTC §408.)

G. **Writing:** The fourth and final *possible* requirement for a valid trust is that it must be in writing. Under the common law approach, whether a trust must be in writing is not a function of the law of trusts per se, but rather a function of the Statute of Frauds and the Wills Act formalities. Absent state statutes expressly requiring all trusts to be in writing (which some states have adopted), whether a trust has to be in writing to be valid is a function of (1) whether the trust is an inter vivos trust or a testamentary trust, and (2) what type of property the trust holds.

1. **Inter vivos trusts:** As a general rule, inter vivos trusts do not have to be in writing unless the trust holds real property. If the trust is to hold real property, under the Statute of Frauds, the declaration of trust or deed of trust must be in writing.

   a. **Common law:** The common law strictly applies the Statute of Frauds regardless of the consequences. Under the Statute of Frauds, the terms of an *oral trust involving real property* cannot be enforced against the transferee because oral conditions are not permitted to vary the terms of a deed.

      Example: Assume *A* conveys real property to *B,* for the benefit of *C,* but (1) the agreement between *A* and *B* that the property is for the benefit of *C* is oral, and (2) the deed from *A* to *B* makes no reference to the agreement. Under the Statute of Frauds, evidence of the oral understanding between *A* and *B* is not admissible to alter the deed. Without the evidence, *B* owns the property outright—not as a trustee, but as a donee, free and clear of any trust. As applied to oral attempts to create inter vivos trusts of land, the common law approach is harsh.

   b. **Modern trend:** The modern trend (adopted by the Restatement (Third) of Trusts §24) finds that the common law outcome constitutes unjust enrichment of the intended trustee. The Restatement corrects the situation by imposing a constructive trust and ordering the purported trustee to distribute the real property to the intended beneficiaries—not in trust, but outright. (Often the settlor is the intended beneficiary, so the constructive trust ends up looking much like a resulting trust.)

   c. **Equitable basis:** Although one could argue that the modern trend should be imposed anytime an oral inter vivos trust of real property fails for want of writing, the courts have shown a greater willingness to impose the constructive trust where there is some additional equitable basis for imposing the constructive trust. In particular, if the purported trustee has procured the transfer as a result of fraud or undue influence, or if the purported trustee stood in a confidential relationship with the transferor, or if the transfer was made with an eye towards the transferor's impending death, the courts will impose a constructive trust.

d. Remedial trusts: The Statute of Frauds does not apply to the remedial trusts (constructive trust or resulting trust) because they are not true trusts in the full sense of the word but rather are judicial, remedial trusts that arise by operation of law. Under the remedial trusts, the original trust is not upheld and enforced; the purported trustee is simply ordered to transfer the real property in question immediately to the appropriate party or parties.

e. Unclean hands: Constructive trusts are an equitable remedy. Equity regards as done that which ought to be done. If the settlor created the oral trust for real property for improper reasons (the settlor was trying to hide his or her assets from creditors or from an impending divorce, and so on), even under the modern trend the courts generally will not come to the aid of one who has "unclean hands." The purported trustee will be permitted to keep the real property free of any trust.

2. Testamentary trusts: Testamentary trusts, which typically are created in a testator's will, must be in writing pursuant to the Wills Act formalities. Where a testamentary trust fails for want of a writing, the issue is whether the relief should be a constructive trust or a resulting trust. The answer turns on whether the failed testamentary trust is deemed a secret trust or a semi-secret trust.

a. Versus inter vivos trust: A trust where the trustee is to deliver personal property at the settlor's death, if funded inter vivos, is an inter vivos trust and does not have to be in writing. In *In re Estate of Fournier*, 902 A.2d 852 (Me. 2006), in 1998 or 1999 Fournier gave $400,000 in cash to a couple with whom he was friends and asked them to hold it until he died and then to deliver it to his sister Fogarty. He had two other sisters, Flanigan and Rose, but he explained to the couple that Fogarty needed the money and the others did not. He died testate, with a will leaving the residue of his estate equally to Fogarty, Flanigan, and his nephew, Curtis King. Fogarty was appointed the personal representative of his estate. Upon learning of the money, she petitioned the court to determine if Fournier had created a valid inter vivos trust. The trial court reasoned that because he had told Flanigan's daughter about the money he must have intended it to pass through probate, but on appeal the court ruled there was clear and convincing evidence he intended to create an inter vivos trust for Fogarty. [Following the initial ruling, Flanigan found a handwritten note in Fournier's house, written by Fournier dated after he gave the money to the couple, that referenced the $400,000 and provided that the money was to "reimburse" Flanigan, Fogarty, and King, though there was a line through King's name. In light of this new evidence, the court emphasized that the note tracked the decedent's residuary clause and ruled that the note sufficiently evidenced that the inter vivos trust was for all three.]

b. Secret trust: A secret trust is a testamentary trust that fails because the terms of the trust are not set forth in the will. On the face of the will, the secret trust looks like an outright gift to a devisee. It is a "secret" trust because there is nothing on the face of the will that indicates that the testator intended the devisee to take the property as a trustee, not as a devisee, with the beneficial interest in some third party. Inasmuch as the courts have to admit extrinsic evidence to determine that the devisee was supposed to take as a trustee, the courts use the extrinsic evidence to impose a constructive trust on the devisee, ordering the devisee to transfer the property to the intended beneficiaries.

c. **Semi-secret trust:** A semi-secret trust is a testamentary trust that fails because the terms of the trust are not set forth in the will. It is a "semi-secret" trust because there is something in the express language of the will that indicates, or at least hints at, the fact that the devisee was not intended to take the property for his or her own benefit. The courts do not need extrinsic evidence to realize that the devisee is not to take the beneficial interest, so the courts **will not take any extrinsic evidence** to identify the intended beneficiaries. The gift to the devisee as trustee fails. The courts impose a resulting trust and give the property back to the settlor/testator. Typically the property then falls to the residuary clause or, if the failed testamentary trust was the residuary clause, to intestacy.

d. **Example:** In *Oliffe v. Wells,* 130 Mass. 221 (1881), the testatrix devised her residuary estate to Rev. Wells "to distribute the same in such manner as in his discretion shall appear best calculated to carry out wishes which I have expressed to him or may express to him." Because the express language of the will indicated that Rev. Wells was to take the property not for himself, but for the benefit of others, but the terms of the trust were not set forth in the will, the "semi-secret" testamentary trust failed. The court imposed a resulting trust on Rev. Wells. Because the failed testamentary trust was the residuary clause of the testatrix's will, the property fell to intestacy where it was distributed to her heirs.

e. **Modern trend:** The modern trend, as reflected in the Restatement (Second) and (Third) of Trusts, §§55 and 18, respectively, takes the position that a constructive trust in favor of the intended beneficiaries should be imposed in both the secret and semi-secret trust situation. The majority of the courts, however, still follows the old common law distinction, imposing a constructive trust on secret trusts and a failed gift/resulting trust analysis on semi-secret trusts.

Quiz Yourself on
TRUSTS: OVERVIEW AND CREATION

57. What are the requirements to create a valid, private trust? _____

58. In front of several witnesses, Sally orally tells Bob that she intends to give him her computer next month. A week later, she dies. Bob claims that Sally's statement constitutes a declaration of trust and that he is entitled to the computer despite her death. Is Bob entitled to the computer? _____

59. In front of several witnesses, Sally declares that she holds her computer for Bob's benefit and that she will deliver it to him next month. A week later, she dies. Bob claims that Sally's statement constitutes a declaration of trust and that he is entitled to her computer despite her death. Is Bob entitled to her computer? _____

60. Charlie's dad gives him $10,000. As he hands the money over, he says, "I hope you use this to help the poor of Malibuville." Instead, Charlie spends the money on Lulu, one of Heidi's friends. Has Charlie misused the money? _____

61. After a rather long and productive night of working very closely with his assistant, Lulu, Prof. Wendel writes her a note that provides in pertinent part, "I want to show my appreciation for your services in helping me finish my contractual obligations to Aspen. I hereby declare myself to be the trustee of the profits of my Wills & Trusts Emanuel's, if I ever finish writing it, with 25 percent of the profits being held in trust for your benefit, Lulu." Prof. Wendel finally finishes the Emanuel's but dies from caffeine poisoning before it is published. Is Lulu entitled to any of the profits, if there are any?

---

62. Prof. Wendel makes a fortune off of his student study aid (obviously a hypothetical). To thank his students, he puts a provision in his will that provides in pertinent part that he gives "$100,000, in trust, to Lulu, my trustee, to distribute equally among my favorite students." Following his death, the takers under his residuary clause sue to invalidate the gift. Who takes the $100,000?

---

63. Michael's will provides in pertinent part that upon his death he leaves $50,000 to his sister, Janet, to use to take care of Bubbles, his pet monkey. Following Michael's death from a mysterious skin ailment, the takers under his residuary clause challenge the gift to Janet. What is the most likely outcome? _____

64. Lisa is engaged to Nicholas. Worried that their relationship might not make it, and concerned that if they divorce the court may award part of her prized possession, Gracelandacres, to Nicholas, she transfers Gracelandacres by deed to her old friend, Michael, shortly before she marries Nicholas. Lisa and Michael orally agree that Michael will hold Gracelandacres while Lisa is married, and that Michael will convey Gracelandacres back to Lisa after five years or following her divorce from Nicholas, whichever comes first. Only months after their marriage, Lisa and Nicholas file for divorce. Following the divorce, Lisa asks Michael to convey Gracelandacres back to her. Michael refuses. Lisa sues to recover Gracelandacres.

a. What is the most likely outcome under the common law approach? _____

b. What is the most likely outcome under the modern trend? _____

65. Richard learns that he has terminal cancer. Accepting the inevitable, he contacts his good friend, Ian, and asks Ian if he will do him a favor. Richard tells Ian that he wants to leave him $25,000 to use to take the cast of his last movie to London where they will have a grand party to celebrate his life. Ian agrees. When Richard dies, his will provides in pertinent part, "I leave $25,000 to Ian to use for the purpose we have agreed upon." The takers under his residuary clause challenge the gift.

---

a. Who takes the $25,000 under the common law approach? _____

b. Who takes the $25,000 under the modern trend approach? _____

Answers

57.   To have a validly created private trust, (1) there must be the intent to create a trust, (2) the trust must be funded with property, (3) there must be ascertainable beneficiaries, and (4) if the trust is an inter vivos trust that holds real property or the trust is a testamentary trust, the trust terms must be in writing.

58. Sally's statement arguably does not constitute a valid declaration of trust, and Bob is not entitled to the computer. Sally's statement arguably constitutes merely a gratuitous promise to make a gift in the future, not a present declaration of a trust. The distinction is a difficult one, but here there is no express reference to a trust or trustee, and the focus of the statement appears to be in the future, not the present. It is unlikely that a court would hold that this statement constitutes the necessary intent to create a trust. It is merely a gratuitous promise to make a gift in the future, a gift that fails for want of delivery.

59. Sally's statement constitutes a valid declaration of trust, and Bob is entitled to Sally's computer. Sally's statement constitutes a present declaration of a trust. She expressed the present intent that she held the property in question for the benefit of another—classic intent to create a trust. Because she is both settlor and trustee, her statement that she held the computer for Bob's benefit constitutes adequate evidence of funding. Pursuant to the statement, she transferred the computer from herself as settlor to herself as trustee. The trust has an ascertainable beneficiary, Bob. And because the trust was created inter vivos and held only personal property, the trust does not have to be in writing to be valid. A trust will not fail for want of a trustee. The courts will appoint a successor trustee who will be bound by the terms of the trust—to distribute the computer to Bob next month.

60. No, Charlie's dad's statement imposes only a moral obligation, not a legal obligation. Where the qualifying language attached to the gift imposes only a moral obligation, there is only a precatory trust, not a true trust. A precatory trust imposes no legal obligations on the donee. The donee is free to use the property as he or she sees fit. It is only a gift with a wish attached. There is no intent to create a trust, no trust, and no breach of trust.

61. Although Prof. Wendel has the intent to create a trust (as evidenced by his declaring himself trustee and declaring that he hold the future profits "in trust"), the beneficiary is ascertainable (Lulu), and the terms of the trust are in writing (the note), under traditional trust law the trust fails for want of funding. Prof. Wendel has attempted to fund this trust with the future profits from his book. Classic trust law holds that future profits are not an adequate property interest to constitute funding. Without funding, the trust fails and the future profits are not subject to the terms of the trust. (Under the law of inter vivos gifts, however, future profits can be an adequate property interest, particularly where the donor has the current means of producing the profits and the gift is in writing and is delivered to the donee, as was the case here. A strong argument can be made that if future profits are an adequate property interest for purposes of making an outright gift inter vivos that they should be an adequate property interest for purposes of funding an inter vivos trust.)

62. Prof. Wendel has the intent to create a trust, as evidenced by the phrase "my trustee, in trust." Prof. Wendel has funded the trust through the clause in his will transferring $100,000 to the trustee of the trust. The trust is a testamentary trust, so the terms must be in writing, which they are by being set forth in the will. The trust fails, however, for want of ascertainable beneficiaries. There must be an objective method of identifying the beneficiaries. Here, the alleged beneficiaries are Prof. Wendel's "favorite students." There is no objective way to ascertain who are the intended beneficiaries. Whenever a trust fails, a resulting trust is imposed and the property is ordered transferred back to the settlor. Here, Lulu will be ordered to return the $100,000 to Prof. Wendel, where the property will fall to his probate estate and to his residuary clause.

63. The gift to Janet arguably was an attempt to create a private trust. (The trust is not a charitable trust because the gift is not for the care of animals generally, just for this particular monkey.) Janet was to hold and manage the property not for her own benefit, but for the benefit of Bubbles. The trust is a testamentary trust, funded via the provision in his will with $50,000. As a testamentary trust, it must be in writing, as it is because its terms are set forth in the will. The problem, however, is that technically the trust fails for want of ascertainable beneficiaries. Where, however, the purpose of a private trust is such that it is impossible to have ascertainable beneficiaries, and the purpose is not capricious or illegal, the courts usually permit the "trust" to continue as an honorary trust as long as the "trustee" is willing to honor the terms of the gift. If Janet is willing to use the money to care for the monkey, the courts will permit the arrangement as long as Janet is willing to carry out Michael's wishes. (There is a Rule against Perpetuities issue, but that is beyond the scope of the material at this point.) The Uniform Trust Code and an increasing number of states specifically recognize and permit a trust for the benefit of pets as distinct from an honorary trust. UTC §408.

64a. Lisa intended to create an inter vivos trust when she conveyed Gracelandacres to Michael. Michael was not to hold the property for his own benefit, but rather he was to hold it for Lisa's benefit. The trust was funded when she transferred the property to Michael, and she constitutes an ascertainable beneficiary. But inter vivos trusts of land must be in writing. The agreement between Lisa and Michael was oral. The common law takes the Statute of Frauds seriously. The deed conveying Gracelandacres from Lisa to Michael cannot be conditioned by any oral understanding between the parties. Any attempts by Lisa to introduce evidence of their oral understanding would be barred by the Statute of Frauds under the common law approach. Michael keeps the property.

64b. The modern trend does not like the notion that the Statute of Frauds could be used to perpetrate what amounts to a fraud. Under the modern trend, extrinsic evidence is generally admissible to prove an alleged oral trust with respect to real property. The attempted trust is still invalid, but once the oral agreement is established, the court can impose a constructive trust and order the property transferred to the intended beneficiaries. Resulting trusts and/or constructive trusts are equitable trusts (remedies) that arise by operation of law and as such are not subject to the Statute of Frauds. But inasmuch as both are equitable remedies, the party seeking relief must not be guilty of unclean hands. Here, Lisa is guilty of unclean hands in that she transferred Gracelandacres to Michael in an attempt to hide the asset in the event of divorce. If the court finds that Lisa is guilty of unclean hands, even under the modern trend Michael will be permitted to keep Gracelandacres.

65a. The agreement between Richard and Ian constitutes the necessary intent to create a trust—Ian has agreed to receive and use the property for the benefit of others, the cast of the movie. The trust is to be funded through the gift in the will, and the beneficiaries are ascertainable, the cast of his last movie. The problem is, because the trust is being funded through the gift in his will, the trust is a testamentary trust. Testamentary trusts must be in writing, and the necessary terms of this trust are not in writing. The trust fails. At common law, if the express words of the will hint at the intent to create a trust but the trust fails for want of writing, the trust is called a "semi-secret" trust. If the failed testamentary trust is a semi-secret trust, the courts impose a resulting trust—the property is ordered back to the decedent's probate estate. Here, the property will be distributed to the residuary takers under Richard's will.

65b. The analysis is basically the same under the modern trend—the trust is still invalid for want of a written instrument. The modern trend, however, no longer distinguishes between secret trusts and semi-secret trusts. In both cases, the courts tend to grant a constructive trust and order the property distributed to the intended beneficiaries. Here, that is the cast of Richard's last movie.

Exam Tips on
TRUSTS: OVERVIEW AND CREATION

Requirements for a valid private trust

☞ Creation of a valid private trust is much easier than the material makes it look. Rarely is creation an issue in the real world. Don't let the material distort your understanding of it.

 ☞ The first requirement, the intent to create a trust, is the most difficult to understand and thus one of the more favorite elements to test. The issue is almost always whether the person has the intent to make an outright gift or the intent to make a gift in trust, but there are a number of different possible intent scenarios.

 ☞ First, if you see a transfer of property from one party to another with qualifying language that is ambiguous, the issue is whether the language constitutes merely a precatory trust or a true trust. The key is who is to have the beneficial interest in the property, the recipient (gift) or someone else (trust).

 ☞ Second, if there is a declaration of intent but no transfer of property, the issue is whether the party has adequately expressed the intent to create a trust, thereby appointing him- or herself trustee, or if the party has merely expressed a gratuitous intent to make a gift in the future (which typically fails for want of delivery). If the party uses classic trust terminology, the intent to create a trust is present. Otherwise, analyze the language very carefully to see if there is a present intent to transfer an interest to a third party (trust) or merely a promise to transfer some property in the future (promise to make a gift in the future).

☞ The second requirement, that the trust be funded with some property interest, is doctrinally simple, but theoretically complicated. Doctrinally, any property interest qualifies, except expectancies and future profits. Theoretically, the distinction is hard to justify.

☞ The third requirement, ascertainable beneficiaries, is simple. There must be an objective method of naming the beneficiaries. If, however, the purpose of the trust is such that it is impossible to have ascertainable beneficiaries, think honorary trust.

☞ The final requirement, writing, is rather straightforward. The wrinkle on this requirement and the area tested most often, is what remedy should be awarded if the trust fails for want of a written instrument. If a testamentary trust, at common law whether the court orders a resulting trust or a constructive trust turns on whether the failed testamentary trust is a secret trust or a semi-secret trust. If an inter vivos trust of land fails, at common law the "trustee" gets to keep the property. Under the modern trend, the courts impose a constructive trust to take the property from the "trustee"—unless the "settlor" was guilty of unclean hands in creating the arrangement.

CHAPTER 9

TRUSTS: LIFE AND TERMINATION

ChapterScope

This chapter briefly examines the key issues of a trust once it is created: who gets what when—i.e., the rights of a beneficiary, creditors' rights, and how a trust can be modified or terminated prematurely. In particular, the chapter examines:

- **Trust life:** Once a trust is validly created, the primary issue during the life of the trust is the extent of each beneficiary's interest in the trust. A beneficiary's interest can be either mandatory or discretionary, and it can be in the principal or income, or both.

  - **Mandatory trust:** If the trustee *must* distribute all of the income on a regular basis, the trust is a mandatory trust.

  - **Discretionary trust:** If the trustee has *discretion* over when to distribute the income and/or principal, or how much to distribute, the trust is a discretionary trust. Because of the trustee's fiduciary duties to the beneficiaries, however, the trustee still has a duty to inquire and a duty to act reasonably and in good faith in exercising his or her discretion.

- **Creditors' rights:** A creditor's rights depend on whether the creditor is a creditor of a beneficiary or of the settlor.

  - **Creditors of beneficiary:** A creditor of a beneficiary steps into the beneficiary's shoes and acquires the same rights the beneficiary had—no more and no less.

  - **Spendthrift trust:** If the settlor includes a spendthrift clause (a clause that prohibits beneficiaries from transferring their interest) in the trust, the general rule is that the beneficiary's creditors cannot step into the beneficiary's shoes—they cannot reach the beneficiary's interest in the trust.

    - **Exceptions:** Not all creditors are subject to spendthrift clauses. As a general rule, children entitled to child support, ex-spouses entitled to alimony, creditors who provide basic necessities, and the government are creditors who are not subject to a spendthrift clause but rather can step into the beneficiary's shoes.

  - **Creditors of settlor:** It is against public policy to permit one to shield one's assets from creditors. Accordingly, creditors of a settlor can reach the settlor's interest in the trust to the full extent that the trustee *could* use the trust for the benefit of the settlor. Moreover, spendthrift trusts in favor of a settlor are null and void.

- **Modification and termination:** A trust ends naturally when all of the trust principal is disbursed pursuant to the terms of the trust. Under special circumstances, however, the terms of the trust may be modified or the trust may be terminated prematurely.

  - **Modification:** At common law, courts order the terms of a trust to be modified if (1) all the beneficiaries consent, and (2) an unforeseen change in circumstances materially frustrates settlor's intent. The trust is modified to promote the settlor's presumed intent under the circumstances.

■ **Termination:** At common law, under the Claflin doctrine, courts order a trust to be terminated prematurely, even if the trustee objects, if (1) all the beneficiaries consent, and (2) there is no unfulfilled material purpose.

I. LIFE OF TRUST: EXTENT OF BENEFICIARIES' INTERESTS

A. **Introduction:** Once a trust has been validly created, there is one principal issue during the life of the trust—the extent of each beneficiary's interest in the trust. When analyzing the beneficiaries' interests in the trust, the trust property has to be bifurcated between the income and the principal (the latter being the property transferred to the trust, and the former being the money the principal generates). In assessing each beneficiary's interest in the income and/or the principal, the beneficiary's interest can be either mandatory or discretionary. Once a trust has been validly created, it is critical that each beneficiary's interest be analyzed.

B. **Mandatory trust:** A mandatory trust is one where the beneficiary's interest in the income is mandatory—the trustee must distribute the income to the beneficiary (typically according to a fixed schedule set forth in the express terms of the trust).

   Overview: Mandatory trusts and mandatory interests cause relatively few problems because either the trustee performs pursuant to the mandatory terms of the trust or the trustee does not. In contrast, discretionary trusts are full of "soft" doctrines that lend themselves to litigation over interpretation and application.

C. **Discretionary trust:** A discretionary trust is one where the beneficiary's interest in the income and/or principal is discretionary. In a pure discretionary trust, the beneficiary has no right to receive payments of income and/or principal. Any such payments are at the discretion of the trustee (typically according to some standard set forth in the express terms of the trust). The trustee's discretion, however, also can be limited by coupling it with an express standard. (For example, a "support trust" is where the trustee's discretion is limited by an ascertainable support standard; and "a discretionary support trust" adds an express statement of absolute discretion to the support trust language.)

   1. **Introduction:** At first blush, it seems somewhat incompatible to say that a beneficiary has an equitable interest in a trust, that the trustee owes the beneficiary a fiduciary duty, and at the same time to describe the beneficiary's interest as merely a discretionary interest. The courts have been very careful to articulate the scope of a discretionary interest to ensure that a beneficiary has more than a mere expectancy.

   2. **Duty to decide:** Where a beneficiary's interest in a trust is discretionary, it is, to a certain degree, at the mercy of the trustee. But the trustee must exercise his or her discretion pursuant to the terms of the trust, even if that decision is not to make a payment to the beneficiary. In assessing the trustee's decision-making process, the courts have kept in mind the fiduciary duty that the trustee owes the beneficiary.

   3. **Duty to inquire:** Consistent with the fiduciary duty the trustee owes the beneficiary, before the trustee can exercise his or her discretion with respect to whether to make a payment to the

beneficiary, the trustee has a duty to inquire as to the beneficiary's status and needs. If the trustee fails to inquire, the trustee is deemed to have breached his or her fiduciary duty to the beneficiary.

Scope of duty: In defining and applying the duty to inquire, the courts are guided by the fact that the trustee owes the beneficiary a fiduciary duty to do all that he or she does in the beneficiary's best interests. Under the duty of inquiry, the trustee must exercise due diligence in attempting to gather the relevant information, and where the initial attempts are unsuccessful or incomplete, the trustee has a duty to follow up. Where the trustee fails to do so, it is relatively easy for the courts to find that the trustee has failed to properly exercise his or her discretionary power.

4. **Scope of discretion:** After having gathered all the appropriate information about the beneficiary, in deciding whether to make a payment, the trustee has a duty to act reasonably and in good faith.

   a. **Duty to act reasonably:** The duty to act reasonably is an objective standard—to act as a reasonable trustee would act. The duty to act reasonably requirement permits a fair degree of judicial oversight of a trustee's discretionary decisions.

   b. **Duty to act in good faith:** The duty to act in good faith is a subjective standard. The trustee acts in good faith as long as he or she honestly thought that he or she was acting in the best interests of the beneficiaries and the trust in making his or her decision.

5. **Absolute discretion:** The trustee's duty to act reasonably and in good faith in making a discretionary decision is a default standard. A settlor may modify the duty by express language in the trust instrument. It is not uncommon for the trust to authorize the trustee to act in his or her "sole discretion," or "sole and absolute discretion." The courts have construed such language as not granting truly absolute and uncontrolled discretion, for if such were the case, there would be nothing left of the trustee's fiduciary duty; and without a fiduciary duty, there would be no trust, just a precatory trust. Instead, the courts have construed such language as virtually eliminating the duty to act reasonably, but the trustee still must act in good faith. UTC §814.

6. **Settlor's purpose:** A settlor can also, and often does, provide a purpose or standard that the trustee must keep in mind when exercising his or her discretion. The standard must be set forth in the express terms of the trust. Each clause granting a beneficiary a discretionary interest must be read carefully to see if there is a statement of a standard, or purpose, that the trustee is to keep in mind when making his or her decision. Such standards, if present, are given great weight when considering whether the trustee properly exercised his or her discretion.

   Comfortable support and maintenance: One of the most common standards that settlors include in their discretionary trusts is that the trustee has the discretion to make whatever payments he or she deems advisable for the beneficiary's "comfortable support and maintenance." The phrase "comfortable support and maintenance" has become a term of art expressing the intent that the beneficiary is to be kept at the standard of living that he or she was accustomed to at the time that he or she became a beneficiary of the trust.

7. **Beneficiary's resources:** Whether a trustee is to consider a beneficiary's other resources in deciding whether to make a payment to the beneficiary is a question of settlor's intent. In essence the issue is whether the settlor intended to provide a floor level of income for the

beneficiary regardless of the beneficiary's other resources or whether the settlor intended to provide a safety net only in the event the beneficiary's other resources were inadequate. Where the settlor's intent is not clear, most courts hold that the presumption is that the settlor intended to provide for the beneficiary regardless of the beneficiary's other resources—the trustee is *not* to take into consideration a beneficiary's other resources absent the trust expressly authorizing it.

8. **Example:** In *Marsman v. Nasca,* 573 N.E.2d 1025 (Mass. App. 1991), Sara created a testamentary trust that provided that the trustees were to pay the income to her husband (Cappy) at least quarterly, and "after having considered the various available sources of support for him, my trustees shall, if they deem it necessary or desirable . . . , in their sole and uncontrolled discretion, pay over to him, . . . such amount or amounts of the principal thereof as they deem advisable for his comfortable support and maintenance." During Sara's lifetime, Sara and Cappy lived well. Following Sara's death, Cappy lost his employment, and his standard of living fell substantially. When Cappy brought his plight to the trustee's attention, the trustee gave Cappy a minimal distribution of principal ($300) and asked Cappy to explain in writing the need for the principal. Cappy failed to reply, and the trustee failed to follow-up. The court ruled that the trustee had breached his duty to inquire into Cappy's situation and had breached his or her discretion in not disbursing more principal to Cappy. Despite the broad discretion in the trust, the court found that Cappy's standard of living had been reduced substantially and that in light of the settlor's intent that the principal was to be used to maintain Cappy's comfortable support and maintenance, the trustee had breached the duty to distribute principal under the trust.

9. **Exculpatory clauses:** Discretionary trusts often include an exculpatory clause protecting the trustee against liability for breach of trust absent "willful neglect" or the like. Such clauses are like no contest clauses in that they are double-edged swords: they can deter frivolous lawsuits by frustrated beneficiaries who do not like a trustee's decision under a discretionary trust; but they can also reduce a trustee's incentive to pay attention to a beneficiary. Such exculpatory clauses are generally upheld, but the courts construe them narrowly. If a court concludes that an exculpatory clause was put in the trust because of the trustee's overreaching or abuse of fiduciary or confidential relationship, the clause will be deemed null and void. Such clauses are also unenforceable if the court concludes that the breach of trust was committed intentionally, in bad faith, or in reckless disregard for the beneficiary's interest. Under the traditional and general rule, a beneficiary challenging the validity of an exculpatory clause bears the burden of proof. Under the Uniform Trust Code, if the trustee drafted the exculpatory clause or caused it to be drafted, the clause is presumed to be invalid "unless the trustee proves the exculpatory clause is fair under the circumstances and that its existence and contents were adequately communicated to the settlor." UTC §1008(b). New York goes even further; it voids exculpatory clauses granting immunity to trustees for failure to exercise reasonable care as against public policy.

Example: In *Marsman v. Nasca*, above, the trustee inserted an exculpatory clause into the trust protecting the trustee absent "willful neglect or default." The trustee testified that he discussed the clause with the settlor during the drafting process, and the settlor approved the clause. Although the trustee drafted the trust and suggested the clause, the court ruled that was insufficient to render the clause null and void. While the trustee's conduct concerning Cappy constituted a breach of duty, the court implicitly found that the breach was not intentional, in bad faith, or in reckless disregard for the beneficiary's interest.

10. **Mandatory arbitration clause:** In an attempt to minimize administrative fees and to expedite resolution of disputes, increasingly trusts contain mandatory arbitration clauses. The cases to date where the clause was challenged tend to invalidated the clause, but a strong argument can be made that such clauses should be subject to the same analysis as exculpatory clauses and should not be per se invalid.

D. **Sprinkle/spray trust:** A sprinkle or spray trust requires the trustee to distribute the property in question, but the payment is to be made to a group of individuals and the trustee has discretion as to whom to make the payments and how much each is to receive. The trustee has the power to "sprinkle" or "spray" the property among the eligible beneficiaries. Sprinkle/spray trusts are something of a hybrid trust. From the beneficiaries' perspective, the trust is discretionary—no beneficiary has a right to receive any of the property. From the trustee's perspective, the trust is mandatory—the trustee must distribute the property, but as to whom and how much, the trust is discretionary.

E. **Unitrust:** Under a unitrust, a life beneficiary is given a fixed annual percentage interest in the total worth of the trust, regardless of whether the property needed to satisfy that fixed interest comes from the income or the principal. The trustee is then free to pursue any investment that he or she thinks will produce the greatest benefit for the trust, regardless of the amount of income the investment produces, because the trustee has the power to disburse not only income but principal to the life beneficiary to satisfy the life beneficiary's fixed annual percentage interest in the unitrust.

F. **Perpetual dynasty trust:** An increasing number of jurisdictions are abolishing the Rule against Perpetuities. This permits trusts to last forever. Where a settlor takes advantage of this and creates a trust that will last forever for the benefit of one's issue, the trust is typically called a perpetual dynasty trust. The standard distributive provisions of such trusts grant the trustee discretionary powers over both the income and the principal, thus granting the trustee the flexibility to manage the trust to permit the corpus to remain intact, if not grow, while creating a stream of income for settlor's descendants.

II. LIFE OF TRUST: CREDITORS' RIGHTS

A. **Introduction:** A creditor's ability to reach a beneficiary's interest in a trust depends on whether the beneficiary is the settlor or someone other than the settlor. As a general rule, it is against public policy to use a trust to try to shield one's assets from one's creditors. Creditors of a beneficiary who is also the settlor have a greater ability to reach that beneficiary's interest in the trust than a creditor would if the beneficiary is not the settlor. When the material refers to a beneficiary, assume the norm—that the beneficiary is not the settlor—unless the material expressly provides otherwise.

1. **Creditors' rights generally:** As a general rule, a creditor can reach a debtor's property as long as the property interest in question is transferable. As applied to trusts, absent special provisions in the trust, generally a beneficiary's interest is freely transferable, whether the beneficiary's interest is discretionary or mandatory.

2. **Scope of creditors' rights:** In light of the fact that a beneficiary's interest in a trust is freely transferable, creditors of a beneficiary can reach the beneficiary's interest in the trust. For all

practical purposes, the creditor steps into the shoes of the beneficiary and receives whatever interest the beneficiary has in the trust—no more, and no less.

    a. Mandatory trust: If the trust is a mandatory trust, the creditor can force the trustee to distribute the income to the creditor pursuant to the terms of the trust just as the beneficiary could have. The trustee must distribute the income to the creditor.

B. Discretionary trust: In a discretionary trust, a beneficiary's right to receive a distribution is subject to the trustee's discretion. How much discretion the trustee has turns on the terms of the trust—the settlor's intent.

    1. Pure discretionary trust: If the trust is a pure discretionary trust, just as the beneficiary could not force a trustee to distribute property to the beneficiary (absent a showing of abuse of discretion), nor can a creditor of a beneficiary of a discretionary trust force a trustee to distribute property (absent a showing of abuse of discretion as applied to the beneficiary in question, not the creditor).

        a. Court order: In some jurisdictions, a creditor of a beneficiary of a discretionary interest can get a court order directing that if and when the trustee decides to exercise his or her discretion in favor of making a payment to the beneficiary, the trustee must make the payment to the creditor. (A settlor can avoid such a court order by an express clause in the trust permitting the trustee to make payments directly to any third parties that provide support to the beneficiary. Such language permits the trustee to choose which creditors will receive any payments the trustee decides to make—current creditors or past creditors.) The Restatement (Third) of Trusts and the Uniform Trust Code disagree over the extent to which creditors can reach a beneficiary's interest in a discretionary trust.

        b. Restatement (Third) of Trusts: A creditor of a beneficiary of a discretionary trust is entitled to receive or attach any distributions the trustee makes or is required to make in the exercise of its discretion.

        c. Uniform Trust Code: A creditor of a beneficiary may not compel a distribution that is subject to the trustee's discretion, regardless of the presence or absence of a spendthrift clause, even if there is a standard limiting the discretion or the trustee has abused the discretion, unless (1) the trustee has not complied with a standard of distribution or there has been an abuse of discretion; and (2) the distribution is ordered to satisfy a judgment or court order against the beneficiary for support or maintenance of a child, spouse, or former spouse.

    2. Support trusts: A support trust is a trust that requires the trustee to pay as much income (and, if expressly provided in the trust, principal as well) as necessary for the beneficiary's support and education.

        a. Transferability: If the trust is a support trust, the beneficiary does not have the right to transfer his or her interest. The effect of saying that the interest is nontransferable is to limit a creditor's right to reach the beneficiary's interest in the trust.

        b. Basic necessities: Because a support trust is to ensure that the beneficiary receives support, creditors who provide basic necessities (whatever is necessary for support) are not subject to the implied spendthrift clause and can reach the beneficiary's interest in the support trust. Increasingly jurisdictions are also permitting children and ex-spouses to assert claims for child support and alimony against a beneficiary's interest in a support trust.

    c. Construction: The key to classifying a trust as a support trust is the formula that controls how much the trustee can distribute to the beneficiary, not the use of the word *support* per se. If the trustee is required to distribute all of the income to the beneficiary for his or her support, the trust is not a support trust because the amount being paid out is not limited to the amount necessary for the beneficiary's support. Where the payment is limited to the amount necessary for the beneficiary's support (and education), the trust qualifies as a support trust.

  3. Discretionary support trust: Increasingly practitioners are combining the aspects of a discretionary trust with a support trust to form what is becoming known as a *discretionary support trust*. From a creditor's rights perspective, the courts tend to treat is more as a pure discretionary trust than as a support trust.

  4. Modern trend/UTC: The modern trend and UTC is to abolish the distinction between pure discretionary trusts and support trusts, giving creditors the same rights over all trusts where the trustee's power to make distribution is discretionary regardless of the extent of the discretion. The Restatement (Third) of Trusts gives creditors the right to reach any distributions the trustee makes or is required to make in the exercise of discretion (§60), while the UTC provides that other than claims for child support or alimony, a creditor cannot reach property subject to the trustee's discretion even if the beneficiary could force a distribution.

  5. Protective trust: A protective trust is something of a hybrid trust. It is mandatory until a creditor attaches a beneficiary's interest, at which point the beneficiary's interest automatically becomes discretionary (to protect it against the claim of the creditor). Such trusts are particularly attractive in jurisdictions which do not recognize spendthrift clauses. (England does not recognize spendthrift trusts, and protective trusts are the norm in England.)

C. Spendthrift trust: A settlor can modify a beneficiary's ability to transfer his or her interest by including what is known as a spendthrift clause in the trust that expressly restricts the beneficiary's power to transfer his or her interest. A standard spendthrift clause bars a beneficiary's ability to transfer his or her interest voluntarily (by sale or gift) or involuntarily (creditors reaching). (In New York, a beneficiary's interest is presumed nontransferable unless the trust expressly provides otherwise.)

  1. Voluntary transfers: A spendthrift clause does not have to restrict both voluntary and involuntary transfers by a beneficiary. A spendthrift clause that bars only voluntary transfers by a beneficiary but leaves open involuntary transfers, thereby permitting a beneficiary's creditors to reach the property, is permitted.

  2. Involuntary transfers: A spendthrift clause that bars only involuntary transfers by a beneficiary, but leaves open voluntary transfers, is deemed against public policy and is null and void. If the beneficiary has the benefit of the right to transfer his or her interest voluntarily, the beneficiary must also have the risk of creditors having the right to involuntarily reach the beneficiary's interest.

  3. Validity: There is an on-going debate over both the validity of spendthrift clauses and the scope of spendthrift clauses.

    a. Arguments against: It is unfair to permit one to enjoy the benefits of being a beneficiary without permitting creditors of that beneficiary to reach that property. Moreover, because the rich are much more likely to use trusts than are the poor, permitting spendthrift clauses in trusts unfairly favors the rich over the poor. (England and most other common law countries do not recognize spendthrift clauses; but they do recognize protective trusts and discretionary trusts.)

    b. Arguments in support: The property in trust is not really the beneficiary's property. The beneficiary has no legal interest in the property, only an equitable interest. The scope of a beneficiary's interest in a trust is purely a question of the settlor's intent, and there is no reason why a settlor should not be permitted to limit a beneficiary's interest by barring the beneficiary's ability to transfer his or her interest. A creditor can still reach the beneficiary's interest once the property is distributed to the beneficiary; the creditor just cannot reach the property while it is still in the trust.

4. General rule: The general rule is that spendthrift clauses are valid and enforceable, even as applied to remainder interests in trust.

5. Exceptions: Although spendthrift clauses are generally valid, most jurisdictions have either statutorily or judicially adopted doctrines that limit their application and effect.

    a. Judicial exceptions: In many jurisdictions, for public policy reasons, courts have held that certain categories of creditors are not subject to spendthrift clauses: (1) ex-spouses entitled to spousal support (alimony), (2) children entitled to child support, (3) creditors who provide basic necessities, and (4) tax claims by the state or federal government. In essence, these creditors can pierce the spendthrift clause and reach the beneficiary's interest in the trust. A majority of jurisdictions, however, still apply spendthrift clauses to tort creditors.

    b. Uniform Trust Code: The Uniform Trust Code limits the exceptions to a spendthrift clause to (1) children entitled to child support pursuant to a judgment or court order; (2) spouses/ex-spouses entitled to spousal support (alimony/maintenance) pursuant to a judgment or court order; (3) a claim by a state or the federal government; and (4) a judgment creditor who has provided services for the protection of a beneficiary's interest in the trust.

    c. Intentional tort example: In *Scheffel v. Krueger*, 782 A.2d 410 (N.H. 2001), Krueger's grandmother set up a trust for his benefit. He had a mandatory interest in the income, discretionary as to the principal (for his maintenance, support, and education), and the trust had a spendthrift clause. Thereafter Krueger sexually assaulted a minor, videotaped it, and broadcast it over the Internet. In addition to being criminally convicted, a tort judgment in the amount of over $500,000 was entered against him. The mother of the victim sought to reach Krueger's interest in the trust to satisfy the judgment. Despite the equities of her claim, the court ruled that the spendthrift clause barred reaching Krueger's interest in the trust.

    d. Child support/alimony example: In *Shelley v. Shelley*, 354 P.2d 282 (Or. 1960), the settlor created a trust for the benefit of his son. The son's interest in the income was mandatory and discretionary as to the principal. The trust also authorized the trustee to disburse principal to the son, or his children, in an emergency. The trust had a standard spendthrift clause. The settlor's son owed both alimony and child support payments to his ex-spouses and children. When the son disappeared, the ex-spouses and children sued seeking to reach the son's interest in the trust. The court ruled that the creditors were not subject to the spendthrift clause. Both the ex-spouses and the children were entitled to reach the son's mandatory interest in the income. Moreover, the ex-spouses and children were entitled to reach the son's interest in the principal, but because the son's interest was discretionary, they could not force the trustee to make disbursements of the principal to them *as creditors*. But because the children were beneficiaries of the principal in their own right, the trustee's failure to disburse principal to them *as beneficiaries* was an abuse of discretion. The children were entitled to payments of the principal in their capacity as beneficiaries, not as creditors.

   e. **Statutory limitations:** A number of states have statutorily limited the amount of the beneficiary's interest in the trust that can be protected against creditors' claims by a spendthrift clause. Such statutes usually take one of three approaches. The first limits the amount of a beneficiary's interest that can be shielded from creditors' claims by a spendthrift clause to the amount necessary for the beneficiary's support and education. The second type of statute permits a creditor to reach a fixed percentage (usually less than a third) of a beneficiary's interest in the income. And the third type of statute typically has a fixed dollar amount cap on the amount of money that can be shielded from creditors' claims by a spendthrift clause.

      i. **ERISA:** An employee's pension benefits, and the employee's ability to depend upon those assets being there when needed, are so important that ERISA mandates that such benefits are nontransferable. Thus, an employee's interest in a pension trust is not reachable by his or her current creditors.

      ii. **Bankruptcy creditors:** The Bankruptcy Code provides that a beneficiary's interest in a trust passes to the bankruptcy trustee only if the beneficiary's interest is transferable. If the trust has a spendthrift clause, the beneficiary's interest is not reachable in bankruptcy.

D. **Settlor as beneficiary ("self-settled asset protection trusts"):** The traditional rule is that one cannot use a trust to shield one's assets from one's creditors. The general creditors' rights rules set forth above assume that the beneficiary is someone other than the settlor. If the beneficiary is the settlor, creditors have greater rights to reach the beneficiary's interest in the trust.

   1. **Mandatory interest:** If the settlor retained a mandatory interest in the trust, creditors of the settlor can reach the mandatory interest in the trust. If the trustee fails to make the payment to them, they can force the trustee to make the payment to them.

   2. **Discretionary interest:** If the settlor retained a discretionary interest in the trust, creditors of the settlor can reach the discretionary interest in the trust to the full extent that the trust permits the trustee to use the trust for the benefit of the settlor. In essence, the creditors can force the trustee to exercise his or her discretion to the full extent permitted under the terms of the trust for the benefit of the settlor.

   3. **Spendthrift clause:** As a general rule, spendthrift clauses are null and void as applied to creditors of a beneficiary who is also the settlor. It is against public policy to permit one to shield one's assets in a spendthrift trust.

   4. **Modern trend:** In an attempt to attract trust business, a number of states recently have adopted statutes authorizing self-settled discretionary trusts (self-settled spendthrift trusts are available in offshore jurisdictions). Alaska and Delaware started the movement, permitting asset protection trusts in favor of a beneficiary who is also the settlor if (1) the trust is irrevocable, (2) the trust interest is discretionary, and (3) the trust was not created to defraud

creditors. Settlors in any state can take advantage of these exceptions as long as the trusts are created in one of these states. This has put economic pressure on other states wishing to keep the revenues associated with trust administration business to adopt similar measures. Increasingly states are doing so. (The Rule against Perpetuities is experiencing a similar state-by-state abolishment in response to economic pressures to attract more trust business. *See* Chapter 14.)

Judicial response: In *Federal Trade Commission v. Affordable Media, LLC*, 179 F.3d 1228 (9th Cir. 1999), Denyse and Michael Anderson created a telemarketing scheme that constituted a Ponzi scheme to defraud investors of millions of dollars which they tucked away in a "Cook Islands" trust (an offshore self-settled spendthrift trust). The Andersons were co-trustees, along with AsiaCiti Trust Limited. The Federal Trade Commission (FTC) brought suit against the Andersons to recover as much money as possible for the defrauded investors and was granted a preliminary injunction ordering the Andersons to account for the funds held offshore and to repatriate the funds. The Andersons faxed AsiaCiti for an accounting and to repatriate the funds to the states, but AsiaCiti concluded that the district court's preliminary injunction constituted duress voiding the Andersons' request, and under the terms of the trust, authorized AsiaCiti to remove the Andersons as co-trustees. The district court held the Andersons in civil contempt for failure to account and repatriate the funds and took them into custody. As a general rule, a party's inability to comply with a judicial order constitutes a defense to a charge of civil contempt. The Andersons argued that the terms of the trust prevented them from complying with the court order. The court expressed skepticism as a legal matter as to the applicability of the defense where the inability to comply is the intended result of the defendants' own actions (here, the creation of the offshore asset protection trust to protect the assets from the reach of U.S. courts). Rather than adopting a per se rule, however, the court ruled that the Andersons had not met their burden of showing "categorically and in detail" that they were unable to comply with the court order—a particularly high burden in light of the possibility that any offered evidence of inability to comply would be a charade rather than a good faith attempt to comply. The court was not convinced that the Andersons had put the money beyond their control, particularly because the Andersons retained the position of "protectors" of the trust. Protectors have significant control of offshore trusts—including the appointment of successor trustees and the power to make the anti-duress provisions of the trust subject to their control. The circuit court affirmed the district court's finding the Andersons in contempt.

Epilogue: The district court freed the Andersons six months after finding them in contempt. The FTC sued AsiaCiti in the Cook Islands for $20 million, but settled for $1.2 million—a recovery of less than 6 cents on the dollar for the defrauded investors.

5. **Transfers in fraud of creditors:** Asset transfers made with the intent to hinder or defraud a creditor's claim (as opposed to transfers made before a creditor's claim arises) constitute actual fraud and are recoverable under the widely adopted Uniform Fraudulent Transfer Act.

6. **Child support and/or alimony:** Those states that permit asset protection trusts are split over whether children asserting child support claims and ex-spouses asserting alimony claims should be able to reach the assets in the trust.

7. **Professional Responsibility:** Inasmuch as a lawyer has an ethical obligation not to "counsel a client to engage, or assist a client, in conduct that the lawyer knows is criminal or fraudulent"

(Model Rule of Prof. Conduct 1.2(d)), a lawyer needs to proceed very carefully in creating an asset protection trust that would delay, hinder, or defraud a client's existing or foreseeable creditors.

E. **Public health benefits:** Public health benefits, such as Medicaid and state-sponsored health programs, are usually limited to people who are without the resources to pay for their own health services. People have tried to use trusts (discretionary trusts in particular) to shield their assets from their medical expenses, thereby qualifying for public assistance. Whether such legal maneuvering is successful turns primarily on whether the applicant who is the beneficiary of the trust contributed to the creation of the trust or whether someone other than the applicant/beneficiary created the trust.

  1. **Applicant created trusts ("self-settled trusts"):** If the applicant created or contributed to the creation of the trust (or the applicant's spouse created the trust), the rules tend to favor including the trust property among the applicant's resources for determining the applicant's eligibility for Medicaid and the state-sponsored health programs. If the applicant has the power to revoke, the whole trust is considered the applicant's property for purposes of determining eligibility. If the trust is irrevocable, the trust property is considered the applicant's property to the full extent that any part of the trust could be used for the applicant's benefit. These rules do not apply if the trust (1) is a testamentary discretionary trust created by the applicant's spouse (by his or her will), or (2) is created for a disabled individual and provides that it will reimburse the government for all unreimbursed medical costs upon the applicant's death.

  2. **Third-party created trusts:** If the applicant had no role in the creation of the trust, the beneficiary's interest in the trust is considered part of the applicant's resources only to the extent the beneficiary could compel the trustee to make a payment of income or principal (typically in a mandatory or support trust, but not in a discretionary trust). As a provider of basic necessities, the government generally is not subject to a spendthrift clause. (Under the Uniform Trust Code, providers of basic necessities generally have no right to reach a beneficiary's interest in a trust, but the state as the plaintiff does.)

    Discretionary trusts: Where the trust is a discretionary trust created by a third party, the state's ability to reach the beneficiary's interest in the trust turns on the settlor's intent generally. Where the discretionary trust is a hybrid with a support standard under which the beneficiary could force distribution, so too can the state under the appropriate circumstances. Where, however, the settlor's intent was to provide benefits only that the state is unwilling or unable to provide, the trust is a ***supplemental needs trust***, and the state cannot reach the beneficiary's interest.

III. TRUST MODIFICATION AND TERMINATION

  A. **Introduction:** A trust ends naturally pursuant to its terms. A trust ends when all of the trust res is completely disbursed. A trust's terms will provide for when the trust res (principal) is to be disbursed. This section deals with the issue of when the trust may be modified or terminated prematurely. The issue of trust modification and/or termination turns on who has an interest in the trust and what the extent of their interest is.

  Revocable trusts: If the settlor retains the power to revoke the trust, the settlor can single-handedly terminate the trust. The power to terminate implicitly includes the power to modify—the settlor can revoke the trust and create a new trust with modified terms and conditions. The settlor can terminate or modify regardless of the objections of the beneficiaries and/or the trustee. The settlor must comply with the requirements for revoking the trust. The doctrines of trust modification and termination presume an irrevocable trust.

B. **Interest in trust:** In theory, there are three parties who could have an interest in a trust: the settlor, the trustee, and the beneficiaries. If all three groups agree to modify or terminate the trust, the trust can be modified or terminated. If any of the parties subsequently changes his or her mind and sues any of the other parties, the suing party will be estopped based on his or her initial consent.

C. **Settlor and beneficiaries consent:** If the settlor and all the beneficiaries consent, even if the trustee objects, the trust can be modified or terminated. The trustee has no beneficial interest in the trust. At best, the trustee can assert the settlor's intent, as expressed in the terms of the trust, as grounds for objecting to modification or termination. If, however, the settlor is alive and consents, the trustee has no right to speak for the settlor.

D. **Trustee and beneficiaries consent:** Assuming the settlor has no interest in the trust (an irrevocable trust), if all the beneficiaries consent and the trustee consents, the trust can be modified or terminated. The trustee owes a fiduciary duty to the beneficiaries to comply with the terms of the trust, and modification or termination arguably constitutes a breach of that duty. But if all the beneficiaries consent, each will be estopped later if one tries to sue the trustee. The settlor has no interest in the trust and as such has no right to sue the trustee if the trustee consents with the beneficiaries to the termination of the trust.

E. **Beneficiaries consent—trustee objects:** If all the beneficiaries consent, but the trustee objects and the settlor is dead, the jurisdictions are split over whether the beneficiaries have the power to modify or terminate the trust over the trustee's objections.

   1. **English approach:** Under the English approach, "dead hand" control generally is not permitted. After the death of the settlor, the beneficiaries are deemed the owners of the trust property for purposes of modification and termination of the trust. If all the beneficiaries consent, the trust is modified or terminated regardless of the terms in the trust or the trustee's objections.

   2. **Traditional American approach:** The traditional American approach is more protective of settlor's intent. Under the general American approach, the trustee has the right, and to some degree, the duty, to object to a modification or termination by invoking the settlor's intent as expressed in the terms of the trust.

      Rationale: The creation of trusts for the benefit of others is considered a good that should be encouraged. The assumption is that by protecting a deceased settlor's intent as expressed in the trust, future settlors will be encouraged to create trusts because they will know that as a general rule the courts will protect and uphold their intent even after their death (if the trustee objects). The trust is a creature of settlor's intent; settlor's intent controls. The trust owns the property, pursuant to the settlor's intent, as set forth in the terms of the trust.

F. **Trust modification:** At common law, even if the trustee objects, if an unforeseen change of circumstances defeats or substantially frustrates settlor's intent, and all the beneficiaries consent, the court will order modification of the trust.

   1. **Settlor's intent:** Under the common law doctrine of modification, the assumption is that the modification is to *further* the settlor's intent.

2. **Unforeseen change:** The requirement that the change in circumstances must be "unforeseen" is a very soft, fact-sensitive inquiry.

    a. **Common law:** At common law, the courts are generally more protective of settlor's intent, even against attempts at modification. The courts tend to apply a rather high threshold for what constitutes an unforeseen change in circumstances.

    b. **Modern trend:** Under the modern trend approach, there is a noticeable shift toward giving the beneficiaries greater control over the property in the trust after the settlor's death. This translates into a low threshold for what constitutes an unforeseen change in circumstances. An unusually high rate of inflation or increased medical costs can be enough to constitute an unforeseen change.

    c. **Beneficiary's advantage:** The mere fact that the proposed modification would be more advantageous to one or more beneficiaries is not enough to warrant modifying a trust even if all the beneficiaries agree.

3. **Substantially impair:** Whether an unforeseen change in circumstances "defeats or substantially impairs" the settlor's intent is a very soft, fact-sensitive inquiry.

    a. **Common law approach:** At common law, the courts are generally more protective of settlor's intent. The courts tend to apply a rather high threshold before finding that the change "defeats or substantially impairs" settlor's intent.

    b. **Modern trend/UTC approach:** The modern trend favors granting beneficiaries greater power over the trust. The modern trend uses a rather low threshold for what constitutes "defeating or substantially impairing" settlor's intent. The Uniform Trust Code authorizes a court to modify the administrative or dispositive provisions of a trust if, because of circumstances not anticipated by the settlor, modification would further the purposes of the trust. There is no requirement that the change in circumstances defeat or substantially impair the settlor's intent.

4. **Beneficiaries' consent:** As a general rule, even if an unforeseen change in circumstances defeats or substantially impairs the settlor's intent, before a court directs or permits modification, *all* of the beneficiaries must consent. There are doctrines facilitating getting consent from beneficiaries who lack the capacity to consent or from future beneficiaries who might not even be born yet.

    a. **Guardian ad litem:** One method of getting the consent of minors or unborn beneficiaries is to petition the court for an appointment of a guardian ad litem to represent the interests of the minor or unborn beneficiaries.

        i. **Traditional approach:** Traditionally, guardians ad litem take a rather strict and conservative approach to representing the minor or unborn beneficiary, asking only whether the proposed modification would increase or decrease the economic value of the interest the guardian was appointed to protect. The guardian typically ignores noneconomic family considerations.

        ii. **Modern trend:** The courts have encouraged guardians ad litem to take into consideration noneconomic factors, such as family harmony and the settlor's apparent primary intent to take care of other family members.

b. **Virtual representation:** Some courts and the Uniform Trust Code have held that under the doctrine of virtual representation, if the interests of the minor or unborn beneficiaries are virtually identical to those of living adult beneficiaries, the living adult beneficiaries are deemed to speak not only for themselves, but also for the interests of the minor or unborn beneficiaries by virtual representation.

c. **Modern statutory trends:** The modern trend has been to either try to facilitate getting the consent of all the beneficiaries by reducing the pool of beneficiaries who have to consent or by permitting the court to order modification even in the absence of all the beneficiaries consenting. The Uniform Trust Code requires the consent of only "qualified beneficiaries" for the removal of a trustee. A qualified beneficiary is one who would be entitled to receive property if the trust was terminated on the day the petition were filed. The UTC also authorizes the court to order modification or termination *without requiring the consent of all the beneficiaries* if (1) the trust could have been modified if all the beneficiaries had consented, and (2) the interests of the non-consenting beneficiaries are adequately protected. UTC §411(e) (2004).

Tax benefits: A handful of states, and both the Restatement (Third) of Property, Donative Transfers, and the Uniform Trust Code, authorize modification of trusts to further a settlor's apparent tax minimizing objectives.

5. **Administrative modification:** As a general rule, courts are more willing to modify administrative provisions under the unforeseen change in circumstances doctrine than they are to modify distributive provisions. The rationale is that the distributive provisions go to the heart of the settlor's intent, while the administrative provisions are merely the means of achieving those objectives. Pursuant to this reasoning, modifying administrative provisions is less violative of settlor's intent. The UTC authorizes a court to modify the administrative provisions of a trust if continuing the current administrative procedures would be impractical or wasteful or impair the trust's administration.

6. **Example:** In *In re Riddell*, 157 P.3d (Ct. App. Wash. 2007), George and Irene created trusts to benefit their only son Ralph and his wife Beverly, and upon the death of the latter of them, to provide benefits to Ralph's children until they reach the age of 35 when the principal would be distributed outright to them. Ralph has two children, Donald and Nancy, both of whom are over age 35, so upon the death of the latter of Ralph and Beverly, the trust res would be distributed outright. Nancy suffers from schizophrenia and lives in a state hospital. Ralph filed a petition to create a special needs trust that would (1) manage Nancy's funds for her benefit, (2) avoid the state seizing the funds to be reimbursed for medical expenses, and (3) avoid Nancy's mismanagement of the money. The Court found that (1) Nancy's special needs constituted circumstances not anticipated by the settlors because Irene and George were unaware of them, (2) the special needs modification will further the purposes of the trust, and (3) the modification was not against public policy. George and Irene's intent was not to lose the money to the state and prevent Nancy from passing the money on to her son. The court recognized that special needs trusts allow disabled persons to continue to receive government assistance for their care and ruled that Ralph, as trustee, should be allowed to modify the trusts.

7. **Trust protector:** A "trust protector" is a relatively new development. A trust protector can be given powers and control over a trust similar to those held by the settlor of a revocable trust, thereby increasing trust administration flexibility in that the trust protector can terminate or modify the administrative or dispositive provisions of the trust in response to changed

circumstances. Whether a trust protector owes the beneficiaries a fiduciary duty is still up for debate. The Uniform Trust Code embraces the use of trust protectors but provides that they constitute a fiduciary who has a duty to act in good faith. UTC §808 (2000).

G. Trust termination: The issue of premature termination of a trust where all the beneficiaries consent, but the trustee objects, troubled the courts. On the one hand, the courts wanted to protect settlor's intent under the theory that the trust owned the property in the trust, not the trust beneficiaries. On the other hand, the courts were somewhat suspicious of the trustee's objection because of the trustee's vested interest in continuing to receive his or her trustee fees. Because of the conflict of interest, the courts developed a doctrine to discern when the trustee was objecting for legitimate reasons as opposed to when the trustee was objecting for illegitimate reasons.

1. **The Claflin doctrine:** Consistent with the traditional American approach of being more protective of settlor's intent, under the Claflin doctrine the trustee can block premature termination of the trust, even if all the beneficiaries consent, if the trust has an unfulfilled material purpose. If, however, there is no unfulfilled material purpose and all the beneficiaries consent to the premature termination of the trust, the trustee cannot block its termination.

2. **Unfulfilled material purpose:** Under the Claflin doctrine, what constitutes an unfulfilled material purpose is whatever the trustee can convince the court constitutes an unfulfilled material purpose. The test is very fact-sensitive, turning on the language and apparent purpose of each trust. There is a handful of scenarios where virtually every court has held the trust intrinsically includes an unfulfilled material purpose: (1) discretionary trusts, (2) spendthrift trusts, (3) support trusts, and (4) trusts where the property is not to be disbursed until the beneficiary reaches a specific age. If the court determines that the dispositive provisions of the trust constitute merely a succession of interests that have no material purpose, premature termination is ordered if all the beneficiaries consent.

   a. **Settlor's consent:** Even if the trust expresses an unfulfilled material purpose that the trustee invokes to block premature termination of the trust, if the settlor is alive and consents with all the beneficiaries, the settlor's consent controls over the trustee's attempt to block. In essence, the settlor's consent constitutes a waiver of the unfulfilled material purpose.

   b. **Example:** In *In re Estate of Brown*, 528 A.2d 752 (Vt. 1987), the decedent's testamentary trust authorized the trustee to use the income and principal to provide an education for the decedent's nephew's children. Upon completion of that purpose, the income and principal were to be used for the care, maintenance, and welfare of said nephew and his wife, so that they may live in the style and manner to which they were accustomed, for the remainder of their lives. Upon the death of the survivor, the trust res was to be distributed to their then-living children equally. When the educational purpose had been fulfilled, all the beneficiaries petitioned to terminate the trust. The trustee objected. The court construed the trust as expressing a material purpose that the nephew and his wife were to be assured of a life-long source of income through the trustee's management of the trust property. The court declined to terminate the trust.

   c. **Modern trend/UTC:** A number of states have statutes that facilitate premature termination of a trust, even where there is an unfulfilled material purpose, under a variety of conditions (for example: for good cause; where a court determines it is in the beneficiaries' best interest; where a court determines unborn or unascertained beneficiaries not adversely affected; and/or where changed circumstances would otherwise defeat settlor's intent). The Restatement (Third) of Property, Donative Transfers, agrees with the common law approach that the presence of a spendthrift clause constitutes an unfulfilled material purpose, but the Uniform Trust Code rejects that position. But the Restatement permits premature termination of the trust over the objection of the trustee, even if there is an unfulfilled material purpose, as long as (1) all the beneficiaries consent, and (2) the court determines *the reasons to terminate outweigh the unfulfilled material purpose*. Restatement (Third) of Property §65. On the other hand, the UTC authorizes a court to order (1) termination if all beneficiaries consent and continuance is not necessary to achieve any material purpose of the trust; (2) modification if all beneficiaries consent and modification *is not inconsistent* with a material purpose; (3) termination or modification *without requiring the consent of all the beneficiaries* as long as (a) the trust could have been terminated if all the beneficiaries had consented, and (b) the interests of the non-consenting beneficiaries are adequately protected. UTC §411 (2004).

d. Probate settlement: Where there is litigation during probate, and the heirs and trust beneficiaries reach a settlement that includes terminating the trust, most (but not all) courts enforce the settlement and terminate the testamentary trust despite its terms (even if there is an unfulfilled material purpose).

e. Trust revocability where trust silent: The majority rule is that a trust is irrevocable unless the trust expressly provides otherwise. The Uniform Trust Code, and a minority of states, however, reverse the presumption and provide that the trust is *revocable* unless the trust expressly provides otherwise. UTC §602 (2000).

Revocation by will: The traditional rule is that a will cannot revoke an inter vivos trust unless the trust expressly authorizes it. The Uniform Trust Code and the Restatement (Third) of Property, Donative Transfers, expressly authorize a subsequent will (or codicil) to revoke a revocable trust, or a provision in a trust, either expressly or implicitly where the will expressly devises the property that otherwise would have passed under the trust, where the trust does not provide (i) for how it is to be revoked, or (ii) that the method provided is to be exclusive. UTC §602 (2000); Restatement (Third) of Property, §63.

H. Trustee's removal: The traditional approach is that settlor's intent controls. If the settlor selected a particular trustee, that trustee cannot be removed, even if all the beneficiaries consent, unless the trustee is unfit to serve or commits a serious breach of trust.

1. Uniform Trust Code: The Uniform Trust Code provides more grounds which authorize a court to remove a trustee. First, under the Uniform Trust Code, a settlor is given standing (along with a co-trustee and a beneficiary) to seek removal. Second, a trustee can be removed if (1) there is a material breach of trust; (2) infighting among co-trustees substantially impairs its administration; (3) the trust has underperformed persistently and substantially relative to comparable trusts; or (4) there has been a substantial change of circumstances or all beneficiaries request a change of trustee, and the court finds removal best serves the interests of all the beneficiaries and it is not inconsistent with a material purpose of the trust. UTC §706 (2000).

2. Example: In *Davis v U.S. Bank National Association*, 243 S.W.3d 425 (Mo. Ct. App. 2007), Ayers created a trust and appointed a Missouri bank as trustee. Ayers's son, Davis, was the beneficiary for life and upon his death the principal would be divided among Davis's children, and if he had no surviving children, then to his heirs who are direct descendants of Ayers, and if none, to Lafayette College. Missouri had adopted the UTC, and on behalf of himself and his two children, Davis petitioned to remove the Missouri bank as trustee, to appoint a trust company in Delaware as successor trustee, and to have the assets transferred to it. Davis lived in Delaware and the transfer would not only be more convenient and avoid out-of-state income tax, it would save the trust money in bank fees. The Missouri bank contested the transfer saying that the failure to join all possible remote beneficiaries violated the requirement that all beneficiaries consent. The court disagreed. The UTC requires that only the "qualified beneficiaries" consent. A qualified beneficiary is one who would be entitled to distribution if the trust were terminated on the date the petition is filed. Davis and his two children were the permissible distributees, the remote remainder beneficiaries did not qualify. The court also found that Davis did not have conflicting interests in representing his two children as they all had similar interests in the transfer. Finally, the bank claimed the transfer was not in the best interest of the beneficiaries and that it was inconsistent with the material purpose of the trust. The bank could not show, however, that the change would injure the beneficiaries or that there was an unfulfilled material purpose in the trust that prohibited such a change. In light of the factually supported beneficial reasons for the change, the removal of the trustee was affirmed.

Quiz Yourself on *TRUSTS: LIFE AND TERMINATION*

66. Robert's father sets up a trust that provides in pertinent part that "the trustee shall distribute the income to Robert quarterly, and the trustee may distribute to Robert as much of the principal as trustee deems necessary, in her sole and absolute discretion, for his comfortable support and maintenance." Each quarter, the trustee mails Robert a questionnaire inquiring as to his situation. Robert is addicted to drugs and is in rehab. He fails to return several questionnaires and claims financial hardship in some of the others, but fails to support his claim with details because he is too embarrassed to admit to his addiction and the financial problems it is causing. The trustee declines to disburse any principal to him. Thereafter, when Robert's condition improves, he sues the trustee claiming abuse of discretion and breach of fiduciary duty in not disbursing any principal to him. The trustee responds that because Robert's interest in the principal is merely discretionary and the trustee has absolute discretion, Robert has no right to any principal so there was no breach of trust or duty. What is the most likely result? _____

67. Father sets up a trust for the benefit of his sons, Alec, Steven, William, and Fred. The trust provides in pertinent part that "the trustee shall distribute the income equally to the sons at least quarterly, and the trustee may distribute principal to any of the sons if the trustee deems it appropriate." Thereafter, Alec divorces Kim. The court orders him to pay alimony and child support. Thereafter, Alec buys a new yacht (dealer-financed) and sets sail, never to be seen again. The yacht dealer, his ex-wife, and his children sue the trustee to reach Alec's interest in the trust to satisfy his debts.

a. What is the most likely result? _____

b. What difference would it make if the trust contained a spendthrift clause? _____

c. What difference, if any, would it make if Alec had created the trust? _____

68. Ted's will establishes a trust for the benefit of his children. The trustee is to pay the income to them for 20 years, and then the principal is to be disbursed to them equally. Shortly after his death, the relationships among Ted's children turn frosty. One of the children proposes terminating the trust and splitting the money. The others agree, but the trustee objects.

a. Can the children force premature termination of the trust? _____

b. What difference, if any, would it make if one of the children objected? _____

Answers

66. Even where a beneficiary's interest in a trust is discretionary, the trustee still owes the beneficiary certain duties. First, the trustee must exercise his or her discretion, and before he or she can do so, he or she must inquire as to the beneficiary's situation and needs. Where the beneficiary fails to reply or returns an incomplete reply, the duty is on the trustee to follow up. Here, the trustee failed to follow up when Robert failed to reply, thereby breaching the duty to inquire. In addition, once the trustee has all the necessary information, the trustee has a duty to act reasonably and in good faith in deciding whether to exercise his or her discretion under the terms of the trust. This standard can be altered by the settlor, but even where the trust purports to grant the trustee absolute discretion, the discretion cannot be absolute (if it were, the trust would be merely a precatory trust). The trustee still must act in good faith with an eye towards the purpose of the trust. Here, the trust specifically provides that the trustee has the power to invade the principal if necessary to maintain Robert's "comfortable support and maintenance." This phrase has become a term of art that means the beneficiary is to be kept at the standard of living he or she had at the time he or she became a beneficiary. The facts say that Robert's addiction has caused him financial problems. If these problems have affected his standard of living, the trustee has abused his or her discretion in not disbursing any of the principal to Robert. The most likely result under the facts is that the court will find that the trustee has breached the duty of inquiry and abused his or her discretion in not disbursing any of the principal to Robert.

67a. The general rule is that creditors of a beneficiary can reach a beneficiary's interest in a trust. The creditors step into the beneficiary's shoes and acquire the beneficiary's interest in the trust, but no more. Here, all of the creditors can reach Alec's interest in the trust. Because Alec's interest in the income was mandatory, the creditors can force the trustee to distribute Alec's share of the income to them, but because his interest in the principal was discretionary, they cannot force the trustee to exercise the trustee's discretion to disburse any of the principal to them. Under the Uniform Trust Code, creditors of a beneficiary can reach his or her interest to the extent it is mandatory but cannot reach the interest to the extent it is discretionary unless (1) the trustee has not complied with a standard of distribution or there has been an abuse of discretion, and (2) the distribution is ordered to satisfy a judgment or court order against the beneficiary for support or maintenance of a child, spouse, or former spouse. The answer is the same under the UTC.

67b. The general effect of a standard spendthrift clause is to make a beneficiary's interest in the trust nontransferable, and thus creditors of the beneficiary cannot reach the beneficiary's interest in the trust. Not all creditors, however, are subject to spendthrift clauses. Here, assuming a yacht is not a basic necessity, the yacht dealer is subject to the spendthrift clause and cannot reach Alec's interest in the trust. His ex-wife entitled to alimony and his children entitled to child support are not subject to the spendthrift clause as a general rule, and they can reach his interest in the trust. They can force the trustee to distribute Alec's share of the income to them, but they cannot force the trustee to distribute any principal to them. The Uniform Trust Code limits the exceptions to a spendthrift clause to (1) children entitled to child support pursuant to a judgment or court order; (2) spouses/ex-spouses entitled to spousal support (alimony/maintenance) pursuant to a judgment or court order; (3) a claim by a state or the federal government; and (4) a judgment creditor who has provided services for the protection of a beneficiary's interest in the trust. The children and ex-spouse are not subject to the spendthrift clause and can reach the beneficiary's mandatory interest in the income, but to reach the beneficiary's discretionary interest in the income they would also have to prove to the court that the trustee's failure to distribute any of the principal was inconsistent with the standard of distribution in the trust or an abuse of discretion. In light of the broad discretion granted the trustee "if the trustee deems it appropriate" it may be tough to convince a court that the trustee's failure is an abuse of discretion.

67c. Where the settlor is also a beneficiary, and the creditors are creditors of the settlor/beneficiary, spendthrift clauses are null and void, and creditors can reach the maximum amount the trustee could pay to the settlor/beneficiary under the terms of the trust. Here, even if the trust had a spendthrift clause, all of the creditors can force the trustee not only to distribute Alec's share of the income to them but, if that is not enough to satisfy the debts, to exercise his or her discretion and disburse principal to them until their debts are satisfied.

68a. Under the Claflin doctrine and the Uniform Trust Code, if all the beneficiaries consent to premature termination of the trust, but the trustee objects, the trustee can block the termination only if the trust has an unfulfilled material purpose. Here, there does not appear to be an unfulfilled material purpose. The children should be permitted to terminate the trust.

68b. If one of the children objected, under the traditional common law approach this would prevent premature termination. All of the beneficiaries must consent. Under the Uniform Trust Code, the court could still order termination if it concluded that: (1) if all of the beneficiaries had consented, termination would have been appropriate, and (2) the interest of the beneficiary who objects can be adequately protected. Although the facts arguably establish the first prong of the UTC test, there is not enough information to analyze the second prong, although on its face it would appear that the interests of the objecting beneficiary could be adequately protected.

Exam Tips on
TRUSTS: LIFE AND TERMINATION

Life of the trust

☞ Once the trust is created, the key issue during the life of the trust is what is the extent of each beneficiary's interest. A beneficiary's interest is either mandatory or discretionary. The extent of a beneficiary's interest depends on settlor's intent as expressed in the terms of the trust. Properly analyzing the extent of a beneficiary's interest requires careful reading of the express language of the trust.

☞ Mandatory interests pose few issues. The trustee must perform as directed.

☞ Discretionary interests contain a whole host of issues and are tested much more often. To say that an interest is discretionary only begins to touch on the subissues involved in discretionary trusts.

 ☞ Know the subduties inherent in discretionary trust: the duty of inquiry; the duty to act reasonably and in good faith in exercising the discretion, unless modified by the settlor in the express terms of the trust (but a trustee cannot have absolute discretion because that makes it a precatory trust); and the duty to take any express purpose set forth in the trust into consideration when deciding.

☞ Creditors' rights are a favorite area to test because they are derivative of beneficiary's interests, so a professor can test both areas at once. The key to analyzing creditors' rights is who is the beneficiary: the settlor or someone other than the settlor.

 ☞ If the beneficiary is someone other than the settlor, the creditor steps into the beneficiary's shoes and acquires the same rights as the beneficiary, but not more. A spendthrift clause blocks a creditor's ability to step into the beneficiary's shoes—the creditor must wait until the property is distributed to the beneficiary. Not all creditors, however, are subject to a spendthrift clause.

  ☞ Support trusts are a favorite area to test because of their wrinkles. First, use of the word *support* does not necessarily make a trust a support trust unless the level of distribution is limited to as much as necessary for support. Second, a support trust inherently includes a spendthrift clause. And third, only creditors who provide basic necessities can pierce the spendthrift clause under the traditional approach.

  ☞ Watch for issues designed to test the differences between the traditional approach and the UTC. The UTC abolishes the distinction between support trusts and discretionary trusts and provides no beneficiary can force a distribution from a discretionary trust, even if the trustee's failure to do so is an abuse of discretion, except for children entitled to child support payments or ex-spouses entitled to alimony/maintenance.

 ☞ If the beneficiary is the settlor, public policy does not permit one to shield one's assets behind a trust. Creditors not only can step into the beneficiary's shoes, they can force the trustee to exercise his or her discretion to the full extent permitted under the terms of the trust, and spendthrift clauses are null and void.

Modification and premature termination

☞ Both of these issues are fairly easy to spot because one or more beneficiaries have to ask the trustee to change the dispositive provisions of the trust. Distinguishing between the two issues is also fairly easy because it goes to the scope of the change the beneficiaries are requesting: if a slight change, modification; if total distribution, termination.

 ☞ For modification, all beneficiaries have to consent and an unforeseen change in circumstances must materially frustrate settlor's intent.

☞ Common law is more protective of settlor's intent and strictly applies the doctrinal requirements. Modern trend favors the beneficiaries and takes a broader interpretation of the doctrinal requirements (which leads to a great theoretical question of who really owns the property in trust).

☞ A wrinkle issue is how can all beneficiaries consent if some are minors or unborn—discuss the guardian ad litem and virtual representation doctrines.

☞ Premature termination is a bit more complicated just because there are different scenarios in which it can arise. First and foremost, at common law, at a minimum all beneficiaries have to consent.

☞ If all the beneficiaries consent and the trustee consents, terminate the trust.

☞ If all the beneficiaries consent and the settlor consents, terminate the trust.

☞ If all the beneficiaries consent, the trustee objects, and the settlor is dead, apply the Claflin doctrine. The trustee can block the premature termination only if there is an unfulfilled material purpose. Anything can qualify as a material purpose, though there are four well-recognized material purposes: discretionary trusts, spendthrift trusts, support trusts, and trusts where the principal is not to be distributed until the beneficiary reaches a specified age.

☞ The Uniform Trust Code greatly facilitates the standard for trust modification, termination, and/or trustee removal. If your professor requires you to know the UTC material, be sure to watch for these areas to be tested as they are a natural target because of the changes they embody as compared to the traditional approach.

CHAPTER 10

TRUST ADMINISTRATION AND THE TRUSTEE'S DUTIES

ChapterScope

This chapter examines the core issues that arise during the administration of the trust—the trustee's duties, the trustee's powers generally, and the trustee's investment powers and duties. In particular, the chapter examines:

- **Trustee's powers:** The scope of the trustee's powers has varied over time.

  - **Common law:** At common law, the office of trustee has no inherent powers, only those that were either expressly granted to the trustee by the deed or declaration of trust or those implicitly provided in light of the express trust powers and/or purpose.

  - **Modern trend:** At first, to simplify the granting of trust powers, states adopted long lists of statutory powers that the settlor could incorporate by reference to the statutory provision. More recently, the trustee has been granted automatically all the powers a prudent person would need to manage the trust in light of its purpose.

  - **Duty of loyalty:** The trustee owes a duty of absolute loyalty to the beneficiaries. Everything the trustee does must be done in the best interests of the beneficiaries.

- **Trust investments:** The issue of what constitutes an appropriate trust investment has, to a large degree, paralleled the issue of the trustee's powers.

  - **Traditional approach:** Traditionally, the presumed purpose of a trust was to *preserve* the trust property. Trustees were authorized to make such investments as a prudent man would with his own property with an eye towards preserving the principal while producing a reasonable income. Only relatively safe investments were deemed appropriate, and each investment decision was viewed individually.

  - **Modern trend:** The modern trend view of a trust is that it is a vehicle for holding and managing assets. The modern trend adopts the prudent investor rule. The risk of loss is assessed on a portfolio basis, not individual investments, and the trustee has a duty to diversify his or her investments. The focus is on total rate of return, not individual investments or investment decisions.

    - **Delegation:** Historically, a trustee could not delegate those activities and responsibilities that he or she reasonably could be expected to perform. Trustees could, however, delegate ministerial activities—those that do not require the exercise of discretion. The modern trend, prudent investor rule, also modifies the duty not to delegate, providing that an unsophisticated trustee has a duty to delegate investment decisions to professionals who are in a better position to make the necessary investment analysis and decisions.

- **Duty of impartiality:** A trustee has a duty of loyalty to all the beneficiaries. The trustee must balance the competing interests of the different beneficiaries. The trustee has a duty to produce a reasonable income for the life beneficiary while protecting the remainder interest for the remainderman.

■ **Principal and income:** The modern trend, prudent investor rule, also modifies the traditional rules concerning allocation of income and principal. Because the focus is on total return, and not on income vs. principal, the trustee is authorized to reassign some of the return, if necessary, to make sure that both categories of beneficiaries are treated fairly.

■ **Duty to care for the property:** The trustee must take proper care of the trust property. The trustee has the duty to take possession of and protect the trust property, to earmark the trust property, and to segregate the trust property from other property (particularly the trustee's own property).

■ **Duty to inform and account to beneficiaries:** The trustee has a duty to provide beneficiaries with complete and accurate information when requested and a duty to account either to the court or to the beneficiaries on a regular basis.

I. INTRODUCTION

A. **Risk management:** The essence of a trust is the separation of the legal ownership from the equitable ownership. The trustee holds the legal title and has the burden of managing the trust property. The beneficiaries hold the equitable title, and they bear the risk of the trustee's actions. If the trustee manages the property well, the beneficiaries benefit; if the trustee manages the property poorly, the beneficiaries bear the loss. Historically the common law regulated this risk by limiting the trustee's powers over the property. Modern trend law regulates this risk primarily by imposing a number of fiduciary duties on the trustee which he or she owes the beneficiaries; the duties of loyalty and prudence in particular; and then a number of subsidiary duties as well.

1. **Historical background:** The trust evolved out of a property-based background. Trusts arose to facilitate transferring real property. Trusts were funded primarily with real property and the primary duty of the trustee was to **preserve** the real property for the parties holding the future interest. The risk of trustee mismanagement was regulated primarily by granting that the trustee had no inherent powers over the trust property and by imposing on third parties interested in dealing with the trustee a high duty to inquire into the propriety of the transaction.

2. **Modern trend:** The contemporary trust typically is funded with an intangible fund of assets (stocks, bonds, mutual fund shares, pension plans, bank accounts, etc.). The primary duty of the trustee is to **manage** this fund of wealth. The trustee is granted by law all the powers a reasonable person would need to manage the trust, and third parties interested in dealing with a trustee have no duty to inquire absent suspicious circumstances. The risk of trustee mismanagement is regulated primarily by imposing a duty of loyalty and prudent administration on the trustee.

3. **Agency theory:** From a theoretical perspective, the risks inherent in the use of a trust are analogous to the risks inherent in the use of an agent. It is impossible **ex ante** for the parties (principal and agent; settlor and trustee; etc.) to anticipate and contract with respect to every

conceivable scenario so the relationship is governed primarily by the more flexible fiduciary principle. In the trust context, however, the beneficiaries do not have the same control over the trustee that a principal typically has over an agent. Hence, traditionally courts were stricter in their application of fiduciary principles to trustees.

II. TRUSTEE'S POWERS

A. **Common law:** At common law, the office of trustee has no inherent powers. The trustee possesses only those powers either expressly granted in the terms of the trust or those necessarily implied in light of the trust purposes.

B. **Judicial authorization:** A trustee can petition a court of equity for authorization to undertake an action not expressly or implicitly authorized under the terms of the trust. If the court authorizes the requested action, in essence, the court grants the trustee the requested additional power.

C. **Modern trend:** The modern trend is to facilitate the granting of powers to the trustee. The modern trend takes two approaches toward this goal.

   1. **Statutory list:** Under this approach, the jurisdiction adopts a statute that sets forth a long list of powers it is presumed a trustee would need, thereby permitting settlors to incorporate the statutory list of powers by simply referring to the statutory provisions (incorporation by reference).

   2. **Inherent powers:** The alternative modern trend approach is statutorily to grant the trustee a broad set of powers unless the settlor expressly provides that the trustee is not to have one or more of the granted powers. Typically, the statute provides that a trustee is presumed to have all the powers a reasonable person would need to perform the acts necessary in light of the purposes of the trust.

D. **Third parties' liability:** A trustee's powers to act are only effective if third parties are willing to deal with a trustee. In light of the fact that third parties can be held liable for participating in a breach of trust, the protection accorded third parties who deal with a trustee affects the practical scope of the trustee's powers.

   1. **Common law:** At common law, it is generally presumed that the purpose of a trust is to preserve the trust property. Hence, the common law discourages third parties from dealing with trustees by imposing virtually strict liability on third parties if the transaction constitutes a breach of trust. Although a third party who qualifies as subsequent bona fide purchaser without notice is not liable if the transaction constitutes a breach of trust, at common law if the party has notice he or she is dealing with a trustee, it is virtually impossible to qualify as a subsequent bona fide purchaser without notice. If the third party knows or should know that he or she is dealing with a trustee, the party has a duty to inspect the trust instrument to see if the transaction is authorized and is charged with proper interpretation of the trust.

   2. **Modern trend:** The modern trend presumes that the purpose of a trust is to hold and manage the trust property. To facilitate trust management, the modern trend grants the trustee broad powers and third parties dealing with a trustee greater protection to facilitate trust transactions. The Uniform Trustee's Powers Act eliminates the duty to inquire into the terms of the trust and

protects third parties unless they have actual knowledge that the transaction constitutes a breach of trust. The Uniform Trust Code requires third parties to act in good faith and give valuable consideration.

III. DUTY OF LOYALTY

A. **Scope:** The golden rule of trust administration is that the trustee owes the trust beneficiaries the duty of absolute loyalty. Everything the trustee does must be done solely in the best interests of the beneficiaries. Many of the other trustee's duties arguably are merely logical subsidiary duties of this one supreme duty—absolute loyalty to the trust beneficiaries.

   1. **Fiduciary:** It should be noted that a trustee is a fiduciary, but that there are other types of fiduciaries; in particular, executors/personal representatives are fiduciaries with respect to the administration of the probate estate. While the material will focus on the trustee and the trustee's duties, there are other fiduciaries who owe similar duties in carrying out the responsibilities inherent in their positions.

   2. **Test:** In applying the duty of loyalty to a particular act undertaken by the trustee, the courts have translated the duty of loyalty into a duty to act reasonably and in good faith. The requirement that the trustee act in good faith is a subjective standard that addresses the trustee's state of mind—the trustee must have thought that what he or she was doing was in the beneficiaries' best interests. The requirement that the trustee act reasonably is an objective standard that permits judicial review and supervision of a trustee's actions even where the trustee acted in good faith.

B. **Duty against self-dealing:** Self-dealing arises where the trust and the trustee engage in a transaction. The trustee has a conflict of interest. The trustee has a personal interest in the transaction while at the same time the trustee has duty to act only in the best interests of the beneficiaries. The beneficiaries' interests must prevail. The duty against self-dealing is usually construed broadly to include transactions involving other members of the trustee's family (spouse, children, parents).

   1. **No further inquiry:** Where a trustee engages in self-dealing, an irrebuttable presumption of breach of the duty of loyalty arises. Once it is established that self-dealing has occurred, no further inquiry of the trustee's reasonableness or good faith is necessary or appropriate—per se it constitutes a breach of the duty of loyalty. The beneficiaries can hold the trustee liable for any loss the trust has sustained, compel the trustee to transfer any profit made to the trust, or undo the transaction.

   2. **Example:** In ***Hartman v. Hartle***, 122 A. 615 (N.J. Ch. 1923), the testatrix had five children. Her will appointed two of her sons-in-law executors of her estate and directed that her real property was to be sold and divided equally among the five children. The land was sold for $3,900 at public auction, and one of the testatrix's sons bought it for his sister, who was the wife of one of the executors. Two months later, the sister sold the land for $5,500. The court ruled that the duty against self-dealing applied to the spouse of the fiduciary. Absent court approval of the transaction, the sale was inappropriate. The sale could not be rescinded because of the subsequent sale to a bona fide purchaser without notice of the breach of trust, but the sister was forced to share one-fifth of the profit upon resale with the complaining beneficiary.

3. **Traditional exceptions:** The duty against self-dealing can be waived either by the settlor in the terms of the trust or by all the beneficiaries, following a full disclosure of the proposed transaction.

   Judicial review: Even where the self-dealing is authorized, the transaction must still be reasonable and fair, and if it is not, the trustee is liable for breaching the duty of loyalty. UTC §802(b).

4. **Modern trend exceptions:** In light of increasing use of institutional trustees, and to permit such trustees to take advantage of economies of scale, a number of statutory exceptions to the traditional no self-dealing rule have been adopted. Many states have statutes permitting a bank trust department to deposit trust assets in its own banking department; institutional trustees are increasingly authorized to combine separate trust accounts into a common trust fund or mutual fund; trustees are authorized to charge a reasonable compensation. UTC §802(f), (h).

5. **Uniform Trust Code:** For the most part the Uniform Trust Code adopts the traditional approach to self-dealing, except transactions by a trustee with a close relative or with the trustee's lawyer are no longer absolutely forbidden but are only presumptively voidable. If the trustee can prove that the transaction was objectively fair and reasonable, and not affected by a conflict, the trustee is not liable.

6. **Trust pursuit rule:** Among the remedies available to trust beneficiaries where there is a breach of trust is the ability of the trust beneficiaries to pursue the trust property and secure its return despite its transfer, unless the property is sold to a subsequent bona fide purchaser without notice of the breach of trust.

C. **Duty to avoid conflicts of interest:** A conflict of interest arises where the trust deals with another party with whom the trustee has an interest that may affect the trustee's assessment of the proposed transaction. If the transaction involves a possible conflict of interest, but not self-dealing, the "no further inquiry" rule does not apply. The transaction is assessed to see if it is reasonable and fair under the circumstances.

1. **Example:** In *In re Rothko*, 372 N.E.2d 291 (N.Y. 1977), testator's will appointed three friends executors of his estate (which consisted primarily of almost 800 paintings). The executors contracted with an art gallery that agreed to purchase 100 of the paintings and to sell the rest on consignment. In analyzing the contracts, the court found that two of the executors had a conflict of interest. One of the executors was a director and officer of the art gallery. The contract resulted in that executor receiving greater financial remuneration and status, and the gallery gave favorable treatment to the executor's own art collection. The second executor had a conflict of interest because he was a struggling artist seeking to curry favor with the gallery so it would buy and sell his paintings, something that in fact happened during the contract negotiations. The court found that the contracts were neither fair nor in the beneficiaries' best interests. The court found that the third executor was aware of the breaches of trust being committed by the other executors and failed to act—a breach of trust, even where the third executor was acting on the advice of counsel. The advice of counsel gave the executor good faith, but the transactions were not reasonable, and the executor did not act reasonably in failing to properly assess the contracts.

2. **Damages:** Where a trustee is authorized to transfer trust property but improperly sells it for too low a price, the trustee is liable for the difference in the actual sale price and the price that should have been realized. Where a trustee sells property he or she was not authorized to sell,

appreciation damages are appropriate. Appreciation damages constitute the difference between the sale price and the value of the property as of the date of the court's decree (thereby putting the beneficiaries back in the position where they would have been but for the unauthorized sale). In *In re Rothko*, the court ruled that where the sale of the trust property constitutes a breach of misfeasance other than just selling the property for too low a price, the fiduciary may be liable for appreciation damages. Transferees who take with notice of the breach of trust are liable for appreciation damages as well. In *In re Rothko*, the court imposed appreciation damages on the two executors who acted with the conflict of interest, as well as the art gallery.

D. Co-trustee liability: A trustee is liable for a breach of trust if the trustee (1) consents to the action that constitutes the breach, or (2) negligently fails to act to stop or try to stop the other trustees from engaging in the action that constitutes the breach. A trustee's fiduciary duties to the beneficiaries include monitoring the conduct of his or her fellow trustees. Failure to monitor the actions of one's co-trustees or delegating one's nonministerial responsibilities to co-trustees constitutes a breach of trust.

Right to contribution: Co-trustees are jointly liable. A trustee generally has a right to contribution from co-trustees where he or she is found liable. Under the Restatement (Second) of Trusts, however, the right to contribution may be limited if the trustee either was more at fault or benefited personally from the breach; and the right to contribution is eliminated if the trustee acted in bad faith.

IV. DUTY OF PRUDENCE—TRUST INVESTMENTS

A. Introduction: The trustee has a duty to administer the trust with such skill and care as a person of ordinary prudence would use in dealing with his or her own property. The duty is an objective standard of care, focusing on what a reasonable person would do, not the trustee's subjective intentions when acting. The Uniform Trust Code adopts this approach. UTC §804 (2000).

B. Trust investments—overview: The issue of what constitutes an appropriate trust investment goes directly to the philosophical question of what is the purpose of a trust. Just as the function of a trust has changed over time from *preserving* property to *managing* the trust property, so too has the notion of what constitutes an appropriate trust investment. The rules limiting trust investments to "safe" investments have given way to permitting an acceptable level of risk to ensure an adequate return on the trust property.

1. **Background:** Historically, the most common approach to what constituted an appropriate trust investment was a judicial and/or statutory list of appropriate investments. The courts and/or legislature would identify categories of investments that were presumptively appropriate, but even then an investment in a particular entity or activity included within the list had to be otherwise reasonable and proper.

2. **Investments analyzed individually:** Under the traditional common law approach, each investment decision is viewed separately. If one investment decision out of a hundred is deemed inappropriate, the trustee is liable for any loss caused by the one inappropriate investment. The risk level of other investments and the profits generated by them are completely irrelevant in assessing the propriety of a particular investment.

3. **Settlor's authorization:** If a settlor expressly authorizes investments that are not on a jurisdiction's statutory list, such investments are appropriate investments as long as otherwise reasonable and proper.

   Judicial construction: As a general rule, courts tend to construe narrowly provisions authorizing a trustee to invest in otherwise inappropriate investments, requiring the trustee to still act reasonably and properly.

C. **Model Prudent Man Investment Act:** The Model Prudent *Man* Investment Act abolishes statutory lists and permits any investment that a prudent man would make, barring only "speculative" investments. The act was first adopted in 1940 and is still followed in some jurisdictions.

   1. **Prudent person:** The most common statement of the prudent person standard is that the trustee should invest with the same care as a prudent person would of his or her own property, taking into consideration the dual goals of preserving the principal while generating a stream of income.

   2. **Criticism:** The prudent man rule has been criticized for putting too much emphasis on how risky investments are. Return on investments corresponds directly with risk. Permitting only nonspeculative investments restricts the potential return for the beneficiaries. Moreover, "safe" investment may have little to no risk of complete loss, but they may subject the trust to a substantial risk of inflation in that if inflation exceeds the rate of return, the real value of the trust property will fall.

D. **Uniform Prudent Investor Act:** The Uniform Prudent *Investor* Act, adopted in 1994, builds on the prudent person approach. The Uniform Prudent Investor Act focuses on the actions that constitute a prudent investor and the duties that go hand in hand with those actions. It adopts a number of express provisions that constitute innovative approaches that repudiate the old common law approach. The Restatement (Third) of Trusts and the Trustee Act of 2000 have adopted the prudent investor standard.

   1. **Duty to diversify:** The prudent investor standard still requires the trustee to spread the risk of loss by diversifying the trust investments, unless it is prudent not to do so.

   2. **Pooling trust funds:** The common law rule strictly requires each trust fund to be segregated from both the trustee's own funds and other trust funds. Segregating trust funds, however, makes diversification of smaller trusts more difficult and increases transaction costs associated with trust investments (increases transaction costs that could be reduced by permitting one transaction for multiple trusts). The modern trend and majority rule permits pooling of trust funds to achieve efficiencies of scale and to facilitate diversifying trust investments. The modern trend likewise permits investments in mutual funds.

   3. **Portfolio approach:** The Uniform Prudent Investor Act expressly adopts the portfolio approach to investments—individual investments are no longer assessed in isolation, but rather the total performance of the trust's investments is the standard. The duty to diversify goes hand in hand with the portfolio approach. A well-diversified portfolio spreads the risk of loss across all the investments so that the aggregate level of risk is acceptable in light of the trust purposes. Under the portfolio approach, an individual investment that might look speculative in isolation can be reasonable if offset by other safe investments with low levels of risk associated with

them. One of the keys to assessing the propriety of an investment under the portfolio approach is whether it is a compensated or uncompensated risk.

a. **Compensated risks:** Compensated risks are investments that are riskier than others but that have a corresponding higher rate of possible return associated with them. The investor is compensated appropriately for the enhanced risk. Compensated risks are appropriate investments under the portfolio approach as long as the overall risk level of the trust's investment portfolio is acceptable relative to the trust purposes. Putting an appropriate amount of a trust's funds into a start-up company with great growth potential is an example of a compensated risk.

b. **Uncompensated risks:** Uncompensated risks are those investments that are risky and do not have a corresponding market-enhanced compensation to reward the investor for taking the risk. Putting all of one's investments in one stock, regardless of the level of risk associated with the stock, is an example of an uncompensated risk (i.e., lack of diversification constitutes an uncompensated risk).

c. **Investment decisions:** Arguably the key considerations in assessing a trustee's investments under the portfolio theory approach are (1) the trustee's investigations and decision-making process in determining the trust's acceptable level of compensated risk, and (2) how that level is achieved through the combination of trust investments.

d. **Duty to delegate:** The prudent investor approach assumes that expert assistance in the investing decision-making process is beneficial, if not required. Delegating the investment process to an expert is viewed with favor, though the trustee still has a duty to properly investigate to whom the power should be delegated, to consult with the agent to ensure that he or she properly understands the trust's terms, purposes, and acceptable level of compensable risk, and to monitor the activities and decisions of the investment agent.

4. **Adequate diversification:** How much diversification is necessary is not addressed in the Act. Apparently that is a fact-sensitive issue to be determined on a trust-by-trust basis, taking into consideration the purpose of the trust and the particular investments in question.

a. **Example:** In *In re Estate of Janes*, 681 N.E.2d 332 (Ct. App. N.Y. 1997), the testator died May 26, 1973, with a probate estate of approximately $3.5 million, $2.5 million of which was held in stock, and 71 percent of that (or $1.79 million) consisted of 13,232 shares of Kodak common stock. His will bequeathed most of his estate to three trusts. The first was a marital deduction trust for the benefit of his wife, Cynthia. The second trust was for the benefit of selected charities. The third trust was for Cynthia's benefit during her life, and upon her death, the principal was to pour over to the charitable trust. Cynthia and Lincoln Rochester Trust Company were appointed co-executors. By August of 1973, the Trust Company's trust and estate officers had determined the estate's expenses and how many shares of stock needed to be sold to cover the expenses. At that meeting the trust officers recommended holding the remaining shares until the trusts were funded. The memo did not otherwise discuss investment strategy. In September of that year, Cynthia consented to the sale of an additional 1,200 shares of Kodak stock. At that time the stock was selling at $139 a share. That was the last time the trust officers discussed the retention of the stock or other investment issues with Cynthia. Thereafter Kodak stock declined steadily—falling to $109 a share by the end of 1973; to $63 a share by the end of 1974; to $51 a share by the end of 1977; and to $40 a share by March 1978. In 1980, the trust company filed its initial accounting covering most of the period in question and sought judicial settlement of it. Cynthia and the attorney general (on behalf of the charitable trust) objected and sought to surcharge the trust company for its imprudent retention of the high concentration of Kodak stock in violation of the prudent person rule of investment. The surrogate court found the trust company had acted imprudently, ruling that the trust company should have divested the estate of the high concentration of Kodak stock by August 1973. The court imposed a $6.1 million surcharge (including a "lost profit" on the money which would have been reinvested if there had been proper divestment). The Appellate Division upheld the finding of imprudence and the date used to calculate damages, but not the inclusion of the lost profits. The surcharge was reduced to $4.1 million. On appeal, the trust company argued that there was no duty to diversify absent additional elements of hazard and argued that a list of factors indicated that no additional elements of hazard existed in this case. The New York Court of Appeals rejected the trust company's argument, ruling instead that no precise formula exists for determining the prudent person standard. Each case turns on its own facts and circumstances, with the trustee's investment decisions to be measured in light of the business and economic circumstances at the time they were made in light of the circumstances of the trust itself rather than the integrity of the particular investment. The court held that the high concentration of Kodak stock (with the other shares primarily in other growth stocks) failed to take into adequate consideration the needs of the testator's 72-year-old widow. The annual return on the Kodak stock at the time of funding was 1.06 percent, thereby jeopardizing the interests of the primary beneficiary, his widow, and the income beneficiary. In addition, the trust company failed to exercise the due care and skill of a corporate fiduciary by: (1) failing to establish an investment plan upon funding; (2) failing to follow its own internal policies of special caution and attention to cases of portfolio concentration exceeding 20 percent; and (3) failing to conduct more than routine reviews of the account in the face of declining values. The court affirmed that the trust company acted imprudently and that a prudent fiduciary would have divested itself of the high concentration of Kodak stock by August 1973. Lastly, the court ruled that where the imprudent conduct is that the trustee ***negligently*** retained assets it should have sold, the measure of damages is limited to the lost capital (though the court noted that lost profits are appropriate where deliberate self-dealing or faithless transfers are involved).

b. **Professional and corporate trustees:** Professional and corporate trustees are usually held to a higher standard of care in investing due to their presumed expertise. Individual trustees are usually held to a lower standard of care.

c. **Exceptions to duty to diversify:** The duty to diversify is not absolute. There are situations where a fiduciary arguably is justified in not diversifying: where the administrative costs of diversifying (including tax consequences) would outweigh the benefits; where there is a family-run business or diversifying would entail loss of a controlling interest; personal assets (family vacation home; personal home). One can even argue that if the trust is but one piece of a larger investment scheme, the trust need not be diversified if the larger investment scheme is. Investment in a single mutual fund may constitute adequate diversification if the mutual fund is diversified.

d. **Inception assets:** Many jurisdictions permit a trustee to have a preference for retaining the trust's "inception assets"—the assets used to fund the trust that the settlor recommends the trustee retain. Such preference, however, is not an absolute right and is subject to the trustee's more general fiduciary duty of prudent administration.

e. **Authorization to retain vs. duty to sell:** Even where the trust instrument authorizes the trustee to retain the trust assets in question, where failure to diversify is inconsistent with the modern portfolio approach, the trustee has a duty to sell the trust property in a timely manner (within a reasonable time period).

f. **Direction to retain vs. duty to sell:** Where the trust instrument directs the trustee to retain the trust assets in question, the issue is more complicated. The general rule is that the settlor's intent controls, so some courts have ruled that the trustee must comply with the retention order. Other courts, consistent with the modern portfolio emphasis on diversification, have approved diversification if there are "changed circumstances," thereby relieving the trustee of the duty to follow the settlor's directions. (The trustee may even have a duty to petition the court for authorization to sell the asset under these circumstances—the Restatement (Third) of Trusts imposes just such a duty; the Uniform Trust Code does not.)

g. **Calculating damages:** Where there is a breach of trust, the trust beneficiaries are entitled to be made whole. There are three ways the beneficiaries can be made whole: (1) charge the trustee with any resulting loss; (2) charge the trustee with any profit made; or (3) charge the trustee with any profit that would have accrued but for the breach.

  i. **The total return damages approach:** The "total return/make whole" damages approach favors including lost profits that would have been made if the proper actions had been taken in a timely manner, including profits on the prudent administration and any profits made by the trustee through the breach. UTC §1002. Where there are several plausible investment strategies, the Restatement (Third) of Trusts favors application of the most profitable unless the trustee can justify why it should not apply.

  ii. **The capital lost plus interest approach:** The "capital lost plus interest" approach does not punish the trustee for lost investment opportunities, awarding interest to the trust beneficiaries rather than possible profits from prudent investment of the lost capital. Under this approach, the rate of interest is critical. Different possible rates include the historic average rate of inflation; the annual return on long-term government bonds; and the legal rate applied to money judgments.

  iii. **Total return approach:** The "total return" approach calculates damages by awarding the difference between how the particular, imprudently managed, portfolio actually performed versus how a hypothetical matching portfolio, prudently managed, would have performed, taking into consideration taxes, expenses, and distributions. This approach requires the testimony of expert witnesses and is somewhat speculative.

h. **Duty to avoid unnecessary costs:** Just as a reasonable person would take all appropriate steps to minimize the expenses associated with his or her own investments, so too a trustee must take all reasonable steps to minimize the expenses associated with the trust, including investment expenses, tax consequences, and inflation.

5. **Settlor authorization:** If a settlor expressly authorizes all investments, regardless of their legality, the courts tend to construe such provisions narrowly, granting a trustee some extra room for lapses in judgment, but not absolute immunity for improper investments under the prudent investor standard. Such exculpatory clauses also do not protect a trustee who acts in bad faith or recklessly in making trust investments.

a. **Example:** In *Wood v. U.S. Bank, N.A.*, 828 N.E.2d 1072 (Ct. App. Ohio 2005), John Wood created a trust that named Firstar Bank (it later became U.S. Bank) as trustee and his wife, Dana, as a beneficiary. When created, 80 percent of the trust assets were in Firstar stock. A provision in the trust allowed Firstar to retain "any securities in the same form as when received, including shares of a corporate Trustee. . . ." Firstar did not diversify but instead unloaded the non-Firstar stock to pay the debts of the estate in a much greater proportion so that soon after John's death, 86 percent of the trust was comprised of Firstar stock. Dana asked (orally, not in writing) Firstar to diversify but the bank still did not comply. A few months later, Firstar's stock plunged and then Firstar made the final distribution to the beneficiaries, costing them an estimated $771,099. Dana alleged Firstar breached its duty to diversify. The trial court had instructed the jury that a trustee was liable for failing to diversify only if there was an abuse of discretion. The Appellate Court reversed, holding that absent special circumstances where *not* diversifying would better serve the purposes of the trust, a trustee has a duty to diversify. The court reasoned that while the boilerplate retention clause waived the duty of undivided loyalty with respect to the trustee's stock, it did not address the trustee's duty to act prudently and to diversify. There were special circumstances that prevented sale of the stock while John was alive (tax considerations), but that special circumstance was removed upon his death. A general authorization, like the clause in John's trust, does not abrogate the duty to diversify absent specific language authorizing the trustee to retain a larger percentage of one investment than would normally be prudent. The case was remanded to the trial court to determine if because of special circumstances (i.e., holdings that are important to a family or a trust), the purposes of the trust were better served without diversifying.

b. **Authorization vs. mandate:** Trust provisions that *mandate* asset retention should be distinguished from those that *authorize* asset retention. The latter do not excuse a trustee's liability for failing to diversify absent good reasons not to, while the former arguably do. The power to retain an asset does not waive the duty to diversify (though some courts have held that the power to retain may excuse slower reallocation of the assets). Even where the trust mandates asset retention, the trustee may have a duty to petition the court for guidance if failure to diversify would harm the beneficiaries, which it typically does, but some states have adopted statutory provisions protecting mandated asset retention provisions from judicial review.

c. **Judicial construction:** Some commentators have criticized the courts as being too narrow in their interpretation of the prudent investor doctrine, complaining that the courts implicitly are still applying the traditional view that trustees have to practice safe investing instead of permitting the broader investments authorized by the Act and/or the express terms of a trust instrument.

d. **Trustee protection:** Attempts at granting a trustee "absolute discretion" and complete protection with respect to investment decisions are analogous to similar clauses granting a trustee absolute discretion and complete protection with respect to discretionary trusts. (*See* Chapter 9.I.C.4 and I.C.9) Such provisions are inconsistent with the fiduciary nature of the trustee's position and therefore are not given full effect.

e. **ERISA:** The prudent investor rule governs trustees managing pension funds regulated by ERISA. ERISA imposes an exclusive benefit rule on the trustee which is analogous to the duty of loyalty. Accordingly, the law of trusts often is invoked in ERISA litigation, and ERISA opinions may end up affecting the law of trusts.

6. **Delegation:** At common law, a trustee cannot delegate any discretionary responsibilities. The reasoning is that the settlor reposed great trust in the trustee and assumed that the appointed trustee personally would hold and manage the trust property. If the trustee delegates discretionary responsibility to another, such delegation violates the settlor's intent.

   a. **Exception—ministerial responsibilities:** Even at common law, there is an exception for ministerial responsibilities. Responsibilities that do not require the exercise of any discretion are generally deemed ministerial (for example, cutting the grass, making repairs, maintaining and cleaning the property).

   b. **Modern trend—duty to delegate:** The modern trend, and overwhelmingly majority rule these days, recognizes that some trustees are unqualified to undertake certain responsibilities inherent in holding and managing trust property—in particular, the duty to invest trust property properly. Under the Uniform Prudent Investor Act §9, the Restatement (Third) of Trusts §171, and the Uniform Trust Code §807 (2000), the trustee may have a duty to delegate those responsibilities if a prudent person would delegate under similar circumstances. The trustee must act in the best interests of the beneficiaries in deciding whether to delegate discretionary responsibilities, including investment-making responsibilities, and to whom to delegate them.

      i. **Duty to supervise:** Even where the trustee is authorized to delegate either ministerial or discretionary responsibilities, the trustee has an on-going duty of care in (1) selecting the agent(s); (2) defining the agent(s)' role and giving proper instructions; and (3) monitoring and supervising the actions of the agent(s) to whom the trustee delegates the responsibilities to ensure that the agent(s) is/are acting within the delegated authority and in the best interests of the beneficiaries. The trustee cannot abdicate or delegate unreasonably.

      ii. **Example:** In *Shriners Hospital for Crippled Children v. Gardiner*, 733 P.2d 1110 (Ariz. 1987), settlor created a trust, income to her daughter, grandchildren, and daughter-in-law, remainder upon the death of the last income life beneficiary to Shriners Hospital. Settlor appointed her daughter trustee and her grandson as successor trustee. The daughter had no investment experience, so she placed the funds with a brokerage house. The grandson was a stockbroker, so he made all the investment decisions. The grandson embezzled $317,234 from the trust. The remainderman, Shriners Hospital, sued the daughter as trustee for breach of trust in delegating the investment responsibilities. The court stated that while an inexperienced trustee has a duty to seek expert advice with respect to the trust investments, the trustee cannot delegate the investment decisions completely, but rather must exercise his or her own judgment after receiving such advice. Here, the daughter turned over the investment decision-making process completely to the grandson in breach of her duty. The court noted that it made no difference that the grandson was the successor trustee.

   c. **Directed vs. delegated trusts:** Under a delegated trust, the *trustee* decides which tasks should be delegated and to whom they should be delegated. The trustee is subject to the duties above inherent in selecting, instructing and supervising the agents. In a directed trust, however, the *settlor*, through the terms of the trust, by directing the trustee to follow the instruction of others, in essence selects the agent to whom certain tasks are to be delegated and the trustee must follow the third parties' directions. Increasingly settlors are creating directed trusts. Developing law tends to be more protective of a "directed" trustee.

V. IMPARTIALITY—ALLOCATING PRINCIPAL AND INCOME

A. **Duty to be impartial:** The trustee's duty of loyalty extends to all beneficiaries, those holding the present interest (typically a life estate in the income) and those holding the future interest (typically a remainder in the principal). Because the beneficiaries have different property interests, their personal interests often conflict. The income beneficiaries prefer the trust principal be invested so that high levels of interest are generated (risky investments); while the remaindermen prefer the trust property be invested in safe investments that protect the principal (but generate little income).

1. **Rule statement:** The trustee's duty of loyalty to both present and future interests translates into a duty of impartiality between the competing interests—historically that meant a duty to invest the property so that it produces a reasonable income while preserving the principal for the remaindermen; increasingly today it is rephrased as striking a balance between the beneficiaries, giving proper consideration for their respective interests.

2. **Waiver:** The duty to be impartial can be waived by the settlor where the trust instrument adequately expresses an intent to favor one beneficiary over another. In ***Howard v. Howard***, 156 P.3d 89 (Ct. App. Oreg. 2007), Leo and Marcene were married. Leo had three children from a prior marriage, Marcene two. They created two trusts, one for each. They transferred 60 percent of their assets to Leo's trust and 40 percent to Marcene's. Each trust provided first for the settlor . . . , then upon the death of the settlor . . . , for the benefit of the surviving spouse, and then upon his or her death, for the benefit of the issue of the respective settlor . . . , resulting in equal shares to the children. Each trust provided for a number of different scenarios under which the trustees may exercise their discretion to distribute income to the different beneficiaries. In most of these, the trust expressly provided that the trustee was to take into consideration the beneficiary's needs and other resources—but that provision was not included in the clause in Leo's trust requiring the income to be distributed to Marcene after Leo's death. Leo's trust also expressly stated that he made no provision for his stepchildren because they are provided for under Marcene's trust, but Marcene's "support, comfort, companionship, enjoyment and desires" shall be preferred over the rights of the remaindermen. Although the statute usually requires a trustee to be impartial between beneficiaries, the court ruled this last clause overrode the rule of impartiality. Leo's son alleged that the trustee should consider Marcene's other assets in making distribution decisions for the trust because if the trustee did not, the trustee could not comply with Leo's intent to pass the remainderman to his children and not his stepchildren. The court disagreed and said the trustee did not have to consider Marcene's other financial resources because Leo's intent was to favor Marcene's desires—as evidenced by the fact that in other parts of the trust, the trustee was required to consider the beneficiary's needs and other income, so the omission in this regard as to Marcene must have been intentional. An investment strategy that took into account preserving assets for the remainder beneficiaries would conflict with the clause giving clear preference to Marcene. Marcene's other resources were not relevant to the administration of the trust.

3. **Inception assets:** Many jurisdictions permit a trustee to have a preference for retaining the trust's "inception assets"—the assets used to fund the trust that the settlor recommends the trustee retain. Such preference, however, is not an absolute right and is subject to the trustee's more general fiduciary duty of impartiality among the beneficiaries.

4. **Duty to sell:** Even where the trust instrument authorizes the trustee to retain the trust assets in question, where failure to diversify is inconsistent with the modern portfolio approach, the trustee has a duty to sell the trust property in a timely manner (within a reasonable time period).

   Judicial authorization: Where one group of beneficiaries objects to the sale, or if a co-trustee blocks the sale, the duty to be impartial requires the trustee (or other co-trustees, as the case may be) to petition the court for authority to sell.

5. **Power to reallocate sale proceeds:** If a trustee does not dispose of underperforming or overperforming property within a reasonable time, the trustee has a duty to re-allocate the sale proceeds so that the beneficiaries adversely affected by the delayed sale are compensated for the damage to their interest caused by the delay.

   a. **Underperforming property:** Where underperforming property is not sold in a timely manner, the income beneficiaries are entitled to a share of the sale proceeds to reflect the income they lost during the delay when the property was not generating the income it should have been. The Restatement (Third) of Trusts §241 calculates their share by subtracting from the sale proceeds the income that would have been generated by that amount from the date the duty to sell arose.

      Revised Uniform Principal and Income Act: The Revised Uniform Principal and Income Act provides that where underperforming trust property is sold, the proceeds must be apportioned between the income beneficiaries and the remaindermen to offset the loss sustained by the income beneficiaries, even if the duty to sell never arose.

   b. **Overperforming property:** Where overperforming property is not sold in a timely manner, the remaindermen are entitled to a share of the income generated during the delay. The share is determined by calculating the value of the property on the date the duty arose, minus the actual sale price when finally sold, multiplied by a percentage to reflect return on the properly invested principal for appreciation and inflation. If the trustee fails to withhold some of the income generated during the delay, the trustee may be liable for the difference.

B. **Allocating principal and income:** Typically, the life beneficiaries of a trust are entitled to the income, and the remainder beneficiaries are entitled to the principal. The bifurcated interests mean that decisions concerning what constitutes income and what constitutes principal are critical to the interests of the different categories of beneficiaries.

   1. **1962 Principal and Income Act:** The 1962 Principal and Income Act sets forth the traditional approach to allocating income and principal.

      a. **Income:** The assumption is that money generated on a regular or irregular basis as a result of the trust property or trust investments constitutes income. Classic examples include interest, rent, cash dividends on stock, net profits from a business, and royalties (though a fraction of royalties are allocated to principal).

b. Principal: The assumption is that money generated as part of a conveyance (voluntary or involuntary) of trust property is considered principal (for example, sale proceeds, insurance proceeds). In addition, stock splits and stock dividends are considered principal because such property has to be retained as principal to maintain the trust's percentage interest in the company. Bond principal payments and part of royalty payments are also considered principal.

2. **1997 Principal and Income Act—the power of equitable adjustment:** Under the modern trend portfolio approach, the focus is on the total return to the trust portfolio. As long as the trust achieves an acceptable rate of return on its investments, it is irrelevant whether that return is generated in the form of income or principal as traditionally defined (though the traditional classification schemes are retained). The trustee has the power and discretion, the power of equitable adjustment, to reallocate the total return between the income and principal beneficiaries to ensure that the two groups are treated fairly while paying particular attention to the larger rate of return regardless of how the return is classified (income vs. principal).

Settlor's intent: The settlor may expressly provide that the trustee does not have the power to reallocate principal and income.

3. **Unitrust:** Under a unitrust, the life beneficiaries are entitled to a specified percentage of the value of the trust principal each year, so there is no need to distinguish income from principal. All property generated by the trust is assigned to principal, and at the appropriate intervals, the specified percentage of the trust principal is distributed to the appropriate beneficiaries. The purpose of the unitrust is to permit the trustee to focus on investing the trust portfolio to maximize total return as opposed to worrying about investing to ensure an appropriate income stream for the income beneficiary.

4. **Unitrust election:** Many states have statutes authorizing a trustee to convert a traditional trust to a unitrust (called adjustment powers). Some states deny this power to a trustee-beneficiary; others permit it but scrutinize the trustee's decision more closely.

Example: In *In re Matter of Heller*, 849 N.E.2d 262 (Ct. App. N.Y. 2007), Jacob created a testamentary trust for the benefit of his wife Bertha and his children from a previous marriage. Bertha was to receive the income from the trust each year, and after her death, the principal was to be distributed to his children. Jacob's two daughters were to receive a 30 percent share each, and his two sons, who were also trustees, 20 percent each. Following Jacob's death, the income to Bertha averaged $190,000 a year for a number of years. In 2001, in order to facilitate overall portfolio performance, New York enacted legislation that created an optional unitrust provision. It allows a trustee to calculate the income to be distributed according to a fixed formula and based on the net fair market value of the trust assets. In 2003, the brothers elected to use this option and apply it retroactively, reducing Bertha's annual income to $70,000. Jacob's sons then were able to make investments that, although they produced low dividend yields, would outperform the alternative in the long-term, creating an overall better return. The court ruled that when an interested trustee elects a unitrust, it is not per se inconsistent with his or her fiduciary duties, and therefore, though the brothers were beneficiaries and trustees, they could elect unitrust treatment. The courts ruled, however, that the lower courts should scrutinize the unitrust election with special care in such cases to ensure that the election is not a violation of the trustee's fiduciary duties to any of the beneficiaries.

VI. SUB-DUTIES RELATING TO CARE OF TRUST PROPERTY

A. **Introduction:** At the macro level, a trustee has a duty to care for the property as a prudent person would care for the property of another.

1. **Duty to secure possession:** Intrinsic in the trustee's job to hold and manage the trust property is the duty to secure possession of the trust property in a timely manner. With testamentary trusts, the trustee has a duty to monitor the executor's actions and ensure that the trust receives what it is entitled to with no unreasonable delays. UTC §809.

2. **Duty to care for and maintain:** Having secured possession, logically the trustee has a duty to care for and maintain the trust property. Where the trust holds real property, the trustee should treat the property as an ordinary owner would treat similarly situated property. The trustee should insure the property, keep the property in good repair, and otherwise take whatever reasonable steps an ordinary owner would take to protect and care for the property. UTC §809.

3. **Duty to earmark:** Where the trust property is personal property, in particular fungible assets (money, stocks, and so on), the trustee has a duty to separate the trust property from all other assets and to properly designate the property as trust assets to ensure that a trustee cannot "switch" trust assets and personal assets after the fact where the former outperform the latter. UTC §810.

    a. **Exception—bearer bonds:** A well-recognized exception to the duty to segregate and identify trust assets is where a trustee invests in bearer bonds.

    b. **Common law—strict liability:** At common law, if a trustee breaches the duty to segregate and identify trust assets, the trustee is strictly liable for any damage the trust property may sustain, even if the damage is not caused by the breach.

    c. **Modern trend—causation:** The modern trend is that a trustee is not liable for a breach unless the breach of the duty causes the damage to the trust property.

4. **Duty not to commingle:** At common law, there was a strict duty not to commingle the trust assets with trustee's assets because commingled assets make it more difficult to assess how the trustee is managing the property. The modern trend keeps this general principle (Uniform Trust Code §810(b) (2000)), but permits commingling with other trust funds (but not the trustee's own funds) to achieve economies of scale and to improve the efficiency of the trust administration. (*See supra* this chapter, IV.D.2, permitting pooling of funds to invest in a common trust fund and where the trust accounts are small.)

    Standard of liability: As with the duty to earmark, at common law if there was a breach of the duty not to commingle, the trustee was strictly liable; under the modern trend the trust beneficiaries must prove the breach caused the damage to the trust property.

VII. DUTY TO INFORM AND ACCOUNT

A. **Duty to disclose:** The beneficiaries are the equitable owners of the trust property. The trustee is merely holding and managing the trust assets. Accordingly, the trust beneficiaries are entitled to receive (1) enough information about the terms of the trust to be able to assess the extent of their rights and to determine if a breach of trust has occurred, and (2) complete and accurate information about the nature and extent of the trust property, including access to trust records and accounts. UTC §8113.

1. **Settlor authorizes withholding info:** Where the settlor expressly provides in the trust that the terms of the trust or information about the trust property are to be withheld from the beneficiary, the law is not clear. At a minimum, each beneficiary arguably is entitled to receive information about his or her interest in the trust (and copies of those pages of the trust), but it is open to debate whether the beneficiaries are entitled to receive a complete copy of the trust.

   a. **Uniform Trust Code:** The Uniform Trust Code provides that the default rule is that a trustee must promptly provide a copy of the trust instrument to the beneficiary if he or she requests a copy, unless the settlor provides otherwise. UTC §813(b)(1).

   b. **California—right to receive:** By statute, the state of California provides that upon the death of a settlor of a revocable trust, all beneficiaries *and heirs* of the settlor have the right to request a complete copy of the trust instrument.

2. **Duty to notify before acting:** The trustee has a duty to give advance notice to the trust beneficiaries where the trustee proposes to sell a significant portion of the trust assets unless the value of the assets are readily ascertainable or disclosure is seriously detrimental to the beneficiaries' interests.

3. **Example:** In *Fletcher v. Fletcher*, 480 S.E.2d 488 (Va. 1997), settlor created a revocable inter vivos trust that provided that upon her death, a number of subtrusts would be created, including one for her adult son James. Following the settlor's death, one of the other sons of the settlor and a corporate trustee were appointed co-trustees. James sued the co-trustees, alleging that they refused to provide him with enough information about the trust (and an alleged "new" trust created upon the settlor's death) to permit him to determine his interests and rights. The co-trustees replied that the settlor expressly indicated (orally; the claimed intent was not in the trust) that the terms and dealings were to be kept confidential, even from beneficiaries. The court ordered the trustees to provide the beneficiaries with complete copies of the trust instrument, despite the claimed settlor's intent, because such information was necessary for the beneficiaries to assess their interests and rights. The court rejected the trustees' argument that the duty to disclose extended only to the provisions of the particular beneficiary's subtrust, holding that all of the trusts were part of one, single, cohesive trust instrument.

B. **Duty to account:** A trustee has a duty to account on a regular basis for the actions he or she has taken as trustee so that his or her performance can be assessed relative to the terms and fiduciary duties created by the express terms of the trust.

1. **Testamentary trusts:** Testamentary trusts are created as part of the probate process, and supervision over the trust is generally accorded to the probate court. Trustees have a duty to account to the probate court so that the court can assess the trustee's performance. Some courts permit a provision in the trust releasing a trustee from his or her duty to account to the probate court (because doing so is burdensome and expensive) as long as the trustee accounts directly to the beneficiaries (typically the income beneficiaries). Some jurisdictions hold that such "no judicial accounting" clauses violate public policy because they fail to adequately protect the interests of the remaindermen.

2. **Inter vivos trusts:** Inter vivos trusts are not created as part of the probate process and hence are not naturally subject to probate court supervision, though judicial accounting is still possible. Because the trust was not created as part of the probate process, however, "no judicial accounting" clauses are usually held valid if the trust is an inter vivos trust. Clauses that give absolute immunity based on accountings accepted by life beneficiaries alone have not been universally accepted.

3. **Uniform Trust Code:** The Uniform Trust Code drops the reference to "accounting" and speaks of the trustee's duty to "report" instead (apparently to increase flexibility as to form and frequency of the duty to report). The Code authorizes the settlor to waive the duty to report to the beneficiaries; and the beneficiaries may likewise waive their right to a report or other information (though a beneficiary cannot *ex ante* and irrevocably waive his or her right to all reports and information). UTC §813. Waiver, however, does not relieve a trustee from liability for misconduct which a report would have disclosed.

4. **Duty to review accounting:** When a trustee makes an accounting, either to the court or directly to the beneficiaries, the beneficiaries have a duty to check the accounting and to object in a timely manner. If the beneficiaries fail to object in a timely manner, they may be barred from complaining later.

5. **Fraudulent accounting:** Where a trustee files a fraudulent accounting and the beneficiaries later discover the fraud, the beneficiaries are not barred from reopening the accounting.

6. **Constructive fraud:** Where an accounting makes factual representations that turn out to be false, if the trustee made the representations without undertaking reasonable efforts to ascertain the accuracy of the factual representations, such false factual representations in the accounting constitute a "constructive" or "technical" fraud. Such a fraud constitutes grounds for reopening an otherwise properly allowed accounting.

   a. **Investigation:** The doctrine of constructive or technical fraud does not make trustees guarantors of all factual representations in an accounting. Where such representations are made in good faith and follow reasonable efforts to ascertain the accuracy of the representations, the trustee has fulfilled his or her duty.

   b. **Factual representations:** The doctrine of constructive or technical fraud applies only to factual representations in the accounting. Statements of judgment or discretion are not factual representations.

   c. **Discoverability:** If the factual falsehood is discoverable from an inspection of all the trust accounts, the trust terms, and the law, the doctrine of constructive or technical fraud does not apply.

7. **Improper payments:** Where an accounting reveals that a trustee has improperly distributed trust property to one who is not entitled to receive such property, the trustee is liable for breach of trust unless the court approves the accounting. Where the court's approval is based upon a fraudulent accounting, reopening such accounting voids the court's approval of the accounting.

8. **Example:** In ***National Academy of Sciences v. Cambridge Trust Co.***, 346 N.E.2d 879 (Mass. 1976), the settlor created a trust for the benefit of his wife as long as she remained unmarried. Upon her death or remarriage, the trusteeship was to be transferred to the National Research Council and converted into the Troland Foundation for Research in Psychophysics. The settlor died in 1932. His wife remarried in 1945, but the trustee did not know it and continued to make

income payments to her until her death in 1967, when it was discovered that she had remarried in 1945. The remainder beneficiary sued the trustee, seeking restoration of all the improperly made payments. The trustee argued that the payments had been disclosed in its annual accounting that were filed with the probate court, provided to the remainder beneficiary, and approved by the probate court. The court held that the representation in the accountings that the settlor's wife remained unmarried was a factual representation that the trustee had never undertaken to verify, not even asking her to certify it. In light of the trustee's failure to attempt to verify the information, the court held the representations constituted a constructive or technical fraud on both the remainder beneficiary and the court. The court reopened the accountings in question and held the trustee liable for the payments made over the course of some 30 years after the settlor's wife had remarried.

Quiz Yourself on
TRUST ADMINISTRATION AND THE TRUSTEE'S DUTIES

69. Nancy sets up a testamentary trust for Ronald's benefit during his lifetime, and, upon his death, the principal is to be distributed to the presidential library. The trust appoints George trustee. George decides that some trust property needs to be sold to help support Ronald. The property is sold at public auction, but the bidding is light, so Jeb, George's brother, purchases the property to help out. Not long thereafter, the property is appraised for significantly more than the sale price. The presidential library sues, claiming breach of fiduciary duty in the sale of the property. At trial, the only expert witness testifies that the sale price was fair and reasonable. Who prevails and why? _____

70. Frank creates a testamentary trust for the benefit of Maria during her lifetime, and, upon her death, any remaining principal is to be distributed to their kids, Robert and Raymond. The trust appoints Raymond trustee. Raymond invests the trust principal in the stock market, diversifying his investment. To facilitate dealing with the stock and to save administrative costs, Raymond takes title to each stock certificate in his personal name. All of his investments go up in value, except for his investment in Ehnron. Robert sues Raymond, claiming breach of duty. Who prevails and why? _____

71. Frank creates a testamentary trust for the benefit of Maria during her lifetime, and, upon her death, any remaining principal is to be distributed to their local church. The trust appoints their sons, Robert and Raymond, as co-trustees. Raymond goes on vacation to San Francisco (to see the new baseball stadium), and on his way out of town he authorizes Robert to administer the trust while he is away. While Raymond is gone, Robert invests all of the money in Worldquom, a telecommunications company that later files for bankruptcy. The church sues Raymond, claiming breach of duty. Raymond's defense is that Robert purchased the stock. Who prevails and why? _____

72. Frank and Marie establish an irrevocable inter vivos trust that is for the benefit of their sons, Robert and Raymond, during their lifetimes, and, upon the death of the survivor, the principal is to be divided equally among their issue. Raymond is appointed trustee, and he invests all of the trust property in a minor league baseball team that makes money at first but then loses money on paper each year. But

the team is appreciating in value (outperforming the market). The trust expressly permits Raymond to invest in any investment he deems appropriate in his sole and absolute discretion, and it expressly permits him to retain any investment even if not otherwise authorized by law. Robert sues, claiming breach of duty. Who prevails and why? _____

73. SpongeBill creates a trust for the benefit of Tom and Jerry. The trust appoints Dexter as trustee. Dexter invests the trust proceeds in a variety of companies, including a start-up biotech company that is considered extremely risky. The company fails rather quickly. Tom and Jerry sue, claiming breach of duty. Who prevails, and why? _____

Answers

69. The presidential library probably will prevail on the grounds that the sale to a family member of the trustee constitutes self-dealing. A trustee owes a duty of loyalty to the trust beneficiaries. To ensure the trustee's undivided loyalty, there is a duty against self-dealing that applies not only to the trustee but, in many jurisdictions, to the trustee's family members as well. Where there is self-dealing, under the "no further inquiry" rule, the fairness and reasonableness of the sale are irrelevant. The court probably will hold the sale illegal and void and order the property transferred back to the trust.

Under the Uniform Trust Code, transactions by a trustee with a close relative are no longer absolutely forbidden but are only presumptively voidable. If George can prove that the transaction was objectively fair and reasonable, and not affected by a conflict, he would not be liable.

70. Robert's strongest argument is to claim failure to earmark the trust property. The trustee has a duty to separate trust property from his or her own property and to clearly indicate which property is the trust property. At common law, if the trustee breaches the duty and the trust property declines in value, the trustee is strictly liable for any loss in the trust property regardless of whether the trustee's breach of duty causes the loss. Under the modern trend, the trustee is not liable for any loss not caused by the failure to earmark. Robert probably would prevail under the common law approach, but he would have a much tougher time and probably would not prevail under the modern trend.

71. At common law, a trustee can delegate ministerial duties but not discretionary duties (such as how to invest the trust property). This duty against delegation includes delegation to co-trustees. Under the modern trend, the trustee may have a duty to delegate investment decisions but only to investment experts (no evidence suggests that Robert qualifies as an investment expert). Raymond arguably is liable under both the common law and the modern trend, though under the modern trend/Uniform Trust Code, he may be entitled to indemnity from Robert because Robert is substantially more at fault.

72. Whether there has been a breach of the duty of impartiality turns on the approach the jurisdiction takes. The general rule is that a trustee has a duty of impartiality that requires the trust to produce a reasonable income while preserving the principal for the remaindermen. The duty is implied even where the trust expressly authorizes the trustee to retain certain property. Here, the trust is no longer producing any income. Continuing to hold on to the investment in the baseball team constitutes an abuse of the duty of impartiality. Following the sale of the investment, a portion of the sale proceeds should be allocated to income and distributed to the income beneficiaries to make up for the delay in selling the investment.

Under the modern trend portfolio approach, the focus is on the annual total return regardless of the form of the return. The trustee is authorized to reallocate receipts to ensure that the income and remaindermen beneficiaries are treated fairly. Under this approach, if Raymond reallocates some of the capital appreciation each year to income and distributes it, there may be no breach of the duty of impartiality.

In addition, if the trust is a unitrust, with the income beneficiaries entitled to a fixed share of the trust principal each year, as long as Raymond distributes to the income beneficiaries their annual share of the trust principal each year, there is no breach of the duty of impartiality.

73. Whether there has been a breach of the trustee's duty with respect to investing the trust assets depends on the approach taken by the jurisdiction. At early common law, trustees were limited in their investment options by a statutory list that expressly listed those investments considered safe and appropriate. Any investment in a company or investment vehicle not listed in the statutory list was considered improper unless expressly authorized by the trust instrument. Under the facts, it is unlikely a start-up company would be on the statutory list, and no express provision appears to authorize the investment in question. If the jurisdiction follows something akin to a statutory list, the court likely will hold that the investment constitutes a breach of the trustee's duty concerning trust investments.

If the jurisdiction has adopted the Uniform Prudent Man Investment Act, the trustee is not limited to those investments listed in a statutory list but rather is authorized to make any prudent investment that is not speculative. A strong argument can be made that an investment in a start-up biotech company is too speculative to be appropriate for a trust investment. If the jurisdiction follows the Uniform Prudent Man Investment approach, the court likely will hold that the investment constitutes a breach of the trustee's duty concerning trust investments.

If the jurisdiction has adopted the Uniform Prudent Investor Act, with its portfolio approach, it is unclear whether the investment in the biotech company is appropriate without knowing more information about the other investments Dexter made. Under the portfolio approach, the total return on the trust investments is the key. High-risk investments, even investments that arguably are speculative, are authorized as long as they constitute a compensated risk and there are offsetting safe investments to balance the overall investment risk of the portfolio.

Exam Tips on
TRUST ADMINISTRATION AND THE TRUSTEE'S DUTIES

Trustee's powers

☛ This material is fairly straightforward. If tested, the issue typically is whether a trustee has the power to do something that appears implicit in light of the express powers and the trust purpose. If there is doubt, a trustee can get court approval for the contemplated act.

☛ Remember, under the modern trend the trustee is automatically granted all the powers a prudent person would need to manage the trust in light of its purpose.

Duty of loyalty

☛ Under the broad duty of loyalty, watch for fact patterns where the trustee or someone associated with the trustee benefits from dealing with the trust. Distinguish between whether it is the trustee or a family member benefiting, in which case the duty against self-dealing probably applies, or whether it is someone else associated with the trustee, in which case the duty against conflicts of interest probably applies (if the trustee might benefit indirectly from the transaction, that is usually a conflict of interest situation).

☞ Under self-dealing, apply the "no further inquiry" rule unless the trust authorizes the self-dealing or the beneficiaries authorize the self-dealing after full disclosure surrounding the transaction. Even then, the trustee is under a duty to act reasonably and in good faith in engaging in the transaction. Remember, the modern trend/UTC modifies the "no further inquiry" rule.

☛ If the transaction involves an alleged conflict of interest, apply only the "reasonably and in good faith" standard.

☞ The beneficiaries may be entitled to appreciation damages if the breach involves some misfeasance other than simply selling the trust property for too low a price.

☛ If the trust has more than one trustee, watch for the issue of co-trustee liability (note the common law vs. UTC split on issue).

Duty of prudence—trust investments

☛ A trustee's powers and duties concerning trust investments are the "hot" area of trust administration (and thus of testing too).

☛ The historical context is important. The law has moved from the common law statutory lists, to the prudent investor standard (duty not to speculate), to the modern trend portfolio theory. Implicit in the historical evolution has been the shift from each investment decision to the overall return on the trust portfolio. Diversification has become increasingly important, as has the trustee's duty to create a paper trail supporting the reasonableness of his or her actions.

☛ One constant is that under all approaches, exculpatory clauses are construed strictly and are not given effect where they appear to protect trustees who act with reckless indifference to the beneficiaries' interest or in bad faith.

Duty not to delegate

☛ The duty not to delegate can be tested two ways. First, if someone other than a trustee performs a function related to the trust property, the issue is whether it is appropriate for that person to perform the function.

☞ At common law, the rule is fairly easy to state and apply; discretionary duties cannot be delegated, while ministerial duties can. While there is some gray area as to what constitutes discretionary vs. ministerial, if the function goes to the heart of the trust or constitutes a critical function concerning the trust property, the function is discretionary and cannot be delegated.

☞ Under the modern trend, the issue is complicated because not only is the trustee permitted to delegate certain investment-making decisions, the trustee may have a duty to delegate the power. But the trustee still must exercise care in selecting the agent and must properly supervise the agent.

☛ The second and subtler way to test the duty not to delegate is where one trustee implicitly or expressly delegates functions to other trustees. The rule is the same for co-trustees—they can delegate ministerial duties to co-trustees, but not discretionary duties.

Impartiality—allocating principal and income

☛ Duty of impartiality issues are easy to spot and analyze. Either the trust principal is appreciating but it is not generating a reasonable stream of income, or the trust is producing a healthy stream of income but the principal is depreciating. In either scenario, the trustee is favoring one class of beneficiaries over the other.

☞ The duty is breached even if the trust expressly permits the trustee to retain the assets in question.

☞ The hard part is to articulate the remedy, particularly where the breach has been on-going for a period of time. Whether a generic statement of reallocating assets suffices or whether you need to know the details of how to reallocate the assets depends upon your professor's coverage of this material.

☞ Under the modern trend and the Uniform Prudent Investor Act, the traditional duty of impartiality is modified to reflect the focus on total return as opposed to principal versus income. The trustee is empowered to reallocate receipts to ensure the beneficiaries are being treated fairly.

☞ The issue is moot under the unitrust, where the income beneficiary is entitled to a fixed percentage of the trust principal each year.

Subduties relating to care of trust property

☛ If the trust property sustains a loss that is not the direct result of a questionable transaction that the trustee entered into, that usually raises the issue of whether the trustee has exercised proper care over the trust property. At common law these duties are strict liability duties. The modern trend requires causation. This split is tested often.

Duty to inform and account

☛ The duty to inform is straightforward. If tested, the wrinkle to watch for is where the trustee claims the settlor authorized withholding information.

☛ The constructive fraud doctrine is an important doctrine to keep in mind when analyzing accounting issues.

CHAPTER 11

CHARITABLE TRUSTS

ChapterScope

This chapter examines the requirements for, and benefits of, charitable trusts. In particular, the chapter examines:

- **Charitable purpose:** A trust is a charitable trust if it has a charitable purpose. A purpose is charitable if it is for (a) the relief of poverty, (b) the advancement of education, (c) the advancement of religion, (d) the promotion of health, (e) governmental or municipal purposes, or (f) any other purposes the accomplishment of which is beneficial to the community at large. Benevolent trusts (trusts that perform kind acts) are not charitable trusts unless they accomplish one of the specific charitable purposes.

- **Benefits:** There are two principal advantages, from a trust law perspective, of classifying a trust as a charitable trust:

  - **Rule against Perpetuities:** Because charitable trusts serve charitable purposes that benefit the community at large, they are not subject to the Rule against Perpetuities.

  - **Ascertainable beneficiaries:** Because charitable trusts have to serve the community at large, or at least a good segment of the community at large, there is no requirement that the trust have ascertainable beneficiaries.

- **Cy pres:** Where a trust with a general charitable purpose expresses a particular charitable purpose and it becomes impossible, impractical, or illegal to carry out that particular charitable purpose, rather than imposing a resulting trust, modify the trust purpose to another particular charitable purpose within the general charitable purpose.

  - **Administrative deviation:** If accomplishing the trust purpose has become impossible or impractical for administrative reasons, apply administrative deviation and modify the administrative provisions to remove the obstacle before modifying the settlor's intent with cy pres.

- **Charitable trust supervision:** The attorney general of each state has the duty of supervising the administration of each charitable trust. This is an extreme burden, so many courts have granted standing to members of the community who have a "special interest" in the trust to bring suit against the charitable trustee for breach of trust.

I. CHARITABLE PURPOSE

A. **Rule statement:** The distinguishing characteristic and key requirement of a charitable trust is that the trust must be for a charitable purpose.

B. **Charitable purposes:** What constitutes a charitable purpose is not a completely fact-sensitive inquiry. The courts have typically limited the concept to one of six delineated purposes. The trust purpose must be (1) to relieve poverty; (2) to advance education; (3) to advance religion; (4) to promote health; (5) for governmental or municipal purposes; or (6) for other purposes that, if accomplished, would benefit the community. UTC §405. (The courts tend to construe this last charitable purpose very narrowly, often requiring an overlap with at least one of the other five charitable purposes.)

1. **Benevolent trusts:** Benevolent trusts are trusts that perform kind acts or do "good things." As a general rule, trusts for "benevolent" or "philanthropic" purposes are not charitable trusts unless the trust references particular types of kind acts that qualify as one of the recognized charitable purposes.

2. **Example:** In *Shenandoah Valley National Bank v. Taylor*, 63 S.E.2d 786 (Va. 1951), settlor's trust provided that the income was to be distributed on the last day of school preceding Easter and Christmas break to the children in the first, second, and third grades at a local elementary school, to be used by the children to further their education. The timing of the payments indicated that the true purpose of the trust was to be a benevolent trust, not a charitable trust. There were no enforceable restrictions on how the children used the money, and, in light of the timing of the payments, the children were unlikely to use it on education. Where a trust conveys mere financial enrichment, the trust qualifies as a charitable trust only if, from a totality of the circumstances, it becomes apparent that the intended beneficiaries are poor or in necessitous conditions. No evidence suggested that these children were poor. As a benevolent trust, the trust failed because it violated the Rule against Perpetuities.

3. **Delegation of charitable purpose:** The settlor may delegate selection of the charitable purpose to the trustee. If *S* transfers property to *T* to use for "whatever charitable purpose(s) *T* selects" a valid charitable trust has been established.

4. **Modern trend:** Traditionally, trusts for "benevolent" or "philanthropic" purposes were deemed to authorize noncharitable purposes and as such typically were invalid. Increasingly the modern trend is to favor constructions that validate trusts as charitable. Increasingly trusts for "benevolent" or "charitable" purposes qualify as charitable trusts. Even where the trust does not qualify as a charitable trust, under the modern trend approach to the Rule against Perpetuities typically such a finding will not automatically invalidate the trust.

C. **Beneficiaries:** While private trusts require that there be ascertainable beneficiaries, a charitable trust, by its nature, must be for the community at large, or at least a significant subset of the community at large. In assessing who benefits from a charitable trust, it is important to distinguish between direct beneficiaries and indirect beneficiaries.

1. **Direct vs. indirect beneficiaries:** A charitable trust can benefit a single or limited number of individuals, as long as a larger pool of the community has a chance to be that individual, or as long as that individual is being supported in an activity that constitutes a charitable service that benefits the larger community.

   Examples: A trust to educate a specific individual is generally not a charitable trust, but where the trust is to put a specific individual through medical school on condition that the individual return to the rural community that is supporting the trust to provide medical care to the community, the trust does constitute a charitable trust. Trusts to educate a group or class of individuals, such as the valedictorians of a particular school, are generally upheld as charitable trusts.

2. **Governmental:** Trusts to improve governmental functions or the structure of the government are charitable trusts, but trusts for the benefit of a political party are not.

3. **Mortmain statutes:** Common law was concerned that deathbed devises to charitable organizations might have been prompted by overreaching men of the cloth—throwing the fear of eternal damnation into the dying unless he or she "bought" his or her way into heaven by making a charitable donation. Most states had "mortmain statutes" that permitted surviving spouses and/or children to void such deathbed charitable donations. Such statutes have been repealed in virtually every jurisdiction.

4. **Failed charitable trust:** Because charitable trusts do not have ascertainable beneficiaries, if a trust fails as a charitable trust it often will fail as a private trust because it will not have ascertainable beneficiaries. An exception to this is if the trust can qualify as an honorary trust. (*See* Chapter 8.II.F.4 for a more detailed discussion of honorary trusts.)

D. **Rule against Perpetuities:** One of the principal benefits of a charitable trust is that it is not subject to the Rule against Perpetuities.

1. **Modern trend:** With most jurisdictions now following the wait-and-see approach to or abolishing the Rule against Perpetuities, this benefit is not as great as it used to be. Because only a handful of jurisdictions have completely abolished the rule, classifying a trust as a charitable trust is still significant because it affects how long the trust can last. Even if the trust fails to qualify as a charitable trust, under the modern trend it should be permitted to continue for a significant period of time.

2. **UPC:** The UPC expressly provides that a trust that fails for want of a charitable purpose may continue for up to 21 years if the trustee is willing to honor the purpose and the purpose is lawful. UPC §2-907(a).

E. **Trustees:** The general rule for private trusts is that they are authorized to act only if all of the trustees consent to the proposed action. (The modern trend is to permit the trust to act upon a vote of the majority of the trustees.) Unlike private trusts, charitable trusts have always been permitted to act based upon a vote of a majority of the trustees.

II. CY PRES

A. **Overview:** Because charitable trusts are not subject to the Rule against Perpetuities, they can last forever. But it is possible that the specific charitable purpose for which they were created may become impossible or impractical (for example, a charitable trust for the cure of a particular illness, and with time, a cure is found). If a trust purpose becomes impossible or impractical, the general trust rule is the trust fails, and a resulting trust is imposed to give the trust property back to the settlor (absent an express clause saying what is to happen if the trust fails). With respect to charitable trusts, however, the courts developed the doctrine of cy pres instead of immediately applying a resulting trust.

B. **Cy pres rule statement:** Where a trust with a general charitable purpose expresses a specific charitable purpose, and it becomes impossible, impractical, or illegal to carry out that specific charitable purpose, rather than imposing a resulting trust, the trust purpose is modified to serve another specific charitable purpose within the settlor's general charitable purpose.

1. **Rationale:** The cy pres doctrine can be justified on the grounds that it is nothing more than modifying the terms of a trust to *promote* the settlor's general charitable purpose. That also helps explain the approach many courts take that the "new" specific purpose should be as close as possible to the settlor's original charitable purpose. Not all courts, however, apply that approach in practice.

2. **Example:** In *In re Neher*, 18 N.E.2d 625 (N.Y. 1939), testatrix's will devised her house to the local town as a memorial to her husband, with the direction that the property be used for a hospital. Six years later, the town petitioned the court to modify the gift because the town lacked the resources to build and run a hospital and a new hospital had been built in a neighboring community. The court held that the testatrix had a general charitable purpose to help the community and that her specific charitable purpose was to have the land used for a hospital. Because that use had become impractical, the court applied cy pres and modified the gift to permit it to be used for another specific charitable community purpose—to erect and maintain an administrative building for the city, the Herbert Neher Memorial Hall.

3. **Philanthropic inefficiency:** A lively academic debate has arisen over whether "inefficient" use of charitable trust resources to support the original trust purpose is grounds to apply cy pres to put the trust resources to more productive use. Implicit in this issue is the question of who really owns the property in a charitable trust—the community or settlor's intent as expressed in the trust. The perpetual nature of charitable trusts contributes to this issue, with the original intent inflexibly set forth despite a possible change in circumstances years after the trust is created.

   a. **Example:** Testatrix devised the residue of her estate (stock worth $9 million) in trust to support the relief of poverty and other charitable purposes in Marin County (one of the richest counties in the country). Within a decade, the stock was worth over $300 million. The trustee, a community trust foundation administering trusts throughout the San Francisco Bay area, petitioned the court to apply cy pres, claiming that the unforeseen change in value of the trust res, coupled with the limited area where the trust funds could be used, constituted inefficient use of the trust income. The court ruled that concepts of inefficiency and ineffectiveness are not relevant to whether a settlor's charitable purpose has become "impractical."

   b. **Modern statutory approaches facilitate application:** Both the Uniform Trust Code and the Restatement (Third) of Trusts (1) presume a general charitable purpose, thereby lessening the burden of proof on those seeking application of cy pres (shifting the burden to those who oppose it to prove that the settlor did *not* have a general charitable purpose); and (2) authorize a court to apply cy pres if the particular charitable purpose becomes unlawful, impractical, impossible, or *wasteful.* UTC §413(a); Restatement (Third) of Trusts §67. The official reporter for the UTC has written that wasteful expenditure of trust resources is where the trust funds available for use so exceed what is necessary for the particular charitable purpose that continued use of all the funds for that purpose only would be wasteful. In such cases he advocates permitting a court to "broaden" the purposes of the trust to permit more efficient uses of the trust funds (typically by broadening *who* can receive the benefits, as opposed to broadening the trust's purposes).

4. **Gift-over clause:** Many charitable trusts contain an express gift-over clause—a clause expressly stating how the property should be used if the specific charitable purpose becomes impossible or impractical. The courts are split over the effect of a gift-over clause. Some hold

it controls and the application of cy pres is inappropriate. Increasingly, however, statutes and courts hold a gift-over clause is simply a factor for the court to consider in determining whether the settlor had a general charitable intent that permits cy pres. UTC §41; Restatement (Third) of Trusts §67.

5. **Administrative deviation:** Where the administrative provisions of a trust cause the purpose to become illegal, impossible, or impractical, the doctrine of administrative deviation provides that the administrative provisions of the trust should be modified before modifying the trust purpose, thereby preserving settlor's intent. The Uniform Trust Code authorizes a court to change the administrative *or dispositive* terms of a trust if necessary in light of changed circumstances not anticipated by the settlor.

6. **Discriminatory trusts:** Many older charitable trusts limited who qualified as an eligible beneficiary based on either gender or race (or both). There has been much litigation over whether such restrictions constitute illegal discrimination. Some courts have applied cy pres to modify the terms of the trust to eliminate the racial or gender restriction; some courts have applied administrative deviation to eliminate the state action involved in the trust administration while permitting the discrimination; and some courts have terminated the trust rather than apply cy pres.

III. ENFORCING THE TERMS OF A CHARITABLE TRUST

A. **Overview:** Private trusts require ascertainable beneficiaries, in part, so that the court knows who has standing to enforce the trust's terms and to whom the trustee owes the fiduciary duty. Charitable trusts, on the other hand, as a general rule cannot have ascertainable beneficiaries because they are for the benefit of the community at large (or at least a large subset of the community). The issue that naturally arises is who has standing to enforce the terms of a charitable trust and the trustee's fiduciary duty.

B. **State attorney general:** The general rule is that the state's attorney general represents the interests of the community and has exclusive standing to enforce the terms of the trust and the fiduciary duty against the charitable trustee.

C. **Individuals with special interest:** Depending upon the trust, some members of a community may receive more direct benefits from a charitable trust than do other members of the community. Some courts have seized upon this point to expand the scope of who has standing to enforce the terms of a charitable trust to recognize that members of the community who have a "special interest" in the trust also have standing to sue to enforce the terms of the trust and the trustee's fiduciary duty. The plaintiff must show that he or she has a special interest in the trust—that he or she is eligible for a benefit that other members of the community are not.

Modern trend: Recognizing that state attorney general offices are overwhelmed with other responsibilities, courts are increasingly defining what constitutes a special interest more broadly, thereby facilitating private parties being able to bring suits against trustees of charitable trusts.

D. **Settlors/donors:** The traditional common law rule is that settlors do not have standing to enforce the terms of their trusts, private or charitable, absent a retained special interest in the property. The modern trend, however, is statutorily to extend standing to donors.

1. **Example:** In *Carl J. Herzog Foundation, Inc. v. University of Bridgeport*, 699 A.2d 995 (Conn. 1997), the Herzog Foundation made a gift to Bridgeport University for need-based merit scholarships to aid disadvantaged students for medical-related education. Thereafter, the foundation sued, claiming that the funds had been commingled with the university's general funds and were not being used for the specified purpose. The university countered that the foundation lacked standing. The general common law rule is that a donor has no standing to enforce the terms of a completed charitable gift unless the donor has expressly reserved a property interest in the gift. Connecticut had adopted the Uniform Management of Institutional Funds Act to give colleges and universities a mechanism for freeing themselves from dated restrictions attached to gifts. One way is by written consent of the donor. The court ruled that the statutory provision giving the donor the power to release the restriction did not give the donor an interest for purposes of suing to enforce a restriction.

2. **Example:** In *Smithers v. St. Luke's-Roosevelt Hospital Center*, 723 N.Y.S.2d 426 (Sup. Ct., App. Div. 2001), Mr. Smithers, a recovered alcoholic, announced in 1971 he was making a gift of $10 million (the "Gift") to the St. Luke's-Roosevelt Hospital Center (the "Hospital") to establish the Smithers Alcoholism Treatment and Training Center (the "Center") in a structure *separate from the Hospital* to provide rehabilitation in a therapeutic community *removed* from the Hospital. The first $1 million was used to purchase a building (the "Building") to house the Center. Over time, the relationship between Mr. Smithers and the Hospital grew strained. Mr. Smithers even declared at one point that because the Hospital was not living up to the agreement, no more funding would be provided. The Hospital assured Mr. Smithers in writing that it would strictly adhere to the conditions of the Gift to entice him to complete the Gift, which Mr. Smithers did. In 1995, just a year after Mr. Smithers' death, the Hospital announced it was selling the Building and moving the Center into the Hospital. Mrs. Smithers objected. She discovered that for years the Hospital had been making interest free "loans" from the Center's endowment to the Hospital. The attorney general sued and the funds were returned to the Center's endowment, but without restoring the lost income. In addition, the attorney general and the Hospital agreed that the terms of the Gift did not preclude the Hospital from selling the Building and moving the Center into the Hospital, and that only $1 million of the sale proceeds had to be used for the Center. Mrs. Smithers, as special administratrix of Mr. Smither's estate, sued to enforce the terms of the Gift. The Hospital moved to dismiss on the grounds she lacked standing—a position which the attorney general supported. (While the suit was pending, the attorney general and the Hospital reached a new agreement requiring the Hospital to restore the income lost during the loans, and to restrict all of the sale proceeds to use by the Center.) The court noted that the general rule is that standing to enforce the terms of a charitable trust is not limited to the attorney general. The court reasoned that a donor is in a better position than the attorney general to be vigilant to ensure that the terms of a charitable gift are being followed. Under the common law of New York, donors have standing to enforce the terms of their gifts and the attorney general has standing to enforce such gifts on behalf of the beneficiaries. As special administratrix of his estate, the court ruled Mrs. Smithers had co-existent standing with the attorney general.

3. **Statutory developments:** The Uniform Trust Code rejects the old common law rule and gives settlors standing to enforce the terms of their charitable gifts even in the absence of an express retention of an interest. UTC §405(c). It is unclear, however, whether this right is a personal right that dies with the donor. The Uniform Management of Institutional Funds Act does not grant donors standing.

Quiz Yourself on CHARITABLE TRUSTS

74. Sammy sets up a trust, the pertinent provisions of which state that the trust is to promote education and that the income from the trust is to be distributed in equal shares to the sixth graders at Mother Theresa's Elementary school (an inner city school located in the poorest part of the city) the day before the end of each semester. Sammy's heirs sue, claiming that the kids use the money to purchase candy and that the trust violates the Rule against Perpetuities. Does the trust qualify as a charitable trust? _____

75. Ali sets up a trust, the pertinent provisions of which provide that the income is to go to the law school Ali attended to pay the salary of "a wills and trust professor who knows what he or she is doing." Ali's heirs sue, claiming that the trust violates the Rule against Perpetuities. Does the trust qualify as a charitable trust? _____

76. Elizabeth funds a trust with the royalties from her movies and perfume. The trust provides in pertinent part that the income is to be used to support research to help find a cure for AIDS. Not long after Elizabeth's death, a leading biotech company finds a cure for AIDS. The takers under Elizabeth's residuary clause sue, asking the court to order a resulting trust that gives the trust principal to them. Are the residuary takers under her will entitled to the property? _____

Answers

74. The trust fails as a charitable trust that advances education, but it qualifies as a charitable trust that relieves poverty. Where a trust conveys mere financial enrichment upon its beneficiaries, to qualify as a charitable trust the court must find, from a totality of the circumstances, that the intended beneficiaries were poor or in necessitous circumstances. Here, Mother Theresa's Elementary school is located in the poorest part of the city. The court should find that the trust has a charitable purpose—the relief of poverty.

75. The trust has a charitable purpose, the advancement of education, but it appears to benefit only one person—the professor whose salary the income will pay. But by helping the law school to hire a qualified wills and trusts professor, the law students will benefit, and by benefiting the law students, the community at large arguably will benefit by being served by better trained lawyers. The indirect beneficiaries are the law students and the community at large. The trust qualifies as a charitable trust.

76. The court could impose a resulting trust and order the property distributed to the residuary takers, but the more likely result is that the court will apply cy pres. Elizabeth had a general charitable purpose (the promotion of health by curing communicative diseases), and although the particular charitable purpose (finding a cure for AIDS) is now impossible because it has been achieved, there are other communicative diseases that need curing. The court will probably apply cy pres and modify the terms of the trust to permit the income to be used to help find the cure of another communicative disease.

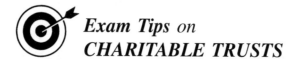

Exam Tips on
CHARITABLE TRUSTS

Charitable trusts: charitable purpose

☛ Whether a trust qualifies as a charitable trust is basically a two-step process. First, the purpose of the trust must be charitable. Just because a trust does "good things" (a benevolent trust), that does not necessarily qualify it as a charitable trust. State and then apply the qualifying charitable purposes.

☛ Second, a charitable trust arguably should not have ascertainable beneficiaries because it is for the benefit of the community at large. Trusts that appear to have a charitable purpose but that benefit a single individual or narrow group of individuals arguably do not qualify as charitable trusts.

  ☞ In assessing whether the trust is for the benefit of the community at large, distinguish between direct and indirect beneficiaries.

Cy pres

☛ If it becomes impossible or impractical to achieve the purpose of a charitable trust, apply the cy pres doctrine before applying the resulting trust doctrine.

☛ Cy pres is a two-step process. First, based on the original specific purpose of the trust, identify its more general charitable purpose (typically one of the five specific charitable purposes). Second, pick another specific charitable purpose within its general charitable purpose that is closely related to the trust's original specific purpose.

  ☞ As a practical matter, many courts appear more likely to apply cy pres the longer a charitable trust has been operating. Some courts apply the doctrine even where the trust has an express gift-over clause in the event the specific charitable purpose becomes impossible or impractical, though that is of questionable practice.

☛ Before applying cy pres, check analytically to see if administration deviation applies.

  ☞ The issue of ineffective philanthropy raises fascinating theoretical issues, but doctrinally the courts have declined to hold it constitutes grounds to apply cy pres.

Standing to enforce terms of charitable trusts

☛ If standing is to be an issue, typically the question will be whether the plaintiff has a "special interest" in the trust. Define what constitutes a special interest and note that the modern trend has been to broaden the definition of what constitutes a special interest, thereby broadening the class of individuals who have standing to enforce the terms of a charitable trust. The UTC gives the settlor standing.

CHAPTER 12

POWERS OF APPOINTMENT: DISCRETIONARY FLEXIBILITY

ChapterScope ────────────────────────────

This chapter examines an important tool that estate planners commonly use to add flexibility to the administration of a trust—giving a power of appointment to a trust beneficiary. In particular, the chapter examines:

- **Power of appointment:** A power of appointment is similar to a power to revoke in the hands of a beneficiary other than the settlor. A power of appointment gives the donee the power to override the distributive terms of the trust and to direct the trustee to distribute some or all of the trust property outright to the appointees.

  - **General power:** A general power of appointment permits the donee to exercise the power (that is, to appoint the property) in favor of the donee, the donee's estate, the donee's creditors, or creditors of the donee's estate.

  - **Special power:** A special power of appointment is one that cannot be exercised in favor of the donee, the donee's estate, the donee's creditors, or creditors of the donee's estate.

  - **Inter vivos vs. testamentary:** In creating the power, the donor can also specify *when* the power may be exercised—only inter vivos, only upon the donee's death (testamentary), or either.

- **Creditors' rights:** Creditors of a donee do not have much right to reach the property subject to the donee's power.

  - **Special power:** Creditors cannot reach the property subject to the power.

  - **General power:** Creditors cannot reach the property subject to the power unless the donee exercises the power. If the donee exercises the power, the creditors can reach the property that was appointed. (In a few states, creditors of a donee holding a general power of appointment can reach the property subject to the power.)

- **Intent to create:** If one party intends to give another party a discretionary power to appoint property, the first party has created a power of appointment. No technical words are necessary to create a power.

- **Exercise:** A power of appointment is exercised anytime the donee intends to exercise the power. The instrument creating the power may stipulate how express the donee must be. The majority rule is that a basic residuary clause does not exercise a general or special testamentary power of appointment, though the jurisdictions are split on the issue.

  - **Allocation:** Where the holder of a special power creates an instrument that purports to (1) blend the appointive property with his or her own property, and then (2) dispose of all the property, the allocation doctrine "unblends" the property to ensure that only eligible appointees take the appointive property.

- **Capture:** Where the holder of a general power creates an instrument that purports to (1) blend the appointive property with his or her own property, and then (2) dispose of all the property, and (3) one or more of the gifts fail, the donee is deemed to have appointed the failed gift to him- or herself (or estate), and the appointive property will be distributed accordingly.

- **Release:** A donee may release the power in whole or in part (either in whose favor the property may be appointed or when the power may be exercised).

- **Failure to exercise:** If a donee fails to exercise the power of appointment, the appointive property is distributed pursuant to the donor's instructions in the event the power was not exercised. Where the donor has not made express provision for such an event, the property is returned to the donor (or the donor's estate), unless the power was a special power of appointment to an ascertainable limited group, in which case the property may be distributed equally among the possible appointees.

I. INTRODUCTION

A. **Conceptual overview:** In the context of a trust, the party who holds a power of appointment has the ability to direct a trustee to distribute some or all of the trust property regardless of the distributive provisions of the trust. While a power of appointment may be given to anyone in the world, if a power to appoint property held in trust is created, the power is usually given to one of the trust beneficiaries.

   1. **Observation:** A power to revoke is a form of a power. It gives the settlor the right to direct the trustee to distribute some or all of the trust property regardless of the distributive provisions of the trust—to direct the trustee to give some or all of the trust res back to the settlor. A power of appointment is similar, except that it is held by someone other than the settlor (typically a trust beneficiary), and the power can be structured so as to limit to whom the property can be distributed (that is, in whose favor the power can be exercised) and when the power can be exercised (inter vivos or testamentary).

   2. **Discretionary:** Like a power to revoke, a power to appoint is purely discretionary. The holder owes no fiduciary duty to anyone. It is the discretionary nature of the power of appointment that helps distinguish it from other legal relationships.

   3. **Purpose:** Powers of appointment add flexibility to an estate plan. When a settlor creates a trust and decides who should take what and when, the settlor is making assumptions about the future. Often the future does not go as one assumes. While the settlor is alive and retains the power to revoke, the settlor can revoke and/or amend the trust to change the trust to reflect the changed circumstances. But after the settlor dies or after the trust becomes irrevocable, this opportunity is lost. By giving a beneficiary a power of appointment, the settlor gives the beneficiary the power to override the terms of the trust if change warrants it or if the holder deems it appropriate.

      Example: Sally creates a trust for her benefit for life, and upon her death, the principal is to be distributed equally among her children. If one of the children were in a bad accident and paralyzed for life, Sally may want to alter her distributive scheme to use more of the property to help that child. If Sally were alive and the trust were revocable, she could revoke the trust, in whole or in part, to make sure she had enough money to provide for the child. If Sally were dead, however, her distributive scheme would be set in stone unless she had granted someone a power of appointment. If she had, the party could exercise the power to override the trust's distributive scheme to ensure that the disabled child had enough resources.

B. Terminology:

There is special terminology that accompanies a power of appointment.

- **Donor:** The party who creates the power of appointment.

- **Donee:** The party who holds and has the right to exercise the power of appointment.

- **Appointive property:** The property that is subject to a power of appointment; the property that the donee may appoint.

- **Objects:** The class of individuals to whom the property may be appointed; the group of eligible appointees in whose favor the power may be exercised.

- **Appointee(s):** The individual(s) to whom the property is actually appointed; the individual(s) in whose favor the power is actually exercised.

- **Takers in default:** The individuals who are identified in the instrument creating the power who are to take the property if the donee fails to exercise the power.

C. Types of powers: There are two key variables with respect to each power of appointment that control the scope of the power. Special attention should be paid to (1) in whose favor the power can be exercised—whether the power is general or special, and (2) when it can be exercised—inter vivos, testamentary, or either.

1. **General power:** A general power of appointment is one that may be exercised in favor of the donee, the donee's estate, creditors of the donee, or creditors of the donee's estate.

   Comment: One way to think about a general power of appointment is that it may be exercised in favor of anyone in the world. Because the donee can appoint the property to him- or herself, the donee can turn around and gift the property to anyone in the world.

2. **Special power:** A special power of appointment is one that the donee can exercise in favor of anyone except the donee, the donee's estate, creditors of the donee, or creditors of the donee's estate.

   Comment: While the definition of a special power of appointment makes the class of objects sound large, as a practical matter, the instrument creating the power typically will identify a rather small class of objects—one that *must* exclude the donee, the donee's estate, creditors of the donee, and creditors of the donee's estate. (But be careful of generalizations. Depending on the facts, a special power can be broader than a general power.)

3. **Inter vivos power:** An inter vivos power of appointment is one that must be exercised, if at all, by a writing or deed executed by the donee inter vivos.

4. **Testamentary power:** A testamentary power of appointment is one that must be exercised, if at all, by the donee at death, typically in his or her will.

D. Creditors' rights: The general rule is that a creditor may reach a debtor's property, if necessary, to satisfy a debt. A power of appointment is generally considered a personal right and not a property interest. Creditors cannot reach the power. Creditors of a donee may, however, be able to reach the appointive property if the power is exercised.

1. **Special power:** A donee of a special power of appointment has no right to appoint the property to him- or herself or to use it for his or her benefit. The donee is merely an agent for the donor, with the power to appoint the property for the benefit of others. Under the traditional *relation-back* doctrine with respect to powers of appointment, the appointee is deemed to have received the property directly from the donor, not the donee. Creditors of a donee of a special power of appointment have no right to reach the appointive property, either before it is appointed or after it has been appointed.

2. **General power:** The traditional common law view of a general power of appointment is that it is not a property interest; it is merely an offer to the donee to have some power over the donor's property. The donor is still considered the owner of the property until the power is exercised. Under the traditional view of a general power of appointment, the donor has offered a gift to the donee, but there is no acceptance until the general power is exercised.

   a. **Failure to exercise:** The appointive property is considered the donor's property until the power is exercised. Under the traditional view, if the donee does not exercise the power, creditors of the donee cannot reach the property subject to the power of appointment.

   b. **Exercised:** If the donee exercises the general power of appointment, the courts treat the exercise as if the property momentarily passes through the donee's hands, and, during that instant, the creditors of the donee's interest attach to the appointive property. If the donee exercises the power in favor of anyone, even if not him- or herself, creditors of the donee can reach the appointed property.

      Modern statutory trend: By some states' statutes (and the Restatement (Third) of Property, Donative Transfers, and the Uniform Trust Code §505(b)(1)), creditors of a donee of a general *inter vivos* power of appointment can reach the appointive property even absent an exercise of the power by the donee. The rationale is that holding a general power of appointment is tantamount to ownership over the assets, thereby subjecting them to creditors' claims. Such statutes often require the creditors to exhaust the donee's other property first. Most of these statutes also permit the creditors of a donee a general *testamentary* power of appointment to reach the appointive property even absent an appointment, but only upon the donee's death (the Uniform Trust Code is silent on this issue).

   c. **Elective share claims:** Under the traditional approach to the elective share and general powers of appointment, the appointive property is not subject to the elective share doctrine. The Uniform Probate Code's augmented estate, however, expressly includes property over which the decedent held a general power of appointment—the surviving spouse is entitled to claim a portion of the appointive property under the elective share. UPC §2-205(1)(i).

3. **Example:** In *Irwin Union Bank & Trust Co. v. Long*, 312 N.E.2d 908 (Ind. App. 1974), as a result of a divorce judgment, Phillip Long owed Victoria Long $15,000. Victoria sued the trustee of a trust in which Phillip Long had an interest in an attempt to satisfy her judgment. The trust granted Phillip the right to withdraw up to 4 percent of the principal per year. The court ruled that the right to withdraw was a general power of appointment over 4 percent of the trust res per year. The court applied the traditional view that a donee of a general power of

appointment has no property interest in the appointive property unless and until the power is exercised. Because Phillip did not exercise the power, Victoria had no right to reach any of the property.

4. **Tax consequences:** The Internal Revenue Code has its own rules for powers.

   a. **General power:** For tax purposes, the holder of a *general* power of appointment is generally treated as the owner of the property over which he or she holds the power. If the property generates income, it is treated as the donee's income for income tax purposes. If the donee appoints the property, the property is subject to gift taxes. If the holder of a general power dies holding the power, the appointive property is included in his or her estate for federal estate tax purposes.

      Life estate in surviving spouse with general power: If the decedent leaves his or her surviving spouse a life estate interest in property, with a general power of appointment, the transfer qualifies for the marital deduction and is not taxable for federal estate tax purposes when the first spouse dies, but the property is taxable as part of federal gross estate of the second spouse to die.

   b. **Special power of appointment:** For tax purposes, the holder of a special power of appointment is generally *not* treated as the owner of the property over which he or she holds the power of appointment. The income generated by the appointive property is not treated as the donee's income, and the appointive property is not included in the donee's estate for federal estate tax purposes.

      i. **Taxes—pre-1986:** For trusts established prior to 1986, a settlor could pass property from generation to generation (subject to the Rule against Perpetuities), without federal estate tax consequences, by giving each new generation of beneficiaries a life estate and special power of appointment. (The settlor could even include (1) a power to consume as long as it was limited to an ascertainable standard relating to the beneficiary's health, education, support, or maintenance, and/or (2) a power to withdraw up to $5,000 or 5 percent of the principal, whichever is greater, annually.)

      ii. **Taxes—post-1986:** The Tax Reform Act of 1986 imposes either an estate tax or a generation-skipping transfer tax following the death of each life tenant at each generation younger than the settlor.

5. **Malpractice liability:** A lawyer who fails to take full advantage of the tax savings opportunities present in using powers of appointments may be liable in malpractice for tax liability that could have been avoided.

II. CREATING A POWER OF APPOINTMENT

A. **Intent:** A power of appointment is created as long as one has the intent to create a discretionary power in one party, over property held by another party, to direct the one holding the property to transfer the property. No technical words are necessary to create a power of appointment, only the intent to create a discretionary power. Precatory words do not constitute the intent to create a power absent additional evidence of such an intent.

B. Donee: A power of appointment can be created only in a living person.

C. Power to consume: If a party is given a life estate with a power to consume the principal, the power to consume is deemed to constitute a general power of appointment if the power to consume is not limited to an ascertainable standard relating to the health, education, support, or maintenance of the holder of the power to consume.

III. EXERCISING A POWER OF APPOINTMENT

A. Intent: The donor's intent controls what is necessary to validly exercise a power of appointment. Assuming the donee complies with the requirements inherent in each type of power (general vs. special; inter vivos vs. testamentary), whether a donee has exercised a power of appointment is a question of the donee's intent. Although no express reference to the power is generally required (unless the instrument creating the power expressly requires), failure to refer to the power expressly constitutes an ambiguity that often results in litigation over whether the donee intended to exercise the power.

B. Residuary clause: The jurisdictions are split over whether a standard residuary clause in the donee's will that does not make any reference to a power of appointment exercises a testamentary power of appointment.

   1. Majority rule: The overwhelming majority rule is that a standard residuary clause that does not make any reference to a power of appointment does ***not exercise*** either a general or a special testamentary power of appointment that the testator may have held.

   Extrinsic evidence: Where the decedent held a power of appointment and his or her residuary clause does not make any reference to the power, the jurisdictions that follow the majority rule are split over whether this constitutes a sufficient ambiguity to permit courts to admit extrinsic evidence as to the decedent's intent that his or her residuary clause exercise the power of appointment.

   2. Minority rule: A small minority of jurisdictions holds that a standard residuary clause adequately expresses the testator's intent to exercise a general power of appointment that the testator held unless a contrary intent affirmatively appears, but not a special power that the testator held.

   Rationale: A general power of appointment is so close to ownership of the property subject to the power that the donee often thinks of the appointive property as if it were his or hers. Hence, the residuary clause should be deemed to exercise a general power but not a special power (because the donee of a special power does not think of the property as his or hers because the donee cannot appoint it to him- or herself).

   3. UPC approach: A residuary clause expresses the intent to exercise a power of appointment the testator held only if (1) the power is a general power of appointment and the creating instrument does not contain a gift-over in the event the power is not exercised, or (2) the testator's will manifests an intention to include the property subject to the power. UPC §2-608.

   4. Choice of law: Where the appointive property is land, the applicable law for interpreting a power of appointment and whether it has been exercised is the jurisdiction where the land is located. Where the appointive property is not land, however, and the donor and donee reside in different jurisdictions, the jurisdictions are split over which state's law controls. The traditional approach and majority rule is the law of the donor's domicile controls, but a number of jurisdictions and the Restatement (Third) of Property: Wills and Other Donative Transfers adopt the minority approach and apply the law of the donee's domicile.

5. **Example:** In ***Beals v. State Street Bank & Trust Co.***, 326 N.E.2d 896 (Mass. 1975), the residuary clause of Authur Hunnewell's will created a trust for the benefit of his wife for life, and upon her death, separate trusts for each of their daughters for life, and upon each daughter's death, the principal in her trust was to be paid as appointed by her will. In default of appointment, the property would be paid to that daughter's heirs. Daughter Isabella asked the trustees to distribute most of the principal in her trust to her husband's office so he could manage it, which the trustees did. Thereafter, Isabella executed a partial release of her power, limiting her power to appoint the property to the descendants of Arthur. When Isabella died, the trustees still held $88,000 in the trust for her. Her will made no express reference to the power of appointment but her residuary clause gave the rest of her property to the issue of her sister Margaret. The court applied the law of the donor's domicile, which followed the minority approach that a residuary clause is deemed to exercise a general power of appointment but not a special power of appointment. The court ruled, however, that although the power was a special power of appointment at the time of Isabella's death by virtue of her partial release, her actions with respect to the appointive property showed that Isabella treated the appointive property as if it were her own and that the rationale for the general power of appointment should be applied—her residuary clause exercised the power.

6. **Generic reference:** The cases disagree over whether a standard residuary clause with a generic reference to any powers of appointment the testator may hold is adequate to exercise a power of appointment (this assumes the document creating the power does not expressly require an express reference to the power when the power is exercised). For the UPC approach, see paragraph III.B.3 above.

7. **Specific reference required:** To avoid unintentional exercise of a power of appointment, a donor can include in the power a requirement that exercise of the power must make specific reference to the instrument creating the power. The courts tend to be very strict in applying specific reference requirements, though a number of commentators have criticized the courts for putting formalities over intent and have argued, under the modern trend intent-based approach, for reforming the donee's instrument under such circumstance.

8. **Blended residuary clause:** A "blended" residuary clause is one that includes within the residuary clause a generic reference to any power of appointment the testator may hold: "I hereby give the rest, residue, and remainder of my estate, including any property over which I hold a power of appointment, to. . . ." Under the UPC, such a generic reference is not enough, in and of itself, to exercise any power of appointment the testator may hold *that requires a specific reference* to the power. It may, however, raise an issue of intent that may permit extrinsic evidence on the question of testator's intent, and if there is extrinsic evidence the testator intended the clause to exercise the power, the blended residuary clause should be deemed to exercise the power.

9. **Lapse and anti-lapse:** Where a donee exercises a testamentary power of appointment, but the appointee predeceases the donee, the issue arises whether lapse and anti-lapse should be applied to the appointment.

a. **General power:** As a general rule, the courts have applied lapse and anti-lapse where the appointee of a general power of appointment predeceases the donee and meets the necessary degree of relationship to the donee.

b. **Special power:** The appointee of a special power of appointment must be an eligible object as defined in the instrument creating the power of appointment. If the effect of applying anti-lapse would be that the appointive property would end up in the hands of issue who were not eligible takers under the express terms of the power, the traditional rule is that anti-lapse cannot be applied. The modern trend applies anti-lapse to objects of the special power of appointment class even if their issue are not express objects of the class.

c. **UPC:** Under the UPC and the statutes in a handful of jurisdictions, anti-lapse applies to appointees of a power of appointment. UPC §2-603.

C. **Limitations:** Although the expectation is that the holder of a power of appointment will appoint the property outright to an appointee, theoretically, that is not the only option. A donee could appoint the property in trust or even create a new power of appointment. Whether such conditional appointments are valid is a question of the original donor's intent.

1. **General power:** The donee of a general power of appointment can appoint the property as he or she wishes: outright, in trust, or even subject to a new power of appointment.

2. **Special power:** Absent express authority in the instrument originally creating the special power, the general rule is that the donee is to appoint the property outright. The modern trend, however, permits the donee of a special power of appointment to appoint either in trust or even subject to a new power of appointment as long as both the donee and objects of the new power are included in the original class of objects.

   Restatement (Second): The Restatement (Second) of Property, Donative Transfers, permits the donee to create either a general power of appointment in an appointee who was a member of the original class of objects, or to create a special power of appointment in anyone as long as the class of objects is the same as the original class of objects.

3. **Appointments:** Where the power is a special power of appointment and the class of objects is relatively small, the issue arises as to whether the donee can appoint all of the property to one member of the class.

   a. **Exclusive:** If the power is exclusive, the donee can appoint all of the property to one member of the class.

   b. **Nonexclusive:** If the power is nonexclusive, each member of the class must receive some distribution of the appointive property (and in some jurisdictions, the amount cannot be a "sham" amount).

   c. **Donor's intent:** In determining whether the power is exclusive or nonexclusive, the starting point is the donor's intent. Particular attention is paid to the language used in creating the power. Words such as *to one or more* indicate an exclusive power, while *among* is usually held to constitute a nonexclusive power.

   d. **Default:** The jurisdictions are split over which approach should be the default that applies where the instrument is ambiguous. The Restatement (Second) of Property §21.1 adopts the exclusive approach as its default.

4. Fraud: A fraud on a special power of appointment occurs where the donee and an eligible appointee agree that the donee will exercise the power of appointment in favor of the class member on condition that he or she share some of the appointive property with a person who is not an eligible appointee.

Remedy: Where the parties engage in fraud on a special power of appointment, the courts tend to hold that the entire appointment is void, even the portion that the eligible appointee was to retain.

D. Attempted appointment that fails

1. Allocation/marshalling: If the donee of a special power of appointment expresses the intent to exercise the power of appointment, but inappropriately attempts to mix the appointive property with the donee's own property in the distributive clause (typically in a blended residuary clause), the doctrine of allocation "unblends" the property to ensure that only eligible objects receive the appointive property.

Rationale: In "unblending" the appointive property from the donee's own property and making sure that the appointive property is allocated only to takers who are eligible takers, the court is simply construing the language in the donee's will so that it gives maximum effect to the intent expressed while honoring the requirement that only eligible takers can take the appointive property.

2. Capture: If the donee of a general power of appointment (1) expresses the intent to exercise the power of appointment, and (2) blends the exercise with the distributive provisions of his or her own will (typically in a blended residuary clause), if any of the appointment gifts fails for any reason, the donee is held to have appointed the failed gifts to him- or herself ("captured the appointive property"), and the failed appointive property is distributed as a part of the donee's general assets.

IV. RELEASE OF A POWER OF APPOINTMENT

A. Release: Because a power of appointment is a discretionary power, with no fiduciary duty attached to it, a donee has no duty to exercise it. Failure to exercise the power occurs if the donee dies without exercising it. Included within the right not to exercise the power, however, is the right to release the power at any time. The release may be complete or partial. If partial, it is important to note whether the release relates: (1) to *the property* that may be appointed; (2) to *whom* the property may be appointed; or (3) to *when* the power may be exercised.

B. Testamentary power: A testamentary power is exercisable only upon the donee's death. The primary purpose of making a power testamentary is to make sure that the donee waits as long as possible before exercising the power of appointment. Waiting until death forces the donee to take into consideration all the changes that occur during his or her lifetime before deciding whether, and how, to exercise the power.

1. Contract to exercise: If a donee of a testamentary power of appointment—or any other power not presently exercisable—enters into a contract, inter vivos, that promises to exercise the testamentary power in a certain way upon the donee's death, the contract is null and void. The contract violates the donor's intent in creating the testamentary power. The effect of the contract, if enforceable, would be to exercise the power inter vivos. Any attempt at exercising a testamentary power inter vivos is null and void. This rule applies to all powers of appointment that are not presently exercisable.

Restitution: Although the inter vivos contract to exercise a testamentary power is unenforceable, the contracting party does have a cause of action against the donee for restitution from the donee's personal assets of the value given.

2. **Release:** Although a testamentary power of appointment may not be exercised inter vivos, a testamentary power of appointment may be released inter vivos.

3. **Contract vs. release:** Although an inter vivos contract to exercise a testamentary power of appointment is unenforceable, if the substantial effect of the contract is the same as the effect of a release of the power, many courts (but not all) will enforce the agreement, not as a contract but as an inter vivos release of the testamentary power.

4. **Example:** In *Seidel v. Werner*, 364 N.Y.S.2d 963 (Sup. Ct. 1975), the decedent held a testamentary power of appointment. The decedent contracted inter vivos to make, and not revoke, a will that exercised his power of appointment in favor of his children, for their support and maintenance until they reached the age of 21, at which time they were to receive the principal equally. Just four months later, the decedent executed a will exercising his testamentary power of appointment in favor of his new wife. The court held the contract to exercise the testamentary power of appointment null and void. The children attempted to characterize the contract as a release of the testamentary power. The court analyzed the effect of a release and the effect of the contract and ruled that the two were not substantially the same. The court declined to construe the contract as a release, but the court held that the children were entitled to restitution from the decedent's probate estate.

V. FAILURE TO EXERCISE A POWER OF APPOINTMENT

A. **Donor's intent:** If a donee fails to exercise a power of appointment, the donor's intent controls what should happen to the appointive property where the power is not exercised.

B. **Takers in default:** If the instrument that created the power identifies one or more express takers in default if the power is not exercised, the expressly identified takers in default take if the power is not exercised.

C. **No takers in default—general power:** If there are no express default takers and the power is a general power of appointment, if the power is not exercised, the traditional and general rule is the property reverts to the donor (or the donor's estate if he or she is dead). The Restatement (Third) of Property: Wills and Other Donative Transfers §19.22, however, shifts the default presumption. It provides that if there are no express default takers (or the clause is ineffective) and the general power of appointment is not exercised, the property defaults to the donee (or the donee's estate) unless the donee "expressly refrained from exercising the power."

D. **No takers in default—special power:** If there are no express takers in default and the power is a special power of appointment, if the class of possible objects is relatively small and ascertainable, the court may imply that the donor intended that the appointive property be distributed equally among the members of the appointive class rather than revert to the donor (or his or her estate).

Example: In *Loring v. Marshall*, 484 N.E.2d 1315 (Mass. 1985), the testator created a trust for her brothers, sisters, and two nephews, with the income to be distributed to them. Upon the death of the last income beneficiary, the trustees were to divide the trust into as many parts as necessary for the benefit of the wife and issue of each nephew as he may appoint by will, and if neither nephew left eligible appointees, the trust fund was to be paid equally to the Boston Museum of Fine Arts, Massachusetts Institute of Technology, and Harvard Medical School. Although the trust gave the last surviving nephew the power to appoint to his "wife and issue," the nephew gave his wife only a life estate in the income. When she died the trustees petitioned the court to determine to whom to distribute the principal. The charities were not entitled to take because they were to take only if neither nephew left eligible appointees. Because the nephew was survived by his wife, he left an eligible appointee, and the charities' only opportunity to take was defeated. The court applied the general rule, that when a special power of appointment is not exercised and the instrument that created the power fails to specify an express default taker, the property not appointed goes in equal shares to the members of the class to whom the property could have been appointed.

Quiz Yourself on
POWERS OF APPOINTMENT: DISCRETIONARY FLEXIBILITY

77. Judy creates a trust that provides in pertinent part that the trustee shall distribute the income quarterly to her daughter Liza, and, upon Liza's death, Liza has the power to appoint the principal as she deems appropriate. In the absence of appointment, the property goes to the Make a Wish Foundation. What is Liza's interest in the trust? Assume at Liza's death her medical bills exceed her probate estate. May her creditors reach the property over which she holds the power to appoint? _____

78. Bill's will provides that he leaves his property to his wife, Yi, "for life, with full power in her to dispose of the property during her life as she may desire, and, upon her death, the remaining property shall go to our kids equally." What is Yi's interest under Bill's will, and what is the significance of that interest at the time of her death? _____

79. Tom's mom creates a trust in which he holds a life estate and general testamentary power of appointment. The trust expressly provides that in the event Tom does not exercise the power of appointment, the property in question will go to his issue. Thereafter, Tom and Nicole divorce. As part of the divorce, Tom executes an agreement that promises to execute a will that properly exercises the testamentary power of appointment that he holds in favor of his children. When Tom dies, his will contains a provision that expressly exercises the power of appointment in his mother's trust in favor of Lulu. Nicole and the kids sue. Who takes the property subject to the power? _____

80. Rosemary's will leaves all of her estate, in trust, to George for life. The will also gives George the power to appoint the property, inter vivos or upon his death, to whomever he desires. Thereafter, George executes a valid will that makes no express reference to the power of appointment under his Aunt Rosemary's will. The residuary clause of George's will leaves "the rest, residue, and remainder of my property to Chicago Memorial Hospital." When family members ask George about the power of appointment in his aunt's will, he assures them that he has taken care of it in his will. Has George validly exercised the power of appointment? _____

81. Tom's mom creates a trust with $1 million in which he holds a life estate and a testamentary power to appoint the property among his relatives, as he deems appropriate. Tom's will provides in pertinent as follows: "I give the rest, residue, and remainder of my estate, including any property over which I hold a power of appointment, as follows: one-quarter to Penelope, one-quarter to Princeton, and one-half to my kids." Assuming Tom's residuary estate consists of $3 million, how will his estate be distributed? _____

82. Barbara creates an inter vivos trust for the benefit of her son, George W., during his life, and she gives him a testamentary power to appoint the property among his issue upon his death. George W. executes a valid will that provides in pertinent part that he gives all of his property, including any property over which he holds a power of appointment, to the Republican Party. Who takes the property subject to the power? _____

_____

Answers

77. Liza's interest in the income is mandatory, and she has a general testamentary power of appointment over the principal. Here, the creating instrument expressly provides that Liza can appoint the property upon her death, making it testamentary, as she deems appropriate. This language permits Liza to appoint it to her estate or creditors of her estate, making it a general testamentary power. The general rule is that the creditors of a donee holding a general power of appointment cannot reach the property subject to the power unless the donee exercises the power. If Liza's will exercises the power of appointment, her creditors can reach the property subject to the power even if Liza appoints the property to someone else. If, however, Liza does not exercise the power of appointment, under the general rule her creditors cannot reach the property.

78. Yi has a life estate and, arguably, a power to consume. A power to consume constitutes an inter vivos general power of appointment. No technical words are necessary to create a power of appointment. Yi's ability to appoint the property in question to herself during her lifetime makes the power to consume a general power of appointment. The significance of that is that for federal estate tax purposes, property over which a decedent holds an unrestricted general power of appointment is included in the decedent's federal gross estate for estate tax purposes.

79. Inter vivos contracts with respect to how a donee will exercise a testamentary power of appointment are null and void as contrary to the donor's intent. Tom's inter vivos agreement that promises that he will exercise the power in favor of the kids is unenforceable as an inter vivos contract. Where the effect of an inter vivos contract is substantially the same as the effect of a release, the inter vivos contract can be construed as an inter vivos release. Here, Tom's issue are the express default takers if the power is not exercised, and they are also the takers under the inter vivos contract. Many courts would hold that the inter vivos contract constitutes an inter vivos release and enforce it as such, giving the property to Tom's children.

80. The general rule is that a bare residuary clause that makes no reference to any powers of appointment does not exercise a power of appointment. Under the majority approach, George's residuary clause would be presumed not to have exercised the power of appointment. (The jurisdictions are split as to whether George's statements to his family members that he has taken care of the power of appointment are admissible as evidence of his intent that the residuary clause did exercise the power.) Under the UPC, a basic residuary clause exercises a power of appointment if the power is a general power of appointment and the creating instrument contains no express gift-over in the event the power is not exercised. Here, George's power is a general power of appointment because he can appoint the property to "whomever he desires"—including himself. In addition, Rosemary's will makes no provision for where the property should go in the event George fails to exercise the power. Under the UPC approach, George's residuary clause would be deemed to have exercised the power of appointment.

81. Because Tom is limited in appointing the property over which he holds a power of appointment to his relatives, Tom's power is a special power of appointment. Yet Tom attempts to blend the property over which he holds the power of appointment with the residue of his probate estate and give the combined property to a group of takers, some of whom are not eligible appointees. The doctrine of allocation provides that the property needs to be "unblended" and the appointive property allocated first to those who are eligible to take. Here, if the property is unblended, the appointive property is $1 million. That property is allocated first to his kids, who are the only eligible takers in the clause, to count towards their share of the combined property (they were to take $2 million of the $4 million). The rest of Tom's property is then allocated to best fulfill his intent—another $1 million to his kids, $1 million to Penelope, and $1 million to Princeton.

82. George's power of appointment is a special power of appointment because he is limited in whose favor he can appoint the property and because the class excludes himself, his creditors, his estate, and creditors of his estate. George has attempted to exercise the power of appointment in his residuary clause, but the taker under the clause is not an eligible appointee. George has not properly exercised the power of appointment. There is no express default taker in the trust creating the power. Before giving the property back to Barbara (or her estate, as the case may be), most courts would find that the class of eligible appointees constitutes a limited enough group to imply a default gift in the class members. George's issue will take in default rather than seeing the gift returned to Barbara.

Exam Tips on
POWERS OF APPOINTMENT: DISCRETIONARY FLEXIBILITY

Powers conceptually

☞ Spend some time getting comfortable conceptually with powers of appointment. One way to think about them is that they are nothing more than a power to revoke in the hands of someone other than the settlor/donor. The party holding the power can override all the other provisions of the instrument (typically a trust) and order the property (typically the principal) distributed immediately pursuant to the exercise of the power.

Powers generally

☞ Every power has two key characteristics: its scope (general vs. special) and when it can be exercised (inter vivos vs. testamentary, or both). Most of the issues and doctrines turn on whether the power is general or special and, to a lesser degree, whether it is inter vivos or testamentary.

Every time you see a power, you should immediately stop and analyze it for its two key characteristics. (Creditors' rights are derivative of the type of power and thus a common area to test because professors can test two doctrines with one issue.)

Creation: Intent-based

☛ No special language is needed to create a power, though proper drafting would expressly refer to the power as a power. A general power to appoint, however, can also be created as a power to withdraw, appropriate, or consume—a more subtle way to raise the issue.

Exercise of a power

☛ Absent express requirements in the instrument creating a power, whether a power has been exercised is a question of the donee's intent. The area where this causes the most problems, and is tested the most, is whether a standard residuary clause with no express reference to any power of appointment exercises a power of appointment.

   ☞ The states are split over this issue, often distinguishing between a general power and a special power. Know which approach you need to know: your state's approach, the general approach, or the UPC approach. If the residuary clause is presumed not to have exercised the power of appointment, address whether evidence of the donee's intent is limited to the face of the will or includes extrinsic evidence.

☛ Where you have a validly exercised power but the property is not appointed outright, you need to discuss whether there are any limitations on how the power can be exercised that affects the purported exercise.

Failed or improper exercise of a power of appointment

☛ An area of powers that is tested often (because it overlaps nicely with other doctrines) is the failed/improper exercise of the power. Watch for blended residuary clauses; they often raise issues of allocation or capture.

   ☞ Under the doctrine of allocation, allocate the property subject to the power to those who are eligible to receive it first, and then allocate the decedent's property as appropriate to fulfill the rest of the decedent's wishes. If there is more property subject to the power to appoint than there are eligible takers, as to that excess appointive property, the property has not been appointed.

   ☞ If the power of appointment is a general power of appointment and the gift to one or more of the beneficiaries fails under the capture doctrine, give the failed gifts to the other takers under the decedent's will (or intestacy) rather than having the property subject to the power of appointment pass under the instrument creating the power.

Release of a power

☛ Whether a power has been released can be raised indirectly by a donee of a testamentary power attempting to contract inter vivos as to how the donee will exercise the power testamentary. The release material can also be raised by a partial release of a general power, turning the general power into a special power or turning a power that could be exercised inter vivos or testamentary into a purely testamentary power. Be on the watch for these overlaps.

Failure to exercise a power

☞ If the power is a general power, if the donee fails to properly exercise the power, and if the capture doctrine does not apply, first check to see if the instrument creating the power expressly provides for a default taker. If not, give the property back to the donor and let it pass as a failed gift.

☞ If the power is a special power and the donee does not properly appoint all of the property, first check again for an express default clause. But if there is none, before giving the property back to the donor, if the class of possible appointees is a fairly limited and defined class, argue that the power constitutes an imperative power and give the property equally to the class of possible appointees.

CHAPTER 13

CONSTRUING TRUSTS: FUTURE INTERESTS

ChapterScope ─────────────────────────────────────

This chapter examines the issue of how to construe the equitable interests that are created when a trust is created. Almost invariably, the interests are some combination of possessory estate and future interests. A future interest is the present right to possession and enjoyment in the future. In particular, the chapter examines:

- **Future interests:** If the settlor retains the future interest, it must be a reversion, a possibility of reverter, or a right of entry. If a beneficiary holds the future interest, it must be a vested remainder, a contingent remainder, or an executory interest.

- **Vested remainders favored:** Remainders can be vested or contingent. The common law courts favor construing an ambiguous remainder as vested.

    - **Benefits:** Vested remainders have several benefits over contingent remainders: (1) vested remainders accelerate to immediate possession regardless of how the preceding estate ends; (2) vested remainders are transferable; (3) if the party holding the remainder dies before the end of the preceding estate, a vested remainder passes to the holder's heirs or devisees; and (4) language divesting vested remainders is construed strictly.

- **Class gifts:** Where a gift is to a class, a variety of construction issues can arise.

    - **Gift of income to class:** A gift of income to a class is presumed to be in joint tenancy with right of survivorship, so if one member dies, his or her share is distributed among the other class members. The presumption is rebutted if the instrument expresses a contrary intent, either expressly or implicitly.

    - **"Issue":** Gifts to "issue" are ambiguous if the instrument fails to indicate whether the gift should be distributed per stirpes, per capita, or per capita at each generation.

    - **"Heirs":** Remainders to a particular party's "heirs" create problems concerning who is included (for example, the surviving spouse) and when the class of heirs should be determined (when the individual dies or when the remainder becomes possessory).

        - **Common law:** Common law rules often void express gifts to "heirs." Under the Doctrine of Worthier Title, if a document purports to create a remainder in the settlor's heirs, the remainder is converted into a reversion in the grantor; and under the Rule in Shelley's Case, if a document purports to create a remainder in real property in the heirs of a life tenant, the remainder is given to the life tenant.

- **Rule of convenience:** Under the rule of convenience, a class closes automatically by operation of law as soon as one member of the class is entitled to possession of his or her interest. No one else can enter the class, even if he or she otherwise appears to be eligible to join the class.

I. FUTURE INTERESTS

A. **Trust's equitable interests:** At the equitable level, a trust is some combination of possessory estate and future interests. At common law, a whole host of technical drafting rules applied with respect to the future interests. If the future interest violates a rule, typically it is null and void (thereby defeating the settlor's intent).

   1. **Possessory estate:** The party who holds the possessory estate holds the present right to possess the property right now.

   2. **Future interest:** The party who holds the future interest holds the present right to possess the property at some point in the future.

   3. **Terminology:** Possessory estates and future interests typically are created in a trust, but they do not have to be. If the interests are not created in a trust, they are called "legal" possessory estates and future interests; if they are created in a trust, they are called "equitable" possessory estates and future interests. The party who creates the interests is typically called the grantor, and any party other than the grantor who receives an interest is a grantee. If the interests are created in a trust, the party who creates the interests is typically called the settlor, and any party other than the settlor who receives an interest is typically called a beneficiary.

B. **Future interests in the grantor/settlor:** If a grantor retains a future interest, it must be one of three future interests: a reversion, a possibility of reverter, or a right of entry. (The most common future interest in the grantor is the reversion.)

   1. **Reversion:** If the grantor has the right to possess the property after a finite estate ends, the grantor holds a reversion.

      a. **Finite estates:** A finite estate is an estate that must end. At common law there are three possible finite estates: life estates, fee tails, and terms of years. (The most common finite estate is the life estate.)

      b. **Implied reversions:** Reversions can arise implicitly (by operation of law) if a grantor does not convey his or her entire interest. Whatever interest he or she does not convey is presumed retained, and if the retained future interest follows a life estate or other finite estate (the most common scenario), it is a reversion.

      Example: Bilbo, who owns Shireacres, creates an inter vivos trust that provides in pertinent part: "To Frodo for life." State the title. Frodo holds a life estate; the settlor, Bilbo, holds a reversion.

      c. **Vested:** Reversions are vested future interests. (Classifying a future interest as vested does not necessarily mean that it will become possessory. But there are benefits associated with vested interests such as transferability, not being subject to destructibility, and so on.)

   2. **Possibility of reverter:** If the grantor conveys a fee simple determinable, the grantor is deemed to have retained a possibility of reverter. (A fee simple determinable is a fee simple that may last forever, but it may end if a specified condition or event occurs, in which case the right to possession ends immediately and automatically. The right to possession reverts to the grantor under the possibility of reverter.)

   3. **Right of entry:** If the grantor conveys a fee simple subject to a condition subsequent, the grantor is deemed to have retained a right of entry in the event the condition subsequent occurs.

(The fee simple subject to a condition subsequent is similar to the fee simple determinable in that the possessory estate is a fee simple that may last forever, but it may end if a specified condition or event occurs. The difference is that if the specified condition or event occurs, the fee simple does not end automatically, but rather the grantor has the right to enter the property and retake possession.)

C. Future interests in a grantee/beneficiary: A beneficiary can hold only two future interests: a remainder or an executory interest.

   1. Remainder: If a beneficiary has the right to possession after a finite estate ends, the beneficiary holds a remainder.

     a. Must be express: Unlike reversions, a remainder arises only if the words of the instrument expressly grant the future interest following a finite estate to a beneficiary. Remainders are not implied.

     b. Example: Bilbo creates an inter vivos trust that provides in pertinent part: "To Frodo for life, then to Sam for life." State the equitable interests created. Frodo holds a life estate. The trust expressly provides that Sam holds the future interest following Frodo's finite estate, so Sam holds a remainder—in life estate. (Because the remainder is not in fee simple, the settlor, Bilbo, retains a reversion following Sam's life estate.)

   2. Vested vs. contingent: Every remainder is either vested or contingent. A remainder is vested if (1) the holder of the interest is ascertainable, and (2) there is no express condition precedent, in the clause creating the remainder or the preceding clause, that has to be satisfied before the remainder can become possessory. If a remainder is not vested, by default it is contingent.

     a. Ascertainable: Ascertainable means that the party who holds the remainder must be identifiable by his or her personal name.

     b. Condition precedent: A condition precedent is an express condition in the instrument creating the remainder that must occur before the remainder becomes possessory. If the condition is set forth in the clause creating the remainder or the preceding clause, the remainder is a contingent remainder.

     c. Destructibility: At common law, if a contingent remainder does not vest before or at the moment the preceding finite estate ends, the contingent remainder is destroyed.

     d. Reversion: Whenever an instrument creates a contingent remainder, there must be a reversion in the grantor (express or implied) in the event the contingent remainder does not vest in time.

       i. Example: "To Frodo for life, then to Frodo's children." Frodo has no children. State the title. Frodo has a life estate. Because his children are not ascertainable, the instrument grants them a contingent remainder. Because the remainder is contingent, the grantor holds a reversion.

       ii. Example: "To Frodo for life, then to Sam if Sam survives Frodo." State the title. Frodo has a life estate. Sam has a contingent remainder because there is an express condition precedent in the clause creating the remainder that must be satisfied before Sam's interest can become possessory—that is, Sam must survive Frodo. Because Sam's remainder is contingent, the grantor holds a reversion.

e. **Alternative contingent remainders:** A remainder that takes possession only if a contingent remainder created earlier in the conveyance fails is called an alternative contingent remainder. The express condition precedent is the condition that the prior contingent remainder must fail.

    i. **Example:** "To Frodo for life, then to Sam if he makes it back from Mordor, but if Sam does not make it back from Mordor, then to Pippin." State the title. Frodo has a life estate, Sam has a contingent remainder, Pippin has an alternative contingent remainder (contingent on Sam not making it back from Mordor), and the grantor has a reversion.

    ii. **Reversion:** With alternative contingent remainders, it looks like one or the other will become possessory. There appears no need to have a default reversion in the grantor. But because contingent remainders cannot accelerate into possession, if the preceding finite estate ends early and the first contingent remainder has not vested by or at that moment, both contingent remainders are destroyed and the property reverts to the grantor. So even when the conveyance does not appear to require a default reversion because of the alternative contingent remainders, one is necessary.

    iii. **Premature termination:** A finite estate can end prematurely (before its natural termination) if there is forfeiture, renunciation, or merger. Under forfeiture, if a party commits certain crimes, the party has to forfeit his or her property. Renunciation occurs where one renounces one's interest. Merger occurs if one party holds successive vested interests (usually as a result of a transfer of one of the interests). The interests merge into the largest possible interest. If a life estate is merged into a larger interest, the life estate is terminated. If a contingent remainder has not vested before or at the moment the preceding finite estate ends, be it naturally or prematurely, the contingent remainder is destroyed.

3. **Remainders and class gifts:** Where a remainder is to a class of beneficiaries, the interest may be (1) vested as to all, (2) contingent as to all, or (3) vested as to some, but still open. If the class is vested as to some but still open so others can join the class, as new members join the class they are entitled to a share of the property (thereby partially divesting those members of the class who previously had vested).

Example: "To Harrison for life, then to Harrison's children." Assume Harrison has two children, Ben and Will. State the title. Harrison has a life estate. Because Ben and Will are ascertainable and there is no express condition precedent, Ben and Will hold a vested remainder. But because Harrison may have more children, Ben and Will hold a vested remainder subject to partial divestment (because the class is still open and if Harrison has more children, they would partially divest Ben and Will of some of their interests).

4. **Vested remainders subject to divestment:** A vested remainder subject to divestment is created when there is an express condition precedent that may affect the remainder's possessory interest, but the condition precedent is set forth in a clause *after* the clause creating the remainder. If the condition occurs, the vested remainder is completely divested. In distinguishing contingent remainders from vested remainders subject to divestment, the key is the location of the condition precedent.

a. **Example:** Compare the following two conveyances:

"To Frodo for life, then to Sam if he returns the ring." State the title. Frodo has a life estate. Sam has a contingent remainder because there is an express condition precedent in the same clause creating the remainder that he has to satisfy before the remainder can become possessory—he has to return the ring first. Because Sam holds a contingent remainder, the grantor retains a reversion.

"To Frodo for life, then to Sam, but if Frodo gives the ring to Paul, then to Paul." State the title. Frodo has a life estate. Reading and analyzing comma to comma, Sam has a vested remainder. Sam is ascertainable and there is no express condition precedent in the clause creating the remainder or the preceding clause. There is, however, an express condition precedent (a condition that could occur prior to the remainder becoming possessory) in the clause subsequent to the clause creating the remainder. If that condition precedent occurs, Sam's remainder would be completely divested and the property would pass to Paul instead. Sam holds a vested remainder subject to divestment.

b. **Powers of appointment:** If a trust creates a life estate, gives someone a power of appointment, and expressly provides for default takers who take in the event the power of appointment is not exercised, the express takers in default hold a vested remainder, and the potential exercise of the power of appointment constitutes a condition, which if exercised, would divest the vested remainder.

5. **Executory interests:** An executory interest is the name of the future interest if it is held by a third party (someone other than the grantor) and it follows either (1) a vested remainder subject to divestment, or (2) a fee simple subject to an executory limitation. (The latter is a fee simple determinable or a fee simple subject to condition subsequent, only the future interest following fee simple defeasible is held by a third party.)

a. **Shifting vs. springing:** The executory interest is a *shifting* executory interest if the party holding the executory interest takes the right to possession from someone other than the grantor. The executory interest is a *springing* executory interest if the party holding the executory interest takes the right to possession from the grantor.

b. **Example:** "To Diana for life, then to Nick, but if Diana sells alcohol on the land, then to Winona." State the title. Diana has a life estate. Nick has a vested remainder subject to divestment. Winona has a shifting executory interest.

c. **Example:** "To Frodo if he destroys the ring." State the title. Normally the first grantee takes the possessory estate. Here, there is an express condition precedent that must be satisfied before the first possessory estate can become possessory. The grantor holds a fee simple subject to an executory limitation, and Frodo holds a springing executory interest.

II. PREFERENCE FOR VESTED REMAINDERS

A. **Vested vs. contingent:** Classifying a remainder as a vested remainder or a contingent remainder has a number of possible consequences.

B. **Destructibility:** Under the common law destructibility of contingent remainders, if a contingent remainder does not vest before or at the moment the preceding estate ends, the contingent remainder is destroyed (it becomes null and void).

1. **Scope:** The destructibility of contingent remainders applies only to legal contingent remainders in real property.

2. **Modern trend:** The modern trend abolishes the destructibility of contingent remainders doctrine.

C. **Accelerate to possession:** A vested remainder accelerates into possession the moment the preceding life estate ends, whether it ends naturally or prematurely. On the other hand, contingent remainders cannot become possessory until all of the express condition precedents are satisfied. If a contingent remainder does not vest in time, at common law it is subject to being destroyed under the destructibility of contingent remainders.

1. **Disclaimers—modern trend:** If a life tenant disclaims, at common law the issue of whether the remainder accelerates into possession turns on whether the remainder is contingent or vested. Under the modern trend, some courts rule that the issue turns on testator's probable intent if he or she had known that the life tenant would disclaim. Because the modern trend involves high administrative costs (whenever a life tenant disclaims, litigation is necessary to determine the testator's probable intent), many jurisdictions have adopted disclaimer statutes that expressly provide that the disclaiming party is treated as if he or she predeceased the decedent. Whether a remainder accelerates into possession then depends on the effect of treating the disclaiming party as if he or she predeceased the decedent.

2. **Example:** In *In re Estate of Gilbert*, 592 N.Y.S.2d 224 (Sur. 1992), testator created a testamentary elective share trust for his wife for life and four discretionary trusts, one each for the benefit of each of his four children and their issue. Upon the death of his surviving wife, the property in her trust was to be added to the residuary trusts for the children and their issue. One of the testator's sons, Lester, renounced his interest in the trust. Lester had no children at the time. With respect to the contingent remainder in Lester's unborn issue, the state had adopted the modern trend—the disclaiming party is treated as predeceasing the decedent, with the effect of accelerating subsequent interests. Because Lester had no issue, the interest in his issue was terminated as well even though that arguably is inconsistent with the testator's intent. The court refused to consider a case-by-case approach to the testator's intent, stating that one of the purposes of the statute was to prevent such costs of administration. Lester was treated as having predeceased his father without issue. Lester's disclaimer, coupled with the acceleration of the remainder interest in his issue, had the effect of also disclaiming any interest his after-born issue might have had.

3. **Disclaimer execution:** The UPC and federal tax laws disagree over when a disclaimer must be executed to be effective.

   a. **Federal tax laws:** Under federal tax laws, for a disclaimer to be effective and not incur a gift tax, the disclaimer must be executed within nine months of the interest in question being created. As applied to a trust, the disclaimer must be filed within nine months of the trust being created, even if the interest is contingent. IRC §2518(b)(2).

   b. **UPC:** Under the UPC, a disclaimer is effective as long as it is executed within nine months of the interest vesting indefeasibly. As applied to contingent remainders contingent upon the remainderman surviving the life tenant, the remainderman can wait until the death of the life tenant to decide whether to disclaim. UPC §2-801.

4. Generation-skipping transfer tax: Under the federal tax code, when an individual dies and passes property on to his or her heirs or devisees, an estate tax may be owed. If the decedent passes his or her property to a life tenant, and then on to more remote descendants (grandchildren or more remote descendants), a generation-skipping transfer tax is imposed when the life tenant dies. If the life tenant disclaims, just as the remainder interest is accelerated into possession, the generation-skipping transfer tax is likewise accelerated and due. If the trust is a testamentary trust, both the estate tax and the generation-skipping transfer tax are due upon the testator's death if the life tenant disclaims, passing the property to a more remote descendant.

D. Transferability: At common law, vested remainders are transferable, but contingent remainders and executory interests are not. The modern trend repudiates the distinction between vested and contingent remainders, making contingent remainders transferable.

1. Spendthrift clause: A settlor can prevent the transferability of both vested and contingent remainders by including a spendthrift clause in the trust. A spendthrift clause prohibits a beneficiary from transferring his or her interest.

2. Transmissibility: A property interest is transmissible if the party holding it has the power to devise it upon death. In the event the interest is not properly devised, the interest is descendible—it passes to one's heirs. Reversions, remainders (vested and contingent, as long as the contingency is not that the remainderman must survive to the time of possession), and executory interests are transmissible.

3. Taxation: A transmissible future interest constitutes a property interest for purposes of the federal estate tax. If a party holds a transmissible property interest when he or she dies, the interest is included in his or her probate estate for purposes of calculating the party's estate tax.

a. Valuation: Where the transmissible interest is vested, its value turns on (1) the life expectancy of the life tenant, (2) discounted to its present value based on interest rates. Where the transmissible interest is contingent, or subject to a power of appointment, or subject to depletion in favor of the life tenant, valuation is much more difficult, turning on the totality of the circumstances.

b. Avoidance: A special power of appointment is not a property interest for purposes of calculating estate taxes. Accordingly, if a grantor wishes to avoid estate taxes being imposed on a transmissible future interest in the event a vested remainderman dies before his or her interest becomes possessory, the grantor can (1) make the remainderman's interest contingent on surviving to the time of possession, and (2) grant the remainderman a special power to appoint the property among his or her heirs. The contingent remainder that the remainderman has to survive the life tenant makes the remainder nontransmissible, so there is no estate tax imposed when the remainderman dies. But giving the remainderman a special power of appointment permits the remainderman to appoint the property interest to the same takers. Because the special power of appointment is not a taxable property interest, the remainderman has the same power at death—to pass it to his or her heirs without an estate tax being imposed.

E. Instrument ambiguous re when remainder vests: Where a remainder is created and the language is ambiguous as to whether the remainder is to vest upon the death of the transferor or upon the death of the life tenant, the preference for a vested remainder means that the gift is construed so that the remainder vests upon the death of the transferor.

1. **Remainderman predeceases life tenant:** If the remainderman dies before the life tenant, the issue that arises is what happens to the remainderman's interest.

   a. **Transmissibility:** The traditional and still general rule is that the remainderman's interest is transmissible—it passes into his or her probate estate where the remainderman has the option of devising it to whomever he or she wishes. In the event the remainderman fails to devise it, it passes to his or her heirs.

   b. **Lapse/anti-lapse:** Historically, the lapse and anti-lapse doctrines were limited to wills. The difference between transmissibility and lapse/anti-lapse is significant. If the interest is transmissible, if a remainderman dies before his or her interest become possessory, he or she can devise the remainder to whomever he or she wants. In the event it is not devised, the interest passes to the remainderman's heirs. Under lapse/anti-lapse, the predeceased remainderman has no interest unless he or she meets the requisite degree of relationship, and even then, the interest goes only to his or her issue; if none, the remainderman's interest lapses (fails).

   c. **UPC revision:** The UPC advocates a new approach to future interests in trust (revocable or irrevocable): a lapse/anti-lapse type approach to all future interests in trust, unless the instrument expressly provides otherwise. UPC §2-707.

2. **Example:** In *First National Bank of Bar Harbor v. Anthony*, 557 A.2d 957 (Me. 1989), settlor created a revocable trust for his benefit for life, then for his wife's benefit for life, then the res was to be distributed equally to his three children. The settlor's wife died, and one of his sons died unmarried but survived by three children. When the settlor died a year later, his will left all of his property to his two surviving children. The children of his predeceased son were expressly omitted from the will. The settlor's surviving children argued that the terms of the trust were ambiguous and offered extrinsic evidence that the settlor did not want any of the property in the trust to go to the issue of the predeceased son. The court ruled that the trust created a remainder interest in the settlor's children, that the interest was vested from the moment the trust was created, and that the presence of the power to revoke made the remainders subject to divestment, not contingent. Because the settlor died without revoking the trust or revising its terms, the court ruled the terms of the trust were clear that the interest should go to the settlor's three children. The court applied the traditional rule that the son's vested remainder interest was transmissible and passed to his children and declined to apply anti-lapse to the revocable trust.

   Transmissible interest: If a party holds a transmissible future interest but dies before the interest becomes possessory, the interest is treated like any other property the party owns. The transmissible property interest falls into probate, where it is subject to the probate process and estate taxes.

   a. **Probate:** Often executors and probate courts overlook a transmissible interest. The interest often is not discovered until the party holding the preceding estate dies. Where the interest is overlooked, courts can order the transmissible interest to be distributed directly to the parties who are entitled to receive the interest without reopening probate.

   b. **Flexibility:** A party who holds a transmissible property interest essentially holds a general testamentary power of appointment. The party can devise the transmissible interest as he or she sees fit. The power to devise the interest means that the party holding the transmissible interest has the flexibility to alter the disposition of the property if circumstances warrant.

If the interest is subject to lapse and anti-lapse, the power to devise is lost, as is the flexibility to take into consideration any change in circumstances that may warrant altering the disposition plan.

c. **Taxation:** Pre-1986, there were tax benefits to making a remainderman's interest contingent upon his or her surviving until the time of possession. If the remainderman died before the life tenant, the property did not pass into the remainderman's estate, thereby avoiding estate taxes. In 1986, however, Congress adopted the generation-skipping transfer tax. The tax applies if, upon the life tenant's death, the property is transferred to a grandchild or more remote descendent of the settlor. The generation-skipping transfer tax eliminates any tax benefits associated with making the remainderman's interest contingent upon surviving the life tenant.

3. **Express survival requirement:** Where a grantor includes an express survival requirement in his or her conveyance, care needs to be taken to indicate whether the party in question must survive the grantor, the life tenant, or one or more of the remaindermen. Whom the party must survive is a question of grantor's intent, and therefore is a fact-sensitive issue. If a general rule exists, however, it appears to be that where a party's interest is qualified by an express survival requirement, more often than not the courts construe the survival requirement to mean the party must survive to the moment he or she is entitled to possession.

Example: Godfather creates an inter vivos trust that provides as follows: "To Godfather for life, then to Michael, but if Michael dies before Godfather, to Michael's surviving children." Assume Michael has two children, Vinnie and Niko. Assume Michael dies, and then Niko dies survived by a child, Rosina. Then the Godfather dies. Under the general rule, the survival requirement on Michael's children is tested when their interest becomes possessory—under these facts, when Michael dies. Because Niko dies before the interest becomes possessory, Niko has no interest in the property, and nor does Rosina.

4. **Implied survival requirement:** Although courts generally do not imply a requirement that the party survive until the time of possession where the gift is to the grantor's children, siblings, or similar "single-generation" gift recipients, they do imply such a survival requirement where the gift is to the grantor's heirs, issue, descendants, or similar "multiple-generation" gift recipients.

5. **Divesting condition:** Where the conveyance contains an express condition that if the remainderman dies without issue his or her interest is divested and transferred to another party, ambiguity often arises as to whether the divesting condition is to apply only if the remainderman dies before the life tenant or if the divesting condition is to apply whenever the remainderman dies. Again, the issue is one of grantor's intent. Absent clear evidence of grantor's intent, most courts rule that the divesting condition applies only if the remainderman dies before the life tenant.

Example: Godfather transfers property in trust as follows: "To Godfather for life, and then to Michael, but if Michael dies without surviving issue, to Sonny." The general rule is that the divesting condition "dies without surviving issue" applies only if the remainderman dies before the life tenant—here, only if Michael dies without surviving issue before Godfather dies.

6. **Rules in Clobberie's Case:** Clobberie's Case is an old English case that established three rules of construction concerning gifts to be paid upon a beneficiary reaching a specific age. The exact wording of the gift is critical to determine which rule applies. Two of the three rules

evidence the common law preference against imposing a survival requirement and in favor of vested interests, but one implies a survival requirement, resulting in a contingent interest.

a. **Rule 1:** Where one conveys (by will or trust) "all the *income* to [a beneficiary], with principal to be paid when she reaches a specific age or upon marriage" and the beneficiary dies before reaching that age or marrying, the beneficiary's interest in the principal is transmissible.

   Rationale: The rationale is that the gift is complete upon execution of the instrument, and only possession is to be delayed. Upon the death of the beneficiary, however, there is no need to delay distribution of the principal. It is paid to the beneficiary's estate upon his or her death.

   Example: In *Goldenberg v. Golden*, 769 So. 2d 1144 (Fla. App. 2000), the testator created a trust for the benefit of his daughter and her two children. The daughter was to receive 75 percent of the income and the two grandchildren were to split the remaining 25 percent. Upon the daughter's death, the principal was to be divided between the two grandchildren, with each receiving half at age 25 and the other half at age 30. While the daughter was still alive, one of the grandchildren died intestate at the age of 44, survived only by his wife. The surviving grandchild and the widow of the deceased grandchild both claimed the interest of the deceased grandchild. The surviving grandchild claimed the interest was contingent and was destroyed; the grandchild's widow claimed the interest was vested and transmissible and so it passed to her through intestacy. The court applied the first rule in Clobberie's Case and construed the gift as vested and transmissible and awarded it to the deceased grandchild's widow.

b. **Rule 2:** Where one conveys (by will or trust) a sum of money "to [a beneficiary] *at*" a specific age, if the beneficiary dies before reaching that age, the gift fails.

   Rationale: The court construes the language that the gift is paid "at" a specific age as constituting an express condition precedent that the beneficiary reaches that age. One way to justify the distinction under this conveyance is that there is no comma between the words identifying the beneficiary and the condition that the gift is to be made "at" a specific age. In contrast, in the other two rules, the gift is made to the person, then typically there is a comma, and then there is the clause indicating that possession is to be delayed until a specific age. An alternative justification is that the language "to be paid at" a specific age more clearly indicates a completed gift, with just possession being delayed until that age, versus a gift "at" a specific age, which appears to indicate an intent that the gift not be made until the person reaches the specific age. The latter does not just delay possession, but the whole gift is contingent upon reaching that age.

   Criticism/modern trend: Too much is being read into the distinction between a gift "*to be paid* at" a specific age and a gift "at" a specific age. Under the modern trend, the courts construe the latter the same as the former—in both the gift is complete, only possession is delayed, and if the beneficiary dies before receiving possession, the gift is paid to his or her estate.

c. **Rule 3:** Where one conveys (by will or trust) a sum of money "to [a beneficiary], to be paid when the beneficiary reaches" a specific age and the party dies before reaching that age, the beneficiary's interest is transmissible.

Rationale: The rationale is comparable to the rationale for the first rule. The language of the gift indicates a completed gift, with possession delayed until a specific age, as supported by the location of the comma.

d. **Class gifts:** The rules in Clobberie's case have been applied to class gifts as well as gifts to individuals.

7. **UPC revision:** The UPC advocates a new, complex approach to future interests in trust (revocable or irrevocable): a lapse/anti-lapse *type* approach to *all* future interests in trust, unless the instrument expressly provides otherwise. UPC §2-707.

a. **Implied survival requirement:** UPC §2-707 requires holders of future interests to survive to the time of distribution. If a remainderman does not survive to the time for distribution, the UPC provides for a gift-over to the remainderman's issue; if there are none, the gift fails and is returned to the grantor's estate unless there is an express default taker who is to take in the event the gift fails.

b. **Rationale:** The UPC provision is based on the typical transferor's presumed intent. The transferor's intent was to give the gift to the person. If the person were to die before receiving the property, the UPC assumes that the transferor would prefer not to make the gift because under the common law approach the interest is transmissible so the donee could devise the gift to anyone—maybe even someone the transferor did not like. If, however, the predeceased beneficiary is survived by issue, the UPC assumes that the transferor would want the gift to go to the beneficiary's issue rather than fail. Otherwise the UPC presumes that the transferor would prefer that the gift fail if the beneficiary dies before receiving possession. (Technically, the UPC does not rest its rationale on the grantor's presumed intent, but rather on avoiding the high administration costs of probating the future interest where the holder dies before distribution.)

c. **Criticism:** The UPC proposal has been heavily criticized and not widely adopted. Critics have offered several arguments against the provision. As for the presumed intent arguments, there is no evidence to support the assumption that the transferor would prefer the gift to fail. Second, the effect of the UPC approach is to favor the transferee's issue over the transferee's spouse (who would take the transmissible interest most likely, under either intestacy or the transferee's will). Third, by eliminating the transmissibility of the interest, the beneficiary loses the flexibility to alter the gift if circumstances warrant. Fourth, the UPC provision also creates complications where the express language of the conveyance requires the beneficiary to survive until the time of distribution. Traditional construction would void the beneficiary's gift completely. The UPC would give the gift to the beneficiary's issue (if any) despite the grantor's express intent. Fifth, under the UPC, if the gift fails, the takers are the settlor's heirs or devisees—even if the settlor is still alive. The gift is not given to the settlor but to the settlor's heirs apparent at the time the gift fails. The ripple effect of the UPC approach raises the concern that its costs are not worth its benefits. Prof. French recommends imposing a survival requirement on future interest holders only as long as the holders also are granted a special testamentary power of appointment, thereby providing flexibility to alter the plan of disposition if circumstances warrant, and saving estate taxes and probate costs. (Lastly, as for the official UPC rationale, to avoid the high costs of administration, the modern trend is not to reopen probate where the beneficiary dies before distribution, but to permit the court to order distribution directly to those entitled to take at distribution.)

III. CLASS GIFTS

A. Definition—review: A class gift is a gift to a group of individuals with a built-in right of survivorship (membership in the class is not fixed). A gift to multiple individuals is a class gift if the transferor so intends, and where the intent is not clear, typically the courts look at several variables (the UPC focuses on how the beneficiaries are described—collectively or individually). (See Chapter 5.II.E for a more detailed discussion of what constitutes a class gift.)

B. Income to class: A gift of income to a class, with a gift-over to others following the death of the last class member, inherently includes an ambiguity. The express gift-over following the death of the last class member indicates that each member of the class takes only a life estate interest in the income. If one member of the class dies, an ambiguity arises as to what happens to that share. If the instrument does not expressly provide for what happens to the income upon the death of a class member, litigation is inevitable.

   1. Default: The general rule is that a gift to a class is presumed to be in joint tenancy with right of survivorship. Under this approach, upon the death of one member of the class entitled to share in the distribution of the income, his or her share of the income is redistributed among the other members of the class entitled to receive the income.

   2. Intent: The issue of what is to happen to the share that was being distributed to the deceased member of the income class is a question of settlor's intent. The instrument creating the gifts may expressly or implicitly indicate an intent that differs from the default general rule.

   3. Example: In ***Dewire v. Haveles***, 534 N.E.2d 782 (Mass. 1989), the testator created a testamentary trust that provided in part that all the income was to go to his grandchildren, and 21 years after the death of his last surviving grandchild, the trust was to terminate. The settlor had six grandchildren. During the time when the trustee was distributing the income to the grandchildren, one of the six died. The trust failed to provide for what was to happen to his share. The court noted the general default rule, but held it inapplicable. The court concluded that the testator must have intended the income to be distributed to the issue of the deceased grandchildren. The court found that the settlor's repeated statements that it was his desire to treat each grandchild equally supported this interpretation.

   4. Restatement (Third) approach: The Restatement (Third) of Trusts and the Restatement (Third) of Property, Donative Transfers, reject the traditional joint tenancy default rule and instead favor the issue of the deceased class member. Where there is a gift of income to a class, and one class member dies, both Restatements adopt the view that the natural inference is that the share of the deceased class member should be paid to his or her surviving issue.

C. Gifts to "surviving children": If a will or trust provides for a gift to one's "surviving children," and the instrument fails to expressly provide for what is to happen upon the death of one of the children before distribution of the property, the general rule is that the gift is expressly limited to the transferor's surviving children, and the surviving issue of any deceased children do not take.

   1. Extrinsic evidence: A few courts have held that where the instrument is homemade, the transferor may not have understood the full legal significance of the phrase "surviving children" and will take extrinsic evidence to determine the transferor's true intent with respect to the use of the term.

2. **Stepchildren:** Although ultimately a question of the transferor's intent, the general rule is that use of the term "children" or "issue" does not include stepchildren absent contrary intent expressed by the transferor.

D. **Gifts to "issue/descendants":** While the use of the terms "issue" or "descendants" indicates the intent that if an issue dies survived by issue, his or her share can be taken by his or her surviving issue, there is still ambiguity as to which approach should be taken to calculate the shares going to each "issue" or "descendant"—per stirpes, per capita, or per capita at each generation.

1. **Majority:** The majority approach is that the court applies whatever is the default approach in the jurisdiction (the intestacy approach).

2. **Restatement (Second):** The Restatement (Second) of Property, Donative Transfers, presumes that the per capita approach applies to gifts to "issue" in written instruments regardless of the state's default approach to intestate distributions to issue (though a gift to "issue per stirpes" expresses an adequate contrary intent to overcome the presumed default; the property would be distributed to the issue per stirpes).

3. **UPC:** The UPC position depends on the language used. If the gift is to "issue" or "issue by representation," the property should be distributed pursuant to the state's default/intestate approach. The latter construction may cause problems.

   "By representation": Historically the phrase "by representation" was construed to mean per stirpes. Restatement of Property §303. The UPC approach construes the phrase "by representation" as meaning the default approach (which under the UPC is per capita at each generation and in most jurisdictions is the per capita by representation approach). This change in construction may cause problems in jurisdictions that used to follow the historical approach. UPC §§2-708, 2-709.

4. **Nonmarital children:** Another ambiguity inherent in the use of the term "issue/descendant" is whether nonmarital children/issue are included.

   a. **Common law:** Common law presumes that the terms "issue" and "descendant" include only children born to a married couple, not nonmarital children. The question is one of transferor's intent, however, and the presumption is rebuttable.

   b. **Modern trend:** The modern trend presumes that marital and nonmarital children are included in the term "issue/descendant" if that term is used in a written instrument. The question is one of the transferor's intent, and the presumption is rebuttable. (In many modern trend jurisdictions, the change in law applies only to written instruments executed after the change in law, not to written instruments created before. In such jurisdictions, attention to the relevant dates is critical.)

E. **Adopted children:** While all states provide by statute that an adopted child constitutes a child of the adoptive parent(s) for intestate purposes, the question of whether an adopted child constitutes a "child" or "issue" for purposes of taking under a written instrument is a question of the transferor's intent. The intestate rule does not necessarily control. Where the written instrument expressly addresses the issue, the transferor's intent controls. In the absence of such a provision, it is a question of transferor's intent.

1. **Common law:** At common law, only blood descendants qualify as "children" or "issue." Under this approach, an adopted child does not qualify as a beneficiary under a written instrument.

    Adopting parent: Where, however, the transferor is the adopting parent, even the common law assumes that when the transferor used the terms "child" or "issue," he or she intended to include any adopted child.

2. **Modern trend:** The modern trend, both judicially and statutorily, is to presume that the use of the terms "child" or "issue" should be construed as including adopted children absent contrary intent. Where the change has been made judicially, however, some states have said that the modern trend applies only when certain terms are used; when adopted legislatively, the change applies only prospectively.

3. **UPC:** The UPC approach provides that adopted children and children born out of wedlock are included in gifts in written instruments to the same extent they would be included if the gift were being distributed through intestacy. Terms that do not differentiate relatives by blood from relatives by affinity (aunts, uncles, nieces, nephews) are construed as excluding relatives by affinity. Terms that do not distinguish between whole and half bloods (brothers, sisters, nieces, nephews) are construed as including both half and whole bloods. UPC §2-705.

4. **Adult adoptions:** Adult adoptions are permitted in almost all states. The issue of whether an adopted adult should receive the same inheritance rights as an adopted minor, however, has split the courts. Although the statutes granting inheritance rights typically do not draw a distinction between an adopted adult and an adopted minor, in a significant number of cases the courts have engrafted an exception on the statute where the adult is adopted solely to try to qualify as an heir under the instrument of a remote ancestor. (See Chapter 2.VI.D.6 for further discussion of this point.)

F. **Gifts to "heirs":** The problem with gifts of future interests to "heirs" is whether who qualifies as an heir should be determined (1) upon the death of the transferor, or (2) at the time of distribution of their interest. The question is one of the transferor's intent.

1. **Common law:** The common law preference for vested interests argues in favor of ascertaining who qualifies as an heir of a denominated person as of the date when the denominated person dies. If thereafter the heir dies before distribution, his or her vested interest is transmissible. The preference, however, is merely a rule of construction. The issue is one of the transferor's intent, not a rule of law.

    a. **Exception:** Where the instrument gives a life estate or defeasible fee to a person who is one of the transferor's heirs, and then goes on to give a remainder or executory interest to the testator's heirs, some authorities and courts have concluded that the transferor's intent was that the term "heirs" should be determined upon the death of the life tenant because the transferor arguably did not intend to give a possessory interest and a future interest to the same party.

    b. **Overall testamentary scheme:** Because the issue of *when* the transferor's heirs should be determined is a question of transferor's intent, the transferor's overall testamentary scheme may be relevant to the issue. Whether such an approach is helpful, however, is extremely fact-sensitive.

2. **Modern trend/UPC approach:** The modern trend approach, as reflected in the UPC and some state statutes, is to determine who qualifies as an heir at the time when the property is to be distributed to the heirs.

   Rationale: If heirs are determined upon the death of the transferor and an heir dies before distribution, his or her transmissible interest is subject to estate tax upon distribution. Under the modern trend, by determining who qualifies as an heir at time of distribution, if a party who otherwise qualifies as an heir dies before distribution, he or she no longer has a transmissible interest—thereby avoiding estate taxes (but depriving his or her devisees or heirs of their interest).

3. **Example:** In *Estate of Woodworth*, 22 Cal. Rptr. 2d 676 (App. 1993), the testator created a testamentary trust, life estate for his wife, and following her death, distribution to Elizabeth (testator's sister), if then surviving, and if not, then to her heirs. Elizabeth died in 1980, survived by her husband who died later leaving all of his estate to the University of California Regents. The testator's wife died in 1991. The issue was whether Elizabeth's heirs should be determined as of the date of Elizabeth's death or as of the date of the life tenant's death. The court applied the common law rule that heirs of a denominated person are to be determined as of the date of death of the denominated person. Elizabeth's husband was alive and qualified as an heir as of the date of her death. His interest was transmissible and passed to the University of California Regents. The fact that some of the transferor's property would pass to nonrelatives was not sufficient to constitute proof of transferor's intent that Elizabeth's heirs be determined at the death of the life tenant so as to keep his property within his family.

4. **Doctrine of worthier title:** Pursuant to the common law doctrine of worthier title, where a grantor purports to create a future interest in the heirs of the grantor, give the future interest to the grantor and reclassify it as a reversion. The doctrine of worthier title is yet another example of the common law's preference for vested interests.

   a. **Rule of construction:** The doctrine of worthier title is a rule of construction, not a rule of law. If there is sufficient evidence to show that the grantor intended to create a future interest in his or her heirs, the doctrine does not apply.

   b. **Modern trend:** Under the modern trend, most jurisdictions have abolished the doctrine of worthier title.

5. **Rule in Shelley's Case:** Where real estate is conveyed by a single written instrument (be it a will, trust, or deed) and the instrument purports to create a contingent remainder in the heirs of a life tenant, give the remainder to the life tenant (which vests the remainder; if there is no other vested interest between the life estate and the remainder, the interests will merge). The Rule in Shelley's Case is yet another example of the common law's preference for vested interests.

   a. **Rule of law:** The Rule in Shelley's Case is a rule of law. The rule applies regardless of the clarity of the transferor's intent to create a remainder in the heirs of the life tenant.

   b. **Modern trend:** Under the modern trend, most jurisdictions have abolished the Rule in Shelley's Case.

G. **Class closing rules:** A class, by definition, is a generic description of a group of individuals who share a common characteristic, for example, a gift "to *A*'s children." Often the description of the common characteristic is such that other people holding that characteristic may enter the class—*A* may have more children. At some point, however, the class must close.

1. **Naturally:** The most common way for the class to close is naturally—if the way for people to enter the class closes naturally. In the example "to *A*'s children," the class closes naturally if *A* dies. No one else can enter the class.

2. **Rule of convenience—introduction:** Common law quickly realized that for administrative purposes, an alternative to closing the class naturally had to be created. For example, if the conveyance is "to *B* for life, then to the children of *A*," if *B* dies and *A* is still alive with two children, what is to be done with the property? Could *A*'s children who are alive take the property, subject to possible partial divestment if *A* has more children? Should the court hold the property and accumulate income, thereby depriving the living children of the benefit of their gift? To avoid these difficult administrative issues, the common law courts created a second method of determining when a class closed—the rule of convenience.

   a. **Rule statement:** Under the rule of convenience, as soon as one member of the class legally has the right to receive, possess, and/or enjoy his or her share of the property, the class closes.

   b. **Rule of construction:** Despite the rationale for the rule, the courts have deemed the rule of convenience a rule of construction based upon the transferor's presumed intent, and not a rule of law. The courts, however, are quick to apply it, making it look more like a rule of law in most cases than a rule of construction.

   c. **Vesting:** Closing a class under the rule of convenience does not mean that all of those who are included in the class will necessarily receive a share of the property. A class may close, but the class may still be contingent as to some members of the class. As to the latter, if any one of them does not satisfy the express condition precedent, they do not share in the property.

   Class closure: Compare the following provisions in a testator's will:

   "to *A* for life, then to the children of *B*, upon reaching the age of 18" vs. "to *A* for life, then to the children of *B* who reach age 18." In the first example, the gift to *A*'s children vests upon the birth of a child, with payment delayed until he or she reaches age 18. If *B* has a child, the class closes as soon as *A*'s life estate ends, regardless of how old the child is. In the second example, the express condition precedent that only *B*'s children "who reach age 18" take means that the interest does not vest until the first child of *B* reaches age 18. The class is *B*'s children, but the class does not close until one of them is entitled to distribution—that is, not until *A* dies and one of them reaches age 18.

3. **Direct gift:** Where a written instrument (typically a will) provides for an outright gift to a class of beneficiaries, the class closes upon the death of the transferor/testator.

   a. **Exception:** The courts have ruled that where no member of the class was born before the transferor's death, it must be presumed that the transferor knew this and yet still made the gift. Accordingly, under these conditions, the rule of convenience does not apply, and the class is held open until it closes naturally—until the death of the designated party who controls access to the class. (In the example "to the children of *A*," if *A* has no children when the testator dies, the class would stay open until it closed naturally—until *A*'s death.)

b. **Rule in Wild's Case:** The devise "to *A* and her children" contains an inherent ambiguity as to who takes what interest. The common law approach established in Wild's Case and based on common law rules of construction, is that *A* and her children take as tenants in common. Under the modern trend, some courts construe this type of gift as conveying a life estate to *A*, remainder to the children.

c. **Posthumously conceived children:** Posthumously born children pose problems for class closing rules. The modern trend is to recognize posthumously conceived children as

children of the decedent as long as they are born within a reasonable time. For purposes of applying class closing rules, the Restatement (Third) of Property proposes treating posthumously conceived children as alive at the time of the decedent's death as long as the children are born within a reasonable time of the decedent's death (in essence, applying a reasonable time delay to class closing rules for posthumously conceived children).

4. **Future interests:** Where a written instrument creates a future interest in a class, the first variable is whether the gift is of income or principal.

   a. **Gifts of income:** Where the gift is a periodic payment of income, the class closes upon each periodic date for distribution of the income. Because no beneficiary is entitled to distribution of any income until the designated date for distribution, the class cannot be closed until the designated date for distribution. The class automatically reopens for the duration of the next payment period.

   b. **Gifts of principal:** Where the gift is a one-time disbursement of principal, the earliest the class will close is upon the end of the preceding estate if at least one member of the class is entitled to distribution—if at least one member's interest has vested (even if that member is dead, if the interest is transmissible or passes via anti-lapse to his or her issue, the future interest has vested). If the gift is to the children of a designated person who has not had any children yet (the scenario for the exception to outright gifts), the rule appears to be that the exception that applies to outright gifts applies to future interests.

   c. **Example:** In *Lux v. Lux,* 288 A.2d 701 (R.I. 1972), testator devised the residue of her estate to her grandchildren, share and share alike. The will provided that any real estate included in the residue "shall be maintained for the benefit of said grandchildren and shall not be sold until the youngest . . . [grandchild] has reached age 21." The court ruled that, in light of the requirement that any real estate be maintained until the youngest grandchild reached the age of 21, the gift was a gift in trust. With respect to when the class closed, the court ruled that testator's intent should control, but indefinite delay of distribution until the date when it was physically impossible for any more grandchildren to be born did not make sense, particularly in light of the common law presumption that one is fertile until death. Instead, the court ruled that when the youngest then-living grandchild reached the age of 21, the class closed under the rule of convenience even if it were possible that more grandchildren could be born.

   Distribution of income: Where a trust fails to provide for how the income is to be treated, the default rule is against holding and accumulating the income. The income is distributable to the beneficiaries on a regular basis as the income accrues. In *Lux v. Lux,* the court applied the rule with respect to the income generated by the principal.

5. **Gifts of a specific amount:** Where a written instrument (typically a will) provides for an outright gift of a specific amount to each class member, the class closes absolutely and completely at the time for distribution (typically the death of the transferor). No exception applies, even if no member of the class has been born by that time.

Quiz Yourself on
CONSTRUING TRUSTS: FUTURE INTERESTS

83. Bilbo funds his inter vivos trust with Shireacres. The trust gives the property "to Frodo for life, then to Frodo's first child." Bilbo's will devises all of his property to Gandalf.

   a. Assuming Frodo has no children, state the future interests. _____

   b. If Bilbo dies and then Frodo dies childless, what happens to the property? _____

   c. If Frodo has a child, Eve, and then Bilbo dies, what happens to the property? _____

   d. If Bilbo dies, Frodo has a child, Eve, Eve dies with a will devising all her property to Ian, and then Frodo dies, what happens to the property? _____

84. Bilbo's inter vivos trust provides as follows: "To Frodo for life, then to Frodo's first child if he or she survives him, otherwise to Gandalf." Assume Frodo has a child, Eve. State the future interests. _____

85. Bilbo's inter vivos trust provides as follows: "To Frodo for life, then to Frodo's first child, but if the child fails to survive him, then to Gandalf." Assume Frodo has a child, Eve. State the future interests. _____

86. Bilbo dies with a will that devises Shireacres "to Frodo for life, then to his firstborn child." Frodo has a child, Eve, and Frodo disclaims his interest. State the title. _____

87. Bilbo dies with a will that devises Shireacres as follows: "To Frodo for life, then to his firstborn child if he or she survives Frodo." Frodo has a child, Eve, and Frodo disclaims his interest. Who holds what interest in the property? _____

88. Godfather transfers Sopranoacres in trust as follows: "To Godfather for life, then to Sonny, but if Sonny dies before Godfather, to Sonny's surviving children." Assume Sonny has two children, Mariano and Vinnie.

   a. Who has what interest in the trust? _____

   b. Assume Sonny dies, and then Vinnie dies survived by Rosina, and then Godfather dies. Who has what interest in the property? _____

89. Bruce transfers Duetacres in trust as follows: "To Bruce for life, then to Gwyenth, but if Gwyenth dies without surviving issue, then to Gwyenth's brother." Assume Bruce dies, and many years later Gwyenth dies, without issue, devising all of her property to the Royale Shakespeare Company. Who takes Duetacres? _____

90. Olivia devises $1,000 "to Selena at age 30." Tragically, Selena dies before reaching age 30. Her will devises her property to Sergio. Who takes the $1,000? _____

91. Olivia transfers property in trust "to Juan for life, then to Selena." Tragically, Selena dies before Juan dies. She dies with a will devising all of her property to Sergio. Who takes the property upon Juan's death? _____

92. Mom sets up a trust that provides as follows: "Income to Brady for life, upon Brady's death, all the income is to be distributed to his children, and upon the death of the last surviving child, the principal is to be distributed equally to his grandchildren then living." Brady dies survived by eight children. Assume one of them, Marsha, dies survived by two children, Izzy and Tom. Who takes Marsha's share of the income? _____

93. Laverne's will bequeaths $15,000 "to the children of Sherlie who reach age 21." At the time of Laverne's death, Sherlie has two children, Andy (age 12) and Betty (age 7). Five years later, Sherlie has another child, Carl, and five years later, Sherlie has yet another child, Deb. Two years later, Betty dies. Carl and Deb both live to age 21. Who takes how much of the property? _____

Answers

83a. The instrument gives the future interest following Frodo's life estate to someone other than the grantor, so it is a remainder. Frodo has no children, however, so his first child is not ascertainable. The remainder in favor of Frodo's first child is contingent, which means Bilbo must hold a reversion.

83b. If Frodo dies without any children, the contingent remainder is destroyed at common law because it did not vest before or at the moment the preceding life estate ended. The reversion becomes possessory, but Bilbo has devised the reversion to Gandalf, so Gandalf owns the property.

83c. Because Eve is ascertainable and there is no express condition precedent that Eve has to satisfy before taking possession, Eve holds a vested remainder. Once the remainder vests, there is no longer any reversion interest in the grantor.

83d. Eve held a vested remainder when she died, so her interest is devisable and inheritable. She devised it to Ian. When Frodo dies, Eve's vested remainder becomes possessory. Ian is entitled to the property following Frodo's death.

84. The trust expressly gives the future interest following Frodo's life estate to someone other than the grantor, so it is a remainder. Although Frodo's daughter is ascertainable, there is an express condition precedent that she has to survive Frodo. The remainder is a contingent remainder. Gandalf takes, if at all, at the end of Frodo's life estate, so he too holds a remainder. It too is contingent, contingent on Frodo's first child not surviving him. Because both remainders are contingent, Bilbo holds a reversion. (If the life estate ends prematurely and the first contingent remainder is not vested at that moment, both remainders are destroyed, and Bilbo's reversion takes possession.)

85. The future interest following Frodo's life estate goes to someone other than the grantor, so it is a remainder. Frodo's daughter is ascertainable and there is no express condition precedent in the clause creating the remainder or the preceding clause, so Eve holds a vested remainder. The express condition precedent in the clause following the clause creating the remainder (that Eve must survive

Frodo) makes the vested remainder subject to divestment, which means that Gandalf must hold an executory interest (shifting because he is taking the right to possession from someone other than the transferor).

The only difference in the conveyance in this problem versus the conveyance in the prior problem is where the express condition that Frodo's first child must survive Frodo is placed in the conveyance. If the express condition precedent is in the same clause as the clause creating the remainder or in the preceding clause, it makes the remainder a contingent remainder. If the express condition precedent is in a clause subsequent to the clause creating the remainder, it makes the remainder subject to divestment.

86. As initially devised, Frodo holds a life estate. His firstborn child, Eve, holds a vested remainder. When Frodo disclaims, his interest is extinguished and the vested remainder accelerates into possession. Eve is entitled to the property.

87. As initially devised, Frodo holds a life estate. His firstborn child, Eve, holds a contingent remainder because of the express condition precedent that the child has to survive Frodo. Because the remainder is contingent, Bilbo holds a reversion. When Frodo disclaims, his interest is extinguished and at common law, contingent remainders do not accelerate into possession. Strict application of the destructibility of the contingent remainder doctrine destroys the contingent remainder, and the property reverts to the transferor, Bilbo. Under the modern trend/UPC approach, the disclaimant is treated as having predeceased the transferor. As applied to the trust, Eve is treated as if she survived Frodo and her interest accelerates into possession. Eve takes the property.

88a. Read and analyze comma to comma, clause by clause. As drafted, Godfather has a life estate, Sonny has a vested remainder in fee simple subject to divestment, and Sonny's children have a shifting executory interest.

88b. The general rule is that where a future interest is given to "surviving children," the condition precedent that the takers have to "survive" is applied at the moment their interest becomes possessory. Here, although Vinnie survives Sonny, he does not survive to the moment of possession (when Godfather died). Vinnie does not share in the property and neither does his issue Rosina. Mariano is the sole taker.

89. The general rule is that where the divesting condition is "if the remainderman dies without surviving issue," the condition is applied only if the remainderman dies before the life tenant. Here, Gwyenth survives Bruce, so even if many years later she dies without surviving issue, the divesting condition does not apply. The Royale Shakespeare Company takes Duetacres.

90. At common law, under the Rule in Clobberie's Case, gifts to a beneficiary "at" a specific age are considered contingent gifts. Under that approach, Selena's gift is contingent upon her reaching age 30. The gift fails and falls to the residuary clause or, if there is none, to intestacy. The modern trend construes such gifts as transmissible. Selena's will devises all of her property to Sergio, so he gets the $1,000.

91. Selena held a vested remainder. At common law and under the prevailing approach, a vested remainder is a transmissible interest. Selena was free to devise her interest to Sergio, so he takes upon Juan's death. Under the heavily criticized and not widely adopted UPC approach, all future interests in trust are subject to the lapse and anti-lapse doctrines. Selena's death constitutes a lapse, and because she has no children, anti-lapse does not apply. Where there is no express alternative taker, the UPC gives the failed gift to the settlor's residuary devisees or heirs. Under the UPC, Selena's remainder fails, and the gift passes to the settlor's residuary devisees or heirs.

92. At common law, where income is gifted to a class and distribution of the principal is delayed until the death of the last member of the income class, upon the death of one member of the income class, his or her share is redistributed among the other members of the income class. Brady's seven surviving children share Marsha's share of the income. Izzy and Tom do not take any of the income. Under the modern trend, the preference is to apply anti-lapse to the share of the income and give it to the issue of the deceased income class member. Izzy and Tom take Marsha's share of the income.

93. The gift is to a class (the children of Sherlie), with an express condition precedent attached (who reach age 21). The class closes under the rule of convenience as soon as the first member of the class is entitled to possession of his or her share. The day Andy turns 21, the class closes. Carl was born before this date, but Deb was born after this date. Deb is excluded from the class even though she meets the class description because of the rule of convenience. When the class closed, there were three members in the class, so Andy is entitled to his share, one-third or $5,000. Betty died at age 19. She did not meet the express condition precedent and does not receive any of the property. Upon her death, the class is reduced to two members, so Andy receives another $2,500 upon Betty's death to reflect that he holds a one-half interest in the class now. When Carl reaches age 21, Carl receives the other half of the gift.

Exam Tips on
CONSTRUING TRUSTS: FUTURE INTERESTS

Classifying future interests

☛ The first key is to identify who holds the future interest, the grantor or someone else. If the grantor holds the future interest, whether the grantor holds a reversion, a right of entry, or a possibility of reverter depends on the preceding estate. For trust purposes, the most common combination is one of the finite estates and a reversion.

☛ If a third party is to take the future interest, there must be an express clause in the instrument giving the interest to the third party. If the instrument is silent as to who takes the future interest, it always reverts to the grantor. If there is an express clause giving the future interest to a third party, the future interest has to be either a remainder or an executory interest.

　☞ Anytime there is a remainder, it must be classified as either vested or contingent. Anytime there is a contingent remainder (or alternative contingent remainders), the grantor must hold a reversion.

☛ The key to applying these rules is to read and analyze comma to comma, clause to clause.

Preference for vested remainders

☛ Watch for life tenants who disclaim their interest. This raises the issue of whether the remainder accelerates into possession. Common law applies the destructibility of contingent remainders, while the modern trend approach treats the disclaimant as having predeceased the transferor, increasing the chances that the contingent remainders are treated as vested.

☛ Watch for fact patterns where the holder of a vested remainder dies before his or her interest becomes possessory. This raises the issue of whether the interest is transmissible or whether anti-lapse should apply.

☛ Watch for express conveyances of future interests to "surviving children (or issue)" and for divesting conditions if the remainderman dies "without surviving issue." Such phrases raise quirky, but easy to test, rules of construction.

  ☞ Where the future interest is to "surviving issue," the general rule is that the survival requirement is applied at the moment the issue have the right to claim possession.

  ☞ Where the vested remainder is divested if the remainderman dies without surviving issue, the general rule is that the condition applies only if the remainderman dies before the life tenant.

☛ Watch for gifts to a beneficiary upon his or her reaching a specific age or event. The key to analyzing such gifts is if the gift expressly provides that it is to be "to *A at* age 30," as opposed to "to *A, upon reaching* age 30" or "to *A, to be paid at* age 30." The Rules in Clobberie's Case provide that the latter gifts are vested (and thus transmissible even if the beneficiary dies before reaching the specific age), while the first gift is considered contingent (and not transmissible if the beneficiary dies before reaching the age). Under the modern trend, all three phases are presumed transmissible unless the language clearly indicates the gift is contingent ("to *A if* she reaches age 30").

Class gifts

☛ Just because a gift is to more than one individual, the gift is not necessarily a class gift. Analyze the conveyance to see if the transferor intended a class gift.

☛ Watch for gifts of income to a class, remainder to the issue of the class, where the instrument fails to provide for what is to happen to the income as the members of the income class die. Apply the common law-modern trend split.

☛ Watch for gifts to "issue" or "descendants." The problem is which approach to apply if one or more of the children predeceases the donor survived by issue: per capita, per stirpes, or per capita at each generation.

☛ Watch for adopted children and class gifts. Apply the common law–modern trend split.

☛ Watch for gifts to "heirs" of a party who holds a remainder. Generally, who qualifies as an heir is determined as of the date of the death of the party holding the remainder, even if the remainderman dies before the interest becomes possessory. The exception to this is if the life tenant is one of the heirs of the party holding the remainder. In such a case, do not determine who qualifies as an heir until the life tenant dies.

☛ An area of class gifts that is often tested is the rule of convenience. Watch for gifts of a remainder to a class, where the class is still open when the preceding finite estate ends. Under the rule of convenience, close the class once one member of the class is entitled to possession.

   ☞ But closing the class does not mean that all members of the class receive property. If there is an express condition precedent that the members of the class must also satisfy, the class members receive property only when they meet the express condition precedent (and they may receive additional property if other class members do not meet the condition).

☛ If the gift is a gift of a set amount to a class, the class closes on the testator's death.

CHAPTER 14

THE RULE AGAINST PERPETUITIES

ChapterScope

This chapter examines the Rule against Perpetuities, the rule that regulates future interests. In particular, the chapter examines:

- **The Rule against Perpetuities:** A future interest must vest, if at all, within the lives in being at the time of its creation plus 21 years, or the interest is void. The rule is applied in the abstract and is not based on probabilities.

    - **The fertile octogenarian:** In applying the Rule against Perpetuities, the common law courts assume conclusively that a person is fertile until death. This presumption often causes problems for future interests in grandchildren.

    - **The unborn widow:** A person's widow cannot be identified until the designated person dies, so any future interest following a future interest to a "widow" needs to be analyzed carefully to see if it violates the Rule against Perpetuities.

    - **The slothful executor:** Because of the potential for delayed and/or prolonged administration of a decedent's estate, gifts made to generic takers upon distribution of a decedent's estate usually violate the Rule against Perpetuities.

- **Perpetuities reform:** Because of the harshness of the Rule against Perpetuities, in particular the fact that it is applied in the abstract regardless of real-life probabilities, the modern trend is to modify the rule. There are several different approaches to such modification:

    - **Saving clause:** Because of the difficulty in understanding the Rule against Perpetuities, the courts will enforce a "saving clause" that provides that despite the other express terms of the trust, the trust will terminate at the latest upon the running of the perpetuities period.

    - **Cy pres:** Under the cy pres doctrine, where a future interest in a trust violates the Rule against Perpetuities, the court is empowered to modify the trust so that it does not violate the rule.

    - **Wait and see:** Instead of applying the Rule against Perpetuities in the abstract, the courts wait and see if the future interest in question actually does not vest until after the perpetuities period.

    - **Abolishing the Rule against Perpetuities:** Some states have abolished the Rule against Perpetuities, permitting trusts to last forever.

- **Class gifts:** If a gift to a class violates the Rule against Perpetuities as to one member of the class, it violates the rule as to all members of the class. The courts, however, have recognized several exceptions to this rule:

    - **Gifts to subclasses:** If the future interest in question can be characterized as a gift to subclasses, apply the Rule against Perpetuities separately to each subclass.

    - **Gifts of specific amounts:** If each class member's share is a specific sum not indeterminate upon the final number of class members, the gift is valid as to those members whose share is definitively ascertainable within the perpetuities period.

■ **Powers of appointment:** A general inter vivos power of appointment must become presently exercisable, if at all, within the Rule against Perpetuities time period or the power is void. General testamentary powers of appointment and special powers of appointment are valid as long as the donee cannot have the ability to exercise the power after the perpetuities period. With respect to any interests created by the exercise of a valid general testamentary power or special power, the interests created are analyzed as if they were created by the instrument creating the power.

I. INTRODUCTION

A. **Overview:** The Rule against Perpetuities is yet another example of the common law's preference for vested interests. The rule was conceived to regulate future interests. Future interests that run far into the future permit "dead hand" control when such control may not be in the best interest of those affected or the community. If the future interests were vested, they could effectively be eliminated through transfer and merger. But if the interests are not transferable, they could clog the title inefficiently for decades to come. The courts developed the Rule against Perpetuities to limit how long "dead hand" control through nonvested future interests would be permitted.

B. **Rule statement:** No interest is good unless it must vest, if at all, within the lives in being at the time of its creation plus 21 years.

C. **Conceptual understanding:** One way to think about the Rule against Perpetuities conceptually is that it is like a statute of limitations.

   1. **Statute of limitations:** Under a statute of limitations, a party who has a cause of action against another party must bring his or her action, if at all, within the statutory period or the cause of action is barred (effectively null and void).

   2. **Rule against Perpetuities:** Under the Rule against Perpetuities, a future interest must vest, if at all, within the perpetuities period (lives in being at the time of creation plus 21 years), or the interest is barred (null and void).

      a. **Vesting:** Just as a statute of limitations does not require that a cause of action be brought within the statutory period (it simply dictates that a cause of action cannot be brought *after* the statutory period), the Rule against Perpetuities does not require that a future interest must vest. It only requires that if the future interest is going to vest, it cannot vest *after* the perpetuities period.

      b. **Perpetuities period:** A statute of limitations sets forth a fixed period of years in which a cause of action must be brought, if at all, or the cause of action is barred. The Rule against Perpetuities sets forth a formula for when the future interest must vest, if at all, or the interest is barred. The formula is any life in being at the time the interest was created plus 21 years.

         i. **Life in being:** The "life in being" prong of the formula is the life of any person who was alive at the time the interest was created, however many years any person who was alive at the time the interest was created lives.

         ii. **Measuring life:** Whoever is picked to fulfill the life in being prong of the perpetuities period is typically referred to as the "measuring life." However long he or she lived, their life is used to measure the number of years that serves as the base period of the perpetuities period, to which 21 years is added under the second prong of the perpetuities period.

D. Scope: Despite the express language of the Rule against Perpetuities that "no interest" is valid unless it must vest, if at all, within the perpetuities period, common law courts apply the rule only to certain future interests.

Interests subject to rule: Common law courts ruled that only contingent remainders, vested remainders subject to open, executory interests, and powers of appointment are subject to the Rule against Perpetuities.

E. Application: Unlike a statute of limitations that waits to see if a party holding a cause of action brings the cause of action within the statutory period, the Rule against Perpetuities is applied abstractly the moment the transferor attempts to create the future interest. If there is even one scenario, no matter how improbable, where the future interest vests, but not until after the running of the perpetuities period, the interest is null and void from the moment the transferor attempted to create it. There cannot be one scenario where the interest vests after the perpetuities period.

F. Vesting requirement: The Rule against Perpetuities requires that the interest must vest, if at all, within the lives in being at the time of the interest's creation plus 21 years. The vesting requirement means something different as applied to the future interests that are subject to the rule.

  1. Contingent remainders: As applied to contingent remainders, the interest can vest by either (a) vesting in interest (but not possession), or (b) vesting in possession.

  2. Executory interests: As applied to executory interests, the interest vests only by vesting in possession.

G. Analytical steps: There are two different analytical approaches that can be used to apply the Rule against Perpetuities to a future interest to see if the interest is valid.

  1. The measuring life approach: Under the measuring life approach, the key is to identify who constitutes the measuring life in analyzing whether the future interest violates the Rule against Perpetuities. Although in theory anyone alive at the moment the interest is created can serve as the measuring life, in practice the only lives that are relevant are those lives that can affect whether the future interest in question vests (either in interest or in possession). By focusing on those lives, one can analytically determine whether the interest must vest, if at all, within the perpetuities period.

  2. The invalidating life approach: Under the invalidating life approach, the analysis is turned on its head. Instead of trying to prove logically that the interest must vest, if at all, within the perpetuities period, the invalidating life approach tries to create a scenario that violates the rule—where the interest in question vests, but only *after* the lives in being plus 21 years perpetuities period. The idea under the invalidating life approach is to see if you can create a person in whom the interest will vest, but only after the lives in being plus 21 years.

  3. Example 1: Assume the following conveyance:

  "To *A* for life, then to *A*'s first child to reach age 15." *A* has two children, *B*, age 10, and *C*, age 13. The contingent remainder in *A*'s first child to reach age 15 is subject to the Rule against Perpetuities.

a. **Measuring life approach:** Using *A* as the measuring life, the interest must vest, if at all, within *A*'s life plus 21 years or fail. If the interest were to vest in either *B* or *C*, the interest must vest within the next 5 years at the latest, so the interest must vest, if at all, within the perpetuities period. Assuming a worst-case scenario, that *B* and *C* both die before reaching age 15, the only other way the interest could vest would be for *A* to give birth to a child, and that event would have to occur during *A*'s lifetime (the measuring life), and that child would have to vest within 15 years of his or her birth, thereby satisfying the requirement that the interest must vest, if at all, within the perpetuities period. The interest is valid.

b. **Invalidating life approach:** Under the invalidating life approach, the first step is to create a party in whom the interest will vest, but not until *after* the perpetuities period. Here, the interest can vest only in a child of *A*, so the invalidating life has to be a new child for *A*. Assume *A* gives birth to a new child, *X*. Then kill all the lives in being named in the problem when the interest was created—*A, B*, and *C*. Then see if it is possible to delay the vesting for another 21 years. The contingent remainder in question must vest, if at all, when *A*'s first child reaches age 15. *X* either will or will not reach age 15 within 21 years of *X*'s birth. There is no way to delay the vesting until after the perpetuities time. The interest is valid.

4. **Example 2:** Assume the following conveyance: "To *A* for life, then to *A*'s first child to graduate from law school." *A* has two children, *B* and *C*. The contingent remainder in *A*'s first child to graduate from law school is subject to the Rule against Perpetuities.

a. **Measuring life approach:** If the interest were to vest in either *B* or *C*, the interest would be valid, because either are lives in being at the time the interest was created. But it is conceivable that neither will attend law school. It is also conceivable that *A* could have another child, *X*. After *X*'s birth, it is conceivable that *A* could die. *X* could graduate from law school, but not until more than 21 years after *A*'s death. It cannot be proved conclusively that the interest must vest, if at all, within the lives in being plus 21 years period. The interest is null and void from the moment of its attempted creation.

b. **Invalidating life approach:** Under the invalidating vesting life approach, the first step is to identify in whom the interest must vest, if at all. The interest here must vest, if at all, in one of *A*'s children. Create a new child for *A*, child *X*. Then kill all the lives in being when the interest was created—*A, B,* and *C*. Now that the lives in being prong of the perpetuities period is accounted for, ask whether it is possible to delay the vesting until more than 21 years after the death of the last life in being. Certainly it is. *X* could graduate from law school more than 21 years after the death of the last life in being. Because a scenario exists under which the interest vests, but not until after the running of the perpetuities period, the interest is void from its attempted creation.

H. **Creation of future interest:** The Rule against Perpetuities requires that the interest must vest, if at all, within the lives in being at the time the interest is *created* plus 21 years. A key step in the analytical process is determining when the interest is created. That varies depending on the nature of the written instrument used to create the interest.

1. **Deed:** If the interests are created in a deed, the general rule is that the interests are deemed created when the deed becomes effective—when it is delivered.

2. **Will:** If the interests are created in a will, the general rule is that the interests are deemed created when the will becomes effective—when the testator dies.

3. **Irrevocable trust:** If the interests are created in an irrevocable trust, the general rule is that the interests are deemed created when the trust is created—when it is funded.

4. **Revocable trust:** If the interests are created in a revocable trust, the general rule is that the interests are deemed created when the trust becomes irrevocable—typically when the settlor dies (assuming the settlor alone holds the power to revoke).

5. **Powers of appointment:** Where the interest is a power of appointment or is created by a power of appointment, special rules apply that are covered later in this chapter.

I. **Periods of gestation:** At common law, a child is considered alive from the moment of conception. For purposes of applying the Rule against Perpetuities, this rule must be kept in mind. A child in utero is considered alive for purposes of determining who qualifies as a life in being, and a child in utero is considered alive for purposes of qualifying as a taker under the terms of a conveyance.

II. CLASSIC RULE AGAINST PERPETUITIES SCENARIOS

A. **Introduction:** There are a handful of Rule against Perpetuities scenarios that have become classics because they evidence the principle that the rule is not concerned with probabilities, but rather with abstract analysis, no matter how unlikely the scenario.

B. **The fertile octogenarian:** The common law presumes that an individual is fertile and capable of having children no matter how advanced his or her age. When coupled with the Rule against Perpetuities' abstract approach, the result is that a future interest that appears valid may be invalid.

1. **Example:** Testator's will provides as follows: "To my wife for life, then to her first child to have a grandchild." When the testator dies, his wife is 80 and has three children, *A, B,* and *C,* and no grandchildren. Under the common law irrebuttable presumption that a person is fertile until death, the testator's wife could have another child, *X,* a year after the testator died. The testator's wife and her children who were alive when the testator died could die without any of them having a child. More than 21 years later, it is conceivable that child *X* could have a child, the first grandchild of the testator's wife. A scenario exists where the interest could vest, but not until after the perpetuities period. The interest is void.

2. **Modern trend:** Under the modern trend, some states have either modified or abolished the common law presumption that an individual is fertile until death. Some states have established statutory ages during which a person is presumed fertile; others permit extrinsic evidence to prove that the designated person is no longer fertile. Some states also provide that the possibility that a person may adopt is not relevant to the Rule against Perpetuities analysis.

C. **The unborn widow:** Where a conveyance refers to a designated person's widow, there is a tendency to assume that the reference to the widow must be to the person's current spouse. Such, however, is not the case. The person could divorce and remarry (or the spouse could die and the designated person could remarry). Moreover, the designated person may remarry someone *who is not even alive when the future interest is created*. Although this scenario is highly improbable, it is conceivable. Where a conveyance grants a future interest to a widow, there is a good chance the future interest *following* the future interest to the unborn widow violates the Rule against Perpetuities.

1. **Example:** In *Dickerson v. Union National Bank of Little Rock*, 595 S.W.2d 677 (Ark. 1980), testatrix's will created a trust that provided that it was to continue until the death of the

testatrix's two sons, Martin and Cecil, and Martin's widow (unnamed), and until the youngest child of either son reached age 25. The court ruled the last interest violated the Rule against Perpetuities because abstractly it was possible that (1) Martin could marry a woman who was not born when the testatrix created the trust (when she died), and (2) one of the sons could have a child, and (3) Martin, Cecil, and all the other lives in being alive when the trust was created could die the next day, and (4) the interest in the youngest child to reach age 25 would not vest until after the lives in being at the time the interest was created plus 21 years.

2. **Alternative contingent remainder:** Where a conveyance creates a contingent remainder and an alternative contingent remainder, inasmuch as both remainders are contingent, both are subject to the Rule against Perpetuities. Each is analyzed separately under the rule. Just because one violates the rule, it does not necessarily mean the other violates the Rule against Perpetuities.

D. **The slothful executor:** It is not uncommon for a beneficiary under a will to die before the gift is distributed from probate. In an effort to avoid this risk, some testators provide that the gift is contingent upon the beneficiary surviving until the time the property is distributed from probate. Although it is reasonable to assume that such a time must occur within the lives in being plus 21 years, it is conceivable that probating an estate can take longer than the lives in being plus 21 years to probate. The phrase "the slothful executor" has arisen to describe this risk. Where such a conveyance is created, the gift may violate the Rule against Perpetuities, and if it does, it is void.

1. **Example:** *T*'s will gifts the residue of her estate to "my issue living when probate of my estate is completed." It is conceivable that one of *T*'s issue living at the time of her death may have a child *X* (another issue of *T*), that all of *T*'s issue living when *T* died may die, and another 21 years may pass before probate of *T*'s estate may be complete. Under this scenario, the interest in *T*'s "issue living when probate of my estate is completed" vests, but not until after the lives in being at the creation of the interest plus 21 years. The gift violates the Rule against Perpetuities and is void.

2. **Modern trend:** Some courts have construed such clauses as implicitly containing a "reasonable time" provision, either closing the class and vesting the interest when distribution reasonably should have been made or leaving the estate open for a reasonable time to see if it closes within a reasonable time. This approach eliminates the Rule against Perpetuities problem.

E. **Other scenarios that can trip the unsuspecting**

1. **The bottomless gravel pit:** *T*'s will gifts her gravel pit to her trustee to work as long as there is gravel to be extracted, remainder to *T*'s issue then living. The future interest in *T*'s issue then living is void because it violates the Rule against Perpetuities. The gravel pit may remain productive for longer than the lives in being plus 21 years, thereby vesting but not until *after* the perpetuities period.

2. **The endless war:** *T*'s will gifts the residue of her estate to her heirs alive when the war in Iraq ends. The war may last longer than the lives in being plus 21 years. The future interest in *T*'s "heirs alive when the war ends" may not vest until *after* the perpetuities period. The interest is void.

3. **The 21st birthday requirement:** *T*'s will gifts the residue of her estate to *A* for life, then to *A*'s children who reach their 21st birthday. The common law ruled that technically one turns

21 the day *before* one's 21st birthday because that is the day the 20th year is completed. Under that reasoning, one's 21st birth *day* is the first day after 21 years. Under that strict reasoning, the gift to *A*'s children would not vest until the day *after* the lives in being plus 21 years. Watch for gifts tied to "the day the party turns 21" or "his or her 21st birthday" as opposed to gifts to an individual upon "turning" or "reaching" age 21.

III. PERPETUITIES REFORM

A. Self-Help—saving clause: A Rule against Perpetuities saving clause is a clause in the instrument creating the future interests that provides that in the event the trust has not yet terminated, it shall terminate 21 years after the death of the last living beneficiary alive when the trust was created, and the property shall be distributed to the then income beneficiaries in the same ratio as they are entitled to receive the income.

    1. Validity: Saving clauses are valid and enforceable, thereby saving a conveyance that would otherwise violate the Rule against Perpetuities.

    2. Malpractice liability: As a general rule, attorneys who draft instruments that violate the Rule against Perpetuities are liable to the intended beneficiaries. Although there is one case that held that violating the Rule against Perpetuities did not constitute negligence because the rule is so hard to understand and apply, the case has been heavily criticized and distinguished by other courts. In particular, the availability of saving clauses makes it even easier to hold an attorney liable for not including such a clause.

B. The cy pres approach: Cy pres is a doctrine that empowers a court to modify a *charitable* trust that otherwise would fail (the doctrine is covered in more detail in Chapter 11). One approach to modifying the *effect* of the Rule against Perpetuities is to extend the doctrine of cy pres to permit courts to modify private trusts that would otherwise fail because they violate the Rule against Perpetuities.

    Application: Many contingent remainders violate the Rule against Perpetuities because of an age requirement greater than 21 years old or an express contingency which could occur more than 21 years in the future. Cy pres would reform such an interest that otherwise would violate the Rule against Perpetuities to reduce any age limit to 21 years old or to assume that any express condition must occur within 21 years. Gifts to a beneficiary's widow could be reformed to refer to the beneficiary's current spouse. (Some states deal with the "fertile octogenarian" scenario by either statutorily assuming an individual is not fertile after a set age or by taking extrinsic evidence on a case-by-case basis.)

C. Modern trend: During the last 50 years or so, the Rule against Perpetuities has come under considerable attack as needlessly complicated and unnecessarily harsh. A number of jurisdictions have statutorily either modified or abolished the rule.

D. The wait-and-see approach: The wait-and-see approach abolishes the abstract application of the Rule against Perpetuities and instead applies the statute of limitations approach. The wait-and-see approach lets the facts unfold and waits to see if the future interest involved is still not vested when the perpetuities period ends. The mere possibility of remote vesting is not enough to invalidate the interest, only if the interest actually has not vested at the end of the perpetuities' period is the interest invalid.

1. **Widely adopted:** A majority of the states now follow the wait-and-see approach. These states, however, are split over (1) how to *measure* the wait-and-see period, and (2) what to do if the interest still violates the reformed perpetuities period.

2. **Traditional perpetuities period:** Some of the states apply the wait-and-see approach for the traditional perpetuities period—the lives in being at the time the interest was created plus 21 years. If it violates the perpetuities period at the end of that period, the states are split yet again on what should be done to the interest.

   a. **Judicial reform:** Some states permit the courts to modify an otherwise violating interest so as to effectuate the transferor's intent as closely as possible.

   b. **Void:** Some states apply the traditional approach to an interest that has not vested after the wait-and-see approach—void the interest and strike it.

3. **The Uniform Statutory Rule Against Perpetuities:** The Uniform Statutory Rule Against Perpetuities adopts the wait-and-see approach but modifies the "life in being plus 21 years" perpetuities period by offering a simpler alternative "90 years" perpetuities period. If the interest has not vested at the end of the 90-year period, the interest is not invalid, but rather the statute authorizes the courts to reform the conveyance to validate the interest in a manner that most closely follows the transferor's intent.

   a. **Traditional period:** The Uniform Statutory Rule Against Perpetuities does not reject the traditional, common law perpetuities period, it just provides an alternative perpetuities period—90 years. As long as the interest vests within *either* perpetuities period, it is valid. As a practical matter, more often than not, the 90-year period will be the applicable period.

   b. **Generation-skipping transfer tax:** Trusts created before the generation-skipping transfer tax was enacted in 1986 are not subject to the tax. If a jurisdiction has adopted the Uniform Statutory Rule Against Perpetuities and applies it to interests created by the exercise of a special power of appointment *after* the adoption of the statute, the effect is to permit the trust to last longer, avoiding taxes longer. Treasury regulations permit such extended tax avoidance only if the special power of appointment is not exercised in a way that attempts to obtain the longer of the two perpetuities periods permitted under the statute.

E. **Abolition:** The third modern trend approach to the Rule against Perpetuities is to abolish it completely. All future interests are valid no matter when they will vest.

   1. **"Dead hand" control:** If one of the principal purposes of the Rule against Perpetuities is to control the risk that a settlor's intent will control well after the time when the settlor could be presumed to have been able to reasonably foresee the future, abolishing the rule creates the potential for inefficient and inflexible "dead hand" control that restricts property for centuries. But under the modern trend, most settlers include powers of appointment, thereby building in flexibility by permitting the life tenants to alter the terms of the trust if circumstances warrant. Moreover, the modern trend grants courts and beneficiaries greater power to modify, if not terminate, trusts prematurely. These developments offset somewhat the risks created by abolishing the Rule against Perpetuities.

   2. **To attract trust business:** A dynasty/perpetual trust is a trust set up to take maximum advantage of the tax savings permitted under the generation-skipping transfer tax. Each person can transfer up to $1.5 million in trust ($1.5 million in 2004—to increase to $3.5 million after 2008). The trust can grow, from generation to generation, through a succession of life estates

(with right to income) with a special power of appointment, for as long as permitted by the state's perpetuities period. Such transfers are exempt from estate taxes, gift taxes, and generation-skipping transfer tax for the duration of the trust. The duration depends on whether the jurisdiction has retained the traditional Rule against Perpetuities period or the Uniform Statutory Rule Against Perpetuities period, or has abolished the doctrine completely. Because the exemption amount applies to the initial contribution, not to the size of the trust, a well-invested dynasty/perpetual trust could grow to hundreds of millions of dollars, with no taxes being imposed until the trust is terminated. In states which have not abolished the Rule against Perpetuities, sooner or later (roughly 90 years) the trust must terminate and taxes will be due. In states which have abolished the Rule against Perpetuities, such trusts can continue forever tax-free. A handful of states abolished the Rule against Perpetuities to attract such trusts—and now all states are feeling pressure to abolish the Rule against Perpetuities to keep their share of the trust business. Increasingly, the Rule against Perpetuities is being abolished not because the state repudiates the policies underlying the Rule, but for economic reasons—to attract trust business.

IV. CLASS GIFTS AND THE RULE AGAINST PERPETUITIES

A. **All or nothing:** As applied to class gifts, as a general rule the Rule against Perpetuities requires that the class close and the interest vest as to *all* members of the class before the running of the perpetuities period or the gift is null and void as to every member of the class. The focus is on whether there is one possible scenario, no matter how implausible, where the interest would vest in a class member but only after the lives in being when the interest was created plus 21 years.

   1. **Rule of convenience:** The rule of convenience applies to class gifts. As soon as one member of the class is entitled to receive his or her interest, the class closes.

   2. **Closing vs. vesting:** Closing the class is not necessarily the same as vesting the class. There may be an express condition precedent that the parties within the class must satisfy before their interest vests.

   3. **Close and vest:** As applied to class gifts, the Rule against Perpetuities analysis requires the class to close and vest with respect to *each* member of the class within the perpetuities period or the gift is void as to the whole class as a general rule.

   4. **Example:** *T*'s will devises Greenacres to *A* for life, then to *A*'s children who reach age 25. At the time of *T*'s death, *A* has two children, *B* age 30 and *C* age 15. The gift in *A*'s children is vested subject to open so it is subject to the Rule against Perpetuities. Create a new child for *A*, child *X*. Kill *A, B,* and *C*. Although killing *A, B,* and *C* would close the class, child *X* is in the class but has not met the express condition precedent—*X* has not reached age 25. The class closing rules do not affect *X*'s interest. Count 21 years. *X* will be 21 years old. Is it possible that *X* could live another four years, thereby vesting the interest but after the perpetuities period? Sure. As long as the interest can vest in one class member *after* the lives in being plus 21 years, the gift is void as to the whole class.

B. **Subclasses exception:** Where a gift to a class can be construed as gifts to subclasses, the Rule against Perpetuities is applied separately to each subclass. If the gift to a subclass closes and vests as to all members of the subclass within the perpetuities period, the gift is valid as to that subclass. As to any subclass where the gift does not close and vest as to all members of the subclass, the gift fails as to all members of that subclass.

1. **Subclass:** A gift to a subclass exists when the conveyance describes the beneficiaries not as a single class, but rather as a group of subclasses. As to each subclass, if the share to which the separate subclass is entitled is determinable within the perpetuities period, the gift to that subclass does not violate the Rule against Perpetuities.

2. **Example:** In ***American Security & Trust Co. v. Cramer***, 175 F. Supp. 367 (D.D.C. 1959), testator's will created a trust for his adopted daughter for life, and upon her death, the trust was to be divided into shares, one share for each of the children of said adopted daughter for their respective lives, and upon the death of each, the share of each to go absolutely to his or her heirs. The adopted daughter had two children before the testator died, and she had two more after the testator died. The interest to the children born after the testator died violated the Rule against Perpetuities. The court held, however, that the gift was a gift to subclasses, each child of the adopted daughter and his or her heirs constituting a separate subclass. The share to go to each subclass was determinable within the Rule against Perpetuities because the shares were calculable upon the death of the adopted daughter (the number of children she had was determinable then). As to the children who were alive when the testator died, the gifts to those two subclasses were valid; as to the two children born after the death of the testator, the gifts to those two subclasses were invalid. The invalid remainders in the heirs of the children did not pass to the life tenants but reverted to the heirs of the settlor/testator.

C. **Specific amount exception:** One of the typical characteristics of a class gift is that the share of each class member cannot be determined until the class closes and each member's interest vests. It is possible, however, to have a class gift with respect to who is to receive, but a fixed amount as to each member who does qualify. In such class gifts, the courts have ruled that because the gift to each member is fixed, as long as the gift to that class member vests before the perpetuities period, as to that class member, the gift is valid, even if gifts to other class members violate the Rule against Perpetuities.

V. POWERS OF APPOINTMENT AND THE RULE AGAINST PERPETUITIES

A. **Introduction:** When studying powers of appointment, the material emphasizes that there are two key variables to each power: (1) in whose favor it can be exercised—general vs. special, and (2) when can it be exercised—inter vivos vs. testamentary. These two variables are also the keys to analyzing powers of appointment under the Rule against Perpetuities.

B. **Application:** The Rule against Perpetuities can apply to a power of appointment in two ways:

   (1) the power itself is treated as a property interest subject to the Rule against Perpetuities, and
   (2) the property interests created by the exercise of a power are subject to the Rule against Perpetuities.

C. **The power:** In applying the Rule against Perpetuities to a power, the analysis turns on (1) ***which type*** of power it is, and (2) ***when*** the power can be exercised.

1. **General power:** In assessing a general power of appointment, the key is whether it is an inter vivos or testamentary power.

   a. **Inter vivos:** For purposes of the Rule against Perpetuities, a donee holding a presently exercisable general power of appointment is treated as if he or she owns the appointive property. As long as a general inter vivos power of appointment becomes exercisable or fails within the perpetuities period, the power is valid, even if it is not actually exercised until after the perpetuities period.

   b. **Testamentary:** For purposes of the Rule against Perpetuities, a donee holding a general testamentary power of appointment is not treated as if he or she owned the property, but rather the donee is treated as an agent of the donor. If the general testamentary power of appointment can be exercised, under any possible scenario, *after* the running of the perpetuities period, the power is void from the moment of its attempted creation.

2. **Special power:** A donee holding a special power of appointment is likewise treated as an agent of the donor. If there is any scenario under which the special power of appointment can be exercised *after* the perpetuities period, the power is void from the moment of its attempted creation.

   a. **Discretionary power to distribute:** If a trustee is granted a discretionary power to distribute income from the trust, for purposes of the Rule against Perpetuities, the discretionary power is treated the same as a special power of appointment.

      Series of powers vs. one power: One of the leading authorities on trusts, John Gray, argued that the discretionary power is not a single power but rather a series of annual powers to distribute the income. The discretionary power would be valid and exercisable for 21 years after the death of the life tenant before it violates the Rule against Perpetuities. Courts that have addressed the issue, however, have not agreed for the most part, holding that the whole power is invalid if it can be exercised at all beyond the perpetuities period.

   b. **Practical effect:** A trustee's discretionary power over income should be limited to persons alive when it is created or the power runs the risk of being invalid.

D. **Exercise of power—interests created:** In analyzing the interests created under the Rule against Perpetuities, the key is the nature of the power that was exercised.

   1. **General inter vivos power:** For purposes of applying the Rule against Perpetuities, a donee holding a general inter vivos power of appointment is treated as if he or she owned the appointed property. In analyzing interests created by the exercise of the power, the perpetuities period starts with the exercise of the power.

   2. **General testamentary power or special power:** A donee holding a general testamentary power of appointment or a special power of appointment is treated, under the Rule against Perpetuities, as if he or she is acting as an agent for the donor. In analyzing the interests created by the exercise of the power, the perpetuities period is deemed to have started when the power was created. The interests created by the exercise of the power must vest, if at all, within 21 years of the death of some life in being when the power was created, or the interest is void. The apparent harshness of his approach is tempered somewhat by the second-look doctrine.

      a. **Second-look doctrine:** Under the second-look doctrine, the courts do not look just at the words of the donee's appointment and read them into the initial instrument creating the power. The courts also look at the facts surrounding the donee at the time of the exercise to see if in applying the Rule against Perpetuities to the actual interests created, the interests must vest, if at all, within 21 years of the death of some life in being when the power was created.

b. **Example:** *T*'s will devises property "to *A* for life, remainder as *A* appoints in her will, outright or in trust." *A*'s will provides that "the appointive property shall be held in trust until the youngest of my children reaches the age of 25, then the property shall be distributed outright in equal shares to those then living." *A*'s power is a general testamentary power of appointment. Reading the terms of *A*'s appointment into the instrument creating the power, the conveyance reads "to *A* for life, then to *A*'s children until the youngest reaches the age of 25, then the property shall be distributed outright in equal shares to those then living." Applying the Rule against Perpetuities in the abstract, the remainder interest violates the Rule and is therefore void. Under the second-look doctrine, however, the courts look at the facts surrounding the donee at the time the power was exercised to see if all of *A*'s children who survived *A* were alive when *T* died. If so, each child would qualify as a life in being at the time the interest was created, and the remainder would not violate the Rule against Perpetuities.

c. **Delaware tax trap:** Life estates and special powers of appointment are not subject to federal estate tax. In most states, the Rule against Perpetuities limits the number of life estates with a special power of appointment one can create. In Delaware, however, there is no limit on the number of life estates with a special power of appointment that can be created. The generation-skipping transfer tax, however, limits the attractiveness of life estates with a special power of appointment as a tax avoidance scheme by imposing a generation-skipping transfer tax of 55 percent. Because that rate is equal to the highest possible estate tax, a donee may want to appoint by giving the next life tenant a general power of appointment, thereby incurring an estate tax that may be lower than the generation-skipping transfer tax.

VI. OTHER RULES REGULATING TEMPORAL RESTRICTIONS

A. **The rule prohibiting suspension of the power of alienation:** The power to alienate is critical to permitting property to be put to its most productive use. A capitalistic approach assumes that property will be transferred until it finds the user who can put it to the most productive use. The issue is to what extent can a property owner suspend the power to alienate the property in question.

1. **Suspension:** The power to alienate is deemed suspended when no one alive, either alone or in combination with others, can convey the property in question in fee simple.

2. **Jurisdictional split:** The jurisdictions are split over when the power to alienate has been suspended.

a. **Wisconsin view:** Under the Wisconsin view, as long as the trustee has the power to sell the trust assets, the power to alienate has not been suspended.

b. **New York view:** Under the New York view, the power to alienate has been suspended if either (1) the trustee lacks the power to transfer legal title, or (2) the beneficiaries, acting together, lack the power to transfer the equitable title. (The New York approach takes the broader view of when the power to alienate has been suspended.)

3. **Future interests:** Under the modern trend, all future interests are transferable, even contingent remainders and executory interests. The only interests that are not transferable, and hence are subject to the rule against suspending alienation, are future interests in unborn or unascertainable holders. In addition, where the law or the instrument expressly restricts the power to transfer, those interests are subject to the rule against suspending alienation as well.

4. **Rule statement:** A suspension of the power to alienate cannot last for a period of time longer than the Rule against Perpetuities' time period.

   Application: A future interest that is valid under the Rule against Perpetuities may be invalid under the rule against suspension of the power to alienate. A person's power to alienate is often limited by a spendthrift clause. If the power to transfer is given or denied to a person, and not to a period of time, a spendthrift clause is usually void if it restricts the power to transfer for more than one life estate.

B. **The rule against accumulations of income:** The rule against the accumulations of income regulates how long a settlor can direct a trustee to accumulate trust income rather than distributing it to beneficiaries. In 1800, Parliament enacted the Thellusson Act which provided that accumulations of income must be limited to (1) the settlor's life; (2) the settlor's life plus 21 years; (3) the remaining years of minority of anyone alive at the time of the settlor's death; or (4) the point in time when a minor beneficiary entitled to receive the income being accumulated reaches the age of majority.

   1. **Modern trend/American approach:** Most contemporary commentators question the merits of a separate rule against accumulations of income. If a state has a rule, most apply the same standard as the Rule against Perpetuities or the rule against suspension of the power of alienation.

   2. **States that have abolished the Rule against Perpetuities:** Most states that have abolished the Rule against Perpetuities also have abolished the rule against the accumulations of income, but not all. At least one state has applied the traditional Rule against Perpetuities period to a provision authorizing perpetual accumulation of 25 percent of the income from a trust. The court voided the accumulation/reinvestment provision and imposed a resulting trust, awarded the property subject to reinvestment clause disbursed to the settlor's heirs.

Quiz Yourself on *THE RULE AGAINST PERPETUITIES*

94. Michael creates an irrevocable inter vivos trust that provides in pertinent part as follows: "To Donald for life, then to my first child to reach age 25." Michael has three children at the time the trust is created, Huey (age 10), Dewy (age 15), and Luey (age 20). Who holds what interests in the trust? _____

95. Michael dies, and his will devises Mickeyacres as follows: "To Donald for life, then to my first child to reach age 25." Michael has three children when he dies, Huey (age 10), Dewy (age 15), and Luey (age 20). Who holds what interests in Mickeyacres? _____

96. Laura deeds her white house as follows: "To Al, but if a woman is ever elected president of the United States, to Hilary." Who holds what interests in the property? _____

97. Laura deeds her white house as follows: "To Al, but if Hilary is ever elected president of the United States, to Hilary." Who holds what interests in the property? _____

98. Martin devises Malibuacres "to the children of Charlie who reach age 25." Who holds what interests in the property if:

a. Charlie is alive and has two children, Andy, age 15, and Betty, age 5. _____

b. Charlie is alive and has two children, Andy, age 30, and Betty, age 3. _____

99. Martin devises "$100,000 to each of Charlie's children, whenever they are born, who reach age 25." Charlie is alive and has two children, Andy, age 15, and Betty, age 5. Two years after Martin's death, Charlie has another child, Sunshine. Who, if anyone, is entitled to receive $100,000?
_____

100. Martin devises Malibuacres "to Charlie for life, remainder to such of Charlie's issue as he appoints by will." Charlie's will provides that Malibuacres is to be distributed "to my children who reach age 25." When Martin dies, Charlie has two children, Andy, age 15, and Betty, age 5. Charlie dies seven years later without having any more children. Is the interest in Charlie's children valid?
_____

Answers

94. The instrument appears to create a life estate in Donald, contingent remainder in Michael's first child to reach age 25. Because the remainder is contingent, Michael retains a reversion. The contingent remainder is subject to the Rule against Perpetuities. Although it appears likely that one of Michael's children will reach age 25 within the perpetuities period, you cannot use any of them to definitively prove it because each could die before reaching age 25. There is no validating life among the lives in being.

Under the invalidating life approach, the interest can vest only in one of Michael's children, so create a new child for Michael, Fred. The next day, kill everyone who was alive when the interest was created (Michael, Donald, Huey, Dewy, and Luey). Then count 21 years. Fred is only 21 years old. It is possible Fred will live another 4 years, thereby becoming Michael's first child to reach age 25—vesting the interest after the Rule against Perpetuities period. The contingent remainder violates the Rule against Perpetuities and is void from the moment Michael attempted to create it.

95. This conveyance is very similar to the one in the prior problem, but here the interests are being created in Michael's will. This difference is critical. Because the interests are created upon Michael's death, the pool of validating lives is limited to Huey, Dewy, and Luey because no one else can satisfy the express condition in the instrument given that Michael is dead and cannot have any more children. Using their lives as validating lives, you can conclusively prove that the interest must vest, if at all, during one of their lives or the interest will fail. The contingent remainder does not violate the rule.

Under the invalidating life approach, the first step is to create (give birth to) a new person in whom the interest can vest. Here, the interest can vest only in one of Michael's sons. Because the interests were created in his will, Michael must be dead, so you cannot create a new son for him. Without being able to create a new son for him, you cannot delay the vesting until after the perpetuities period. The interest must be valid.

96. Al and his heirs hold the property until a woman is elected president of the United States, at which time his interest is divested and Hilary or her heirs or devisees take the property. There is no validating life that definitely proves that Hilary's interest must take possession, if at all, during the perpetuities period. Many generations from now, well after the lives in being at the time the interests were created, a woman may be elected president, thereby divesting Al's heirs or devisees of the property and transferring it to Hilary's heirs or devisees. The key is that both Al's interest and Hilary's interest are transmissible. Under the invalidating life approach, create heirs for both Al and Hilary, kill Al and Hilary, count 21 years, and ask if it is conceivable that a woman may be elected president. Obviously. You have created a scenario where the executory interest becomes possessory but not until after the perpetuities period. The executory interest violates the Rule against Perpetuities and is void.

97. The express divesting condition ("if Hilary is ever elected president") is tied to a life in being. Hilary can be used as the validating life. The executory interest must become possessory, if at all, during Hilary's life. Alternatively, it is impossible to conceive of a scenario where the executory interest would become possessory, but only after the perpetuities period. Although you can create heirs for Al and Hilary, the moment you kill the lives in being at the time the interest was created you make it impossible for the executory interest to become possessory after the perpetuities period. The executory interest does not violate the Rule against Perpetuities and is valid.

98a. The gift to Charlie's children who reach age 25 is void as against the Rule against Perpetuities. Both of Charlie's living children could die before the age of 25. Charlie could have another child after Martin's death. Charlie could die shortly after that child's birth, and that child could be the first to reach age 25—but this would be after the perpetuities period. There is not a validating life, and it is easy to conceive of a scenario where the interest vests but only after the perpetuities period.

98b. The gift to Charlie's children who reach age 25 does not violate the Rule against Perpetuities. Under the rule of convenience, as soon as one member of the class is entitled to receive possession of his or her share of the property, the class closes. Here, when Martin dies Charlie's oldest child is 30. The class closes immediately upon Martin's death. Although Charlie could have more children, they would not be able to get into the class. It is impossible then to create a scenario where a share would vest but only after the perpetuities period. Although it will be longer than 21 years before Betty's interest vests, she counts as a life in being, and therefore her interest must vest, if at all, during the perpetuities period.

99. Where a set gift is given to each member of a class, the Rule against Perpetuities is not applied to the whole class but rather is applied individually to each gift to each class member. Here, Andy and Betty constitute lives in being when the gift was made, so the gifts to them are valid. The gift to Sunshine, however, is invalid. She was not alive when the gift was made, and it is easy to conceive of a scenario where if all the parties died shortly after her birth her interest would not vest until after all the lives in being at the time the gift was made plus 21 years.

100. Charlie holds a special, testamentary power of appointment. The power is valid because Charlie was a life in being when the interest, the power, was created. Because the power is a special, testamentary power of appointment, when Charlie exercises the power, treat the interests created by the *exercise* of the power as if they were created by the instrument *creating* the power. The original instrument can be rewritten to read: "To Charlie for life, then to his children who reach age 25." At first blush, the future interests in Charlie's children who reach age 25 appear to violate the Rule against Perpetuities because it is possible to conceive of a scenario where Charlie has another child whose interest would vest after the perpetuities period. But under the second-look doctrine, in applying the Rule against Perpetuities, the court will take into account the facts that existed when the power was exercised. Charlie died without having any more children. As applied to that factual situation, the interests in Charlie's children who reach age 25 do not violate the Rule against Perpetuities because the only children alive when he died were the same children alive when Martin created the power. As applied to those children, the interest does not violate the Rule against Perpetuities.

Exam Tips *on*
THE RULE AGAINST PERPETUITIES

The Rule against Perpetuities

☞ Under the measuring life (or validating life) approach, a validating life is a person who was alive at the time the interests were created whose life can be used to prove logically and definitively that under the terms of the conveyance, the interest in question must vest, if at all, within the perpetuities period. If you can find such a life, the interest must be valid. If you cannot find such a life, the interest is invalid.

☞ Under the invalidating life approach, if you can create one scenario, no matter how preposterous, where the interest in question vests in someone who was *not* alive at the time the interest was created, but not until *after* the perpetuities period, the interest violates the Rule against Perpetuities and fails.

> ☞ The Rule against Perpetuities is applied in the abstract the moment the interest is created. In applying the invalidating life approach, do not apply the common law destructibility of contingent remainders rule.

☞ Watch for *when* the interest is created. The rule applies the moment the interest is *irrevocably* created (wills vs. revocable trusts vs. irrevocable trusts vs. powers of appointment). This is a favorite area for professors to test because the answer turns on the instrument used to create the interest, not so much on the Rule against Perpetuities.

Spotting Rule against Perpetuities issues

☞ There is a Rule against Perpetuities issue anytime you see, and only when you see, a contingent remainder, a vested remainder subject to open (or subject to partial divestment), an executory interest, or a power of appointment.

☛ If the condition or power is tied to someone who is alive at the moment the interest is created, the interest does not violate the Rule against Perpetuities. If the interest or power is not tied to someone who is alive when the interest or power is created, that is when there is a potential problem with the Rule against Perpetuities.

    ☞ Be particularly suspicious of contingent remainders where there is an express time period that is greater than 21 years and contingent remainders where the future interest in question is more than two generations removed from the transferor.

    ☞ When analyzing executory interests, if the divesting condition is not tied to a life in being, almost invariably the interest is void (unless it is limited to parties who are alive when the interest is created and when the divesting condition occurs).

Class gifts and the Rule against Perpetuities

☛ Remember the general rule that the interest is valid as to the whole class or void as to the whole class, and the two exceptions: (1) if the class can be construed as subclasses, apply the rule separately to each subclass; (2) if the gift is a specific amount to class members, apply the rule individually to each member (what constitutes a subclass is often difficult to delineate and open to too much debate).

Powers of appointment and the Rule against Perpetuities

☛ If the power is presently exercisable general inter vivos power of appointment, the power is valid. The only issue is whether the interests created by the exercise of the power are valid. Treat the exercise of the power as a new conveyance and analyze the future interests created by the power as you would any other conveyance.

☛ If the power is a general testamentary power of appointment or a special power of appointment, two issues need to be analyzed: (1) whether the power is valid, and (2) whether the interests created by the exercise of the power are valid.

    ☞ In analyzing whether the power is valid, if you can conceive of a scenario where the power in question can be exercised beyond the perpetuities period, the power itself is void from the moment the donor attempted to create it.

    ☞ In analyzing whether the interests created by the power are valid, treat the interests as if they were created by the instrument creating the power. Analytically, rewrite the instrument creating the power to include the interests created by the power. In applying the rule to that "rewritten" conveyance, the courts take into consideration the facts that exist when the power is exercised. If those facts limit the possible scenarios that would violate the rule, limit your analysis of the rule likewise.

Saving clauses

☛ If the instrument contains a savings clause, the interests do not violate the Rule against Perpetuities. Focus on who would take if the savings clause were applied.

Modern trend approaches to the Rule against Perpetuities

☞ If the fact pattern tells you that the jurisdiction has adopted one of the modern trend reformations of the Rule against Perpetuities, you should apply that approach.

☞ Cy pres is tantamount to reading a savings clause into the conveyance.

☞ Under the wait-and-see approach, which adopts the statute of limitations approach, it is important to note the distinction between the common law approach and the Uniform Statutory Rule Against Perpetuities flat 90-year approach. Under either, however, if the interest is invalid at the appropriate time, the general rule is to permit the court to reform the interest to best carry out the transferor's intent.

CHAPTER 15

ESTATE AND GIFT TAXES

ChapterScope ━━

This chapter examines the principal provisions of the gift and estate tax system and some of the more common methods of trying to avoid or minimize such taxes. In particular, this chapter examines:

- **Federal gift tax:** Inter vivos gifts that exceed the annual gift tax exclusion constitute a taxable gift during that year. Depending on the amount of cumulative taxable gifts, a donor may owe federal gift taxes.

- **Federal estate tax:** Depending on the value of a decedent's net property holdings at death and the amount of his or her inter vivos gifts, a decedent may owe federal estate taxes at death. There are several steps in determining whether a decedent owes a federal estate tax.

  - **Calculate decedent's gross estate:** The decedent's gross estate consists of the value of virtually all property the decedent owned and transferred at time of death via probate or nonprobate means. The nonprobate property includes property transferred by right of survivorship, transfers where the decedent retained a life estate or control of the beneficial rights, revocable transfers, transfers where the decedent retained a reversionary interest, selected transfers within three years of death, and property over which the decedent held a general power of appointment.

  - **Calculate decedent's taxable estate:** To calculate the decedent's taxable estate, miscellaneous deductions are allowed from the decedent's gross estate. The principal deductions are for charitable contributions; a decedent's debts, loans, mortgages; and the marital deduction.

    - **Marital deduction:** One spouse can transfer an unlimited amount of property to the other spouse without any gift or estate tax as long as the transfer meets the requirements for the marital deduction, the key requirement being that the interest must be something other than a life estate or other terminable interest.

  - **Calculate estate tax before credits:** The estate tax is calculated on a "cumulative" basis, taking into consideration the decedent's taxable estate and inter vivos gifts. The tax is computed utilizing a graduated rate schedule with various adjustments to make sure that inter vivos gifts are not taxed twice.

  - **Apply tax credits:** A variety of tax credits are applied to the tentative estate tax to determine if the decedent owes a federal estate tax. The most important tax credit is the unified estate/gift tax credit.

- **Generation-skipping transfer tax:** Where a transferor attempts to transfer property to a transferee who is more than one generation below the transferor, a federal generation-skipping transfer tax is imposed. The tax imposed is the highest possible federal estate tax rate, but various exemptions and exclusions apply.

I. OVERVIEW

A. Gift vs. estate taxes: The government imposes a number of different taxes on an individual or on property, depending on the situation. The focus here is on those taxes imposed as part of the dying process that affect the transfer of property at death. It is important that up front one has at least a conceptual understanding of each.

1. Gift tax: The gift tax system focuses on inter vivos transfers that lack consideration—inter vivos gifts. The tax is imposed where a donor makes a taxable gift. IRC §2501(a). The tax is imposed on the donor, but if the donor is unable to pay the tax, the donee is liable for the tax. The tax is implicated if there is a taxable gift. Each donor is entitled to make annual gifts up to a set amount to each individual donee before there are gift tax implications. Under the Tax Reform Act of 1976, the annual exclusion per donor was $10,000. This annual exclusion is "indexed for inflation" in $1,000 increments. The annual exclusion increased, due to inflation, to $13,000 in 2009. Depending on the amount of cumulative taxable gifts, a donor may owe federal gift taxes. While the actual system of computing gift taxes is unnecessarily complex, the general scheme is that an individual will not incur a gift tax until his or her cumulative lifetime gifts (after applicable annual exclusions) exceed $1 million. Technically, this is done through a somewhat unified gift and estate tax credit (see below for more information regarding exemptions vs. credits).

2. Estate tax: The estate tax system focuses on testamentary transfers that lack consideration—at-death transfers. The tax is imposed on the decedent's taxable estate at time of death. The taxable estate is the decedent's gross estate less deductions. The gross estate includes (1) the property in his or her probate estate, (2) most nonprobate transfers, and (3) other transfers if the decedent retained sufficient control and/or power over the property even after its apparent inter vivos transfer. Deductions to arrive at the taxable estate include charitable devises; decedent's debts, loans, and mortgages; and the marital deduction. The estate tax is calculated on a "cumulative" basis, taking into consideration the decedent's taxable estate and inter vivos gifts. The tax is computed utilizing a graduated rate schedule with various adjustments to make sure that inter vivos gifts are not taxed twice. Each individual, however, is granted a unified estate/gift tax credit that has the effect of permitting an individual to pass up to a set amount of property at death (and/or during life) free of any estate (or gift) tax. For many years this unified tax credit permitted each individual to pass $600,000 before any taxes were due. President Bush's 2001 Tax Act legislation, however, gradually increased the effective estate tax-free amount from $1 million in 2002 to $3.5 million in 2009. As of this writing, President Obama's 2009 budget proposals will retain, for 2010 and future years, the $3.5 million that can be passed, tax free, per person at death (effectively permitting $7 million for a married couple with proper estate planning).

3. Exemption vs. credit: Although it is often easier to think and speak of the amount of property that one can pass tax-free at death as an exemption from the estate tax system, technically the IRS calculates the exemption by granting a tax credit to the decedent. For example, a per-person $3.5 million tax exemption (the 2009 amount) is not really an exemption that is used in computing a decedent's net/taxable estate. Rather, the estate tax is calculated based on the decedent's full net/taxable estate, and that computed tax is reduced by a credit—the credit being equal to what would be the tax on the "exemption" amount. The current $3.5 million "exemption" is really a $1,455,800 credit (the tax on a $3.5 million net/taxable estate). The same is true for the gift tax calculation, with the $1 million lifetime gift "exemption" really being a tax credit of $345,000.

4. **Estate tax repeal, gift tax continuance, anticipated changes:** The major tax legislation during the George W. Bush presidency was the Economic Growth and Tax Relief Reconciliation Act of 2001 (the 2001 Tax Act). Among other things, this act gradually increased the effective estate tax exemption (the credit, as discussed above) to the $3.5 million amount for 2009 (but made static the $1 million effective lifetime exclusion for gift taxes). A major piece of the 2001 Tax Act was to abolish the estate tax (but not the gift tax) beginning in 2010. Accompanying this repeal of the estate tax was a little-known provision that would generally repeal a hugely beneficial income tax provision relating to the "step-up" in basis of appreciated property received from a decedent (this is an income tax concept and beyond the scope of this book). The 2001 Tax Act contained a sunset clause, however, that, unless affirmatively changed by future legislation, will make all these provisions, including the repeal of these taxes, evaporate after 2010 (returning the tax laws to the way they were prior to the 2001 Tax Act). President Obama, in recent 2009 budget release information, has called for legislation that would prevent the 2010 repeal of the estate tax and retain both the gift and the estate tax systems (and accompanying income tax provisions relating to basis) in their current, 2009, form (with applicable exclusions/credits remaining at 2009 levels).

5. **Inheritance tax distinguished:** An inheritance tax system also focuses on testamentary transfers that lack consideration—at-death transfers. Unlike an estate tax, however, an inheritance tax is imposed on the amount a recipient receives, not on the decedent. The amount of the tax depends not only on the amount the recipient receives but in many jurisdictions, it also depends on the relationship between the recipient and the donor—the closer the relationship, the lower the inheritance tax. There is no federal inheritance tax, but some states have inheritance taxes.

   a. **Liability:** The personal representative is personally liable for the estate tax, but he or she is entitled to reimbursement from the estate.

   b. **Death tax:** Some use the term "death tax" to refer to both estate and inheritance taxes.

6. **Unified gift and estate tax scheme:** The Tax Reform Act of 1976 unified the gift and estate tax schemes. Inter vivos and testamentary transfers are generally taxed at the same rates, and the estate tax exemption/tax credit amount is applicable to an individual's inter vivos taxable gifts and the decedent's taxable estate. Large inter vivos gifts that trigger gift taxes do not result in the donor paying a gift tax that year, but rather the tax due as a result of the inter vivos gift is charged against the individual's unified estate/gift tax credit. Charging inter vivos gift tax amounts against the individual's unified credit means that the practical amount that the individual can pass at death free of the estate tax is reduced. While the gift and estate tax schemes are still unified, the 2001 Tax Act created a divergence between the two, starting in 2004, with differing amounts transferable before the actual payment of taxes (i.e., the effective exclusions, which are really credits—see above).

7. **Generation-skipping transfer tax:** Prior to 1986, it was possible to pass property in trust from one generation to another, via a series of life estates and special powers of appointment, with the property being passed from generation to generation escaping both estate tax and gift tax for as long as permitted under the Rule against Perpetuities (commonly called "dynasty

trusts"). The Tax Reform Act of 1986, however, closed this loophole. It imposes a generation-skipping transfer tax on transfers where the beneficiary is more than one generation below the transferor's generation. As applied to dynasty trusts, it imposes a transfer tax upon the death of a life tenant if the next-in-line taker is a grandchild of the settlor or a more remote descendant. The Tax Act of 1986 imposes a tax on generation-skipping transfers at a flat rate equal to the highest estate tax rate after the effective application of various exemptions and exclusions.

Scheduled repeal: As with the estate tax, the 2001 Tax Act set out to repeal the generation-skipping transfer tax system for generation-skipping transfers that occur after December 31, 2009. While subject to the same "sunset clause" discussed above, the current federal budget materials are likely to retain the generation-skipping transfer tax in its 2009 form.

II. THE FEDERAL GIFT TAX SCHEME

A. **Taxable gift:** Two variables need analyzing when calculating whether an inter vivos gift triggers gift tax consequences: (1) whether the transfer is a gift, and (2) whether the amount exceeds the annual gift tax exclusion (or is otherwise excluded from gift tax).

1. **Gift defined:** The Internal Revenue Code does not fully define what constitutes a gift, but it is *not* determined by the intent of the transferor at the time of transfer. Rather, a gift for gift tax purposes is one where the transferor has not received adequate consideration in money or money's worth and when the transferor has abandoned sufficient dominion and control over the property being transferred to put it beyond recall or the right to demand the beneficial enjoyment of the property.

2. **Retained interest:** Where the transferor retains an interest in the property, for example where the settlor is also a beneficiary, the issue is whether the interest is mandatory or discretionary.

   a. **Mandatory:** Where the settlor grants him- or herself a mandatory interest in the property in trust, there is no gift.

   b. **Discretionary:** Where the settlor grants him- or herself a discretionary interest in the property in trust, the issue is how discretionary the trustee's discretion is.

      i. **Ascertainable standard:** Where the trustee's discretion is governed by an express ascertainable standard, no gift has been made for gift tax purposes.

      ii. **Unfettered discretion—majority view:** In most jurisdictions, even where the trustee has unfettered discretion, it is still not a completed gift for gift tax purposes. The reasoning is that creditors of a settlor can force a trustee to exercise his or her discretion in favor of the creditors, and a settlor can voluntarily put him- or herself in a situation where his or her creditors would sue the trustee.

      iii. **Unfettered discretion—minority view:** In a minority of jurisdictions, if the discretion is unfettered and without any express standard that the settlor could use to facilitate an abuse of discretion claim, the gift is considered complete for gift tax purposes.

   c. **Example:** In *Holtz's Estate v. Commissioner*, 38 T.C. 37 (1962), the settlor created an inter vivos trust and retained a life estate. The trustee had a mandatory duty to pay the income to the settlor for life, and the trust gave the trustee the discretion to invade the principal for the settlor's benefit if necessary for the settlor's "welfare, comfort, and support, . . . or hospitalization or other emergency needs." The court ruled that the inclusion of the standard of guidance for the trustee meant that the standard was not truly discretionary and there was no completed gift. This holding was reinforced by testimony that the trustee assured the settlor the principal would be at his disposal if reasonably necessary.

    d. Gifts of future interests: Where the holder of a future interest transfers his or her interest to a donee, a gift is made. The fact that the gift is a future interest and not a possessory interest does not defeat the fact that the transferor has relinquished dominion and control over the property interest. The fact that it is a future interest affects its valuation, but not the fact that a gift was made.

    Contingent future interests: Likewise, if the future interest is a contingent future interest or if the future interest is subject to divestment, the future interest is still a property interest subject to being transferred as a gift. Its uncertain nature affects its valuation, but not its status as a property interest subject to being gifted to another.

    e. Disclaimers: A disclaimer has the effect of transferring a property interest. The party disclaiming is not treated as having made a gift as long as the disclaimer complies with the IRS requirements for a valid disclaimer: (1) the disclaimer is in writing; (2) the disclaimer is executed within 9 months of the party receiving the property interest (or within 9 months of the disclaimant reaching age 21); (3) the disclaimant accepted no interest in the disclaimed property prior to disclaiming it; and (4) the disclaimant does not designate to whom the disclaimed property is to go, but rather the property passes to the next eligible takers under the applicable law. IRC §2518.

3. Retained powers: If the transferor retains the power to revoke, appoint, or change the owner, the transferor has not abandoned sufficient dominion and control over the property for the transfer to be deemed a completed gift. (These powers usually arise, if at all, where the transfer is the creation of a trust.)

    a. Third-party consent required: Where the transferor retains the power to revoke, appoint, or change the owner or beneficiary only upon the consent of a third party, for gift tax purposes the issue is whether the third party is an adverse party (a beneficiary who would be adversely affected). Where the third party is adverse, the gift is complete despite the retained power. Where the third party is not adverse, the transferor has not relinquished sufficient dominion and control over the property for the transfer to be a gift.

    b. Limited by ascertainable standard: Where the transferor retains the power to appoint or change the owner or beneficiary (for example, the transferor has the power to invade the principal and use it for another's benefit), but such power is limited by an express ascertainable standard (for example, only for purposes of the person's health, education, support, or maintenance), the transferor has relinquished sufficient dominion and control over the property for the transfer to be considered a gift.

    c. Termination of power inter vivos: If the transferor terminates or releases the power inter vivos and the effect is that the transferor is now deemed to have abandoned dominion and control over the property, the act of terminating or releasing the power constitutes the act that triggers gift tax consequences, valuing the amount of the gift at such time.

d. Termination of power upon death: Where the transferor retains the power to revoke, alter, or appoint, and the power is not exercised but terminates with the death of the transferor, the termination of the power does not give rise to gift tax consequences. The property in question, however, is considered part of the transferor's gross estate for estate tax purposes, thereby possibly implicating estate taxes (but not gift taxes), valuing the property at the transferor's death.

e. Tax implications: If a gift has not been made, the transferor is still liable for the income generated by the property. If the settlor creates a revocable trust and the trust provides that the income is to be paid to someone other than the settlor, the power to revoke means that no gift has been made. The settlor is liable for the income tax on the income generated by the property in trust. IRC §§676, 677.

f. Joint tenancy with non-spouse: Where a spouse enters into a joint tenancy with a non-spouse, the first issue is whether both parties contributed valuable consideration. If not, if one party puts up all the consideration for the joint tenancy property, that party is generally treated as having made a gift of the appropriate share of the property owned by the other joint tenant or tenants (because each tenant has the power to unilaterally sever his or her share). A common example of this is a parent placing a child's name on property as a joint tenant with the parent. If the value of the share exceeds the annual gift tax exclusion, inter vivos gift tax consequences result. (The same holds true if the parties purchase the property as tenants in common.)

Exception: Because each joint tenancy bank account or government bond has the right to withdraw all of the funds or cash the bond, no gift occurs until the noncontributing party withdraws some of the money or cashes the bond.

g. Basis: Where property is sold, an income tax is typically levied on any gain realized (sale price minus basis). Where a donee sells property he or she received as a gift, the donor's basis is used (unless a loss is involved, in which case the value of the property on the date of the gift is used). Where the donor is a decedent, however, the value of the property gets a *stepped-up basis*—the value is stepped up to its fair market value at time of death—for a subsequent sale involving either a gain or loss.

B. Gift tax annual exclusion: Not all gifts trigger a gift tax. The tax code provides that each donor can give up to $10,000 a year to each donee before a gift is considered a taxable gift (with the requisite duty to file a gift tax return). IRC §2503(b). The annual amount that can be gifted to a donee tax-free is commonly referred to as the annual gift tax exclusion. In 1997, Congress legislated that the size of the exclusion will increase in $1,000 increments to keep pace with inflation. The amount increased to $13,000 in 2009.

1. Future interests: Where a donor makes a gift of a future interest, no part of the gift qualifies for the annual gift exclusion. The whole present value of the future interest is subject to the gift tax analysis.

Gift to a minor: Because a minor lacks legal capacity to manage property until he or she reaches the age of majority, the issue arises whether a gift of property to a minor is, in substance, a gift of a future interest (the minor is to receive the property when the minor reaches the age of majority). The gift of property to a minor does not constitute a gift of a future interest and therefore qualifies for the annual gift exclusion, as long as: (1) the property is given to the minor despite his or her age; (2) the property is given to the guardian for the minor; or

(3) if the property (and all interest generated by the property) can be used for the minor's benefit, and any unexpended property will either pass to the donee upon reaching age 21 or to the donee's estate if he or she dies before reaching age 21 (or by exercise of a general power of appointment held by the donee). IRC §2503(c).

2. **Right or power to receive trust property:** As a general rule, when a trust beneficiary is not receiving at least trust income presently, there is no present interest and, therefore, no annual exclusion. If, however, the trust contains a provision that allows the beneficiary to immediately demand, at time of contribution to the trust, a certain dollar amount (usually equal to the amount of the annual exclusion), then for gift tax purposes, this is deemed to be a present interest and therefore qualifies for the annual exclusion (to the donor). This is commonly known as a Crummey withdrawal right, named after the case *Crummey v. Commissioner*, T.C. Memo. 1966-144, aff'd in part and rev'd in part, 397 F.2d 82 (9th Cir. 1968). These withdrawal rights usually are designed to last for only a limited period of time and then expire. It does not matter that the beneficiary actually exercises his or her right of withdrawal but, rather, that he or she has the right to do so, thus facilitating the availability of the annual exclusion(s) to the donor.

   a. **Sham power:** Where the parties have an agreement or understanding that the person having this withdrawal right (Crummey power) will not exercise it, the power is a sham and is not considered a gift of a present interest, and the annual exclusion is not available to the donor.

   b. **Holder's interest a contingent future interest:** Crummey withdrawal rights are usually given, pursuant to the trust instrument, to primary beneficiaries. The trust instrument, however, can give such powers to remote contingent beneficiaries, thereby increasing the number of annual exclusions available.

   c. **Example:** In *Estate of Cristofani v. Commissioner,* 97 T.C. 74 (1991), the settlor created a trust to which she transferred her interest in a parcel of real property, one-third a year over three years (valued at $70,000 a year). The trust expressly granted her two children and her five grandchildren the power to withdraw principal, up to the amount of the annual gift tax exclusion, for a limited time period each year (if exercised within 15 days of the contribution of the one-third interest of the property to the trust). The court held that the transfers of the presently exercisable rights of withdrawal constituted a general power of appointment that constituted a present interest in the property qualifying for the annual gift tax exclusion of $10,000. The court rejected the argument made by the IRS that the test for what constitutes a present interest for gift tax purposes should be whether there was a likelihood that the beneficiary would actually receive present enjoyment of the property. The court held there was a present interest as long as the beneficiaries had the legal ability to exercise the right to withdraw the property and the trustee did not have the legal ability to resist such an attempt. Applying this test, the court held that the grandchildren had such a right and that there was no evidence of an understanding among the parties that the power would not be exercised.

   d. **Failure to exercise:** Where a donee holds a Crummey withdrawal right or general power of appointment, failure to exercise the right or power may constitute a gift of the property subject to the power by the donee to the remainderman. IRC §2041(b)(2). This is referred to as a lapsing right of withdrawal or general power of appointment, and the specific rules regarding taxability are very complex.

C. **Other gift tax exclusions:** In addition to the annual gift tax exclusion, certain amounts paid by an individual on behalf of another individual for education and medical items are not considered taxable gifts. IRC §2503(e). This exclusion is in addition to the annual exclusion.

   1. **Educational tuition payments exclusion:** In addition to the annual gift tax exclusion, any and all payments one person makes directly to an educational institution to cover tuition and fees for another person are excluded from gift tax considerations, regardless of the size of the payments. IRC §2503(e).

      Tuition and fees only: The exclusion applies only to tuition payments and to no other types of payments (books, supplies, room and board, and so on).

   2. **Medical expenses exclusion:** In addition to the annual gift tax exclusion, most payments one person makes for another person's medical care are excluded from gift tax considerations, regardless of the size of the gift payments. IRC §2503(e).

   3. **Must be paid directly to provider:** The exclusion for education and medical payments apply only to amounts paid directly to the provider of the education or qualifying medical services (the school, university, the hospital, doctor, and so on). Amounts paid to an individual who then uses the money for tuition and fees or for qualifying medical care do not qualify for this exclusion (but the payment to the individual does qualify for the annual exclusion).

D. **Deductions in computing taxable gifts:** Generally, gifts made to charity and to a spouse are deducted (in effect, not counted) in computing taxable gifts.

   1. **Marital deduction—gifts between spouses:** As a general rule, spouses are permitted to make an unlimited number of gifts to each other, inter vivos or testamentary, outright or in a qualifying marital trust, regardless of the amount, without incurring gift tax or estate tax consequences. (The details of the marital deduction are set forth later in this chapter in section V.) Where one spouse makes a gift to a third party, for gift tax purposes the gift can be split between the two spouses as long as the non-donor spouse consents.

   2. **Gifts to charity:** As a general rule, gifts to qualified charities do not result in taxable gifts and thereby do not result in the imposition of gift taxes.

III. THE FEDERAL ESTATE TAX: AN OVERVIEW

A. **Overview:** The federal estate tax system is a complicated system that imposes a graduated tax on an estate calculated by adding and subtracting a number of different categories of property interests and deductions.

   First step—calculate taxable estate: At the macro level, the first step in determining a decedent's federal estate tax is to calculate the decedent's taxable estate. The decedent's taxable estate is (1) the decedent's *gross estate* (the value of all property that the decedent owned, had a beneficial interest in, or retained dominion and control over at time of death, and certain transfers made and gift taxes paid within three years of death), *minus* (2) *various deductions* (for death-related expenses, charitable deductions, and the marital deduction).

   Second step—calculate the estate tax: The estate tax is based on applying the tax rate schedule to the decedent's taxable estate. (It is a bit more complex than that, however, because of the unified nature of the estate and gift tax schemes. Actually, the estate tax is cumulative in nature and takes into consideration, for purposes of applying the graduated estate tax rates, the decedent's inter vivos taxable gifts made after 1976. Through a somewhat complex mechanism, taxable gifts are not taxed twice—that is, again as part of the estate tax—but are used in determining the decedent's rate of estate tax.)

Third step—apply credits to determine estate tax liability: Once the estate tax "before credits" is calculated, this amount is reduced by various credits including, most notably, the unified estate tax credit.

IV. CALCULATING THE DECEDENT'S GROSS ESTATE

A. **Decedent's gross estate—an overview:** The decedent's gross estate includes the value of property that the decedent owned, had a beneficial interest in, or retained dominion and control over at the time of his or her death.

   Inter vivos gifts: Inter vivos gifts not only reduce the decedent's gross estate, but they can use the annual exclusion to avoid or minimize gift taxes, any subsequent appreciation is not included in the decedent's gross estate, and the gift tax is tax-exclusive while the estate tax is tax-inclusive.

B. **Property includible in decedent's gross estate:** The Internal Revenue Code expressly identifies the different types of property interest that are includible in the decedent's gross estate for federal estate tax purposes.

   1. **Decedent's probate property:** All property that passes into the decedent's probate estate (transmissible property) is part of the decedent's gross estate for federal estate tax purposes. IRC §2033. It is not reduced by the value of the surviving spouse's elective share rights.

      Nontransmissible property generally excluded: If the decedent owned a terminable interest (that is, a life estate) *created by someone else,* the interest does not pass into the decedent's probate estate and is not included in the decedent's gross estate. The terminable interest can even be coupled with a limited power to invade the principal and a special power of appointment without the property being included in the decedent's gross estate.

      a. **Nontransmissible property included if coupled with power of appointment:** If, however, the terminable interest, created by someone else, is coupled with a general power of appointment over the property vested in the decedent, the property constitutes part of the decedent's gross estate for federal estate tax purposes. IRC §2041.

      b. **Decedent created life estate included:** If inter vivos the decedent transferred the property but retained a life estate, the property is included in the decedent's gross estate. IRC §2036.

   2. **Concurrently owned property:** There are four possible ways a spouse can own property concurrently with another person: (1) joint tenancy, (2) tenancy in common, (3) tenancy by the entirety, and (4) community property. The decedent's interest in tenancy in common and community property are probate assets and, as such, are includible in the decedent's gross estate for that reason. Because the joint tenancy and tenancy by the entirety involve the right of survivorship, they involve special consideration.

      a. **Joint tenancy with non-spouse—estate tax:** At time of death, the entire value of the joint tenancy property, as of the date of death, is included in the decedent's gross estate, minus a number calculated by multiplying the date of death value times the percentage of the original purchase price contributed by the surviving joint tenant. The burden of proof is on the decedent's personal representative to prove what percentage of the original purchase price the surviving joint tenant(s) contributed. IRC §2040(a).

No double taxation: If the other co-tenant made no contribution either in kind to the property (joint tenancy bank account) or no contribution to the original purchase, and a gift tax resulted when the other co-tenant was placed on title (for example, a parent placing a child's name on title as a joint tenant), this gift tax will effectively be credited against the estate tax (when computing the estate tax) to make sure there is no double taxation.

b. **Joint tenancy/tenancy by the entirety with spouse:** A joint tenancy or tenancy by the entirety created between spouses qualifies for the marital deduction even if one spouse puts up all of the consideration or property. There is no inter vivos gift tax, and there is no estate tax upon the death of the first spouse if the spouses are the only parties to the co-tenancy. One-half of the joint tenancy/tenancy by the entirety date of death value is included in the deceased spouse's gross estate, but it qualifies for the marital deduction, so there are no estate tax consequences.

3. **Payable-on-death property included:** Property that the decedent had control over via a contract with a payable-on-death (P.O.D.) clause is included in the decedent's gross estate for federal estate tax purposes. IRC §2033.

a. **Employee death benefits:** If the decedent had the right to receive a benefit from an employment-related benefits program that also included a P.O.D. component, the property interest is includible in the decedent's gross estate for federal estate tax purposes even if the decedent never actually received any direct benefit from the program. IRC §2039.

b. **Life insurance:** Where a life insurance policy (term or whole life) was taken out on the decedent's life, the value of the proceeds of the policy is included in the decedent's gross estate for federal estate tax purposes if the decedent had any of the usual incidents of ownership over the policy at the time of death or if the proceeds were payable to the insured's executor or probate estate. The usual incidents of ownership include the right to cancel the policy, the right to change the beneficiary, the right to transfer the policy, the right to borrow against the policy, and so on. The insured need not make the payments on the policy for it to be included in his or her gross estate. IRC §2042.

4. **Beneficial interest or control:** Where the decedent transfers legal title interest but retains sufficient beneficial interest in or retained dominion and control over the property, the property is includible in the decedent's gross estate for federal estate tax purposes. IRC §2036.

a. **Possession, enjoyment, or right to income:** Where the decedent transfers legal title to property inter vivos, but retains (1) the right to possess the property, (2) the enjoyment of the property, (3) the right to the income generated by the property, or (4) the right to control, either alone or in conjunction with others, who shall possess, enjoy, or receive the income from the property, the decedent has retained sufficient interest in or control over the property that his or her interest in the property is includible in his or her gross estate for federal estate tax purposes. IRC §2036(a)(1), (2).

b. **As trustee:** If the transferor creates an irrevocable trust but appoints him- or herself trustee (sole or co-trustee), and the trust is a discretionary trust, the transferor retains control over who receives the enjoyment of the property over which the transferor has discretion. Such property is includible in the transferor's gross estate for federal estate tax purposes.

c. **Right to possession:** Where the transferor retains actual possession or the right to possession for life, a presumption arises that the property is includible in the transferor's gross estate unless the transfer was a bona fide transfer for full consideration. In determining whether the transfer was a bona fide transfer for full consideration, the intent of the parties as to whether the consideration will ever be paid is a legitimate inquiry in determining whether the transaction is bona fide.

> **Example:** In *Estate of Maxwell v. Commissioner*, 3 F.3d 591 (2d Cir. 1993), the transferor sold the property for $270,000 and leased it back at a rate remarkably close to the interest payments due on the mortgage. The lease payments cancelled out the interest payments, and the purchasers never paid any principal. Upon the transferor's death, the transferor's estate listed only the outstanding balance on the purchase price in the gross estate. The Commissioner characterized the decedent's interest as a retained life estate and included the full value of the property in the decedent's gross estate. The court held that there was no real expectation that the purchase price would ever be paid and that the parties had an understanding that the note would be forgiven, so the transfer was not a bona fide transfer for full consideration. The full value of the property was includible in the decedent's gross estate.

d. **Reciprocal trust doctrine:** Where two parties (typically husband and wife) set up trusts that give each other a life estate interest in the other's trust, the value of the trust in which each holds the life estate interest is includible in each party's gross estate for federal estate tax purposes.

> **Example:** In *Old Colony Trust Co. v. United States*, 423 F.2d 601 (1st Cir. 1970), settlor created an inter vivos trust for the benefit of his son for life and, upon his death, for the benefit of his widow and issue. The settlor was one of the initial trustees. The trust provided that 80 percent of the income was payable to the son, but the trustees had the absolute discretion to increase the amount of the income if needed in case of sickness or changed circumstances, and the power to stop all payments completely if in the son's best interests. The trust also gave the trustees unusually broad administrative and investment powers as if there were no trust, including the absolute power to allocate between income and principal. The court rejected the argument that the unusually broad administrative powers gave the trustees the ability to shift the economic benefits of the trust between the life tenant and the remaindermen. Because the trustees have a duty to be impartial between the two groups of beneficiaries, the court held that the broad powers were not tantamount to continued ownership by the settlor. The court ruled that no aggregation of purely administrative powers could rise to the level of sufficient dominion and control to constitute ownership for estate tax purposes. The distributive powers over the income, however, expressly permitted the trustees to prefer one group of beneficiaries over the other, and, in the absence of an ascertainable standard, such control constitutes an incident of ownership for estate tax purposes. There is no ascertainable standard where the standard is too loose. Continuing a beneficiary's standard of life is ascertainable, while the power to provide for the beneficiary's happiness, pleasure, or use and benefit are not. While permitting altering the allocation for the beneficiary's "sickness" or "changed circumstances" arguably is

ascertainable, "best interests" is not an ascertainable standard. The settlor's retained power over the property in the trust warranted including it in the settlor's gross estate.

e. **Family limited partnerships ("FLP"):** In an FLP, the decedent transfers the bulk of his or her assets to a limited partnership receiving shares in the partnership in exchange, and the decedent's other family members transfer relatively small amounts to the limited partnership receiving shares in the partnership in exchange. A corporation formed and owned by the family is the general partner. The logic behind creating FLPs as estate planning arrangements is that because the limited partners lack control over the assets and have limited power to transfer their interests, the value of their interests are discounted for estate tax purposes. The courts have generally held that where the FLP is motivated solely by estate tax savings (i.e., the FLP serves no real business or commercial purpose, profits are passed through to the parties in proportion to their interests, and there is an implicit understanding that the limited partners can obtain whatever resources they need from the FLP for support), the transfers to the FLP are not a bona fide sale for adequate consideration and the full value of the assets transfers are included in the decedent's gross estate (not the discounted limited partnership value). Where, however, the FLP is a bona fide arrangement (the transfers were for adequate consideration and/or the FLP was formed for and/or conducted legitimate business and commercial activity), the discounted limited partnership value was the appropriate value to include in the decedent's gross estate.

f. **Control over trustee:** Where the settlor creates a discretionary trust and does not appoint him- or herself trustee, if the settlor retains control over the trustee through the power to remove and appoint a friendly or subordinate trustee, the settlor is deemed to have retained dominion and control over the trust property for federal estate tax purposes. In some instances, the property is included in the settlor's estate when a mere possibility exists that the settlor could have appointed him- or herself as trustee, even though such power could occur only if the trustee resigned, died, stepped down as trustee, and so on, and such contingency did not occur before the settlor's death.

5. **Power to revoke, appoint, or modify:** If at the time of his or her death, the transferor retained the power to revoke, appoint, or modify who has the right to enjoy the property or when a party has the right to enjoy the property, the property is includible in the transferor's gross estate for federal estate tax purposes. If the transferor retained such power but released it within three years of the transferor's death, the property is still includible in the transferor's gross estate. The rule applies whether the transferor retains the power alone or in conjunction with others (friendly or adverse). If the power to revoke or modify the right to enjoy is given to a third party, friendly or adverse, the property is not includible in the transferor's gross estate unless the transferor retains control over that party. IRC §2038.

6. **Reversion:** If a transferor transfers a finite estate (life estate typically), retains a reversionary interest, and transfers an alternative future interest to a third party whose possession or enjoyment is conditioned on surviving the transferor, and the value of the reversionary interest immediately before the transferor's death exceeds 5 percent of the value of the property, the value of the property (less the possessory estate) is included in the transferor's gross estate. IRC §2037.

Reversionary interest: If a transferor transfers a finite estate (life estate typically) and reserves a reversionary interest, with no express alternative gift over in the event the transferor predeceases the holder of the finite estate, only the reversionary interest is included in the transferor's gross estate. IRC §2033.

7. **Powers relinquished and transfers made within three years of death:** Discussed above are certain powers that, if held by the decedent at the time of his or her death, cause inclusion of property in his or her estate. Typically these are powers retained with respect trusts and include the power to revoke, alter, and amend (IRC §2038), the power retained for life to enjoy trust income or determine who gets the trust property or income (IRC §2038), or certain retained reversionary interests (IRC §2037). When an individual who retained such powers relinquishes them and dies within three years, IRC §2035 generally requires treating the decedent as if he or she still retained such powers, implicating the requisite inclusion of property in the gross estate. In addition, transfers of ownership of life insurance within three years of death nonetheless require inclusion of the full proceeds in the insured's/transferor's estate. Finally, gift taxes paid on any gifts within three years of death are artificially "brought back" into the decedent's gross estate. IRC §2035(b).

8. **General power of appointment:** If the decedent held a general power of appointment when he or she died, testamentary or inter vivos, that was created by another, the property subject to the power is included in the decedent's gross estate for federal estate tax purposes (whether the power is exercised or not). IRC §2041. If, however, the power is a special power of appointment, the property is not included in the donee's gross estate, even if the donee exercises the power.

   a. **Given to beneficiary/trustee:** A power to invade held by a beneficiary/trustee for the benefit of the beneficiary/trustee constitutes a general power of appointment even if there are other co-trustees who must consent to the exercise of the power, unless the other co-trustees have an interest that is adverse to the exercise of the power. IRC §2041.

   Exception: A power vested in a trustee to invade for his or her own benefit is not included in the trustee's gross estate if the power is limited by an ascertainable standard relating to health, education, support, or maintenance.

   b. **Example:** In *Estate of Vissering v. Commissioner*, 990 F.2d 578 (10th Cir. 1993), decedent was co-trustee of a trust created by his mother. The trust authorized the trustees to invade the principal for limited purposes. The co-trustees were not adversely affected by the exercise of the power, so the decedent was charged with holding a general power of appointment. Although the power to invade for one's comfort generally is not an ascertainable standard, here the language was qualified that the power could be exercised if "required for the continued comfort." The court ruled that the trust's language was tantamount to maintaining the beneficiary's standard of living, an ascertainable standard. As such, the property subject to the general power of appointment was not includible in the decedent's gross estate.

   c. **Power limited to $5,000 or 5 percent annually:** A power to invade the principal for up to the greater of $5,000 or 5 percent of the property annually results in only up to $5,000 or 5 percent of the property being included in the donee's gross estate for federal estate tax purposes (but if the power was fully exercised in the year the donee died, the power is not included in the donee's gross estate).

d. Example: In *Estate of Kurz v. Commissioner*, 68 F.3d 1027 (7th Cir. 1995), the decedent was the beneficiary of two trusts, a marital trust and a family trust. Under the marital trust, she had an unlimited right to invade the principal. Under the family trust, she was limited to 5 percent a year and only if the marital trust was exhausted. The issue was whether the sequence of withdrawal rights prevents a power of appointment from being deemed "exercisable." Although the tax regulations expressly provide that a power expressly exercisable upon the occurrence of an event that did not occur is not a power in existence at the decedent's death, the decedent must not have had control over such conditions. Here, the decedent had control over whether the marital trust was exhausted. The decedent held a general power to appoint 5 percent of the family trust, and that 5 percent is also includible in the decedent's gross estate for federal estate tax purposes.

V. THE MARITAL DEDUCTION

A. Introduction: As a general rule, spouses are permitted to make an unlimited number of gifts to each other, inter vivos or testamentary, regardless of the amount, without incurring gift tax or estate tax consequences. IRC §2056.

B. Requirements: Property qualifies for the marital deduction as long as (1) the transferor is either a citizen or resident of the United States at the time of his or her death; (2) the property "passes" from the transferor to his or her spouse, inter vivos or at time of death; (3) the donee spouse survives the transferor; (4) the value of the property otherwise would have been includible in the transferor's gross estate for federal estate tax purposes; and (5) the property is not a nondeductible terminable interest. IRC §2056(b).

1. Passing requirement: The requirement that the property must "pass" from the transferor to the transferor's surviving spouse has been broadly construed to cover virtually all forms of passing a property interest—inter vivos or testamentary (probate testate, probate intestate, and nonprobate transfers).

2. Not a nondeductible terminal interest requirement: To qualify as a deductible interest, the property interest must be one that (1) will end up in the surviving spouse's estate (and thus subject to taxation at the time), or (2) the surviving spouse can transfer to third parties (and thus be subject to taxation at that time). If the property interest is a terminable interest, an interest that may fail or be extinguished during the donee's spouse's lifetime, or an interest that will be extinguished upon the donee spouse's death (a life estate to surviving spouse with remainder to others), the property transfer to the donee spouse does not qualify for the marital deduction.

3. Exceptions: There are a handful of exceptions to the requirement that the property being passed to the surviving spouse cannot be a life estate or other terminable interest.

a. Estate trust exception: An interest does not qualify as a nondeductible terminable interest only if upon the termination of the spouse's interest the property passes to someone other than the surviving spouse or his or her probate estate. If the conveyance expressly provides that upon the death of the party, the property is to pass to his or her estate, the property qualifies for the marital deduction. (This exception is typically used only if the trust holds unproductive property that makes it difficult to qualify under the other exceptions.)

b. Limited survival requirement: If the gift to the surviving spouse is conditioned upon the surviving spouse surviving the decedent by a specific period of time not to exceed 6 months, the interest being transferred qualifies for the marital deduction as long as the surviving spouse meets the survival requirement. IRC §2056(b)(3).

c. **Marital deduction power of appointment trust (life estate + general power of appointment):** If the donee spouse is given a life estate interest in a trust but is also given the power to appoint to him- or herself, or his or her estate, this is considered a general power of appointment, causing inclusion of the property in the donee spouse's gross estate for estate tax purposes. Because the property is taxable upon the death of the donee spouse, the transfer to the donee spouse qualifies for the marital deduction as long as the additional statutory requirements are satisfied: (1) the donee spouse has a mandatory interest in the income, payable annually, if not more frequently; (2) the power of appointment can be exercised, at a minimum, in favor of the surviving spouse or his or her estate; (3) the power is exercisable alone and in all events (that is, the exercise of the power does not require anyone else's consent and is not contingent on anything such as not remarrying); and (4) no other party can have a power to appoint the property unless it is in favor of the surviving spouse. IRC §2056(b)(5).

d. **QTIP trust exception:** The qualified terminable interest property (QTIP) trust exception provides that if the surviving spouse is given a life estate interest in a trust, with a mandatory interest in the income, payable annually, if not more frequently, and no one (including the surviving spouse) has the power to appoint the property during the surviving spouse's lifetime to anyone other than the spouse, the property qualifies for the marital deduction (even if the surviving spouse is given a special testamentary power of appointment over the property, though it is not required that the surviving spouse be given this power). In addition, a qualified election (on the estate tax return of the first spouse to die) must be made in a timely manner (on a timely filed estate tax return). IRC §2056(b)(7). If the transfer qualifies as a QTIP trust, the property is included in the surviving spouse's gross estate for estate tax purposes, but the tax is paid by the persons receiving the property upon the surviving spouse's death (or, if the interest is in trust, as is the norm, the tax is paid out of the trust corpus before the next interest is given effect). IRC §§2044, 2207A.

e. **Judicially reformed trusts:** Increasingly, courts are reforming trusts to achieve tax benefits, including to qualify as marital deduction power of appointment trusts, estate trusts, or QTIP trusts. Where a trust qualifies for the marital deduction as the result of judicial reformation, however, the state court proceedings are not binding for purposes of determining federal estate taxes owed unless the judicial proceedings are approved by the state's highest court. *See Commissioner v. Estate of Bosch*, 387 U.S. 456 (1967).

  i. **Example:** In *Estate of Rapp v. Commissioner*, 140 F.3d 1211 (9th Cir. 1998), the decedent devised his one-half of the community property to a trust, with a life estate to his surviving spouse. The children, as co-trustees, were given the power to invade the principal, if they deemed necessary, for the benefit of the surviving spouse. The trust did not qualify as a QTIP trust. The surviving spouse claimed the deceased spouse intended to create a QTIP trust and petitioned the court to reform the trust to qualify as a QTIP trust. The probate court did reform the trust, amending the trust so that it provided that all income was to be paid to the surviving spouse at least annually, and the court eliminated the power to invade the principal. The tax court noted that the California

Supreme Court had not approved the probate court's reformation. The tax court ruled that under California law, the trust should not have been reformed, and thus the trust did not qualify as a QTIP trust.

ii. **Example:** In ***Pond v. Pond***, 678 N.E.2d 1321 (Mass. 1997), the trustee of the Sidney Pond trust petitioned the probate court to reform the trust. The trust provided that during the settlor's life, all of the income and as much principal as the trustee deemed necessary were to be paid to the settlor. The trust, however, made no provision for income or principal to be paid to his wife were she to survive him. His will, however, appointed her personal representative and authorized her to elect to qualify the trust for the federal estate tax marital deduction. To qualify, however, the trust must provide the surviving spouse with a "qualifying income interest for life." Without the marital deduction, the settlor's estate would have to pay $70,000 in otherwise avoidable taxes. The trustee claimed the error was due to scrivener's error and petitioned the court to reform the trust (1) to qualify it for the marital deduction, and (2) to permit the trust's assets to be used to support his surviving spouse. The court noted when a trust fails to reflect settlor's intent due to scrivener's error, it should be reformed as long as there is clear and decisive proof of the mistake. The court concluded there was clear and decisive proof that (1) the settlor intended the trust to qualify for the marital deduction based on the provisions in the will, and (2) the settlor intended his wife to have discretionary access to the principal during her lifetime as was the case during his lifetime. The court ordered the trust to be reformed.

4. **Noncitizen surviving spouse:** The marital deduction does not apply if the surviving spouse is not a citizen of the United States.

   Qualified domestic trust exception: If the surviving spouse is not a U.S. citizen, the transfer to the surviving spouse may still qualify for the marital deduction if the transfer qualifies as a qualified domestic trust. IRC §2056(d)(2). The trust must qualify as a marital deduction power of appointment trust, an estate trust, or a QTIP trust, and at least one of the trustees must be a U.S. citizen or domestic corporate trustee, and the trustee must be authorized to withhold the deferred estate tax.

5. **Estate planning considerations:** Although the marital deduction permits transfer of property from one spouse to another without incurring estate tax consequences upon the death of the first spouse, the marital deduction only ***delays*** estate taxation until the death of the second spouse—it does ***not*** necessarily ***avoid*** estate tax. Each individual, however, has a unified credit that permits a set amount of property to be passed without any estate tax. Proper estate planning is important to ensure that each spouse's unified credit is fully utilized. The availability of the marital deduction may cause some to overlook the tax benefits of taking advantage of the unified credit that is available upon the death of the first spouse. Any property given outright to a surviving spouse, while avoiding estate tax upon the death of the first spouse, is included in the second spouse's gross estate for estate tax purposes if the second spouse still owns it upon death. To minimize estate taxes, the first spouse to die might want to give the surviving spouse a life estate interest in as much property as qualifies for the deceased spouse's unified credit, thereby avoiding estate taxes on the death of either spouse as to that amount, and use the marital deduction only for property above and beyond the amount available for the unified credit. This ensures maximum use of the combined unified credit available for a couple.

6. **Unlimited charitable tax deduction:** In calculating a decedent's taxable estate, the Code permits unlimited deductions for qualifying charitable transfers. IRC §2055. Twice a year the IRS publishes a list of corporations that have qualified as charitable organizations. Outright transfers to such organizations qualify for the charitable tax deduction as a matter of course. Transfers of remainder interests are more complicated.

VI. THE GENERATION-SKIPPING TRANSFER TAX

A. **Historical background:** Prior to adoption of the generation-skipping transfer tax in 1986, it was possible to transfer equitable property interests in trusts, from one generation to another, tax-free until the trust had to terminate pursuant to the jurisdiction's Rule against Perpetuities.

B. **Generation-skipping transfer tax:** The Tax Reform Act of 1986 attempted to close the generation-skipping transfer loophole by requiring a transfer tax on any generation-skipping transfer. IRC §2611(a). A generation-skipping transfer is one that skips a generation, where the transferee is two or more generations below the transferor's generation. Such transferees are known as skip persons under the Internal Revenue Code. Transfers to one's spouse or children do not skip a generation and are not subject to the generation-skipping transfer tax. Transfers from a grandparent to a grandchild or a more remote descendent are subject to the generation-skipping transfer tax.

1. **Applies post-1986:** The generation-skipping transfer tax does not apply to irrevocable trusts created prior to adoption of the Tax Reform Act of 1986.

2. **Abolished 2010?:** Pursuant to the Tax Act of 2001, as mentioned above, the generation-skipping transfer tax does not apply to transfers made after December 31, 2009. Also, as mentioned above, this repeal, along with the 2001 Tax Act's sunset clause, is likely to disappear pursuant to legislation implementing President Obama's 2009 federal budget proposals. Thus, it is anticipated that the generation-skipping transfer tax will continue on past 2009 in its current form (as of 2009).

C. **Generation-skipping transfers:** The Code identifies three generation-skipping transfers that are subject to the generation-skipping transfer tax.

1. **Direct skip transfers:** If a transferor transfers property directly to a skip person, the generation-skipping transfer tax applies. If it is a testamentary transfer, an estate tax may also be due. If it is an inter vivos transfer, a gift tax may also be due.

   a. **Exception—multiple skips:** Where a direct transfer skips more than one generation, only one generation-skipping transfer tax is imposed.

   b. **Exception—predeceased intervening descendent:** Where a direct transfer skips a generation because the descendant at that generation has predeceased the transfer, no generation-skipping transfer tax is imposed.

2. **Taxable terminations:** If property is held in trust and an interest in the property is terminated by whatever means (death, lapse of time, release, or other), a taxable termination has occurred unless (1) immediately after such termination a nonskip person is entitled to the property, or (2) at no time after such termination may the property be distributed from the trust to a skip person. IRC §2611(a).

3. **Taxable distributions:** If property is distributed from a trust to a skip person, a taxable distribution has occurred. IRC §2611(a).

4. **Scope:** Taxable terminations and taxable distributions also apply to trust equivalents—legal life estates and remainders, terms of years and remainders, and insurance and annuity contracts.

5. **Imposition of tax:** If the taxable transfer is a direct skip transfer, the generation-skipping transfer tax is imposed on the date the transfer is effective. If the taxable transfer is a taxable termination or distribution, the generation-skipping transfer tax is imposed when the transfer occurs.

D. **Rate:** The generation-skipping transfer tax rate is the highest possible estate tax rate.

E. **Property covered:** If a generation-skipping transfer occurs, the property subject to the tax and who pays the tax depend on which type of generation-skipping transfer it was.

1. **Direct skip:** If the transfer is a direct skip, the entire amount of the transfer is subject to the generation-skipping transfer tax. The transferor pays the tax.

2. **Taxable termination:** If the transfer is a taxable termination from a trust, the entire property that is subject to the terminated interest is subject to the generation-skipping transfer tax. The trustee pays the tax.

3. **Taxable distribution:** If the transfer is a taxable distribution from a trust, the property subject to the generation-skipping transfer tax is the entire distribution. The beneficiary who receives the distribution pays the tax.

F. **Exemption:** Each individual can transfer up to $1 million that is exempt from the generation-skipping transfer tax. IRC §2611(a). This exemption amount increases with inflation and is $1.1 million in 2002.

G. **Exclusions:** The Code excludes a number of transfers from the scope of the generation-skipping transfer tax.

1. **Annual gift tax exclusion:** Transfers that are not subject to gift taxes due to the annual gift tax exclusion are excluded. IRC §2612(c).

2. **Tuition/medical payments:** Direct payments of tuition and/or medical expenses of an individual are not subject to either gift taxes or generation-skipping transfer taxes. IRC §2611(b)(2).

3. **Trust transfers subject to estate or gift taxes:** Any transfer from a trust that is subject to estate or gift taxes with respect to a nonskip person is not subject to the generation-skipping transfer tax. IRC §2611(b)(1).

H. **Terminology:** When applying the generation-skipping transfer tax scheme, keep the following terms of art in mind.

1. **Transferor:** A party who has control over who takes the property.

2. **Skip person:** Any person who is two or more generations below the transferor. This applies to direct descendants and to remote relatives based on the table of consanguinity.

I. **Property interests subject to the tax:** A party must have a right (other than a future interest) to receive income or principal from the trust or the party must be currently eligible to receive income or principal from the trust. Future interests, whether vested or contingent, do not qualify as an interest for purposes of the generation-skipping transfer tax. A person who is an eligible object of a presently exercisable power of appointment, however, does have an interest for purposes of the generation-skipping transfer tax.

VII. STATE DEATH TAXES

A. **Overview:** All states, except Nevada, have one form or another of a death tax (though only a few have a gift tax on inter vivos transfers). The different types of state death taxes can loosely be grouped into three categories.

1. **Pick-up death tax:** Prior to 2005, the federal estate tax allowed a credit against the federal estate tax for estate taxes paid to a state, up to a certain amount. This federal estate tax mechanism effectively gave states the opportunity to implement a very simple estate tax that "piggybacked" on this credit system, allowing a state to "pick up," as a state estate tax, the federal statutory credit. The total estate tax obligation of a decedent would not increase, but, rather, a portion of the computed federal estate tax would go to the state via this "pick-up" type of state legislation. Many states enacted this method of estate tax because it was simple and inexpensive to administer, being based almost entirely on an already-established federal estate tax reporting system. However, the 2001 Tax Act contained a provision that eliminated, after 2004, the credit for state estate taxes, thus effectively eliminating a state estate tax based on this "pick-up" mechanism. As a result, some states have passed legislation adopting a different form of state estate tax which does not rely on this currently non-existent federal state tax credit. As previously indicated, the 2001 Tax Act contains a sunset clause that, if allowed to occur, would reinstate the federal credit for state estate tax and thus automatically reinstate a state "pick-up" estate tax. Recent materials accompanying President Obama's 2009 federal budget provisions, however, would seem to indicate that anticipated legislation would retain the estate tax system in its 2009 form. Unless the federal estate tax credit for state estate taxes is reinstated, state estate tax systems designed as a "pick-up" tax will not be viable.

2. **Inheritance tax:** An inheritance tax is a tax imposed on a gift being transferred at death to a taker, whether the transfer is an intestate, probate testate, or nonprobate transfer. The tax depends on the size of the gift the taker is receiving and the taker's relationship to the decedent. Takers who are more closely related to the decedent pay a lower rate compared to those who are remotely related or not related at all. The tax typically is paid out of the gift.

3. **Miscellaneous other state death taxes:** The remaining state death tax schemes do not follow any particular pattern, though they often borrow heavily from the federal estate tax approach.

Quiz Yourself on *ESTATE AND GIFT TAXES*

101. Liz creates an inter vivos trust that provides that the trustee is to distribute the income to Michael, and, upon his death, the principal is to be distributed to her foundation for the cure of AIDS. The trust grants Liz a special testamentary power to appoint the property among her ex-spouses. Liz did not exercise the power upon her death. Should the property in the trust be included in her gross estate for federal estate tax purposes? _____

102. Will purchases securities worth $20,000, taking title in the name of Will and Grace, his friend, as joint tenants with right of survivorship. Ten years later, when Will dies, the securities are worth $50,000.

   a. Were there any gift taxes due upon Will's purchase of the securities; and how much, if any, of the value of the securities should be included in Will's gross estate for federal estate tax purposes? _____

   b. What difference would it make, if any, if Will and Grace were married at all times during the hypothetical? _____

103. Frank creates an irrevocable inter vivos trust. The pertinent provisions of the trust provide that all of the income is to be paid to his sister Sally for her lifetime, and, upon her death, the principal is to be paid to Frank's son, Raymond.

   a. What are the gift tax consequences of the transfer that creates the trust? _____

   b. What are the estate tax consequences, if any, when Frank dies? _____

   c. What are the estate tax consequences, if any, when Sally dies? _____

104. Donald creates an irrevocable inter vivos trust. The pertinent provisions of the trust provide that all of the income is to be paid to Daisy, and, upon her death, the principal is to be paid to her children, if any. Donald retains a special inter vivos power of appointment to appoint the property among his nephews.

   a. What are the gift tax consequences of the transfer that creates the trust? _____

   b. What are the estate tax consequences, if any, when Donald dies? _____

105. Godfather creates an irrevocable inter vivos trust. He gives his son, Michael, a life estate interest, remainder to Michael's children who survive Michael, if any, or, if not, to Godfather's issue per stirpes. The trust also gives Michael a testamentary power to appoint any portion or all of the trust to anyone, including Michael's estate and the creditors of his estate. Michael dies intestate, survived by two children. Is any part of the trust included in Michael's gross estate for federal estate tax purposes?

106. Bill creates a testamentary trust that provides in pertinent part as follows: "All the income to my wife, Camille, and, upon her death, the property is to be distributed equally to our children." The trustee is given the power to invade the principal, if necessary, during Camille's lifetime for her health. Camille is also given a testamentary power of appointment to vary the shares to the children if she deems appropriate.

   a. What are the estate tax consequences, if any, upon Bill's death? _____

   b. What are the estate tax consequences, if any, upon Camille's death? _____

107. Charles's will provides that upon his death his property is to be distributed equally to his sons, Harry and William. William predeceases Charles but is survived by Elizabeth (William's daughter). Harry survives Charles but disclaims his interest in his father's estate. Harry has two children, Anne and Diana, who are the default takers of Harry's interest under Charles's will. What are the tax consequences of the transfers? _____

108. Homer's will creates a testamentary trust that provides in part as follows: "All to my son Bart for life, and, upon his death, to Bart's children equally." The trust also gives Bart a special power to appoint the property among Homer's heirs. What are the tax consequences upon Bart's death assuming a son, Homer II, survives him and Bart does not exercise the power of appointment?

_____

Answers

101. First, the facts fail to indicate whether the trust is revocable or irrevocable. If the trust is revocable, Liz has not relinquished dominion and control over the property inter vivos, so the property is included in her estate. If the trust is irrevocable, the issue of Liz's testamentary special power of appointment remains. The power allows her to change the beneficiaries. Even if she does not exercise the power, the mere retention of the power is enough dominion and control over the property that it does not constitute a gift. The property is included in her gross estate for estate tax purposes.

102a. When Will purchased the securities and took title in both parties' names as joint tenants, he made an inter vivos gift to Grace of one-half of the value of the securities. The $10,000 gift, however, is well below the current annual gift tax exclusion amount ($13,000 in 2009), so no gift tax is due. Upon death, because Grace is not Will's spouse, the percentage of the value of the property that is included in his estate is the percentage of the money he put towards the purchase price. Because Will contributed 100 percent of the purchase price, 100 percent of the value of the securities at the time of his death is included in his gross estate—here, the full $50,000 value at Will's death.

102b. If Will and Grace were married, Will made a gift to his wife in the amount of $10,000, but the gift qualifies for the marital deduction and is not taxable even if it exceeds the annual gift tax exclusion. Upon death, one-half of the value of the property at Will's death is included in his gross estate, but the transfer to his wife (through the right of survivorship) gives rise to a marital deduction of the same amount. Thus, no federal estate tax results from including it in Will's gross estate.

103a. When Frank creates the trust, he is making an inter vivos gift of the life estate interest to Sally and of the remainder to Raymond. The value of these interests is determined by government-provided life expectancy tables—the aggregate of the two equal the value of the gift when made. The gift to Sally is considered a "present interest" and therefore qualifies for the annual exclusion. The gift of the remainder to Raymond is not a present interest and does not entitle Frank to an annual exclusion with respect to this gift. Gift taxes are computed on Frank's total taxable gifts for the year. Whether he owes any taxes depends on how much of his unified credit he has used in prior years.

103b. Because Frank does not retain any interest in the trust, no part of it is included in his gross estate for federal estate tax purposes when he dies.

103c. When Sally dies, because she held only a life estate interest created by Frank and she did not hold a general power of appointment, the property is not included in her gross estate for federal estate tax purposes. There is no generation-skipping transfer tax either because Raymond does not qualify as a skip person.

104a. There is no gift if the transferor retains the power to revoke or the power to appoint over the property (that is, change beneficiaries without an ascertainable standard) because the donor has not relinquished sufficient dominion and control to make the gift complete. Here, although the trust is irrevocable, because Donald retained the power to appoint the property inter vivos among his nephews, no gifts, for gift tax purposes, result.

104b. Because Donald retained control over who has the right to enjoy the property, the property (full amount of the trust) is included in his gross estate for federal estate tax purposes (valued as of Donald's death) even if the power to appoint is not exercised.

105. The general rule is that if a party holds only a life estate interest created by another party, the property is not included in the life tenant's gross estate. If, however, the party also holds a general power of appointment, a party holding a general power of appointment is treated as owner of the property for estate tax purposes, even if the party does not exercise the power. Here, Michael held a general power of appointment over the property. The property therefore is included in Michael's gross estate upon his death. Because the property is included in Michael's gross estate upon his death, there is no generation-skipping transfer tax issue upon his death.

106a. Because the trust is a testamentary trust, all of the property used to fund the trust is included in Bill's gross estate for federal estate tax purposes. The issue is whether the property qualifies for a marital deduction for the full amount of the property in trust. The general rule is that testamentary transfers to spouses qualify as long as the interest is a nonterminable interest. Life estates are a terminable interest unless coupled with a general power of appointment or unless the interest qualifies as a QTIP life estate. Camille's interest is limited to a life estate. She is given a power of appointment but only to vary the shares among the children, so the power is a special power. The interest, however, qualifies as a QTIP interest because she is given all of the income during her lifetime and no one has the power to appoint any of the property during her lifetime to anyone other than the spouse. The fact that she is given the testamentary special power of appointment does not affect the analysis. Upon Bill's death, the property is included in his gross estate, but it also qualifies for the marital deduction (assuming a valid QTIP election is made on his timely filed estate tax return), thereby resulting in no net estate tax.

106b. When Camille dies, the full value of the trust property is included in her gross estate because Bill's estate was entitled to a full marital deduction. The extra estate tax associated with this inclusion is paid out of this trust before the property is distributed to the trust beneficiaries, here, the children.

107. When Charles dies, his property is included in his gross estate for federal estate tax purposes, and in the event the tax thereon exceeds the unified credit, there will be estate tax liability. William's death constitutes a lapse, and under anti-lapse his half is distributed to his child, Elizabeth. Because William actually predeceases Charles, his child moves up to his generation for purposes of the generation-skipping transfer tax; there is no generation-skipping transfer tax on the transfer to Elizabeth. In contrast, because Harry actually survives Charles but disclaims, Harry is treated as alive for purposes of applying the generation-skipping transfer tax, and because Anne and Diana are two generations removed from Charles, they constitute skip parties for purposes of the generation-skipping transfer tax. In addition to a possible estate tax, a generation-skipping transfer tax may be due upon the transfer to Anne and Diana. Lastly, Harry's disclaimer may be considered a gift to his children unless it meets the requirements of a qualified disclaimer pursuant to IRC §2518.

108. Bart holds a life estate interest in Homer's trust that is not enough to constitute a property interest for purposes of his gross estate. If the life estate is coupled with a general power of appointment, the property is included in the life tenant's gross estate. Here, Bart has the power to appoint the property among Homer's heirs only, making it a special power. The property is not included in

Bart's gross estate. Because Bart does not exercise the power of appointment, however, the property passes to his son, Homer II (Homer's grandson). Homer II is two generations removed from Homer, making Homer II a skip person. Bart's death and the transfer to Homer II constitute a taxable termination triggering a generation-skipping transfer tax if the amount put in the trust exceeds Homer's exemption.

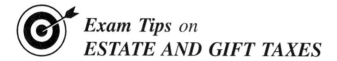

Exam Tips on
ESTATE AND GIFT TAXES

The federal estate and gift tax scheme

☛ Most schools have a separate course on estate and gift tax, so this chapter is but a short introduction to the area. The overlaps, however, are obvious, and so some professors bring some of the estate and gift tax considerations into the basic wills and trusts course.

☛ This material has become more difficult to teach in the basic wills and trusts course, however, because of all the recent changes in the tax code. It is not uncommon to have supplements to update the material, with more changes pending as of the date this book went to press.

The federal gift tax

☛ If this area is tested, the issue is usually whether a valid inter vivos gift has been made. If so, the property generally is not included in the decedent's gross estate for federal estate tax purposes; if not, the property is included.

   ☞ Where the settlor creates a trust and retains a power over the property in the trust, the settlor has not relinquished sufficient dominion and control. Where the donor creates a trust but reserves in him- or herself an interest in the principal, the general rule is the gift is not complete.

☛ Watch for gifts of future interests. They do not qualify for the annual gift tax exclusion. If, however, the future interest is coupled with a present right to demand the property (a Crummey power or general power of appointment or right to withdraw), that right constitutes a present interest that does qualify for the annual exclusion.

The federal estate tax

☛ There are four major steps to determining a decedent's federal estate tax: (1) compute his or her gross estate, (2) subtract various deductions, (3) apply the estate tax rate schedule to determine the tentative estate tax, and (4) apply the credits (principally the unified credit).

☛ In calculating the decedent's gross estate, the issues that arise concern nonprobate property. All probate property, whether testate or intestate, is included.

☞ If the decedent owned property in joint tenancy or tenancy in common, there usually are both gift tax and estate tax issues. In particular, watch for when the other joint tenant is *not* the decedent's spouse. Ask who provided the consideration to see if there are gift tax issues (for both tenancy in common and joint tenancy). Upon death of one joint tenant, distinguish between tenants in common (where the value of the decedent's share of the property at time of death is included in the decedent's gross estate) and joint tenants (where the percentage of the time of death value of the property included in decedent's gross estate is based on the percentage of the purchase price the decedent contributed when the property was purchased).

☞ If the fact pattern includes employee death benefits, they are included in the decedent's gross estate if the decedent had the right to receive the benefits had he or she lived long enough (that is, retirement benefits such as an annuity or a pension). If, however, the statute requires that the death benefits be paid to the decedent's surviving spouse or children, then the benefits are not included in the decedent's gross estate. (Bottom line—employee death benefits typically are included in the gross estate.)

☞ The value of insurance proceeds on the life of the decedent are included in the decedent's gross estate if the decedent possessed even one of the usual incidents of ownership (control over the policy or who were the beneficiaries) or the policy is payable to the decedent's executor or estate. It does not matter who pays the premiums. If the beneficiary is the decedent's surviving spouse, include the proceeds in the gross estate but deduct the proceeds under the marital deduction.

☛ Lifetime transfers pose the most challenging issues with respect to a decedent's gross estate because on the face of the transfer including the property in the decedent's gross estate appears inconsistent with the inter vivos transfer. Be on the watch for those lifetime transfers that still qualify for inclusion in the decedent's gross estate.

☞ If the decedent retains a life estate, the property is included in the decedent's gross estate. If the decedent transfers title but retains possession, the decedent retains a life estate unless there is a bona fide transfer of the property for full consideration.

☞ If the decedent retains control over who gets to enjoy the property, the property is included in the decedent's gross estate. The most common ways of retaining control over who gets to enjoy the property are (1) to retain a power over the property, or (2) to create a discretionary trust and appoint the decedent trustee (or co-trustee) (though if there is an ascertainable standard controlling the trustee's discretion, then the settlor does ***not*** retain control over who gets to enjoy the property).

☞ If the decedent retains the power to revoke or amend, the property is included in the decedent's gross estate.

☛ Watch for fact patterns involving powers of appointments. If the decedent holds a general power of appointment over property, the property is included in the decedent's gross estate, regardless of whether the decedent ever exercised the power. If, however, the decedent has a power to invade for his or her own benefit that is limited by an ascertainable standard relating to health, education, support, or maintenance, the power is not a general power of appointment.

☞ If the power is a special power, the general rule is that it is not included in the decedent's estate (even if the decedent held a limited power to appoint some of the property to him- or herself during his or her lifetime).

The marital deduction

☞ Although there are a number of requirements for a transfer from one spouse to the other to qualify for the marital deduction, the most important requirement is the requirement that the interest transferred must be a nonterminable interest—an interest that will last longer than the spouse's lifetime and hence be taxed upon the spouse's death. The classic example of a terminable interest that does not qualify is a life estate.

> ☞ Although life estates generally do not qualify for the marital deduction, note the two exceptions to this rule. First, a life estate coupled with a general power of appointment is taxable upon the spouse's death and thus qualifies for the marital deduction. Second, a QTIP trust qualifies for the marital deduction if (1) the surviving spouse was entitled to all the income for life, and (2) no one had the power to appoint or apply the property inter vivos (a special testamentary power over the property can be given to anyone without affecting the QTIP status). The donor or the donor's spouse's executor must elect to have the property taxed in the surviving spouse's gross estate, though the tax is paid by those who receive the property.

> ☞ In either case, if the life estate ends upon remarriage, the property does not qualify for the marital deduction.

The generation-skipping transfer tax

☞ The generation-skipping transfer tax is one of the more difficult issues conceptually. As an issue, however, it is fairly easy to spot in that you have to see a transfer where the transferee is at least two generations removed from the transferor. (Use proper terminology: the transferee is called a skip person to reflect that at least one generation has been skipped over in the transfer.)

☞ The classic generation-skipping transfer scenario that you should watch for is a life estate to the transferor's child or children, remainder to their children. Because the transferor's children have only a life estate, their interest is not included in their gross estate, so there is no tax upon the death of the life tenants; but a generation-skipping transfer tax is due because the grandchildren are the skip persons.

☞ The generation-skipping transfer tax arises regardless of what triggers the transfer to the skip person (taxable termination—termination of preceding interest; taxable distribution—exercise of power or discretionary distribution; or a direct skip—a direct gift).

> ☞ The generation-skipping transfer scenario can be raised more subtly by a transferee only one generation below the transferor (who does not constitute a skip person) predeceasing the transferor (either actually or by disclaimer). If the transferee *actually* predeceases the transferor, the descendants of the predeceased transferee are moved up a generation so there is not skip transfer. If, however, the transferee merely *disclaims,* the disclaiming party is treated as alive for purposes of applying the generation-skipping transfer tax. If the disclaimed property goes to the children of the disclaiming transferee, they qualify as skip persons.

Essay Exam Questions and Answers

QUESTION 1: Assume that Hal and Wendy are married. They own Greenacres as "true joint tenants with right of survivorship and not as tenants in common." Wendy has $100,000 in a savings account from her earnings acquired after she married Hal. She also has 100 shares of Amgen stock she inherited after she married. Wendy's brother, Bill, is dying of AIDS, so in 2007 Wendy and Hal adopt Bill's young son, Sam. Bill dies shortly thereafter. Several years later, Wendy is killed in a car accident. She is survived by her mother, Maude, by Hal, by Sam, and by Daisy, a grown daughter who years ago joined a religious cult and who has not contacted Hal or Wendy since. Following her death, they find an old business supply store form document titled "Last Will & Testament." Wendy had dated the document (December 2005) and had filled in some of the blanks on the form by hand so the document reads as follows:

> I, *Wendy Smith*, leave my property as follows: *all my property to my loving husband, Hal.*

No other part of the form document was filled in or completed, and she did not sign the signature block at the bottom of the document. There are no witnesses to the writings on the form.

Analyze who gets Wendy's property. Be sure to raise and analyze the arguments any party to the fact pattern could raise in court.

1. Assume that the jurisdiction has a typical intestate scheme, a probate code that recognizes attested wills and holographic wills, and that the jurisdiction applies the strict compliance judicial approach to the Wills Act formalities. Who takes Wendy's property under strict compliance?
2. To what extent, if any, would your analysis be any different if instead of strict compliance the jurisdiction applies the harmless error approach to the Wills Act formalities?

QUESTION 2: Tess, a single woman with three children, validly executed duplicate original wills. She took one copy home and left the other with her lawyer. The will provided in pertinent part as follows:

5. I leave my personal property to those individuals listed on a piece of paper that will be found with this will when I die. Any personal property not distributed by that list, or elsewhere in this will, I leave to my personal representative, as trustee, to hold and distribute among my children who reach age 25, as he deems appropriate, when the youngest reaches the age of 25.
6. I give 100 shares of Genentech (a publicly traded company) to my good friend, Lulu Lava.
7. I give the rest of my property to State University Law School.

Later in the document, the will set forth a generic set of trust administration provisions.

Thereafter, Tess typed up a document she titled "Tess's Personal Property List," which provided as follows: "I give all of my Genentech stock to my mom, Maude, and my car to my dad, Dave. In addition, I give my jewelry to my sister, Sally." She dated the document, but did not sign it. She paper-clipped the document to her will. Thereafter, Genentech declared a two-for-one stock split. Tess owned 200 shares when she executed the will (so she owned 400 shares at the time of her death). Thereafter she executed a valid will that provided in pertinent part as follows: "I hereby revoke paragraph 7 of my original will and instead give all the rest, residue and remainder of my property to Loyola Law School." Thereafter, she died. The duplicate original will that was left with her lawyer could not be found, but the one last in Tess's possession was found among her papers. Tess is survived by her three children, Alicia (age 24), Javan (age 20), and Taurean (age 15).

Who takes Tess's property? Please raise and analyze all possible arguments.

SAMPLE ANSWER TO QUESTION 1:

1. Who takes Wendy's property under strict compliance?

  a. Nonprobate property—Greenacres: First, Wendy and Hal owned Greenacres as true joint tenants. The essence of a joint tenancy is the right of survivorship, which means that, upon one joint tenant's death, his or her interest is extinguished, and the shares of the remaining joint tenants are recalculated. Because the decedent's interest is extinguished, no property interest passes to the other joint tenant(s). The property is nonprobate property. Upon Wendy's death, her interest is extinguished, and Hal alone now owns Greenacres.

  b. Wendy's probate property: Assuming a non-community property jurisdiction, Wendy's $100,000 and 100 shares of Amgen stock would fall into her probate estate.[1] Who takes her probate property depends first on whether she has a valid will.

  c. Testate succession—the business supply store form document: Hal will offer the business supply store form document and try to probate it as Wendy's last will and testament.

  i. Attested will—strict compliance: Although the requirements of an attested will vary from jurisdiction to jurisdiction, the basic requirements are that there must be a writing, that the testator signed or acknowledged the writing (or that it was signed by another at the direction of the testator and in her presence), and that the testator's signing or acknowledging of the will was witnessed by two witnesses, present at the same time that the testator signed or acknowledged the instrument. Under the traditional strict compliance approach, the will's execution must comply 100 percent with the Wills Act formalities. Any little shortfall will invalidate the will. Here, the facts state that the business supply store form document is a writing, but there are no witnesses and it is unclear whether it is properly signed (see below). Under strict compliance, however, the signature issue is moot because the absence of witnesses in and of itself invalidates the document as an attested will under strict compliance.

  ii. Holographic will—strict compliance: To have a valid holographic will, there must be a writing in the testator's handwriting, it must be signed, and the writing must have testamentary intent. Some jurisdictions also require the writing to be dated. Here, the fact pattern expressly says that Wendy dated the document (December 2005) so that is not at issue, even if required by the jurisdiction. How much of the document must be in the testator's handwriting also varies from jurisdiction to jurisdiction. Some jurisdictions require the whole document to be in the testator's handwriting. Under this approach, the document is not a valid holographic because Wendy used a commercially printed form will that contains quite a bit of printed material not in her handwriting.

---

1. If the jurisdiction were a community property state, this would affect how much property would fall into probate. Community property is any property acquired during the marriage as a result of the labor and effort of either spouse. Upon the death of a spouse, each community property asset is owned 50-50 by each spouse. The surviving spouse owns his or her share outright, while the deceased spouse's share goes into probate. Here, because the $100,000 in the savings account was from Wendy's earnings during her marriage, it would be classified as community property. Hal would own $50,000 outright, and the remaining $50,000 would fall into Wendy's probate estate. Separate property is any property acquired by either spouse before marriage or during marriage by gift, descent, or devise. Here, even though Wendy acquired the 100 shares of Amgen after she married Hal, she inherited the shares so they would be her separate property. All 100 shares would fall into her probate estate as her separate property.

If the jurisdiction requires only the material provisions to be in the testator's handwriting, it is likely the document meets this requirement. At a minimum, jurisdictions define the material provisions to constitute the "who" gets "what." Here, Wendy has expressed in her own handwriting "who" gets "what:" *all my property to my loving husband, Hal.*

Another issue with respect to the requirement that the material provisions be in the testator's handwriting is whether the required testamentary intent is also a material provision, i.e., whether it must be expressed in the testator's handwriting. The traditional test for testamentary intent is whether the testator intended this document to constitute his or her last will and testament, i.e., that the decedent intended this document to be taken down to the probate court and probated as his or her will. Here, if the jurisdiction considers testamentary intent to be a material provision, meaning it must be expressed in the testator's handwriting, it is unlikely that a court would find it present. Although the handwritten provisions express Wendy's intent to convey her property to her husband, Hal, it lacks the necessary temporal component to know *when* that conveyance was to occur—inter vivos or at time of death. Absent evidence that the conveyance is intended to be when Wendy dies, it is unlikely that a court would conclude that the handwriting evidences testamentary intent. Many jurisdictions, however, do not limit the court's examination to the handwritten provisions. In many jurisdictions, the court can take into consideration the context in which the handwritten words are written—the printed words of the commercially printed form will—in evaluating whether there is testamentary intent. Some jurisdictions permit the court to take any extrinsic evidence into account when evaluating whether there is testamentary intent. If the jurisdiction permits the court to consider the printed material in addition to the handwritten material, or if the jurisdiction permits the court to take into account any relevant extrinsic evidence, it is likely the court would conclude that the document expresses the intent that it be a will. It is a form will and no doubt, as such, there is language in it expressing that the document is intended to be the person's will. In fact, the document is titled "Last Will & Testament." Whether the decedent actually intended this document to be his or her last will, however, overlaps with the remaining requirement—the requirement that the document be signed.

The next issue is whether Wendy signed the form will. A signature is any mark the testator makes that he or she *intends* to be his or her signature. Hal will argue that since Wendy filled in her name on the document, her full name, the will was signed and should be probated. The counterargument is that she did not sign the signatory block at the end of the document, she merely wrote her name in the middle of the document where the name is requested for identification purposes, not signatory purposes. Hal will counter that in most jurisdictions there is no requirement that a holographic will be subscribed or signed at the end.

If the jurisdiction does require that the document be signed at the end, Wendy's act of writing her name would not qualify. But assuming the jurisdiction does not require the document to be signed at the end, there is a real issue as to whether Wendy intended her name to be for signatory or for identification purposes. The will opponents will argue that Wendy did not complete any other part of the will, and this indicates that she had not finalized the document as her will. Hal will argue that in light of what she did write (all to Hal), there was no need for her to complete any other part of the will since her handwritten provisions adequately expressed her testamentary intent and her whole testamentary scheme.

Assuming the jurisdiction applies strict compliance, it is unclear whether a court would conclude Wendy's name would constitute her signature. If the court truly applies strict compliance, the likely outcome is that the court would rule that her handwritten name was not intended to constitute her signature but rather was written for identification purposes. Strict compliance errs on the side of invaliding a will if there is any doubt as to whether the will is valid. Here, there is ambiguity as to why Wendy wrote her name when she did, so the court would likely conclude that the will was invalid. In some strict compliance jurisdictions, however, some courts, while paying lip service to strict compliance, take into consideration that holographic wills typically are homemade wills and therefore cut testators some slack in determining whether the document is a valid will. If the court were of this philosophy, there is a chance that the court might conclude that when Wendy wrote her name she meant it not only for identification purposes but also for signatory purposes. Such a court would probate the will as Wendy's last will and testament, and Hal would claim all of Wendy's property under the will.

iii. **Omitted/pretermitted child doctrine:** Assuming, arguendo, the document is held to be a valid holographic will, Sam will claim that despite the terms of the will, he is entitled to a share of Wendy's estate under the omitted/pretermitted child doctrine. Although the details of the doctrine can vary a bit in different jurisdictions, the traditional and general approach to the omitted child doctrine is that where a testator executes a valid will, and thereafter the testator has a child, and thereafter the testator dies without revoking or revising the will, a rebuttable presumption arises that the testator intended to amend the will to provide for the new child but accidentally failed to get around to doing so – i.e., that the child was accidentally, not intentionally, disinherited.[2] The classic scenario for the doctrine is when the testator or the testator's spouse gives birth to a child after the valid execution of the will, but the doctrine also applies to situations where the parent-child relationship is created legally instead of naturally – where the testator adopts a child. Here, Sam was legally adopted in 2007, two years after the date of the holographic will. If the holographic will is deemed a valid will, Sam can successfully invoke the omitted/pretermitted child doctrine to create a presumption that he was accidentally omitted from Wendy's will. If the presumption is not rebutted, the general rule is Sam is entitled to his intestate share of Wendy's estate. In most jurisdictions, the presumption can be rebutted only if one can show: (1) the testator's failure to provide for the child was intentional and that intent is expressed in the will; (2) the testator provided for the child by transfer outside of the will and the intention that the transfer be in lieu of a provision in the will is shown by statements of the decedent or from the amount of the transfer or by other evidence; or (3) the testator had one or more children and devised substantially all the estate to the other parent of the omitted child. Here, there is no evidence, in the will or elsewhere, that Wendy intentionally disinherited Sam. There is no evidence here that Wendy otherwise provided for Sam outside of the will in lieu of his taking under the will. At the time Wendy executed the holographic will, however, she did have another child (Daisy) and under the terms of the holographic will she devised all of her estate to Hal. Hal can successfully rebut the presumption that Sam was accidentally omitted from the will. Sam is not entitled to any of Wendy's estate under the omitted/pretermitted child doctrine.

d. **Intestate succession—failure of the business supply store form document:** If the court were to apply strict compliance literally, it would likely hold that the document does not constitute a valid will, and Wendy's property would fall to intestacy. Under intestacy, the first taker is the surviving spouse. Here, Wendy has a surviving spouse, so Hal would take first. How much he would take varies by jurisdiction, but in most jurisdictions, if there are surviving issue, there is a good chance

---

2. In some jurisdictions, the doctrine has been expanded to apply not only to wills, but also to inter vivos revocable trusts. Here, however, there is no inter vivos revocable trust, so the analysis will focus on the traditional approach to the doctrine that focused only on a decedent's will.

they would share in the intestate estate. This raises the issue of whether Daisy and Sam qualify as issue of Wendy. To qualify as an issue, one has to establish a parent-child relationship, either naturally or legally (typically through adoption). Daisy is Wendy and Hal's natural child. She qualifies as an issue. The fact that neither Wendy nor Hal has had contact with Daisy in years is irrelevant. Daisy still qualifies as Wendy's child and is entitled to her share of Wendy's intestate property. Sam is not a natural child of Wendy, but Wendy legally adopted Sam. The general rule is that adoption severs the parent-child relationship between the adopted child and his or her natural parents and creates a parent-child relationship between the adopted child and his or her adoptive parents. Full inheritance rights attach themselves to this parent-child relationship. Sam has the right to inherit from and through Wendy and Hal; and Wendy and Hal have the right to inherit from and through Sam. Wendy is survived by a spouse and two children. The share that Hal and the children would receive would depend on the details of the state's intestate distribution scheme.

2. **What difference, if any, would it make if the jurisdiction applies the harmless error approach?**

   a. **Nonprobate property—Greenacres:** If the jurisdiction applied the harmless error doctrine, it would not affect who takes Greenacres. Greenacres is still nonprobate property that Hal would own immediately upon Wendy's death pursuant to the right of survivorship implicit with joint tenancy.

   b. **Testate succession—the business supply store form document:** The issue is whether the harmless error doctrine would make any difference with respect to whether the business supply document constitutes a valid will. Under the harmless error doctrine, a document can still be probated as the decedent's last will and testament, even it were not properly executed under strict compliance, if there is clear and convincing evidence that the testator intended the document to be his or her last will and testament. The issue is whether there is clear and convincing evidence the testator intended the document to be her will in light of the ambiguity surrounding whether the document was properly signed. Absent additional information, it appears difficult to establish that there is clear and convincing evidence that Wendy intended the document to be her last will and testament when the signatory block of the form will was not completed. It is unclear whether she wrote her name for identification purposes or for signatory purposes. In light of this ambiguity, it is unlikely that a court would conclude that the document constitutes Wendy's will, even under the harmless error doctrine. The outcome should be the same as it most likely was under strict compliance.

SAMPLE ANSWER TO QUESTION 2:

Who takes Tess's property?

   a. **Revocation by presumption:** The first issue is whether revocation by presumption applies. Revocation by presumption provides that where a will is last in testator's possession, and it cannot be found following her death, a presumption arises that the testator destroyed the document with the intent to revoke it. Where there are duplicate originals, some jurisdictions apply the presumption doctrine only if *none* of the duplicate originals can be found. Here, although one of the duplicate originals cannot be found following Tess's death, it was the duplicate original that was last in her attorney's possession. The one in Tess's possession was found, and there is no evidence that she directed her attorney to destroy that other duplicate original with the intent to revoke it. The presumption doctrine does not apply under these facts. Tess died testate.

   b. **The personal property list:** The facts state that Tess validly executed her will. The first issue is whether the court can give effect to her intent (and the gifts) expressed in Tess's Personal Property List consistent with paragraph 5 of her will. The list cannot qualify as a valid will. An attested will requires a writing that is signed and witnessed. A holographic will generally requires a writing that is signed, with either all or the material provisions in the testator's handwriting, and testamentary intent. The list does not qualify as either type of will because it was not signed (nor does it have testamentary intent in that Tess did not intend for it to be a will, she intended it to be an addition to her will—a tangible personal property list).

If the jurisdiction has adopted the modern trend/UPC approach, the list can probably be given effect as a tangible personal property list. The UPC's tangible personal property list permits a testator to give away his or her tangible personal property via a list not executed with Wills Act formalities, even if the list is created *after* the will is executed, as long as the will expressly states such an intent. UPC §2-513. In essence, the doctrine modifies incorporation by reference by waiving the requirement that the document be in existence at the time the will is executed as long as the document only disposes of the testator's tangible personal property (other than money). The exact requirements vary by jurisdiction, but under the UPC, the writing must be signed and it must describe the items and devisees with reasonable certainty to be given effect. Other jurisdictions, such as California, do not require the list to be signed by the testator but do cap the value of permissible devises made in the list. Here, paragraph 5 of Tess's will adequately expresses the intent to create a tangible personal property list. The list does not qualify under the UPC tangible personal property list doctrine, however, because it was not signed by the testator. Other jurisdictions, however, may not require the list to be signed, and, as such, the list may be valid. Either way, however, the list can dispose of Tess's tangible personal property only. Here, the gift of Genentech stock would not qualify as tangible personal property. Stock is an intangible property interest and therefore is invalid. The list may, however, be given effect to transfer the car to Tess's dad, Dave, and the jewelry to her sister, Sally. The rest of her tangible personal property is given to her personal representative, as trustee, to hold in trust for the benefit of her children. This testamentary trust will be discussed below.

At common law, there are two other possible doctrines that could be asserted in an attempt to give effect to *all* the writing in the list. The first possible common law doctrine that one could assert in an attempt to give effect to the gifts in the list is acts of independent significance. Acts of independent significance require the will to reference an act that will affect either who takes or how much they take, and the referenced act must have its own "independent significance"—significance independent of its effect upon the will. Here, the referenced act is the making of the list. The problem is the list has no independent significance. The only reason the list exists is to affect the distribution of Tess's property upon her death. The list cannot be given effect under acts of independent significance.

The second common law doctrine that might apply to give effect to *all* the writing in the list is incorporation by reference. It requires the will to express the intent to incorporate the writing, the will to describe the document with reasonable certainty, and proof that the document being incorporated was in existence at the time the will was executed. Here, the express reference in paragraph 5 to the Personal Property List constitutes an adequate intent to incorporate the document by reference, and the name of the document in paragraph 5 permits it to be identified with reasonable certainty, but the document was not in existence at the time *the original will* was executed. The facts specifically state that the list was created after Tess executed her will. The intent expressed in the document could not be given effect under incorporation by reference – at the time the list was created.

But after executing the tangible personal property list, the testator validly executed another will that validly revoked paragraph 7 of the original will and substituted a new paragraph 7. A validly executed will that is executed later in time can either expressly revoke or revoke by inconsistency a prior will. The new will expressly revokes paragraph 7 of the original will. Express revocation of part of a duplicate original is effective to revoke that part of both duplicate originals. The new will revokes by writing paragraph 7 in both duplicate original wills. Because the new will only *partially* revokes the original will—and amends it by substituting a new paragraph 7—the new will is a codicil. Under republication by codicil, a codicil is presumed to re-execute, re-publish, and re-date the original will. Re-dating the original will to the date of the codicil, all of the 'list of personal property' can now be given effect under incorporation by reference. The re-dated will expresses the intent to incorporate the list because it references the list. The will describes the list with reasonable certainty because there is no evidence that there is another list. The list is in existence at the time of the codicil—which re-dates the underlying will—so the list can be given effect under incorporation by reference. If the court is so inclined, all gifts in the list can be given effect because there are no longer any restrictions on the nature or amount of gifts that can be given effect under incorporation by reference.

c. **Number of Genentech shares made in the gift:** Paragraph 6 of Tess's will devises 100 shares of Genentech stock to her friend, Lulu Lava. This is a general gift: a gift of a general pecuniary value. Lulu will gladly take any 100 shares of Genentech. The issue is whether Lulu gets the benefit of the stock split that occurred after execution of the will and before Tess died. The jurisdictions are split. The traditional common law approach was that the beneficiary received the benefit of the change in stock only if the change was initiated by a corporate entity and the gift was a specific gift. A specific gift is a gift of a specific item. Typically, a specific gift is modified by the word "my." Here, if the common law approach were the rule, although the change in the number of shares Tess owned at the time of her death was the result of Genentech's actions (declaring a two-for-one stock split), based on the language of the gift, it is not likely a specific gift but rather a general gift since it was not modified by the word "my." Lulu could argue, however, that since Tess owned 200 shares of Genentech stock at the time she executed the will, Tess was implicitly referring to 100 of the shares she owned at that time, thus arguing that Tess had in mind that Lulu take a specific gift—100 shares of Tess's personal collection of the stock. If a court were to accept this argument, the gift could be treated as a specific gift, and Lulu would get the benefit of the stock split. Whether Lulu received the benefit of the stock split (200 shares) or merely the gift in the will (100 shares) depends on whether the court puts more emphasis on the language of the gift or Lulu's argument of Tess's likely intent based on her ownership of matching shares.

Some jurisdictions have adopted a more modern trend approach to stock splits that focuses on the intrinsic nature of stock. Under the modern trend, the assumption is that the testator is attempting to give a percentage interest in the company and that percentage interest can be achieved only by giving the beneficiary the benefit of the stock split regardless of whether the gift is characterized as specific or general. The beneficiary receives the change in the stock regardless (as long as the change is initiated by the corporate entity). If that were the rule in this jurisdiction, Lulu would receive the benefit of the stock split. She would receive 200 shares of Genentech under the modern trend.

Whatever shares do not go to Lulu will go to Wendy's mom, Maude, under the terms of the personal property list and not to the trustee of the personal property trust under the terms of the residuary clause. Maude is entitled to the remaining shares not under the tangible personal property list but instead under incorporation by reference, as analyzed above.

d. **Residuary clause:** Paragraph 7 of Tess's will is a valid residuary clause—a clause that devises any and all probate property that was not previously validly given away in her will to the residuary beneficiary. The provision is valid, and under the original will State University Law School would have taken the rest, residue, and remainder of her property. But a later will can expressly revoke a prior will. Here Tess' later will expressly revokes paragraph 7 of her original will and substitutes a new residuary clause, one that leaves all her property to Loyola Law School. The codicil is valid and Loyola Law School would get her residuary property.

e. **Testamentary trust:** There is an issue as to whether the trust Tess attempted to create in paragraph 5 is valid. A valid trust requires intent to create a trust, funding, ascertainable beneficiaries, and possibly a writing. The intent to create a trust exists when one party gives property to a second for the benefit of a third. Here, Tess, the settlor, gives property to her personal representative, as trustee, for the benefit of her children, the trust beneficiaries. The will adequately expresses the intent to create a trust. Second, funding requires that an adequate property interest be transferred to the trust/trustee. Here, Tess is funding the trust with her personal property that is not disposed of in her tangible property list or elsewhere in the will. Her personal property is an adequate property interest, and the will's gift of the property to the trustee will constitute funding. Third, there must be ascertainable beneficiaries so that the court knows who has standing to come into court and enforce the terms of the trust. For the beneficiaries to be ascertainable, there must be an objective means of identifying the parties in question. Here, although the language in the will does not expressly name the beneficiaries, the term used to describe the class of beneficiaries—"my children"—permits a court objectively to ascertain to whom the testator is referring. There are ascertainable beneficiaries. Fourth, the trust must be in writing if it is an inter vivos trust that is to hold and manage real property or if it is a testamentary trust. A trust is created when it is funded.

Here, the trust is funded through paragraph 5 of the will so it is a testamentary trust. Pursuant to the Wills Act formalities, all testamentary trusts must be in writing. Here, the trust is in writing in Tess's will. The trust is properly created.

f. **Rule against Perpetuities:** There is a potential Rule against Perpetuities issue with respect to the beneficiaries' interest, however. It is a class gift where the interest of each class member does not vest until he or she reaches age 25. Where there is a class gift that is vested as to some members but not as to others, the general rule is that if the gift violates the Rule against Perpetuities as to even one class member, it is void as to the whole class. Does the gift violate the Rule against Perpetuities as to even one member? If the trust were an inter vivos trust, the answer would be "yes." If Tess were still alive, it would be possible to envision a scenario where she could have another child. Then all of the lives in being at the time the interest was created could die the next day, and yet that child could live another 25 years, thereby creating a scenario where the interest in question would not vest until after the Rule against Perpetuities' statutory period: the lives in being plus 21 years. But here, the trust is a testamentary trust. Tess is dead. All of her children are alive at the time the trust is created. Their interests must vest, if at all, during their lifetimes. Because it is a testamentary trust, the interests in her children do not violate the Rule against Perpetuities.

g. **Sprinkle trust:** A sprinkle trust is a hybrid trust, one that is both mandatory and discretionary. It is a trust that *requires* the trustee to distribute all of the property in question among a limited group of individuals, but the trustee has *discretion* as to who is to receive how much. Here, Tess's trust is a sprinkle trust because it specifically requires the trustee to distribute all of the trust property among Tess's children when the youngest reaches age 25, but it gives the trustee to discretion to distribute the property among the children "as he deems appropriate." Tess's trust is a valid sprinkle, or spray, trust.

Table of Cases

Subject Matter Index